LAW
ENFORCEMENT *in*
the UNITED STATES

James A. Conser, PhD, CPP
Professor Emeritus
Criminal Justice and Forensic Sciences Department
Youngstown State University
Youngstown, OH

Rebecca Paynich, PhD
Associate Professor of Criminal Justice
Co-Director, Master of Arts in Criminal Justice
Curry College
Milton, MA

Terry E. Gingerich, PhD
Associate Professor
Department of Criminal Justice
Western Oregon University
Monmouth, OR

JONES & BARTLETT
LEARNING

World Headquarters
Jones & Bartlett Learning
5 Wall Street
Burlington, MA 01803
978-443-5000
info@jblearning.com
www.jblearning.com

Jones & Bartlett Learning books and products are available through most bookstores and online booksellers. To contact Jones & Bartlett Learning directly, call 800-832-0034, fax 978-443-8000, or visit our website, www.jblearning.com.

Substantial discounts on bulk quantities of Jones & Bartlett Learning publications are available to corporations, professional associations, and other qualified organizations. For details and specific discount information, contact the special sales department at Jones & Bartlett Learning via the above contact information or send an email to specialsales@jblearning.com.

Production Credits
Publisher: Cathleen Sether
Acquisitions Editor: Sean Connelly
Editorial Assistant: Caitlin Murphy
Director of Production: Amy Rose
Production Assistant: Alyssa Lawrence
Associate Marketing Manager: Lindsay White
Manufacturing and Inventory Control Supervisor: Amy Bacus
Cover and Title Page Design: Scott Moden
Permissions and Photo Researcher: Amy Mendosa
Composition: Cenveo Publisher Services
Cover Image: © Konstantin Sutyagin/ShutterStock, Inc.
Printing and Binding: Edwards Brothers Malloy
Cover Printing: Edwards Brothers Malloy

Library of Congress Cataloging-in-Publication Data
Conser, James A. (James Andrew), 1948-
Law enforcement in the United States / James Conser, Rebecca Paynich, and Terry Gingerich. — 3rd ed.
    p. cm.
Includes index.
ISBN-13: 978-0-7637-9938-0 (pbk.)
ISBN-10: 0-7637-9938-6 (pbk.)
1. Law enforcement—United States. 2. Police—United States. I. Paynich, Rebecca. II. Gingerich, Terry. III. Title.
HV8139.C647 2013
363.2'30973—dc23
                       2011023562
6048

Printed in the United States of America
17 16 15   10 9 8 7 6 5 4 3

DEDICATION

To the law enforcement officers, firefighters, EMS providers, security personnel, and all other public servants who lost their lives in the attacks of September 11, 2001. May your lives and service never fade from the memories of the people of the United States. May your loss never be taken for granted.

Table of Contents

Acknowledgments

The authors want to specifically acknowledge and thank the editors and staff of Jones & Bartlett Learning—Sean Connelly, Caitlin Murphy, Alyssa Lawrence, and Amy Mendosa, for their excellent work on this third edition. Their professionalism was evident throughout the process from the outline to the final proofs—we thank all of you.

Jim Conser wishes to acknowledge his wife, Linda, who has supported his various projects and endeavors over the last 41 years. She helped to instill honesty and integrity in their three daughters, Nicole, Jami and Jodi; and now influences their grandchildren, Tyler, Caleb, Alexis, and Justus.

Rebecca Paynich wishes to express her gratitude to her loving husband, Jason, who has supported her in many ways throughout the writing process for all of her projects and to her children, Spencer, Dylan, and Jack, whose curiosity about the world around them continually amazes her.

Terry Gingerich wishes to thank his wife Tracy for her love, encouragement, and support; his children, Matthew, Peter, Ethan, Annemarie, and April; and his grandchildren, Chad, Troy, Ella, Riley, Travis, and Mackenzie, for the enormous pride and joy they bring to his life.

We would also like to thank the following reviewers for their input in the revision of this text:

Wayne L. Babish, University of Pittsburgh and University of Phoenix
Carol Mathews, Century College
Larry W. Robinson, Oklahoma State University-Oklahoma City
Daniel Simone, Saint Peter's College
Arnold R. Waggoner, Rose State College
Francis M. Williams, Plymouth State University

About the Authors

James (Jim) Conser is Professor Emeritus at Youngstown State University, Youngstown, Ohio. He earned an A.B. degree in Law Enforcement Administration from Youngstown State University, an M.S. degree in Criminal Justice from Michigan State University, and a PhD in Higher Education Administration from Kent State University. He began his career as a police officer in Arlington County, Virginia in 1972. He has held academic and university administrative positions (instructor, professor, department chair, and assistant dean) since 1975. Dr. Conser was an Assistant Executive Director of the Ohio Peace Officer Training Commission (OPOTC) from 1999 through 2002. Jim is a Certified Protection Professional through ASIS International. He is coauthor of two textbooks: *Law Enforcement in the United States, Second Edition* (Jones & Bartlett, 2005) and *The Police Personnel System* (John Wiley & Sons, 1983); and has contributed several chapters to other texts. He is a lifetime member (and former National Secretary) of Police Futurists International and the Academy of Criminal Justice Sciences; a member of the American Society for Industrial Security, the World Future Society, the Ohio Crime Prevention Association, and the Ohio Council of Criminal Educators. Jim serves his local community as a volunteer firefighter. He and his wife have three married daughters, and four grandchildren.

Rebecca Paynich earned a Master of Arts in Criminal Justice (2000) and a Ph.D. in Political Science (2003) from Washington State University, and currently teaches at Curry College, in Milton, MA. Dr. Paynich's teaching skills take a generalist approach toward the Criminal Justice field. She holds classes in statistics, crime mapping, corrections, police, criminal justice ethics, criminology, criminal justice policy, and many others. Dr. Paynich has been involved in several research projects throughout her academic career including work as a researcher on the Project Safe Neighborhood grant for the state of North Dakota. While her primary research interests revolve around law enforcement, she also does work in the areas of criminal justice theory and policy, and crime mapping. She has coauthored two books with Jones & Bartlett, *Law Enforcement in the United States, Second Edition* (Jones & Bartlett, 2005), and *The Fundamentals of Crime Mapping: Principles and Practice* (Jones & Bartlett, 2009). She has also published in *Police Practice and Research: An International Journal* and *Journal of Contemporary Criminal Justice*. She is married and has three children.

Terry E. Gingerich earned his Ph.D. from Washington State University in 2002. He also holds an MA from California State University in Los Angeles and a BA from the University of San Francisco. Prior to entering academia, Dr. Gingerich served 25 years with the Los Angeles County Sheriff's Department, retiring in 1996 as a sergeant. He worked a variety of assignments with the LASD, including tours in custody, patrol, administration, and detective divisions. Prior to joining the LASD, he was a police officer with the Metropolitan Police Department, Washington DC. He served four and half years in the USMC (1963-1968). He holds basic, intermediate, advanced, and supervisory certificates from the California Commission on Police Officer Standards and Training. Dr. Gingerich has coauthored one book: *Law Enforcement in the United States, Second Edition* (Jones & Bartlett, 2005) and has published articles in the *Asian Journal of Criminology*, the *Justice Policy Journal* and *Asian Politics and Policy*. He is a member of the Police Administration Committee of the International Association of Chiefs of Police, the Academy of Criminal Justice Sciences, and the Asian Association of Police Studies. Dr. Gingerich's research interests include: police history, criminal justice policy, comparative criminal justice, and police management. He is married and has five children and six grandchildren.

Preface

American law enforcement, at all levels, has undergone a tremendous change in the past 50 years. Indeed, it has undergone dynamic change in the past 15 years alone, some as a result of the terrorist attacks of September 11, 2001; some as a result of technological improvements; and some as a result of political and social pressures on law enforcement to become more engaged with the public.

This text is designed to help students of the criminal justice system understand the birth, emergence, and current status of American law enforcement by examining the social, political, institutional, and cultural forces that have shaped this critical institution. Law enforcement has undergone four major stages since its formal inception in the United States. First, its creation during the "political era" of American governance—a period characterized by corruption, violence, and political cronyism, and one in which law enforcement was largely the arm of a given political party. Second, the progressive reform movement's reaction to that legacy and the creation of an infant civil service system which, by the 1930s and 1940s, gave at least the hint of some professional demeanor and the absence of political influence. Third, the adoption of many recommendations of a presidential commission report issued in 1967; changes that have taken over 40 years to come to fruition, but they ushered in the "community era" of policing—one characterized by local community policing, problem oriented policing, and policy driven by community demands rather than the demands of those in command of law enforcement. The fourth major stage emerged from the Terror Attacks of September 11, 2001 and the additional responsibilities of homeland security. The latter focus has impacted federal and state law enforcement agencies the greatest, along with the largest metropolitan areas of the country; but local agencies have experienced their own issues related to homeland and national security. Additionally, the economic downturn has had a negative effect on state and local resources, and can be only marginally relevant to state law enforcement agencies. Hence, there is division between discourse in those sectors of law enforcement and those that include municipal police and sheriff's departments. Federal agencies have been radically altered by the events of 9/11. The effects on local enforcement are less clear, but no less certain.

To appreciate the organizational challenges that the future holds, it is essential to understand the history of organizational evolution; the creation, maintenance, and transmission of organizational culture across time; and how law enforcement officers see their role—that is, *their perspective on their role* rather than the perspective of others. In short, reform of any sort—structural reform or reform created through policy directives—requires the support and assistance of the officers and agents whose task it is to carry out organizational policy.

We offer the student a glimpse into not only the historical imperatives that helped shape law enforcement, but also the institutional dynamics, the social movements, and political events that have driven law enforcement to its current status. Law enforcement was not created instantaneously—it evolved in response to a multitude of forces. The *system* of law enforcement must be seen for what it is—an interlocked set of institutional structures, behaviors, and conditions, all responding to the external environment and its demands; hence our choice to view law enforcement from a systems perspective.

In closing, a word about conducting further research and viewing the Internet links throughout the text. Several additional links are provided at the end of each chapter for students to "dig deeper" into the topics presented. Occasionally, websites change their addresses or are temporarily unavailable. If a cited address is not found, don't give up—try again later or use a search engine to locate more information about the topic, agency, association, or document. You may find the site you were originally seeking or an alternative site that contains related information. There is a wealth of criminal justice information on the Internet and more is added daily; use this text to determine key words for searches.

SUPPLEMENTS

This textbook is accompanied by a series of valuable supplements. An instructor's manual (with Microsoft® PowerPoint® Lecture Outlines) is available to assist instructors in teaching introduction to policing and other law enforcement courses. Additionally, a TestBank containing discussion questions and practical exercises is provided to stimulate the critical thinking skills.

The Field of Law Enforcement

KEY TERMS USED IN THIS CHAPTER

representative democracy	full enforcement
law enforcement	zero tolerance
police powers	public policy perspective
policing	proactive
police officials	systems theory
social control	global perspective
socialization	diplomatic immunity
legal perspective	Vienna Convention on
discretion	Consular Relations
selective enforcement	

THE BASIC CONCEPT OF LAW ENFORCEMENT

In our society, as in all modern societies, the enforcement of the law is vital—without some type of law enforcement, a society would eventually cease to exist. Generally speaking, the function called law enforcement is a society's formal attempt to obtain compliance with the established rules, regulations, and laws of that society. Without law enforcement, society as we know it would probably succumb to social disorder and chaos.

The United States is a **representative democracy**, which places great emphasis on the protection of individual freedoms and liberties; as such, its institutions must reflect those principles upon which the country was founded. Because the United States is predominately an open and free society—in the political sense, with freedom to disagree from region to region, state to state, and city to city about how to design and direct law enforcement and develop policy—it is common to have disagreements about how to enforce the law. Historically, our country's citizens have often questioned the actions of government officials. As citizens, we may not always agree with what happens on the street, in police stations, in courtrooms, in jails, or in prisons, but people in the United States possess the freedom to criticize and protest governmental actions (or inactions) because of the structure of our criminal justice system. That structure and the Constitution may occasionally appear to be in conflict with one another, but that may also be evidence that the system works. The debate over civil liberties and national security that has emerged since the 9/11 terrorist attacks on the United States is another example of our principles at work. Inevitably, such issues prompt us to ask two significant questions: (1) how can the law enforcement community function to preserve the civil liberties and freedoms that are cherished and protected by the Constitution?, and (2) how do we balance our constitutional rights with public safety and national security concerns?

The purpose of this book is to help you answer these questions by providing information about the field of law enforcement, so that you have an understanding and appreciation for both its objectives and activities. Such a background is necessary for you to develop *informed* opinions about the field, rather than opinions based on limited knowledge and experience. Everyone has opinions; some are more informed than others. Informed persons have a foundation (facts and evidence) for their arguments and reasons for doing things, making choices, and advocating changes. Society needs informed, knowledgeable citizens that understand the field of law enforcement and its impact on social behavior.

Law enforcement is one means of formally supervising human behavior to ensure that the laws and regulations of a society are followed and that there is a certain amount of security and stability in society. The enforcement of law in all of its forms (statutes, regulations, administrative codes, ordinances, zoning laws, etc.) is legally authorized by

Different uniforms, same mission

Source: © David Hiller/Photodisc/Thinkstock

the concept of **police powers**, which is the government's lawful authority to enact regulations and laws related to health, safety, welfare, and morals. Police powers are carried out by the various levels of government in the United States, including the establishment and regulation of water and sewer systems, highway and transportation systems, fire protection, monetary regulatory systems, health and medical systems, park and recreation areas, general assistance to the economically deprived, and food processing. In short, police powers provide the authority for law enforcement officials to act.

The process of law enforcement is a formal one sanctioned in the United States by the people (voters) through their elected governmental bodies. Of the three branches of government in the United States, the law enforcement function is the responsibility of the executive branch. Executive branch officials include the President of the United States at the federal level, governors at the state level, and mayors at the local level. These officials and their representatives use their governmental authority in the appointment of law enforcement officials and the establishment of philosophies and general policies under which they will operate. The other branches of government also affect the ability of law enforcement officials

FIGURE 1-1 The U.S. Government's Involvement in Law Enforcement

BRANCH	Legislative	Executive	Judicial
OFFICES or TITLES	Congress	President	Courts
	Legislatures	Governors	Justices
	Boards	Trustees	Judges
	Councils	Mayors	Magistrates
LAW ENFORCEMENT ROLE	Enacts statutes, codes, ordinances and resolutions	Enforces legislative enactments	Reviews enforcement actions
	Establishes policy	Operates law enforcement agencies	Adjudicates legal disputes
		Initiates criminal prosecutions	Tries criminal cases
		Establishes agency procedures/rules	Issues orders and sanctions

to perform their jobs. The legislative branch provides the statutory authority under which law enforcement officials operate. This authority includes the lawful right to use different levels of force to achieve law enforcement goals and objectives, and it is the authorized use of this force that sets law enforcement officials apart from other occupations. Also, the legislative branch is formally responsible for defining behavior that is to be considered criminal in a particular jurisdiction. The judicial branch of government reviews the actions of law enforcement officials according to the established rules of constitutional law, civil law, criminal procedure, and evidence. This review normally occurs during judicial proceedings, such as initial hearings, preliminary hearings, suppression of evidence hearings, and trials (civil and criminal). The judicial branch, through the review process, creates rules for how law enforcement may operate in a given context; examples include the rules of interrogation, arrest, and the use of force. **Figure 1-1** summarizes the role of the three branches of government regarding the law enforcement function of the United States.

LAW ENFORCEMENT AND POLICING

The concept of law enforcement encompasses all levels (federal, state, and local) of the executive branch of government. It includes agencies that enforce administrative

codes and regulations (rules of agencies) and criminal laws related to the health, safety, and welfare of the people. A broad spectrum of officials with titles such as inspector, compliance officer, deputy, special agent, trooper, auditor, investigator, ranger, marshal, constable, or police officer can be found in law enforcement agencies. These officials may be employees of agencies that inspect the food supply (Department of Agriculture) and places of employment (Occupational Safety and Health Administration), investigate the causes of fires (State Fire Marshal), protect abused and neglected children (County Children Services), investigate airplane accidents (Federal Aviation Administration), conduct audits of government expenditures (State Auditor's Office), investigate criminal complaints (federal, state, and local law enforcement), and/or apprehend offenders (any agency with arrest authority).

The term **policing**, on the other hand, refers to a subset of law enforcement that applies to the process of regulating the general health, safety, welfare, and morals of society as it relates to criminal behavior. The policing function in the United States is primarily observed through the operations of the criminal justice system in the prevention, detection, investigation, and prosecution of crime. The personnel affiliated with agencies who are engaged in policing functions can be referred to as law enforcement personnel; however, in the United States, **police officials** are a unique group of law enforcement officials because they are armed and are authorized to use coercive and physical force, under certain conditions, when carrying out their duties. They are non-military, armed, governmental personnel who are granted the authority to prevent, detect, investigate, and prosecute criminal behavior and to apprehend alleged offenders. **Figure** 1-2 illustrates the policing agencies as a subset of the law enforcement community.

The focus of this text is on the policing agencies of the law enforcement community as identified in

Figure 1-2. However, it must be understood that the entire law enforcement community is quite extensive. The term law enforcement is also used to describe one of the many functions within policing agencies; in fact, the local policing agency personnel normally spend less than 20–30% of their time engaged in crime-related law enforcement functions (Greene and Klockars 1991, 279). Most of their time is spent on prevention, general public service, and order maintenance functions. This relationship is depicted in **Figure 1-3**. Today's professional police officials often do not want to emphasize their law enforcement functions; they prefer to be thought of for

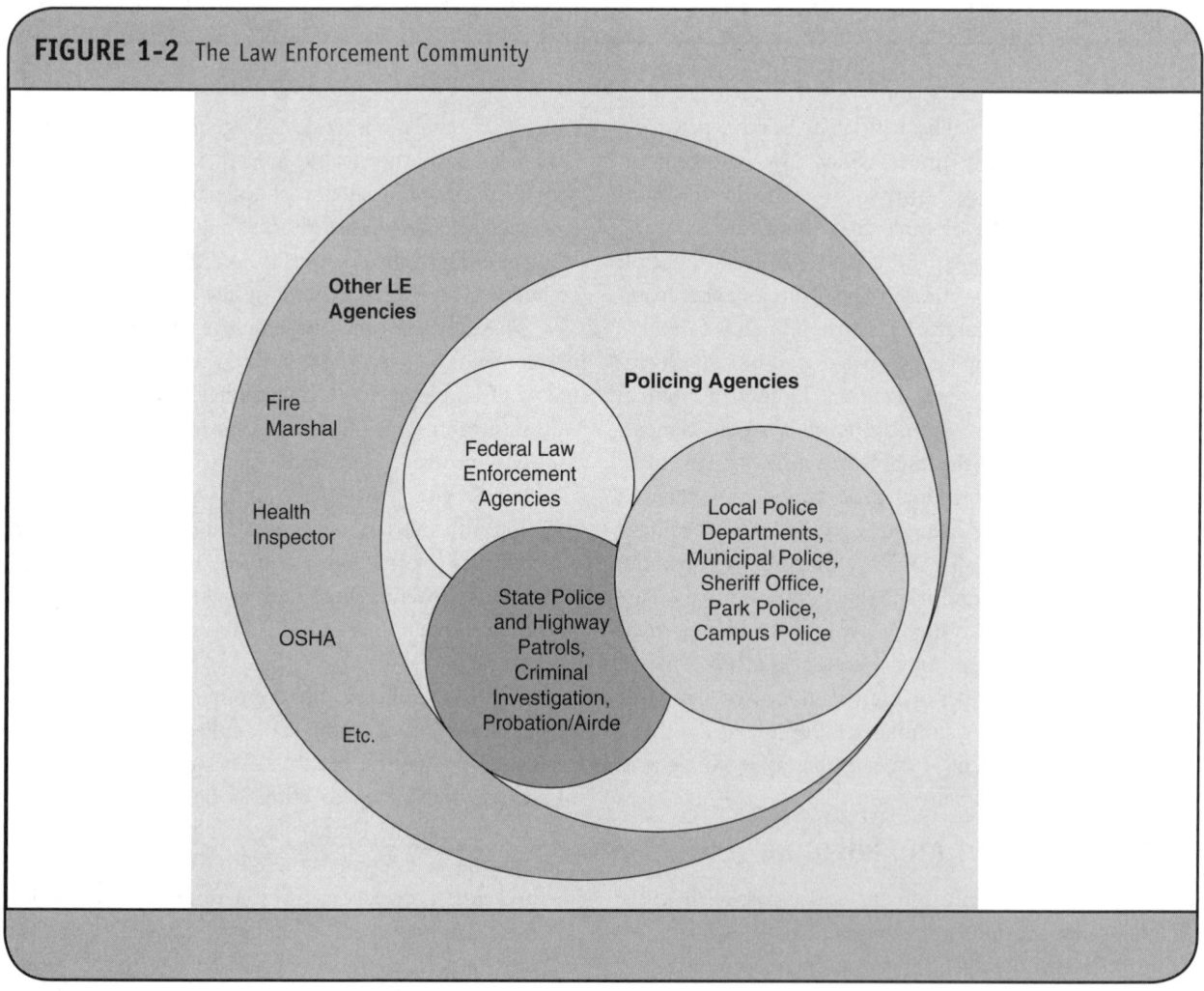

FIGURE 1-2 The Law Enforcement Community

Other LE Agencies

Fire Marshal

Health Inspector

OSHA

Etc.

Federal Law Enforcement Agencies

Policing Agencies

State Police and Highway Patrols, Criminal Investigation, Probation/Airde

Local Police Departments, Municipal Police, Sheriff Office, Park Police, Campus Police

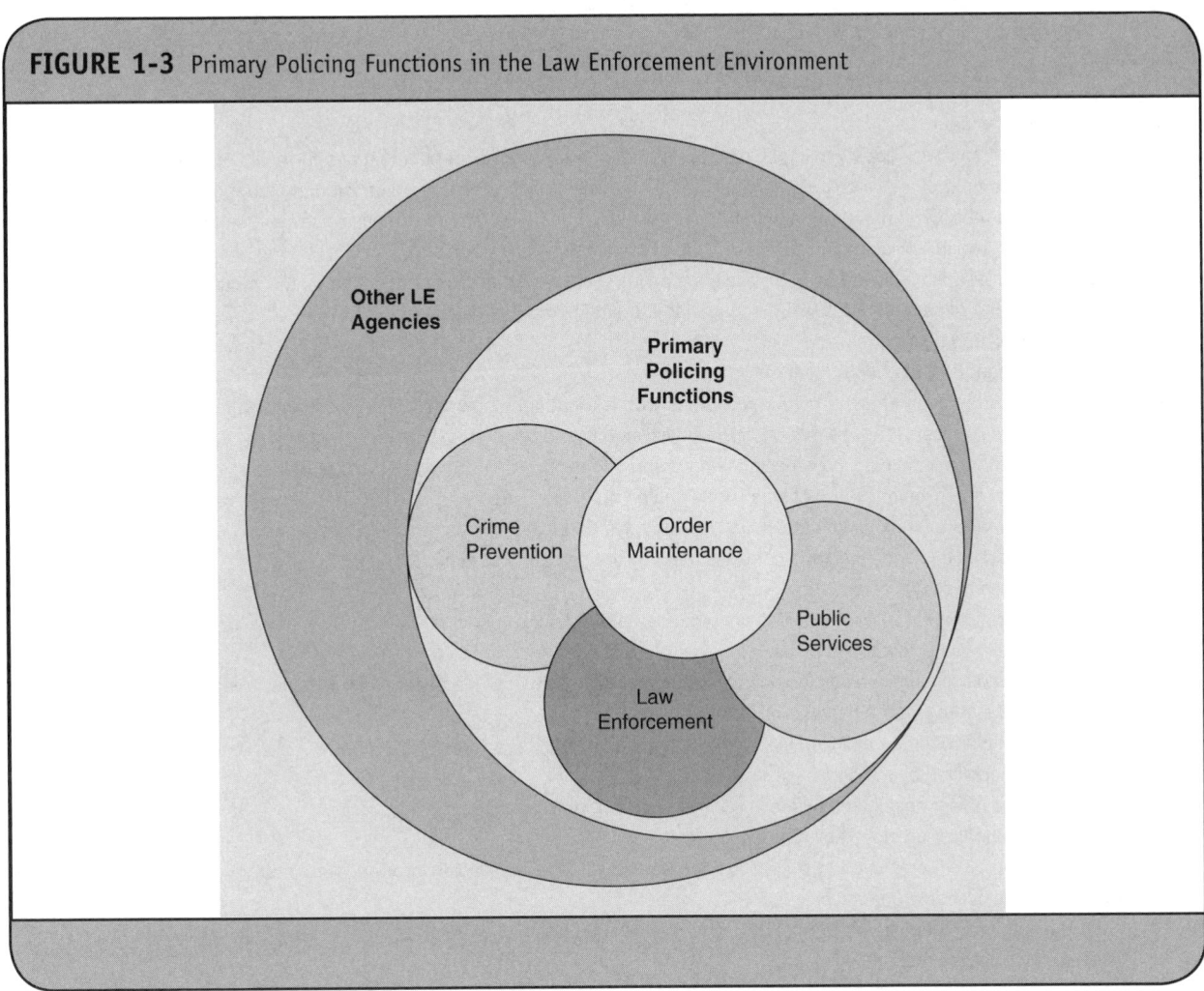

FIGURE 1-3 Primary Policing Functions in the Law Enforcement Environment

their service, especially the public safety functions which do not involve enforcement activities.

Some states add to the confusion of terms by using the phrase "peace officer" to refer to an entire class of policing officials who generally are authorized by statutory law to make arrests and serve warrants. A sample of such statutory language for the state of Ohio is reprinted in **Figure 1-4**. Notice that the state has 23 different types of peace officers. (It is also interesting to note that, for definitional purposes in Ohio, "sheriffs" and "state troopers" are not peace officers. However, there are other statutes that describe their authority as "law enforcement officers.")

As a student of the policing function, you should know that the terminology associated with police officials and their agency affiliations is important and occasionally confusing. Several terms (police powers, law enforcement, policing officials, and peace officer) have been used above and may appear to be very similar. It is essential to know that titles in the law enforcement field are important, and to know the different titles that distinguish policing officials. At the federal level, such officials are usually referred to as "agents" or "special agents," although members of the U.S. Marshal's Office are called "deputy marshals." At the state level they may be called "troopers," "state police officers," and/or "agents." At the local level,

FIGURE 1-4 The Definition of Peace Officer in Ohio

(A) "Peace officer" means:

(1) A deputy sheriff, marshal, deputy marshal, member of the organized police department of a township or municipal corporation, member of a township police district or joint township police district police force, member of a police force employed by a metropolitan housing authority … or township constable, who is commissioned and employed as a peace officer by a political subdivision of this state or by a metropolitan housing authority … ;

(2) A police officer who is employed by a railroad company and appointed and commissioned by the secretary of state … ;

(3) Employees of the department of taxation engaged in the enforcement of Chapter 5743 … ;

(4) An undercover drug agent;

(5) Enforcement agents of the department of public safety … ;

(6) An employee of the department of natural resources who is a natural resources law enforcement staff officer … a park officer … a forest officer … a preserve officer … a wildlife officer … or a state watercraft officer … ;

(7) An employee of a park district who is designated pursuant to section 511.232 or 1545.13 of the Revised Code;

(8) An employee of a conservancy district who is designated pursuant to section 6101.75 of the Revised Code;

(9) A police officer who is employed by a hospital that employs and maintains its own proprietary police department or security department, and who is appointed and commissioned by the secretary of state … ;

(10) Veterans' homes police officers … ;

(11) A police officer … employed by a qualified nonprofit corporation police department … ;

(12) A state university law enforcement officer … ;

(13) A special police officer employed by the department of mental health … or the department of developmental disabilities … ;

(14) A member of a campus police department … ;

(15) A member of a police force employed by a regional transit authority … ;

(16) Investigators appointed by the auditor of state … ;

(17) A special police officer designated by the superintendent of the state highway patrol … ;

(18) A special police officer employed by a port authority … ;

(19) A special police officer employed by a municipal corporation … at a municipal airport, or other municipal air navigation facility, that has scheduled operations … ;

(20) A police officer who is employed by an owner or operator of an amusement park that has an average yearly attendance in excess of six hundred thousand guests … ;

(21) A police officer who is employed by a bank, savings and loan association, savings bank, credit union, or association of banks, savings and loan associations, savings banks, or credit unions, … appointed and commissioned by the secretary of state … ;

(22) An investigator … of the bureau of criminal identification and investigation … commissioned … as a special agent … ;

(23) A state fire marshal law enforcement officer … ;

(24) A gaming agent employed under section 3772.03 of the Revised Code.

Source: Section 109.71(A) of the Ohio Revised Code, 2010; specific details omitted.

members of the county sheriff's office are "deputies" or "deputy sheriffs," and members of municipal and village police departments are called "police officers." The terms "constable" and "marshal" may be used in some jurisdictions at the local level, particularly in townships and villages. Members of federal and state forestry, park, or wildlife divisions may have the title of "ranger" or "warden." It does get confusing, but personnel in the law enforcement field do make these distinctions for reasons of courtesy, respect, and clarification of responsibilities. An analogy might be that most of us drive vehicles, but some insist on referring to their vehicles by name—Focus, Camry, Civic, Tacoma, and so on; not all vehicles are created equal, and some people want you to know that! In this same vein, police officials are of different types and serve different jurisdictions, and may also possess different legal authority under the law. All police officials are law enforcement officers, but not all law enforcement officers are called "police." It is possible that you may encounter some police officials who are sensitive about their titles. If you plan to become an employee in the criminal justice field, it is recommended that you pay attention to titles and job classifications.

The Courtroom—formal social control.

Source: © scoutingstock/ShutterStock, Inc.

Law enforcement personnel occupy unique positions in American society. They act with the authority of the state, meaning that they have been entrusted with the lawful right to enforce the law. Few people in the United States are given the authority (under certain carefully defined conditions) to use coercive force to carry out that duty. Some of these officials are uniformed (and therefore easily visible), and others are not. Regardless of the title or whether they wear a uniform or not, police officials in our society serve in a formal social control capacity. **Social control** is the process whereby a society encourages or enforces compliance with social norms, customs, and laws. There are various viewpoints regarding how limited or extensive this social control function should be. Let us examine in greater depth some of the aspects of the concept of social control.

LAW ENFORCEMENT AS SOCIAL CONTROL

Law enforcement is a societal function necessary for internal stability and security. Through the process of law enforcement, society exercises a form of social control of behavior, deviant or otherwise. Every society has social control mechanisms because they serve as a means of **socialization**, or the process of teaching the culture and norms of the society to its members.

Social control mechanisms are either formal or informal. Formal mechanisms generally refer to the units of the governing authority of the country; formal social control units in the United States include the executive, legislative, and judicial components of the governmental structure at all levels of government. Informal mechanisms include family, peers, religious organizations, significant others, and so on. **Figure 1-5** depicts a simplified version of selected social control mechanisms.

Social control mechanisms are not as simple to classify as Figure 1-5 might indicate. For example, where should education be placed? The educational process can be considered a formal control mechanism because it is often supported (via taxes) by government institutions. What you learn in school, however, is not simply the formal curriculum, but many other things as well (such as social skills, teamwork, manners, customs, etc.). Thus, it would fit equally well as an informal mechanism.

The social control mechanisms of a society do not exist in a vacuum. Social, economic, and political influences impact social control. These influences cause shifts in attitudes and values over time, in that they can cause a society to become more conservative or more liberal in its approach to controlling behavior. Social influences come mainly from the interaction between people and groups

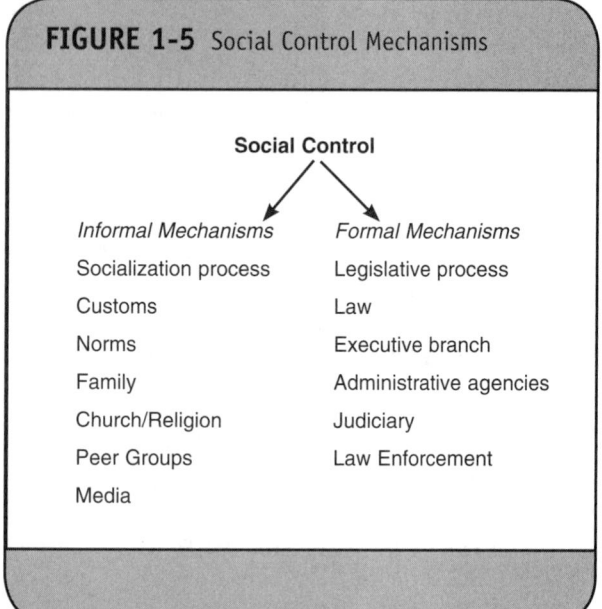

FIGURE 1-5 Social Control Mechanisms

Social Control

Informal Mechanisms	*Formal Mechanisms*
Socialization process	Legislative process
Customs	Law
Norms	Executive branch
Family	Administrative agencies
Church/Religion	Judiciary
Peer Groups	Law Enforcement
Media	

that is, the government's influence on controlling behavior? Or should the informal control mechanism be emphasized for guiding and influencing behavior? Ultimately, the question becomes one of how much influence the police should have on controlling people's behavior. A person who believes that the police should not have much of a role in controlling societal behavior would probably believe that there should be greater emphasis placed on the informal mechanisms (e.g., family, church, peer group), while one who believes the police should play an active role in controlling social behavior may emphasize tough policing measures to control behavior and greater use of the courts and formal punishments to influence behavior. Let us examine four common perspectives (viewpoints) on social control and their impact on policing in the United States. These perspectives are important because they reflect the diversity of ideas and beliefs of how our government agencies should function. They reflect how citizens view crime and influence government policies related to preventing and controlling criminal behavior.

and include forces such as customs, values and religion. Economic influences refer to resources (employment, income, and inflation) and the distribution of goods and services (transportation systems and businesses). Political factors include the policy-making process (elections, legislative actions, lobbying) and its related institutions (Congress, legislatures, and city councils). **Figure 1-6** identifies a number of examples of these influences upon society.

As with the placement of formal and informal social control mechanisms, the influencing factors are not easily categorized into social, economic, or political ones. For example, the factor of "poverty" is listed in all three categories. Is poverty a social condition? Is it an economic one? What influence do politics and public policy have on poverty? You could persuasively argue each of these positions, and there is validity to each. Likewise, "terrorism" is listed under political influences, but doesn't it also influence social and economic issues?

Social control issues raise several questions for law enforcement. How much of a role should policing have in the social control function in society? Should there be greater emphasis placed on formal control mechanisms,

FIGURE 1-6 Influences upon Social Control

Social	Economic	Political
Fads/Trends	Inflation/Recession	Major Parties/
Social	Unemployment	Elections
Movements	Welfare	Party in Power
Morality	Interest Rates	Wars/Conflicts
Religion	Poverty	Arms Race
Poverty	Energy Costs	Poverty
Homelessness	Consumer	Congress
Race Relations	Confidence	Patriotism
Abortion Debate	National Debt	Government
Crime	Crime Control	Regulation
Mass Media	Costs	Government Policy
Entertainment	Credit Rate	Foreign Relations
	Advertising	Foreign Aid
	Imports/Exports	Terrorism

FOUR PERSPECTIVES ON LAW ENFORCEMENT

There are several ways to view the world in which we live. Some people take a narrow viewpoint of certain issues, while others take a broader approach in perceiving situations. For example, in a verbal description about the design of a building, the architect may have one mental image or perspective, the builder a different one, and the prospective resident yet another. The architect may be concerned about how the building "fits" into the landscape or with the surrounding buildings. The builder is possibly thinking about cost and what types of materials are to be used. The resident could be concerned about the location of internal features, the size of rooms, utilities costs, and how soon it can be built. Each viewpoint is valid in and of itself, but the focus of the discussion can become very confusing if the three persons do not attempt to see the other person's approach to the building. In this example, a comprehensive set of blueprints and architectural drawings could help each person better perceive the others' concerns. In the following discussion, various approaches to viewing the field of law enforcement are presented. If a person is an advocate of one of these approaches and is discussing law enforcement with a person who holds a different viewpoint, there could be confusion or heated debate. The purpose here is to increase your understanding of each approach to help you reduce confusion and conflict over issues in policing, as sometimes situations are improved when one can see the other person's point of view. It must be remembered that these approaches are not totally independent of one another; occasionally some aspects overlap with other perspectives. It is also possible that a person can hold one perspective on a particular issue and a different perspective on another issue.

The Legal Perspective

One common approach to policing is that "the law is the law." The **legal perspective** is an approach that views behavior from a rule-based philosophy, in that the law is paramount and it is the guide for behavior that everyone must follow. Strong advocates of crime control and severe punishment for infractions often adopt this perspective. While there is merit in holding the law in high regard, one must be careful to evaluate a particular law's purpose and whether it is too restrictive. The legalistic approach is evident when someone says, "there should be a law against that." The person is implying that making the behavior a crime will stop people from doing it, or at least allow the authorities to intervene.

Most people in the United States obey the majority of laws. According to the 2009 crime victimization survey, about 6.6% of the population were victimized that year (Truman and Rand 2010) and there were approximately 13.6 million arrests made in the United States (Federal Bureau of Investigation 2010). It is believed that 20% of offenders commit 80% of the offences, at least for some types of crime (Clarke and Eck 2005). Of course, we cannot know who breaks the law when a crime is not officially reported (which happens, on average, nearly 50% of the time) or when there is no suspect to arrest (which happens almost as often, depending upon the type of crime), but evidence suggests that most of these crimes are committed by repeat offenders who will eventually be caught unless they "age out" and stop offending. As such, we can say the vast majority of men, and nearly all women, obey the law. This probably occurs for two reasons: (1) the majority of laws are deemed appropriate, and/or (2) most people respect the law. However, not everyone believes all the laws are appropriate. There also are different levels of legality. For example, gambling is generally against the law in most places, but certain types (e.g., bingo, horse racing, and lotteries) may not be, and some people believe that all forms of gambling should be legal. Some believe that crimes related to certain sexual actions (e.g., prostitution or having sex with children) should not be against the law, while others believe that the law should enforce traditional sexual morality. As any society becomes more diverse in terms of ethnic (national origin), racial, religious, and social backgrounds, agreement on what should be legal and illegal diminishes. This lack of agreement leads to many problems for policy makers as well as law enforcement officials, as too many laws against too many behaviors can reduce respect for the law.

In this perspective, police officials are placed in an awkward position, since they have sworn to enforce the laws of the nation and the state. They know that if they strictly enforce the law, many, many people would be arrested or given summonses; therefore, these officials must evaluate behavior in terms of "the letter-of-the-law" and "the spirit-of-the-law." If the letter-of-the-law is adhered to, then any violation of law results in official intervention by the police. If the spirit-of-the-law is followed, degrees of seriousness and contextual factors may be considered. Some laws may not be enforced at all, and some people who non-flagrantly violate the law may be handled informally (e.g., verbal reprimand, warnings) or with no intervention at all.

This evaluative process leads to the use of **discretion** and **selective enforcement**. Discretion is the process of making a choice among appropriate alternative courses of action. Although most state codes do not give peace officers the lawful right to use discretion, it has been professionally and judicially acknowledged. (Discretion is described in greater detail in Chapter 6.) The police simply cannot enforce every law that has been enacted; selective enforcement refers to enforcing those laws deemed appropriate to the situation or related to the priorities of the agency and the community. The opposite of selective enforcement, **full enforcement,** is enforcing all laws all the time, which, again, is not possible. One major drawback of the legal perspective is the belief that simply passing and enforcing criminal laws can solve most social control problems. A type of full enforcement directed toward certain problems, such as gang, drug, or traffic offenses, is called **zero tolerance**. It is exemplified when officers use every violation for justification to intervene in situations. It often occurs for targeted problem areas (driving under the influence) or types of offenses within a jurisdiction (gun violence). The empirical evidence, to date, fails to support this approach except in limited and rare circumstances, such as "hot spot" enforcement with directed patrols (Mazerolle et al. 2000), and if the efforts are not maintained after the initial implementation, the targeted problem usually resurfaces shortly after the zero tolerance

Terrorism here and abroad—the global perspective

Source: Courtesy of Photographer's Mate 2nd Class Bob Houlihan/U.S. Navy

Use of released U.S. Navy imagery does not constitute product or organizational endorsement of any kind by the U.S. Navy

approach goes away. Some recent studies related to school discipline and violence indicate ineffective results from current zero tolerance policies (American Psychological Association Zero Tolerance Task Force 2008; McNeal and Dunbar 2010).

The Public Policy Perspective

Public policy, broadly defined, is made up of the rules and regulations legislative bodies and agencies choose to establish. For example, if drug or spousal abuse requires regulation, a city council or state legislature may pass a law or an ordinance regarding domestic violence and drug dealing. Similarly, a bill might be passed to provide counseling for those charged with spousal abuse or drug use. Both of these actions are examples of public policy developed to address societal problems (Cochran and Malone 1995). This approach is similar to the legal approach we just discussed; however, greater emphasis is placed on the political process and on internal agency operations in the public policy approach.

Policy also is established in administrative organizations such as law enforcement agencies. A departmental policy regarding citizen complaints might set out the procedure for reviewing a complaint and detail the possible alternative solutions. Policy can also be made simply by consistently doing something in a particular way. For example, some police departments may tend to avoid domestic violence arrests or ignore concealed weapons found on citizens who have no criminal record. In both cases, a policy has been constructed and followed, even if it is not written.

Using a public policy approach to study law enforcement is important for a number of reasons. First, as the field of law enforcement evolves and becomes more **proactive** in community problems, more policy will be made at the department level. (A proactive response to problems is one that anticipates potential problems and tries to prevent the worst consequences from occurring.) Second, law enforcement managers may need legislative assistance in enacting policy because of current legal restrictions or because they lack the proper authority. Therefore, it is important to understand the political nature of the policy-making process and the importance of defending or justifying a policy in an appropriate manner.

Formal policy making at the agency level is a function of the executive team. The chief of police, sheriff, or department head is generally the final authority on policy (although it might be a safety director or city manager). Policy cannot be made without considering internal procedure and management, legal and political influences, and community expectations. Internal management issues might include union reactions, current contract language, and officer morale or resistance. Community expectations might come from meetings held with civic groups or from public meetings on selected issues (e.g., curfew enforcement, treatment of juveniles, or rumors of a growing gang influence). Political influences can relate to local politics and the campaign promises of elected officials who have some influence over the department's budget. Other forces that impact policy development and evaluation are pending litigation over the actions taken by officers and severe fiscal problems that may cause layoffs or a cut in agency services (Gilmour and Halley, 1994). Issues related to political concerns and their impact on law enforcement agencies are discussed in later chapters.

Border patrol agents and a detainee

Source: Courtesy of CBP Border Patrol, photo by Geral L. Nino

Establishing policy within an agency is a three-step process. The first step is the identification of the need for policy. This often becomes apparent when things do not function properly or serious problems have developed, such as an officer who used deadly force when not authorized to do so. However, identification of policy needs also occurs during agency evaluations and reviews of existing policies when compared to model (suggested) policy. The professional literature and associations often publish the experiences of other agencies in terms of policy.

The second step involves implementation, or putting the policy into action. Obviously, this relates to how the written word is translated into practice by the persons affected; this means that policy must be properly interpreted, conveyed, and practiced by the agency's personnel. This often involves meetings and training sessions to explain the policy, its rationale, and significance. Policy implementation is a complex interaction of organizational and environmental variables, and frequently policies will fail not because they were bad policies, but because they were poorly implemented. This is particularly true in the justice system inasmuch as there are so many different institutions with an interest in policy outcomes (Lemley and Russell 2002).

The third step in establishing policy is evaluation. In the current law enforcement environment, it is critical to evaluate the effectiveness of all law enforcement policies to ensure that the anticipated improvements have actually occurred. Policy effectiveness can be evaluated through periodic assessment of officer performance, critical incidents, threatened litigation, selected agency measures, and current vulnerability. For example, the policy under Tennessee law prior to 1985 permitted police officers to fire upon fleeing suspects regardless of the threat the suspect posed to officers or others. In *Tennessee v. Garner* (471 U.S. 1), the U.S. Supreme Court struck down the policy, setting a common law "defense of self or others" when facing an "imminent threat" as the new standard. Subsequent analysis demonstrated that these changes caused the Memphis Police Department to substantially alter its behavior in regard to officer-involved shootings (Sparger and Giacopassi, 1992). It should be noted that the evaluation process also leads to the identification of weaknesses and needs for future policy; therefore, the process becomes cyclical and permits continuous updating of policy. Each aspect of policymaking—identification,

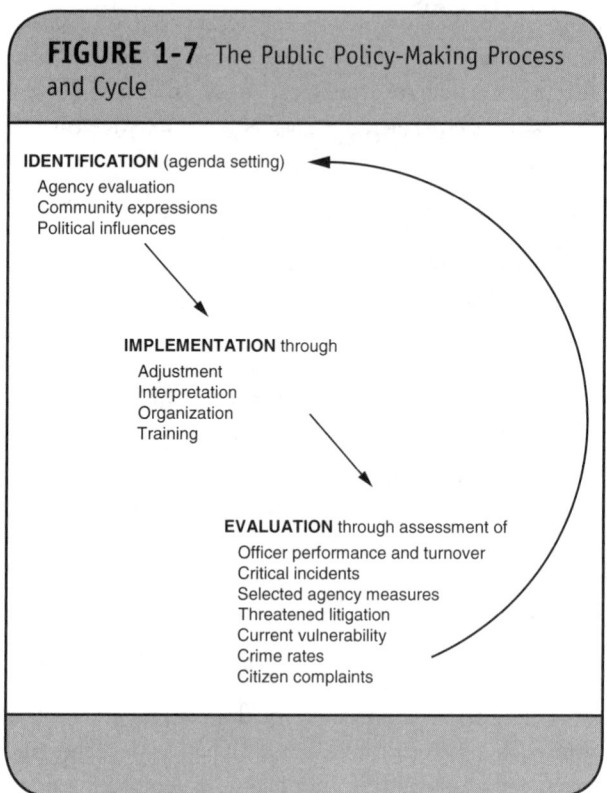

FIGURE 1-7 The Public Policy-Making Process and Cycle

IDENTIFICATION (agenda setting)
Agency evaluation
Community expressions
Political influences

IMPLEMENTATION through
Adjustment
Interpretation
Organization
Training

EVALUATION through assessment of
Officer performance and turnover
Critical incidents
Selected agency measures
Threatened litigation
Current vulnerability
Crime rates
Citizen complaints

implementation, and evaluation—must be understood for an agency to function effectively as we enter the next century (Fischer 1995). **Figure 1-7** summarizes the policymaking process.

The Systems Perspective

Law enforcement can also be viewed from the context of **systems theory**. This approach views the entire context (environment) in which an issue exists by analyzing all the forces or influences (or drivers) impacting on it; in other words, law enforcement or a particular agency is perceived by analyzing all the influences upon it from the environment in which it operates. Systems theory is more easily understood if one understands the concept of subsystems. As an example, let us consider a person sitting at home in an air-conditioned room. If the focus of discussion is on the person's body, we could use systems theory to examine the situation. The body itself is made up of subsystems—the nervous subsystem, the respiratory subsystem, the cardiovascular subsystem, the skeletal subsystem, and the digestive subsystem, for example. When all of the subsystems function properly, the body as a whole functions well. But, if something affects one subsystem, it can impact the others. If some external force frightens the person, say a bolt of lightning striking the tree outside the room, various subsystems can be affected: fright causes the heart to beat faster, breathing may become shallow and rapid, digestive juices are released by the nervous system, and the stomach may become upset, or the sudden jolt and noise may additionally cause the body to jump or swing around quickly, bumping into a table and breaking a finger bone, causing pain. The subsystems are interconnected, and their functions impact the others. In organization theory, the "biological model" is often employed to compare organizational functioning with that of a biological system, such as the ecosystem or the human body. In this regard, internal and external influences are all considered, producing a much more robust and complete view of organizational functioning in the real world.

In this example, the systems theory approach would describe the person's body and the immediate surroundings of the room and house as the "environment." This approach attempts to consider the forces or influences of the environment and their impact upon the entity or issue being considered. Taking a systems perspective to the earlier discussion of social control and its influences (Figures 1-4 and 1-5) would mean viewing each factor as having a possible impact on the others as well as an impact on social control. In other words, the various types of social control and the different types of social, economic, and political influences that impact it are interrelated. The best symbol to illustrate the systems approach is that of the atom. The nucleus becomes the issue being considered (e.g., the concept of social control or the police agency as an organization), and the orbiting electrons and their paths become the factors that influence the issue being discussed. **Figure 1-8** is a systems approach illustration of the concept of social control with its various influence subsystems, and **Figure 1-9** is a systems representation of a law enforcement agency (LEA) with its various subsystems in today's society.

All of the subsystems interrelate and influence each other. When applying this model to policing, try to think of the illustrations as three-dimensional.

Viewing law enforcement from a systems perspective is important because it ensures that we consider the impact and influence of other environmental forces in our society. It assists in understanding the impact and possible implications of decisions and to anticipate their impact on other subsystems. We say that, in a systems approach, everything affects everything else. It is a view that makes one consider issues that otherwise might be overlooked. For example, what if a neo-Nazi or Ku Klux Klan group seeks a permit to hold a rally in a city? City officials must consider all the implications (forces) and outcomes (effects) to the decision. Examples of questions to be considered regarding this matter include:

- If denied, might the group have standing to sue the agency for a breach of constitutional rights of freedom of expression?
- Is the city willing and financially capable of fighting the matter in court?
- If the permit is granted, will the rally be orderly or will there be opposition groups present seeking a confrontation?
- Might people get injured and need medical attention?
- Will officers have to work overtime to provide necessary security?
- Will the budget of the department permit overtime to be used?
- Does the city policy require such groups to have insurance coverage for any damages that may be incurred as a direct result of the rally?
- Does the permit require the group to pay overtime to the officers providing security to the group?
- Will the group provide any security of its own?
- What are the public media/community relations ramifications?
- Who protects the rest of the city when most of the officers are protecting the rally?
- Can you enlist the assistance (mutual aid) of state and neighboring law enforcement agencies? If so, what formal process must be undertaken to do so?

FIGURE 1-8 The Systems Theory Applied to Social Control

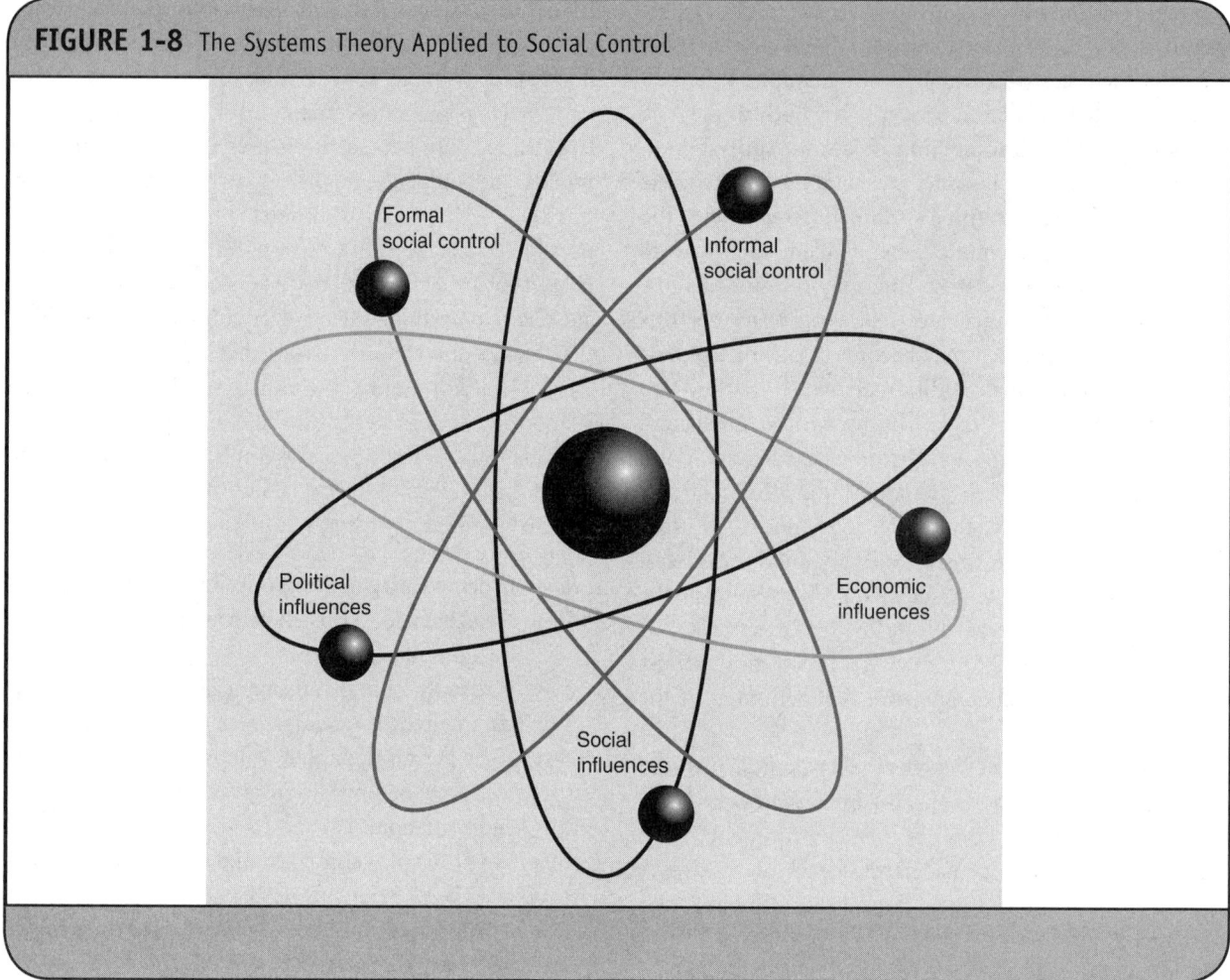

In short, the systems approach assists in analyzing issues from a broader perspective, one in which the agency is just one entity (subsystem) among many in the total environment. In this example, the total environment includes several city officials such as the mayor, law director or prosecutor, council members, the fire department, ambulance/medical services, and the city services director.

The Global Perspective (or Extended Systems Approach)

The **global perspective** is an extension of the systems approach. In addition to recognizing the immediate environmental influences, it gives significant recognition to world events and the international influences upon the agency. The instability of a government can cause problems for other countries. Many great societies and nations have risen and fallen during the last 3000 years. During the twentieth century, for example, many government officials in powerful countries have lost their right to govern. Some lost that right as a result of war (e.g., World Wars I and II, the war in Vietnam), and some as a result of internal conflict and unrest (e.g., East Germany and the former Union of Soviet Socialist Republics during the early 1990s). Changes continue to occur in trouble spots

FIGURE 1-9 Systems Approach Applied to Law Enforcement Agencies

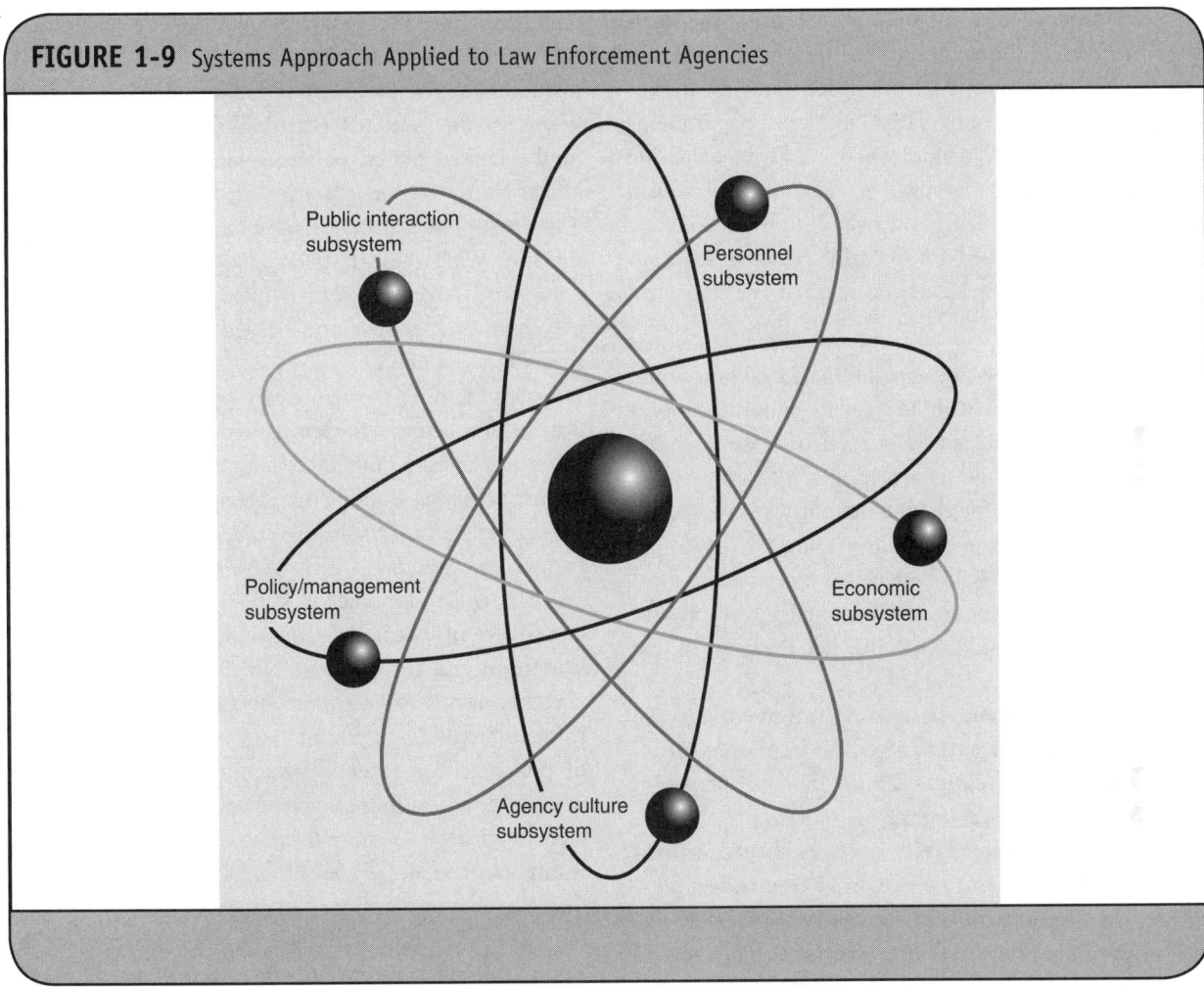

around the world. Events in the Middle East, Africa, and East Asia are a constant threat to regional and even world peace. The terrorist attacks of the 1990s and post-9/11 are changing the way people and governments view the world. Over $1.5 billion was spent on security and law enforcement protection at the 2004 Olympic Games in Greece, and the estimated cost for the 2012 London Olympics is $2.3 billion (Merrick, 2008). The 2003–2004 Iraq War and the security struggle that followed drew the world's attention to terrorism and the effects of overthrowing a harsh dictator; the international and national divide about the actions of the United States in Iraq will continue for years.

According to the National Defense Council Foundation (2004), during 1995 there were 71 "little wars" across the globe, which was double the tally of 1989, while in 2002 the number of conflicts had dropped to 53. According to the United States Institute of Peace (2010), there were over 100 active conflicts around the world by 2010, and the U.S. State Department reported that during 2009, "ethnic, racial, and religious tensions led to violent conflicts and serious human rights violations and fueled or exacerbated more than 30 wars or internal armed conflicts" (U.S. Department of State 2010). According to the State Department, in 1999 there were 1649 U.S. law enforcement personnel permanently assigned overseas for crime fighting, intelligence, liaison, and training purposes; that number has risen since 9/11 but exact numbers are not made public. Today, some large city police departments in the United States have officers overseas for gathering intelligence related to investigative and counter-terrorism activities. Currently, figures on overseas assignments are not generally published for security reasons; however, some statistics recently have been released (Fuentes 2007 and Ford 2007):

- The FBI has 60 fully-operational Legal offices and 15 sub-offices, with 165 agents and 103 support personnel assigned for a total of 268 employees stationed around the world.
- At least 696 officials in 63 countries work for the Drug Enforcement Administration.
- The U.S. Marshal's Service has a permanent presence in three countries with a total of seven agents. In addition, USMS currently has 16 agents in Iraq and 5 in Afghanistan.
- Immigration and Customs Enforcement had 298 investigative agents in 52 offices in 41 countries.
- Customs and Border Patrol has 943 personnel deployed to 28 countries.
- The U.S. Secret Service operates abroad with 54 agents staffed to 19 offices in 15 countries.
- The Department of State has approximately 590 Regional Security Officer special agents assigned to 202 Foreign Service posts throughout the world, making it the most widely represented U.S. law enforcement agency overseas.
- The Container Security Initiative (staffed by unarmed personnel) is in place at 58 ports overseas in 35 countries.

One may ask what world events in other countries have to do with policing in the United States? The answer is a great deal, depending on where you are. The United States, as a prosperous world leader, is often called upon to provide military and humanitarian aid to those in need. Although the country's success to date places it in this position, continuing this role in the future may become more challenging. The opportunity exists to assist many people in their struggles to survive and to relieve their pain and suffering, but realizing these goals reduces the resources available for American needs of all types, including the enhancement of public safety. For example, whenever the National Guard or Reserves is activated in the United States, police departments are adversely affected since officers are often members of these forces. The call-up of thousands of military reservists during the Iraq Wars created staffing hardships for many law enforcement agencies in the United States. By law, agencies cannot replace personnel called to active duty, and if they fill the spot temporarily, the agencies pay for training knowing (as does the temporary officer) that when the other officer returns, the temporary officer is out of a job. When you consider that more than 50% of agencies in the United States have fewer than 50 officers to cover three shifts over seven days, losing even one person, let alone two, is devastating.

The global approach is very similar to the systems perspective in that it views the situation in terms of outside forces and environmental impact. The major difference between the two is that the global approach places primary focus on the international influences on the field of policing. The federal law enforcement community, without doubt, is more involved and concerned with the global approach than are local police, but this approach is important to all U.S. law enforcement officials because they must be alert for possible trouble in the United States because of situations in foreign countries. Terrorist activities are no longer confined to other countries, as witnessed by the 9/11 attacks in the United States. Immediately following the attacks, many U.S. agencies assigned additional personnel to protect Muslim neighborhoods, businesses, and mosques. Other examples of international incidents include the bombing of Pan Am flight 103, returning to the United States from Europe in 1988, killing 270, and the 1993 bombing of the World Trade Center in New York City that killed six and injured more than 1,000. On March 29, 2010, two female suicide bombers killed 38 passengers in two attacks, timed 30 minutes apart, on the Moscow subway system; U.S. transit systems were put on high alert and passengers on New York City and Washington, D.C. subway systems were subject to random inspections (CBS/AP 2010). Alerts also were triggered by an attack on a train in Spain in 2004 that killed 191 people, and by four attacks on the London subway system in July 2005 that killed 52.

These kinds of events have increased the cautionary measures law enforcement must take to protect national security and local public safety. For example, since 9/11, the Transportation Security Agency has replaced private screeners at airports, the Department of Homeland Security was created, and the number of FBI/state/local joint terrorism task forces has risen from 34 to 106 (U.S. Department of Justice 2010).

The global approach to social control realizes that law enforcement is a global challenge and is impacted by global events. While most law enforcement personnel in the United States are probably not affected greatly by global events, more have been affected in the last decade than in previous decades. The professional law enforcement officer understands the importance of world events and their possible impact on policing domestically.

There were 55 million international visitors to the United States in 2009 (U.S. Department of Commerce 2010) and, unfortunately, some of them have contact with law enforcement and criminal justice officials in their official capacities. The top ten cities for overseas visitors are listed in **Table 1-1**, along with their market share of the visitors and the approximate number of visitors to the city.

Officers in larger cities also often have contact with persons possessing (and claiming to possess) **diplomatic immunity**. Diplomatic immunity means that the person enjoys certain privileges and immunities from the laws of the United States and its political subdivisions. The legal basis for diplomatic immunity and other issues relating to consular affairs stems from a multilateral agreement called the **Vienna Convention on Consular Relations** (VCCR), which was completed in 1963. The provisions of the VCCR became effective in the United States in December of 1969. Currently, over 165 different countries are party to the VCCR. The provisions related to actions by law enforcement officials in the United States are summarized in **Table 1-2**. While some people have difficulty understanding why members of the foreign diplomatic corps should not be subject to our country's laws, we must remember that U.S. diplomats abroad also enjoy diplomatic immunity from the laws of other countries. It should be remembered that most diplomats enjoy their assignments in the

TABLE 1-1 Overseas* Visitors to Select U.S. Cities in 2009

2009 Rank	City	2009 Market Share	Visitors (thousands)
1	New York City	32.8%	7792
2	Miami	11.2%	2661
3	Los Angeles	10.6%	2518
4	Orlando	10.1%	2399
5	San Francisco	9.4%	2233
6	Las Vegas	7.8%	1853
7	Washington, D.C.	6.5%	1544
8	Honolulu	6.3%	1497
9	Boston	4.8%	1140
10	Chicago	4.7%	1117

Source: U.S. Department of Commerce, Office of Travel and Tourism Industries, May 2010.

*Excludes Canada and Mexico.

United States and seldom are a problem for public law enforcement. Diplomats are not immune from their home country's laws, and generally, they do not want to be sent home for what is considered serious criminal behavior in the United States.

The VCCR also affects every local, state, and federal law enforcement agency and every U.S. citizen that travels abroad. Other provisions of the treaty address the duties and responsibilities of law enforcement agencies when a foreign national is detained or arrested. In short, persons who are not citizens, including foreign visitors, legal permanent aliens, and illegal aliens, have the right to have their consulate notified of their detention or arrest. These treaties also give consular officers the right to have access to their citizens in these situations. Criminal justice officials are obligated by law to comply with the provisions of the VCCR. The U.S. State Department provides publications and training materials on such matters. Failure to comply can cause an

TABLE 1-2 Diplomatic and Consular Privileges and Immunities from Criminal Jurisdiction

Summary of Law Enforcement Aspects

Category	May Be Arrested or Detained	Residence May be Entered Subject to Ordinary Procedures	May Be Issued Traffic Citation	May Be Subpoenaed as Witness	May Be Prosecuted	Recognized Family Member
Diplomatic						
Diplomatic Agent	No[1]	No	Yes	No	No	Same as sponsor (full immunity and inviolability).
Member of Administrative and Technical Staff	No[1]	No	Yes	No	No	Same as sponsor (full immunity and inviolability).
Service Staff	Yes	Yes	Yes	Yes	Yes	No immunity or inviolability.[2]
Consular						
Career Consular Officers	Yes, if for a felony and pursuant to a warrant.[2]	Yes[4]	Yes	No—for official acts. Testimony may not be compelled in any case.	No—for official acts. Otherwise, yes.[2]	No immunity or inviolability.[2]
Honorary Consular Officers	Yes	Yes	Yes	No—for official acts. Yes, in all other cases.	No—for official acts. Otherwise, yes.	No immunity or inviolability.
Consular Employees	Yes[2]	Yes	Yes	No—for official acts. Yes, in all other cases.	No—for official acts. Otherwise, yes.[2]	No immunity or inviolability.[2]
International Organizations						
International Organizations Staff[3]	Yes[3]	Yes[3]	Yes	No—for official acts. Yes, in all other cases.	No—for official acts. Otherwise, yes.[3]	No immunity or inviolability.
Diplomatic-Level Staff of Missions to International Organizations	No[1]	No	Yes	No	No	Same as sponsor (full immunity and inviolability).
Support Staff of Missions to International Organizations	Yes	Yes	Yes	No—for official acts. Yes, in all other cases.	No—for official acts. Otherwise, yes.	No immunity or inviolability.

1. Reasonable constraints, however, may be applied in emergency circumstances involving self-defense, public safety, or the prevention of serious criminal acts.
2. This table presents general rules. Particularly in the cases indicated, the employees of certain foreign countries may enjoy **higher** levels of privileges and immunities on the basis of special bilateral agreements.
3. A small number of senior officers are entitled to be treated identically to "diplomatic agents."
4. Note that consular residences are sometimes located within the official conular premises. In such cases, **only** the official office space is protected from police entry.

Source: U.S. department of State: http://state.gov/documents/organization/20047.pdf

"international incident" over a person's detention or arrest. In April 2010, three Houston Police Department officers arrested and injured a Chinese diplomat following a traffic stop. The officers were placed on desk duty during the investigation, and within a few weeks, local law enforcement personnel attended a special training session on dealing with representatives of foreign governments (Turner, 2010). One summary of the requirements pertaining to foreign nationals provides the following six guidelines (U.S. Department of State 2010, 2):

- When foreign nationals from most countries are arrested or detained, they may, upon request, have their consular officers notified without delay of their arrest or detention, and may have their communications to their consular officers forwarded without delay. In addition, foreign nationals must be advised of this information without delay. (See examples in **Figures 1-10** and **1-11**.)
- For foreign nationals of some countries, consular officers must be notified of the arrest or detention of a foreign national even if the foreign national does not request or want notification.
- Consular officers are entitled to communicate with and have access to their nationals in detention, and to provide consular assistance to them, including arranging for legal representation.
- When a law enforcement or other government official becomes aware of the death, serious injury, or serious illness of a foreign national, consular officers must be notified.
- When a guardianship or trusteeship is being considered with respect to a foreign national who is a minor or an incompetent adult, consular officers must be notified.
- When a foreign ship wrecks or a foreign aircraft crashes in U.S. territory, consular officers must be notified.

THE APPROACH OF THIS TEXT

The field of law enforcement is one component of the process of social control. The focus of this text is on crime-related law enforcement services provided by those agencies commonly referred to as the police. The approach taken in our presentation is primarily the systems approach, which encompasses all the forces or influences in society that impact policing. Among those influences are issues related to politics, public policy, social trends, international events, and national issues. The text describes the background of the field of policing: where it has been, where it is now, and where future challenges remain. Basic elements of management and organizational principles are also included.

The systems approach to policing recognizes the significant involvement of government and public policy makers in setting goals and objectives for law enforcement. By taking a systems perspective to policing, the text incorporates selected aspects from the other perspectives of law enforcement. In the systems approach, it is understood that sometimes the other perspectives have merit in certain situations. Sometimes public policy issues are very important to the issues being discussed, and sometimes an officer must have a global perspective to understand the "big picture" of the events that he or she is managing. Whatever the situation, professional law enforcement personnel must understand the power and influence of their office. They make policy-related decisions and/or carry out policy every day they are on duty. They affect the lives of people they encounter, and they possess some of the most powerful discretion of any person working in the criminal justice system.

The chapters that follow should be viewed from a systems perspective. For example, the history of policing influences present-day mindsets; it has an effect on public policy, and it helps shape our culture. Law enforcement was first formed during the emergence of political influence in the administration of governmental affairs. Police from the 1830s to the early 1900s were brutal, untrained, and politically controlled. In reaction to that, policing organizations became more professional and more separated from communities, and this produced its own set of problems in the 1960s. The result was the reform movement now known as the "community era," which involved community policing, problem-oriented policing, and similar themes. These changes influenced the design of organizations and their relationship with the surrounding environment. Those structures and external political forces influence the selection and training of law enforcement

FIGURE 1-10 Suggested Statements to Arrested or Detained Foreign Nationals

*Statement 1: For All Foreign Nationals Except Those
from "Mandatory Notification" Countries*

As a non U.S. citizen who is being arrested or detained, you may request that we notify your country's consular officers here in the United States of your situation. You may communicate with your consular officers. A consular officer may be able to help you obtain legal representation, and may contact your family and visit you in detention, among other things. If you want us to notify your consular officers, you can request this notification now, or at any time in the future. Do you want us to notify your consular officers at this time?

YES   NO

Printed name: _____   Witness: _____
Signature: _____   Date: _____

*Statement 2: For Foreign Nationals
from "Mandatory Notification" Countries*

Because of your nationality, we are required to notify your country's consular officers here in the United States that you have been arrested or detained. We will do this as soon as possible. In addition, you may communicate with your consular officers. You are not required to accept their assistance but your consular officers may be able to help you obtain legal representation, and may contact your family and visit you in detention, among other things. Please sign to show that you have received this information.

Printed name: _____   Witness: _____
Signature: _____   Date: _____

Source: U.S. Department of State (September 2010). Consular Notification and Access, 3rd Edition. Washington, D.C.: U.S. Department of State, p. 75.

personnel and help to further influence the internal cultures of organizations. History, culture, and politics influence our legal mechanisms that place limitations on the policing community. All of the social, economic, and political forces within our complex society affect the type of policing services delivered to the public, and these forces shape the future challenges and influence the professionalism of law enforcement personnel. Everything affects everything else; nothing is simple in today's society. This may sound either too simplistic or horribly complex. Organizations are not isolated from financial crises (e.g., loss of a major employer in the community), political events (e.g., a police shooting and subsequent calls for reform), or social change (e.g., patterns of migration and immigration). The list of potential sources of influence is endless, requiring the United States to have a global and systemic perspective.

SUMMARY

This chapter introduced you to the field of law enforcement. It described law enforcement as one of the formal processes of social control, which means that it is one of society's attempts to obtain compliance with the law. The common term "policing" is defined as one form of law enforcement that emphasizes the prevention, detection, investigation, and prosecution of crime, as well as providing numerous other services to society. Policing officials are distinguished from other law enforcement officials by the fact that they are non-military government personnel who are armed and may use coercive and physical

---

FIGURE 1-11 Arrest and Detention of Foregin Nationals

SPANISH
*Statement 1: For All Foreign Nationals Except Those
from "Mandatory Notification" Countries*

Por no ser ciudadano de los Estados Unidos, y estar arrestado o detenido, usted puede pedirnos que notifiquemos de su situacion a los funcionarios consulares de su país en los Estados Unidos. Tambien puede commuicarse con los funcionario consular de su país puede ayudarle a conseguir asesoramiento legal, y tambien puede ponerse en contacto con su familia y visitarle en el lugar de detencion. Si usted desea que notifiquemos a los funcionarios consulares de su país, puede solicitarlo ahora o en cualquier oportunidad en el futuro. ¿Desea que notifiquemos a los funcionarios consulares de su país?

SÍ (YES)	NO (NO)
Nombre _____	Testigo: _____
Printed Name	Witness
Firma: _____	Fecha: _____
Signature	Date

*Statement 2: For Foreign Nationals
from "Mandatory Notification" Countries*

Debido a su nacionalidad, estamos obligados a notificar a los funcionarios consulares de su país en los Estados Unidos que used ha sido arrestado o detenido. Haremos esta notificacion lo mas pronto possible. Ademas, usted puede comunicarse con los funcionarios consulares de su pais. Usted no está obligado a aceptar su ayuda, pero esos funcionarios pueden ayudarle, entre otras cosas, a conseguir asesoramiento legal, y tambien pueden ponerse en contacto con su familia y visitarle en el lugar de detencion. Sirvase firmar para indicar que ha recibido esta informacion.

Nombre _____	Testigo: _____
Printed Name	Witness
Firma: _____	Fecha: _____
Signature	Date

Source: U.S. Department of State (September 2010). Consular Notification and Access, 3rd Edition. Washington, D.C.: U.S. Department of State, p. 92.

---

force under certain conditions. Since policing is a form of social control, the differences between formal (government sponsored) and informal control mechanisms have been presented here as well. Of particular concern are the many influences upon social control, which have been presented as social, economic, and political factors. These factors influence the police function in every community within the country.

The chapter described the various perspectives to law enforcement in a social control context. The four approaches—legal, public policy, systems, and global—have each been presented and applied to the field of law enforcement. The legal approach emphasizes the enforcement of the law; however, since full enforcement is not possible, discretion and selective enforcement becomes prevalent. The public policy approach emphasizes the process of developing and implementing policy, which can have consequent effects on the delivery of police services to the community. The systems approach recognizes the importance of all the environmental influences in society, including international influences. The global approach is an extension of the systems perspective; however, it places greater emphasis and priority on international events and influence. Although global issues are very important, they do not yet dominate the daily operation of the 17,000-plus law enforcement agencies in the United States.

The recognition and identification of the multiple influences upon social control is vital to providing effective policing to a complex, democratic society. While there is some overlap among the four approaches to policing, the differences are significant. The legal approach recognizes the formal and informal influence of law and sanctions on members of society. The public policy approach emphasizes the systematic approach to policing (among other things) through the governmental policy-making process. The systems approach attempts to understand how the environmental forces of politics, law, community, and economics effect policing. The global perspective emphasizes the larger impact of world events on the law enforcement function. While each approach has merit, the focus of this text is primarily from a systems approach, which, in essence, recognizes the impact and contribution of all the other approaches as they relate to one another.

Critical Thinking Questions

1. Using the concepts described in this chapter, explain the following statement: "All police officials are law enforcement officials, but not all law enforcement officials are police officials."

2. How does policing relate to the concept of social control? Which is the broader concept?

3. Using the four perspectives (approaches) on the law enforcement function presented in this chapter, identify the similarities and differences among them.

4. Using the systems approach to policing, what are two social factors, two economic factors, and two political factors that influence policing at your local level of government?

5. What is the significance of the Vienna Convention on Consular Relations?

CHAPTER SPECIFIC INTERNET LINKS

Department of Commerce, Office of Travel and Tourism Industries: http://tinet.ita.doc.gov/

International Crisis Group: http://www.crisisgroup.org/.

Federal Bureau of Investigation, Legal Attaché Offices: http://www.fbi.gov/contact/legat/legat.htm.

Flashpoints: Guide to World Conflicts: http://www.flashpoints.info/start.html.

Legal Aspects of Diplomatic Immunity and Privileges: http://www.state.gov/documents/organization/20047.pdf

United States Institute of Peace. Countries & Continents. http://www.usip.org/countries-continents.

CHAPTER GLOSSARY

Diplomatic immunity—a phrase used to describe certain privileges of foreign government representatives who are not subject to the laws of the United States and its political subdivisions. The legal basis for diplomatic immunity and other issues relating to consular affairs stems from the Vienna Convention on Consular Relations.

Discretion—the process of making a choice among appropriate alternative courses of action.

Full enforcement—enforcing all laws all of the time.

Global perspective—an extension of the systems approach that, in addition to recognizing the immediate environmental influences, gives significant recognition to world events and the international influences upon the agency.

Law enforcement—a society's formal attempt to obtain compliance with the established rules, regulations, and laws of that society.

Legal perspective—an approach that views behavior from a rule-based philosophy, in that the law is paramount and is the guide for behavior that everyone must follow.

Police officials—a special group of non-military law enforcement officials who are armed and authorized to use coercive and physical force (under certain conditions) when carrying out their duties to prevent, detect, investigate, and prosecute criminal behavior.

Police powers—refers to the government's lawful authority to enact regulations and laws related to health, safety, welfare, and morals.

Policing—the process of regulating the general health, safety, welfare, and morals of society.

Proactive—a response that anticipates the direction of problems and tries to prevent the worst consequences from occurring.

Public policy perspective—a viewpoint that emphasizes the rules and regulations that legislative bodies and agencies choose to establish for social control.

Representative democracy—a form of government where the people choose or elect others to make legislative and executive decisions, particularly at the state and national levels of government.

Selective enforcement—enforcing those laws deemed appropriate to the situation or related to the priorities of the agency and the community.

Social control—the processes whereby a society encourages or enforces compliance with social norms, customs, and law.

Socialization—the process of teaching the culture and norms of the society to its members.

Systems theory or systems approach—an approach that views the entire context (environment) in which an issue exists by analyzing all of the forces or influences impacting on it.

Vienna Convention on Consular Relations (VCCR)—a multilateral agreement among world nations that establishes the legal basis for diplomatic immunity and other issues relating to consular affairs.

Zero tolerance—a type of full enforcement usually directed toward certain problems, such as gang, drug, or traffic offenses; it is exemplified when officers use every violation for justification to intervene in situations.

CHAPTER REFERENCES AND ADDITIONAL READING

Clarke, Ronald V. and John E. Eck (2005). *Crime Analysis for Problem Solvers in 60 Small Steps.* Washington, D.C.: U.S. Department of Justice.

Cochran, Charles L. and Eloise F. Malone (1995). *Public Policy: Perspectives and Choices.* New York: McGraw-Hill.

Federal Bureau of Investigation (2010). Crime in the United States, 2009. Washington, D.C.: U.S. Department of Justice.

Fischer, Frank (1995). *Evaluating Public Policy*. Chicago: Nelson-Hall.

Flashpoints: Guide to World Conflicts (2010). http://www.flashpoints.info/start.html.

Ford, Jess T. (2007). Combating Terrorism: Law Enforcement Agencies Lack Directives to assist Foreign Nations to Identify, Disrupt, and Prosecute Terrorists. Washington, D.C.: Government Accounting Office, Report # GAO-07-697, released June 25, http://www.gao.gov/htext/d07697.html, accessed July 27, 2010.

Fuentes, Thomas V. (2007). Statement before the Subcommittee on Border, Maritime, and Global Counterterrorism House Homeland Security Committee, October 4, 2007. http://www.fbi.gov/congress/congress07/fuentes100407.htm.

Fyfe, James J. (2004). Stops, Frisks, Searches, and the Constitution. *Criminology and Public Policy* 3 (July, 3): 379–398.

Gaouette, Nicole (2010). State Department investigating Houston police incident with Chinese diplomat. Statesman.com. April 30. http://www.statesman.com/news/texas/state-department-investigating-houston-police-incident-with-chinese-654460.html.

Gilmour, Robert S. and Alexis A. Halley (1994). *Who Makes Public Policy*. Chatham, N.J.: Chatham House.

Gould, Jon B. and Stephen D. Mastrofski. Suspect Searches: Assessing Police Behavior under the U.S. Constitution. *Criminology and Public Policy* 3 (July, 3):315–362.

Greene, Jack R. and Carl B. Klockars (1991). What Police Do. In Klockars, Carl B. and Stephen D. Mastrofski (eds.) *Thinking About Police*, 2nd edition. New York: McGraw-Hill.

Harcourt, Bernard E., (2004). Unconstitutional Police Searches and Collective Responsibility. *Criminology and Public Policy* 3 (July, 3): 363–378.

International Crisis Group (2010). http://www.crisisgroup.org/.

Lemley, Ellen C. and Gregory D. Russell (2002). Implementing Restorative Justice by Groping Along: A Case Study in Program Evolutionary Implementation. *Justice System Journal,* 23(2):157–190.

Mazerolle, Lorraine Green, Justin Ready, William Terrill, and Elin Waring (2000). Problem Oriented Policing in Public Housing: The Jersey City Evaluation. *Justice Quarterly,* 17 (March, 1):129–158.

National Defense Council Foundation (2004). http://www.ndcf.org/.

Parmer, Raymond R. (2010). Visa Security and Passenger Pre-Screening Efforts In The Wake Of Flight 253. Hearing before The U.S. House of Representatives, Committee on Homeland Security, Subcommittee on Border, Maritime and Global Counterterrorism, March 11.

Sparger, Jerry R. and David J. Giacopassi (1992). Memphis Revisited: A Reexamination of Police Shootings After the Garner Decision. *Justice Quarterly,* 9 (June, 2): 211–225.

Truman, Jennifer L. and Michael R. Rand (2010). Criminal Victimization, 2009. Washington, D.C.: Bureau of Justice Statistics, NCJ 231327, October.

United States Institute of Peace (2010). Countries & Continents. http://www.usip.org/countries-continents.

U.S. Department of Commerce, ITA, Office of Travel & Tourism Industries (2010). Overseas Visitation Estimates for U.S. States, Cities, and Census Regions: 2009. Washington, D.C.: U.S. Department of Commerce, May. http://tinet.ita.doc.gov/outreach-pages/download_data_table/2009_States_and_Cities.pdf.

U.S. Department of Homeland Security (2007). Fact Sheet: CSI. Washington, D.C.: Customs and Border Protection, October 2.

U.S. Department of Justice (2010). The Accomplishments of the U.S. Department of Justice, 2001–2009. Washington, D.C.: U.S. Department of Justice.

U.S. Department of State (2010). 2009 Human Rights Report: Introduction http://www.state.gov/g/drl/rls/hrrpt/2009/frontmatter/135936.htm.

U.S. Department of State (June 2004). Consular Notification and Access Reference Card: Instructions for Arrests and Detentions of Foreign Nationals. Washington, D.C.: U.S. Department of State.

U.S. Department of State (2003). Consular Notification and Access. Washington, D.C.: U.S. Department of State.

U.S. Department of State (September 2010). Consular Notification and Access, 3rd Edition. Washington, D.C.: U.S. Department of State. http://travel.state.gov/pdf/cna/CNA_Manual_3d_Edition.pdf.

U.S. Department of State (2010a). Diplomatic and Consular Privileges and Immunities From Criminal Jurisdiction (chart). http://www.state.gov/documents/organization/20047.pdf.

CHAPTER 2

A Brief History of Early Policing

LEARNING OBJECTIVES

A broad understanding of the history and evolution of policing is important, as without this knowledge, we cannot appreciate the contemporary state of policing nor fashion its future. After studying this chapter, you should be able to:

- Explain why the study of history is important to the field of criminal justice.
- Discuss the contributions of various ancient civilizations and societies to the development of policing.
- Identify historic law codes and Commandments and explain why they are still important today.
- Identify the contributions to policing made by the French from the Middle Ages to the early 1800s.
- Describe the contributions to policing made by the English, as well as the circumstances leading to the establishment of the London Metropolitan Police in 1829.
- Identify the principal English architects of modern policing.

KEY TERMS USED IN THIS CHAPTER

Code of Hammurabi	Surete
lex talionis	tything (or tithing) system
Mosaic Law	hundred
Laws of the Twelve Tables	shire
Praetorian Guards	reeve
Urban Cohort	Peace Guilds
Vigiles	praepostus
frankpledge	vicecomes
constable	Courts of Leet
feudalism	Magna Carta
sergeant	Statute of Winchester
Commune juree	An Act for Improving
Lieutenant of Police	the Police in and near
	the Metropolis

CHAPTER OUTLINE

THE SIGNIFICANCE OF HISTORY

This chapter offers a selected summary of policing as it was practiced at various times in ancient history. It also reviews the contributions to policing made just prior to the founding of our nation. Because this chapter is limited in scope, we encourage you to consult additional historical sources, including those in the references and selected sites on the Internet. We begin this section by discussing three reasons for studying history.

First, history is the study of the past. It is a record or narrative description of events that directly or indirectly define the values that underlie contemporary society. Consequently, we study the past to gain a better understanding of our current state-of-affairs.

To illustrate the significance of history, we need look no further than the evening news. For example, we are currently involved in two wars, one in Iraq and one in Afghanistan. These conflicts have cost our nation billions of dollars, caused untold suffering, and ended the lives of many of our young men and woman in uniform, not to mention the lives of many innocent citizens in our nation and around the world. The reasons for these conflicts are complex and deeply rooted in Middle Eastern political, social, and religious history.

Because of the global nature of terrorism and crime, the international nature of our economy, and the ease of international travel, it is vital that police officers have a working understanding of world history. For example, without an understanding of world history, it would be impossible to successfully respond to the attacks of September 11, 2001. Let us take this example one step further. Imagine for the moment that you are one of the hundreds of federal, state, and local agents assigned to investigate the attacks of September 11 and to prevent further attacks on our citizens. Your usefulness would be greatly impaired without a broad understanding of Middle Eastern history, the history of terrorism, and American history. Think of your embarrassment if you were attending an investigative briefing given by a counter-terrorism expert and you had no clue that opium had been grown and traded in the Middle East since antiquity, or who she was talking about when she discussed Yasser Arafat, or what she was talking about when she mentioned the Mossad. There may have been a time when the average police officer could function without an in-depth understanding of historical events beyond his or her beat, but that luxury is now over. It is imperative, given the international nature of crime, terrorism, and the global economy, that law enforcement officers acquire a worldview of their beats. As the 9/11 Commission report (2004) states, "The enemy is not just 'terrorism,' some generic evil. This vagueness blurs the strategy. The catastrophic threat at this moment in history is more specific. It is the threat posed by Islamist terrorism—especially the al-Qaida network, its affiliates, and its ideology" (362).

As a student of policing, the second reason for studying history is to gain a better understanding of the social, political, and economic forces that have (and continue) to shape American society. We are a culturally diverse nation blessed with many ethnic groups, each with their own subset of cultural histories and contributions to our development. Consequently, our history is replete with the influences fashioned by immigration, urbanization, and industrialization, and interspersed within these forces have been the tempering influences of revolution, slavery, civil war, world wars, depression, cold wars, and the challenge of securing civil rights for every citizen. Throughout our history, police officers have played important roles in our nation's development: sometimes they have been part of the problem, and at other times they have been part of the solution. As you study the history of policing, try to picture yourself as a working-class citizen of the period; think how economic, political, and social conditions might have influenced your life.

The third reason for studying history is that criminal justice professionals must understand the history of their field. "Knowing from whence you came" is an important aspect of professional growth. George Santayana (1905) made a similar point in his now famous quotation, when he observed that, "Those who cannot remember the past are condemned to repeat it" (284). Many people misunderstand this statement, suggesting that it is saying that history repeats itself, which is not the true basis of the quote; in fact, history sometimes repeats itself because people fail to correctly remember events and the underlying circumstances that produced the event. Consequently, professionals in the criminal justice field must have an understanding and sense of history to avoid past mistakes, to build on successes, and to plan for the future.

CONTRIBUTIONS TO LAW AND POLICING FROM SELECTED ANCIENT CIVILIZATIONS

Most ancient civilizations created laws and institutions to control their citizens, protect the ruling class, and/or to secure a civil society. In all cases, these institutions and laws were a response to social, political, and economic conditions that posed a threat to the status quo. Because of their historical importance, in this section we briefly review the contributions to law and policing of five ancient civilizations or peoples: Babylon, Egypt, the Hebrews, the Greeks, and the Romans.

Babylon

Babylonian civilization prospered from 1800 to 600 BC in the ancient lands of Mesopotamia, the fertile plain between the Tigris and Euphrates rivers, in what is present-day Iraq. It is often referred to as the "cradle of civilization". A long succession of rulers presided over the region, which was noted for its diverse agriculture and urban trading centers. Over time, the region prospered and merchants became more powerful as they collected wealth from trading and banking. Yet, the king's power was absolute, maintained through a system that included dividing land and then placing loyal noblemen in charge of the sections (as you will see, the concept of dividing responsibility and authority for the security of a selected area will continue throughout the ages). The noblemen occupied the land at the will of the king and, in return, they paid him tribute and military service. The nobility, in general, were the king's counselors, assistants in government, governors, judges, and military officers. Society below the king and the nobility consisted of the common people: artisans, tradesmen, and slaves, none of whom played any role in government or public life (Goodspeed 1904; Brandon 1970; Grun 1991).

One of the most important Babylonian rulers was King Hammurabi, who reigned from about 1728 to 1686 BC. Under his leadership, Babylonian civilization reached the zenith of its cultural development and political power. King Hammurabi is primarily remembered for his extensive legal code. The **Code of Hammurabi** contained some 282 regulations and evidenced a sense of justice built on personal responsibility and accountability (refer to **Figure 2-1**). Historian Mitchel Roth (2005) observes that although Hammurabi "is often credited with conceiving the first law code," archaeologists now believe that "he borrowed extensively from [the law codes of] earlier rulers" (4–5). Nevertheless, he was astute enough to assemble a collection of both civil and criminal laws that were, in the words of Roth (2005), "more complex and comprehensive than any law code previously attempted" (5). The code included forms of punishment, fines, or obligations for offenders, although fines were not paid to the state, and it was was more advanced than tribal custom in that it recognized no blood feud, private retaliation, or marriage by capture. One of its main legal principles was **lex talionis**,

Oblisk with the Code of Hammurabi

1. *Partie supérieure du Code de Hammourabi. Vers 2000 av. J. C. (Louvre).*

Source: © National Library of Medicine

or the law of retaliation. The death penalty was common punishment for offenses against the state and criminal negligence, yet the Code's provision went far beyond criminal offenses; it essentially addressed all aspects of family, social, and business life, as well as property transactions (Gadd 1971).

Why is the Code of Hammurabi still important today? The answer is simple: it sets a benchmark from which to measure the progress of civil society. As Roth (2005) states, "By codifying both criminal and civil laws and creating specific penalties for breaking these tenets, for the first time in recorded history a connection was established between crime and its punishment" (6).

FIGURE 2-1 Historical Legal Codes on the World Wide Web

The principal source of the Code of Hammurabi is the stone monument made of black basalt on which the code is inscribed. Part of the code on the lower portion of the monument was erased by an Elamite king who captured the stela around 1200 BC. The stone was discovered in 1901 and is preserved in the Louvre in Paris. For a translation of the Code of Hammurabi, log on to the website at http://www.duhaime.org/LawMuseum/LawArticle-105/1760-BC—Hammurabis-Code-of-Laws.aspx. For another view of the stone monument, log on to this website: http://www.abu.nb.ca/ecm/photo/vhamurab.gif.

There are a number of excellent sites on the World Wide Web related to the history of legal codes, history, and philosophy. Examples include the University of Chicago's D'Angelo Law Library at http://www.lib.uchicago.edu/e/law/history.html and the Avalon Project at Yale Law School: http://avalon.law.yale.edu/default.asp. Other sites can be located by using the search terms "legal history," "ancient codes," and "history of law."

Egypt

When we think of ancient Egypt, we think of the great pyramids at Giza, the Sphinx, the pyramid complexes at Saqqara and Memphis, the temples of Luxor and Karnak, and the Valley of the Kings. We are awed by their sheer size, majesty, and complexity. We also think of the long procession of Egyptian dynasties and their pharaohs, remembering that most of this history occurred over 4000 years ago. What we seldom ponder is the day-to-day lives of the people who built these great monuments. Certainly, nothing of this magnitude and majesty could have been built without a significant degree of social stability, advanced mathematical and engineering skills, law, and public administration—in other words, government.

Historians Zaky Iskander and Alexander Badawy (1965) report that as early as the First Dynasty (3200–2980 BC), Egypt had acquired "a highly developed system of centralized government" supported and directed by written laws and a corps of public servants (28). There was also "a vast middle-class" of skilled craftsmen, which included painters, masons, scribes, and sculptors. By the Second Dynasty (2980–2778 BC), there is ample evidence that most citizens of Egypt enjoyed a comfortable lifestyle. Furthermore, they had developed three scripts (forms of writing): hieroglyphic; a cursive known as hieratic; and later, a simplification of the hieratic know as demotic, which served to transcribe the popular tongue. They also had advanced knowledge of, among other things, crop irrigation, seafaring, shipbuilding, surgery, and medicine, and, as we now marvel, a sophisticated knowledge of engineering and architecture.

As Egypt continued to prosper during the "pyramid building period" (from the Third through the Sixth Dynasty, 2778–2680 BC), we find abundant evidence in the archaeological record indicating "that the government was very powerful and well organized" (Iskander and Badawy 1965, 37). For example, there is mention of prime ministers, ministers of public works, tax collectors, local governors, and "vizirs," persons who acted as both the head of the entire government and at the same time as the "chief of justice and chief archivist of the state" (Iskander and Badawy 1965, 49). Adding to this list, historian Roger Bagnall (1977) describes another agency of government: the police. He states that, "The police, called *Medjay*, in the new Kingdom, were organized and dressed in much the same way as the army, but they formed a distinct organization; the provision of such police goes as far back as the Old Kindom" (67).

Additional archaeological evidence reveals that members of the civil police force lived in their own quarters in many ancient Egyptain cities (Samuel 1999), worked from police posts or stations (Fairman, 1949), patrolled the frontier, and collected taxes (Gardiner, 1920). Historian Carol Trojan (1989) reports that internal security officials known as "Judges Commandment of the Police" existed during the Fourth Dynasty (circa 2900 BC) and that Hur Moheb created an organized police force around 1340 BC to protect commerce and ensure safe navigation along the Nile. Trojan also states that:

> Ramses III (1198–1166 BC) invested the police with much authority in an effort to establish peace and security. He produced laws that dealt severely with criminals and punishment being awarded in public. The most important police units were those responsible for the security of the tombs, where valuables were placed with the dead. The Egyptians claim that they were the first to use dogs for police purposes, using them for guarding property. The police of ancient Egypt were also vested with judicial powers; they not only tried the cases, but they passed judgment and executed the sentences (Trojan 1989, 238).

As people traveled in ancient times for purposes of conquest and trade, there was also a transfer of knowledge, culture, and religion. For example, early contact between ancient civilizations in the Middle East and Mediterranean exerted tremendous influence on the empires and people that followed. Brandon (1970) states that the debt owed to Egypt by Western civilization is immense:

> The ancient Greeks, probably the most intelligent race that has ever lived, acknowledged this debt freely. From the time when their merchants began setting up trading posts in Egypt in the seventh and sixth centuries BC they were fascinated by Egypt.... Archaic Greek art was clearly influenced by Egyptian sculpture, which at its best has few equals anywhere in the world. The Greeks copied Egyptian medicine and surgery and in many other fields of knowledge looked upon the Egyptian priests as their mentors (127).

The Greeks in Egypt

It seems the Greeks were also impressed with other aspects of Egyptian society besides art, medicine, and surgery. After Alexander (356–323 BC) liberated Egypt from the Persians in 332 BC, he and the other Greek rulers that followed adopted a policy of tolerance toward Egyptian civilization, which they held in high regard. This included "paying tribute to their religious and social customs" and affording certain rights to property owners (Iskander and Badawy 1965, 118).

We know that a well-organized and developed police system existed during Greek rule in Egypt. Every Egyptian village and town had a police unit commanded by a police chief; in fact, law enforcement responsibilities were divided into divisions and sections. A mounted police corps patrolled the desert areas, another guarded the borders, there was a special unit to patrol the canals and rivers, another unit was responsible for buying goods for the government, and still another unit was responsible for inspecting the harvest on royal lands. In addition to these services, some officers were assigned to tax collection duties, while others were assigned special duties in the offices of high officials, including acting as bodyguards. In summary, the police were a professional (as opposed to ad hoc) volunteer force that occupied permanent positions and received regular pay. Some officers were even given a plot of arable land for their service (Iskander and Badawy 1965; Bagnell 1977). Consequently, we see that policing is certainly not a new concept.

The Hebrews

Between 1650 and 1300 BC, groups of wandering tribes, the Hebrews (later known as the Israelites), migrated into Egypt. They claimed a common ancestor, Abraham, and shared a common religion, Judaism. Eventually, the Israelites left Egypt under the leadership of Moses (about 1250 BC) and wandered through the "wilderness" (the Sinai desert) for 40 years. In time, they established a homeland in Palestine along the northern shores of the Dead Sea. The significance of this to the modern-day world was the introduction of **Mosaic Law**, meaning "the law of Moses." Besides the biblical Ten Commandments, the Law of Moses are recorded in the Old Testament books of Genesis, Exodus, Leviticus, Numbers, and Deuteronomy. At the heart of Mosaic Law is the covenant between man and God. Historian Mitchel Roth (2005) observes that Mosaic Law was "committed to the elimination of class distinctions," placing it in sharp contrast "with Hammurabi's code by repudiating the notion of a rich man's law by applying a uniform moral standard applicable to all people" (6). Under Mosaic Law, people abide by the law out of an obligation to a higher authority (God) and not to an earthly ruler. It is from this Hebrew foundation and its principles that Judaism and Christianity evolved. The impact of these laws upon cultures and moral beliefs is referred to as the "Judeo-Christian influence". Its influence, codified in the Ten Commandments, forms the "foundation of law systems throughout much of the Western world" (Roth 2005, 6).

From about 1050 to 930 BC, the Kingdom of Israel was a major power in the Middle East. King David, who reigned from 1003–1070 BC, established his capital at Jerusalem, built up an army, and made its influence felt throughout the region. He was followed by King Solomon, who reigned from 971 to 931 BC; during King Solomon's reign, alliances were established with other powers in the region, including the Phoenicians and Egyptians (Brandon 1970).

The Greeks

The tribes of the eastern Mediterranean expanded their trade and commerce into other nearby regions, including that of Asia Minor (Turkey), the Aegean Sea, and into the Balkan Peninsula. The influence of the Egyptians, the Assyrians, the Phoenicians, and the Hittites upon the Greeks allowed them to gain great power and influence of their own by 1500 BC. The Greek conquest of the Aegean area occurred between 1500 and 1200 BC, but their influence declined shortly thereafter because of invading groups (barbarians) from the north. Greeks migrated back toward their homelands, where they prospered in limited geographical colonies called city-states (*poleis* or *polis* in Greek).

Each city-state was an independent, close-knit entity that formed its own political and social life. It was in these self-contained city-states that the principle of democracy, "the rule of the people," was born (Breasted 1916, 300). The early city-states were ruled originally by aristocrats who had accumulated great wealth and, therefore, were able to rule as a king would, but as their influence grew weaker, they used unjust and despotic methods to maintain their positions. One of the major complaints of the people about this time was that only the ruler knew all the laws; consequently, the people began demanding that the laws be written down. According to Goodspeed (1904), the Greek custom became one of commissioning "the best man in the state, to whom all power was given that he might prepare,

publish and administer a code of law which should be binding upon the people" (100). One such lawgiver, Draco, was appointed around 624 BC in Athens. He codified the oral law and customs of the land; unfortunately, the law of Draco was considered very harsh and punitive, with some saying it was "written in blood." Subsequently, another lawgiver, Solon, modified the law and was responsible for giving political power to all citizens of the state. Because of this, Solon is known as the "Founder of the Athenian Democracy" (Goodspeed 1904, 109–110).

Interestingly, it was the age of tyrants, a term which originally meant a high office held by a ruler not of aristocratic lineage, that led to the development of a more democratic society. One such tyrant, Pisistratus of Athens, was known for looking after the rights of the people; curbing the nobles; giving great attention to public works like harbor improvements, state buildings, and temples; and cultivating art, music, and literature (Breasted 1916, 317). He expanded the basic principles of political rights of the masses established by Solon. It was during this period that Homer's poems were written, and other cultural advances in the theater prospered.

During the early fifth century BC, many of the larger Greek city-states banded together to successfully ward off invasions by the Persians, which led to a stronger Greek influence in the Aegean Sea. Following the defeat of the Persians, Athens and Sparta became the predominant city-states and soon began to rival each other. Sparta represented the tradition of military might and limited privileges to citizens, and Athens represented the seeds of democracy and culture (Breasted 1916, 347). Unfortunately, this rivalry and domination of other cities and lands saw some curtailments in democracy. Citizenship was no longer granted to foreigners, and people with legal disputes were forced to travel to Athens to present their case to the citizen juries; this was a great inconvenience to the people of the Athenian Empire. Also, meetings of representatives from all states of the Empire were discontinued. Athens was being viewed as increasingly dictatorial and was losing the favor of people outside her immediate borders.

By 404 BC, following a 27-year war with Sparta, the Athenian Empire had crumbled; democracy had failed to overcome the fragmented nature of the Athenian Empire and unite the Greek world. In conquered lands, the Spartans set up a form of government known as an oligarchy (a term meaning "rule of a few") which consisted of the upper class or nobility, supported by military force (Breasted 1916, 400–401). The Spartan rule of the area, however, ended following a military defeat in 371 BC. As the Athenian Empire was crumbling, the Macedonians to the north were gaining power. Alexander of Macedonia was thirteen (around 343 BC) when he studied under the great philosopher Aristotle, and only 20-years-old when he became King of Macedonia. He believed that the Greeks should submit to his leadership, but they did not. Eventually, Alexander would conquer the major Greek city-states, as well as the Persian, Phoenician, and Egyptian empires before he turned 26. During the following 6 years (circa 323 BC), he conquered what is today's Iran, India, and parts of China, and he died shortly thereafter at the age of 33. Although his empire was maintained for some time by his heirs, other communities of the region (e.g., the Greek city-states) were beginning to regain their identity and history, and others (e.g., the Romans) were gaining power and expanding their borders (Breasted 1916, 430–438).

The Romans

Rome, founded between 800 and 750 BC, was first ruled by aristocratic kings. From 500 to 133 BC, the government of Rome experienced great change. People gradually secured the right to have laws published, the power to elect magistrates, and the establishment of a republican form of government. Around 450 BC, the **Laws of the Twelve Tables** became the foundation of the early Roman legal system. These laws were inscribed on twelve tablets of brass displayed for public inspection on the walls of the Temple of Jupiter. Although only fragmentary portions of the laws remain, they were essentially a collection of Roman maxims of universal application from which formal laws were later developed. The Twelve Tables were like crude chapters of procedures of conduct (see **Figure 2-2**).

During the reign of Augustus (28 BC–14 AD), the Roman Empire stretched to England and the city of Rome had a population of over 1.25 million people, which included large numbers of slaves and indentured servants from conquered lands. The city was built largely of wood and brick, and buildings were close to one another, causing major problems when fires broke out. Moreover, there was constant

---

FIGURE 2-2 Selected sections of the Laws of the Twelve Tables

Table I
  1. If a man call another to law, he shall go. If he go not, they shall witness it; then he shall be seized.
  2. If he flee or evade, lay hands on him as he goes.
  6. If they settle the matter, let it be told.
  7. If they settle not, they shall join issue in the assembly or in the Forum before midday, then they shall plead and prove, both being present.

Table II
  3. He who needs a witness shall within three days go to his house and notify him.

Table VIII
  2. If a man has broken the limb of another and does not settle with him, let there be retaliation.
  3. If a man with fist or club breaks the bone of another, he is liable to penalty, of 300 (pence) if done to a free man, 150 if done to a slave.
  12. If by night a man have done a theft, and (the owner) kills him, let him be (as if) killed by law.

Table X
  1. A dead man you shall not bury or burn within the city.
  4. Women shall not tear their faces, nor make excessive lamentation for the dead.

Source: Adapted from Albert Kocourek and John H. Wigmore (1915). Sources of Ancient and Primitive Law. Boston: Little, Brown, and Company, 465–468.

fear of insurrection because of social class distinction, limited civil rights for non-citizens, and discrimination against non-Romans. Crime in the streets was rampant. Moreover, there was no law enforcement agency or street lighting system; consequently, gangs controlled large areas of the city (Brandon 1970; Kelly 1973, 56–60).

In an attempt to address these threatening conditions, Augustus established two entities, the **Praetorian Guards**, to act as his personal bodyguards, and the **Urban Cohort** as protectors of the peace throughout Rome. Both were military units and part of the regular army under the control of the emperor. However, around 14 BC, and in partial response to political opposition, he appointed a force of freedmen called **Vigiles**, or night watchers, to act as Rome's first fire-fighting unit. The Vigiles eventually numbered approximately 9000 and were divided into seven cohorts (districts). Besides their fire-related duties, they were eventually assigned policing duties charged with making arrests for theft, burglary, and assault; capturing runaway slaves; and serving as guards at the public baths. **Figure 2-3** lists terms associated with the Vigiles.

Overlooking the Egyptian experience with policing, historians often cite the Vigiles as the first large civilian unit in a metropolitan setting used for law enforcement and social control purposes (refer to the previous sections of this chapter). In any event, the Vigiles were the first known public safety unit appointed to serve both the fire-fighting and

policing needs of a city. Because of Augustus' creation of the Vigiles, he is referred to by some as the "Father of Policing". Most historians believe that policing did not see an equivalent force until the establishment of city police in nineteenth century Europe and England (Kelly 1973, 56, 60).

THE FRENCH POLICE SYSTEM

After the fall of the Roman Empire, the next major developments in policing occurred during the Middle Ages in France, under the rule of Charlemagne (who reigned as King of the Franks from 768 to 814). Charlemagne consolidated power into a centralized government and required all free men to take an oath of fidelity to him. He also united the whole area of Gaul (an area that today encompasses most of Western Europe, including France, Belgium, western Switzerland, and parts of the Netherlands and Germany). This oath is sometimes referred to as a **frankpledge**, which is a system of social control supported by oath to obey the law of the land. Charlemagne divided his staff of servants into areas of service, one of which was the position of **constable**, or count of the stable, an important position of trust (Seignobos 1932, 58–59).

By the ninth century, the area of Gaul was again fragmented into large centers of authority, each consisting of a king and his subjects. **Feudalism**, the practice of providing basic needs to those under a leader's control or subject to a leader's authority, was established as a system of social life. Under this arrangement in France, the king or lord placed trusted agents, known as mayors in every village, who policed the village with the aid of armed **sergeants**:

> *The mayors of towns . . . exercised all the powers enjoyed by the town, dispensing justice, both civil and criminal, levying taxation, controlling public order, leading the militia composed of the burgesses, providing for the defense of the walls, and keeping the treasure, the archives and the keys to the town gates* (Seignobos 1932, 126).

By the twelfth century, many towns in France had formed a mutual defense association known as **commune juree**, where an oath formed a bond between a large number of men of equal status for the defense of a collective interest (Seignobos 1932, 103–126). France's first efforts to establish a centralized police force occurred during the

---

FIGURE 2-3 Terms associated with the Vigiles of Rome

Excubitorem—the substation located in the districts; it housed the Vigiles and the equipment needed to fight fire. It also had cells for prisoners.

Karcerarius—the Vigile assigned to jailor duty.

Quae-stionarius—the interrogator and/or torturer.

Sebaciarii—believed to be the plain clothes men or early form of detective.

Saint Sebastian—Patron Saint of the police; was an officer in the Vigiles.

Source: Adapted from Martin A. Kelly, "The First Urban Policeman," Journal of Police Science and Administration, (March 1973, 58–59).

reign of Louis XIV; in 1666, he appointed a council under the direction of Jean-Baptiste Colbert to develop a plan for police organization and administration. The edicts of the council (1666–1667) established police powers and procedures, restricted the private ownership of arms, and created the **Lieutenant of Police** for the City of Paris, which by the mid-1700s had the most advanced system of police of any city in Europe (Fairlie 1901). The Lieutenant of Police was granted seven distinct areas of authority by Louis XIV:

1. The security of Paris, including the repression of civil disorders, making arrests, and surveillance of foreigners
2. The cleaning and lighting of streets, fire fighting and prevention, and flood control
3. Regulating and upgrading the moral behavior of the citizens
4. Regulating social affairs in matters of abandoned children, unfaithful wives, organization of hospitals, and inspection of prisons and jails
5. Assuring adequate food supplies for the city
6. Protecting the city in times of epidemics and general maintenance of health conditions
7. Regulating the economy, which included surveillance of worker's associations and policing the marketplace (Arnold, 1979, 14–15)

Louis XIV later set up Lieutenants-General of Police in all the principal cities of France. The idea of a royal police continued for over 100 years, until the French people's growing distrust of the monarchy and its government led to the French Revolution of 1789. Following the Revolution of 1789, power was transferred from the king to the Assembly, which reorganized the government based on the uniformity of institutions and not obedience to the king. The monarchy, however, was retained, with Louis XVI on the throne. Every region became autonomous, having an elected administration with the power of maintaining order, policing its own area, and even collecting taxes; in other words, power was decentralized (a concept that was adopted in America following our own Revolution in 1776). However, conflict between the monarchy and the Assembly led to another revolution in France in 1792 and years of civil strife. During this period, the Committee of General Security was responsible for

police power, and centralization of the police became a primary issue. In 1796, the Ministry of General Police was established for the "execution of the laws relative to the police, security, and general tranquility of the Republic" (Arnold 1979, 23–24).

With Napoleon Bonaparte's rise to power in 1799, the police system in France became an integral part of his regime. His initial Minister of General Police was Joseph Fouche, who maintained an elaborate intelligence system that kept the Emperor well-informed (Arnold 1979, 33–35, 161). Additionally, a former convict, Eugene Francois Vidocq, became the head of a small detective unit of the Paris police. He staffed his unit with former criminals, under the philosophy that "it takes a thief to catch a thief," and paid them according to their performance (see **Figures 2-4** and **2-5** for additional information

Eugene Francois Vidocq

VIDOCQ, THE CELEBRATED FRENCH DETECTIVE.
(From the Engraving by Mlle. Coignet.)

Source: © Mary Evans Picture Library/Alamy Images

FIGURE 2-4 Eugene Francois Vidocq

Historically, Eugene Francois Vidocq's legendary crimesolving reputation was lauded in Poe's Murders in the Rue Morgue and in Herman Melville's Moby Dick. The fugitive in Charles Dickens' Great Expectations is also inspired by Vidocq's real-life exploits. As a fugitive from French justice he first offered his services as a police spy and informer, later becoming a master of disguise who was so successful at catching criminals that, in 1811, he was named the first chief of the Surete. In time he directed a force of 28 detectives, all of whom were also former criminals.

Eugene Francois Vidocq is considered by historians and those in law enforcement to be the father of modern criminal investigation. Vidocq's accomplishments and contributions to law enforcement were many. He introduced record keeping (i.e., a card index system) and criminalistics, introduced the science of ballistics, was the first to make plaster-of-paris casts of foot/shoe impressions, was a master of disguise and surveillance, held patents on indelible ink and unalterable bond paper, and founded the first modern detective agency and credit bureau, Le Bureau des Renseignements. After resigning from the Surete, he published Memoires de Vidocq (1828), a book which became a bestseller in Europe and firmly established Eugene Francios Vidocq as the world's greatest detective.

Vidocq's regard for his fellow man also was legendary. He was a philanthropist who also helped the poor and abandoned of Paris; at the same time that he was pursuing the guilty, he was also freeing the innocent.

Source: The Vidocq Society, 1998. *Used by permission.*

FIGURE 2-5 The Vidocq Society

One of the most unusual crimesolving organizations in the world meets in the historic area of Philadelphia next to Independence Hall. The Vidocq Society is named in honor of Eugene Francois Vidocq, the brilliant 18th century French detective who founded the Surete. Vidocq Society Members ("V.S.M.s") and their guests draw upon years of forensic skills used each day at work to evaluate, investigate, and endeavor to solve unsolved crimes, particularly murder. When requested, members participate in the investigation and prosecution of the person or persons who are eventually charged with the murder. Members are motivated purely by public service. They are forensic professionals who eagerly donate centuries of deductive and scientific talent for the common good. The Vidocq Society credo is "Veritas Veritatum." The phrase, in Latin, means "Truth Begets Truth." The Vidocq Society was founded in Philadelphia in 1990 by worldrenowned sculptor and forensic reconstructionist Frank Bender; internationally known forensic psychologist and crime "profiler" Richard Walter, M.A.; and Bill Fleisher, a former Philadelphia Police Officer, and then FBI Special Agent who later became the Assistant Special Agent in Charge of the U.S. Customs Service in Philadelphia.

Vidocq Society membership represents 17 states and 11 foreign countries. It is a rare privilege and has been bestowed upon less than 150 men and women; new members must be sponsored by existing members. Most members are employed in public service by federal, state and local law enforcement either behind badges or at prosecutors' tables. Some Vidocqians consult regularly with federal, state, or local law enforcement; attorneys in private practice and entrepreneurs are also members.

A longunsolved homicide or disappearance is usually the centerpiece of each Vidocq Society meeting. The crime and its evidence are disclosed to members and invited guests, with an eye towards rekindling or refocusing the investigation. The presenter of a coldcase murder or disappearance at a Vidocq Society luncheon could be a law enforcement professional who has investigated the murder over the years and continues to carry it on his caseload, a Vidocq Society member, or a private investigator hired by the murder victim's family. The spirited, synergistic question-and-answer period that follows each formal case presentation becomes a collaborative effort that involves members and invited guests in the search for a solution to a previously unsolved crime. If substantial interest is shown by Vidocq Society members following the case presentation, a "working group" is assembled (an investigative team of Vidocq Society members and volunteers that is tailored to advance that specific investigation).

Additional information about the Society can be found on the world wide web at: http://www.vidocq.org.

Source: The Vidocq Society. *Used by permission.*

about Vidocq's legacy). Vidocq developed an elaborate system of informants and intelligence-gathering networks that became the model for the **Surete**, or criminal investigations division of the police, which evolved into La Surete Nationale, or what is today the French National Police (Holden 1992). France has undergone a number of changes in governmental structure since Napoleon, but the centralization of the police has remained a major feature of most of these governmental reforms.

THE BRITISH EXPERIENCE

Early History

As mentioned earlier, the Roman Empire once stretched to England, and during much of its early history parts of England were occupied by other groups as well. However, by fifth century social control in England had become an individual and group responsibility. Known as the **tything (or tithing) system**, it consisted of a group of ten families (normally an extended family) living in close proximity to each other to provide self-protection and security. In effect, the people were the police; if an infraction of the common law happened, members of the tything were expected to raise the "hue and cry", prompting others to come to their aid. A territory containing 10 tythings was called a **hundred**, and several hundreds covered an area called a **shire**. Using today's terms, a tything would be a village, a hundred a township, and a shire a county. The chief law enforcement officer or magistrate of the shire was called a **reeve**. It was from this early terminology that the word "sheriff" (shire-reeve) originated (Lee 1971, 3–7).

The shire-reeve was responsible for conducting annual inspections of the tythings and holding court. However, at the end of the 10th century, a period referred to as the "Dark Ages," England and Europe fell into a time of cultural, intellectual, and economic deterioration following the decline of the Western Roman Empire. It was at this time that **Peace Guilds** become popular as a local means of social control. These guilds were private, voluntary associations, arranged in 10 groups under 10 headmen, one of whom acted as a chief and treasurer. The guilds were mutual assurance societies, and the contributions made to them went toward apprehension of offenders.

Following the Norman conquest of 1066, some traditional titles of positions associated with the tything system

changed. The headman of the tything became the **praepostus**, and the shire-reeve was replaced by **vicecomes** who went on the circuit to hold court (known as the police courts). The Normans also established a feudalistic form of social control. By the 12th century, **Courts of Leet** (local police courts) had been instituted as a substitute for the sheriff's courts. In fact, they became so popular that the sheriff eventually "ceased to trouble the village communities with his annual visit of inspection" (Lee 1971, 6–17).

During the 1100s, the kings of England continued the slow process of judicial reform, yet these measures did not satisfy a growing sense of injustice in England's feudal society. In 1215, King John, who had succeeding in alienating every segment of English society due to his ineptness, was forced by a number of barons to sign the **Magna Carta** (Latin, meaning "the great charter"). This profoundly important document, today considered a foundational statement of democratic principles, limited the power of the king and granted the citizens of England certain guarantees, including a church free from domination by the monarchy, reforming the justice system to make it more equitable, and greater political liberties and rights for citizens. For example, Section 20 of the document rebukes the alleged abuses by officials in rendering justice and penalties: "We will not make men justiciaries, constables, sheriffs or bailiffs, unless they understand the law of the land, and are well disposed to observe it" (Lee 1971, 20).

The importance of the Magna Carta cannot be overstated, not only to the citizens of England when it was signed in 1215, but to all peoples who would subsequently come to live under a democratic form of government. As Roth (2005), observes, "It was a turning point in legal history" (36). Its powerful concepts of due process, justice, and the restraint of unchecked government serve as "one of the foundations of modern democracy," evidenced in the fact that the framers would turn to the Magna Carta for "…basic principles that would be incorporated in the American Constitution 500 years later…" (Roth 2005, 36).

During the reign of Edward I, the **Statute of Winchester (1285)** was enacted in response to increasing incidents of crime brought on by the urbanization of

English society. According to Roth (2005) it was "one of the most important pieces of criminal justice legislation to come out of the Middle Ages…" (36). It created, as historian Melville Lee (1971) observes, a policing system that continued for nearly 500 years. Among other things, it provided for:

- A "watch and ward" system of protection (a night watch system, made up of all eligible males who took turns serving on the watch)
- A duty to inform others of offenses and offenders (the "hue and cry")
- The arming of all males aged 15 to 60 to defend the kingdom and to maintain order
- The removal of brush and most trees 200 feet on each side of the king's highway (to prevent surprise attacks from robbers) (Lee 1971, 24–28)

Consequently, it added new meaning to the French word "frankpledge," which the English had adopted into their language. As Lee (1971) observes, by the end of 12th century the term "frankpledge" meant recognition of the responsibility of every citizen to play his part in maintaining peace in the state, or the liability that all men share to render police services when called upon to do so.

The 1700s and 1800s

The watch system served the English people well until the 1700s, when numerous social, economic, and political circumstances combined to change the character of English society. As the century progressed, England became less and less an agrarian country. The advent of international trade and commerce, the discovery of new lands, the expansion of the British Empire, and war with Spain and France changed England's posture in the world. At home, religious protests and calls for social reform, as well as civil war within its Empire, created a social environment wherein unpaid, unskilled watchmen were no longer effective agents of social control.

These challenges were compounded by the Industrial Revolution, which brought increased urbanization and a new social class—factory workers and miners. Working conditions in the new factories and mines were often harsh, unsafe, and unhealthy. Following their men in

an exodus from the farms of rural England, women and children also entered the workforce in large numbers. They, too, faced a harsh and unsafe working environment. Moreover, living conditions in the new industrial centers, like Manchester, Liverpool, and London, were crowded, crime-ridden, and unsanitary. These conditions produced a myriad of social problems, including an increase in crime and riots, which were becoming common. The Riots Acts of 1715 made rioting a felonious act and extended powers of the Justices of the Peace but unfortunately, new laws would not address the underlying social problems of the period, which would continue to fester. Nevertheless, in 1736, Parliament enacted a law allowing London's city council to raise monies for all police purposes and constables were empowered to make arrests (Lee 1971, 147–151).

In 1746, Henry Fielding, an English writer, playwright, journalist, and lawyer, was appointed magistrate of the Bow Street Magistrates Court, which was located in a particularly crime-ridden and rowdy section of London. Beyond his accomplished writing abilities and his sense of justice from the bench, he is noted for his research and insights into crime and police reform. He authored one of the first treatises on police reform in 1751, *Enquiry into the Causes of the Late Increase of Robbers*, which addressed the social context of crime. He also established a police office (the Bow Street Police Office) as part of his court. He staffed the office by hiring six constables who were charged with responding to criminal incidents and with apprehending known thieves. These officers, who were very successful at their duties, became known as the Bow Street Runners, and they were paid for their services from the fines levied against wrongdoers. Fielding supported the idea of a 24-hour patrol by officers, and even recommended horse patrols for the city. Some have called him the "Father of the Police of London". His brother, John Fielding, who succeeded him as magistrate of the Bow Street court, continued the police reform movement. Foot patrol officers were assigned in 1782, a horse patrol was added in 1805, and a dismounted horse patrol was established in 1821 (Tobias 1979, 44–52).

Patrick Colquhoun, a Middlesex magistrate, was another police reformer of this time. He published several works about policing, including *Treatise on the Police of* the Metropolis (1796), *The Commerce and Policing of the Thames River* (1800), and *Treatise on the Functions and Duties of the Constable* (1803) (Lee 1991, 177, 218–219). These publications helped to inform the public about alternatives to the antiquated watch and parish constable systems that served the city. Within the next two decades, police reform was to occur on a much larger scale.

Historian Charles Reith (1956) notes that Henry and John Fielding's and Patrick Colquhoun's progressive ideas about police reform were just one component of a larger campaign of social reforms to address the underlying problems of urban life in London and other cities. They believed that "police reform was a preliminary and absolute necessity, as without it social reform laws could not be enforced" (Reith 1956, 123). Many of their ideas to reform policing would become reality under the leadership of a young chief secretary for Ireland by the name of Robert Peel (1788–1850). From 1812 through 1818, Peel governed Ireland during a period marked by civil disorders, increasing crime, and religious conflict. Shortly after passage of the Peace Preservation Act of 1814, he was able to establish a new form of policing—the Royal Irish Constabulary. The Constabulary was a civil (as opposed to military) police force designed to assist in reducing crime and disorder (Stead 1985, 62). Consequently, by the time Peel was appointed Home Secretary of England in 1821, he had gained valuable experience organizing police. Upon his return to England, he inherited five distinct classes of police officers:

1. Parochial Constables, elected annually in parish or townships, serving gratuitously
2. Their substitutes for deputies serving for a wage voluntarily paid by the principals
3. Salaried Bow Street officers and patrols charged with the suppression of highwaymen and footpads
4. Stipendiary police constables attached to the public officers established under the "Middlesex Justices Act"
5. Stipendiary Water-Police attached to the Thames Office, as established by act of Parliament in 1789 (Lee 1971, 177)

In 1829, Sir Robert Peel, in his role as home secretary, introduced a bill to create a "new police". **The Act for Improving the Police in and near the Metropolis** established a centralized police force for the metropolitan London area. According to Roth (2005), "Peel had originally hoped to create a nationwide police force, but to his constituency this suggested oppression and totalitarianism" (104). Consequently, he settled on a more focused mission in London. What today seems like a good idea did not meet with universal approval in 1829. Reith (1956) explains that while crime and riots were becoming uncontrollable in London in the early 1800s, "accompanying these events was the growth of hostility to the idea of establishing police" (122) These fears were wide spread among business owners and "men of good-will in all classes who genuinely believed," given the example of French police, "that police of any kind were synonymous with tyranny and the destruction of liberty" (Reith 1856, 122)

Keenly aware of these concerns, two co-commissioners were appointed to help Peel: Charles Rowan, a former

Sir Robert Peel

Source: © Thinkstock

military colonel, and Richard Mayne, an attorney. The new management team recruited and trained over 1000 new officers, who would come to form the new Metropolitan Police Department. The force they created was, "A preventative rather than reactive force; it replaced the ages-old night watch with professional, paid, full-time officers" (Roth 2005, 104). Early decisions about the force are summarized below:

- The force would function on a 24-hour basis.
- Officers would wear a uniform and a top hat.
- Officers would carry no weapons beyond a truncheon.
- Officers would carry a small staff with a crown on one end to symbolize the royal authority (Tobias 1979, 44–46).

Based on the *First Instructions* issued by Rowan and Mayne (and approved by Sir Robert Peel), historians have devised various listings of what is known as "Peel's Principles," or "Principles of Peelian Reform." **Figure 2-6** shows two different lists derived from the many versions of the list. The wording has been modernized somewhat.

The new police force did not immediately replace the existing classes of peace officers mentioned earlier. However, by 1839, following the recommendations of a number of select committees to establish the English police system, especially in London, most of the other police forces in London had been "absorbed" into the New Police. Although the new force was not popular at first, because of the fear of centralized police authority, it eventually won wide public support and became a popular model for municipal police forces worldwide (Emsley 1991), especially in the United States. Peel's contributions to policing have earned him recognition as the "Father of Modern Policing."

SUMMARY

This chapter presented an overview of nearly 3800 years of the history of policing. We have reviewed selected examples of social control in the form of laws and various manifestations of policing from the Babylonian to the British Empires. The chapter emphasized the evolutionary nature of policing, pointing out that laws and policing

---

FIGURE 2-6 Peel's Principles of Policing

Version 1—General Principles

1. Prevention of crime is the basic mission of the police.
2. Police must have full respect of the citizenry.
3. A citizen's respect for the law develops respect for the police.
4. Cooperation of the public decreases as the use of force increases.
5. Police must render impartial enforcement of the law.
6. Physical force is used only as a last resort.
7. The police are the public and the public are the police.
8. Police represent the law.
9. The absence of crime and disorder is the test of police efficiency.

Version 2—Organization Principles

1. Police must be stable, efficient, and organized along military lines.
2. Police must be under government control.
3. The efficiency of the police should be judged by the absence or presence of crime.
4. Distribution of crime information is essential.
5. The police should be deployed by time and area.
6. Qualities such as the command of temper, a quiet determined manner, and so on are indispensable to police officers.
7. Good appearance commands respect.
8. Efficiency is premised on securing and training the proper persons.
9. Public security demands that every police officer be given a number.
10. Police headquarters should be centrally located and easily accessible to the people.
11. Police officers should be hired on a probationary basis.
12. Police records are necessary to the correct distribution of police strength.

Source: Reprinted with permission from J.A. Conser and G.G. Frissora, *Peel's Principles Revisited.* Paper presented at the annual conference of the Midwestern Criminal Justice Association, Chicago, 15 September, 1994.

---

evolved in response to social, political, and economic conditions. With the exception of the Egyptians and the Vigiles in Rome, policing in ancient civilizations was carried out by the military and the elite forces of the aristocracy. This slowly changed in the 17th and 18th centuries as France and England developed the fundamental outlines of modern policing—concepts, which you will learn in the next chapter, were adopted as America begin to establish police departments in the late 1830s.

History is the study of past events. It reconstructs and identifies the social, political, and economic forces that have, and continue to, shape our society. An appreciation and understanding of history helps us make informed decisions about contemporary conditions. Importantly, as George Santayana (1905) warns, "Those who cannot remember the past are condemned to repeat it."

Critical Thinking Questions

1. Why is history an important field of study for a criminal justice professional?

2. Why is the Code of Hammurabi important today?

3. What was unique about the establishment of the Vigiles in ancient Rome? What social and political forces affected their creation?

4. Why is the Magna Carta an important document, both in England and the United States?

5. What key contributions did the French make to the field of policing between the Middle Ages and the early 1800s?

6. Explain why some citizens of England did not support the establishment of the Metropolitan Police of London in 1829.

7. Who were some of the early police reformers in England during the late 1700s and early 1800s?

CHAPTER SPECIFIC INTERNET LINKS

Law of the Twelve Tables: http://www.umass.edu/wsp/comparative/law/rome/twelve/index.html

The Code of Hammurabi: http://www.constitution.org/ime/hammurabi.htm

The Vidocq Society: http://www.vidocq.org

The London Metropolitan Police Department: http://www.met.police.uk/history/index.htm

Henry and John Fielding and Victorian Era policing: http://www.devon-cornwall.police.uk/v3/about/history/vicpolice/intro.htm

CHAPTER GLOSSARY

An Act for Improving the Police in and near the Metropolis—introduced and enacted by Sir Robert Peel, Home Secretary of England, in 1829, it established a centralized police force for the metropolitan London area.

Code of Hammurabi—the legal code of ancient Babylon, codified under King Hammurabi around 1750 BC; it contained some 282 statutes and evidenced a sense of justice built on personal responsibility and accountability.

Commune juree—a 12th century French mutual defense association where an oath formed a bond between a large number of men of equal status for the defense of a collective interest.

Constable—an important position of trust in France during the Middle Ages; a count of the stable.

Courts of Leet (local police courts)—instituted as a substitute for the sheriff's courts.

Feudalism—the practice of providing the living needs of those under a leader's control or subject to a leader's authority.

Frankpledge system—a form of social control where all free men took an oath of fidelity to the king; it was introduced in France during the reign of Charlemagne. Later the word was adopted by the English, where its meaning evolved to include recognition of the responsibility of every citizen to do his part in maintaining peace in the state, or the liability that all men share to render police services when called upon to do so.

Hundred—a collection of 10 tythings.

Laws of the Twelve Tables—a set of twelve brass tablets describing proper conduct that became the foundation of the Roman Empire's legal system (around 450 BC).

Lex talionis—the law of retaliation.

Lieutenant of Police—established by the edicts of the council in France (1666–1667) for the city of Paris.

Magna Carta—the great charter of England signed by King John in 1215; it granted certain guarantees toward a fairer justice system and rights to the people.

Mosaic Law—the law of Moses as found in the Old Testament books of Genesis, Exodus, Leviticus, Numbers, and Deuteronomy.

Peace Guilds—local means of social control in 10th century England; private and voluntary associations, arranged in 10 groups under 10 headmen; mutual assurance societies.

Praepostus—the title of the headman of the English tything following the Norman conquest of 1066.

Praetorian Guards—personal bodyguards of Caesar Augustus; an elite military unit.

Reeve—the chief law enforcement official and magistrate of the shire in the English tything system (known as the shire-reeve, or later as the sheriff).

Sergeant—armed police assistants to early French village mayors.

Shire—a geographical area roughly equivalent to a county.

Statute of Winchester—enacted in 1285 during the reign of Edward I; it created a policing system that continued for nearly 500 years.

Surete—the criminal division of the Paris Police (which in 1913 became the Police Judiciaire).

Tything (or tithing) system—early English system of social control.

Urban Cohort—Roman military units used as protectors of the peace throughout Rome.

Vicecomes—title change of the shire-reeve following the Norman conquest of 1066; responsible for going on the circuit to hold court (known as the police courts).

Vigiles—a civilian force of freedmen created by Emperor Augustus around 14 BC to act as night watchmen; it was the city's first fire-fighting and police unit.

CHAPTER REFERENCES AND ADDITIONAL READINGS

Arnold, Eric A. Jr. (1979). *Fouche, Napoleon, and the General Police*. Washington, DC: University Press of America.

Bagnell, Roger S. (1977), Army and Police in Roman Upper Egypt. *The Journal of the American Research Center in Egypt*, 14, 67–86.

Brandon, S.G.F. (ed.) (1970). *Ancient Empires*. New York: Newsweek.

Breasted, James Henry (1916). *The Conquest of Civilization*. New York: Harper & Brothers Publishers.

Conser, J.A. and G.G. Frissora. *Peel's Principles Revisited*. Paper presented at the annual conference of the Midwestern Criminal Justice Association, Chicago, IL. September, 1994.

Cottrell, Leonare (1970). Gift of the Nile. In Brandon (ed.) *Ancient Empires*. New York: Newsweek, 13.

Emsley, Clive (1991). *The English Police: A Political and Social History*. New York: St. Martin's Press.

Fairlie, John A. (1901). Police Administration. *Political Science Quarterly*, 16:1, 1–23.

Fairman, H.W. (1949). Town Planning in Pharaonic Egypt. *The Town Planning Review*, 20:1, 32–51.

Gadd, Cyril John (1971). "Code of Hammurabi." In Benton, W. (publisher). *Encyclopaedia Britannica*, 11, 41–43.

Gardiner, Alan H. (1920). The Ancient Military Road Between Egypt and Palestine. *The Journal of Egyptain Archaeology*, 6:2, 99–116.

Goodspeed, George S. (1904). *A History of the Ancient World*. New York: Charles Scribner's Sons.

Grun, Bernard (1991). *The Timetables of History: The New Third Revised Edition*. New York: Simon & Schuster.

Holden, Richard N. (1992). *Law Enforcement: An Introduction*. Englewood Cliffs, NJ: Prentice Hall.

Iskander, Zaky and Alexander Badawy (1965). *Brief History of Ancient Egypt*. Cairo, Egypt: Madkour Press.

Kelly, Martin A. (1973, March). The First Urban Policeman. *Journal of Police Science and Administration*, 1(1):56–60.

Kocourek, Albert and John H. Wigmore (1915). *Sources of Ancient and Primitive Law*. Boston: Little, Brown, and Company.

Lee, W.L. Melville (1971, originally published in 1901). *History of Police in England*. Montclair, NJ: Patterson Smith.

National Commission on Terrorist Attacks Upon the United States (2004). "The 9/11 Commission Report." Authorized Edition. New York: W.W. Norton & Co.

Reith, Charles (1956), *A New Study of Police History*, London, Oliver and Boyd Company.

Roth, Mitchel P. (2005). *Crime and Punishment: A History of the Criminal Justice System*. Belmont, CA: Thomson Wadsworth.

Samuel, Delwen (1999), Bread Making and Social Interactions at the Amarna Workman's Villige. Egypt. *World Archaeology*, 31:1, 121–144.

Santayana, George (1905). *The Life of Reason Volume 1*. New York: Charles Scribner's Sons.

Seignobos, Charles (1932). *The Evolution of the French People*, translated by Catherine Alison Phillips. New York: Alfred A. Knopf.

Stead, Philip John (1985). *The Police of Britain*. New York: MacMillan.

Tobias, J.J. (1979). *Crime and Police in England, 1700–1900*. New York: St. Martin's Press.

Trojan, Carol (1986). "Egypt: Evolution of a Modern Police State." *Comparative Criminal Justice*. Chicago, IL: Office of International Criminal Justice, University of Illionois at Chicago, pp. 235–242.

CHAPTER 3

The Evolution of Law Enforcement in the United States

LEARNING OBJECTIVES

This chapter presents a brief history of law enforcement in the United States. As you read the chapter, refer to Appendix II, *Timelines in American Policing*, to help you place events in historical perspective. You will learn that police departments were established as a supplement to traditional forces of social control: family, religion, and the community. The introduction of organized uniformed police in the late 1830s was an acknowledgement that traditional forces of social control, supplemented by a haphazard and amateurish system of night watches, constables, and sheriffs, were no longer an effective bulwark against social disorder and crime; this became especially apparent as America experienced waves of immigration coupled with industrialization and urbanization. American policing, from its inception in the late 1830s and continuing into the early 1900s, struggled to deal with crime and disorder. Its inefficiencies rested almost exclusively on one fact: from its inception as an institution, big-city police fell under the corrupting and pervasive influence of partisan politics, a blight that infected policing well into the 1930s. Reform proved to be a slow, stubborn, and halting process. After studying this chapter, you should be able to:

- Describe a colonial night-watch patrol and its duties.
- Describe how the combined forces of family, religion, and community influenced social control in colonial America.
- Describe a southern slave patrol and its duties.
- Describe how immigration, industrialization, and urbanization influenced the development of American policing.
- Explain how a national culture of racism influenced the development and enforcement of laws and the staffing of law enforcement agencies in American history.
- Explain how the Progressive Movement changed American policing.
- Identify those individuals most responsible for reforming policing from the 1890s through the 1950s.
- Identify the major writers and historians of American policing.
- Discuss the evolution of state police.
- Explain how crime commissions and presidential commissions changed law enforcement in the United States.

KEY TERMS USED IN THIS CHAPTER

Frame of Government

slave codes

slave patrols

paddyrollers

night watch

rattlewatch

wardens

Judiciary Act of 1789

Whiskey Rebellion

vigilantism

vigilante committees

antebellum

Emancipation Proclamation

Reconstruction

Black Codes

freedmen

Ku Klux Klan (KKK)

Jim Crow laws

Plessy v. Ferguson

Progressive Movement

International Association of Chiefs of Police (IACP)

police benevolent associations

Fraternal Order of Police (FOP)

Lola Greene Baldwin

Alice Stebbins Wells

International Association of Women Police (IAWP)

National Commission on Law Observance and Enforcement (Wickersham Commission)

President's Commission on Law Enforcement and Administration of Justice

Law Enforcement Assistance Administration (LEAA)

Omnibus Crime Control and Safe Streets Act of 1968

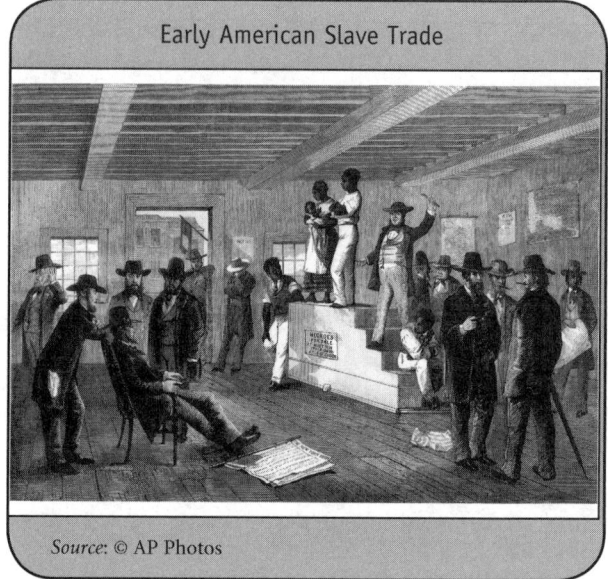

Early American Slave Trade

Source: © AP Photos

POLICING & SOCIAL CONTROL IN COLONIAL AMERICA: 1585 TO 1776

Beginning in 1585, with the founding of the first colony on Roanoke Island, successive groups of settlers from Germany, Holland, Scandinavia, and England began new lives along North America's eastern seaboard. The British would lead this migration in both numbers and influence; in fact, they would become the dominant presence in North America and would have the most influence in establishing, among other things, a common language, social norms, and political institutions, including the new institutions of criminal justice. As historian Samuel Walker (1998) explains, "American criminal justice begins with the first European colonists," especially the English, who introduced "criminal codes, law enforcement agencies, courts, and various modes of punishments" (14).

The colonization of America, which lasted for more than 150 years, is one of the great sagas of human history. Between 1607 and 1733, a kaleidoscope of social, political, and economic forces, turned by the hands of time and geography, led to the founding of 13 American colonies. While variations in time and place make comparison difficult, there were important similarities in the early characteristics of colonies. For example, according to historian James Cox (2003), American colonies "were autocratic and theocratic, with a patriarchal system of justice: magistrates and religious leaders, sometimes one and the same, made the laws, and the burden of obeying them fell on the less exalted—the tradesmen, soldiers, farmers, servants, slaves, and the young" (1). While harsh and undemocratic by today's standards, these arrangements met little resistance. It was a time, as Walker (1998) observes, when crime and sin were seen as one aberration; when social control rested within three closely connected institutions: the church, the family, and the community; and when obedience to authority, especially the church and the male head of the household, was paramount.

By 1770, over two million people of European heritage lived in the 13 colonies, yet not all who arrived came willingly. Between 1718 and 1776, England shipped approximately 30,000 convicts to the colonies, a practice called transportation. While life in the colonies was difficult, it was better than a London prison cell. The young, and mostly male, convicts traded prison for a four to seven-year contract of hard labor as indentured servants. In doing so, they became America's first source of low-cost labor, many destined for tobacco plantations in Virginia and Maryland. However, as the supply of convict labor began to decline, another source of low-cost labor—African slaves—quickly replaced indentured servants, and thus began a long and tragic chapter in American history, one that would cast a shadow over our system of justice, particularly the institution of policing.

Regional Differences: New England, Pennsylvania, and Virginia

Historian Mitchel Roth (2005) observes that from their rudimentary beginnings, the agencies of criminal justice were local creations "resembling those of England, Holland, Spain, and France," depending on the colonists' country of origin (50). Their development took on a local (if not regional) character in response to particular social problems, political circumstances, and/or economic enterprise, and so a visitor to colonial America would note differences in the organized mechanisms of social control as he traveled from New England, south through Pennsylvania and Maryland, and down to the plantations of Virginia and the Carolinas. **Figure 3-1** identifies several informative sites on the World Wide Web that contain histories of selected agencies.

An early visitor to a New England village would find scant evidence of an organized system of social control. While a county sheriff or constable may have provided an image of justice, they were appointed, or elected armatures who performed very little law enforcement as we understand it today. Social circumstances (i.e. crime and disorder) had not yet produced the political will for a more robust law enforcement presence. In many ways, this can be attributed to the ". . . high level of homogeneity and consensus on basic values that prevailed in American communities at that time" (Walker 1998, 2). Consensus and obedience to authority were common. In fact, as Walker (1998) notes, obedience to authority

was an accepted condition of daily life, offered "first to God, then to the clergy, and finally to the male head of the household" (15). Lesser violations of community norms or church doctrine—swearing, for instance—were attended to quickly by the voice of public criticism. If the violation was more serious—for example, failing to observe the Sabbath—the offender would be made to suffer the spectacle of public shaming, which included being placed in the stocks, flogged or branded, or even banished from the community. Only in the rare case of rape or murder was a person put to death (Roth 2005; Cox 2003; Walker 1998).

Overall, public order in the villages of New England was generally easy to maintain. This can be attributed to a simple fact: the villages of New England were homogeneous communities where shared assumptions of proper conduct were common, predatory crimes were uncommon, and the influences of church, family, and community were the primary forces of social control. There was little need for the formal agencies of social control that we know today. The church, the family, and the community (formalized in the town meeting) were all that was generally necessary to maintain social order (Roth 2005; Cox 2003; Walker 1998).

In many ways, colonial Pennsylvania was much like New England. A visitor there would also find a strong religious influence and consensus on community values, and yet there were differences. In 1682, the Quakers (the Society of Friends), under the leadership of William Penn (1644–1718), introduced a very different and more tolerant philosophy of Christian teaching and political thought. For example, the Quakers believed that every person was blessed with certain religious and civil rights; rights that were granted by their creator, not the crown (i.e. the British government). Therefore, it was the duty of government, in the opinion of Quakers, to protect these rights, which Penn detailed in a now seminal document, the ***Frame of Government***. In a prophetic announcement, Penn assured the settlers of Pennsylvania that, "You shall be governed by the laws of your own making . . ." (Wallace and O'Brien 1995, 1).

William Penn had introduced elements of a political philosophy that would find great appeal and meaning in America's future. In less than 100 years, the core

---

FIGURE 3-1 Selected histories of law enforcement agencies found on the World Wide Web

By reviewing the histories of several selected law enforcement agencies, you will be able to identify various similarities and differences.

Federal Agencies
Bureau of Alcohol, Tobacco, and Firearms:
  http://www.atf.gov/about/history/atf-from-1789-1998.html
United States Marshals Service
  http://www.usmarshals.gov/history/index.html
United States Bureau of Prisons
  http://www.bop.gov/about/history/first_years.jsp

Southern Region
Miami (FL) P.D.
  http://www.youtube.com/watch?v=MlaDmI2I6JA
Houston (TX) P.D.
  http://www.hpou.org/history/history_1940.cfm
Winston-Salem (NC) P.D.
  http://www.cityofws.org/Home/Departments/Police/PoliceHistory/Articles/WSPDHistory

Northeastern Region
Boston (MA) P.D.
  https://www.cityofboston.gov/police/about/history.asp
Baltimore County (MD) P.D.
  http://www.baltimorecountymd.gov/Agencies/police/history.html
Buffalo (NY) P.D.
  http://bpdthenandnow.com/homepage.html

Midwestern Region
Boone County (MO) Sheriff's Department
  http://www.showmeboone.com/sheriff/history.aspx
Pennsylvania State Police
  http://www.psp-hemc.org/history/psp.html
Xenia (OH) P.D.
  http://www.ci.xenia.oh.us/police-division/history-3.html

Western Region
Colorado Springs (CO) P.D.
  http://www.springsgov.com/units/police/history/history1.asp
Phoenix (AZ) P.D.
  http://phoenix.gov/POLICE/histor1.html
Los Angeles County (CA) Sheriff's Department
  http://www.lasd.org/aboutlasd/history.html

---

principles enumerated in Penn's *Frame of Government* (e.g. trial by jury, freedom of the press, and religious tolerance) would reappear in the Constitution and Bill of Rights (see Appendix I) of a new nation. It was a philosophy based on the rule of law, a principle that would come to guide American justice. Yet, for many, it was a hopeful but hollow promise, conflicting with the realities of the American experience, especially those individuals held in bondage.

William Penn

Source: © Getty Images/Thinkstock

Traveling south, an early visitor to Virginia or the Carolinas would find a somewhat different society. Unlike Pennsylvania and New England, which were founded primarily by family units for religious reasons, Virginia was established as a business venture. Moreover, its early settlers, according to Roth (2005), were a loose "assortment of gentlemen, servants, and vagrants" attracted by the opportunities of business (52). Religion, in the form of the Church of England, was important, though it played a lesser role in Virginia than it had in New England or Pennsylvania. Also, the southern colonies quickly developed an economy based on the cultivation of a single crop: tobacco. Unfortunately, tobacco farming was labor-intensive and required a large labor force; according to Roth (2005), this need was initially satisfied by indentured servants, but a new source of cheap labor would soon emerge to replace this uncertain workforce—slaves.

Slavery and Slave Patrols

Wherever a visitor might travel in the colonies by the late 17th century, the institution of slavery would be apparent. It had become a dominant presence in the southern colonies, an unpleasant fact in the northern colonies, and a brooding fixture in the American experience. In fact, the introduction of large numbers of African slaves would eventually lead to a general fear of slave revolts and "insurrection, real or imagined" among white plantation owners and settlers (Roth 2005, 55). Consequently, in 1705, Virginia passed the first **slave codes** in an attempt to regulate and control the behavior of the growing numbers of slaves; South Carolina followed suit in 1740 when it established a basic slave law. These laws were intended to protect whites from runaway slaves, inhibit insurrection, and authorize the recapture of fugitive slaves. The laws also created an enforcement mechanism, **slave patrols**, which were empowered to visit every plantation and to search all "Negro-houses for offensive weapons and ammunition," and to inflict corporal punishment if any slave was found to have left his owner's property without permission (Wood 1984, 123–124). (For an excellent and informative account of slave patrols, see Sally E. Hadden's book (2001) *Slave Patrols: Laws and Violence in Virginia and the Carolinas*.)

According to Walker (1998), "Charleston, South Carolina and New Orleans both established slave patrol systems that preceded northern city police departments by many decades." (23) This is not to suggest that northern colonies (and later northern states) were havens for slaves or freedmen; for example, in 1702, New York passed an Act for Regulating Slaves, and this was followed in 1703 by a law in Massachusetts that "forbade Indians, Negroes, and mulatto slaves and servants from being away from their homes after 9 pm, unless on a specific errand for their master" (Walker 1998, 24). By 1837, the Charleston slave patrol, which included about 100 officers, was possibly the country's largest single "police force" (Wintersmith 1974, 19–21). However, the control of slaves was not just a state issue or something that occurred in colonial America. As late as 1861, U.S. Marshals were arresting and returning fugitive slaves to their southern masters in compliance with the Fugitive Slave Act, which was passed by Congress in 1850.

Historian Sally Hadden (2001) observes that early slave patrols were semi-organized groups of volunteers who worked at the behest of an individual plantation owner or a local group of slave masters; these early volunteer patrols were erratic and proved ineffective, thus prompting the legislatures of Virginia, North Carolina, and South Carolina to replace voluntarily patrols "with colony-sanctioned authority figures who would monitor slave movement and behavior" (38). This created an institution of government (hundreds of slave-patrols that operated throughout the South) that was specifically designed to regulate the activities of a class of "citizens" based on the explicit criteria of race.

Individuals appointed to slave patrols were officially referred to as "constables, searchers, overseers, or patrollers," but were less affectionately labeled by those they sought to enslave as "**paddyrollers**." Beyond undergirding the entire structure of slavery, slave patrol membership brought authority, status, camaraderie, and social interaction with other whites. Consequently, it helped institutionalize the prevailing culture of racism (Hadden 2001).

Social, political, and economic forces had coalesced in the colonies, especially the southern colonies, to create a three-headed monster: slavery, the apparatus to maintain it, and a culture that tolerated it. This would have grave ramifications for the future development of southern law enforcement, law enforcement more generally, and the nation as a whole. For example, Hadden (2001) believes that as political conditions in the South changed following the Civil War, many slave patrollers moved to employment in city police departments throughout the South, bringing the culture and practice of racism with them. Some historians even maintain that the slave patrols of the South were America's first modern-style police forces (Williams and Murphy 1990).

Racism and discrimination were not confined to southern police; it was, and still is, a national problem (see **Figure 3-2**).

Night Watch, Constables, and Sheriffs

Let us continue our historical journey by stepping back in time again and visiting some of America's large cities. An early visitor to a major colonial city would find a great deal of commerce and activity, but little in the way of organized law enforcement. As the nation grew in the mid-1600s and early 1700s, cities like Boston, New York, and Philadelphia would soon grow too large, diverse, and transient to be effectively controlled by the influences of church, family, and community. Urbanization, accelerated in years to come by immigration and industrialization, would lead to and compound the problems of social order in American cities (Walker 1998). The first organized attempt to police cities came in the form of a constable and a **night watch**, comprised of volunteers or men drafted to serve.

Police historian Eric Monkkonen (1981) reports that constables (who were generally elected) were assisted by a system of night watch, and eventually day watch volunteers, although some cities did, in time, pay for their service. If someone was detained by a watchman, they would be turned over to the constable, who would take the accused before a justice of the peace. However, the night watch (or patrol, as they were sometimes called) was held in low esteem by the citizens they served. This can be attributed to several conditions: wages, when paid, were low, and working conditions were unattractive, tedious, and at times demanding, if not dangerous. Moreover, the patrol was generally ineffective in controlling crime or providing real security.

An early visitor to a colonial city would note that a night watchman's duties included "walking rounds crying the time of night and the state of weather in a moderate tone" (Roth 2005, 64). First introduced in Boston in 1631, the concept would soon be introduced to other cities. Service as a night watchman was an obligation of all adult males in the community, but it was an unpleasant and onerous duty. For example, historian Roger Lane (1971) reports that night watchmen were required to "see that all disturbances and disorders in the night shall be prevented and suppressed;" they were also given the "authority to examine all persons, whom they have reason to suspect of any unlawful design, and to demand of them their business abroad at such time, and wither they are going; [and to] to enter any house of ill-fame for the purpose of suppressing any riot or disturbance" (10).

Although some communities experimented with paid night watch, most colonists relied on volunteers to staff

FIGURE 3-2 Breaking the color and gender barriers: Selected appointments of African-American and female officers

Boston, MA

Horotio J. Homer was Boston's first African-American police officer and the first appointed in the United States. He was hired in 1878 and promoted to sergeant in 1895. In 1919, after 41 years of service at age 71, he was forced to retire due to illness.
Source: Taylor, Erica (June 23, 2010).

New York, NY

In 1891, Wiley Overton was hired by the Brooklyn Police Department, becoming their first African-American police officer. In 1898, the five boroughs of New York were incorporated to become New York City. In 1911, Samuel J. Battle became the first African-American police officer hired by New York City. He was also the city's first sergeant (1926), lieutenant (1935) and parole commissioner (1941). In 1920, Lawon R. Bruce became the first African-American NYPD policewoman.
Source: Lower Manhattan Construction Command Center (February 18, 2003).

Wichita, KS

In 1894, Sam Jones was elected as a constable, becoming the first African-American voted to county office in Kansas. He also worked as a lather, printer, fireman, and served as a soldier in the Spanish American War, reaching the rank of Major. He later became the Deputy State Fire Marshal. In 1952, he became a history consultant with Historic Wichita, Inc. where he worked until two days before his death at the age of 93 in 1960.
Source: City of Wichita (2010).

Los Angeles, CA

In 1899, J.P. Loving was hired as a deputy sheriff by Los Angeles County Sheriff William A. Hammel, making Loving the first African-American deputy sheriff to serve on the sheriff's department.
Source: Los Angeles County Sheriff's Department (2010).

Los Angeles, CA

In 1909, Los Angeles social worker Alice Stebbins Wells petitioned Mayor George Alexander and the City Council, requesting that an ordinance providing for a Los Angeles Policewoman be adopted. Not only was the measure passed, but on September 12, 1910, Mrs. Wells was appointed as the nation's first female policewoman with arrest powers.
Source: Los Angeles Police Department (2010).

Washington D.C.

In 1919, the Metropolitan Police Department hired three policewomen to form the nucleus of the Women's Bureau. The Women's Bureau handled all matters pertaining to female adults and juveniles coming into official contact with the police. Policewomen investigated causes of delinquency and recommended solutions using either legal action or social treatment.
Source: Metropolitan Police Department, District of Columbia (2010).

Massillon, OH

In 1955, the Massillon Police Department hired its first black police officer, Lemie Gibson, under Chief Switter's administration. The first female police officer for the city of Massillon, Pam Whitmyer, was hired on August 9, 1980.
Source: City of Massillon Ohio (2010).

Source: Adapted from the multiple sources listed.

their novice agencies of law enforcement well into the 1700s (Johnson 1981, 5). Some variations existed; for example, in New Amsterdam (later renamed New York when the British took over the city in 1674), a group of volunteer citizens equipped with rattles to warn of their watchful presence was referred to as the **rattlewatch**. However, in 1658, New Amsterdam appointed eight paid watchmen to replace the volunteers.

Constables and night watchmen were assigned a number of duties other than law enforcement. For example, Joshua Pratt, the constable in Plymouth, Massachusetts in 1634, was the sealer of weights and measures, surveyor of land, jailer, and announcer of marriages (Whitehouse 1973, 88). In addition to night watchmen who patrolled city streets, county governments copied the English precedent of appointing sheriffs as their primary law enforcement officials. Sheriffs, like their British counterparts, were appointed through the political system (usually the colonial governor's office) and were not elected. In some locations, sheriffs had oversight responsibilities for constables, who performed much of the day-to-day law enforcement activity. Despite their official status, early sheriffs and constables were essentially untrained amateurs who ". . . played a relatively minor role in maintaining law and order" (Walker 1998, 13).

During the 1700s, policing in most colonial cities changed little, although Johnson (1981) notes that the reliance on volunteer watchmen was becoming strained:

> By the middle of the eighteenth century the colonists faced a dilemma, which some residents felt they could no longer ignore. The towns had become large enough to need reliable police, but their best citizens habitually refused this duty and the men who did serve were not as effective as they needed to be. Circumstances, not incompetence, dictated this ineffectiveness. Watchmen who worked all day at other jobs could hardly stay awake, let alone maintain order at night. Some cities did pay their watchmen, but not enough to allow someone to earn his living by law enforcement. The idea of citizen participation in policing was breaking down, and something was needed to replace it (6–7).

According to Walker (1998), "Philadelphia had so much trouble finding people to serve [as night watchmen] that a special law was passed in 1712 fining anyone who refused to serve" (27), yet many people simply paid the fine rather than serve. In 1749, the city of Philadelphia was permitted to levy a tax and appoint **wardens** with the authority to hire watchmen as needed. Only those interested in working on the watch for pay applied to the wardens, and watchmen could now be dismissed for inefficiency (Johnson 1981, 7).

The British Military

A visitor to colonial America would also encounter another peacekeeping mechanism: the British military, which loomed ominously over the colonists. Its presence became an unsettling factor as massive social and political discontent grew stronger toward the latter part of the 1700s. From 1765 through the end of the Revolutionary War (1783), colonists faced riots and disturbances in their cities, economic depression, and the ever-increasing imperial policies of Britain. In many cases of mob violence, especially in important coastal cities like Boston, New York, and Baltimore, the duties of public safety were given to British military forces. However, their heavy handedness, evident in incidents like the Boston Massacre, left a lasting hostility to the idea of a uniform/military institution of social control.

Following the Revolutionary War, policing, what little there was of it, returned to civilian control, so as America began its great experiment with democracy, it lacked an effective police force, or even the concept of a police force as we know it today (Lane 1971, 35; Walker 1998, 45–46; Roth 2005, 78). However, two things were certain: citizens were not interested in imposing a military model of policing on themselves, and they were very reluctant to impose additional taxes to pay for any other form of policing.

EARLY DEVELOPMENTS & MODELS OF POLICING: 1780s TO 1880s

Appointment of Federal Marshals

At the national level, the new nation found itself in a curious situation: Congress could pass laws and institute policies, but it could not enforce their mandates if citizens refused to comply. In 1789, 13 years after the American Revolution, Congress passed the **Judiciary Act of 1789**, which established the federal judiciary. This act also created the first federal law enforcement position, the federal marshal. Almost immediately, President George Washington appointed 13 marshals. Their duties were to support the federal courts and to carry out all lawful orders issued by Congress, the president, or judges, including carrying out death sentences. They were also charged with taking the national census every 10 years. Throughout their early years, they were assigned to enforce unpopular federal laws, which included collecting taxes on whiskey. Evidence of their unpopularity became apparent when U.S. Marshal Robert Forsyth was murdered in 1794 while serving papers on distillers in western Pennsylvania. Before the incident ended, 13,000 state militiamen had to be summoned to put down what is known as the **Whiskey Rebellion** (Jackson, 1989). (See **Figure 3-3**)

Some of the duties of marshals seemed to work at cross-purposes, duties rooted in the social chasm that would eventually bring the country to war again. For example, marshals enforced the Slave Trade Act of 1794 and the 1807 Act of Congress, both of which forbid the importation of slaves. Later, they enforced the Fugitive Slave Act of 1850, which required the return of runaway slaves to their owners.

Before the Civil War, marshals also tracked down counterfeiters (since the Secret Service did not exist until 1865). However, they may be best remembered for their efforts to bring some justice to the Wild West. Marshals pursued now infamous outlaws including Billy the Kid, Jesse James, and Butch Cassidy. Marshals such as Heck Thomas, Chris Madsen, and Uncle Billy Tilghman patrolled the Oklahoma Territory. It also appears that Wyatt Earp had an overstated reputation as a marshal and instead may have used the law as a way to make money and avenge his brother's murder (Jackson 1989).

Establishment of Police Departments

The decades from 1820–1850, sometimes referred to as the Jacksonian Era (in reference to President Andrew Jackson), were "a period when Americans first perceived crime as a threat to the order and security of the Republic" (Roth 2005, 121). To compound the problem, the decentralized system of policing comprised of night watch, day watch, part-time and armature constables and sheriffs

---

FIGURE 3-3 First U.S. Marshal killed in the line of duty

On January 11, 1794, Robert Forsyth, U.S. Marshal for the District of Georgia, was shot and killed while attempting to serve civil papers. He was the first civilian official of the United States government and the first of as many as 400 marshals killed in the line of duty over the past 200 years. He was shot while trying to serve civil process on Beverly Allen.

Marshal Forsyth may have expected trouble. He took two of his deputies with him to Mrs. Dixon's house in Augusta, Georgia on January 11, 1794, because the Allen brothers, Beverly and William, had reportedly been seen there.

The forty-year-old Forsyth, a veteran of the Revolutionary War, knew how to take care of himself, but in the four years he had served the new federal government as the first marshal in the District of Georgia he had experienced little, if any, difficulty or resistance.

Most of his work had consisted of routine administrative duties in support of the federal court. His search for the Allen brothers was no different. The marshal merely wanted to serve them with some court papers in a civil suit. Nonetheless, Forsyth took the precaution, for whatever reason, of taking two of his deputies with him. When the three officers entered Mrs. Dixon's house, they found the Allens talking with friends. Wishing to spare the brothers embarrassment, Forsyth asked to speak to them privately outside. Instead of following the marshal, however, the brothers ran up to the second floor and darted into the nearest room, bolting the door behind them. While they waited for Forsyth and his deputies to come after them, Beverly Allen loaded, primed, and cocked his pistol.

Forsyth and his deputies went after the brothers. Hearing their approach, Beverly Allen aimed his pistol toward the door and squeezed the trigger. Before the sound of the gunshot could echo off the walls, the ball splintered through the wooden door and struck Forsyth fair in the head. He was dead before his body hit the floor, the first of 400 or more marshals killed performing their duties.

Source: U.S. Marshal's Service, http://www.usmarshals.gov/history/forsyth/in_line_of_duty.htm.

(which, by design, had been in keeping with traditional fears of despotic government) were no longer capable of dealing with society's fear of crime and social disorder. For many Americans, the general decline in law and order was attributed to "the declining authority of the church and family" (Roth 2005, 121), compounded by the destabilizing influences of immigration, urbanization, and industrialization. Politicians and citizens "groped for ways to maintain order in cities that were increasingly divided by ethnic, religion, lifestyle, and social class" (Walker 1998, 49).

The problems of social disorder eventually outweighed the public's fear of a centralized institution of social control and the kinds of liberties they would have to surrender to a vigorous police, not to mention the additional taxes it would require. Cautiously, beginning with Boston in 1838, and followed by New York in 1845, cities began establishing paid police forces structured after the Metropolitan Police of London. The institution of American policing was born.

Boston's new municipal police force, like all that would follow, was intended to be a preventive force. Specifically, in the words of historian Roger Lane (1971), its members were expected to actively seek out trouble "before it had time to reach serious proportion" (35). First among these duties, they were expected to suppress crime and riot. They were also expected to enforce city ordinances, respond to fires and accidents, and deal with vagrant children. In what would become standard practice across the country, the new police would be paid regular wages, they would work shifts on a 24-hour, 7-days-a-week basis, and they would be divided into divisions (or precincts) to cover geographic sections of their cities (Lane 1971).

While some early police departments simply absorbed the hapless night watch and day watch bureaucracy and personnel that already existed, others began on more solid footing. In 1802, Washington DC organized a centralized auxiliary police watch, which consisted of a captain and 15 policemen. However, this organization eventually proved ineffective, and in 1861:

> President Abraham Lincoln took personal interest in founding a regular police department for the District of Columbia. It was a time of constant danger in the nation's Capital. With the beginning of the Civil War, an army was billeted in the city, government employees were increased by 10-fold, and hordes of unsavory elements descended upon the District's few square miles. President Lincoln personally dispatched an emissary from the newly-created Board of Metropolitan Police Commissioners to New York City to become familiar with that system, which itself was based on the world-acclaimed Metropolitan London Police Department (Metropolitan Police Department).

Based on their study of the NYPD, the District of Columbia established a police force in 1861, comprised of one superintendent (paid $1500 annually), 10 sergeants (each paid $600 annually), and approximately 150 officers (each paid $480 annually).

The new agencies, despite many organizational and staffing problems, offered some hope for the challenges that troubled America's cities. Consequently, as George Kelling and James Steward (1991) report,

> the idea of a "bureaucratic police department spread throughout the United States between 1840 and 1860 [Monkkonen (1992) sets these dates between 1850 and 1880]. Either immediately or eventually, U.S. police resembled their English counterparts in many respects: they were organized on a quasi-military basis; they wore uniforms; they patrolled the streets 24 hours a day; they embodied Peel's spirit of 'peace' officers; their mission was to prevent crime, disorder, riot; and they investigated crimes." (3)

The new agencies presented four important innovative features. First, they were hierarchically organized. Second, they were assigned to the executive branch of government with regular salaries and lines in the city budget. Third, they wore uniforms, making them visible to the public and easier for their superiors to control. Finally, they actively patrolled their beats, where they were expected to discover and prevent crime (Monkkonen 1992). Consequently, they became the most visible arm of

The original nine of the LaPorte Police Department

Source: Courtesy of LaPorte County Historical Society Museum

government and institution of urban service. Monkkonen (1992) explains, that:

> Once in place, city police almost immediately began doing things unexpected by their original creators, whose expectations were more along the lines of crime prevention. Along with arresting offenders, the police took in tramps, returned lost children by the thousands, shot stray dogs, enforced sanitation laws, inspected boilers, took annual censuses, and performed myriad other small tasks. Their unique communications organization and street presence virtually forced them to become city servants as well as crime-control officers (554).

(For an excellent and informative narrative that chronicles the creation of America's first police department, see Roger Lane's book (1971), *Policing the City: Boston, 1822–1885*.)

Vigilantism and Private Detectives

Very different from big-city police, an improvised form of law enforcement called **vigilantism** was common between 1767 and the 1930s. According to historian Richard Brown (1969), there were 326 confirmed and possibly as many as 500 "organized, extralegal movements, which [took] the law into their own hands" to suppress and punish crime summarily (121). While the concept of vigilantism offers a negative connotation in contemporary society, it arose out of necessity in the absence of effective law and order in frontier areas of almost every state in our pioneer history. **Vigilante committees** were organized by community leaders, usually business owners and professionals, and comprised of the industrious and honest men of the community, generally men of average means like farmers, artisans, tradesmen, and teachers, to address specific problems (Brown 1969).

Vigilante committees, which generally functioned under a Constitution signed by committee members, were organized to deal with a wide range of problems, including

Badge worn by a member of the Aurora, Nevada Vigilante, 1864

Source: Courtesy of Doug Gist, Silver State National Peace Officers Museum

rowdies, common criminals, outlaw gangs, cattle and horse thieves, counterfeiters, and gamblers. They appeared in boomtowns like San Francisco and Denver, mining camps, cattle towns, and rural communities. Most vigilante committees were short lived, lasting only long enough to address the problem at hand, which was generally a few days to a few months. Their extralegal actions, which included flogging, expulsion, and hanging, were meant to send a clear message to unruly inhabitants of a community that "the newness of the settlement would provide no opportunity for eroding the established values of civilization." In other words, absent the "foundations of a stable society—churches, schools, cohesive community life," vigilante committees were organized in an attempt to maintain or "reestablish the conservative values of life, property, and law and order" that had existed in the communities were the settlers had once lived (Brown 1969, 123).

In 1767, South Carolina citizens organized the South Carolina Regulators (another name for a vigilante committee) in an attempt to defend themselves against criminals and Indian attacks. It was one of the earliest vigilante organizations, lasting until 1769, when legislators passed the Circuit Court Act authorizing sheriffs, jails, and circuit courts (Walker 1998, 36). Eastern vigilantism (occurring

in areas bordering the Appalachian Mountains, Mississippi Valley, Great Lakes, and Gulf Coast) ended in the 1860s; western vigilantism (occurring in areas west of the Appalachian Mountains, including the Great Plains, Rocky Mountains and Pacific coast), which began in the 1850s, and followed the migration west, lasted until about 1910 (Brown 1969). According to historian Michelle Jolly (2003), "widespread theft and arson, largely unchecked by the courts, provoked the formation of the San Francisco Vigilance Committees of 1851 and 1856" (1). These committees, which numbered about 700 citizens, were possibly the best organized and most powerful of any committees, serving as an organizational model and leaving "an immense impact on American vigilantism" (Brown 1969, 127).

Generally, most vigilante committees were small, but quite effective. After capturing a suspect, public trials were quickly held before juries comprised of committee members, the accused was almost certain to be found guilty, and punishment was public, swift, and certain. In cases where the guilty were to be hanged, they were usually given one hour to pray before the sentence was carried out. In addition to reactive committees, some vigilante committees were organized as a preventive measure. This fact is captured in a letter written by a Denver, Colorado resident, Thomas G. Wildman, on September 8, 1859 to friends back home:

> There is to be a Vigilance Committee organized in the town this evening. All of the leading men of the town have signed the Constitution, and its objective is a good one…. It is thought that stabbing and drunkenness will be rampant here this winter, and we think that the rowdies and gamblers will be more careful when they find out that we are organized and that all the first men of the town are determined to punish crime (Cited by Brown 1969, 133).

Along with the vigilante movement, the private police (detective) field was taking shape in the mid-1800s, as private industry and the railroads needed to protect their assets from criminals, disgruntled employees, and competitors. One early private protection agency was founded by Allan Pinkerton in 1855. Known as Pinkerton's North West Police Agency, its initial task was to investigate criminal activity against railroads. Earlier, in 1850, Henry Wells and William Fargo established the American Express Company, a freight service company. They had to provide their own protection, known as "shotgun riders," as they transported goods and valuables, including payrolls (Green and Fisher 1987, 11). (Chapter 4 describes the private police movement in the United States in greater detail.)

Policing, the Civil War, & Reconstruction (1861 to 1877)

Racial discrimination has been a perpetual feature of the American experience, one that has certainly affected policing in a myriad of ways; this has been especially true for Americans of African descent. For example, in **Antebellum** America, every new state admitted to the union after 1819 restricted voting to whites only. Many states prohibited black testimony in court if whites were a party to the proceeding. One of the duties of early police departments was to capture fugitive slaves (See **Figure 3-4**). Even after the Civil War (1861–1865) and the **Emancipation Proclamation** (signed by President Lincoln on September 22, 1862), discrimination against blacks was endemic.

During **Reconstruction** (1863–1877), as former confederate states were in the process of rebuilding following the Civil War, white politicians began to enact discriminatory laws that limited basic human rights and civil liberties of blacks. The laws, known as the **Black Codes**, were eventually enacted by every former confederate state. According to Historian Eric Foner (1988), the entire complex of Black Codes was enforced "... by a police apparatus and judicial system in which blacks enjoyed virtually no voice whatever. Whites staffed urban police forces as well as state militias, intended, as a Mississippi white put it in 1865, to 'keep good order and discipline amongst the Negro population'" (203).

Moreover, during Reconstruction, whites victimized blacks with near total immunity. Equality, while championed by some quarters of society, was an elusive goal. For example, when southern whites were prosecuted, their

FIGURE 3-4 Boston Caution Poster (c.1851)

CAUTION!!
COLORED PEOPLE
OF BOSTON, ONE & ALL,
You are hereby respectfully CAUTIONED and advised, to avoid conversing with the
Watchmen and Police Officers of Boston,
For since the recent ORDER OF THE MAYOR & ALDERMEN, they are empowered to act as
KIDNAPPERS
AND
Slave Catchers,
And they have already been actually employed in KIDNAPPING, CATCHING, AND KEEPING SLAVES. Therefore, if you value your LIBERTY, and the Welfare of the Fugitives among you, Shun them in every possible manner, as so many HOUNDS on the track of the most unfortunate of your race.
Keep a Sharp Look Out for KIDNAPPERS, and have TOP EYE open.
APRIL 24, 1851.

Source: © AP Photos

sentences were less harsh than sentences given to blacks who committed the same offense. In an attempt to address the injustices of slavery and protect the rights of **freedmen** (freed slaves), the federal government passed the Civil Rights Act of 1866, which specified the rights of citizens regardless of race. It also allowed for lawsuits against persons who deprived a citizen of a civil right. This law led Congress to adopt the Fourteenth Amendment to the Constitution, which provided "equal protection" under the law. Shortly thereafter, the Fifteenth Amendment was adopted, securing voting rights of blacks. Additionally, the Civil Rights Act of 1875 outlawed the exclusion of blacks from hotels, theaters, railroads, and other public accommodations (Williams and Murphy 1990, 7). However, violent opposition to many of the policies of Reconstruction by the **Ku Klux Klan** (which was founded by veterans of the Confederate Army in 1865) undercut

African-American early group photo, Kansas City (MO) PD

Source: Courtesy of Kansas City Police Historical Society

the ability of freedmen to enjoy the rights and protections of these laws.

Reconstruction did bring some progress to policing as politicians began appointing blacks to police departments. For example, black officers were hired in Selma, Alabama in 1867; Houston and Galveston, Texas in 1870; Jackson, Mississippi in 1871; Chicago, Illinois in 1872, Columbia and Charleston, South Carolina in 1873; and Philadelphia, Pennsylvania in 1874. In fact, by 1870, the city of New Orleans had 177 black officers, and three of the five police board members were black. However, just because agencies began appointing blacks did not mean that they were equal to their white counterparts. In many cities, the scope of their duties was restricted. For example, in some cities, black officers were not permitted to arrest whites,

and other cities even refused to put them in uniform, having them wear plain clothes instead. Other cities (e.g., Chicago) assigned black officers to black neighborhoods (remember that communities were very segregated) and even marked the cruisers "Negro Police" (Williams and Murphy 1990, 7; Thale 2005).

The Compromise of 1877 ended Reconstruction and southern states began passing "**Jim Crow**" laws, which separated the races and discriminated against blacks. The term "Jim Crow" is believed to have originated around 1830, when it was first used in a minstrel show that mocked the mannerisms of blacks. Eventually, the term became a racial slur used to describe stereotypical images of black inferiority. Unfortunately, Jim Crow laws created and perpetuated a discriminatory and segregated society in the south, where inferior treatment of blacks was a widely accepted cultural practice, a situation that lasted well into the 1970s (Griffin 1996; Klarman 2004).

The Supreme Court added to this disparity in the case of **Plessy v. Ferguson** (1896), which upheld the constitutionality of state laws under the doctrine of "separate but equal." Among other things, these laws allowed segregation in schools and public accommodations. After the *Plessy* decision, some cities even began firing black officers; for example, New Orleans dropped to only five black officers by 1900 and did not appoint another black officer until 1950 (Williams and Murphy 1990, 9). Figure 3-2 (see page XX) identifies the dates of the appointments of black and female officers (discussed previously in this text) in selected cities in the United States.

THE FIRST WAVE OF REFORM & DEVELOPMENTS IN POLICING, 1890s TO 1920s

Two overlapping waves of reform would join to shape American policing between the 1890s and 1970s. The first wave, spearheaded by individuals outside of policing, emerged in the 1890s and continued through the 1920s. The second wave, stimulated by the intellectual energy generated within the first wave, began in the early-1900s and continued in successive surges through the 1970s. The second wave was different in one important aspect: it came from individuals within policing. The final sections of this chapter review these developments.

The Need for Reform

For better or worse, by the late-1800s police and sheriff's departments had become established fixtures in all of America's big-cities and urban areas. Policing had even developed a small body of literature, which, although partisan, defended and detailed the histories and activities of some police departments against their political opponents. According to Walker (1977), "These histories marked the dawning of organizational self-conscience among the American police." (35). Moreover, a traveler would notice great standardization in organization, personnel, and practices; in the 1890s, policing in New York City was similar to policing in Portland, Oregon or New Orleans in its general

applications. For example, historian Robert Fogelson (1977) reports that police officers in these (and other cities) "passed their time resolving domestic disputes, giving street directions, rendering emergency assistance, calming incendiary situations, and otherwise responding to calls from citizens" (96). Additionally, departments were comprised almost exclusively of white males, many of Irish or Germanic decent, recruited from working or middle-class society, which meant that they held and supported middle-class values. Importantly, by the late-1800s, the police had also developed "a clearly defined job-conscience," which was good for purposes of organizational identity and morale, but which sometimes fostered resistance to change and innovation (Monkkonen 1982, 580).

Unfortunately, the institution of policing was mired in the corrupting influences of partisan politics. Appointments and terms of office for officers were often dictated by elected officials of the party in power for political advantage and personal gain. Not only did "political machines" influence the selection of officers, they interfered with the effective management of police departments in cities across the country, including Philadelphia, Chicago, Kansas City, San Francisco, Los Angeles, and New York, to name a few (Fogelson, 1977). According to Walker (1998), New York City many have been the best example, as it was a place where "corruption was not only rampant but, according to some historians, was the principal activity of the police" (61).

The Progressive Reform Movement

The prevalence of corruption and its inevitable path to inefficiency prompted angry calls for reform. Beginning in the 1890s, a procession of reformers would lead this charge; first among them was the Reverend Charles Parkhurst, who denounced corruption within New York City's Tammany Hall government, including the police department (NYPD). Parkhurst's crusade galvanized the city and the state, focusing great attention on the problem, and his efforts eventually led to a New York State Senate probe of the NYPD, headed by State Senator Clarence Lexow. The Lexow Commission (1894–1895) was the first in the United States to investigate police corruption. Its findings led to the appointment of a new "reform-minded" police commissioner for New York City in 1895, Theodore Roosevelt. (See **Figure 3-5**)

Theodore Roosevelt

However, by the end of the 1890s, little had changed within the NYPD, and "corruption, inefficiency, and brutality continued for decades" (Walker, 1998, 65). It would take a concerted effort to produce real change within American policing. Fortunately, reform would slowly emerge through the efforts of many dedicated citizens, commonly associated with the **Progressive Movement** (1890s to 1920s).

Progressive reformers, in the words of Robert Fogelson (1977), were part of a diverse

> "movement, which began at the turn of the century and thrived for the next two decades, [it] sought to shore up the position of the upper middle and upper classes by reforming the courts, schools and other urban institutions. It attempted to reorganize their structure, upgrade their personnel, and redefine their function in ways that would . . . destroy the system of machine politics, which had developed in the mid- and late-nineteenth century." (44)

Reformers embraced two objectives for policing. First, they wanted to free city government, and the police, from the corrupting influences of partisan politics.

FIGURE 3-5 Police Commissioner Theodore Roosevelt

During his three years as police commissioner of New York City (1895–1897), Roosevelt gained international acclaim for his reforms. He pioneered a bicycle squad, a telephonic communications system, and training for new recruits. He routed out corrupt elements within the department and instituted promotion based on merit rather than on politics. Later, he enthusiastically supported the Pennsylvania State Constabulary (State Police) and, in 1908, as President, he organized the Bureau of Investigation in the Department of Justice, the forerunner of the FBI.

Source: Law Enforcement Assistance Administration (LEAA) (1976), *Two Hundred Years of American Criminal Justice*, Washington, D.C.: U.S. Department of Justice, p. 20.

Second, they wanted to improve police efficiency. Several strategies were offered to accomplish these goals. For example, reformers wanted to increase the power and responsibility of police chiefs and subsequently establish centralized control over police departments. They suggested establishing special units to deal with vice, traffic regulation, and other matters. They introduced civil service regulations. They fought against the formation of unions. Reformers wanted to change the police from a reactive to a preventive orientation; they wanted to remove the police from activities not directly related to crime. They wanted to improve the working conditions of police and, first and foremost, reformers wanted to improve the quality of police personnel (Fogelson 1977).

Attempts at Unionization: The Boston Police Strike (1919)

In the early 1900s, with the growth of corporations and trade unions, some rank-and-file members of police departments toyed with the idea of unionizing to secure better working conditions and salaries. Never before had police officers attempted to unionize. On August 15, 1919, the idea of collective action moved in a new direction when rank-and-file officers in Boston unionized under a charter from the American Federation of Labor (AFL). However, the city of Boston refused to recognize the union, which prompted 1134 rank-and-file members of the police force to vote in favor of a strike, to begin on September 9, 1919. Subsequently, 1117 officers from the 1544-member department failed to report for duty on that day.

The Boston Police Strike left the city's 700,000 residents in a "panic" and resulted in several days of random acts of violence by mobs and hooligans, the mobilization of the state militia, and the subsequent firing of all strikers. Massachusetts Governor Calvin Coolidge expressed the nation's sentiment concerning police unions, when he stated, "There is no right to strike against the public safety by anybody, anywhere, any time" (Russell, 1975, 191). The strike, which attracted national attention and united public opinion, curtailed police unionization efforts for nearly 40 years (refer to Chapter 8 for a more detailed discussion of the unionization movement).

THE SECOND WAVE OF REFORM & DEVELOPMENTS IN POLICING: 1900s TO 1945

Early in the 1900s, a second wave of reformers—police executives—began to reshape the tattered structures of American policing. Their innovations were tied to the ideas offered by earlier reformers outside of policing. Expanding on these ideas, the second wave of reformers operated under the crusading issue of professionalizing policing. Six general assumptions guided their efforts. First, they believed that police chiefs should have more autonomy when commanding their departments. Second, they believed that the primary purpose of the police was to provide the best possible service, as efficiently as possible, but at the lowest possible cost. Third, they believed that police officials were in a better position than politicians or municipal-officials to design police policies and service strategies. Fourth, they believed that law enforcement's proper role was addressing crime, not as a catchall social service agency. Fifth, they felt that police should enforce conventional standards of morality. Finally, they believed that police practices and law enforcement decisions should apply to all citizens equally (Fogelson 1977). Unfortunately, this final assumption often succumbed to a national culture of discrimination, based on one's race, social stature, or political connections.

August Vollmer

Source: Courtesy of the City of Berkeley Police Department Historical Unit

During this period, leading figures in the development of policing, like August Vollmer (Chief of Berkeley, California from 1905–1932) and Superintendent Richard Sylvester (Washington, D.C.), campaigned against inefficiency, low standards, and political interference in policing. They, and many others, formed a vanguard that pressed for greater efficiency, better personnel and practices, and the use of science and technology in policing. Importantly, an emerging body of academic literature concerning police administration supported them. Scholars like Leonhard F. Fuld (1909), who wrote *Police Administration*, and Raymond B. Fosdick (1920), who wrote *American Police Systems*, pressed for police reform through the introduction of strong management, centralization, and administrative efficiency.

Each of the aforementioned books gained wide readership in police reform circles, helping to usher in the concept of professional policing. Progressive police leaders, and now line officers, were also turning to a new body of professional literature that sought to improve the art, craft, and science of criminal investigation and police strategies. For example, Charles W. Fricke's book, *Criminal Investigation* (1930), gained wide use as a "how-to" book for uniformed officers and detectives. Another important book of the period, written by Harry Soderman and John O'Connell (1934), *Modern Criminal Investigation*, was also widely read. In the Forward, New York City Police Commissioner Lewis J. Valentine offers a little insight on the mood of policing at the time. He opined that

> Police practice has long felt the inadequacy of mere experience and is now reaching out for all the help that can be obtained from the growing sciences. Prevention of crime and the detection and apprehension of criminals are rapidly becoming technical processes (Soderman and O'Connell 1934, v).

Building on these works, in 1936 August Vollmer published *The Police and Modern Society*; it would become one of the most important contributions to the literature of policing. It was followed, in 1940, by Bruce Smith's influential book, *Police Systems in the United States*, which guided several post-World War II generations of police leaders, becoming the blue print for modern police organization and management. (See **Figure 3-6** for additional information about August Vollmer.)

The Birth of Professional Associations

As we see from the preceding paragraphs, a new self-consciousness was beginning to emerge in American policing. It was a professional self-consciousness, which could trace its roots to 1893, when a group of innovative police chiefs established the National Chiefs of Police Union. The group changed their name in 1902, becoming the **International Association of Chiefs of Police** (IACP), which today is the world's preeminent voice of law enforcement. The original purpose of the association was to share ideas and provide mutual assistance.

From its inception, the IACP became the authoritative voice of American policing, establishing standardized procedures for many police functions. It advocated the adoption of civil service standards, pioneered national procedures for arresting persons based on telegrams (a forerunner of the National Crime Information Center, NCIC), and established a police telegraph code and uniform system for identifying criminals. Also, in 1905, they addressed the issues of suspect rights (see **Figure 3-7**).

Early reformers within the IACP included: Chief August Vollmer of Berkeley; Major Richard Sylvester, Superintendent of the District of Columbia Police; Chief William S. Seavey of Omaha; Superintendent Robert McLaughrey of Chicago; Chief W.C. Davis of Memphis; Chief Roger O'Mara of Pittsburgh; Chief L. Harrigan of St. Louis; and Chief Harvey O. Carr of Grand Rapids (Dilworth 1976, 3–6; Walker 1977, 48). Importantly, the IACP's annual conventions allowed police executives from across the country and around the world to exchange ideas and keep current on the latest technology and legal developments in the profession. The IACP was to become the driving force behind police professionalization.

Police executives were not alone in reforming policing. **Police benevolent associations**, comprised mainly of rank-and-file police, began to appear as early as 1867, when the city of St. Louis, Missouri organized the Police Relief Association to assist disabled officers and the widows of officers. Their appearance gradually spread to police departments across the country (e.g., Cleveland in 1881 and

FIGURE 3-6 The contributions of August Vollmer (1876–1955)

Recognition:　America's Greatest Cop
　　　　　　　Father of Modern Police Science
　　　　　　　Dean of American Law Enforcement

August Vollmer served the city of Berkeley, California for 27 years, first being elected town marshal in 1905 and then as police chief until his retirement. In 1907, he was elected president of the California Police Chiefs Association, and by 1922 he had ascended to the presidency of the International Association of Chiefs of Police.

He was a strong advocate of college educated police officers. He established one of the first police training schools in the United States and initiated the first college-level law enforcement courses at San Jose State College in 1916. He became a full professor of police administration at the University of Chicago (in 1929 while on leave from Berkeley P.D.), which was followed with an appointment as Professor of Police Administration at the University of California at Berkeley. He served as the Police Consultant to the National Law Observance and Enforcement Commission and was the primary author of its Report on Police (1929–1931). He was instrumental in many other state and national professional associations. He acted as a consultant to over 75 police departments throughout the world during his career. He promoted police professionalism through his many writings, which included books, articles, reports, and correspondence with academic and police leaders throughout the country.

Vollmer was an ardent innovator and advocate of the use of technology. He instituted bicycle patrols (1905), a red light recall system (1906), police records and modus operandi systems (1906), motorcycle patrol (1913), automobile patrol service (1914); installed a fingerprint system, handwriting system, and deception detection system (1921); and installed the first aluminum street signs (1924).

He believed in stringent recruiting standards, emphasized ethical conduct, and advocated freedom from political interference. At times, his views were unpopular with contemporaries. He considered crime prevention a priority, opposed capital punishment, supported decriminalization of victimless crime, and advocated probation for the first-time offenders.

Plagued by ill health in his later years, he ended his own life on 4 November 1955.

Source: Adapted from Gene E. Carte and Elaine H. Carte (1975, 125–128); D.E.J. MacNamara (1955); and Bancroft Library, University of California, Berkeley (n.d.).

FIGURE 3-7 Flashback to 1905: The "rights" warning

Chief Benjamin Murphy of Jersey City, New Jersey, addressed the 12th annual convention (1905) of the IACP about a system adopted in his department some TEN years earlier.

　　It is one of the standing rules of force . . . we have what we term a statement. This statement is typewritten and is furnished to each station house. Just as soon as a person is arrested on the charge of having committed a felon, rape, robbery, burglary, murder, etc., it is the duty of the superior officer present to bring that defendant into a room. This statement is picked up and read to him in the presence of the arresting officer, and, if possible, some other witness." The statement reads in this way: "I am John Brown, a sergeant of police. I am going to ask you some questions concerning the crime for which you are arrested. You are arrested for _____ on _____ street a short time ago. You may answer these questions or not just as you please, but what you do say will be taken down in writing and used at your trial. It must be a free, voluntary statement. Do you understand that?"

Source: Reprinted with permission from Donald C. Dilworth (ed.), *The Blue and The Brass: American Policing 1890–1910*, p. 66, Gaithersburg, MD: International Association of Chiefs of Police, 1976.

Denver in 1883) and marked an important milestone in American policing—the self-consciousness of the rank-and-file police officer. Through these associations, officers organized and advanced their collective interests. Benevolent associations also performed charitable work in their respective cities (Kuechler, 2003). By the 1890s, as rank-and-file police officers started to see police work as a career, they began turning their attention to political and labor issues, and consequently, many benevolent associations took on a fraternal character (Walker 1977, 48–49; Fogelson 1977, 193–218). For example, in 1915, two Pittsburgh patrol officers founded the **Fraternal Order of Police** (FOP) as a social benevolent association that included all ranks in the police organization. In 1917, the FOP opened lodges in other cities, becoming a national organization.

As the nation's cities grew, communities turned to their police departments to assist in all types of issues emerging from an ever more diverse and complex society. Female officers were needed to assist with problems related to women and juveniles. In 1908, the City of Portland, Oregon hired **Lola Greene Baldwin**, a 48-year-old social worker, "to perform police service" as a "police detective," thus, according to historian Gloria Myers (1995), becoming America's first policewoman (1). Lola Baldwin was an effective and energetic police officer during her 16-year career, gaining international recognition for her pioneering work with women and children. Among her many accomplishments, she helped to organize the "municipal policewomen's division; juvenile, morals, and domestic relations courts; a citizens' vice commission; a state institution for sexually delinquent girls; a city venereal detention hospital for prostitutes; and pushed a variety of state and local protection legislation for women and children" (Myers 1995, 3). Lola Baldwin was a member of a small but important group of early police professionals.

In 1910, **Alice Stebbins Wells** became the first policewoman with full police powers in the city of Los Angeles. She became a national advocate of women in policing, and helped organize, and was the first president of, the International Association of Policewomen (today known as the **International Association of Women Police**, see **Figure 3-8**). In 1912, Mrs. Margaret Q. Adams was sworn in as a deputy sheriff with the Los Angeles County Sheriff's Department, making her the first female deputy in the country. By the end of World War I, over 200 cities and counties employed female officers, frequently operating out of separate "women's bureaus."

Crime Commissions

Despite some progress, policing still faced many challenges. In the latter part of the 1920s, several state and local commissions began looking into corrupt and inefficient police practices, as well as the other issues surrounding the administration of criminal justice. Three of these investigations are important because they had a significant influence on police reform in their respective locations. Included in the list are the Cleveland Survey of 1922, the Chicago Crime Survey of 1926, and the Missouri Crime Survey of 1926. These city and state investigations were followed in 1929 by a national investigation, when President Herbert Hoover appointed Attorney General George W. Wickersham to chair the **National Commission on Law Observance and Enforcement**. The **Wickersham Commission**, as it is commonly known, undertook the first national study of the criminal justice system in the United States. August Vollmer was placed in charge of surveying the condition of American policing; his now seminal document, *Report on Police*, which was released in 1931, offered ten recommendations:

1. The corrupting influence of politics should be removed from the police organization.
2. The head of the department should be selected at-large for competence, a leader, preferably a man of considerable police experience, and removable from office only after preferment of charges and a public hearing.
3. Patrolmen should be able to rate a "B" on the Alpha test, be able-bodied and of good character, weigh 150 pounds, measure 5 feet 9 inches tall, and be between 21 and 31 years of age. The chief for good and sufficient reasons could disregard these requirements.
4. Salaries should permit decent living standards, adequate housing, eight hours of work, one day off weekly, annual vacation, fair sick leave with pay, just accident and death benefits when in performance of duty, and reasonable pension provisions on an actuarial basis.

FIGURE 3-8 International Association of Women Police

The International Association of Women Police was originally organized in 1915 as the *International Policewomen's Association*. The International Association of Chiefs of Police lent their support to the newly formed organization by helping to draft the original constitution and outline the association's objectives. The charter was adopted and was incorporated in Washington, D.C. in 1926.

Unfortunately, in 1932, the *International Policewomen's Association* became a "depression casualty." Not having had a chance to be fully implemented, the programs set into motion by the Association went by the wayside. However, its programs and ideals remained only temporarily dormant. Mrs. Wells lived to see the rebirth of the organization.

In 1956, at a meeting of the *Women Peace Officers of California*, in San Diego, California, the Association was reorganized and recognized as the *International Association of Police Women*. Several years later the organization changed its name to the *International Association of Women Police* (IAWP). Under the direction of Doctor Lois Higgins, its newly elected President, IAWP began to change and grow. Dr. Higgins, a thirty-year member of the Chicago Police Department, held the position of IAWP President for eight years and then served twelve more years as its Executive Director.

Speaking at the first biannual meeting of the IAWP held at Purdue University in 1957, Dr. Higgins commented, *"The advent of women into [police] departments brought into existence the crime prevention and juvenile bureaus...These women brought a social viewpoint into police work."*

The IAWP, through its constitution and activities, promoted separate women's bureaus. Many women felt this was their only opportunity for advancement within the department. Before 1969, women were never assigned to patrol, and many did not even own a uniform. Their duties were still restricted to those performed in the early 1900's by Mrs. Wells.

Though IAWP membership remained small through the 1960's, the IAWP began to hold annual three-day conferences in 1963. Attendance at the conferences was minimal. In 1973, by general membership vote, the clause [...to encourage] was deleted from the IAWP Constitution in the section that dealt with "the establishment of women's bureaus in police departments . . ." IAWP began working toward promoting the assignment of women officers into other areas of law enforcement within police departments.

While originally established primarily for women officers, IAWP members recognized that cohesiveness, professionalism, and communication must exist between men and women in all aspects of the criminal justice system. Therefore, in 1976, IAWP began actively recruiting male officers to join its ranks as active IAWP members.

Source: International Association of Women Police (2004), "Past & Present, 1915–today," http://www.iawp.org/history/pastpresent.htm

---

5. Adequate training for recruits, officers, and those already on the roll is imperative.

6. The communication system should provide for call boxes, telephones, a recall system, and (in appropriate circumstances) teletype and radio.

7. Records should be complete, adequate, but as simple as possible. They should be used to secure administrative control of investigations and of department units in the interest of efficiency.

8. A crime-prevention unit should be established if circumstances warrant this action, and qualified women police should be engaged to handle juvenile delinquents and women's cases.

9. State police forces should be established in states where rural protection of this character is required.

10. State bureaus of criminal investigation and information should be established in every state (140).

While some of these points were eventually adopted, political machines continued to exert strong influence over municipal government in many cities. Nevertheless, the recommendations of the Wickersham Commission set the groundwork for a later generation of reform efforts that began soon after World War II.

The Evolution of State Police

The establishment of State Police and Highway Patrol agencies between the early 1900s and 1930s is linked to America's new mobility—the automobile—and the inability of local jurisdictions to effectively respond to regional or statewide problems associated with crime, traffic, and labor disputes. By the early 1900s, America's emerging middle-class was becoming more affluent and mobile. The patterns of American life where changing, generally in a positive direction. However, patterns of crime were also changing. August Vollmer and Alfred Parker (1935) note these changes in the following observation:

> It is no longer possible to say that major crimes are committed only in cities; the countryside, with its quietude, has become the criminal's new world, a realm in which, so far, he has been able to operate almost unmolested because of inadequate and inefficient police service (25).

Traffic, flowing across regional boundaries and jurisdictions, was another problem. According to insurance company records, in 1932 in the United States, approximately 29,000 persons were killed in automobile accidents and 904,800 were injured (Vollmer and Parker 1935, 25). State governments often found themselves without an agency to enforce state traffic laws, as only Texas and Massachusetts had created state agencies prior to the twentieth century. The Texas Rangers were officially formed in 1835, originally to protect the life of American frontier settlers, primarily from Indian raids. Although Massachusetts created its first state police agency in 1865 to focus on vice laws, the force was abolished in 1875 because of the lack of public acceptance (Johnson 1981, 157–158).

In 1905, Pennsylvania established the first modern state police force. Rural crime and violence associated with union strikes, especially in the state's coal fields, led Governor Samuel Pennypacker to create the force of 228 men. Between 1908 and 1923, 14 states (mostly in the northern industrial regions) established similar organizations. Eventually, state police forces turned most of their attention to rural policing, traffic enforcement, and investigating

crimes that crossed regional or state jurisdictions. In 1931, Governor Julius L. Meier of Oregon stated that, "Probably the three principal factors which are fostering the creation of State Police Departments, are the use of automobiles and paved highways in the commission of crimes, the necessity for cooperation in rural communities in the apprehension of criminals, and the need of organized preventive factors" (Vollmer and Parker, 1935, 5). Consequently, during the 1930s, 8 more states added state police forces, while 18 established highway patrol agencies.

State involvement in policing also included establishing communication systems and bureaus of criminal identification. By 1934, 24 states had bureaus of criminal identification, and by the early 1930s, telephone systems and two-way radio technology were sufficiently developed to permit their widespread use by all police jurisdictions, which greatly enhanced efficiency. Generally free of partisan political interference from their inception, state troopers enjoyed good reputations across the United States, achieving elite status in the law enforcement community well ahead of their municipal brothers (Johnson 1981, 158–164).

POST-WORLD WAR II DEVELOPMENTS: 1946 TO 1990s

A Changing Society and Its Police

Following the Second World War, policing in the United States continued its march toward professionalism. Walker (1977) summarized this period best, stating that

> From the 1940s through the early 1960s police reform continued along the lines that were already well established. Police professionalism was defined almost exclusively in terms of managerial efficiency, and administrators sought to refine techniques that would further strengthen their hand in commanding and controlling rank-and-file patrolmen (167).

These efforts were headed by a new post-World War II generation of police leaders. They were better educated than earlier police leaders, many had distinguished military service records, they exerted greater public influence, they were fiercely independent and resistant to political interference, and they spoke forcefully about problems within policing, including the abysmal and unprofessional conditions and conduct of lesser departments. Importantly, they took decisive action to set policing on its contemporary course. For example, they spearheaded the movement to increase hiring standards, improve basic and in-service training, increase efficiency and professionalism, and create police science and criminology programs in colleges and universities. They wrote books and authored articles about the police profession (for example see *Police Chief Magazine*); they began to establish a systematic body of knowledge about the field to accept (and act on) the scholarly critiques of law enforcement's techniques and practices from the academic community.

When the relatively tranquil 1950s turned into the tumultuous 1960s, this generation of police leaders listened to community complaints, surveyed failed policies, and searched for answers that would refocus the traditional model of policing and move it toward a community-policing model. Most importantly, they hired and then mentored a new generation of police officers, who have subsequently passed the torch to another generation—the officers we see today. (See **Figure 3-9** for a brief narrative about four of the post-WWII police leaders)

During the 1950s and early 1960s, police departments across the country successfully completed the marriage of three technologies: the telephone, the patrol car, and the two-way radio. This arrangement led to a basic model in policing—the rapid response to calls-for-service. Moreover, it established the American mind-set that, "if you call, they will come." While some larger cities maintained foot patrols, the die was cast. The tacit relationship between police officer and citizen had changed forever. Rapid mobility and effective communications, coupled with the promise that the police would attempt to solve any problem, created a new dynamic: short duration, but professional intervention and enforcement strategies. Today, the enhanced-911 system has simply improved on this promise. While some have criticized this dynamic, claiming it is impersonal, it remains a basic feature of American policing.

Despite a great deal of progress, the 1950s, 1960s, and 1970s also presented many challenges to American policing. Most communities in America were still segregated and unequal—some were prosperous and relatively free of crime while others were deteriorating and crime-infested.

Riots of the 1960s

Source: © Janine Wiedel Photolibrary/Alamy Images

At the same time, urban life was becoming more chaotic, fast-paced, and burdened with racial/ethnic tensions. Black migration from the rural south had increased during the 1940s as workers moved north to fill wartime factory jobs. Conversely, during the 1950s and 1960s, there was an exodus of whites from the inner city and investment capital followed as they fled to the new suburbs that would come to ring the old cities of their parents and grandparents. Social service agencies and institutions were ill-prepared to serve the needs of those caught in the hopeless poverty and blight of inner city decay. Moreover, political violence in the United States was producing recurring shock waves. Roth (2005) notes that, "no era in American history was marked by the murder of as many public figures as the 1960s. Leaders as diverse as Martin Luther King Jr., John F. Kennedy, Medgar Evers, Robert F. Kennedy, and Malcom X were silenced by assassin's bullets" (293).

Domestic troubles were compounded by the ever-increasing involvement of the United States in foreign affairs (the Korean Conflict, the "cold war," the Cuban missile crisis, and Vietnam). The baby-boomer generation began questioning the country's social and political

FIGURE 3-9 Selected Reformers of the 1950s–1970s

Orlando Winfield Wilson (1900–1972)
O.W. Wilson is best known for authoring several major texts in the police field, especially *Police Administration*, which was first published in 1950 and became the unofficial "bible" for police managers (and students). In 1921, he began his police career as a patrolman in Berkeley, California. He served as chief in Fullerton (CA) and later at Wichita (KS). He taught at Harvard and in 1939 became professor of police administration at the University of California at Berkeley, replacing August Vollmer who retired. He served with the military and also assisted in reorganizing the police forces in Europe following WWII. He served as Superintendent of the Chicago Police Department from 1960–1967.

Vivian Anderson Leonard (1898–1984)
V.A. Leonard joined the Berkeley Police Department in 1925. He went on to earn a BA and MA in colleges in Texas and a Ph.D. from Ohio State (1949). He served as superintendent of the records and identification division of the Ft. Worth Police Department from 1934–1939. From 1941 to 1963, he was affiliated with the Washington State University and became a full professor of Police Science and Administration. He authored *Police Organization and Management* in 1950, as well as six other texts: *Police Communications Systems*, *Police Records Systems*, *The Police of the Twentieth Century*, *The Police*, *Police Personnel Administration*, *Criminal Investigation and Identification*, and *Police Crime Prevention*. He was active in several national organizations, was a founder of what later became the Academy of Criminal Justice Sciences, and was founder of Alpha Phi Sigma (the national criminal justice honor society).

John Edgar Hoover (1895–1972)
Born and educated in Washington, D.C., Hoover spent his career there as well. During WWI, he worked as a special assistant on counterespionage activities to the U.S. Attorney General. In 1924, at age 29, he was appointed the director of the FBI following a major reorganization of it. He reformed the agency into a highly effective and efficient organization. By the 1930s, the agency was a modern crime fighting organization that was aggressively pursuing major criminals throughout the U.S. He adopted modern crime lab technology (in addition to fingerprinting), detailed criminal records and statistics, and later computerization (the National Crime Information Center). The National Police Academy was established to help train state and local managers in the latest methods and techniques. Under Hoover's leadership, the FBI became one of the most effective and respected law enforcement agencies in the world. Unfortunately, some of Hoover's methods and constitutional rights abuses tarnished his latter years of service. He served as director until his death in 1972.

William H. Parker (1902–1966)
Parker is best known for his professional leadership of the Los Angeles Police Department from 1950 to 1966. During that time, he took the agency to national and international prominence by demanding excellence and efficiency, and by projecting a positive public image. He began his career in LA in 1927 and rose through the ranks. During WWII, he served in the U.S. Army and was highly decorated, receiving the American Purple Heart, the French Croix de Guerre with Silver Star, and the Italian Star of Solidarity. He served under Colonel O.W. Wilson and assisted in the reorganization of European police forces following the war. As Chief of LA, he demanded that highly qualified personnel be employed and that they receive only the best training. He reorganized the department and modernized the agency in terms of procedures, buildings, and equipment.

direction—questions that often went unanswered by government. Consequently, vocal segments of citizens across the country began to engage in civil protest.

From the mid-1950s through the 1960s, political protest, racial unrest, and demands for racial equality sparked violent incidents and major riots in cities across the United States, all captured and aired on America's new medium: television. The police, who now prided themselves as professionals, were put to the test. In nationally-televised incident after incident (e.g., school desegregation in Alabama, civil rights marches, riots in major cities, and the "police riot" of the Democratic

National convention in 1968), it became apparent to many citizens, and a growing number of progressive police managers, that there was still a great divide between the rhetoric of professionalism and actual professionalism. Walker (1998) summarized these feelings best when he observed, ". . . never before had the day-to-day operations of the police and prisons been as seriously challenged; and never before had there been such a pervasive sense that something was fundamentally wrong with the criminal justice system" (181). Bob Dylan, a popular songwriter and singer of the period, captured the nation's mood best in the lyrics of a best-selling song titled "The Times They are A-Changin.'" This would certainly be true for American policing.

Presidential Commissions and LEAA

By 1965, social unrest and crime had become a national crisis, forcing President Lyndon Johnson to declare a "war on crime" and appointed a commission to examine every facet of crime and law enforcement in America. Following a two-year investigation, in 1967 the **President's Commission on Law Enforcement and Administration of Justice** issued their summary report, *The Challenge of Crime in a Free Society*. Their critical assessment of the American criminal justice system became the benchmark for reform. In the report, the Commission made numerous recommendations, which they believed would improve police service and lead to a more professional institution. The Commission suggested that:

- Departments should participate in community planning activities
- Departments should establish community-relations units
- As a vehicle for resolving problems, departments should participate in neighborhood citizen advisory committees
- Departments should actively recruit more minority officers
- Departments should institute adequate citizen grievance and complaint procedures
- Departments should develop and enunciate situational guidelines that officers must follow as they work through discretionary decisions

- Departments should divide police functions among three kinds of officers: "community service officer," "police officer," and "police agent"
- Departments should eventually require that a baccalaureate degree become the minimum educational requirement for entry into police service, and immediately make it a requirement for promotion to supervisor and/or executive positions
- Departments should conduct background investigations on all candidates, supplemented with intelligence tests and personal interviews, and the decision to hire a candidate should ultimate rest on their education, background, character, and personality
- Funding authorities should increase police salaries, as higher salaries would attract better candidates
- Promotions should be based on ability, prior performance, character, educational achievement, and leadership potential
- Lateral entry should be permitted
- Training should be enhanced at all levels of service
- A probation period of at least one year, and preferably 18 months, should be established
- Each state should establish a commission on police standards and training
- Departments should retain a legal adviser
- Departments should form a unit specifically responsible for developing, enunciating, and enforcing department policies and guidelines
- Departments should develop a program that fosters integrity and should also establish an internal investigations unit
- Departments should adopt the team policing model
- Departments should adopt a basic "imminent danger" policy that dictates when an officer may use his firearm (91–123)

The above recommendations, in whole or in part, would serve as a roadmap for a generation of police leaders. If you study these recommendations closely, you will see the outlines and seed ideas for a whole host of contemporary police policies, procedures, and strategies. The Commission also published nine additional reports, each dealing with a different field of criminal justice: *The Police*,

The Courts, Corrections, Juvenile Delinquency and Youth Crime, Organized Crime, Assessment of Crime, Narcotics and Drug Abuse, Drunkenness, and *Science and Technology*. These reports make for interesting reading, since each elaborates on the conditions found in the criminal justice system during the mid-1960s.

After the publication of the Commission's findings, Congress created the **Law Enforcement Assistance Administration** (LEAA) to assist state and local law enforcement agencies with implementing the recommendations set forth by the Commission. The enabling legislation, the **Omnibus Crime Control and Safe Streets Act of 1968**, commonly referred to as the "Safe Streets Act" or the "Crime Control Act" of 1968, provided billions of dollars of assistance to the criminal justice community until its funding was removed in 1980.

During the late 1960s and continuing through the 1970s, crime—much of it related to drugs and civil disobedience—grew to become a federal issue. To gain a better understanding of the causes of crime and to develop policies that might address it, various presidents established commissions to study specific problems or incidents, including:

- Commission on Civil Disorders, 1968
- Commission on Causes and Prevention of Violence, 1969
- Commission on Campus Unrest, 1970
- Commission on Civil Rights, 1970
- Commission on Obscenity and Pornography, 1970
- Commission on Marihuana and Drug Abuse, 1972
- National Advisory Commission on Criminal Justice Standards and Goals, 1973
- Commission on Gambling, 1976
- Commission on Disorders and Terrorism, 1976
- Commission on Private Security, 1976
- Commission on Organized Crime, 1976

The recommendations offered in these and other reports would help police leaders as they developed local strategies to address crime and disorder in their communities. By the 1970s, the federal government (with its vast funding), the IACP, and local police leaders were united in a common effort to professionalize policing.

The 1980s and 1990s

Since the late 1970s, policing in the United States has continued to undergo cycles of scrutiny and reform. According to Walker (1992), at the beginning of this period the police were "caught between old problems and new ideas" (26–28). The traditional model of policing (professional, but detached) was not adequately addressing old problems associated with crime and the public's fear of crime. New ideas like problem-oriented policing and the philosophies underlying community policing meant changing traditional concepts and models of police service. Building on these solid platforms of professionalism, American law enforcement slowly, but steadily, transformed itself throughout the 1980s and 1990s. It moved from a traditional model to a customer service model of policing.

The issues, debates, and trends in policing of the last two decades are incorporated throughout the rest of this text. As you study these chapters, pause for a moment and reflect on this chapter, as the profession has made tremendous progress over the course of its history.

SUMMARY

During America's colonial period, volunteer watchmen provided communal security. Gradually, however, as cities grew more populated and diverse, law enforcement services were shifted to full-time, paid police forces, forces that remained inefficient and amateurish for years. The founding of a new nation created the need for federal law enforcement, which was first performed by federal marshals. In many regions of the country, vigilantism augmented or even replaced established police departments with their own brand of justice. Private security agencies arose in areas where law enforcement was ineffective or did not exist.

The early stages of professional policing can be traced to the Progressive Movement. Undaunted by the many problems that faced them and captured by the ideas of professionalism and applying scientific principles to organization, investigation, and crime prevention, a long list of scholars and police leaders pressed for reforms. The goal of creating a police profession moved one step closer with the founding of the International Association of Chiefs of Police (IACP). It took another step forward when rank-and-file officers began to establish associations like the Fraternal Order of Police and the International Association of Women Police, organizations that emerged to address concerns of the working officers. Following the lead of city and state investigations conducted in the 1920s, the Wickersham Commission issued the first national study of the criminal justice system in 1931. Its recommendations became the basis for future reform.

Following the Second World War, policing evolved from an informal, even casual, bureaucracy to a formal rule-governed command and control bureaucracy. By the 1980s, it was successfully moving from a law enforcement model to a community service model, supported by the newest technologies and communications systems. By the 1990s, as you will learn in the following chapters, policing wins recognition as one of America's most professional, trusted, and innovative institutions.

Critical Thinking Questions

1. The influences of family, religion (i.e., a moral compass), and community combine to create the basic institutions of social control in our lives. These influences were so strong in colonial America that there was no need for a supplemental institution of social control, like the police. A number of factors combined to change this arrangement in American history. Identify and then explain how these factors influenced America society and led to the establishment of police departments.

2. Explain why it was necessary to create slave patrols in southern colonies/states and not in northern colonies/states.

3. Citing examples, explain how a national culture of discrimination has influenced the development of laws, the enforcement of laws, and the staffing of law enforcement agencies in American history.

4. Explain how and when American police departments fell under the corrupting influence of partisan politics and then explain how, and approximately when, this corrupting spell was broken.

5. Explain how the "Progressive Movement" changed American policing.

6. Citing examples, what were the objectives of individuals associated with the "first" wave of reform in American policing? What were the objectives of individuals associated with the "second" wave of reform? While they worked toward a common objective, what made individuals in the second wave different?

CHAPTER SPECIFIC INTERNET LINKS

The National Humanities Center: http://nationalhuman-itiescenter.org/pds/maai/index.htm

Library of Congress: http://memory.loc.gov/cgi-bin/query/d?mesnbib:0:./temp/~ammem_w6BJ (for information on slavery and slave patrols)

San Francisco Trolley Dash Cam Footage, 1909: http://www.youtube.com/watch?v=9CaeV88S0Pg

The Boston Police Department Virtual Community: http://www.bpdnews.com/about/history/

The Great Society and Urban Riots: http://scholar.library.miami.edu/sixties/urbanRiots.php

U.S. Marshals Service: http://www.usmarshals.gov/

CHAPTER GLOSSARY

Alice Stebbins Wells—the second policewoman employed in the United States. Hired by the City of Los Angeles in 1910, Officer Wells gained international recognition for her work advocating for policewomen. She helped found the International Association of Women Police.

Antebellum—Latin for "pre-war," generally refers to the period following the American Revolution and the beginning of the Civil War (1776–1861)

Black Codes—laws that specifically spelled out the rights and responsibilities of former slaves and their descendents. They were enacted at the local and state level in southern states after the Civil War in an attempt to regulate the lives of former slaves and their descendents. In many cases, they were simply a revision of earlier slave codes.

Emancipation Proclamation—two executive orders signed by President Abraham Lincoln, one on September 22, 1862 and another on January 1, 1863, that freed slaves in all Confederate States. However, it did not free slaves in states that had not seceded from the Union. Slavery would exist in several states and regions of states until December 18, 1865, when the 13th Amendment was enacted.

Frame of Government (also known as *The Great Law* or *Charter of Liberties*)—a constitution written by William Penn and adopted by Pennsylvania colonists in 1701. It spelled out the rights and liberties for Pennsylvania colonists, including the right to trial by jury, freedom of the press, and religious freedom, among others. It would later serve as a guiding document for the *Constitution* and *Bill of Rights*.

Freedmen—a term that referred to former slaves who had been released from slavery, usually by some form of legal process. The term was used often in legislation and reports during the time of slavery and after the Civil War.

Fraternal Order of Police—an association formed in 1915 by two Pittsburgh patrol officers as a social benevolent association that included all ranks in the police organization.

International Association of Chiefs of Police (IACP)—originally the National Chiefs of Police Union; established in 1893, the IACP is the world's oldest and most respected body of police executives. It has more than 20,000 members in 89 countries. Its administrative and operational standards, publications, training, and research are recognized as the most authoritative source of police information in the free world.

International Association of Women Police (IAWP)—originally organized as the International Association of Policewomen in 1915 to advocate for and advance the employment of women in law enforcement. Today, its mission is to strengthen, unite, and raise the profile of women in criminal justice.

Jim Crow laws—a collection of state and local laws enacted between 1876 and 1965 to segregate blacks from whites in public schools and public places, including transportation, restrooms, and dining facilities. They were eventually declared unconstitutional following the landmark case *Brown v. Board of Education* (1954), and by passage of the Civil Rights Act of 1964 and the Voting Rights Act of 1965.

Judiciary Act of 1789—a landmark statute that established and described the powers of the federal judiciary. It also created the office of U.S. Attorney and the position of U.S. Marshal.

Ku Klux Klan (KKK)—a white supremacy group founded in 1865 by former confederate soldiers.

Law Enforcement Assistance Administration (LEAA)—a federal agency created in 1968 to assist criminal justice agencies at all levels of government to implement some of the recommendations set forth by the President's Commission on Law Enforcement and Administration of Justice.

Lola Greene Baldwin—the first policewoman employed in the United States. Hired by the City of Portland, Oregon in 1908, Officer Baldwin gained international recognition for her work advocating for policewomen, the rights of children, and the rights of women.

National Commission on Law Observance and Enforcement—established by President Herbert Hoover in 1929 to survey the criminal justice system and causes of crime in the United States; commonly referred to as the **Wickersham Commission**. The Commission issued 14 reports, including *Report on Police*, which offered a scathing assessment of the condition of American policing and made 10 recommendations to correct core problems.

Night watch—an untrained organization of men (generally volunteers but sometimes paid) who patrolled the streets of American cities at night from colonial time to the early 1800s. They were charged with a number of tasks, including—maintaining and lighting street lamps; challenging, questioning, and detaining suspicious persons; suppressing disorder and riot; and sounding the alarm in case of fire. They were generally ineffective, not respected, and comprised of the lowest class of citizens.

Omnibus Crime Control and Safe Streets Act of 1968—the enabling legislation for the LEAA; commonly referred to as the "Safe Streets Act" or the "Crime Control Act" of 1968.

Paddyroller—a word used to descript a member of a slave patrol by slaves or freedmen.

Plessy v. Ferguson—the Supreme Court decision in 1896 that sanctioned the doctrine of "separate but equal;" the decision focused on segregation in public accommodations.

Police benevolent associations—organizations formed to assist injured or disabled officers and widows of officers. Through these organizations, officers organized and advanced their collective interests.

President's Commission on Law Enforcement and Administration of Justice—established by President Lyndon Johnson in 1965 to investigate the causes of crime and the condition of the criminal justice system. The Commission issued its findings in 1967, with the publication of *The Challenge of Crime in a Free Society*, which today is considered one of the most important documents on American criminal justice.

Progressive Movement—a movement in the United States, beginning at the turn of the 20th century and thriving for the next two decades that attempted to remove the corrupting influences of partisan politics from local government and reform the police, courts, schools, and other urban institutions by reorganizing their structures, upgrading personnel, and redefining their functions.

Rattlewatch—a group of citizens in colonial New Amsterdam (New York City) equipped with rattles to warn of their watchful presence; a form of night-watch.

Reconstruction—an era in American history from 1865 to 1877 when southern (former Confederate) states underwent a tense period of social, political, and economic reconstruction following the Civil War. During some of this period, southern states were under the rule of the U.S. Army.

Slave codes—laws enacted to regulate and control the behavior of slaves prior to the Civil War; they were intended to protect whites from runaway slaves, inhibit insurrection, and authorize the recapture of fugitive slaves.

Slave patrols—groups that operated in southern states between 1705 and approximately 1865 to protect whites from slaves, to capture runaway slaves, and to inhibit insurrection or other irregularities by slaves. Some scholars consider slave patrols an early form of American police.

Vigilante committee—an impromptu group of citizens, generally the "better class" of the community, formed to protect frontier boarder communities from crime and disorder.

Vigilantism—an improvised form of extralegal law enforcement in America occurring between 1767 and about 1910; the philosophy of vigilantism was premised on organized self-protection in the absence of effective local government law enforcement.

Wardens—early supervisors of night watchmen in various American cities.

Whiskey Rebellion—a tax protest that occurred in western Pennsylvania after the federal government imposed an excise tax on whiskey. It reached a climax in July 1794, when U.S. Marshal Robert Forsyth was killed, becoming the first U.S. marshal killed in the line of duty. Before the incident ended, 13,000 state militiamen had to be summoned.

CHAPTER REFERENCES AND ADDITIONAL READINGS

Bancroft Library (n.d.). Biographical Sketch, August Vollmer Papers. BANC MSS C-B 403.

Brown, Richard M. (1969). Historical Patterns of Violence in America. In Hugh D. Graham and Ted R. Gurr (Editors), *Violence in America: Historical and Comparative Perspectives, Vol. 1*, A Report to the National Commission on the Causes and Prevention of Violence, pp. 35–64, U.S. Government Printing Office, Washington, D.C.

Carte, Gene E. and Elaine H. Carte (1975). *Police Reform in the United States*. Berkeley: University of California Press.

City of Massillon, Ohio (2010). Welcome to the Massillon Police Department History. http://www.massillonohio.com/police/history.htm

City of Wichita (2010). 1890's Excerpts from "Wichita Police Department 1871–2000. http://www.wichita.gov/CityOffices/Police/History/1890s.htm.

Cox, James A. (2003). Bilboes, Brands, and Branks: Colonial Crimes and Punishment. The Journal of the Colonial Williamsburg Foundation, Spring 2003.

Dilworth, Donald C. (ed.) (1976). *The Blue and the Brass: American Policing 1890–1910*. Gaithersburg, MD: International Association of Chiefs of Police.

Fogelson, Robert M. (1977). *Big-City Police*. Cambridge, MA: Harvard University Press.

Foner, Eric F. (1988). *Reconstruction: America's Unfinished Revolution: 1863–1877*. New York: Harper and Row.

Fosdick, Raymond B. (1920). *American Police Systems*. New York: The Century Company.

Fricke, Charles W. (1930). *Criminal Investigation*. Los Angeles, CA: O.W. Smith Law Books.

Fuld, Leonhard F. (1909). *Police Administration*, reprint edition, Montclair, NJ: Patterson Smith, 1971.

Green, Gion and Robert Fisher (1987). *Introduction to Security*, 4th Edition. Boston: Butterworths.

Hadden, Sally E. (2001). *Slave Patrols: Law and Violence in Virginia and the Carolinas*. Cambridge, MA: Harvard University Press.

Jackson, Donald Dale (April 1989). Take the oath, put on the badge and do the job. *Smithsonian*, Vol. 20, No. 1:114–125.

Johnson, David R. (1981). *American Law Enforcement: A History*. St. Louis, MO: Forum Press.

Jolly, Michelle (2003). Sex, Vigilantism, and San Francisco in 1856. *Common-place: The Interactive Journal of Early American Life*, Vol. 3, No. 4, July. (Available online at http://www.common-place.org).

Kelling, George L and James K. Steward (1991). The Evolution of Contemporary Policing. In William A. Geller (Editor), *Local Government Police Management* (3rd.Ed.), International City Management Association, Washington, D.C. pp. 3–21

Klarman, Michael J (2004) *From Jim Crow to Civil Rights: The Supreme Court and the Struggle for Racial Equality*, New York: Oxford University Press.

Kuechler, Lori S. (2003). *The Portland Police Sunshine Division: An Early History*. Portland, OR: Sunshine Division, Inc.

Lane, Roger (1971). *Policing the City: Boston, 1822–1885*. New York, NY: Atheneum Press.

Law Enforcement Assistance Administration (1976). *Two Hundred Years of American Criminal Justice*. Washington, D.C.: U.S. Department of Justice.

Los Angeles County Sheriff's Department (2010). History of The Los Angeles County Sheriff's Department (1849-1871). http://www.lasdhq.org/aboutlasd/history.html.

Los Angeles Police Department (2010). Women in the LAPD. http://www.lapdonline.org/history_of_the_lapd/content_basic_view/833

Lower Manhattan Construction Command Center (February 18, 2003). Museum Honors NYPD's First Black Commissioner. http://www.lowermanhatton.info/news/museum_honors_nypd_s_27751.asp.

MacNamara, D.E.J. (1955). August Vollmer. In T*he Encyclopedia of Police Science*, Second Edition, W. Bailey, ed., Garland Publishing, Inc., New York, NY.

Metropolitan Police Department, District of Columbia (2010). Brief History of the MPDC. http://mpdc.dc.gov/mpdc/cwp/view,a,1230,q,540333,mpdcNav_GID,1529,mpdcNav,|31458|.asp.

Monkkonen, Eric (1992). History of Urban Police. *Crime and Justice*, Vol. 15, 547–580.

Monkkonen, Eric (1982). From Cop History to Social History: The Significance of the Police in American History. *Journal of Social History* 15:4, 575–591.

Monkkonen, Eric (1981). *Police in Urban America, 1860-1920*. New York, NY, Cambridge University Press

Myers, Gloria E. (1995). *A Municipal Mother: Portland's Lola Greene Baldwin, America's First Policewoman*. Corvallis, OR: Oregon State University Press.

National Commission on the Causes and Prevention of Violence (1968). *Rights in Conflict: The Chicago Police Riot*. New York, NY: New American Library, Inc.

National Commission on Law Observance and Enforcement (1931). *Report on Police*. Washington, D.C.: U.S. Government Printing Office. The President's Commission on Law Enforcement and the Administration of Justice (1967).

The Challenge of Crime in a Free Society. Washington, D.C.: U.S. Government Printing Office.

Roth, Mitchel (2005). *Crime and Punishment: A History of the Criminal Justice System*. Belmont, CA: Thomson Wadsworth.

Russell, Francis (1975). *A City in Terror*. The Viking Press, New York.

Taylor, Erica (June 23, 2010). Little-Known Black History Fact: Horatio Homer.

The Tom Joyner Morning Show. http://www.blackamericaweb.com/?q=articles/news/the_black_diaspora_news/19686

Thale, Christopher (2005). "Police," *The Electronic Encyclopedia of Chicago*, Chicago Historical Society.

Thayer, George (1967). *The Farther Shores of Politics: The American Political Fringe Today*. New York: Simon and Schuster.

Trojanowicz, Robert and Samuel Dixon (1974). *Criminal Justice and the Community*. Englewood Cliffs, New Jersey: Prentice Hall.

Trojanowicz, Trojanowicz, and Moss (1975). *Community Based Crime Prevention*. Englewood Cliffs, New Jersey: Prentice Hall.

U.S. Marshals Service (May 1994). The United States Marshals Service: Past and Present. U.S. Marshals Service, Publication Number 3.

U.S. Marshals Service (2010). History: In the Line of Duty. http://www.usmarshals.gov/history/forsyth/in_line_of_duty.htm

Vollmer, August and Alfred E. Parker (1935). *Crime and the State Police*. Berkeley, CA: University of California Press.

Walker, Samuel (1998). *Popular Justice: A History of American Criminal Justice*. New York, NY: Oxford University Press.

Walker, Samuel (1992). *Police in America: An Introduction*. New York, NY: McGraw Hill.

Walker, Samuel (1977). *A Critical History of Police Reform*. Lexington, MA: Lexington Books.

Wallace, Paul A.W. and James P. O'Brien (1995). "William Penn in Pennsylvania," a document retrieved on October 3, 2004, from the Pennsylvania Historical and Museum Commission web page (www.dep.state.us/dep/PA_Env-Her/William_Penn.htm).

Whitehouse, Jack E. (March 1973). Historical Perspectives on the Police Community Service Function. *Journal of Police Science and Administration*, Vol. 1, No. 1, 87–92.

Williams, Hubert and Patrick V. Murphy (1990). The Evolving Strategy of Police: A Minority View. *Perspectives on Policing, No. 13*. Washington, D.C.: National Institute of Justice and Harvard University.

Wintersmith, Robert F. (1974). *Police and the Black Community*. Lexington, MA: Lexington Books.

Wood, B. (1984). *Slavery in Colonial Georgia*. Athens, GA: University of Georgia Press.

CHAPTER 4

The Public Law Enforcement Community in the United States

LEARNING OBJECTIVES

In Chapter 3, you learned about the evolution of policing in the United States. This chapter presents the governmental framework for the authority and existence of law enforcement agencies. It also describes the type and number of agencies that operate in the country. The major responsibilities and functions of these agencies are presented as well. (The private sector law enforcement community will be described in Chapter 12.) After studying this chapter, you should be able to:

- Understand where policing fits in the governmental structure of the United States.
- Explain the basic principles of U.S. government, such as federalism, checks and balances, three branches of government, implied powers doctrine, and judicial review.
- Describe what is meant by "political subdivision" and explain its legal significance.
- Cite the approximate number of law enforcement agencies and the number of law enforcement personnel in the United States.
- Distinguish between "specific police authority" and "general police authority" and be able to give examples of each.
- List the major federal law enforcement agencies and their organizational placement in the federal government structure.
- Describe agencies that have both rehabilitation and law enforcement responsibilities.

CHAPTER OUTLINE

KEY TERMS USED IN THIS CHAPTER

fragmented system

federalism

states' rights amendment

supremacy clause

checks and balances (or separation of powers)

judicial review

political subdivisions

concurrent or overlapping jurisdiction

county police departments

specific police authority

general police authority

implied powers doctrine (or the necessary and proper clause)

pre-sentence investigation/ pre-trial investigation report

THE U.S. GOVERNMENTAL FRAMEWORK APPLIED TO POLICING

The agencies responsible for criminal law enforcement in the United States vary significantly in size, scope of responsibility, and authority. The model of law enforcement that has evolved in the United States can be referred to as a **fragmented system,** since there is no national police force. The country's law enforcement community is decentralized—made up of many independently-organized agencies. In comparison, some countries (e.g., France and Italy) utilize a centralized system of law enforcement, in which all agencies' policies and procedures are controlled by a national or governmental headquarters (Hunter 1990).

Basic Organizing Principles

A review of basic organizing principles of U.S. government is appropriate in examining the authority of U.S. law enforcement agencies. By ratifying the Constitution, the American colonies adopted a form of representative democracy known as **federalism**. This established a "dual system" of government, made up of the federal and state

systems. The authority, powers, and limitations of the federal government were framed in the Constitution and the Bill of Rights (reprinted in Appendix I for reference). The 10th Amendment (also referred to as the **states' rights amendment**) clearly indicated that there would be a sharing of power in the United States: "The powers not delegated to the United States by the Constitution, nor prohibited by it to the states, are reserved to the states respectively, or to the people." This meant that the states were permitted to establish their own governmental structures as long as they did not violate or interfere with the federal Constitution. This permitted the formation of various state structures that could deviate somewhat from the federal system (see **Figure 4-1**).

When a conflict of laws (between state and federal law) exists, the federal judicial system may be asked to clarify and interpret the law in order to resolve the conflict. Such conflicts fall under the **supremacy clause** of Article IV of the United States Constitution, which states:

> *This Constitution, and laws of the United States which shall be made in pursuance thereof…shall be the supreme law of the land; and the judges in every state shall be bound thereby, any thing in the constitution or laws of any state to the contrary notwithstanding.*

Throughout the federal and state governments, there is a system of **checks and balances**. By establishing three branches of government—executive, legislative, and judicial—the United States Constitution provided a mechanism to prevent any one branch from becoming too powerful. This principle is also referred to as **separation of powers.** Once the legislative branch enacts legislation, it is the responsibility of the executive branch to enforce it. The judiciary supervises judicial proceedings, including trials, and through the process of **judicial review** rules on the constitutionality of laws enacted by the legislative branch and procedures used by the executive branch in enforcing laws.

Multiple Jurisdictions

The framework outlined above has led to many geographical jurisdictions, not just those of the federal and state governments. Although the federal level of government

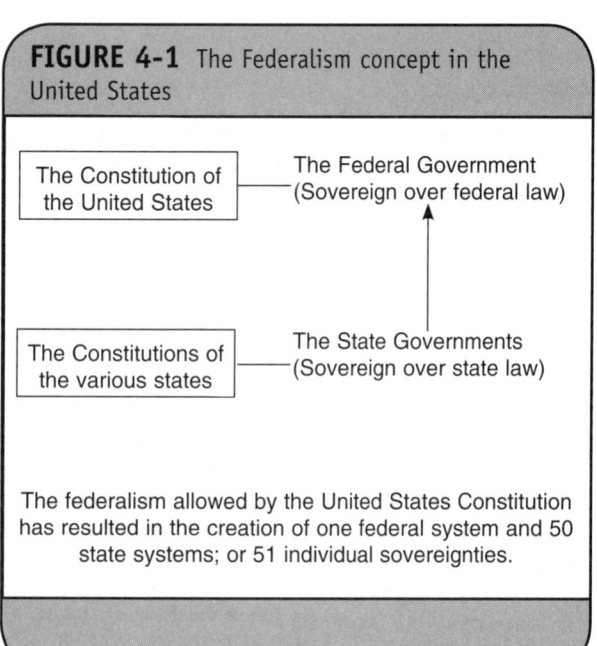

FIGURE 4-1 The Federalism concept in the United States

The Constitution of the United States → The Federal Government (Sovereign over federal law)

The Constitutions of the various states → The State Governments (Sovereign over state law)

The federalism allowed by the United States Constitution has resulted in the creation of one federal system and 50 state systems; or 51 individual sovereignties.

U.S. Supreme Court Building, Washington, D.C.

Source: © Ken Hammond/USDA

maintains a single national jurisdiction, the states have created political subdivisions. The most common names for these political subdivisions include: county, municipality or city, village, borough, and township. However, park districts, school districts, public colleges and universities, and port authorities can also be subdivisions of states. **Political subdivisions** may have the authority to establish law enforcement agencies if the legislative body that created the subdivision granted such authority; as a result, often more than one law enforcement agency can have jurisdiction over the same geographical territory. For example, township police officers have police authority within their township, but so do members of a sheriff's department of the county wherein the township lies. Additionally, state law enforcement agencies would have jurisdiction within both the county and the township. Based on this example, the possible complications and conflicts over jurisdiction become evident. When this situation exists, it is referred to as **concurrent** or **overlapping jurisdiction.** Usually, when agencies have overlapping jurisdiction, there is an understanding (perhaps formal, but usually informal) as to which agency is the "primary" responding agency and which is the "secondary" or "supportive" agency.

Executive Authority

Every law enforcement agency has a chief executive official. The most common title is "police chief," though other titles include "sheriff," "director," "superintendent," "colonel," "commissioner," "warden," "marshal," or "chief constable." The chief executive has the authority and responsibility to guide the organization and direct its members. Duties include establishing and enforcing policy, managing the budget, recommending personnel for employment and for dismissal, scheduling resources, addressing community concerns, and evaluating the overall daily performance of the agency. In addition to these responsibilities, the agency's chief executive official also reports and is accountable to another jurisdictional official or board. If the chief executive is elected by popular vote, he or she is accountable to the people. The law normally describes how the chief executive is appointed (or elected). For example, in many large cities in the United States, the mayor appoints the police chief. In some cases, however, the chief is promoted from within the agency and occupies the position regardless of who is mayor. In some jurisdictions, a board of three or more members chooses the chief executive, and once appointed, the chief executive official might occupy the position until retirement, resignation, removal by a new mayor, or removal at any time. Any action for removal depends on the appointment authority within the jurisdiction and the specific law related to removal or dismissal. (See Chapter 7 for additional information about personnel issues and civil service systems.) The Las Vegas Metropolitan Police Department is a rather unique jurisdiction in that it is called a police department, but its chief executive officer is the elected sheriff; the department's uniforms resemble sheriff deputies but they are referred to as police officers.

STATISTICAL PROFILES AND FUNCTIONS

How many law enforcement agencies are there in the United States? Although this is a straightforward question, it is extremely difficult to answer. Because of the fragmented nature of the governmental system, no one agency or office is responsible for maintaining accurate lists of information on the U.S. law enforcement community. Also, the accuracy of state statistics regarding their agencies varies. Smaller agencies "come and go" at the deliberation of executive and legislative boards; an agency can be formed in one community and abolished in another during the same week. Central registries of this activity are rare, although some reliable data are maintained by state regulatory agencies responsible for the training and certification of officers. Thus, any count of the number of law enforcement agencies is an estimate and not an exact figure.

Since 1987, the Bureau of Justice Statistics (BJS) in the Office of Justice Programs within the U.S. Department of Justice has been collecting data from law enforcement agencies throughout the country. The BJS Law Enforcement Unit maintains more than a dozen national data collections, covering federal, state, and local law enforcement agencies and special topics in law enforcement. This program conducts surveys of the law enforcement community every two to three years, but unfortunately, because the survey consists of several thousand questionnaires and considerable amounts of data, there is considerable delay in reporting the results. Data on police employees can also be found in the annual publication of *Crime in the United States*. The data reported in this chapter are the most recent available when the text was updated, but the websites of BJS, the Federal Bureau of Investigation, and individual agencies should be consulted periodically for the most accurate information (see **Figure 4-2**).

FIGURE 4-2 Primary Sources for Agency and Personnel Statistics

Bureau of Justice Statistics: http://bjs.ojp.usdoj.gov/index.cfm?ty=tp&tid=7

Bureau of Labor Statistics: http://www.bls.gov/

FBI, Crime in the United States (police employee data): http://www.fbi.gov/about-us/cjis/ucr/ucr

Government Accountability Office (search for reports using key terms): http://www.gao.gov/

International Association of Directors of Law Enforcement Standards and Training: http://www.iadlest.org/

Also search individual agency web pages.

TABLE 4-1 Estimated Full-Time Employment by State and Local Law Enforcement Agencies in the United States

Type of Agency	Number of Agencies	Number of Full-time Employees		
		Total	Sworn	Civilian
Local Police	11,218	584,672	452,037	132,635
Sheriff/County	3,067	337,390	190,605	146,785
Primary state	49	97,196	68,038	29,158
Special jurisdictions[a]	1,376	67,972	46,221	21,751
Constables/ Marshals	513	2,823	2,323	500
Total	16,223	1,090,053	759,224	330,829

[a]The special police category includes state-level, local-level, tribal, and campus agencies.

Source: Adapted from FBI (2010a); Reaves (2007); and BLS (2009a).

Local Agencies

Table 4-1 summarizes the number of state and local law enforcement agencies, number of employees, and operating expenses at the various levels of government by type of agency.

Obviously, of the 16,223 state and local agencies, the large majority (over 11,000) are the general policing agencies that include the municipal, village, town, and township departments in the United States. These agencies employ over 452,000 full-time sworn officers and over 132,000 full-time civilians. When the local agencies' totals are added to the other categories, it yields almost 760,000 sworn officers and over 330,000 civilians in full-time positions. These numbers had been growing at a rate of about 1% every year prior to 2000, but since then growth has been less than 1%, and since the economic recession of 2008–09, the increases have been negligible. Many individual agencies have actually laid off personnel during the last few years.

The largest local level police department in the country is New York City, with over 53,774 personnel, of which over 35,000 are sworn. FBI data for 2009 indicated the following approximate staffing levels (full-time sworn officers) for the ten largest municipal departments in the United States:

New York	35,000	Washington, D.C.	4,052
Chicago	13,088	Dallas	3,577
Los Angeles	9,980	Phoenix	3,279
Philadelphia	6,722	Baltimore	3,013
Houston	5,371	Detroit	2,930

The exact number of sworn officers for any agency changes from month to month because of new hires, retirements, layoffs, suspensions, and dismissals, so these staffing levels are approximate.

only one officer. Of all the local police departments in the United States, only 5% of the departments employ 100 or more officers. It is noteworthy that, since 1993, the number of "one officer" agencies has dropped approximately 20%, as this may be indicative of the realization that a minimum staffing level is needed to function effectively and efficiently. The issue of agency consolidation and/or merger is a controversial one in the United States because of the desire for home rule. See **Figure 4-3** for some "what if" statements regarding the impact of possible consolidation based on a minimum number of officers.

Officers on patrol

Source: © Corbis

A more revealing finding from the BJS data is the relationship between the number of agencies and the size of an agency in terms of sworn personnel. **Table 4-2** lists the breakdown of local agencies by number of sworn personnel. Notice that about 20% of the agencies have fewer than five sworn officers, about 45% employ less than 10, and about 88% employ fewer than 50 officers. Also notice that there are about 500 agencies that employ

Although there are many small agencies in the United States employing only a few officers, 60% of all full-time sworn officers at the local level are employed in agencies with 100 or more sworn employees. These sworn officers are employed in only 549 agencies, or about 5% of all local agencies. This means that there is an inverse relationship between the number of agencies and the number of persons employed by those agencies.

TABLE 4-2 Local Police Departments and Total Full-Time Sworn Personnel by Agency Size

Total number of full-time Officers in agency by size*	Estimated Number	Percentage**	Cumulated percentage
1,000 or more	50	0.4	100
500–999	50	0.4	99.6
250–499	90	0.8	99.2
100–249	359	3.2	98.6
50–99	785	6.7	95.2
25–49	1,458	13.0	88.5
10–24	3,365	30.0	75.5
5–9	2,916	25.9	45.5
2–4	1,682	15.2	19.6
1	490	4.4	4.4
Total	11,218	100	100

* Total full-time sworn officers only per agency; data do not include Sheriff, County Police, County Constables/Marshals, or Special Jurisdiction Departments.

** Percentages based on 2004 distributions

Source: Adapted from Hickman and Reaves (2006) with 2009 data from FBI (2010).

of 10,000 to 250,000, 80–90% of departments have primary responsibility for homicide investigation, but 34% of those serving a population of 2500 to 9999 and 54% of those serving fewer than 2500 residents report that they do not have primary responsibility for such investigations. As expected, the percent of local police departments responsible for traffic-related issues is quite large: enforcement of traffic laws: 100%; investigation of traffic accidents: 97%; traffic direction and control: 89%; and parking enforcement: 86%. The size of agencies does have some relationship to their primary function and responsibilities (Hickman and Reaves 2006a). The major functions carried out by law enforcement agencies are also discussed in Chapter 6.

Sheriff's Departments

One unique type of local agency is the county sheriff's department. The BJS surveys treat these departments as a separate category, and for the year 2004 identified 3067

Local law enforcement (the uniformed officer on the beat) is what most Americans observe on a daily basis. It is the local police who respond to street crime and most of the traffic accidents. Local police authority is general in scope. They can enforce the general criminal code of the state, plus appropriate county or city ordinances, and they often are responsible for initiating federal charges in many jurisdictions (these situations, however, are usually referred to federal authorities or investigated jointly). Nearly all local police departments have primary responsibility for investigating at least some types of crimes occurring in their jurisdiction. All departments in jurisdictions with populations of 250,000 or more have primary responsibility for investigating homicides and other violent crimes such as rape, robbery, or assault. For jurisdictions serving a population

FIGURE 4-3 What if agencies had to be a minimum size?

What if the United States undertook an agency consolidation effort? Based on recent data (see Table 4-2), if a federal law were enacted to require a minimum of 10 full-time officers in an agency in order to exist, how many agencies would be affected? At least 5,088 agencies would be affected (about 45% of all local agencies). If the law were to require a minimum of 25 full-time officers, 8,456 agencies would be affected (about 75.5% of all local agencies). If the law required a minimum of 50 full-time officers, 9,911 agencies would be affected (about 88% of all local agencies). Not all of the affected agencies would be eliminated. They could consolidate or merge with other small agencies to form new ones or they could merge with larger existing agencies. Based on estimated data, from 2000 to 2009, roughly 640 agencies with 1-4 officers both gained officers and moved to higher categories or they ceased operations. The point is that the vast majority of jurisdictions in the United States have small law enforcement agencies providing services to their communities.

such agencies (Hickman and Reaves 2006b). However, the National Sheriff's Association (2010) puts the number of sheriffs at 3085. The sheriff's departments in the United States are predominately operated by county governments, except in the states of Alaska, Connecticut, and Hawaii (Reeves 2007). Most sheriff's departments are small in terms of the number of employees, with nearly 60% of the departments employing fewer than 25 sworn personnel. Of all the sheriff's departments, 65% of the full-time sworn personnel work in the largest 11% of the sheriff's departments (i.e., those that employ 100 or more full-time sworn personnel).

Unlike local agencies, sheriff's departments often have primary responsibilities for jail operations and court-related duties. Generally speaking, about 76% of the sheriff's departments have jail operations responsibilities, over 98% serve the civil process of the local county court systems, 92% have criminal investigative responsibilities, and nearly 95% provided court security (Reaves and Hickman 2006, 15–17). The 10 largest county sheriff's offices in the United States, based on their full-time sworn personnel, are the following (Federal Bureau of Investigation 2009, Table 80):

Los Angeles Co. (CA)	9,567	Orange Co. (CA)	1,807
Harris Co. (TX)	2,370	San Bernardino Co. (CA)	1,790
San Diego Co. (CA)	2,261	Broward Co. (FL)	1,584
Cook Co. (IL)	2,227	Palm Beach Co. (FL)	1,549
Riverside Co. (CA)	2,049	Orange Co. (FL)	1,442

Notice that five of these large county-sheriff's department are in the state of California and three are in Florida. Also, two counties not listed, Clark County, Nevada (2735 officers) and Duval County, Florida (1746 officers), have merged with municipalities (Las Vegas and Jacksonville, respectively) and are considered police departments in the BJS surveys.

Some counties (in Delaware, Georgia, Illinois, Maryland, Missouri, New York, Pennsylvania, and Virginia)

TABLE 4-3 Sheriff's Departments by Number of Sworn Personnel

Number of Full-Time Sworn Personnel in Agency	Number of Agencies	Percent of Agencies	Full-time Sworn Personnel	Percent of Sworn
1,000 or more	13	0.4	34,118	17.9
500–999	28	0.9	20,014	10.5
250–499	91	2.9	32,784	17.2
100–249	222	7.2	36,596	19.2
50–99	325	10.6	24,779	13.0
25–49	533	17.4	20,204	10.6
10–24	926	30.2	16,392	8.6
5–9	613	20	4,740	2.5
2–4	291	9.5	953	0.5
1	25	0.8	25	*
Totals	3067	99.9	190,605	100

*Less than 0.5%.

Source: Adapted from Hickman, Reaves (2006, 2); Reaves (2007); and FBI (2010a).

have a **county police department** as well as a county sheriff's department. Where this occurs, any sheriff's department of that county usually has no police patrol or criminal investigation responsibilities. These police departments operate much like municipal police departments. The 10 largest county police departments based on full-time sworn personnel are the following (Federal Bureau of Investigation 2010a, Table 80):

Miami-Dade (FL) PD	3,074	Fairfax County (VA) PD	1,422
Nassau County (NY) PD	2,580	Montgomery Co. (MD) PD	1,164
Suffolk County (NY) PD	2,537	DeKalb County (GA) PD	1,055
Baltimore County (MD) PD	1,902	St. Louis County (MO) PD	784
Prince George's Co. (MD) PD	1,564	Gwinnett County (GA) PD	677

State Agencies

Every state except Hawaii has at least one state-level policing agency. Usually, this major agency is known as the "state police," "state patrol," or "department of public safety." Other state agencies exist, however, and may have responsibilities for specific areas of enforcement such as alcoholic beverage control, fish and wildlife protection, parks protection, healthcare fraud, and environmental crimes. As with other governmental levels, the jurisdiction and authority of state agencies depend on legislative mandate. The terms used to describe and distinguish police authority are **specific police authority** and **general police authority**. As the terms imply, agencies with limited or specifically-stated responsibilities (such as highway patrols) possess specific police authority. Those with policing authority over a broad range of criminal offenses or those that can enforce any statutory laws possess general police authority (see **Figure 4-4**). For example, in Ohio, the state highway patrol is authorized to exercise specific police authority to (a) enforce the traffic code on all roads and highways of the state, (b) enforce the criminal code on state property, (c) investigate accidents and incidents involving aircraft, and (d) protect the governor and other dignitaries. As such,

the Ohio Highway Patrol does not have jurisdiction over common criminal offenses such as robbery, burglary, and murder, unless they are committed on state property. Local or county agencies, which have general police authority, must investigate those offenses. In contrast, in Pennsylvania (and in most states with a "state police" agency), the state police are authorized to exercise general police authority to investigate any criminal offense anywhere in the state.

Table 4-4 lists each primary state agency in the United States and gives information about the number of full-time employees, the number of sworn officers, and the number of civilians. Full-time sworn personnel range from 132 in North Dakota to 7532 in California; however, if you adjust for population, you would find that North Dakota has 2.1 officers per 10,000 residents and California has 2.2 officers per 10,000 residents. Obviously the more populated states have larger agencies, but the ratio of officers to population can vary significantly. For example, the Delaware State Police has 668 officers, or 7.7 officers per 10,000 residents.

Of the 49 primary state law enforcement agencies, 35 (71%) have more than 500 full-time officers, while 19 (38.7%) have more than 1,000 officers. The ratio of full-time officers per 10,000 residents ranges from 1.0

FIGURE 4-4 Specific versus General Police Authority*

Agencies with *Specific Police Authority*	Agencies with *General Police Authority*
Highway Patrols	State Police
Environmental Enforcement Units	County Police
Bureau of Liquor Control	Municipal Police
Fish & Wildlife	County Sheriff's Depts. (most)
State Narcotics Units	Townships/Villages (most)

* The concept of Specific and General Police Authority applies to all levels of policing, not just state agencies.

TABLE 4-4 Full-Time State Employees by Primary State Agency, 2009

State	Agency	Total law enforcement employees	Total Officers	Total Civilians
Alabama	Highway Patrol	1,438	788	650
Alaska	State Troopers	608	363	245
Arizona	Depart. of Public Safety	2,065	1,210	855
Arkansas	State Police	963	559	404
California	Highway Patrol	11,182	7,532	3,650
Colorado	State Patrol	1,010	736	274
Connecticut	State Police	1,679	1,144	535
Delaware	State Police	893	668	225
Florida	Highway Patrol	2,226	1,682	544
Georgia	Depart. of Public Safety	1,515	804	711
Idaho	State Police	468	256	212
Illinois	State Police	3,413	2,077	1,336
Indiana	State Police	1,921	1,293	628
Iowa	Depart. of Public Safety	991	658	333
Kansas	Highway Patrol	845	542	303
Kentucky	State Police	1,694	886	808
Louisiana	State Police	1,692	1,204	488
Maine	State Police	435	318	117
Maryland	State Police	2,184	1,495	689
Massachusetts	State Police	2,774	2,247	527
Michigan	State Police	2,539	1,669	870
Minnesota	State Patrol	808	566	242
Mississippi	Highway Patrol	1,100	581	519
Missouri	State Highway Patrol	2,336	1,087	1,249
Montana	Highway Patrol	278	223	55
Nebraska	State Patrol	720	485	235
Nevada	Highway Patrol	911	498	413
New Hampshire	State Police	496	342	154
New Jersey	State Police	4,392	3,040	1,352
New Mexico	State Police	1,132	542	590
New York	State Police	5,929	4,827	1,102
North Carolina	Highway Patrol	2,307	1,737	570
North Dakota	Highway Patrol	183	132	51

(*continued*)

TABLE 4-4 Full-Time State Employees by Primary State Agency, 2009 (*Continued*)

State	Agency	Total law enforcement employees	Total Officers	Total Civilians
Ohio	Highway Patrol	2576	1522	1053
Oklahoma	Depart. of Public Safety	1521	828	693
Oregon	State Police	767	574	193
Pennsylvania	State Police	6146	4510	1636
Rhode Island	State Police	308	258	50
South Carolina	Highway Patrol	1032	836	196
South Dakota	Highway Patrol	261	164	97
Tennessee	Depart. of Safety	1586	811	775
Texas	Depart. of Public Safety	8196	3504	4692
Utah	Highway Patrol	561	426	135
Vermont	State Police	431	316	115
Virginia	State Police	2551	1863	688
Washington	State Patrol	2254	1094	1160
West Virginia	State Police	1044	684	360
Wisconsin	State Patrol	646	496	150
Wyoming	Highway Patrol	366	203	163

Source: Adapted from FBI (2010a, Table 76).

(Florida Highway Patrol) to 8.1 (Vermont Department of Public Safety). The major functions performed by state policing agencies include the following:

- Accident investigation and traffic enforcement
- Patrol and first response
- Communications and dispatch
- Narcotics/vice enforcement and training academy operations
- Homeland Security-related activities
- Fingerprint processing
- Death investigation
- Property and violent crime (rape, robbery, serious assault) investigation
- Ballistics/laboratory testing and search/rescue operations

It's not always an action job; it can be boring at times

Source: © UpperCut Images/age fotostock

Special Law Enforcement Agencies

Recent surveys identified 1376 special police agencies at both the state and local agency levels. Such agencies employed 67,972 full-time personnel, of which over 46,221 were sworn officers (see Table 4-1). These special police agencies constitute about 8% of all local and state agencies in the United States. This category of agency is very difficult to describe and tabulate because of the variety of special law enforcement agencies. Such agencies usually have names that describe their uniqueness, such as transit police, park district, alcoholic beverage control, metropolitan housing authority, campus police, port authority, amusement park police, or airport police. Officers working in such special law enforcement agencies usually possess general police authority only within the geographical limitations of their jurisdiction, though some of these agencies possess specific police authority over a large geographical area (for example, a state liquor control agent has authority throughout a state, but only over liquor-related offenses and regulations).

Of all the special law enforcement agencies, approximately 50% are college/university (campus) law enforcement agencies. The findings of a 2005 survey of campus police agencies clearly indicate that as size of campus enrollment increases, the percentage of campuses using officers with arrest authority and on armed patrol also generally increases. The survey verified that about 93% of public institutions utilized sworn and armed officers, while only about 42% of private institutions did (Reaves 2008,1).

Table 4-5 indicates the major categories and types of special jurisdictions having full-time sworn officers. Tribal police are included in this section. According to the Bureau of Indians Affairs, there are 565 federally recognized American Indian and Alaska Native tribes

---

TABLE 4-5 Special Law Enforcement Agencies, State, Local, and Tribal Jurisdictions – Major Categories

<u>Government buildings/facilities</u>
4-year college/university
Public school district
2-year college/university
State capitol/government buildings
Medical school/facility
Public housing

<u>Enforcement in Indian Country</u>
Tribal Police

<u>Conservation laws/parks/recreation</u>
Fish and wildlife
Parks and recreational areas
Waterways and boating
Environmental laws
Forest resources
Sanitation laws
Water resources

<u>Criminal investigations</u>
County/city
State bureau
Fire Marshal

<u>Transportation systems/facilities</u>
Mass transit system/railroad
Airports
Transportation centers—multiple types
Port facilities
Commercial vehicle enforcement
Roadways, bridges, tunnels

<u>Special enforcement</u>
Alcohol enforcement
Agricultural
Gaming/racing laws
Drug enforcement
Business regulation

Source: Adapted from Reaves (2007) Perry, (2005).

and villages. Tribes "possess the right to form their own governments; to make and enforce laws, both civil and criminal; to tax; to establish and determine membership (i.e., tribal citizenship); to license and regulate activities within their jurisdiction; to zone; and to exclude persons from tribal lands" (U.S. Department of Interior 2010).

THE FEDERAL AGENCIES AND THEIR RESPONSIBILITIES

Federal employment is often a goal of many college students. It is evident that the number of agencies involved in the law enforcement function is considerably large. Many of the agencies with investigative and criminal responsibilities often require three years of full-time experience (not necessarily in law enforcement) before being considered for an armed agent or investigative position. Persons graduating from college may want to consider seeking employment with other federal agencies and then transferring to one of the major policing agencies after gaining qualifying experience. Following the terrorist attacks of September 11, 2001, considerable discussion ensued about the complexity and number of federal agencies involved in intelligence gathering and national security (see Chapter 12). One result of these debates was Public Law 107-296, signed on November 25, 2002, which established the Department of Homeland Security (DHS), effective January 24, 2003. The creation of the DHS was the largest reorganization effort of the federal government in nearly 50 years. It combined, in whole or in part, 22 agencies and included over 170,000 existing employees. Several changes have occurred in the DHS since its original organization and some additional readjustment is expected in the near future. Criminal justice students should attempt to keep abreast of the ongoing changes to the department and the many opportunities that will exist in terms of career pursuits.

Currently, the executive branch of the U.S. federal government consists of 15 departments and 62 independent agencies. The executive branch is primarily responsible for national security, homeland security, public safety, and the delivery of most national services. Criminal law enforcement responsibility at the federal level in the United States is shared among approximately 38 agencies and 27 offices of the inspector general. These agencies and offices have been created by Congress under the authority

of the **implied powers doctrine** or **the necessary and proper clause** of Article I, Section 8 (Paragraph 18) of the U.S. Constitution, which states:

> [Congress shall have power...] To make all laws which shall be necessary and proper for carrying into execution the foregoing powers, and all other powers vested by this Constitution in the Government of the United States, or in any Department or Officer thereof.

"Foregoing powers" refers to the powers of Congress specifically enumerated in the first 17 paragraphs of Section 8 (see Appendix I of this text). These powers include the right to lay and collect taxes and duties, provide for the general welfare, regulate commerce with foreign nations and among the states, establish a uniform rule of naturalization, coin money and provide for the punishment of counterfeiting, establish post offices and roads, declare war, and raise and support armies and a navy. These specific powers and others of the Constitution are important because they provide the federal authority under which law enforcement agencies are created and operated by the federal government. Generally, when Congress enacts a criminal offense or law enforcement responsibility, it specifically designates which agency is responsible for its enforcement. **Figure 4-5** lists major federal agencies with some type of enforcement responsibility. They are listed according to the department in which they are found in the federal government's organizational structure.

The extent of federal law enforcement is very broad and diverse, as is evident from Figure 4-5. There are many opportunities existing for employment in the federal sector. As of June 2002, federal agencies employed about 93,000 full-time law enforcement officers (LEOs) authorized to make arrests and carry firearms, according to a Bureau of Justice Statistics (BJS) survey. The number of LEOs grew to 105,000 by 2004 (Reaves 2006) and to 127,000 by September 2008. The Government Accountability Office estimated that the growth in federal LEOs from fiscal years 2000 to 2008 rose 55% (Government Accountability Office 2009, 1). There are about 65 federal agencies that employ LEOs; the major agencies with primary criminal investigative responsibilities in terms of size (number of agents) are listed in **Table 4-6**. They are the most commonly thought

---

FIGURE 4-5 Federal agencies employing law enforcement officers (LEOs)

Department of Agriculture
Animal and Plant Health Inspection Service
Forest Service, Law Enforcement and Investigations

Department of Commerce
Bureau of Industry & Security, Office of Export Enforcement
National Institute of Standards and Technology
National Marine Fisheries Service
Office of Security

Department of Defense
Defense Intelligence Agency
Defense Security Service
Criminal Investigation Command, Army
Defense Criminal Investigative Service
Intelligence and Security Command, Army
Military Police Corps, Army
Naval Criminal Investigative Service, Navy
Air Force Security Police Forces,
Office of Special Investigations, Air Force
Pentagon Force Protection Agency

Department of Energy
Office of Health, Safety and Security, Office of Security Operations
National Nuclear Safety Administration, Office of Secure
  Transportation

Department of Health and Human Services
Food & Drug Administration, Office of Criminal Investigation
National Institutes of Health, Police

Department of Homeland Security
Citizenship and Immigration Services
Customs and Border Protection, Office of Customs and Border
Protection Air and Marine
Customs and Border Protection, Border Patrol
Customs and Border Protection, Office of Field Operations/
  CBP Officers
Federal Emergency Management Agency, Security Branch
Federal Law Enforcement Training Center
Transportation Security Administration, Federal Air Marshals
U.S. Coast Guard, Law Enforcement Boarding Officers
U.S. Coast Guard, Investigative Service
U.S. Immigration and Customs Enforcement, Office of
  Detention & Removal
U.S. Immigration and Customs Enforcement, Office of Federal
  Protective Service
U.S. Immigration and Customs Enforcement, Office of
  Intelligence
U.S. Immigration and Customs Enforcement, Office of
  Investigations
U.S. Immigration and Customs Enforcement, Office of
  Professional Responsibility
U.S. Secret Service

Department of Interior
Bureau of Indian Affairs
Bureau of Land Management

Bureau of Reclamation, Hoover Dam Police
National Park Service, Rangers
National Park Service, U.S. Park Police
Office of Law Enforcement, Security and Emergency
  Management
U.S. Fish and Wildlife Service, National Wildlife Refuge System
U.S. Fish and Wildlife Service, Office of Law Enforcement

Department of Justice
Bureau of Alcohol, Tobacco, Firearms and Explosives
Drug Enforcement Administration
Federal Bureau of Investigation
Federal Bureau of Prisons
U.S. Marshals Service

Department of Labor
Employee Benefits Security Administration
Office of Labor-Management Standards

Department of State
Bureau of Diplomatic Security

Department of Transportation
Maritime Administration, Academy Security Force
National Highway Traffic Safety Administration, Odometer Fraud
Office of the Secretary, Executive Protection

Department of the Treasury
Bureau of Engraving and Printing, Police
Internal Revenue Service, Criminal Investigation Division
U.S. Mint, Police Division

Department of Veterans Affairs
Office of Security & Law Enforcement

Non-Departmental / Independent Agencies
Administrative Office of the U.S. Courts, Office of Probation &
  Pretrial Services
Environmental Protection Agency, Criminal Investigations
  Division
Federal Communications Commission
Federal Maritime Commission
Federal Reserve Board,
    Chairman's Protection Unit
    Reserve Banks Security
    Security Unit
Government Accountability Office
    Office of Security & Safety
    Forensic Audits and Special Investigation
National Gallery of Art
National Railroad Passenger Corporation, AMTRAK Police
National Science Foundation, Polar Operations, Antarctica
Nuclear Regulatory Commission, Office of Investigations
Smithsonian Institution, Office of Protection Services
Tennessee Valley Authority, TVA Police
U.S. Postal Service, Postal Inspection Service & Postal Police
U.S. Capitol Police
U.S. Government Printing Office, Police
U.S. Supreme Court Police

Note: This list does not include the various Offices of Inspector General found in 27 federal agencies/departments, employing over 2,867 investigators.

Sources: Adapted from Government Accountability Office (2006) and (2007) and Government Accountability Office (2007).

TABLE 4-6 Major Federal Agencies/Units Employing 100 or More Full-Time Law Enforcement Officer Personnel

Agency	Number of full-time personnel
Customs and Border Patrol	42,389
Federal Bureau of Prisons (correctional officers)	37,504
Federal Bureau of Investigation	13,847
Immigration and Customs Enforcement	10,482
Drug Enforcement Administration	5,235
U.S. Secret Service	4,827
Administrative Office, U.S. Courts (includes probation officers)	4,560
U.S. Coast Guard	3,972
U.S. Marshals Service	3,439
Veterans Health Administration	2,800
Internal Revenue Service, Criminal Investigation Division	2,751
Bureau of Alcohol, Tobacco, Firearms, and Explosives	2,450
National Park Service (Park Rangers and Park Police Officers)	2,158
U.S. Postal Inspection Service	2,150
U.S. Capitol Police	2,003
Bureau of Diplomatic Security, Diplomatic Security Service	1,800
Federal Reserve Board, Reserve Banks Security	1,607
Federal Protective Service	924
USDA Forest Service, Law Enforcement and Investigations	800
U.S. Fish and Wildlife Service, Division of Law Enforcement	590
Pentagon Force Protection Agency	482
AMTRAK	416
U.S. Mint	360
Bureau of Indian Affairs	343
Department of Energy, Office of Secure Transportation	307
Bureau of Engraving and Printing	277
Bureau of Land Management, Law Enforcement and Security	270
Tennessee Valley Authority Police	204
Food and Drug Administration	177
Environmental Protection Agency	173
National Marine Fisheries Service	163
U.S. Supreme Court	139
Veterans Affairs, Office of Security & Law Enforcement	131
Federal Reserve Board, Security Unit	130

Note: This list does not include the various Offices of Inspector General found in 27 federal agencies/departments, employing over 2,867 investigators.
Source: Compiled by authors from data on agency websites, November 2010, and Government Accountability Office (2006); and Government Accountability Office (2007).

of agencies when one mentions federal agents with law enforcement responsibilities. Federal LEOs primarily are employed by the executive branch of the government, but they can also be found in the legislative branch (Capitol Police) and the judicial branch (U.S. Supreme Court Police).

The federal law enforcement community is very fragmented in terms of jurisdictional authority, as each agency has specific authority by statute. The primary duties for federal officers, according to a 2004 BJS survey (Reaves 2006), include criminal investigation (38% of LEOs), police response and patrol (21%), corrections (16%), non-criminal investigation and inspection (16%), court operations (5%), and security and protection (5%). In terms of gender and racial composition, women accounted for 16.1% of federal officers in 2004, while minority representation was 33.2% in 2004, up from 30.5% in 1998. Hispanic or Latino officers comprised 17.7% of officers in 2004, with African American or black officers at 11.4%. Prior to the creation of the Department of Homeland Security in November 2002, the Department of Justice employed 58% of all federal law enforcement personnel and the Treasury Department employed 23%. By 2004, the Department of Homeland Security employed 42% of LEOs and the Justice Department 36% (Reaves 2006). Agencies with 500 or more officers employed about 98,500, or 94%, of the federal law enforcement officers.

The following sections contain brief descriptions of several selected law enforcement agencies of the federal government. It is not our purpose here to describe all the federal agencies, but students are encouraged to use the list of agencies in Figure 4-5 to review additional details of agencies not emphasized here. The number of officers, special agents, or investigators reported in Table 4-6 is probably less than current personnel levels because most federal agencies are increasing their staffs.

Bureau of Customs and Border Protection Agency

In 2003, the Bureau of Customs and Border Protection Agency (CBP) was established in the Directorate for Border and Transportation Security in the newly created Department of Homeland Security. It now includes the Border Patrol, Office of Field Operations/CBP Officers, and the Office of Customs and Border Protection Air and Marine. Fiscal year 2009 data indicate that the CBP employs over 42,000 officers with an estimated 21,000 CBP Officers, 20,000 Border Patrol agents, and 1212 Air and Marine agents (Bureau of Customs and Border Protection 2010a). The Bureau also has over 2200 Agriculture Specialists, but they do not have federal law enforcement officer status. The agency employs over 58,000 personnel nationwide and overseas—it is the largest uniformed, federal law enforcement agency in the country, and the CBP is now the largest employer of federal officers authorized to carry firearms and make arrests. The budget for the CBP for FY 2010 was about $11 billion. The Bureau is responsible for securing the nation's borders and facilitating the legitimate flow of commerce and travel across those borders. The border with Mexico is about 1900 miles long, and that with Canada is about 5000 miles long, with about 327 total *Ports of Entry*, or official entry or crossing points into the country (CBP 2010a). During FY 2009, some of the major accomplishments of the agency included the following (Bureau of Customs and Border Protection 2010b):

- Seized more than 4.75 million pounds of narcotics.
- Personnel encountered more than 224,000 inadmissible aliens and apprehended more than 556,000 at and between air, sea, and land ports of entry.
- At ports of entry, apprehended more than 9500 people wanted for a variety of charges, to include serious criminal crimes such as murder, rape, and child molestation.
- Seized almost 15,000 cargo shipments.
- Inspected 361.2 million travelers and more than 108.5 million cars, trucks, buses, trains, vessels, and aircraft at point of entry.
- Agriculture specialists seized more than 1.5 million prohibited meat, plant, or animal products, including 166,727 agricultural pests, at ports of entry.
- Completed a total of 279 miles of new fencing, in addition to 338 miles of pedestrian fence and 298 miles of vehicle fence already completed.
- Completed construction on 13 communication and sensor towers on the southern border and began construction on 11 Remote Video Surveillance Systems (RVSS) in the Detroit Sector of the northern border.

- Processed 2857 forensics cases, including 2195 cases of controlled substances, 240 fingerprint lifts and examinations, 60 audio/video duplications, 55 audio/video recoveries/enhancements, and 53 crime scenes and DNA developments.
- Implemented the US-VISIT 10-Print processing system—over 90 percent of all US-VISIT fingerprint transactions of visitors entering the United States are now completed through this system.

The CBP Officer's primary responsibility is:

to detect and prevent terrorists and weapons of mass destruction from entering the United States, while facilitating the orderly flow of legitimate trade and travelers. This requires enforcing laws related to revenue and trade, seizure of contraband, interdiction of agricultural pests and diseases, and admissibility of persons. CBP Officers perform the full range of inspection, passenger and cargo analysis, examination and law enforcement activities relating to the arrival and departure of persons, merchandise and conveyances such as cars, trucks, aircraft, and ships at the ports of entry (U.S. Border and Customs Protection 2010c).

Border Patrol Agents and CBP Officers work in tandem with other federal agencies to prevent terrorists and terrorist weapons from entering the United States. Agents also detect and prevent the smuggling and unlawful entry of undocumented aliens into the United States, and apprehend those people found to be in violation of immigration laws. They are the primary drug-interdicting agency along the land border between the ports of entry. The description of federal Border Patrol Agents states that one of the most important duties performed by a Border Patrol Agent is known as "linewatch," which involves the

detection and apprehension of undocumented aliens and their smugglers by maintaining surveillance from a covert position, pursuing leads, responding to electronic sensor alarms, utilizing infrared scopes during night operations, using low-light level television systems, sighting aircraft, and interpreting and following tracks, marks, and other physical evidence (Transportation Security Administration 2010).

In summary, the Bureau of Customs and Border Protection has a very serious responsibility in terms of protecting the nation's borders, screening visitors and cargo and preventing illegal entry and various forms of smuggling. The task is huge, and the agency is large and appears to be growing.

Mexico-U.S. border marker

Source: © Caitlin Mirra/ShutterStock, Inc.

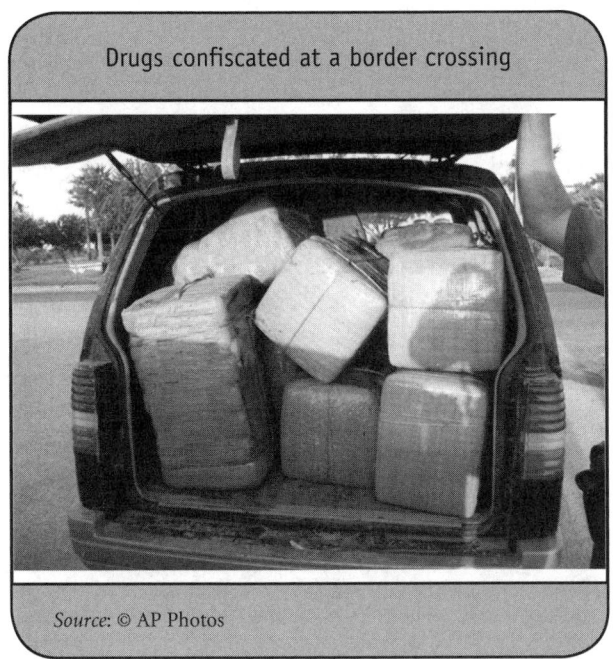

Drugs confiscated at a border crossing

Source: © AP Photos

Immigration and Customs Enforcement

The U.S. Immigration and Customs Enforcement (ICE) agency includes the enforcement and investigation components of the former Immigration and Naturalization Service and Customs agencies. The Department of Homeland Security, in 2003, absorbed the former Immigration and Naturalization Service from the Department of Justice and the US Customs Service from the Department of Treasury to create ICE. Its primary mission is to "promote homeland security and public safety through the criminal and civil enforcement of federal laws governing border control, customs, trade, and immigration." The agency's annual budget is more than $5.7 billion (Immigration and Customs Enforcement 2010) and has over 10,482 agents and officers (Government Accountability Office 2007). Its major divisions include:

- Office of Investigations: responsible for immigration crime; human rights violations and human smuggling; smuggling of narcotics, weapons and other types of contraband; financial crimes; cyber-crime; and export enforcement issues

- Office of Detention and Removal Operations: responsible for identifying, apprehending, detaining, and deporting removable aliens, including convicted criminals, fugitives and recent border entrants
- Federal Protective Service: responsible for policing, securing, and ensuring a safe environment in which federal agencies can conduct their business, by reducing threats posed against more than 9000 federal government facilities nationwide
- Office of Intelligence: responsible for the collection, analysis, and dissemination of strategic and tactical intelligence data for use by the operational elements of ICE and DHS.

The Agency's Strategic Plan for 2010–2014 includes four key priorities (Immigration and Customs Enforcement 2010):

1. Prevent terrorism and enhance security
2. Protect the borders against illicit trade, travel, and finance
3. Protect the borders through smart and tough interior immigration enforcement
4. Construct an efficient, effective agency

One major responsibility for ICE agents is worksite enforcement to identify, arrest, and remove illegal immigrants working in the United States. Inspections are conducted under the administrative authority of I-9 Form audits. During 2008, approximately 6000 persons were arrested, of which 135 were employers. Some cases of such enforcement uncover smuggling operations, the production of fraudulent documents, and improper employment practices by employers. Worksite enforcement often leads to workplace raids and can be controversial. Immigration and Customs Enforcement strategy regarding worksite enforcement appears to be threefold: 1) penalize employers who willfully hire illegal workers, 2) deter employers who are tempted to hire illegal workers, and 3) encourage all employers to take advantage of compliance tools (Forman 2009). One such compliance tool, "E-Verify," is an Internet-based system that allows an employer to determine the eligibility of an employee to work in the United States. By using information on an employee's Form I-9 (Employment Eligibility Verification), an employer can check a federal database operated by the Department of Homeland Security in partnership with the Social Security Administration. As of 2010, more than 216,000 employers were enrolled in the program and over 13 million queries were run through the system (U.S. Department of Homeland Security 2010c).

U.S. Secret Service

The Secret Service is part of the Department of Homeland Security; it was formerly part of the Department of the Treasury. The agency has about 3483 special agents, 1344 uniformed officers, and about 2000 support personnel who have investigation and enforcement duties primarily related to counterfeiting, financial crimes, computer fraud, and threats against dignitaries (U.S. Secret Service 2010, 55). The Uniformed Division provides protection for the White House complex and other presidential offices, the main treasury building and annex, and foreign diplomatic missions. The Secret Service was created originally in 1865 to combat counterfeiting, but it became the general investigative and law enforcement arm of the federal government until 1908 when Congress restricted its authority. Today, its mission is to safeguard the nation's financial infrastructure and payment systems; to preserve the integrity of the economy; and to protect national leaders and visiting heads of state and government, designated sites, and national special security events. The Secret Service is well known for protecting the president and vice president and their immediate families, a task that was not officially performed until the early 1900s, but their responsibilities extend much further, including the protection of (U.S. Secret Service 2010b):

- The president, the vice president (or other individuals next in order of succession to the Office of the President), the president-elect and vice president-elect
- The immediate families of the above individuals
- Former presidents and their spouses for their lifetimes, except when the spouse remarries. However, in 1997, congressional legislation became effective limiting Secret Service protection to former presidents for a period of not more than 10 years from the date the former president leaves office.

- Children of former presidents until age 16
- Visiting heads of foreign states or governments and their spouses traveling with them, other distinguished foreign visitors to the United States, and official representatives of the United States performing special missions abroad
- Major presidential and vice presidential candidates and their spouses within 120 days of a general presidential election
- Other individuals as designated per Executive Order of the President
- National Special Security Events, when designated as such by the Secretary of the Department of Homeland Security

Canine units are used to detect drugs and explosives, and to track persons

Source: © Getty Images/Thinkstock

The Secret Service plays a major role in the modern digital world; its investigation of financial crimes "include, but are not limited to, access device fraud, financial institution fraud, identity theft, computer fraud, and computer-based attacks on our nation's financial, banking, and telecommunications infrastructure" (U.S. Secret Service 2000b). Supporting the overall mission of the agency is its forensic services division and its advanced forensic laboratory, which includes the world's largest ink library. Secret Service forensic analysts examine evidence,

FIGURE 4-6 Electronic Crimes Task Forces and Working Groups

On October 26, 2001, President Bush signed into law H.R. 3162, the USA PATRIOT Act. The U.S. Secret Service was mandated by this Act to establish a nationwide network of Electronic Crimes Task Forces (ECTFs). The concept of the ECTF network is to bring together not only federal, state, and local law enforcement, but also prosecutors, private industry, and academia. The common purpose is the prevention, detection, mitigation, and aggressive investigation of attacks on the nation's financial and critical infrastructures.

The Secret Service's ECTF and Electronic Crimes Working Group initiatives prioritize investigative cases that involve electronic crimes. These initiatives provide necessary support and resources to field investigations that meet any one of the following criteria, a) Significant economic or community impact, b) Participation of organized criminal groups involving multiple districts or transnational organizations, and c) Use of schemes involving new technology. The U.S. Secret Service Electronic Crimes Task Forces are located in the following twenty-four locations:

- Atlanta
- Baltimore
- Birmingham
- Boston
- Buffalo
- Charlotte
- Chicago
- Cleveland
- Dallas
- Houston
- Las Vegas
- Los Angeles
- Miami
- Minneapolis
- New York/New Jersey
- Oklahoma
- Orlando
- Philadelphia
- Pittsburgh
- San Francisco
- Seattle
- South Carolina
- Washington, D.C.

Source: Extracted from U.S. Secret Service (2010d).

develop investigative leads, and provide expert courtroom testimony and forensic/technical assistance in matters involving missing and exploited children (U.S. Secret Service 2010c). See **Figure 4-6** for information related to the Electronic Crimes Task Forces and Working Groups of the Secret Service.

Federal Bureau of Investigation

The Federal Bureau of Investigation (FBI) is part of the Department of Justice. As of 2010, the Bureau had approximately 13,847 special agents and 21,678 support professionals, such as intelligence analysts, language specialists, scientists, information technology specialists, and other professionals. The FBI is responsible for criminal investigation and the enforcement of more than 200 categories of federal crimes, including bank fraud, embezzlement, kidnapping, and civil rights violations. It also has concurrent jurisdiction with the Drug Enforcement Administration (DEA) over drug offenses under the Controlled Substances Act. The mission of the FBI is to protect and defend the United States against terrorist and foreign intelligence threats, to uphold and enforce the criminal laws of the United States, and to provide leadership and criminal justice services to federal, state, municipal, and international agencies and partners. To accomplish this mission, in fiscal year 2010, the FBI received a total of $7.9 billion, including $618 million in net program increases to enhance counterterrorism, counterintelligence, cybercrime, information technology, security, forensics, training, and criminal investigation programs (Federal Bureau of Investigation 2010b).

FBI Evidence Response Vehicle

Source: Courtesy of FBI

Since the September 11, 2001 terrorist attacks on the United States, the FBI has undergone major internal reorganization, which modified the priorities of the agency to the following (Federal Bureau of Investigation 2010b):

1. Protect the United States from terrorist attack
2. Protect the United States against foreign intelligence operations and espionage
3. Protect the United States against cyber-based attacks and high-technology crimes
4. Combat public corruption at all levels
5. Protect civil rights
6. Combat transnational/national criminal organizations and enterprises
7. Combat major white-collar crime
8. Combat significant violent crime
9. Support federal, state, local, and international partners
10. Upgrade technology to successfully perform the FBI's mission

Figure 4-7 lists the national security and criminal priorities established by the FBI. This listing can be found on the agency's website with links to additional information for each item listed. National security issues are discussed in greater detail in Chapter 12.

FBI personnel operate out of 56 field offices and over 400 satellite offices in the United States, with an additional 60 Legal Attaché (Legats) offices around the world (Federal Bureau of Investigation 2010b). The role of legal attachés is primarily one of coordination (they do not conduct foreign intelligence gathering or counterintelligence investigations); "Typical duties of a legal attaché include coordinating requests for FBI or host country assistance overseas; conducting investigations in coordination with the host government; sharing investigative leads and information; briefing embassy counterparts from other agencies, including law enforcement agencies, as appropriate, and ambassadors; managing country clearances; providing situation reports concerning cultural protocol; assessing political and security climates; and coordinating victim and humanitarian assistance" (Federal Bureau of Investigation 2010c).

FIGURE 4-7 The National Security and Criminal Priorities of the FBI

National Security Priorities (Items 1–3)	Criminal Priorities (Items 4–8)	
1. Terrorism • International Terrorism • Domestic Terrorism • Weapons of Mass Destruction	**4. Public Corruption** • Government Fraud • Election Fraud • Foreign Corrupt Practices	**7. White-Collar Crime** • Antitrust • Bankruptcy Fraud • Corporate/Securities Fraud • Health Care Fraud • Insurance Fraud • Mass Marketing Fraud • Money Laundering • Mortgage Fraud • More White-Collar Frauds
2. Counterintelligence • Counterespionage • Counterproliferation • Economic Espionage	**5. Civil Rights** • Hate Crimes • Human Trafficking • Color of Law • Freedom of Access to Clinics	
3. Cyber Crime • Computer Intrusions • Online Predators • Piracy/Intellectual Property Theft • Internet Fraud • Identity Theft	**6. Organized Crime** • Italian Mafia/LCN • Eurasian • Balkan • Middle Eastern • Asian • African • Sports Bribery	**8. Violent Crime & Major Thefts/** • Art Theft • Bank Robberies • Cargo Theft • Crimes Against Children • Cruise Ship Crime • Gangs • Indian Country Crime • Jewelry and Gems Theft • Retail Theft • Vehicle Theft

Source: Extracted from FBI (2010c).

Drug Enforcement Agency

The DEA is also part of the Department of Justice and its 5235 special agents investigate major narcotics violators, enforce regulations governing the manufacture and dispensing of controlled substances, and perform other functions to prevent and control drug trafficking. The DEA's budget for fiscal year 2010 was about $2.3 billion, which included a total staff of about 10,700 (Drug Enforcement Agency 2010a). The agency's primary responsibilities include the following:

- Investigating and preparing for prosecution major violators of controlled substance laws operating at interstate and international levels
- Investigating and preparing for prosecution criminals and drug gangs who perpetrate violence
- Management of a national drug intelligence program, done in cooperation with federal, state, local, and foreign officials, to collect, analyze, and disseminate strategic and operational drug intelligence information
- Seizure and forfeiture of assets derived from, traceable to, or intended to be used for illicit drug trafficking
- Enforcing the provisions of the Controlled Substances Act as they pertain to the manufacture, distribution, and dispensing of legally-produced controlled substances
- Coordination and cooperation with federal, state, and local law enforcement officials on mutual drug enforcement efforts
- Coordination and cooperation with foreign governments, in programs designed to reduce the availability of illicit abuse-type drugs on the United States market through non-enforcement methods such as crop eradication, crop substitution, and training of foreign officials
- Responsibility, under the policy guidance of the Secretary of State and U.S. Ambassadors, for all programs associated with drug law enforcement counterparts in foreign countries
- Liaison with the United Nations, Interpol, and other organizations on matters relating to international drug control programs

The DEA State and Local Task Force Program is a major function of the agency. By 2009, this program had expanded to 381 state and local task forces, staffed by 1890 DEA special agents and over 2200 state and local police officers. Participating state and local task force officers are deputized to perform the same functions as DEA special agents. (A map of DEA Task Forces operating in the United States can be found at http://www.justice.gov/dea/programs/taskforces_map.html.) In 2009, the DEA made 39,567 arrests and seized the following amount of drugs: 49,339 kg of cocaine, 642 kg of heroin, 666,120 kg of marijuana, 1703 kg of methamphetamine, and 2,954,251 dosage units of hallucinogens (see http://www.justice.gov/dea/statistics.html#arrests for other arrest and seizure data, along with links to data for the specific states) (Drug Enforcement Agency 2010c). The DEA also has a foreign presence, with 87 offices in 63 countries (Drug Enforcement Agency 2010a).

U.S. Marshals Service

The Marshals Service is part of the Department of Justice. The responsibilities of its 3439 Marshals, deputy marshals, and criminal investigators include the following:

- receipt, custody, and transportation of all persons arrested by federal agencies
- fugitive matters concerning escaped federal prisoners, probation and parole violators, persons under DEA warrants, and defendants released on bond
- management of the Federal Witness Security and Federal Asset Seizure and Forfeiture Programs
- security for Federal judicial facilities and personnel (Reaves 2006).

The Marshals Service is the oldest federal law enforcement agency; its authority was established in 1789. For nearly 75 years, it was the primary enforcement agency of the federal government.

The Director, Deputy Director, and 94 U.S. Marshals—appointed by the President or the Attorney General—direct the activities of 4942 total personnel across the United States and three foreign offices (U.S. Marshals Service, 2010). The Marshals Service is involved in virtually every federal law enforcement initiative. The service operates the Justice Prisoner and Alien Transportation System (JPATS) for transporting prisoners and criminal aliens. JPATS is one of the largest transporters of prisoners in the world, handling hundreds of requests every day to move prisoners between judicial districts, correctional institutions, and foreign countries.

For FY 2010, the U.S. Marshals Service budget was $1.125 billion. Recent statistics indicate more than 349,000 federal prisoner movements were completed by JPATS via coordinated air and ground systems. About 36,000 federal fugitives were apprehended because of investigations carried out by deputy marshals; the Marshals Service arrests more federal fugitives than all other law enforcement agencies combined. (Since 1983, the Marshals Service has maintained the "15 Most Wanted" fugitives list of high-profile, dangerous career criminals in the United States; of the individuals who have appeared on the list, 211 have been captured.) During 2009, Marshals Service-sponsored task forces arrested more than 90,800 state and local fugitives wanted on felony charges, and the service successfully completed 874 extraditions from around the globe. The U.S. Marshals Service currently manages approximately 18,000 assets (real estate, cash, financial instruments, and vehicles) with a value of more than $2.0 billion, and approximately $5.2 billion has been shared with state/local agencies since fiscal year 1985 (U.S. Marshals Service 2011).

Bureau of Alcohol, Tobacco, Firearms, and Explosives

The Bureau of Alcohol, Tobacco, and Firearms (ATF) has about 5008 total personnel, which includes 2450 agents and 789 investigators, who enforce federal laws related to alcohol, tobacco, firearms, explosives, and arson (Bureau of Alcohol, Tobacco, and Firearms 2010a). Its FY 2009 budget was over $1 billion. In January 2003, the ATF became a Justice Department agency and its name was changed to include the word "explosives"; the Agency, and most others, still refer to it as ATF, which we will do so here as well. Although established in 1972 as a separate agency within the Treasury Department, many of its tax-related enforcement responsibilities have been carried out since 1789 and remain with the Treasury Department (Bureau of Alcohol, Tobacco, and Firearms 2010b).

The ATF's mission goals and strategic plan focus on illegal firearms trafficking, criminal organizations, explosives, and fire/arson (Bureau of Alcohol, Tobacco, and

Firearms 2010c). The major programs and operations of the ATF working to accomplish the illegal firearms trafficking goal include Project Gunrunner, National Tracing Center (NTC), and the National Integrated Ballistic Information Network (NIBIN). Project Gunrunner is the ATF's primary Southwest Border initiative to "stem the trafficking of illegal weapons across the border and to reduce the firearms-driven violence occurring on both sides of the border" (Bureau of Alcohol, Tobacco, and Firearms 2010c). The ATF's National Tracing Center (NTC), created in 2001, provides nationwide firearms tracing capability. It allows the ATF to "trace" each firearm from its point of manufacture or importation to the point of its first retail sale. The NTC traces crime guns for federal, state, local, and international law enforcement agencies to provide investigative leads. By tracing firearms recovered by law enforcement authorities, the ATF is able to discern patterns of names, locations, and weapon types (Bureau of Alcohol, Tobacco, and Firearms 2010c). NIBIN provides investigative support to the nation's state and local partners by comparing ballistics information from criminal incidents across the country. It provides quick discovery of links between crimes, and provides law enforcement agencies with access to a valuable intelligence tool. In 2009, over 187,000 bullets and casings were imaged, with about 5350 resulting matches (Bureau of Alcohol, Tobacco, and Firearms 2010a).

Regarding the criminal organizations goal, the primary tactic is the Violent Crime Impact Teams (VCIT) initiative, which involves working with local law enforcement to identify, arrest, and prosecute the most violent criminals (often gang members) in designated cities. VCIT teams consisting of ATF and other federal agents, state and local police, and federal and state prosecutors have achieved significant success in reducing homicide rates in the cities where they operate. VCIT currently is under way in about 22 cities (Bureau of Alcohol, Tobacco, and Firearms 2010c).

The ATF maintains four National Response Teams (NRT), comprising highly-trained and well-equipped special agents, forensic chemists, and professional support staff that can be deployed within 24 hours to major explosion and fire scenes anywhere in the United States. Approximately 99% of all bombings in the U.S. are under the jurisdiction of the ATF; since 1978, over 25,000 bombings and attempted bombings have been investigated.

The National Center for Explosives Training and Research (NCETR) is a specialized research and education center whose divisions develop, coordinate, conduct, and facilitate the delivery of basic and advanced training courses for law enforcement and military personnel in the United States and for international partners. The ATF also operates Forensic Science Laboratories to provide expert examination of explosive materials. In addition, the agency staffs an International Response Team that participates with the Diplomatic Security Service of the U.S. Department of State to provide technical and investigative assistance at international explosive and fire incidents (Bureau of Alcohol, Tobacco, and Firearms 2010c).

Earlier we mentioned that students wanting to work for federal agencies should search for employment openings in some of the lesser known agencies; the competition may be considerably less but the job may be just as rewarding. Many federal agency job-seekers may only be familiar with the well known larger agencies and don't realize that once in the federal system they can often transfer to the larger agencies. **Figure 4-8** describes one of the lesser known, but very important, federal agencies.

OTHER LAW ENFORCEMENT ENTITIES

When you hear the term law enforcement, you usually think of uniformed officers or criminal investigators, most of who carry a firearm and have the authority to make arrests. These are not the only entities with law enforcement responsibilities, and we will discuss some more in this section.

Probation Officers

Probation officers are usually thought of as part of the corrections field; however, they have several law enforcement duties and responsibilities. They have the dual role of assisting convicted individuals in monitoring their behavior and referring them to treatment, education, financial, and employment services, but they also have a responsibility to keep their communities safe. If the person on probation violates the terms of his or her release, the law enforcement role may take priority. Some probation officers are authorized by law to carry firearms, though this is dependent on the jurisdiction.

At the federal level, probation officers serve the federal court system and are not only authorized to carry weapons, but are classified as law enforcement officers. There are over 5550 LEOs assigned to the Office of Probation and Pretrial Services, which serves the 94 federal district courts across the United States. Their primary emphasis is on providing treatment to offenders and encouraging them

---

FIGURE 4-8 Consider a career with the Federal Protective Service

The federal agency responsible for providing security for federal buildings and grounds nationwide is the Federal Protective Service and is part of the Immigration and Customs Enforcement agency of the Department of Homeland Security. Its personnel design security features and programs at over 9,000 federal facilities. Its 1,200 personnel (including 900 law enforcement security officers, criminal investigators, and police officers) and over 15,000 armed contract security officers provide police response and patrol services to over one million tenants and daily visitors to all federally owned facilities. The U.S. Marshals Service additionally provides security at federal courthouses. The FPS provides the following protective services:

- Conducting Facility Security Assessments
- Designing countermeasures for tenant agencies
- Maintaining uniformed law enforcement presence
- Maintaining armed contract security guards
- Performing background suitability checks for contract employees
- Monitoring security alarms via centralized communication centers
- Conducting criminal investigations
- Sharing intelligence among local/state/federal
- Protecting special events
- Working with FEMA to respond to natural disasters
- Offering special operations including K-9 explosive detection
- Training federal tenants in crime prevention and Occupant Emergency Planning

Positions with the FPS combine law enforcement responsibilities with crime prevention and security functions. Its personnel participate in national disaster recovery efforts, special national events such as president inaugurations and economic summits, conducting background investigations, responses to riots, and attending facility security meetings.

Source: Adapted from Department of Homeland Security (2010a) and (2010b).

to change their behavior. They also provide judges with needed information (usually referred to as a **pre-sentence investigation** or **pre-trial investigation report**) to make sound decisions when deciding whether a person should be placed on probation. Federal probation officers partner closely with the major federal law enforcement agencies and often assist on investigations, task forces, and special operations.

At the state and local levels, probation services usually are administered through the judicial system; however, it may be part of the executive branch and administered through a department of corrections. Recent data indicate that over 4,203,967 persons were on community probation in the United States, with 72% under active supervision (Glaze, Bonczar, and Zhang 2010, 2, 26). Again, the authority to carry firearms and to make apprehensions will vary. The duties and authority of probation officers may be dictated by state law. For example, in Ohio, Section 2151.14 of the Revised Code states the following for probation officers under the direction of a juvenile judge:

> [the probation] department shall make any investigations that the judge directs, keep a written record of the investigations, and submit the record to the judge or deal with them as the judge directs. The department shall furnish to any person placed on community control a statement of the conditions of community control and shall instruct the person regarding them. The department shall keep informed concerning the conduct and condition of each person under its supervision and shall report on their conduct and condition to the judge as the judge directs. Each probation officer shall use all suitable methods to aid persons on community control and to bring about improvement in their conduct and condition.
>
> …A probation officer may serve the process of the court within or without the county, make arrests without warrant upon reasonable information or upon view of the violation of this chapter…detain the person arrested pending the issuance of a warrant, and perform any other duties, incident to the office, that the judge directs. All sheriffs, deputy sheriffs, constables, marshals, deputy marshals, chiefs of police, municipal corporation and township police officers, and other peace officers shall render assistance to probation officers in the performance of their duties when requested to do so by any probation officer (Ohio Revised Code 2010).

Note that probation officers may serve papers to, arrest, and detain persons for violating conditions of probation. This often extends to searches of the probationer's premises as well.

Parole Officers

The distinction between probation officers and parole officers is one of timing and jurisdiction. Probation implies community control or treatment in lieu of being sent to jail or prison, while parole refers to community monitoring and assistance after the individual has served the jail or prison sentence. Congress abolished federal parole in 1984 for any offense that occurred after November 1, 1987 with the Sentencing Reform Act. The Federal Parole Board still exists, however, for those convicted of offenses prior to that date, and any offender who is released on parole will be supervised by a federal probation officer (U.S. Parole Commission 2010).

At the state and local levels, parole systems vary greatly. Thirty-eight states administer parole under their department of corrections or rehabilitation (i.e., prison system), and 11 utilize an independent parole agency or other system (Bonczar, 2008, 1). The Adult Parole Authority is often the title given to branch that carries out the functions associated with those on parole. In 35 states, parole and probation duties may be assigned to the same office or officer (Bonczar 2008, 1). In Pennsylvania, parole may be decided at the state or county level:

> Which system an offender is in depends on the length of the sentence given when the offender was convicted. If the sentence was 24 months or longer, it is a state sentence and the Parole Board makes the decision whether to grant parole and determines the conditions of parole. If the sentence is less than 24 months, it is a county sentence and the sentencing judge makes the decision (Pennsylvania Board of Probation and Parole 2010).

One law enforcement role of parole officers is to initiate parole revocation of a parolee—essentially sending the person back to prison. One study found that from 1977 to 2000, there was seven-fold increase in the number of parole violators returning to prison (Travis and Lawrence 2002, 21–23). According to recent BJS surveys, by the end of 2009 there were 819,308 persons on parole in the United States, with 16% of them under active supervision. Nationwide, about 24% of parolees returned to prison by revocation, an additional 9% were reincarcerated under a new sentence; and 9% absconded (Glaze, Bonczar, and Zhang, 2010, 6).

Corrections Officers

Another unique law enforcement officer is the corrections officer. Again, we usually do not think of their law enforcement role, but there are approximately 454,500 correctional officers and jailors employed in the United States (Bureau of Labor Statistics 2009b). The vast majority of correctional officers, jailors, and their supervisors are employed by state and local government in correctional institutions such as prisons, prison camps, and youth correctional facilities. At the federal level, Bureau of Prisons employees (over 37,000) are considered law enforcement officers (refer to Table 4-6) because all employees are trained in the use of weapons, defensive tactics, and riot strategies.

At the state and local level, corrections officers usually do not carry peace officer status. It is possible, and very probable in many jurisdictions, that local jails are staffed with peace officers or sheriff's deputies with the same authority as other law enforcement officials. With over 767,600 inmates being held in custody in local jails and admissions totaling 13 million on an annual basis (Todd 2010), corrections officers play an important role in processing offenders through the criminal justice system and keeping communities safe.

Inspectors and Fire Marshals

Chapter 1 mentioned that the law enforcement community included others such as various inspectors (fire, building, agricultural, health, safety, etc.) who may have enforcement authority based on state statutes or local ordinances. For example, in California, Division of Forestry Law Enforcement officers are trained and certified in accordance with the state's Peace Officer Standards and Training (Office of the State Fire Marshal 2010). In Ohio, the state fire marshal may appoint a state fire

marshal law enforcement officer who has peace officer status (see Chapter 1, Figure 1-4). In other states, such as Arkansas, Maryland, Oregon, and Pennsylvania, the state fire marshal's office may be a division of the state police and investigators may possess peace officer status.

Since our primary focus in this text is on policing, we will not elaborate on this category. It is important to note that such individuals play a significant role in keeping people safe, whether they test or inspect food supplies, check on safety practices at worksites, or search fire scenes for evidence of arson. Some of these inspector-type positions have authority to issue citations that may result in fines or corrective actions. Their offices often have authority to issue permits and collect fees for various services.

SUMMARY

The public law enforcement community of the United States consists of over 16,000 separate agencies employing over 1.2 million personnel (about 886,000 full-time sworn and 381,000 full-time civilian employees). Those agencies are found throughout the political subdivisions of each state and of the federal government. Consequently, the law enforcement system of the United States is fragmented and non-standardized. Each agency operates within its own jurisdiction; each agency has its own chief executive official; and each agency operates within its own structure, rules, and regulations. Some of these agencies possess general police authority, while others are restricted to specific police authority, such as offenses related to the traffic code, fish and wildlife, or narcotics. Some officers' authority is restricted to their place of employment (i.e., Capitol Police, Supreme Court Police, prison corrections officers). The combined cost of public policing expenditures in the United States for all levels of government is now over $100 billion (up from $98 billion in 2006, according to BJS figures). The law enforcement community is quite fragmented among the various jurisdictional levels and some have called for consolidation, restructuring, and mergers of agencies. By reviewing this chapter, one observes that there are considerable areas of possible restructuring. The current economic constriction in the United States has caused renewed interest in these issues. The next chapter discusses some management issues and other chapters address some of these issues as well.

Critical Thinking Questions

1. Explain the major features of the U.S. governmental structure and why the division of powers among the three branches is significant.

2. Why is the implied powers doctrine so important when analyzing the legislative enactments of Congress?

3. What is meant by a "political subdivision" of a state? How does it contribute to the multitude of policing agencies across the United States?

4. What are the advantages and disadvantages of having so many law enforcement agencies in the United States?

5. Compare and contrast "specific police authority" and "general police authority."

6. After reviewing the major federal law enforcement agencies with investigative and criminal responsibilities, critique their organizational placement in the federal government structure. Do any seem "out of place?"

7. After reading this chapter, explain how the concept of law enforcement is broader in scope and more complex than most people realize.

CHAPTER SPECIFIC INTERNET LINKS

To review additional data, analyses, graphs, and updated statistics about law enforcement and criminal justice issues in the United States—Bureau of Justice Statistics: http://www.ojp.usdoj.gov/bjs/

Secret Service Electronic Crimes Task Forces: http://www.secretservice.gov/ectf.shtml

National Association of State Fire Marshals: http://www.firemarshals.org/links/state-fire-marshals-websites/

CHAPTER GLOSSARY

Checks and balances (or separation of powers)—a mechanism for preventing any one branch of government (executive, legislative, or judicial) from becoming too powerful.

Concurrent or overlapping jurisdiction—when two or more law enforcement agencies, often from different levels of government, have jurisdiction (the right and authority) or are empowered to respond to and investigate criminal complaints in a given geographical area.

County police department—an law enforcement agency with county-wide jurisdiction; it may exist alongside a sheriff's department or operate in place of one.

Federalism—a form of representative democracy establishing a "dual system" of government made up of the federal and state systems.

Fragmented system—one that is not centralized; it refers to the multiple law enforcement agencies at each level of government, as opposed to a national police system.

General police authority—police responsibility extends to most any criminal offense committed within the jurisdiction.

Implied powers doctrine (or the necessary and proper clause)—Article I, Section 8 (Paragraph 18) of the United States Constitution, which grants Congress the right to enact laws in order to properly carry out the specific rights of Congress enumerated in the Constitution.

Judicial review—the authority of the courts to review cases from lower courts and rule on the constitutionality of laws.

Political subdivisions—jurisdictions or entities created by the state that possess authority and control over local matters. The most common names for these political subdivisions include: county, municipality or city, village, borough, and township.

Pre-sentence investigation/pre-trial investigation Report—a report written by probation or pre-trial services personnel for a judge, to assist in determining appropriate sentences and/or treatment of adjudicated offenders

Specific police authority—police responsibility and the right to investigate are limited by law to certain matters.

States' rights amendment—refers to the 10th Amendment to the U.S. Constitution, which states that the powers not delegated to the federal government by the Constitution, nor prohibited to the states, are reserved to the states or the people.

Supremacy clause—refers to Article IV of the U.S. Constitution, which states that the laws of the United States (federal government) shall be the supreme law of the land.

CHAPTER REFERENCES AND ADDITONAL READINGS

Bonczar, Thomas P. (2008). *Characteristics of State Parole Supervising Agencies 2006*. Washington, D.C. : Bureau of Justice Statistics.

Bureau of Alcohol, Tobacco, Firearms, and Explosives (2010a). ATF Fact Sheet. http://www.atf.gov/publications/factsheets/factsheet-facts-and-figures.html

Bureau of Alcohol, Tobacco, Firearms, and Explosives (2010b). ATF's History. http://www.atf.gov/about/history/

Bureau of Alcohol, Tobacco, Firearms, and Explosives (2010c). Strategic Plan—Fiscal Years 2010–2016. http://www.atf.gov/publications/general/strategic-plan/

Bureau of Customs and Border Protection Agency (2010a). Snapshot: A summary of CBP facts and figures. http://www.cbp.gov/linkhandler/cgov/about/accomplish/snapshot.ctt/snapshot.pdf

Bureau of Customs and Border Protection Agency (2010b). Securing America's Borders: CBP Fiscal Year 2009 in Review Fact Sheet. http://www.cbp.gov/xp/cgov/newsroom/news_releases/archives/2009_news_releases/nov_09/11242009_5.xml

Bureau of Customs and Border Protection Agency (2010c). GS-1895-5/7 Customs and Border Protection Officer. http://www.cbp.gov/linkhandler/cgov/careers/customs_careers/officer/officer_fact_sheet.ctt/officer_fact_sheet.pdf

Bureau of Labor Statistics (2009a). Occupational Outlook Handbook, 2010-11 Edition, Police and Detectives. http://www.bls.gov/oco/ocos160.htm

Bureau of Labor Statistics (2009b). Occupational Outlook Handbook, 2010-11 Edition, Correctional Officers, http://www.bls.gov/oco/ocos156.htm

Commission on Accreditation for Law Enforcement Agencies, Inc. (2010). Client Database. http://www.calea.org/content/calea-client-database

Drug Enforcement Administration (2010a) History. http://www.justice.gov/dea/history.htm

Drug Enforcement Administration (2010b). DEA Mission Statement. http://www.justice.gov/dea/agency/mission.htm

Drug Enforcement Administration (2010b). Stats and Facts. http://www.justice.gov/dea/statistics.html#arrests

Federal Bureau of Investigation (2010a). Crime in the United States, 2009. Washington, D.C.: U.S. Department of Justice.

Federal Bureau of Investigation (2010b). "About Us – Quick Facts," http://www.fbi.gov/about-us/quick-facts.

Federal Bureau of Investigation (2010c). Overview of the Legal Attaché Program. http://www.fbi.gov/about-us/international_operations/overview

Federal Bureau of Investigation (2007). "What We Investigate," http://www.fbi.gov/hq.htm

Forman, Marcy M. (April 30, 2009). Worksite Enforcement Strategy (memorandum). Washington, D.C. : U.S. Immigration and Customs Service.

http://www.ice.gov/doclib/foia/dro_policy_memos/worksite_enforcement_strategy4_30_2009.pdf

Government Accountability Office (2006). Federal Law Enforcement: Survey of Federal Civilian Law Enforcement Functions and Authorities. Report to the Chairman, Committee on the Judiciary, House of Representatives, GAO-07-121, December.

Government Accountability Office (2007). Federal Law Enforcement: Results of Surveys of Federal Civilian Law Enforcement Components, GAO-07-223SP, an E-supplement to GAO-07-121.

Government Accountability Office (2009). Federal Law Enforcement Retirement. Washington, D.C.: Government Accountability Office, GAO-09-727, July.

Glaze, Lauren E., Thomas P. Bonczar, and Fan Zhang (2010). *Probation and Parole in the United States, 2009*. Washington, D.C.: Bureau of Justice Statistics.

http://bjs.ojp.usdoj.gov/content/pub/pdf/ppus09.pdf.

Hickman, Matthew J. and Brian A. Reaves (2006a). *Local Police Departments, 2003*. Washington, D.C.: U.S. Department of Justice.

Hickman, Matthew J. and Brian A. Reaves (2006b). *Sheriffs' Offices, 2003*. Washington, D.C.: Bureau of Justice Statistics, U.S. Department of Justice.

Hunter, Ronald D. (Fall 1990). Three Models of Policing. Police Studies, Vol. 13, No. 3:118–123.

Immigration and Customs Enforcement (2010). ICE Overview. http://www.ice.gov/about/overview/

Office of the State Fire Marshal (2010). Law Enforcement. State of California. http://osfm.fire.ca.gov/lawsenforcement/lawenforcement.php.

Ohio Revised Code (2010). Section 2151.14.

Perry, Steven W. (2005). *Census of Tribal Justice Agencies in Indian Country, 2002*. Washington, D.C.: Bureau of Justice Statistics, U.S. Department of Justice.

Pennsylvania Board of Probation and Parole (2010). Understanding Pennsylvania Parole. http://www.pbpp.state.pa.us/portal/server.pt/community/understanding_pennsylvania_parole/5356.

Reaves, Brian A. (2006). *Federal Law Enforcement Officers, 2004*. Washington, D.C.: Bureau of Justice Statistics, U.S. Department of Justice.

Reaves, Brian A. (2007). *Census of State and Local Law Enforcement Agencies, 2004*. Washington, D.C.: Bureau of Justice Statistics, U.S. Department of Justice.

Reaves, Brian A. (2008). *Campus Law Enforcement, 2004–05*. Washington, D.C.: Bureau of Justice Statistics, U.S. Department of Justice.

Reaves, Brian A. and Lynn M. Bauer (2003). *Federal Law Enforcement Officers, 2002*. Washington, D.C.: Bureau of Justice Statistics, U.S. Department of Justice.

Reaves, Brian A. and Matthew Hickman (2003). *Census of State and Local Law Enforcement Agencies, 2000*. Washington, D.C.: Bureau of Justice Statistics, U.S. Department of Justice.

Todd, Minton D. (June 2010). Jail Inmates at Midyear 2009 - Statistical Tables.

http://bjs.ojp.usdoj.gov/index.cfm?ty=pbdetail&iid=2195

Travis, Jeremy and Sarah Lawrence (2002). *Beyond the Prison Gates: The State of Parole in America*. Washington, D.C.: Urban Institute, Justice Policy Center.

Transportation Security Administration (2010). Border Patrol Agent. http://www.tsa.gov/join/benefits/soar/cbp/bpa.shtm.

U.S. Courts (2010). Probation and Pretrial Services – Mission.

http://www.uscourts.gov/FederalCourts/ProbationPretrialServices/Mission.aspx.

U.S. Department of Interior (2010). Indian Affairs. http://www.bia.gov/FAQs/index.htm.

U.S. Department of Homeland Security (2010a). About the Federal Protective Service. http://www.dhs.gov/xabout/structure/gc_1253889058003.shtm.

U.S. Department of Homeland Security (2010b). A Day in the Life of the Federal Protective Service. http://www.dhs.gov/files/programs/gc_1273177025622.shtm.

U.S. Department of Homeland Security (2010c). E-Verify. http://www.dhs.gov/files/programs/gc_1185221678150.shtm

USA.gov (2010). Federal Executive Branch. http://www.usa.gov/Agencies/Federal/Executive.shtml.

U.S. Marshals Service (2010). Fact Sheets: Facts and Figures. http://www.usmarshals.gov/duties/factsheets/fugitive_ops-2011.html.

U.S. Parole Commission (2010). History of the Federal Parole System. http://www.justice.gov/uspc/history.htm.

U.S. Secret Service (2010a). Fiscal Year 2009 Annual Report. http://www.secretservice.gov/FY09_SecretService_Annual%20Report-Web.pdf.

U.S. Secret Service (2010b). Special Agents. http://www.secretservice.gov/whoweare_sa.shtml

U.S. Secret Service (2010c). Forensic Services. http://www.secretservice.gov/forensics.shtml

U.S. Secret Service (2010d). Electronic Crime Task Forces and Working Groups. http://www.secretservice.gov/ectf.shtml.

CHAPTER 5

Organizational Structure and Its Impact

LEARNING OBJECTIVES

This chapter addresses the questions of how organizational structure relates to the effectiveness of the police and its ability to meet society's challenges. How an organization is structured affects how people do their work, and thus how the agency functions. By studying and understanding these ideas, you will be able to:

- State why law enforcement agencies across the country are organized in similar ways.
- Identify the reasons why traditional organizational structure is now being called into question.
- Describe the newer organizational strategies being implemented nationally.
- Explain the benefits that can be derived from organizational change.
- Identify the importance of the patrol officer and supervisor in contemporary law enforcement management approaches.
- Define the benefits and limits of both traditional and contemporary law enforcement organizational designs.
- Understand the role information and communication technology plays in contemporary management theory.
- Explain the basic concepts of Cellular and Net-Centric organization.

CHAPTER OUTLINE

KEY TERMS USED IN THIS CHAPTER

organization theory

organization behavior

human relations/humanistic

human resource

spoils system

rationalization

hierarchy

bureaucracy

Scientific Management Theory

span of control

unity of command

dominance of an idea

structuring by authority

classical organization theory

organize by product

organize by function

task force

stable environment

dynamic environment

goal displacement

trained incapacity

organizational dysfunction

organize by time

organize by place

organize by clientele

motivation

leadership

motivators

hygiene factors/maintainers

satisfaction

job enrichment

traits

contingent leadership

systems theory

contingency theory

matrix organization

problem-oriented policing

team policing

Community-oriented policing (COP)

flat design/flat organization

net-centric

ORGANIZATION THEORY, ITS DEVELOPMENT, AND ITS IMPACT ON LAW ENFORCEMENT

Law enforcement agencies are, above all else, organizations. In law enforcement, as in all other areas of government, questions about size, function, and role are directly related to how law enforcement agencies are organized and the reasons for a particular form of organization. Another word for organization is organizational arrangement—how the various pieces of the organization relate to one another, what function they play, and the goals they seek. We organize to do work, and the nature of the work determines how best to organize; for example, a fast food restaurant is typically organized in a production-line fashion in order to get orders out fast. Every person has a specialized job and the work (order taking and processing) is passed from one "specialist" to the next. Efficiency is the goal or value sought in that organizational arrangement. Similarly, law enforcement organizations are organized around their work. However, in law enforcement, there is not a single important value, but multiple and often competing values that are sought, including efficiency, effectiveness, and equality, to name a few. After discussing some general concepts of organization theory, we will address the challenges facing law enforcement in the early 21st century as the world rapidly changes.

This chapter introduces students to law enforcement organizational structure. It proceeds from the assumption that students are prepared to discard preconceived notions of how an organization should be structured, and this chapter invites the student to consider multiple options of organization accordingly. As this material is read and pondered, memories of organizational experiences should be called upon for examples. Every one of us has been in organizations, even if we did not think of them as such. The Girl Scouts and Boy Scouts, church groups, political parties, schools, our employment location, fraternities and sororities, the military, colleges, universities, and even neighborhood watch groups provide examples of organizations. Each is slightly different, and they are different for a reason. The student should examine those

differences as we discuss law enforcement organizations, which also differ greatly.

Generally, there are two fields of theory and practice of which law enforcement students should be aware. First is **organization theory**, which is a body of research and practice that looks at organizational arrangements in a structural sense, much like a map. The subjects of organization theory include how an organization should be structured, how tasks should be divided, how personnel should be assigned to those tasks, and the level of control or supervision over their work. The second field of study and practice is **organization behavior**, which examines how people act within an organization and their relationships with others. This field includes motivation, leadership, group dynamics, and organizational change and development. Sub-fields include the **human relations** and **human resource** movements; the former addresses the needs of individuals in an organization, while the latter views the individual as an organizational asset. Both are treated here in the context of human-relations theory as a single topic. Each of these sub-fields and topics will be examined in turn, together with their importance to law enforcement personnel.

Organizations have been a part of social life from the beginning of recorded history. The Romans, for example, had very complex bureaucracies over 2000 years ago, and the Greeks did as well, even before the Romans. Still, very little theory about organization design survived. There is evidence, however, that thought was given to the problem of how to organize. Aristotle, for instance, wrote in 360 BC of some organizational issues influenced by culture. Even earlier, the Chinese philosopher Sun Tzu, in his classic work *The Art of War*, discussed the need for hierarchy in organizing armies (see **Figure 5-1**). An early Muslim scholar, Abu Yusuf, discussed the administrative problems of Islamic government, including finance and criminal justice (Shafritz and Ott 1992). What emerged from these early efforts are scattered general ideas about the organization of large entities. Heavy duty, "industrial strength" organization theory really did not arrive until the advent of the industrial revolution.

FIGURE 5-1 *The Art of War* by Sun Tzu

Sun Tsu said:

The art of war is of vital importance to the state. It is a matter of life and death, a road either to safety or to ruin. Hence under no circumstances can it be neglected.

The art of war is governed by five constant factors, all of which need to be taken into account. They are: the Moral Law; Heaven; Earth; the Commander; method and discipline.

The Moral Law causes the people to be in complete accord with their ruler, so that they will follow him regardless of their lives, undismayed by any danger.
Heaven signifies night and day, cold and heat, times and seasons.
Earth comprises distances, great and small; danger and security; open ground and narrow passes; the chances of life and death.
The Commander stands for the virtues of wisdom, sincerity, benevolence, courage, and strictness.
By *method and discipline* are to be understood the marshaling of the army in proper subdivisions, the gradation of rank among the officers, the maintenance of roads by which supplies may reach the army, and the control of military expenditure.

These five factors should be familiar to every general. He who knows them will be victorious; he who knows them not will fail.

Source: Clavell, James (ed.)(1983), *The Art of War by Sun Tzu*. Delaconte Press.

CLASSICAL ORGANIZATION THEORY

Throughout most of the early history of the United States, the postal department was the largest governmental organization, and as a highly decentralized organization, the postal system gave little thought to its structure. Moreover, from the earliest days of the nation there was virtually no permanent army or navy. The nation also was largely agricultural; as such, there was little experience with permanent, large-scale organizations anywhere in the United States. Indeed, the first law enforcement organizations were created at a time in our nation's history when little thought was given to organizing an enterprise of any sort—public or private. Also, formal law enforcement formed at a time when local governments (cities, towns, and counties) were generally run by political parties for the primary benefit of the party members.

In 1829, President Andrew Jackson came into office with a unique perspective on government in a democracy. He argued that elections should be employed not only to elect officials, but to fire those who worked for the loser: in short, "To the victor belong the spoils," a system that came to be called the **spoils system**. If you wanted a job as a police officer, you joined the party, and voted and donated a portion of your salary to the party. In return, the party took care of you. Because there was no training and the only criteria for selection was party support, police were little more than political hacks. Because they were known to be nothing but politicians, they employed violence and brutality to maintain order—if they did anything at all. Teddy Roosevelt, the newly appointed Commissioner of Police in New York City in the early 1900s, set out one day to see where his officers were. He found them drunk in bars, gambling in alleys, and in houses of ill repute. He quit in frustration after trying to bring some semblance of order to what was essentially a uniformed mob (Knott and Miller 1987; Walker 1998). This system of political patronage was partially responsible for the development of civil service systems (see **Figure 5-2**) as reform measures.

In the late 1800s, the Progressive reform movement rose in the Midwest as backlash to the political machines that had come to dominate local and state government. One of the main concerns of this movement was the improvement of public works. The objective was to hire by merit, train people for specialized jobs, promote by merit (rather than by social connections), and discipline by rule. If the earlier period can properly be called the "political" era in policing, the emerging era in the 1900s was the beginning of the "professional" era—one in which law enforcement came to look more and more like a profession with standards for performance and training.

FIGURE 5-2 The Spoils System and Civil Service

When the United States began as a nation, the process of hiring for government positions was generally political. There was no standing army or navy and very little in the way of administrative agencies. There were not many jobs. As the nation grew, it became clear to some that only the elite were serving in government either by election or appointment. These were generally white males with money and education. They were the same citizens who controlled the new states as well as the new federal government. In the 1820s General Andrew Jackson ran for the presidency and vowed that "the common man" should run government. He also vowed that if elected the person being elected should take only friends into office. For him, this was democracy. Who ever wins the election should run the entire government. It was said, "To the victor belong the spoils." Hence it came to be called the spoils system. By the 1880s, as cities grew and city services expanded to police, fire, road, and sanitation services, nearly every city was run by one party. Some cities were democratic while other were republican. But if you did not work for that party, you could not get a job (and sometimes, services). When President Garfield was assassinated by a job seeker who did not get a job in 1881, Congress passed a major civil service bill in 1883. As the use of civil service merit hiring grew, political machines died. However, civil service also places employees beyond political control which makes government respond more slowly. Political hiring and merit hiring both have benefits and detriments.

At the head of the charge for professionalization were some of the most important leaders in law enforcement, including August Vollmer, O.W. Wilson, and V.A. Leonard (see Chapter 3). The influence of organization science, particularly in the case of Vollmer, who was one of the first presidents of the International Association of Chiefs of Police (IACP), presented the first major change in law enforcement management. Vollmer was a fan of Frederick Taylor and his notion of "scientific management," and he adopted Taylor's ideas from beginning to end. Vollmer's leadership, teaching, and writing influenced others, who in turn adopted Taylorism and other

aspects of what came to be called "classical organization theory," or sometimes, just "orthodoxy."

The creation of police departments, schools, sanitation districts, fire departments, and prisons required greater attention to the organization and management of large-scale systems. The models for organizational design were drawn from the military model (hierarchy and chain of command), the Roman Catholic Church (principle of subsidiarity), or the newly emerging economic model (mass production lines). **Figure 5-3** illustrates a typical organizational chart for a large agency and **Figure 5-4** explains the rationale for "interpreting" the meaning of the lines connecting the boxes and the relationships that can be determined by such charts. (Also, see Appendix III of the text for additional organizational charts for selected agencies.)

In the following sections, we discuss the development of classical organization theory and its direct impact on law enforcement. We describe, particularly in relation to local law enforcement, how it produced organizational culture, structure, and goals that in the minds of some were not wholly consistent with major law enforcement policy shifts of the 21st century (most notably community policing and problem oriented policing). We also discuss the conflicts, possible solutions, and misconceptions associated with organization science.

Max Weber

The evolution of early organization practices led several theorists to develop highly-articulated theories about organization design. Max Weber, writing in the late 1800s (but not published in English until 1922), suggested that organizations represented the natural trend in society toward what he called **rationalization**. Drawing upon early theory and his observations about world social development, Weber concluded that the essential aspect of organization was **hierarchy**, represented by the emergence of **bureaucracy**; this meant a division of labor, clear lines of authority, specialization and communication between superior and subordinate, a single unifying authority at the top of the hierarchy producing a clear chain of command, and, most importantly, hiring and promotion based upon merit and productivity, not personality or politics (Gortner, Mahler, and Nicholson 1987).

FIGURE 5-3 Typical Traditional Organizational Chart Design

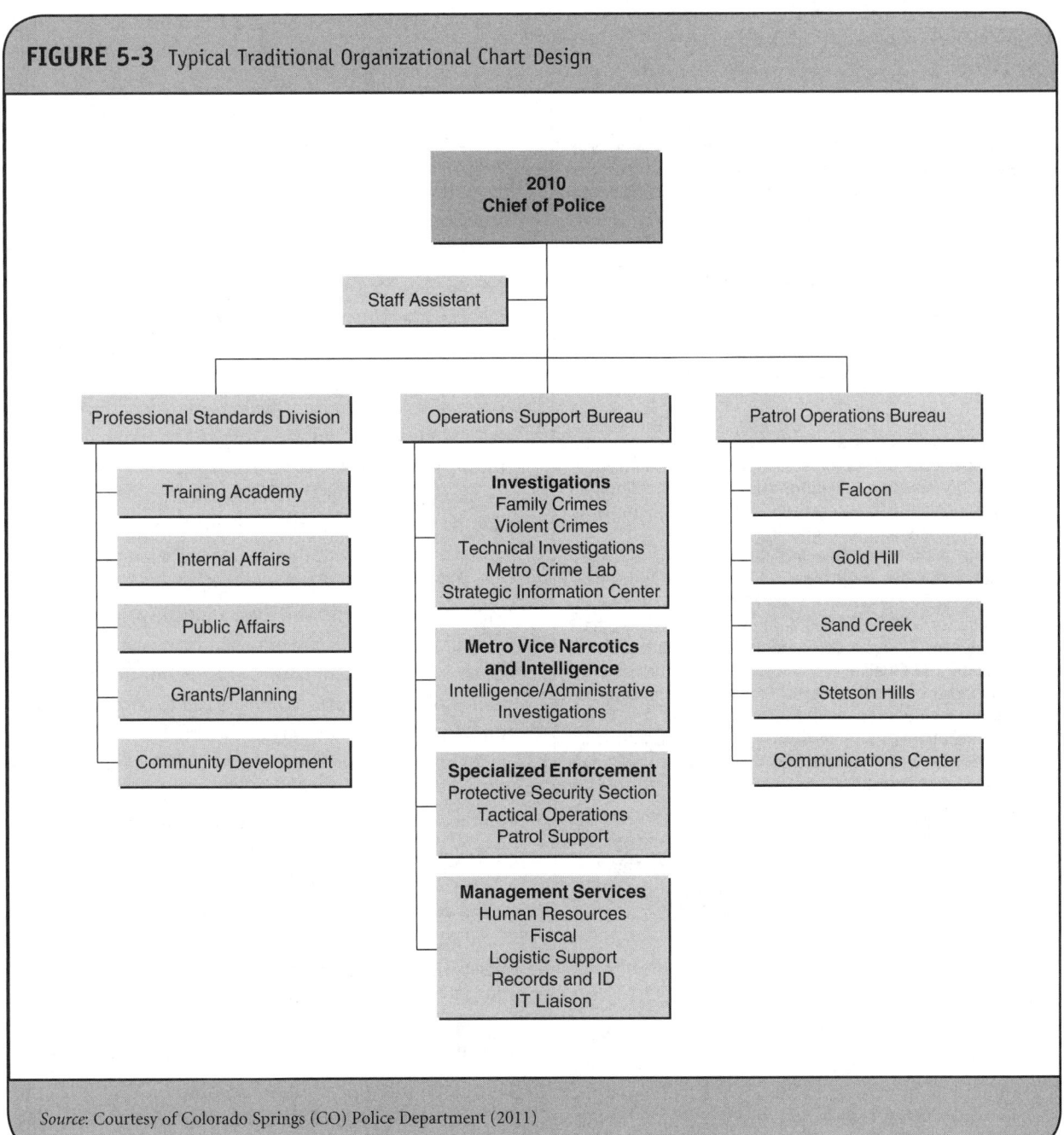

Source: Courtesy of Colorado Springs (CO) Police Department (2011)

FIGURE 5-4 Reading a Traditional Organizational Chart

A table of organization is a chart that shows the positions in an organization and the prescribed interaction between those positions. Each little box on such a chart represents a position or a category of positions. Height on the page is a measure of status. Vertical lines represent the interaction of superiors and subordinates. Horizontal lines represent the interaction of equals.

Any table of organization resembles any other in representing the structure of the organization to consist of positions and interactions. Positions are identified by activity and status. The title of the position on the chart ordinarily identifies its activity. Its distance from the bottom or the top of the chart measures its status. The lines that are drawn between positions indicate prescribed (or occasionally observed) interaction with other positions. Most tables of organization emphasize interaction between superiors and direct subordinates. They minimize or omit interaction between equals and between widely separated positions.

It is sometimes objected that the table of organization does not tell us how an organization works, only how it is *supposed* to work. Informal interaction accounts for part of the discrepancy, but there are other reasons too, such as the tendency for information to lag behind the small social changes that occur continuously and the tendency for desirable conditions to be hopefully included as facts. . . . Nevertheless, the table of organization always tells us a great deal, and it is doubtful whether we can talk sensibly about a particular organization without it.

Source: From Caplow. Principles of Organization, 1E. © 1964 Global Rights & Permissions, a part of Cengage Learning, Inc. Reproduced by permission. www.cengage.com/permissions

Weber was a social scientist (sociology by trade) and examined what he saw as emerging patterns of behavior in society. He neither recommended nor dismissed organizations so designed, but rather argued that society was getting progressively more "rational"—that is, choices were made on the basis of criteria, not on the basis of charisma (personal power), or tradition ("this is how we have always done it"). That society generally was becoming rational held certain effects for public organizations, including law enforcement. Rules and criteria would replace personality and habit. This single condition would lead to a trend to remove direct political influence from law enforcement organizations, and hence remove public contact from public organizations. There were other theorists, however, who had far greater direct impact on police organizations, and none was more important than Frederick Winslow Taylor.

Frederick Winslow Taylor

Another theorist of the same era as Weber, Taylor examined both the way people work (job design) and the way the organization is structured. His **Scientific Management Theory** centered on understanding the work to be done by breaking it down into its smallest parts to determine the most efficient way of performing the task; by understanding the work better, you could scientifically train a worker to do exactly what the job required. He also developed the organizational idea of a planning staff to give management direction (Fry 1989). These notions, together with those of Weber, gave organizations a model for structuring work: define the job, train to the tasks of that job, hire the best trained, promote on the same basis, and have a strong and clear hierarchy—all of which were consistent with the themes of the Progressive reform movement and Vollmer's call for professionalization. Taylor's purpose was to directly link skill and productivity to pay. He reasoned that if skill was in place and properly applied, productivity should follow. Hence, the notion of "job design" contributed to organization theory as well as the nature of organizational arrangement concerns. The fact that Vollmer and other leading executives in the emerging field of police science regarded Taylor's scientific management so highly would deeply impact the structuring and managing of law enforcement organizations for three generations, well into the 1970s.

Luther Gulick

During the late 1930s, other organization theorists added to the growing body of thought about how to most effectively structure work. The most famous, Luther Gulick, a trusted advisor to then-President Franklin Roosevelt, noted that there were limits to the ways work could be divided. He argued that effective communications were essential, and thus the **span of control**—the number of employees supervised—should be small; this meant that no single individual should control more than a few (three to seven) people. Further, the notion of **unity of command** should apply from the top of an organization to the bottom, meaning that every individual should report to only one individual in the organization, and the line of authority (or chain of command) was traceable from any person to the top of the organization.

Most interestingly, he started the debate over whether one should organize by function or organize by product (both of which will be discussed later), a concept very important to current designs for law enforcement organizations. He also noted that you could control an organization either by **dominance of an idea** or by **structuring authority** (Shafritz and Ott 1992). Dominance of an idea meant that a set of values (such as a mission statement or agency goals) could dominate the management of an organization and direct its activities, while structuring by authority was simply the use of hierarchical authority to impose management's desires by orders and supervision.

The primary problems in organizations are control and coordination (Marsden et al. 1994). The cause of these concerns is the need to direct members of the organization toward policy goals set by the organization, not individuals. Complex organizations, those that carry out many tasks with ambiguous processes, are particularly in need of controlling and directly organizing members. Law enforcement is no different, and we need look no farther than use-of-force questions to understand management's need to control and coordinate. Thus, while structuring by authority is important, so are values, ideas, mission statements, and policies and procedures—dominance by ideas.

Classical Theory Applied to Policing

The body of concepts and philosophy from Weber, Taylor, and Gulick, among others, is frequently called **classical organization theory** (see **Figure 5-5**), which took hold in policing for three major reasons. The first was political reform. Prior to the early 1900s, police forces were quite political and hiring was politically influenced, as positions of rank such as captain were literally bought and sold (Knott and Miller 1987). The so-called spoils system of politics controlled government. The previously-mentioned Progressive reform movement of the late 1800s and early 1900s sought to end these abuses, in part

by advocating reliance on a civil service system, which employed objective testing for employment and promotion. However, reformers also wanted to maintain some political accountability, as a democracy should have some way to control government agencies. An organization run much as Weber and Taylor suggested would theoretically achieve these competing goals. Political control would come from carefully designing the jobs to be performed and the manner of performance, while single executive, merit hiring, and promotion would, at least in theory, ensure that the most qualified would be employed and be responsible to one person.

The second reason for the hold that classical theory had on policing was the use of the paramilitary model of command, which fit well into a classic hierarchy. As was discussed in chapter two, law enforcement in many countries came out of a military background, and although the U.S. military and police are distinct entities, one can see they share many of the same job duties. As such, if much of the work that the police and the military do is similar, it is understandable how they would organize in similar ways (although it is important to note that there are key differences in police and military work that have serious implications for organization). Third, the effort to professionalize

---

FIGURE 5-5 Tenets of Classical Organization Theory

One Executive

Unity of Command

Chain of Command

Short Span of Control

Merit Hire (qualifications)

Scientifically Designed Jobs

Merit Promotion (performance)

Division of Labor and Specialization

Line and Staff Functions Defined by Position

law enforcement reinforced the importance of merit and, therefore, hierarchy. The professionalization movement, as noted earlier, was the focus of teaching and writing on law enforcement management, hence the influence of the likes of Vollmer and Leonard.

Classical writers in organization theory often referred to their observations as the "principles of management." These principles were applied to law enforcement agencies throughout the United States just as professionalization and political reform were taking hold; as a result, most existing police departments tend to emulate the traditional hierarchical model of an organization. The organizational chart in Figure 5-3 is an example of what resulted from the application of classical organization theory. The trademarks of classical organizations included distinct levels, the differentiation between units (specialization), progressive promotion from within based upon merit, and a single line of authority from top to bottom. The following sections examine some of the ways in which classical principles were applied to policing organizations, which is followed by a discussion of more contemporary designs.

Organization by Product and Function

When Luther Gulick observed that an enterprise could organize by function or by product, he concluded that the most effective means was to organize by function (a function being a narrow job orientation) (Gulick 1937). This was the prevailing belief in most government agencies, and, as Figure 5-3 demonstrates, this became the accepted organization method in police agencies. In early application, **organization by product** was ignored in law enforcement agencies. Organization by product means that all officers needed to produce a result, such as drug arrests, and it has more of an end result focus (which works best in manufacturing an item), rather than a task focus (such as the service of policing). **Organization by function** is characterized by grouping employees together according to the major functions that they perform. The number of functions grew as administrative and service demands grew. A listing of typical functions serviced by police agencies is indicated in **Figure 5-6**.

The most obvious function associated with law enforcement is patrol. In an agency that was organized solely by function, patrol units would be unrelated to

FIGURE 5-6 Functional Activities

Criminal investigation	Budgetary control
Personnel	Purchasing
Criminal identification	Crime prevention
Communications	Transportation
Traffic regulation and control	Property control
Planning	Follow-up control
Police records	Jail administration
Statistical operations	Public relations
Supply	Intelligence
Criminalistics	Internal affairs
Patrol	Community relations

other units except by chain of command (see Chapter 6 for a detailed discussion of patrol). In some departments, specialized patrol teams using helicopters, bicycles, motorcycles, boats, or horses may be organized as separate units or deployed as part of the general patrol unit. In larger departments, there may be traffic units that are separate from general patrol. Others may have specialized patrol functions, such as park patrol, harbor or river patrol, or border patrol. In each case, the method or design of organization is related to function. The organization of each department is related to the variety of functions identified by that department. Many functions, such as general patrol, are common to nearly all departments, while others, such as harbor patrol or school patrol, are employed in only a few places. **Figure 5-7** identifies the typical line and staff functions within local policing agencies. Keep in mind, however, that in some agencies distinctions between line and staff operations can be a little fuzzy—especially in small agencies where resources are tight and officers are asked to wear many hats.

Similarly, while all law enforcement agencies perform investigations, most have designated investigators or detectives, but the use of personnel is defined by local circumstances. There is usually a separate detective bureau

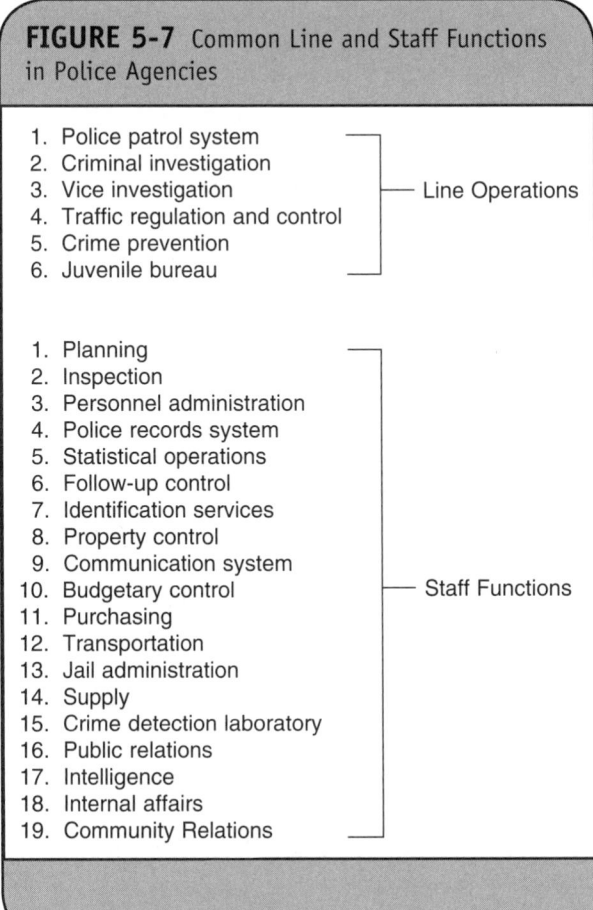

FIGURE 5-7 Common Line and Staff Functions in Police Agencies

1. Police patrol system
2. Criminal investigation
3. Vice investigation — Line Operations
4. Traffic regulation and control
5. Crime prevention
6. Juvenile bureau

1. Planning
2. Inspection
3. Personnel administration
4. Police records system
5. Statistical operations
6. Follow-up control
7. Identification services
8. Property control
9. Communication system
10. Budgetary control — Staff Functions
11. Purchasing
12. Transportation
13. Jail administration
14. Supply
15. Crime detection laboratory
16. Public relations
17. Intelligence
18. Internal affairs
19. Community Relations

(rape and domestic violence), gangs, and white collar crime. Newer problems have introduced new functional demands, such as environmental crime, terrorism, computer (cyber) crime, and growing levels of official corruption. Whether these are given specialized status or not depends solely upon the need and priorities of the agency, which accounts for the wide variation in organizational applications across the country. For example, white collar crime is more likely in communities with high concentrations of banking, insurance, or securities activities, while environmental crimes are more likely in communities with industrial facilities using toxic materials, agricultural facilities, and concentrations of transportation such as railroads and major truck routes. Federal agencies mostly focus on investigations and issues of national significance such as terrorism, homeland security, intelligence, interstate criminal activity, fugitives, etc.

Other organizational functions are relatively similar from agency to agency, such as records, personnel, and purchasing. In larger agencies, these are usually separate offices or units, but in smaller agencies, functions are frequently combined. For example, criminalistics may be part of the investigations unit, while crime prevention, public relations, and community relations may be combined into one unit. The organization principle, however, is generally the same—personnel functions determine organizational placement.

There are both benefits and limitations to this organizational principle. One benefit is that the organizational chart indicates who to contact for a given question or problem. Another benefit is the clarity it brings to the organization, as individual duties and responsibilities are more easily defined, making it simpler to train and integrate new personnel. Politically and administratively, this approach produces clear accountability and also encourages an organizational identification, or esprit de corps. For the administrator and legislative policymaker, it makes budgeting decisions much easier. In short, organization by function is a classical organizational model because divisions are based upon specialization of task.

The classical model, as useful as it is, has its limitations (Franz and Jones 1987). The problems induced by this traditional form of organization are as numerous as the benefits, and the impact of benefits and limitations

or investigations unit, and in larger agencies, these may be further broken down into heavily-specialized investigative units (e.g., burglary, robbery, sex crimes, and homicide squads). Sometimes specialized units are given the name task force, though technically, a **task force** is really a temporary organizational unit that is created for a limited purpose, examples of which include organized crime task forces or narcotics task forces, which may be inter-agency units (e.g., composed of members from several different law enforcement agencies).

Still, other departments create permanent units and give them a title that conveys permanency. Such units often specialize in organized crime, narcotics, auto theft, vice (gambling and prostitution), crimes against women

varies according to the environment in which the organization operates. Obviously, a police department in a town of 20,000 people, surrounded by farmland, operates in a different environment than does one in a city of 800,000 that is surrounded by urban sprawl. Similarly, budget and economic conditions, social upheavals, and changing population patterns alter an organization's environment. Issues related to rural crime are mentioned in **Figure 5-8**.

In a **stable environment**, traditional structures are able to predict future needs and demands and rationally plan for those needs. For example, if you can reasonably predict the amount of crime you expect to see in an area over a certain period of time, you can plan patrol and investigation staffing to meet those needs. You can determine your deployment needs by shift, by area, and by day. But, in a turbulent and chaotic environment, a condition that organization theorists refer to as a **dynamic environment**, the situation is different: it is more difficult to predict adequately the demands that will be placed on an organization. Surprises are more frequent, and in this environment, results are more unpredictable if things are done the way they "always were." The organization and its members feel as if they are in chaos. Classical organizational models assume stable conditions—a constant supply of raw resources, for example, to make steel (or control crime). These models do not do well in turbulent times, especially for public service agencies.

Herbert Simon, a Nobel laureate and one of the most influential social scientists of the 20th Century, recognized that one of the primary functions of an organization is to make decisions, but he argued that organizations and decision makers are "bounded" by limitations of time, money, knowledge, and other resources (Fry 1989). Classical or traditional organizational structures are designed to limit the amount of information that flows to the top decision-making levels, and these limitations mean that organizations make decisions with imperfect knowledge. In a stable environment, this can be harmful to organizational decisions, but in a turbulent or dynamic environment, the consequences may be quite severe.

FIGURE 5-8 Rural Crime and Policing

- Compared with urban areas, little is known about rural crime or rural policing. It appears, however, that crime is less frequent in rural areas, and that "community policing," to which many urban departments now aspire, has been a long-standing practice in rural police agencies.
- While the terms "rural" and "urban" are used frequently in everyday language, there are no precise meanings of these terms upon which everyone can agree. Despite this, it is clear that the idea of rural is useful.
- Differences between rural and urban cultures have implication for rural crime and rural policing. For example, both rural and urban areas have pockets of extreme poverty, but the effects of poverty on crime are different in the two areas.
- Differences across rural areas are large and vary by region of the country, across counties within a State, and sometimes even within a county. For example, illegal immigrants may be a concern in the Southwest, vandalism in the Midwest, and the smuggling of tobacco and liquor in areas along the Canadian border. Thus, national policies uniformly covering rural areas may be a mistake, unless those policies can be tailored to fit local needs.
- There are contradictions across studies that need to be explained. For example, some authors report that homicide is higher in rural areas, while others (including UCR data) suggest the opposite. It is unclear whether these differences are the product of sampling, the definitions used, or regional variations.
- Studying these issues across rural areas and between urban and rural areas is useful in the same way that studies of crime across countries tell us much about larger patters and suggest what works and what does not work in policing and crime prevention.

Source: Weisheit, Ralph, David Falcone, and L. Edward Wells (1994), "Rural Crime and Rural Policing," Research in Brief. Washington, D.C.: U.S. Department of Justice, National Institute of Justice.

Conditions for law enforcement today are changing. Concentrated pockets of violent crime are increasing even while much traditional crime is decreasing. The emergence of crack and designer drugs, proliferation of automatic weapons, escalation of drive-by shootings, threats of terror attacks, and increased juvenile violence have changed the environment for law enforcement. Cities are growing ever more diverse; many neighborhoods are physically deteriorating and becoming highly transient. Conditions such as these are the perfect pre-conditions for increases in violent crime (Short 1997). These conditions are not suitable to rigid organizations because they warrant quick decision making and responses that are flexible.

Another limitation of classical organization theory is **goal displacement**. This happens when those who work in the organization learn to focus on rules rather than service or function. Similarly, members of the organization are likely to respond to requests for assistance with phrases like, "it's not in my job description." This is called **trained incapacity,** because people are also trained what not to do, even if it makes sense to do it. The result of these limitations, called **organizational dysfunctions**, is that organizations are not inclined to be imaginative or innovative. They will not use information about the environment properly and are inclined to rigidity. Retreating to "the book" serves to further isolate the organization from its clients, which in the case of policing is the public. Structure and rule rigidity prevent flexibility, and the public may view it as a lack of professionalism. All of these problems suggest that law enforcement may need to reassess its current approach to organizational design. This holds important implications for the patrol officer. In classical organizations, patrol officers are at the "bottom" of the structure; their role, more or less, is to follow orders within a narrow range and engage in a limited set of predefined tasks.

In alternative organizational formulations, the role of patrol officers would change dramatically. For example, many law enforcement agencies recognized some of the limitations of classical organization structure relatively early in the development of modern policing. Many also realized the limitations built into the organization by function approach. Minor changes in organizational principles resulted. These included the **organize by time** and **organize by place** (or area) approaches (Wilson 1950). For example, many law enforcement agencies, such as the state highway patrol, are inherently spread out over large distances, which require time to cover. Such agencies may be divided into relatively self-contained units called posts, regions, or districts. Similarly, municipal police agencies may cover vast amounts of territory and hundreds of thousands or millions of people. Usually, these agencies are divided into precincts, which may have not only patrol and investigation units, but other specialized units such as Special Weapons and Tactics (SWAT) teams. The typical arrangement is for each such precinct to include all of the line functions (refer to Figure 5-7) and some of the staff functions (such as records, jail administration, and community relations, for example) in one unit. In this arrangement, a department is organized by area and divided into precincts, while each precinct is organized by function. Another kind of organizational approach is to **organize by clientele** (Leonard and Moore 1987). A relatively common example of this approach is the creation of juvenile units. Similarly, state highway patrol agencies normally have a special unit assigned to truck safety.

Each of these organizational approaches can temporarily address some of the limitations of classical hierarchy, but they have their own built-in limitations, since each approach is similar to organization by function. In order to understand the reasons why policing is changing and how it is changing structurally, it is important to understand these prior forms of organization. These examples represent the cumulative effects of merit service, professionalization of law enforcement, and specialization. From the 1880s to the 1920s, the mission of law enforcement agencies was relatively clear: patrol, much of it on foot, was the primary function. Crimes were largely theft and personal assaults, and keeping the peace primarily explained law enforcement's mission. Poor communication, little training, and limited education among officers required close supervision and, therefore, a very short span of control. Law enforcement organizations were thus shaped by the social and environmental forces that surrounded them. When the problems of control and command were largely settled by the 1960s, the external conditions—crime, city structure, and economic stability—were largely unchanging. The impression was that traditional law enforcement, and hence traditional structures, were working.

By the late 1960s that perspective was dispelled. A significant increase in crime, riots, demonstrations, and other disorder left the impression that society was falling apart and law enforcement could not seem to react to or correct these conditions. In 1966, a presidential commission was appointed to study both the increase in crime and the incapacity of the criminal justice system to respond effectively. The reports of this commission, published largely in 1967, argued for a number of things regarding policing: better education and training, a closer connection to the community, and more research on policing, for example.

Research on policing produced several organizational effects. First, it became clear that random patrol did not prevent crime (Kelling et al. 1974). Similarly, the process of investigation came into question for its overall effectiveness (Chaiken et al. 1975). However, subsequent research showed that *focused* patrols (e.g., focusing on identified "hot spots") did work. Research also found that patrol had a role in investigations and that certain techniques of investigation improved the process. The impact of these and other findings called into question the traditional role of specialization, hierarchy, and command decision making. This propelled the discussion of community policing and problem-oriented policing as both a product and structural fix to law enforcement's perceived problems (Skogan and Roth 2004).

Organizations are structured as a response to different task demands made by society and by the environment surrounding the organization (Zhao 1996). If either changes, the organization must change too; this is why so many private sector organizations are altering their business structures. Each kind of organizational design has certain benefits, but each also has limits. Organizations that fail to accommodate changes in demand will invariably falter. Attempts at more flexible organizational approaches began to appear as a consequence of the need to adapt to rapidly changing conditions.

HUMAN RELATIONS THEORY

Another set of researchers and practitioners in organizations looked beyond the mere structure of an organization and examined the impact of individuals and small groups

for ways to make organizations more efficient and effective. Experiments in industrial psychology led theorists in the 1930s to examine how human beings worked in organizations. The collected body of research and concepts associated with this approach is called the Human Relations, or Humanistic, Theory of management, The basic tenets of this perspective are listed in **Figure 5-9**.

Despite more than 60 years of research, real change in organization theory and in organizations themselves has only come about in the last 30 years. For law enforcement agencies, we can generally reduce these to two major areas: motivation and leadership. **Motivation** is a broad field of study that focuses on why people want to work (Conser 1979; Katzell and Thompson 1990). The field of **leadership** is closely related, and focuses on how management is able to get employees and organizations to follow a defined path. Line and staff employees frequently see both concepts differently than do leaders or managers in an organization. This chapter attempts no detailed analysis of these very complex concepts; we leave that for a course on human resources or organizational behavior. However, it is important for the entry-level officer to be aware of the issues in these areas and how they are developing. The trends hold important implications for both patrol officers and supervisors.

Motivation

Researchers addressing motivation focused on human needs and found that while some aspects of work motivate

---

FIGURE 5-9 Tenets of Human Relations Theory

Needs and Desires of Employees Matter
Group Dynamics Affect Productivity
Job Satisfaction
Three-way Communications
Participative Decision Making
Motivation is a Complex Concept
Leadership Styles Matter

people (**motivators**), others only prevent dissatisfaction (so called **hygiene factors** or **maintainers**) (Herzberg 1968). These researchers also found that motivation is the product of a calculated process in which individuals arrive at the probabilities of acquiring certain needs (Campbell, Dunnette, Lawler, and Weick 1970). The central thrust of the Motivation-Hygiene Theory is that people in organizations have two general drives related to their performance.

The first driver is motivation. People are motivated to perform tasks if three conditions exist: (1) they believe that rewards are tied to performance, (2) they value the rewards, and (3) performance is thought to be achievable. Motivation is enhanced if people are permitted to participate in the setting of organizational goals, are given interesting tasks, and are permitted to participate in deciding how to perform those tasks. Taken together, this means people can be motivated in an organization if they see clear, achievable goals that they value and to which there is a clear path (Rainey 1993). The second distinct drive is **satisfaction**, or the degree to which employees feel satisfied with their work and the rewards for that work. So, while motivation is a response to the expectation of future rewards, satisfaction is a response to past rewards. They are also distinct in that satisfaction is related to turnover and absenteeism. More importantly, satisfaction improves as participation in decision making increases (Lawler 1986; Wagner 1994). These are important factors for both leaders and subordinates to understand. For law enforcement organizations, the known sources of motivation and satisfaction pose a problem. The single most common reward (motivator) is monetary compensation and promotion (Ledford 1995). In civil service systems, these two are tied together in a way that they are not in private business; that is, pay for performance is common in business, while pay for longevity (length of tenure) is common in civil service systems such as law enforcement. Moreover, law enforcement agency pay is set by legislative bodies, not by managers, and promotion is largely controlled by civil service rules. Hence, managers in law enforcement are left to find other means to motivate officers, including special training, special assignments, shift assignment, and over-time consideration.

In order to do this, however, they need information. Patrol officers, supervisors, and staff must communicate the level of morale in the agency to managers in order to permit effective decisions. You will recall that traditional hierarchical organization structures restrict effective communication. One solution is to use an alternate organizational structure; an additional solution is for law enforcement managers to adopt leadership approaches which seek out information and participation in decision making.

Alternative motivators are numerous. One is the degree to which leaders listen to subordinates and communicate reasons for actions; others include job definition, temporary job assignments, reassignments, and the creation of task forces or teams. Jobs can be redefined to permit subordinates to focus on areas of their own interest. Reassignment of patrol officers to highly desired assignments is normally within the authority of managers, but does not involve pay or promotion.

Task force and team approaches also address satisfaction. As temporary assignments outside of the normal hierarchy, these approaches overcome the limitations of classical structure and permit employees to take advantage of specialized skills and interests. More importantly, they encourage cooperative decision making. Employees who are allowed to provide active input into their roles are more motivated and more satisfied (Russell and MacLachlan 1999).

Issues of motivation and satisfaction are also important because of the high levels of job burnout and stress in law enforcement. Sources of stress are organization practices, criminal justice system practices, public attitudes, and factors intrinsic to the job, including danger, differential social treatment, and unusual working hours (stress will be discussed in Chapter 6). These combine to create personal, social, and family difficulties for officers. Not all stress is negative, of course—it may make officers more cautious in dangerous situations or work harder when the stakes are exciting. However, negative stress may cause officers to react to outside stimuli in ways that are not positive (Gaines 1993). Strategies such as exercise can be employed to avoid debilitating stress. Also, officers need to feel free to communicate personal problems to their superiors who, in turn, must reduce the role that the organization plays in creating stress. Participative decision making and the use of **job enrichment** to increase levels of motivation and satisfaction will have a beneficial effect. Finally, fellow officers must discuss problems and solutions with one another.

Leadership

Theories about leadership demonstrate the close relationship that exists between organization structure, motivation, and leader behavior. Initially, theories of leadership focused on **traits** that "good" leaders have, but this is a very limited view, since it implies that certain people are born to be leaders and others are not. The more likely possibility is that leaders are people who can use certain skills to obtain information and act in a circumstance-appropriate way. This **contingent leadership** model suggests everyone can learn to be a leader and employ learned skills where conditions permit. More importantly, it does not limit leadership to only top positions in an organization. Rather, it implies that patrol officers and supervisors are leaders and can learn skills to become more effective at leading. Research demonstrates that the most effective leaders were those who employ teams, show a high level of concern for people as well as for results, and are able to show others in the organization how to achieve goals (Hersey, Blanchard, and Johnson 1996; Rainey 1991).

This leadership approach produces high performance, high satisfaction, and high levels of motivation. Some argue that this is why community policing is particularly suited to law enforcement organizations, as a salve for both community relations problems and organizational problems (Langworthy and Travis 2003). However, we think that is an incorrect read of the theory. As Hersey, Blanchard, and Johnson make clear, we do not yet have solid empirical evidence that any of the theories of leadership work. We have some evidence that they all work if certain conditions exist, but some organizations simply are not mature enough to avoid orthodox management styles and are thus not ready to transform their decision-making systems (1996). Recent evidence suggests that even after extensive efforts of community policing and problem-oriented policing, there is little evidence of attitudinal or behavioral change among line officers (Gingerich and Russell 2005).

Clearly, patrol officers are equally important in developing good leadership. Training for leadership roles begins at the patrol level as the use of task forces, teams, community policing, and similar concepts requires leadership at the lowest levels of the organization. Leaders in teams and task forces learn to invite participation and cooperation and discover that every member of the group can lead and can teach others or learn from others. This produces the so-called "learning organization."

Leadership roles may only be temporary. This is very different from a definition of leadership that is dependent upon position in the organization. Top managers must be leaders, yes, but all officers must exercise leadership. Because diverse skills, backgrounds, and knowledge increase leadership resources in the organization, patrol officers can contribute dramatically to the leadership of the department.

The key is to see leadership not as controlling or commanding, but rather as assisting, helping, guiding, facilitating, and contributing knowledge to others. Traditional "authority" is produced not by demand, but by demonstrating an ability to command an organization's resources. Command, therefore, is not obtained merely by giving orders.

CONTEMPORARY MANAGEMENT THEORY

As the previous discussion suggests, the classical paramilitary hierarchy employed in most law enforcement agencies is not very adaptive to rapidly changing conditions. It is also clear from other chapters in this book that environmental conditions surrounding law enforcement are changing rapidly. Furthermore, classical organization structures do not enhance motivation, increase satisfaction, or reduce stress, yet law enforcement organizations are faced with emerging demands from their communities, complex social problems related to crime, shifting crime patterns, shrinking budgets, terror threats, and slipping morale.

These internal and external environmental forces play a unique role in contemporary management perspectives. Two particular theoretical approaches that are concerned with environmental and situational conditions are the **systems theory** and the **contingency theory**.

Systems Perspective

Systems theory was described in some detail in Chapter 1, where we stated that it views the entire context (environment) in which an issue exists by analyzing all the forces or influences impacting it. When focused on organizational and management issues in the law enforcement field, it is particularly interested in analyzing all the influences from the environment that affect the agency. Such influences in the environment have been identified by Stojkovic, Kalinich, and Klofas (2003, 47) as including legal, political, cultural, economic, demographic, ecological, and technological forces. See **Figure 5-10** for a brief explanation and examples of each of these environmental forces. This approach emphasizes that administrators and managers need to consider the influence and effect of these multiple forces upon the agency and its operations.

Contingency

The contingency theory perspective is one that recognizes multiple factors within the organization. It is an attempt to identify which factors are most relevant and the impact of these factors. Organizations are viewed as open systems and much of the systems approach is accepted by contingency advocates. However, contingency theorists maintain

that they cannot rely on any one theoretical approach to address all issues because of the differences in organizations and situations. Decisions are "dependent upon" and "subject to" the evaluation and interaction of several factors, the primary ones being (a) organizational size, (b) technology, (c) environment, and (d) life cycle stage.

In our modern society, the application of classical hierarchy is not very adept at satisfying employees. Low employee satisfaction levels produce burnout, stress, and high rates of turnover. Law enforcement officers who are burned out or who are operating under high levels of stress are likely to make poor decisions and work with a low degree of effectiveness. Costs to the organization are not just financial and performance-related; poor decisions also lead to lower public confidence and trust in the police. Turnover is costly because organizations have tremendous investments in employees, as not only are the costs of training replacements significant, but the loss of experienced officers is damaging from a performance perspective. Indeed, the greater the experience of the

FIGURE 5-10 Environmental Forces – Systems Theory Perspective

Forces	Description	Examples
Legal	The various types of law and lawful authority of the federal, state, and local governments	Statutes, administrative code, agency policies, and case law
Political	The quest for influence by individuals, groups, and governmental actions	Interest groups, the electorate, unions, professional associations
Cultural	The collective norms, values, mores, behaviors, and expectations of a society or group	Male/female roles, ethnic identity and customs, morality
Economic	The financial resources of a community and an agency	Budget, tax base, employment, and business conditions
Demographic	The characteristics of the population – federal, state, and local levels	Population statistics by age, race, ethnicity, sex, educational level
Ecological	Climate, geological, and geographical conditions and related patterns	Weather, rivers, coastline, tourism, agriculture, industrial base
Technological	The practical application of any science or tool to common endeavors	Communications, computerization, vehicle video, forensic science

Source: Adapted from Stojkovic, Stan, David Kalinich, and John Klofas (2003), *Criminal Justice Organizations: Administration and Management, Third Edition*, Belmont, CA: Wadsworth/Thompson Learning, Chapter 3.

lost employee, the greater the cost to the organization in terms of performance. For each of these reasons, law enforcement agencies find themselves questioning the current practice of organizing by hierarchy (Greene 2004; Langworthy and Travis 2003; and Roberg and Kuykendall 1997).

The first approach to take advantage of multiple talents in a given project or operation was the use of **matrix organization** (**Figure 5-11**) (Swanson, Territo, and Taylor 1993). In this approach, a number of personnel are assigned to a given problem regardless of their permanent duty assignment. In this manner, the organization is able to take advantage of the best personnel for a given problem without permanent structural changes. However, it is very difficult to manage day-to-day operations and achieve accountability in matrix organizations. In many respects, this is not very different from special task force operations, because typically a task force takes 20% of an employee's time (i.e., about one day a week). A matrix assignment involves only part of an employee's time, so an officer could be involved in two or three matrix-based projects any day and be reporting to more than one supervisor.

A variation of this form is **problem-oriented policing**, where efforts are organized around a particular problem (Goldstein 1990). This means that entire operations are mounted against a particular problem. Participant officers may be temporarily or partially assigned to the problem. This is a form of organization by product, but it may be considered a team design, depending upon the specific situation. For example, in Santa Rosa, California, the police department detailed all patrol officers to spend some of their time working on community problem solving. To do so, all officers in a given beat (all shifts) would meet periodically to discuss problems and solutions. For beat operations they reported to their beat sergeant, and for community policing operations they reported to a community-policing sergeant. In this manner, their time was distributed by a matrix orientation.

An organizational form similar to the matrix form is **team policing**. In this organizational approach, teams are created based upon specific areas, which may be geographic or focused on a specific problem (similar to problem-oriented policing). Team members are selected from various line operations and assigned full-time to the team. Teams are fully responsible for the assigned area or problem and typically are given wide discretion.

Each of these approaches (matrix, task force, problem-oriented, and team-oriented policing) is very similar from the perspective of an organization theorist. They differ only in organizational permanence, level of discretion, and complexity of problems assigned. The point of each of these methods is an attempt to overcome some of the serious limitations of classical hierarchy so deeply representative of law enforcement organizations. For patrol officers, each of these methods offers varying degrees of increased responsibility and discretion. In effect, these models give more freedom to patrol officers and supervisors to use a wider variety of skills and possible solutions than those permitted by traditional organizational structure. Still, each model is essentially based upon the functions that each individual performs in the organization.

In some respects, these determinations are being made independently of the effort to move toward the use of community policing models as a theory or philosophy of policing. In practical terms, both the move toward **community-oriented policing** (**COP**) and the move away from hierarchy are linked (Bayley 1994). Community policing redefines the roles of officers, the targets of law enforcement activities, and the assignment of resources in the organization, and the result is an organization with a very different focus than before. Many argue that traditional structures are ill designed to meet the needs of this new approach. As policing becomes broader in its concerns, with a focus on employees with multiple skills, the narrow design of traditional hierarchy ceases to hold relevance. As such, law enforcement agencies are redefining management in order to respond to environmental challenges to the organization, advances in organization, and human relations theory, and also respond to the developing theory of community policing (Greene, Bergman, and McLaughlin 1994). Evidence suggests that COP might improve officer satisfaction and motivation, though there is insufficient evidence to be certain (Wilkinson and Rosenbaum 1994). However, we do know that research generally supports the notion that participation improves performance and satisfaction levels (Russell and MacLachlan 1999; Wagner 1994).

In addition, Toch and Grant (2005) show how the problem-solving approach can be used as a change agent in police organizations with line officers at the front line.

What should modern law enforcement organizations look like, and how should they work to meet each of the challenges and satisfy the needs of community policing? In terms of look, modern organizations are developing very "flat" structures (**Figure 5-11**). These are called **flat designs** or **flat organizations** because there are very few levels of hierarchy. Compare Figure 5-3 with Figure 5-12. The most obvious differences between the two designs are, first, the number of levels of organization and, second, the number of units that report to any one person or office above. The so-called span of control is much broader in a flat organization structure.

This form of organization improves communications within organizations as management obtains information with fewer "filters"; information is less likely to be "sanitized," a process by which only good information percolates to the top. Most people hate to be the bearer of bad news, and multiple levels increase the probability that negative information will be blocked. Similarly, orders, instructions, and goals are more easily communicated to lower levels in a flat organization.

In flat organizations, accountability for actions becomes more certain. Previously, it was thought that accountability was best achieved with someone looking over an employee's shoulder at all times. This required a good deal of looking and many people to do it, so large bureaucracies grew to satisfy the need for accountability. We now know, however, that bureaucracy actually allows individuals to escape personal accountability, as responsibility can be pushed to lower or higher levels. In flat organizations, however, accountability is especially localized and forces individuals to take personal responsibility for performance.

Flat organizations also respond to the need for new ways to motivate and satisfy employees. In flat organizations, the

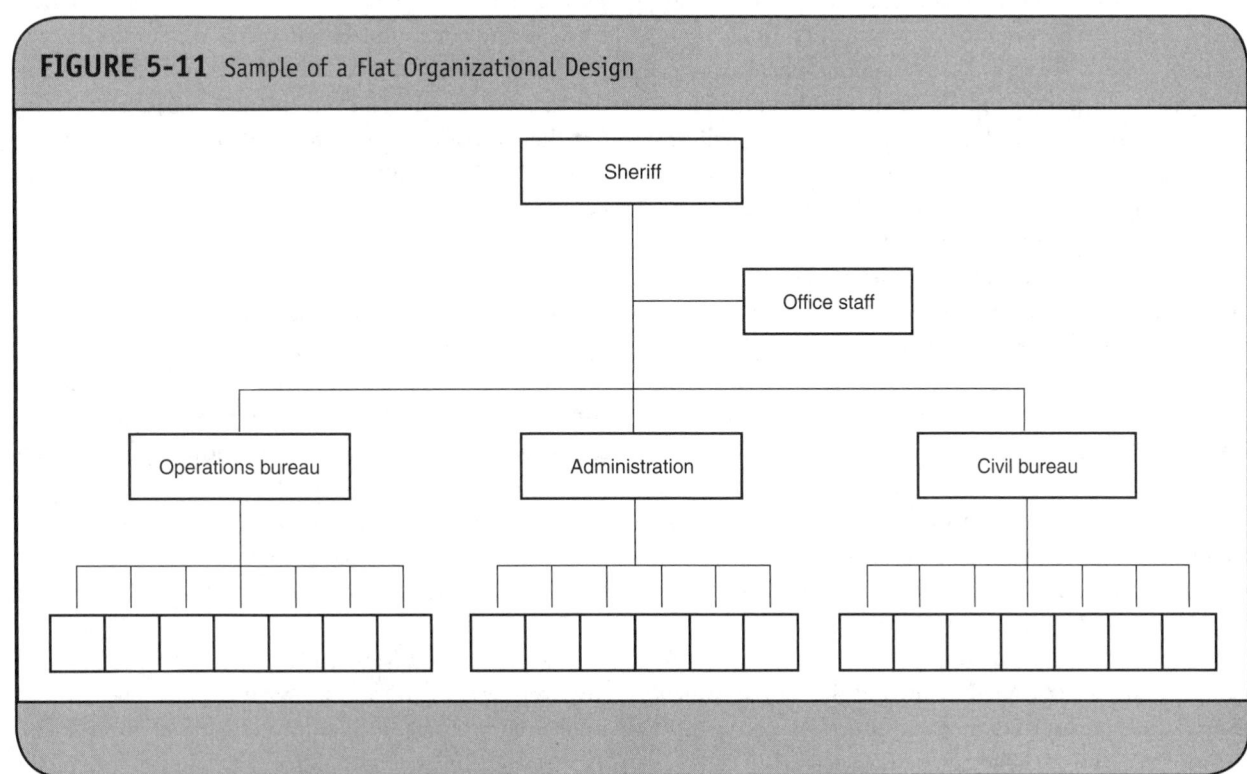

FIGURE 5-11 Sample of a Flat Organizational Design

possibility of job enrichment, a process where employees are given more discretion, flexibility, and authority for performance of assigned duties, is greater. Employees are given freedom to determine how best to carry out their tasks. This does not mean more work; it means more responsibility for deciding how to do tasks and how to achieve goals set by management. This approach produces both higher levels of motivation and higher levels of job satisfaction.

Flat forms of organizational design also offer the possibility of organizational flexibility, fluidity, and rapid problem response. More resources are directly under the control of management, and fewer people are required for agreement. Employees are given more freedom in how to accomplish tasks and management is thereby free to set goals and evaluate performance without a need to micromanage. As employees are given more responsibility, their skill inventory increases; coupled with the increase in communications, this leads to greater overall organizational flexibility to respond to rapidly changing conditions.

An agency that is organized in this manner will also reduce the costs of bureaucracy. Previously, one role for mid-level positions was information analysis. In flat organizations, there is less need for organizational positions dedicated to acquiring and analyzing information. These positions will be merged into patrol and other delivery positions, which will become "enlarged." Rapidly improving computing, communications, and data analysis technologies make this not only possible, but necessary. Each employee, from patrol officer to deputy chief, now has access to tremendous amounts of information and the tools for analysis, thereby reducing the need for supervision. Employees must, however, be skilled in how to use the information to make decisions that are in the best interests of the organization.

The negative aspects of flat organizations are few, but significant. First, this form of organization relies heavily upon a well-trained and educated work force. This includes training in and commitment to basic organizational values and goals. Among these would be the mission statement of the organization, as well as the values in the Constitution of the United States and the state in which the agency is located. Training and education become the basis for decision-making that is decentralized.

A second drawback is the likelihood that divisions or groupings of employees will not be headed by individuals of the same "rank," though they may report to the same superior. In a flat organization, where cooperative decision making at lower levels combines with job enrichment to produce new forms of motivation and satisfaction, rank holds a reduced role. This reduction in rank influence will have negative consequences in the short run, until the correct "rank mix" is established. A third drawback is related to recruitment. Flat designs require the ability to recruit and retain individuals who have the desire and skill to become "self-starters," but the available talent pool is shrinking for every employer in terms of skills and education (Clark 1998).

Net-Centric

Information and communication technology (ICT) has advanced rapidly in the previous decades and is continuing to do so at an exhausting pace. Both public and private organizations are capitalizing on ICT advances and increasingly utilizing them as part of their organizational structure. This is also true for law enforcement agencies. Advances in technology have changed the way police departments can collect, store, analyze, and share the massive amounts of information necessary to carry out their mission. In the **net-centric** (network-centric) approach, the primary assumption is that knowledge is power and that better information sharing and collaboration will enhance both the quality of information and the effectiveness of problem-solving efforts. In a net-centric organization, rather than having a traditional hierarchical structure, the nature of the work determines how the organization structures itself. Technology enhances the connections between people in the organization and, in theory, taps into the knowledge of workers who otherwise would not be connected (Abrams 2009). Thus, especially in large organizations, persons who may not have ever crossed paths or worked together in the past may work together on a weekly basis under this model.

The concept of Net-Centric Policing (NCP) has been advanced by some who view policing as just one network among many others, such as the networks of government, society, economics, and politics. Likewise, the members that make up the policing agency are members of networks also: family, social, employment, religious, recreational, and so on. Net-Centric Policing also recognizes "that crime occurs in the context of social networks: victims, witnesses, other criminal associates. Terrorists operate in networks, and use the network approach to identify targets in order to maximize disruption" (Jackson, Myers, and Cowper 2010, 141). Net-Centric Policing is premised on the agency's acceptance and utilization of all the information technologies available—"computer networks, email, text messages, social networking, wikis, blogs, RSS publishing, geotagging, and video blogging ("vlogging")" to keep agency members informed and responsive to problems" (Jackson et al. 2010, 141). According to Jackson, Myers, and Cowper (2010, 144):

> In the net-centric organization, leadership is dispersed throughout the network. It takes many forms based on a person's position in the organization. Taken to the extreme, net-centric organization allows for completely flat organizations… NCP seeks to create an environment supportive of the development and exercise of leadership throughout all levels of the network, at all levels of its organizations. In effect, NCP seeks to create leadership networks. Such networks are "peer-to-peer" and operate with specialized roles, each with intrinsic social protocols that result in robustness and effectiveness in combination.

They also indicate that the "challenge for police executives is to clearly define the operational mission and behavioral boundaries, to organize agencies around the proper set of values, and to shape the culture so that peer-discipline functions in a manner appropriate to a democracy" (Jackson et al. 2010, 143).

Future organizing perspectives (whatever they may be called) will be tied to advances in technology and its ability to connect people in interesting and innovative ways. For law enforcement, the ability to collaborate with other agencies and utilize regional and national databases for local applications has enormous potential. We will dive more deeply into this topic in Chapter 12.

FIGURE 5-12 Tenets of Modern Management Theory

Systems Perspective
Broad Discretion
Situational Analysis
Open Communications
Value Adherence and Ethics
Participative Decision Making
Cooperative Decision Making
Team and Matrix Assignments
Flat Organizational Structure

To summarize the modern perspective: In order to motivate and satisfy employees, avoid burnout, and remain flexible, law enforcement leaders and their organizations must innovate. Law enforcement agencies cannot avoid the imposed hierarchy of civil service, but they can employ alternative structures to avoid the limitations of classical structure and gain the benefits of modern managerial approaches. The field must invite job enrichment, cooperative and decentralized decision making, and organizational flattening. Each of these changes is essential to the effective implementation of community policing. To get effective, efficient, satisfied, and motivated employees, organizations must be redesigned. Entry-level officers and veterans alike must accommodate themselves to the implications of these changes and the demands they will make. **Figure 5-12** summarizes the tenets of modern management theory.

SUMMARY

In this chapter we briefly reviewed the development of organizational theory typically applied to law enforcement organizations for the better part of the past 100 years. In most respects, we found that traditional or classical structures still dominate law enforcement. We examined the benefits and problems of that organizational approach and found that in a rapidly changing world, traditional structures suffer. However, structures operate better when they allow lower-level employees to make decisions and participate in leading organizations.

We also examined some of the ways in which law enforcement organizations may be able to take advantage of this new organizational form, including task groups, teams, matrix organizations, and net-centric operations. In each case, the effort increases the span of control, increases individual officer responsibility, and invites innovation and participation in problem solving. We also found that motivation achieves higher levels in this design when management sets clear goals and permits small teams to determine how to achieve those goals.

Leadership in such an organization arises from all levels of an organization, so patrol officers must see themselves as both leaders and followers. Emerging forms of policing theory and organizational principles place patrol officers in the role of leader and decision-maker rather than being passive receivers of orders. While adhering to the command structure that is important for political accountability in a democracy, officers must understand the direction of their organizations as we continue through the 21st century, even though the police function seemingly has changed little in the past 25 years (Gaines and Cordner 1999).

Critical Thinking Questions

1. How has history shaped current (traditional) law enforcement?

2. What are the benefits and limitations of the classical organizational structure?

3. What are the benefits and limitations of modern organizational approaches?

4. What motivates employees, and what motivating factors can be used in the field of law enforcement? How?

5. What are the primary causes of stress in law enforcement?

6. What is leadership, and who are leaders?

7. What are the basic characteristics and beliefs of contemporary (modern) management organization theory?

8. What is net-centric organization and what are its potential advantages and disadvantages?

CHAPTER SPECIFIC INTERNET LINKS

International Association of Chiefs of Police: http://www
.theiacp.org/

Net-Centric Warfare: http://www.au.af.mil/au/awc/awcgate/
transformation/oft_implementation_ncw.pdf

CHAPTER GLOSSARY

Bureaucracy—term used to describe large, complex organizations that have several layers of supervisors representing the largest portion of the hierarchy; they tend to be characterized as closed systems with significant division of labor, and predicated on a routine demand for services.

Classical organization theory—the body of theory from Weber, Taylor, and Gulick, among others, which relies upon hierarchy, merit hiring, small spans of control, and a single command authority.

Community-orientated policing (COP)—an attempt by law enforcement agencies to form a partnership with the residents of the area to reduce crime victimization and to improve the overall quality of life; also generally referred to as community policing.

Contingency theory—theoretical perspective that recognizes multiple factors within the organization; it is an attempt to identify which factors are most relevant and what their impact is. This perspective recognizes that one cannot rely on any one theoretical approach to address all issues because of the differences in organizations and situations.

Contingent leadership—a theory of leadership that suggests that everyone can learn to be a leader depending upon the circumstances and the abilities of that person in that situation.

Dominance of an idea—managing an organization by mission statements, values, and goals.

Dynamic environment—a changing environment; a condition that prevents predicting future problems or needs with certainty, and one which produces constantly changing organizational challenges.

Flat design/flat organization—an organizational design that limits the number of levels of an organization, increases the span of control, increases individual responsibility for performance, relies upon teams and task groups, increases communications flows, and increases individual discretion for judgment.

Goal displacement—a behavior of employees who work in the organization and learn to focus on rules rather than service.

Hierarchy—a form of organizational structure that includes a division of labor, clear lines of authority between superior and subordinate, and a single unifying authority at the top of the hierarchy.

Human Relations/Humanistic—a theory of management that focuses on the needs of the individual and assumes that these matter in terms of organizational performance.

Human Resource—a theory of management that looks at individuals as an organizational asset and recommends organization based on their needs and talents.

Hygiene factors/maintainers—aspects of a job that will maintain satisfaction, but which do not motivate greater performance.

Job enrichment—a process where employees are given more discretion, flexibility, and authority for performance of assigned duties so that they have freedom to determine how to best carry out their tasks.

Leadership—a field of study closely related to motivation that focuses on what makes organizations able to get people to follow a path set by management.

Matrix organization—a number of personnel are assigned to use a portion of their time for a given problem, regardless of their permanent duty location.

Motivation—a broad field of study that focuses on what makes people want to work.

Motivators—those things that can increase motivation.

Net-Centric organization—a theory of organization based on acceptance and utilization of all the information technologies available to enhance collaboration and problem solving; it anticipates a flatter structure with leaders being located throughout the organization.

Organization behavior—a body of research that examines organizations at the micro, or small group, and individual levels.

Organization theory—the body of research that explores the ways in which people organize themselves to do work.

Organizational dysfunction—problems inherent in the design of an organization.

Organize by clientele—structuring an organization according to the people to be served or targeted by organizational activities.

Organize by function—characterized by grouping employees together according to the major functions or tasks that they perform.

Organize by place—structuring according to the location of tasks; precincts are an example.

Organize by product—structuring an organization according to what people are producing or making; an outcome-centered means of organization.

Organize by time—structuring an organization according to the time it takes to carry out tasks; shifts, for example, are organizing structures based on time.

Problem-oriented policing—a method where teams of officers are organized around a particular problem.

Rationalization—the process by which Weber felt society was organizing itself; a social system using rules and criteria as the basis for all judgments.

Satisfaction—happiness with one's job, workplace, and performance.

Scientific Management Theory—a theory of work organization that holds that if you understand and analyze a job by breaking it down into its smallest parts, you can train workers to the exact task without wasting time or effort.

Span of control—the number of individuals that one person directly supervises or who otherwise directly report to that person.

Spoils system—the practice of making appointments to loyal supporters, friends, and cronies rather than basing appointments on merit; "to the victor belong the spoils."

Stable environment—the conditions of an organization that do not change and therefore permit the organization to predict future needs and demands and rationally plan for those needs.

Structuring by authority—the use of hierarchical authority to impose management's desires by orders and supervision.

Systems theory—theoretical perspective that views the entire context (environment) in which an issue exists by analyzing all the forces or influences impacting it. When focused on organizational and management issues, it is particularly interested in analyzing all the influences from the environment that affect the organization.

Task force—a temporary organizational division that is created for a limited purpose.

Team policing—an organizational approach in which teams are created based upon specific areas which may be geographic or problem-oriented in nature.

Trained incapacity—a behavior that results when employees are trained not only what to do, but what not to do, and thus refuse to go beyond the limited role of their predefined jobs.

Traits—aspects of a person once thought to be related to leadership.

Unity of command—one person is in command of an organization, and all individuals report to only one person, who can then trace a line of command to the single unifying command at the top.

CHAPTER REFERENCES AND ADDITIONAL READINGS

Abrams, R.S. (2009). "Uncovering the Network-Centric Organization." Ph.D. Dissertation, University of California, Irvine.

Bayley, David H. (1994). *Police for the Future*. New York: Oxford University Press.

Campbell, J.P., M.D. Dunnette, E.E. Lawler, and K. Weick (1970). *Expectancy Theory*. New York: McGraw-Hill.

Caplow, Theodore (1964). *Principles of Organization*. New York: Harcourt, Brace & World, 50–62.

Chaiken, Jan, Peter Greenwood, and Joan Petersilia. (1975). *The Criminal Investigation Process, in Police Operations: Analysis and Evaluation (1996)*. Cincinnati: Anderson Publishing, 161–184.

Clark, Jacob R. (1998). Is Anybody Out There? Stiff Competition for Recruits Fuels Agencies' Personnel Woes. *Law Enforcement News* 24(488):1.

Clavell, James (Ed.) (1983). *The Art of War*, by Sun Tzu. New York: Delacorte Press.

Chicago Police Department (2003). 2002 Annual Report, Chicago PD, p. 38.

Conser, James A. (1979). Motivational Theory Applied to Law Enforcement Agencies. *Journal of Police Science and Administration* 7(3):285–291.

Franz, V. and D.M. Jones (1987). Perceptions of Organizational Performance in Suburban Police Departments: A Critique of the Military Model. *Journal of Police Science and Administration* 15(2):153–161.

Fry, Brian R. (1989). *Mastering Public Administration: From Max Weber to Dwight Waldo*. Chatham, NJ: Chatham House.

Gaines, Larry K. (1993). Coping with the Job: Stress in Police Work, in Critical Issues in Policing: *Contemporary Readings*, Second Edition, edited by Roger G. Dunham and Geoffrey P. Alpert. Prospect Heights, IL: Waveland, 535–550.

Gaines, Larry K. and Gary W. Cordner (1999). The Function of the Police, in *Policing Perspectives*, edited by Larry K. Gaines and Gary W. Cordner. Los Angeles, CA: Roxbury Publishing Co, 1–2.

Gingerich, Terry E. and Gregory D. Russell (2005). Accreditation and Community Policing: Are They Neutral, Hostile, or Synergistic? An Empirical Test Among Street Cops and Management Cops. Unpublished manuscript currently under review.

Goldstein, Herman (1990). *Problem-Oriented Policing*. New York: McGraw-Hill.

Gortner, Harold F., Julianne Mahler, and Jeanne Bell Nicholson (1987). *Organization Theory: A Public Perspective*. Chicago: The Dorsey Press.

Greene, Jack R. (2004). Community Policing and Police Organizations, in *Community Policing: Can it Work*, by Wesley G. Skogan, Belmont, CA: Thompson/Wadsworth, 30–54.

Greene, Jack R., William T. Bergman, and Edward J. McLaughlin (1994). Implementing Community Policing: Cultural and Structural Change in Police Organizations, in *The Challenge of Community Policing: Testing the Promises*, edited by Dennis P. Rosenbaum. Thousand Oaks, CA: Sage Publications, 92–109.

Gulick, Luther (1937). Notes on the theory of organizations, in *Papers on the Science of Administration*, edited by Luther Gulick and Lyndall F. Urwick. New York: Institute of Public Administration, 3–13.

Hersey, Paul, Kenneth H. Blanchard, and Dewey E. Johnson (1996). *Management of Organizational Behavior: Utilizing Human Resources, Seventh Edition*. Upper Saddle River, NJ: Prentice Hall.

Herzberg, Frederick (1968). One More Time: How Do You Motivate Employees? *Harvard Business Review* 46(1):36–44.

Jackson, John, Richard Myers, & Thomas Cowper (2010). Leadership In The Net-Centric Organization, in Joseph A. Schafer and Sandy Boyd (eds). *Advancing Police Leadership: Considerations, Lessons Learned, and Preferable Futures*. Volume 6: Proceedings of the Futures Working Group. Quantico, Virginia. 2010: 138–149.

Katzell, Raymond A. and Donna E. Thompson (1990). Work Motivation: Theory and Practice. *American Psychologist* 45(2):144–153.

Kelling, George E, Tony Pate, Duane Dieckman, and Charles E. Brown (1974). *The Kansas City Preventative Patrol Experiment, in Police Operations: Analysis and Evaluation 1996* Cincinnati: Anderson Publishing, 71–104.

Knott, Jack H. and Gary J. Miller (1987). *Reforming Bureaucracy: The Politics of Institutional Choice*. Englewood Cliffs, NJ: Prentice Hall.

Langworthy, Robert H. and Lawrence F. Travis (2003). *Policing in America: A Balance of Forces, Third Edition*. Upper Saddle River, NJ: Prentice Hall.

Lawler, Edward E. (1986). *High Involvement Management*. San Francisco: Jossey-Bass.

Ledford, Gerald E., Jr. (1995). Pay as an organization development issue. Newsletter of the Organizational Development and Change Division. Academy of Management, Summer.

Leonard, V.A. and Harry W. Moore (1987). *Police Organization and Management, Seventh Edition*. Mineoloa, NY: Foundation Press.

Marsden, Peter V., Cynthia R. Cook, and Arne L. Kallenberg (1994). Organizational Structures. *American Behavioral Scientist*, 37: 539–563.

Rainey, Hal G. (1991). *Understanding and Managing Public Organizations*. San Francisco: Jossey- Bass.

Rainey, Hal G. (1993). Work Motivation, in *Handbook of Organization Behavior*, edited by Robert T. Golembiewski. New York: Marcel Dekker, 19–39.

Reid, Darryn J., Goodman, Graham, Johnson, Wayne and Ralph E. Giffin. (2005). All that Glisters: Is Network-Centric Warfare Really Scientific? *Defense and Security Analysis* 21(4):335–367.

Roberg, Roy R. and Jack Kuykendall (1997). *Police Management*, Second Edition. Los Angeles: Roxbury Publishing Co.

Rosenbaum, Dennis P. and Deanna L. Wilkinson (2004). Can Police Adapt? Tracking the Effects of Organizational Reform Over Six Years. In Wesley G. Skogan (Ed.), *Community Policing: Can it Work*? Belmont, CA: Thompson/Wadsworth, 79–108.

Russell, Gregory D. and Susan MacLachlan (1999). Community Policing, Decentralized Decision Making, and Employee Satisfaction. *Journal of Crime and Justice*, 22(2):33–54.

Shafritz, Jay M. and J. Steven Ott (1992). *Classics of Organization Theory, Third Edition*. Pacific Grove, CA: Brooks Cole.

Short, James F., Jr. (1997). *Poverty, Ethnicity, and Violent Crime*. Boulder, CO: Westview Press.

Skogan, Wesley G. and Jeffrey Roth (2004). Introduction. In Wesley G. Skogan (Ed.), *Community Policing: Can it Work*?. Belmont, CA: Thompson/Wadsworth, xvii–xxxiv.

Stojkovic, Stan, David Kalinich, and John Klofas (2003). *Criminal Justice Organizations: Administration and Management, Third Edition*. Belmont, CA: Thomson/Wadsworth Learning.

Swanson, Charles R., Leonard Territo, and Robert W. Taylor (1993). *Police Administration: Structures, Processes and Behavior, Third Edition*. New York: Macmillan Publishing, Co.

Toch, H., and D. Grant. (2005). *Police as Problem Solvers: How frontline workers can promote organizational and community change, 2nd Edition*: Washington, D.C.: American Psychological Association.

Wagner, John A. III (1994). Participation's Effects on Performance and Satisfaction: A Reconsideration of Research Evidence. *Academy of Management Review* 19(2):312–330.

Walker, Samuel (1998). *Popular Justice: A History of American Criminal Justice*. New York: Oxford University Press.

Weisheit, Ralph, David Falcone, and L. Edward Wells (1994). *Rural Crime and Rural Policing*. Research in Brief. Washington, D.C.: U.S. Department of Justice, National Institute of Justice.

Wilkinson, Deanna L. and Dennis P. Rosenbaum (1994). The Effects of Organizational Structure on Community Policing: A Comparison of Two Cities, in *The Challenge of Community Policing: Testing the Promises*, edited by Dennis P. Rosenbaum. Thousand Oaks, CA: Sage Publications, 110–126.

Wilson, O.W. (1950). *Police Administration*. New York: McGraw-Hill.

Wilson, Woodrow (1887). The Study of Administration. *Political Science Quarterly*, June:197–222.

Zhao, Jihong (1996). *Why Police Organizations Change: A Study of Community-Oriented Policing*. Washington, D.C.: Police Executive Research Forum.

CHAPTER 6

Law Enforcement Tasks, Roles, and Styles

LEARNING OBJECTIVES

In the preceding chapters, you explored the history and extent of the law enforcement function in the United States. Now we turn our attention to the somewhat complex and occasionally controversial matter of the role of law enforcement in our modern society. After studying this chapter, you should be able to:

- Identify the five basic tasks required of law enforcement personnel in the United States.
- Define the concept of "role."
- Identify eight influences upon role and role perceptions.
- Explain why there is debate as to what the role of law enforcement is.
- Cite three examples of the research that examines role.
- Distinguish between "role" and "style."
- Identify 11 influences on "law enforcement style."
- Distinguish how the research on role differs from that of style.
- Compare and contrast the basic organizational roles of the Patrol Officer, the Patrol Supervisor, the Detective, and the Chief Executive Officer.
- Describe the four categories of law enforcement stressors.

CHAPTER OUTLINE

KEY TERMS USED IN THIS CHAPTER

role

popular justice

role conflict

Project STAR

temporal order maintenance

sustained order maintenance

full neighborhood management

officer style

stress

discretion

THE ROLE OF LAW ENFORCEMENT PERSONNEL

The **role** of law enforcement personnel in U.S. society is defined by five important tasks: (1) protecting life and property, (2) preserving the public peace, (3) preventing crime and terrorist activity, (4) detecting and arresting violators of the law, and (5) enforcing the law. To help accomplish these tasks, they are given wide discretionary authority guided by the rule of law. Certainly, given the magnitude of their mission, they are entrusted with one of the most important and challenging roles in U.S. society.

observes, policing personnel are sometimes "called upon to do the impossible or to attempt to provide services they have not been adequately prepared to perform." Because this dilemma is unlikely to change in the near future, "crime control," as Chief Darrel W. Stephens[1] (2003, 31) notes, "remains the central mission of the police, but how it should be accomplished and whether it should be the exclusive focus of police is less clear."

Because of its great importance, the role of the law enforcement personnel is one of the most commonly

California Department of Insurance detective leads subject away after arresting her

Source: Courtesy of California Department of Insurance

For those interested in taking up the call, the field offers a direct and rewarding opportunity for individuals to advance the public good. Yet crime control is a difficult role to play, by definition, and none of these five mandated policing tasks can be entirely achieved. No matter how efficient or professional the personnel are in fulfilling their varied tasks, their situational efforts are at best temporary solutions to chronic social problems. As James Fyfe (2001, 161), a noted policing professional and scholar,

discussed topics in policing literature. While few advocate discarding any of the mandates mentioned above, scholars, public officials, and law enforcement professionals continually search for ways to make policing more

[1] Darrel W. Stephens is the retired chief of police of Charlotte-Mecklenburg, North Carolina and has over 40 years of law enforcement experience.

responsive to the public's safety needs. In the larger search for improvement, the reform debate usually centers on the policies and procedures that facilitate aspects of the policing role, not on its core mandates. For example, some researchers have questioned the usefulness of random patrol, suggesting that this traditional tactic is not as effective as once believed (Wilson and Kelling 1982). Other researchers suggest a better result could be secured through a more focused or problem-oriented approach to policing (Goldstein 1977; 1979; 1990; Toch and Grant 2005). Sometimes major events drive the debate. For example, since the terrorist attacks of September 11, 2001, there has been a heightened awareness of the importance of law enforcement's role in protecting society. As one noted author observed, "communities have started looking to their police departments to assume a new role in identifying and countering potential terrorist activity—creating new challenges for police executives and local government managers" (O'Neill 2003).

Because it is one of the most visible and important services of government, most people have a general understanding of the law enforcement role in our society. From a citizen's perspective, it is that omnipresent helping hand ready at our beck and call when everything else has failed. From an applied perspective, it can be described as three major spheres of simultaneous activity: calls for service, tactical operations to suppress crime, and strategic problem solving (Sweeney 2003). People have come to expect certain actions from officers when they are summoned. It makes no difference what the officers are asked to accomplish; they are expected to perform these functions decisively, professionally, and courteously. Consequently, an officer's performance (the application of role) ranges from the most critical to the most mundane, and it is scrutinized by the public, the media, and by concerned agencies of government, including the officers themselves.

Building on this general introduction, we will now turn our attention to several related topics, including the concept of role, forces that influence role and role perception, controversies and dilemmas surrounding this role, and, finally, research on role.

This chapter contains some conceptual material that may be difficult to grasp at first. Do not become frustrated if you need to re-read sections and contemplate the points being stressed.

What is Meant by Role?

Instead of relying on any one perspective of what is meant by role, we prefer to define it as a multidimensional concept consisting of expected behaviors performed by a person in a given situation or position for the purpose of achieving certain objectives or goals. In other words, role is a blend of behaviors (what one does), expectations and perceptions (what one thinks should be done), and outcomes (what is to be accomplished). Certainly, in an abstract sense, role is difficult to define in concrete terms; it is a concept, and like all concepts, it must be worked out in the mind. It is not a tangible object (such as a pen or table) that physically exists and can be described.

As a practical matter, we can simply state that each officer develops a role perspective based on his or her training, socialization, and experiences within a law enforcement agency. These factors are then accentuated to the degree that performance measures and department values are established, maintained, and reinforced (Nowicki 2003).

The concept of role is very complex and relational (see **Figure 6-1**). Role can be viewed from a social (interpersonal) perspective, such as the role of a parent, brother, sister, or neighbor. Role, as we have discussed above, can also be viewed from an occupational perspective, such as the role of a doctor, lawyer, judge, teacher, nurse, fire fighter, or police officer. Importantly, social roles and occupational roles often overlap and even influence the way we behave while performing a role. For example, a mother may also have roles as a wife, a sister, a daughter, an aunt, and an employee of an agency or company. In her role as an employee, she also may occupy the role of colleague, confidante, supervisor, detective, and so on. The role component in each of these is actually the *behavior* involved and not the status that the person occupies (e.g., mother, sister, detective). What is achieved (outcome) by way of that behavior is a significant determinant in role performance and is the basis of evaluation by others.

The relational aspects of role include the perspectives, personalities, and perceptions of the persons who are in the process of determining their proper role for

FIGURE 6-1 The Complexity of Role

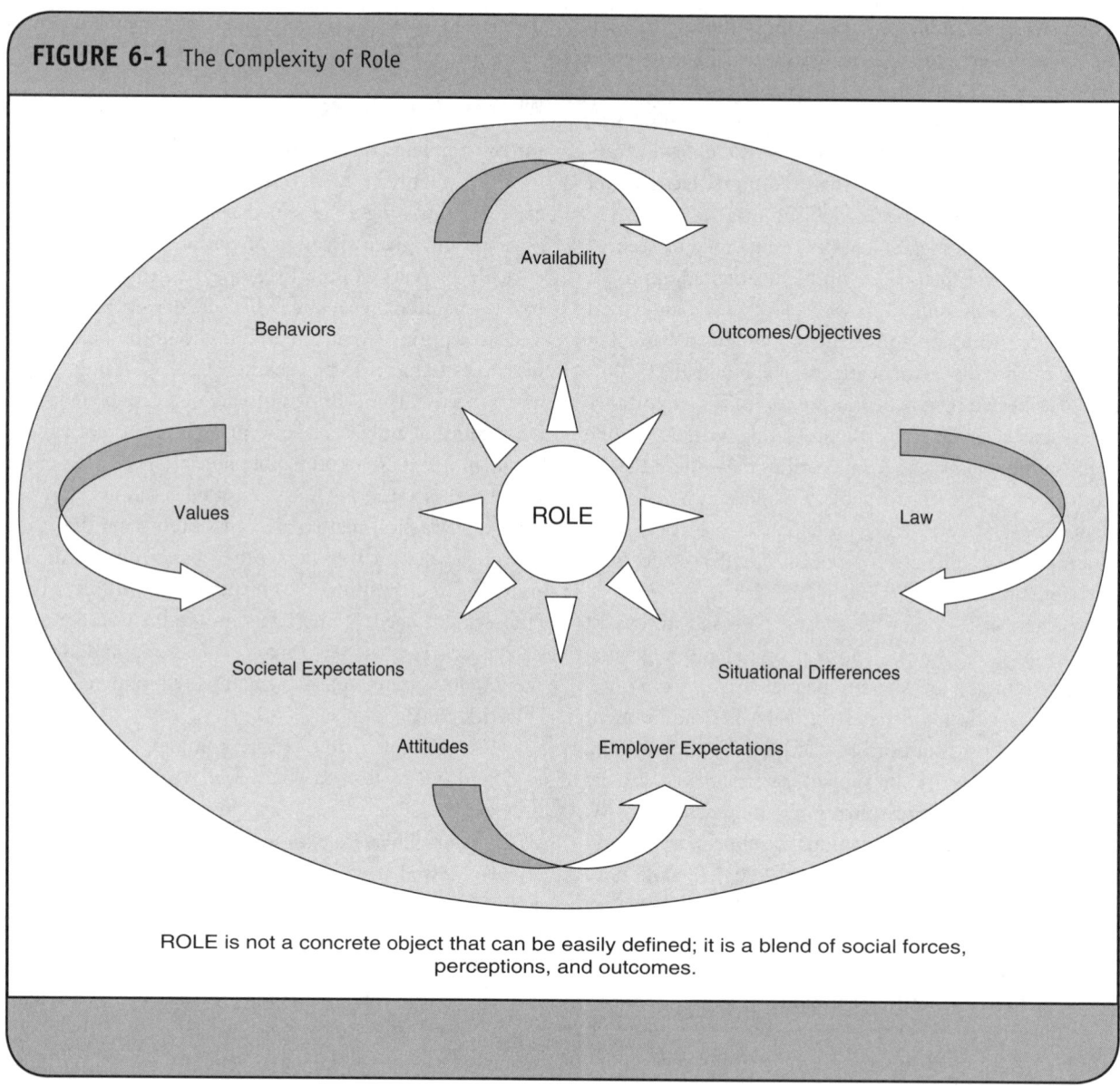

ROLE is not a concrete object that can be easily defined; it is a blend of social forces, perceptions, and outcomes.

a given situation. Interpersonal relationships affect how role is interpreted, and so there are sociological and psychological variables at work during the process of role determination. People interpret their role by viewing and communicating with others, evaluating their surroundings, and gauging their progress toward a desired objective. This process becomes very dynamic, which may cause persons to modify their behavior while they interpret situations as they unfold.

Applying the concept of role to law enforcement is very challenging. The common question is, "What is the role of the police in a democratic society?" The answer depends on who is asked. To some, the role of the policing personnel is to *enforce the law*, to others it is to *prevent crime*, while still others will say it is to *maintain order*. The point is that all of these responses are correct because the role of policing in the United States is multifaceted (remember the five tasks that we introduced in the first paragraph of this chapter) and varies according to place, time, and the objective to be accomplished. Notice that all of these responses are actually objectives (often referred to, interchangeably, as outcomes, functions, or tasks) to be accomplished by the various behaviors of officers. Practically speaking, whether one refers to them as functions, outcomes, or tasks, they are still the goals to be accomplished through the behaviors of officers. Over the years, the law enforcement personnel have acquired or were assigned many different functions. The duties of the officers have changed dramatically over the last 190 years (see **Figure 6-2**).

FIGURE 6-2 Early Police Officer Duties

The local police officer's role has included the following duties:

1820s—cared for common sewers, cared for vaults, and whatever else affected the health, safety, and comfort of the citizens.

1830s—emptied privies, conducted cholera checks.

1850s—removed obstructions from the street, put out fires, tested doors, turned off running water, took drunks home, gathered in stray horses, helped the unemployed find jobs, sheltered the homeless.

1870s—assisted and advised immigrants and strangers, supervised licenses of all types.

1880s—called upon and escorted physicians for patients, inspected tenements and lodging houses for sanitary conditions, tested boiler operators.

1910s—assisted probation officers, were called "welfare" officers, entertained children at Christmas, initiated Junior Police programs, assisted ex-cons to find work, became probation and parole officers.

Source: Modified from Law Enforcement Assistance Administration (LEAA), *Two Hundred Years of American Criminal Justice*, 1976, U.S. Department of Justice.

What Influences Role and Role Perception?

A number of factors, including the democratic process, occupational culture, ethics, training and socialization, availability, technology, and laws, combine to influence the role of policing in American society, or an officer's perception of that role. Some factors are more influential than others. Some factors are universal and influence both the institution of policing itself and the individual officer, like technology. Other factors, like ethics, are only apparent when demonstrated in appropriate behavior or the lack thereof. With the exception of ethics (personal character), we make no attempt to order their importance; we simply assert that it is important to have an understanding of how these forces, conditions, products, and mandates influence both the role of policing and an officer's perception of that role.

Democracy

The first influence on the role of law enforcement personnel is democracy itself, or more accurately, the democratic process. Since the introduction of policing personnel in the United States, their role has reflected society's prevailing customs, values, and beliefs. For better or worse, law enforcement agencies have taken on a distinct and often local presentation, based on popular social and political demands. Samuel Walker (1998) referred to this phenomenon as **popular justice**. He observes that "the administration of criminal justice in the United States reflects the highly democratic character of American politics and society" (6). For example, the forces of democracy, marching under the banner of progressive reform, have long since cast out the dark shadows of inefficiency, corruption, and partisan politics, afflictions that characterized policing in the 1800s and well into the early 1900s. A review of Chapter 3 will help make this historical observation more apparent.

Today, popular justice—the will of the people—is more apparent than at any other time in our history. For example, popular justice is often brought into play through a sequential process that follows a predictable course: unwanted social conditions/events/behaviors give rise to social indignation, which is channeled into political action, which prompts a government response that manifests itself in one (or a combination) of three ways: (1) laws are passed in an attempt to control the unwanted behavior, (2) law enforcement organizations introduce new administrative policies to correct an internal problem or to improve an aspect of service, or (3), as is most likely to occur, law enforcement agencies respond directly to citizen complaints and develop policies or strategies to address a specific problem. Through these processes, the public defines and redefines the policing mandate, especially in their local communities.

In the traditional scenarios described above, we see the policing role as dynamic, pushed or pulled into action by an alignment of unwanted social conditions that lead to political demands for action. These circumstances repeat themselves over and over again in different locations and for different reasons. Sometimes the conditions and events take on national prominence. For example, advocacy groups like Mothers Against Drunk Driving (MADD), and victims' rights groups like the National Organization for Victim Assistance and the National Center for Missing and Exploited Children (to name just a few), address national issues of social concern. A series of child abductions, in some cases followed by sexual abuse and murder, in 1994–2009 led to the enactment of child predator laws and development of sex-offender registration laws (e.g., Jacob Wetterling Act, Megan's Law, Jessica's Law, and the Adam Walsh Child Protection and Safety Act).

Organizations are formed and new laws are enacted when citizens band together in a common effort to correct a social injustice or to improve the government's response to the plight of victims. However, in the vast majority of cases, problems remain a local concern. To correct a specific problem, community leaders, elected officials, citizens' groups, and individual citizens appeal to their local police or sheriff's department for help. Their requests have a direct influence on criminal justice policy and consequently officer behavior. If, on occasion, the problem is not answered in a timely or appropriately manner, political and/or media attention moves the agency into reactive action. Again, even in a reactive mode, we see evidence of democracy at work and the policing role being defined.

Officer conducting sobriety tests

Source: © Doug Menuez/Photodisc/Getty Images

Occupational Culture

Occupational culture also influences role perceptions; in fact, there are three separate cultures operating concurrently within a law enforcement organization. Each culture can be seen as a hidden force that seeks to maintain the status quo. The first force is the omnipresent culture of policing itself. This is a formal force championed and maintained by the mission, traditions, customs, and myths that define the organizations and the profession of policing in general (Selznick 1947). The second force influencing role perceptions is a work culture associated with rank or position. Scholars have suggested that there are two distinct perceptions of one's working role in policing: a management perspective and a street or line officer/agent perspective. On occasion, antagonistic relationships can development between the two perspectives when individuals (usually at the line level) attach themselves to philosophies that are in conflict with the department's mission or goals (Guyot 1979; Reuss-Inni 1984). The third force influencing an individual's perception of role is the subculture of policing. Here, role perceptions are established and defined informally, but profoundly, by one's collective peers who have established a parallel set of traditions, customs, and myths that are not always in sync with those of the organization (Crank 1998).

Ethics

Ethics, or more specifically one's character, has a fundamental influence on role perceptions. No matter what rank or position an officer holds, behavior is still an individual choice. Individual perception and interpretation of expectations are very significant aspects in determining a person's behavior. An officer, for example, will engage in certain behavior because he or she believes it to be the appropriate behavior for that given situation. However, the degree to which officers attach themselves to a value system will have an overarching bearing on all other aspects of behavior, as well as perceptions of proper behavior, both on and off duty (Pollock 2004). Edwin Delattre (2002, 15), an eminent scholar of police ethics, summarized this point best when he observed, "The mission of policing can safely be entrusted only to those who grasp what is morally important and who respect integrity.

Without this kind of personal character in police, no set of codes or rules or laws can safeguard that mission from the ravages of police misconduct." Therefore, we suggest personal ethics is the most influential determinant of role perceptions in policing.

Training and Socialization

Just as we expect each officer to possess a moral compass, we also expect him or her to be competent. This brings us to two closely related influences on role and role perceptions—training and socialization. These are the primary ways officers learn their role and the craft of policing. Training takes many forms and occurs in a variety of settings: classroom instruction, role-playing, field training programs, role-call briefings, and after-action incident debriefings. Training also occurs in a less formal but equally important setting when officers contemplate and/or critique their own actions or omissions. Often these critiques occur in the company of trusted peers and more experienced officers and can be quite candid, informative, and influential.

Training is an important part of the socialization process, yet socialization within a law enforcement agency is more than training: It is the purveyor of culture and the architect of attitudes and behaviors. According to policing scholars, socialization occurs when less experienced officers learn and then mimic the values and behavior patterns of experienced officers (Roberg et al. 2005). David Carter (2002, 398) suggests that "Formal socialization occurs when specific information is directed toward an individual with the intent of shaping values and belief." Since every officer begins his or her career at the same point, as a rookie on the streets, a common socialization occurs. It produces a universal rite of passage leading to a brotherhood among all officers. As John Van Maanen (1985, 155) observes, "One of the most distinctive characteristics of American police agencies is that virtually everyone in the organization, from station house broom to chief, shares the common experience of having worked the streets as a patrol officer." These experiences are essential if one is to master the craft of policing and fulfill its service role. (See Chapter 7 for additional details about training and Chapter 8 for more about socialization issues.)

Availability

Availability factors also help define an officer's role. Samuel Walker (1992) focused on this when he stated, "The most important factor shaping the role of the police [from a purely physical perspective] is their twenty-four-hour availability." Because they are readily available, officers are often called upon to perform various tasks. This seems like an obvious statement of reality, and one hardly worth mentioning. However, sometimes officers feel stressed when they are not available because of being on non-serious service-type calls or when short staffed and calls for service are "stacking up." In some rural communities, an officer's availability may be 30–45 minutes away because of distance. In some urban communities, citizens complain of waiting hours for officers to respond to their calls.

Technology

The role of officers has been affected by various advances in vehicles, telephony, radio, computing, and weaponry. Improved communications and response capability ties in with the availability factor mentioned above, making it easier to contact and summon law enforcement personnel. Likewise, technologies have improved officer safety (protective vests and semi-automatic pistols), response (computers and cameras in vehicles), and investigations (forensic sciences). Chapter 11 describes advances in law enforcement technologies in greater detail; here we mention its importance as one of the influences on role.

Laws

A final influence on role is the legal provision by which a society lives and prospers. Of course, the legal precepts in the United States are both stable and ever-changing: stable in the sense that most of our legal principles are grounded primarily upon British Common Law and the Constitution, but ever-changing in that they are constantly being evaluated, interpreted, expanded, or modified by the legislative and judicial branches of the government. In any case, it is important to remember a seminal concept underlying and guiding the policing role: "Law cannot rule; only men and women, judges and police officers, and human beings in other roles can rule. The rule of law means that decisions taken by these individuals will be determined by a set of general principles that have been established in advance by some authority, social group or agent" (Skolnick et al. 2005, 135). Consequently, an officer's reverence for the law, including an organization's administrative and operational policies, is critical in ordering and fulfilling the policing role.

Our presentation of the major influences upon policing roles is summarized in **Figure 6-3**.

Concepts, Dilemmas, and Controversies

The concept of role and its complexities has led to several dilemmas and controversies as far as policing is concerned. One of the major dilemmas is that of definition and context of the concept. For instance, some practitioners and researchers focus on and debate the mission, goals, and values of the law enforcement community. Are those the same as role? Others refer to the functions of law enforcement officers, such as preventing crime, guaranteeing constitutional rights, resolving conflict, or

FIGURE 6-3 The Major Influences upon the Policing Role: A Summary

AVAILABILITY—twenty-four-hour service

DEMOCRACY (specifically the democratic process)—the will of the people

OCCUPATIONAL CULTURE—the formal culture of the policing organization, the culture of rank and position, and the informal subculture of policing

ETHICS—an officer's value system and character

SOCIALIZATION—the transfer of values, beliefs, and knowledge from one generation of officers to the next

TRAINING—classroom instruction, role-playing, field training programs, role-call briefings, after-action incident debriefings, and personal critiques

LAW—the formal rules, regulations, statutes, ordinances, and court decisions

TECHNOLOGY—innovations and equipment that facilitate officer efficiency

responding to emergencies. Is it any wonder that students of policing become confused when asked, "What is the police role in the United States?" Does the person asking the question want a "conceptual" response that focuses on the definition, or does she want a "functional" response that relates to a process of doing something (behaviors or duties)? Does she want an "outcome" response in terms of what is desired regarding the goal or objective of the role?

Because of the inconsistent use of terms and phrases such as role, mission, objective, function, and task, a certain vagueness clouds the quest for role definition. In 1931, August Vollmer stated that the "police were organized to suppress crime, protect life and property, and preserve the peace" (National Commission on Law Observance and Enforcement 1931, 17). This should be considered a functional statement because of the infinitive verb phrases (to suppress . . . [to] protect . . . [to] preserve). A behavioral statement (sometimes called "tasks"), on the other hand, would include such phrases as "officers engage in community policing activities," "officers arrest offenders," "officers engage in preventative patrol," and "officers conduct investigations." Role statements that focus on outcomes usually point to the desired result of a policing activity such as crime prevention, crime suppression, the protection of property, protection of rights, and so on (see **Figure 6-4**).

Therefore, it is very important in any discussion of role to clearly understand the differences in perspective—whether one is speaking about the functional, behavioral, or outcome aspects of the job of policing. There are subtle but significant differences in language, and that is part of what leads to confusion over the definition of role.

The following observation might help to explain the confusion and frustration sometimes encountered by officers who experience competing, and sometimes opposite, values and expectations. It is referred to as **role conflict** and was explained this way by James S. Campbell in 1970:

> Perhaps the most important source of police frustration, and the most severe limitation under which they operate, is the conflicting roles and demands involved in the order-maintenance, community-service, and crime-fighting responsibilities of the police. Here both the individual officer and the police community as a whole find not only inconsistent public expectations and public reactions, but also inner conflict growing out of the interaction of the policeman's values, customs, and traditions with his intimate experience with the criminal element of the population. The policeman lives on the grinding edge of social conflict, without a well-defined, well-understood notion of what he is supposed to be doing there (291).

FIGURE 6-4 Types of Role Statements

FUNCTIONAL	BEHAVIORAL (task example)	OUTCOMES
To prevent crime	Community policing activity	Crime suppression
To protect life and property	Preventative patrol	Protection of life and property
To detect and arrest violators	Arrest offenders	Bring the accused to justice
To preserve the peace	Counsel/warn/advise	Order maintenance
To serve the public	Assist motorists	Public service

More recently, Carter and Radelet stated:

>...the role conflict has been complicated with the addition of quality-of-life issues as a police responsibility. Certainly, this goes beyond the traditional view of the police as either law officer or peace officer. What is more apparent is the police officer in the role of problem solver. Officers are being asked to be "proactive," that is, to aggressively look for broad solutions to crime, disorder and quality-of-life problems in the community (1999, 118).

We define role conflict as the confusion and frustration brought on by competing and sometimes opposite values and expectations experienced by officers while performing their job tasks. While role conflict has been recognized for decades, it is still very prevalent in some (if not all) agencies. The issue is really how officers deal with it, rather than whether it exists. It will probably always exist because the various forces influencing it (Figure 6-3) will seldom be in total agreement. Role conflict is one factor that influences the level of stress on officers. (Stress is addressed in greater detail later in the chapter.)

Research on Role

The quest to define or determine the appropriate role of law enforcement personnel in the United States has been a focus of scholars for many decades. The purpose of this section is to identify several of the major systematic attempts to observe and analyze the role of officers; it is not to report the many statements that appear in the literature of what that role is or is not. The role of officers has always been a subject of concern, as evidenced by the statements of voices from the past, which appear in **Figure 6-5**.

We believe that one of the most comprehensive statements regarding the role and expectations of police is that of James Currant:

>A simple answer to the question as to what the urban policeman does is that he does everything. Clichés abound concerning the fact that the policeman is a combination

psychiatrist, medical doctor, lawyer, marriage counselor and crime-stopper. The truth of the matter is that he is all of these things, yet none of them.... In broad general terms, it can be said that police deal with virtually every kind of emergency, human problem, and, moreover, appear to spend more of their time dealing with problems not related to crime than with crime-related human problems (1972, 112).

Throughout the 1960s and early 1970s, criminal justice scholars attempted to explain the role of officers by examining what they did and how they did it. Some focused on the question of "why police behave the way

---

FIGURE 6-5 Notable Quotes on the Role of Officers

"A policeman's duties are numerous, and he is brought in contact with the very best as well as the very worst element of the community. He is called upon to settle family difficulties; arbitrate differences between neighbors; regulate the ubiquitous small boy; act in the capacity of sanitary officer when contagion stalks about, and perform a thousand other offices that are never made public . . . . "

—Chief D.S. Gaster, New Orleans, 1900

"The police were organized to suppress crime, protect life and property, and preserve the peace. Where they have commanded the respect and receive the support of the people they have had little difficulty in carrying out their duties. Under our form of government and, more especially, due to the attitude of the American people generally, law enforcement agencies are usually held in contempt and law enforcement is one of our national jokes. Crime, despite the magnitude of the problem, is but one of the many difficulties confronting the police."

—National Commission on Law Observance and Enforcement, Report on Police, 1931.

Source: National Commission on Law Observance and Enforcement, Report on Police, Washington, D.C.: U.S. Government Printing Office, 1931: 17.

they do." One text summed up much of these early find-ings this way:

> If the police are not sure whether their prin-
> cipal function is to prevent crime or serve
> the public, the researchers are no more con-
> sistent in their conclusions.... In truth the
> ambivalence of the police is built into the very
> structure of law enforcement by the variety
> of duties imposed upon police practitioners
> by the law, custom, and ethical requirements
> of the society they live in (Niederhoffer and
> Blumberg 1976, 64).

The major research efforts of the President's Crime Commission on Law Enforcement and Administration of Justice in the mid-1960s established that the role of the law enforcement officer was not well understood in the United States. **Figure 6-6** clearly depicts a finding that was inconclusive, but exemplifies the complexity of the issues. What is most interesting in these historical sentences is that they appear to coincide with the 1990s explanation of the philosophy of community policing (discussed in more detail in Chapter 13).

One of the most comprehensive research efforts on role was the 3.5-year **Project STAR**, which began in 1971. The project involved agencies in four states (California, Michigan, New Jersey, and Texas) and attempted to iden-tify appropriate roles for six key positions (police officer, prosecuting attorney, defense attorney, judge, caseworker, and correctional worker) in the criminal justice system. In this study, role was defined as "the personal characteristics and behavior expected in a specific situation of an individ-ual occupying a position" (Smith et al. 1974). Although the project is over 40 years old, its findings included excellent discussions and qualitative data related to understanding the concepts associated with the policing role.

The project also identified tasks and performance objectives that were defined respectively as follows (refer to **Figure 6-7**):

Task—an activity to be accomplished within a role that usually involves a sequence of steps and can be measured in relation to time.

Performance objectives—statements of operational behavior required for satisfactory performance of a task, the conditions under which the behavior is usually performed, and the criteria for satisfactory performance.

Within the research, findings indicated that for the position of police officer: (a) each role involved the per-formance of several tasks and (b) each task involved the performance of more than one role (Smith et al. 1974, 2).

FIGURE 6-6 The Community Service Role—
Reflections from the Past

In the course of inquiring into police activities, the Commission encountered many differences of opinion among police administrators as to whether the primary police responsibility of law enforcement is made easier or more difficult by the many duties other than enforcing the law that policeman ordinarily perform. . . . They are services somebody must perform, and policemen being ever present and mobile, are logical candidates . . . . Moreover, it is natural to interpret the police role of "protection" as meaning protection not only against crime but against other hazards, accidents or even discomforts of life. . . .

The community's study of the role of the police should cover additional ground. It should examine whether it is desirable, or possible, for the police to devote more time than they now generally do to protect-ing the community from social injustices . . . . They are in constant contact with the conditions associated with crime. They see in minute detail situations that need to be and can be corrected. If a park is being badly main-tained, if a school playground is locked when it is most needed, if garbage goes uncollected, if a landlord fails to repair or heat his building, perhaps the police could make it their business to inform the municipal authori-ties of these derelictions. In this way, police would help to represent the community in securing services to which it is entitled.

Source: Reprinted from President's Commission on Law Enforcement and Administration of Justice, *The Challenge of Crime in a Free Society*, pp. 97–98, 1967, Washington, D.C.: U.S. Government Printing Office.

FIGURE 6-7 Project Star's 33 Tasks Performed by Police Officers in Carrying out the Roles of their Job

Advising	Participating in Community Relations and Education Programs
Booking and Receiving Inmates	Participating in Trial Preparation Conferences
Collecting and Preserving Evidence	Patrolling and Observing
Communicating	Preparing Reports
Conferring about cases	Preparing Search Warrant Requests
Contacting Families of Suspects and Clients	Recovering Property
Controlling Crowds	Referring
Defending Self and Others	Regulating Traffic
Deterring Crime	Responding to Offender Requests
Engaging in Legal Research	Reviewing Case Materials
Engaging in Professional Development	Searching and Examining
Interacting with Other Agencies	Searching for Fugitives
Interviewing	Testifying as a Witness
Investigating	Testing for Drug and Alcohol Use
Making Arrests	Training
Managing Interpersonal Conflict	Using and Maintaining Equipment
Moving Inmates	

Source: Smith, Charles P., Donald E. Pehlke, and Charles D. Weller (1974), *Role Performance and the Criminal Justice System, Volume II: Detailed Performance Objectives*. Project STAR, Cincinnati, OH: Anderson Publishing Company and Santa Cruz, CA: Davis Publishing Company, pp. 9–12.

The 13 roles of police officers identified by Project STAR were:

1. Assists criminal justice system and other appropriate agency personnel
2. Builds respect for law and the criminal justice system
3. Provides public assistance
4. Seeks and disseminates knowledge and understanding
5. Analyzes and communicates information
6. Manages cases
7. Assists personal and social development
8. Displays objectivity and professional ethics
9. Protects rights and dignity of individuals
10. Provides humane treatment
11. Enforces law impartially
12. Enforces law situationally
13. Maintains order

To further illustrate the research of Project STAR and the analysis related to each of the identified roles, **Figure 6-8** details the finding for the role labeled "provides public assistance."

In 1973, the National Advisory Commission on Criminal Justice Standards and Goals addressed the issue of officer role in what today is considered one of the seminal studies of American policing—*Report on Police*. The report began by defining the "functional police role" concept; it emphasized the idea that an agency must prioritize the expectations placed on its officers in terms of serving the community. Because these expectations are so important, the report suggested that they should be put in writing to guide officers' performance. It was expected that the chief executive officer would develop such a policy in consultation with department employees, the community,

FIGURE 6-8 Relationship of Tasks and Performance Objectives to Role

Roles for police officers can be placed into categories; the roles can be described and performance objectives (or outcomes) identified; roles can involve several tasks and each task can relate to more than one role. The relationship among these aspects is illustrated here for the single role of "Provides Public Assistance."

ROLE:

Provides Public Assistance

ROLE DESCRIPTION:

Treating all needs for assistance, requested by the public or observed, in a serious and helpful manner regardless of the appropriateness of the requests. Providing services or appropriate referrals, including any needed arrangements for special assistance, expeditiously and courteously.

PERFORMANCE OBJECTIVES:

— To respond courteously and expeditiously to requests for assistance
— To obtain information about public and private community resources for use in helping people
— To make referrals to other public and private agencies
— To take advantage of opportunities to provide assistance based on an assessment that the need exists

TASKS:

— Advising
— Communicating
— Interacting with other agencies
— Interviewing
— Patrolling/observing
— Referring
— Using equipment

Derived from: Smith, Charles P., Donald E. Pehlke, and Charles D. Weller (1974), *Role Performance and the Criminal Justice System, Volume II: Detailed Performance Objectives*. Project STAR, Cincinnati, OH: Anderson Publishing Company and Santa Cruz, CA: Davis Publishing Company.

and government officials. It was suggested that the policy on role be central to other written policies that guide the department. Other recommendations concerning role included the assurance that every officer understand his or her role (Standard 1.5) and that the public also be informed of the agency's defined policing role (Standard 1.6). Other standards related to role addressed the recognition of the use of force and the use of discretion by officers (National Advisory Commission 1973).

During the 1970s, several scholars published texts that included discussions about the policing role in the United States and how it was multifaceted (Broderick 1977; Goldstein 1977; Manning and Van Maanen 1978; Muir 1977; Skolnick and Gray 1975; Staufenberger 1980). In essence, most agreed that it was a very complex matter to conceptualize and dissect. The role is heavily influenced by officer perceptions of the job, the demands placed upon them by the public, and by legislative enactment. Coupled with this is the need to occasionally use force, the need to often use discretion, and the expectation that the job be carried out under strict constitutional protection of rights and liberties. One researcher put it this way in describing what makes a good officer: "Intellectually, he has to grasp the nature of human suffering. Morally, he has to resolve the contradictions of achieving just ends with coercive means" (Muir 1977, 4).

Another attempt to describe a policing role was made in 1991 when researchers reviewed the statutory language of all 50 states to determine whether the role of officers was clear or specified. The study indicated that only one state (New York) specifically mentions a service function (assists citizens) as part of the formalized role of officers. Order maintenance and law enforcement were the most prevalent roles indicated in the state codes (Burton, Langworthy, and Barker 1991).

Hoover (1992) classified the policing role in the United States into three models: the **temporal order maintenance** role mainly associated with crime-specific models of policing, the **sustained order maintenance** role associated with problem-oriented policing, and the **full neighborhood management** role linked with community-oriented policing. As community policing tends to expand in its application, roles will become more committed to long-term relationships with citizens (full neighborhood management) as opposed to the short-term involvement (temporal order maintenance) of answering single incident calls or solving short-lived crime-related problems (sustained order maintenance). These models of policing are more directly associated with the strategies of law enforcement that are discussed in Chapter 13.

Essentially, what the literature describes about the policing role in the United States is that it is unsettled, subject to ongoing societal change, and is continually evolving because of the democratic processes that shape and reshape its activities. The role of officers cannot be static; it cannot remain constant because society is always changing. As new problems surface, the local police are called to deal with them because there usually is no other agency "out there" to respond. Consider for example the additional demands placed on law enforcement personnel since the September 11, 2001 terrorist attacks, such as homeland security information sharing, preparation for response to the threat of weapons of mass destruction (WMD), and greater security of the nation's infrastructure.

OFFICER STYLES

What is sometimes not distinguished in discussions of role is the difference between an officer's role and an officer's style. Simply stated, **officer style** is the manner in which an officer carries out his or her role. It includes the various techniques, mannerisms, vocabulary, body language, etc., employed by an officer to achieve an objective. An effective law enforcement officer probably will utilize several styles of behavior to accomplish tasks. Officers' styles will reflect their training, role expectation, values, skills, personality, and/or experience. Officers may develop a primary style (the one used most often) and a secondary style or styles (those used as alternatives to the primary style); in short, these styles may be situationally based. For example, officers may be very direct and shout out specific commands to a person they are attempting to control, but they may be very soft spoken when addressing children who need comforting, or they may attempt to reason logically and rationally with a couple during a domestic disturbance. So, regardless of the role and tasks being performed, the officer's style (demeanor and manner) becomes the most observable behavior to the public.

What Influences Style?

As we mentioned in our discussion of role, there are several factors that influence an officer's policing style. In part, style will be dependent on the nature of the complaint, the type of service needed, the environment, the person or persons present, the objective to be achieved, the agency's philosophy and values, supervisory styles, and peer pressure. Other elements may influence an officer's style as well, such as the quality of training received; the levels of knowledge, education, and skills possessed; backgrounds of the subjects involved in the encounter; the officer's knowledge of available alternatives; and the officer's experience. However, underlying and guiding all of this is an officer's character—his moral compass. **Figure 6-9** identifies many of the sub-elements of these influencing factors. Without question, style is influenced by a number of critical factors, which collectively, and sometimes individually, determine the quality of officer service rendered.

Research on Style

Several scholars in recent decades have started to label various types of officer styles. One of the most noted is the work of James Q. Wilson, *The Varieties of Police Behavior*,

FIGURE 6-9 Influences on Officer Styles

NATURE OF THE COMPLAINT — Criminal, civil; misdemeanor, felony

TYPE OF SERVICE NEEDED — Emergency, public assistance, investigation

THE ENVIRONMENT — Rural, suburban, urban; house, apartment, outdoors

PERSON OR PERSONS PRESENT — One-on-one contact, crowds, rioters

GOAL/OBJECTIVE OF CONTACT — Identify offender, arrest, referral

AGENCY PHILOSOPHY AND VALUES — Department policies and procedures

PEER PRESSURE — Expectations of other officers

QUALITY OF TRAINING — Depth of training; sensitivity/ cultural skills

OFFICER ABILITIES — Communication, evaluation, and empathy skills

EXPERIENCE — Skills and insights learned from doing the job

CHARACTER — a moral compass that guides each decision

All of the above factors, and possibly others, can impact an officer's choice of style in handling contacts with citizens and complainants.

published in 1968. Wilson identified three predominant policing styles, which can be summarized as follows:

Watchman—emphasis is on maintaining order by invoking the "path of least resistance." Officers often ignore minor violations unless their authority is challenged.

Legalistic—stresses authority and control mechanisms with emphasis on the letter of the law; generally does not ignore even minor violations.

Service—all calls for service are approached in a serious manner regardless of their nature, and alternatives to formal arrest are emphasized.

Wilson's typologies are widely cited, but the important part of his work is that he developed these styles based upon analysis of eight police departments across the country. In essence, his research was an attempt to show that the ways in which officers perform their tasks are influenced by the nature of the community and political systems of that community. His focus was primarily on the predominant style of the organization and its influence upon the officers.

Several other scholars have contributed to the discussion of style by identifying their own conceptual categories of officer types. Two scholars (Muir and Broderick) have developed style typologies for individual officers, not the organization. William Muir (1977) categorized four types of officers in his research on coercive power and the policing function:

Enforcer—emphasizes legal authority and makes quick decisions as to whether arrest is necessary. Crime control is the major objective.

Reciprocator—adopts an extreme helping pose trying to reach a solution in all problems. Attempts accommodation with vice operators and undesirables.

Avoider—an officer who attempts to avoid all involvement in situations.

Professional—officer understands the complexities of the job and attempts to do the best he or she can, using verbal skills, knowledge, and experience.

Muir's work has influenced others to pursue similar research on the policing styles of officers. Sometimes such research focuses on personality types instead of styles. It should be remembered that, to a large degree, an officer's style is a reflection of his or her personality. Consequently, this line of research reveals the psychological dimension of role development. John J. Broderick (1987) classifies police personalities into four ideal types that reflect officers' values and styles of behavior:

Enforcers—a high value is placed on social order and peace, and a low value on individual rights and due process of law; tend to stress need for authority and respect for law.

Realists—place low value on both social order and individual rights; tend to be less frustrated than other officers, apparently having found a way to come to terms with a difficult job.

Idealists—individual rights and due process of law receive high value; preservation of social order is viewed as a major role; generally suffers from frustration and lack of job satisfaction.

Optimists—job seen as people-oriented, placing a high value on individual rights, less emphasis on crime fighting.

Broderick's 1987 book, *Police in a Time of Change*, presented an excellent discussion of the conceptual styles of policing identified by Muir and similar styles developed by other researchers. Broderick mentioned that many of the conceptual styles developed by researchers were similar and overlap each other's categories (see **Table 6-1**). A detailed discussion of each of these research efforts is beyond our purpose here; however, the reader is encouraged to review additional material for more in-depth analysis of officer styles (Brown 1968; Coates 1972; Hatting et al. 1983; Walsh 1984; White 1972).

A recent study of supervisory styles found evidence that the style of a patrol officer's supervisor also affected that patrol officer's style. Research findings also shed light on how "frontline supervisory styles can influence such patrol officer behavior as making arrests, issuing citations, using force, and engaging in community policing" (Mastrofski et al. 2003, 2). The study identified four main

supervisory styles: traditional, innovative, supportive, and active. A brief summary of each reveals the differences among the various styles (2–6):

Traditional supervisors: expects aggressive enforcement, more likely to take over officer encounters with citizens or tell officers how to handle the situation, task oriented, prefers measurable outcomes, less likely to reward and more likely to punish officers, their ultimate concern is to control subordinates.

Innovative supervisors: more likely to form relationships with officers; low task orientation; more positive toward subordinates; encourages new ideas, philosophies and methods of policing; prefers to have officers think for themselves; and fosters community policing and problem solving approaches.

Supportive supervisors: provides inspirational motivation, protects officers from unfair discipline, acts as a buffer between officers and management, encourages officers through praise and recognition.

Active supervisors: lead by example; involves themselves in the field with their officers; less likely to encourage team building, coaching, or mentoring; prefers to control subordinates through constant direct supervision; has a relatively positive view of subordinate.

TABLE 6-1 A Comparison of Officer Styles from Research

Researcher	Overlapping or Similar Styles			
Coates (1972)	Abusive	Community	Task Officer	Service
White (1972)	Tough Cop & Crime Fighter	Problem Solver	Rule Applier	
Muir (1977)	Enforcer	Reciprocator	Avoider	Professional
Broderick (1977)	Enforcers	Idealists	Realists	Optimists
Brown (1968)	Old Style & Clean Beat Crime Fighter	Service Style I Helper	Service Style II Avoider	Professional
Hatting, et al. (1983)	Blue-Collar	True Blue	Jaded Blue	
Walsh (1984)	Medium Arrest	Low Arrest	Zero Arrest	High Arrest

Source: A minor revision of Table 3 from Broderick, John J. (1987), *Police in a Time of Change, 2nd Edition*. Prospect Heights, IL: Waveland, p. 12. Used with permission.

ORGANIZATIONAL ROLES OF SELECTED POSITIONS

Law enforcement organizations consist of many levels (ranks) and positions. Every person working in the organization occupies a position and has certain job functions to perform. These job functions tend to define, within limits, the role of that particular position. Of course, occasionally new job functions (duties) may develop or appear, and they must be assigned to someone to perform. This demonstrates the fluctuating nature of a person's occupational role when working in an agency whose functions and obligations are not static.

Patrol Officers

Patrol officers are the "eyes and ears" and the "backbone" of all municipal, county, and state policing organizations.

Patrol forces comprise the largest component of a department, and all other units in the organization are designed to directly or indirectly support their operations. Importantly, all local officers and deputy sheriffs began their careers as patrol officers. This is where the craft of policing is learned. Officers usually patrol within assigned beats or districts while in uniform as they tend to the immediate needs of the community. They are usually the first responders to most complaints, which in the vast majority of cases are non-emergency calls for service for both criminal and non-criminal issues. However, calls (and patrol observations) are prioritized by their service nature, with emergencies receiving first attention. In emergencies, officers temporarily abandon routine calls and redirect their attention to the emergency.

In fulfilling their daily routines and assignments, officers are given wide discretion in deciding enforcement and service activities. Other than making general work

Officer assisting a road safety audit team

Source: Courtesy of the Federal Highway Administration

assignments, supervision, when it is present, usually comes in the form of review and critique of work performed, not work in progress. Specifically, most reports and all arrests are reviewed and approved by a sergeant or the watch commander. Only on rare occasions, for example during and following major crimes or incidents, will officers have direct supervision, and this comes more in the form of coordinating efforts than supervision. In terms of doing the work for which a local police agency generally exists, much, if not most of it, is done by patrol officers.

Detectives (Investigators)

In most departments, a patrol officer at the scene conducts the initial investigation of a crime or incident. If the initial officer can appropriately handle the incident or crime (usually decided by department policy), no further investigation, beyond the continuing work of the initial officer, generally occurs. However, if the incident or crime requires a more intensive investigation (e.g., major burglary, high value theft, fatal accident, etc.), or the initial officer lacks the expertise (e.g., arson, rape, child abuse, homicide, etc.), the report is forwarded to a detective for follow-up or subsequent investigation.

Detectives are officers who have been promoted or assigned to the investigative function on a full-time basis. It should be noted that smaller agencies often do not have full-time investigators, so the duties may be assigned as necessary to a patrol officer. In larger agencies, detectives are either appointed by the chief executive or selected through competitive examination. The role of the detective is to conduct follow-up investigation of assigned cases with the objective of developing a case suitable for prosecution of the alleged offender. This may involve crime-scene analysis, evidence collection, photography, interviewing, interrogating, record searches, interpreting crime lab and autopsy reports, preparing reports, preparing affidavits for search and arrest warrants, executing search and arrest warrants, preparing documents for prosecutors, and testifying in court. Investigators spend at great deal of time at their desks using the telephone or computer or evaluating reports, records, and miscellaneous stores of information. Much of this activity is unfruitful, yet they must continue to probe for elusive answers. From this activity, they glean various bits of information, all of which must be culled for the useful tidbit, and all their work must be accurately summarized into an investigative report. Unlike television shows, the detective may have a dozen or more active cases being pursued simultaneously. One aspect of investigative work is "managing the case," which means keeping things organized and progressing toward the desired objective of identifying a suspect and prosecuting the guilty offender.

In state and federal agencies where uniformed officers do not exist, the personnel are often all investigators (some agencies refer to them as agents). Their primary function is to investigate specialized crime such as fraud, embezzlement, liquor violations, counterfeiting, homicides, robberies, kidnapping, computer crime, and so on. These investigators may be assigned their cases hours or days after the incident occurred and may not work on some cases unless local agencies request their assistance; in crimes where specialized knowledge or equipment is needed, local agencies often call for the assistance of county, state, and/or federal agents. These cooperative arrangements have helped to improve and professionalize service outcomes (bring the accused to justice) across the country.

Supervisors

The organizational role of a supervisor is one of coordinating and managing a group of personnel for which he or she is responsible. This means that supervisors are

Mobile command center

Source: © Denise Kappa/ShutterStock, Inc.

responsible for leading and guiding the work accomplished by the unit. The role of the supervisor includes general assignment of duties or cases, scheduling personnel, answering questions, making decisions, advising others, evaluating and documenting performance, approving leave and vacation requests, and receiving complaints from the public about unit personnel. Supervisors usually hold the rank of sergeant or above, unless they are civilian personnel, in which case their title could be supervisor, officer-in-charge (OIC), agent-in-charge (AIC), coordinator, manager, or director. Supervisors are assigned throughout the agency in both operational and staff units.

Specialized Units

Specialty functions within law enforcement agencies include units such as special weapons and tactics (SWAT), crime prevention, public information, internal affairs, training, personnel, fiscal control, identification, detention services, planning and research, vehicle maintenance, parking control, and so on. Usually, the primary functional role of each of these units can be deduced from their titles. It must be remembered that the roles of personnel will vary according to their assigned unit. The priority tasks performed by many specialists do impact the total functioning of the agency; however, these personnel may not be very visible to the public in carrying out the daily policing role of the agency.

The Chief Executive Officer

The primary task and role of the chief executive officer of any law enforcement agency is to lead, coordinate, guide, and manage all the units and personnel employed within the agency. This person is responsible for the

SWAT Officers in training

Source: © Larry St. Pierre/ShutterStock, Inc.

agency's operation on a daily basis. Law enforcement officials occupying this position may have various titles besides the common Chief of Police, including Sheriff, Commissioner, Director, Superintendent, Colonel, Marshal, and Chief Constable. The chief executive officer's role usually includes determining the mission and goals of the agency and communicating these to the department personnel and the community. Of course, it has long been recommended that the community, the elected officials, and the officers of the department should be involved in determining the mission and goals of the agency (President's Commission 1968).

Chief executive officials are generally either appointed or promoted to that position (the sheriff is usually an elected position, however). Appointed officials generally have little or no job security or specified term of office. For example, in the early 1990s, one report indicated that "The average length of time in office for 'big-city' chiefs has dropped to 3.5 years. In Houston the average for a 25-year period was calculated to be 2.3 years" (Frankel 1992). The reasons for such short periods include politics (the election of different mayors who appoint the chief), scandals or public incidents that forced resignation, mandatory retirement ages, and personal reasons. Promoted officials usually occupy positions where a civil service or promotion exam of some type determines who obtains the job. Often these positions have job security or tenure, meaning that the official cannot be removed except for cause. The job may be theirs for the rest of their working career. Systems vary from state to state and often depend on state law and city charter.

UNDERSTANDING THE ROLE DEBATE

How do the concepts discussed in this chapter relate to policing today? Why are the issues of role and styles of concern? Many officers go about their jobs every day and do not express any problems with their role or the various tasks they perform. Others, however, are vocal about the frustrations they have from the job. They make statements like, "I'm a cop, not a social worker!," "I joined this force to enforce the law, not to play games with the neighborhood youth," and "I don't have time to worry about overgrown vacant lots, condemned buildings, and abandoned cars." It is statements like these that provide

evidence that some officers do not understand their role in a today's society. Research clearly shows that enforcement of laws or response to crime-related activities consumes between 20 and 50% of an officer's time (Greene and Klockars 1991). Of course, there are exceptions to this figure in some areas within some cities, but that does not negate the fact that the role of today's officer goes beyond law enforcement. It includes public assistance on many matters, order maintenance, community problems, traffic control, and crime prevention.

As discussed in earlier segments of this chapter, the role of officers in the United States is unsettled, subject to ongoing societal change, and is continually evolving. As new problems surface, the local police are called to deal with them because there often is no other agency to respond. Over time, officers have been caretakers of common sewers, lamplighters, the issuers of licenses, health inspectors, housing inspectors, probation officers, parole officers, employment counselors, animal wardens, and child welfare agents; other social service agencies came into existence because some of the duties became too time-consuming for officers to continue. Recently, other concerns related to homeland security, intelligence gathering, cybercrime, human trafficking, and illegal immigration have been added to the role of officers. In the future, other positions (or agencies) may be created to assume some of the non-law enforcement tasks done by officers today. Until that happens, the role of officers is to do whatever society calls upon them to do.

Those who can accept this responsibility can make excellent law enforcement officers. It is the acceptance of this role ambiguity that impacts the officer's style. Those who accept the changing demands of society, who accept the social service requests from the public, who understand the complexity of social disorder and frustration, and who can acknowledge the rights of all persons should be officers who are accepted by the public. It is this type of officer who exhibits concern for people from all walks of life and learns to treat people with respect and dignity.

So that there is no misunderstanding, an officer can accept this multifaceted role and still be a law enforcer when necessary. Today's role requires the "wearing of many hats" and the willingness to adjust one's demeanor and style as necessary for the tasks at hand. The ability of officers to understand the complexity of their role is the challenge facing them today. In 1977, Herman Goldstein discussed the impact of recognizing the multiple functions of officers and he described one ramification this way:

> …in recruiting personnel to be police officers we need individuals who will not only perform well in dealing with serious crime, but will also be capable in many other areas: resolving conflicts, protecting constitutional guarantees, and handling an incredibly wide range of social and personal problems; and most important who will have the ability to shift with ease from performing one of these functions to performing another (42).

STRESS AND DISCRETION IN LAW ENFORCEMENT

Two other concepts are worthy of mention in the overall discussion of the role of policing in today's society. **Stress** and **discretion** are factors that influence the daily lives of many professionals. Both can influence decisions he or she makes and, therefore, both affect behavior. It is not our purpose here to give a detailed analysis of either of these concepts, but we would be remiss not to mention their relationship to issues in this chapter.

Stress

Stress has been broadly defined as "the body's non-specific response to any demand placed on it" (Selye 1974). Policing is often thought to be a high-stress job compared to other occupations; the conventional wisdom holds that law enforcement personnel face perilous conditions, tedious tasks, and hostile work environments, all of which lead to high stress. Stress, it is thought, produces lower productivity, higher levels of physical and mental illness, suicide, and misconduct. Empirical evidence, however, has been mixed, and there appears to be little evidence that officers are any more stressed than employees in other occupations, including some with similar jobs characteristics. Still, there is some evidence to support the idea. One stressor common among occupations is the loss of job discretion, which officers face organizationally (Lennings 1997). As such, the one stressor that appears to have a significant impact in law enforcement is the organizational restrictions on work, including standard operating procedures and legal rulings (while these stressors can affect an officer's abilities, levels of stress do appear to relate to certain negative health outcomes [Golembiewski et al. 1992]). Clearly, this is an area of concern and one that has led to further research. A different report (Morash et al. 2006) found that among workplace factors, "dealing with bias among coworkers" was most predictive of stress. "Officers reporting high stress said they felt stress from racial or ethnic bias and they spent considerable time and energy dealing with and helping other officers deal with prejudice and bias." The study found that the second strongest predictor of stress in the workplace was "feeling a lack of influence on how police work is accomplished." The officers stressed about this indicated "they could not influence the way policing was done and could not influence department policies and procedures" (35–36).

A memorial tribute to fallen officers

Source: Courtesy of the National Law Enforcement Officers Memorial Fund

An excellent treatise and guide for law enforcement managers on the topic of stress, published in 1990, is Ayers and Flanagan's *Preventing Law Enforcement Stress: The Organization's Role*. It divides law enforcement stressors into four categories: (1) those external to the organization, (2) those internal to the organization, (3) those in law enforcement work itself, and (4) those confronting the individual officer. **Figure 6-10** depicts many of the stressors in each of the four categories.

Stress cannot be avoided when carrying out law enforcement duties. Research can identify stress factors and some of those factors (i.e., related to organization and administration) can be better managed, but some research today is also focusing on the "resilience" capability of individuals (Levin 2007, 443). This approach is more proactive in that it can include training to improve resilience and can better screen in applicants who possess good levels of resilience, thus reducing the negative effects of stress on law enforcement personnel.

Discretion

Discretion is not a role. Rather, discretion means that law enforcement officers have wide latitude in choosing which role to assume and which tactics, approaches, or behaviors to employ while acting within a given role. In most respects, officer discretion is an essential component of the job; in fact, discretion is the essence of policing. Discretionary choices are normally made without direct supervision due to the decentralized and distributed nature of patrol and investigative work.

Discretion can be defined as "the use of individual judgment by officers in making decisions as to which of several behavioral responses is appropriate in specific situations" (Cox 1996, 46). According to Sykes, Fox, and Clark (1976, 171), "discretion exists whenever an officer is free to choose from two or more task-relevant alternative interpretations of the events reported, inferred, or observed in a police-citizen encounter." In other words, discretion is the process of making a choice among believed appropriate alternative courses of action. Although most state codes do not give officers the specific right to use discretion, it has been professionally and judicially acknowledged. As mentioned in Chapter 1, the police simply cannot enforce every law that has been enacted. They must, instead, use prudent

FIGURE 6-10 Stress Factors in Policing by Category

External Stressors

- Frustration with the American judicial system
- Lack of consideration by the courts in scheduling officers for court appearances
- The public's lack of support and negative attitudes toward law enforcement
- Negative or distorted media coverage of law enforcement

Internal (Agency) Stressors

- Policies and procedures that are offensive to officers
- Poor or inadequate training and career development opportunities
- Poor economic benefits and working conditions
- Excessive paper work
- Inconsistent discipline

Stressors in the Work Itself

- The rigors of shift work, especially rotating shifts
- Role conflicts between enforcing the law and serving the community
- Frequent exposure to life's miseries and brutalities
- Fear and dangers of the job
- Work overload

Stressors Confronting the Individual Officer

- Fears regarding job competence, individual success, and safety
- Necessity to conform
- Necessity to take a second job or to further education
- Altered social status in the community due to attitude changes of others because he or she is now an officer.

Source: Ayres, Richard M. and George S. Flanagan (1990), Preventing Law Enforcement Stress: The Organization's Role, Washington, D.C.: U.S. Department of Justice and the National Sheriffs' Association, pp. 4–5.

discretion and enforce only those laws that are reasonable to enforce given the totality of the situation and the interest of justice. They must also use prudent discretion in their non-enforcement or service decisions, again basing their professional judgments on the best interests of the community and the goals and mission of their department. By way of definition, we might add that selective enforcement refers to enforcing those laws deemed appropriate to the situation or related to the priorities of the agency and the community. The opposite of selective enforcement is full enforcement, which means enforcing all laws all the time—a condition that most Americans simply do not want.

According to Cox (1996), there are a number of factors influencing discretion, such as the law, officer attitude and character, department policy, political expectations, public expectations, the situation/setting, and the occupational culture in which they operate. The process of making decisions involves the evaluation of all of these factors. In other words, the officer must evaluate the "totality of circumstances." (Review Figure 6-1 again; think of all of the interrelated factors mentioned there and compare them to the ones influencing discretion.)

The lack of guidelines in law enforcement agencies gives individual officers the opportunity to inject their own prejudices and legal interpretations into their job performance. This can lead to the abuse of discretion. In making a decision, officers must understand that the decision should be appropriate and defensible. They may be asked to explain their decision in the reporting process or in court. In today's litigious society, decisions made by officers are subject to review by others and can result in suits for damages. This adds to the levels of stress an officer endures in his or her career.

One study found that in responding to disturbances, officers engaged in 13 distinct contact actions (e.g., request separation, physical restraint, or forced dispersal), 17 processing actions (e.g., follow complainant's request, restrain someone, or admonish disputants), and 17 distinct exit actions (e.g., just leave, arrest, or warn alleged offenders). Similar patterns were observed in traffic stops (Bayley 1986). Discretion is a large part of law enforcement, a major issue in law enforcement reform, and it produces the most significant dilemma in policing (Brown 1968). Discretion is essential to job performance because of the nature of the work and the geographic dispersal of decision-making officers. Indeed, community policing and various related approaches expect higher levels of discretion, and yet it is also the case that discretion leads to opportunities for misconduct of all sorts. As such, standard operating procedures, orders, written directives, skill training, incident reviews, and supervisory approval of reports all operate to restrain discretion, reduce the likelihood of misconduct, and standardize operations. It is worth noting that, largely due to the high level of inherent danger in such operations, special operations teams operate with very low levels of discretion in tactical terms.

Some agencies recognize the need for and use of discretion by developing policy and official guidelines. One such policy includes a list of factors that should be considered in exercising discretion (University of Texas Police Department at Austin 2007):

> In exercising discretion, an officer must be able to assess the situation or incident, analyze the facts or information, and then determine a reasonable and appropriate course of action. These factors include, but are not limited to:
>
> 1. Department policy, procedures, mission statement, values, vision, goals, and objectives.
> 2. Availability of a supervisor or other officers for guidance and/or consultation.
> 3. Facts and circumstances which will subsequently justify the decision.
> 4. Range of available alternatives.
> 5. Seriousness of the incident.
> 6. Officer safety concerns.
> 7. Other factors such as staffing availability, impact on the University community, humane considerations, and potential for recurrence.

This list of factors related to the use of discretion clearly indicates that the term does NOT mean "Do anything you want to"—you have to perform tasks within policy and procedures, and you must be ready to justify your actions.

SUMMARY

This chapter examined the relationships among the concepts of role, tasks, and style. Role was defined as a multidimensional concept consisting of expected behaviors performed by a person in a given situation or position for the purpose of achieving certain objectives or goals.

Since there are multiple objectives to policing (public safety, homeland security, law enforcement, protection of constitutional rights, etc.), there are multiple roles. These roles require the performance of different tasks. Style, on the other hand, referred to how these tasks were carried out—the officers' demeanor, approach, and technique. Since these concepts are interrelated, they are difficult to discuss separately. The many factors or influences upon role determination and the development of one's style compound the issues. Some of the more relevant research was presented regarding role and style. Additionally, organizational roles of selected positions (assignments) were described. The important factors of stress and discretion were briefly discussed in relation to their general impact on role determination and actions taken in the field.

So what is the role of the officers in a democratic society? It is essentially what society says it is (defined by the community, not the officer). Since reaching a consensus is extremely difficult and there are so many different communities across this country, there cannot be just one role for law enforcement personnel to perform. There are many roles for officers in our society. What sets policing apart from other occupations in society may be the fact that the state has given officers the authority to use force if necessary to carry out their duties (Bittner 1990; Klockars 1985). The fact that officers have this authority and power must not be forgotten, since we ask individual officers to come to our rescue when needed and do what has to be done to protect us, but society also expects them not to be excessive when they have to use force.

Critical Thinking Questions

1. List five influences on role determination and briefly explain how these factors influence role determination.

2. Describe how the democratic process, occupational culture, ethics, socialization, training, availability, technology, and laws combine to influence the role of policing in American society, or an officer's perception of that role.

3. What is meant by "role conflict?" Give two examples.

4. Compare and contrast the concepts of "officer role" and "officer style."

5. Why is it difficult to precisely and definitively answer the question, "What is the role of the police in the United States?"

6. Why are the concepts of "stress" and "discretion" related to the issues of role and style?

CHAPTER SPECIFIC INTERNET LINKS

Bureau of Labor Statistics, Police and Detectives: http://www.bls.gov/oco/ocos160.htm

International Association of Chiefs of Police: http://discoverpolicing.org/

National Criminal Justice Reference Service: http://www.ncjrs.gov/ (use key terms or phrases from this chapter to find related documents)

University of Texas Police Department: http://www.utexas.edu/police/manual/

Shields of Gold: DNRE Conservation Officers, State of Michigan: http://www.youtube.com/watch?v=T6Tp1rUu9sM&feature=player_embedded

Kingsport (TN) Police Department, Residents tackle crime in the community: http://www.youtube.com/watch?v=Rj9k3wWwZwU

Video: http://www.youtube.com/watch?v=2WGNAwdkoGo-Role Conflict During Hurricane Katrina.

CHAPTER GLOSSARY

Discretion—individual judgment by officers in making decisions as to which of several behavioral responses is appropriate in specific situations.

Full neighborhood management—a commitment and philosophy to allow officers to intervene in any problem in a community that requires a response by police officers or other government personnel.

Officer style—the manner in which officers carry out their police role; it includes the various techniques, procedures, mannerisms, vocabulary, body language, and so on, that are available to them.

Popular justice—a term used to describe how police departments have taken on a distinct, and often local, presentation throughout their development, based on popular social and political demands (sometimes referred to as "the will of the people").

Project STAR—a comprehensive 3.5-year research effort (1971–1974) that involved the federal government and agencies in four states; it attempted to identify appropriate roles for six key positions (police officer, prosecuting attorney, defense attorney, judge, caseworker, and correctional worker) in the criminal justice system.

Role—a multidimensional concept consisting of expected behaviors performed by a person in a given situation or position for the purpose of achieving certain objectives or goals.

Role conflict—the confusion and frustration brought on by competing and sometimes opposite values and expectations experienced by officers while performing their job tasks.

Stress—broadly defined as "the body's nonspecific response to any demand placed on it" (Selye 1994).

Sustained order maintenance—a phrase referring to intervention by police that has required greater problem-solving analysis and possibly a greater commitment of resources than for short-term intervention.

Temporal order maintenance—a phrase referring to the short-term intervention by police officers in situations of interpersonal conflict and social disorder.

CHAPTER REFERENCES AND ADDITIONAL READINGS

Ayres, Richard M. and George S. Flanagan (1990). *Preventing Law Enforcement Stress: The Organization's Role.* Washington, D.C.: U.S. Department of Justice and the National Sheriff's Association.

Bayley, David (1986). The tactical choices of police patrol officers. *Journal of Criminal Justice* 14(4):329–348.

Bittner, Egon (1990). *Aspects of Police Work.* Boston: Northeastern University Press.

Broderick, John J. (1977). *Police in a Time of Change.* Morristown, NJ: General Learning Press.

Broderick, John J. (1987). *Police in a Time of Change,* Second Edition. Prospect Heights, IL: Waveland Press, Inc.

Brown, Michael K. (1968). *Working the Street: Police Discretion and the Dilemmas of Reform.* New York: Macmillan.

Burton, Velmer S., Jr., Robert H. Langworthy, and Troy A. Barker (1991). The prescribed role of police in a free society: A national survey of state legal codes. Paper presented at the annual conference. Chicago: Midwest Criminal Justice Association.

Campbell, James S., Joseph Sahid, and David Stang (1970). *Law and order reconsidered: Report of the task force on law and law enforcement to the National Commission on the Causes and Prevention of Violence.* New York: Bantam Books.

Carter, David L. (2002). *The Police and the Community,* Seventh Edition. Upper Saddle River, NJ: Prentice Hall

Carter, David L. and Louis A. Radelet (1999). *The Police and the Community,* Sixth Edition. Upper Saddle River, NJ: Prentice Hall

Coates, Robert B. (1972). The dimensions of police-citizen interaction: A social psychological analysis. Ph.D. dissertation. College Park, MD: University of Maryland.

Cox, Steven M. (1996). *Police: Practices-Perspectives-Problems.* Boston: Allyn and Bacon.

Crank, John P. (1998). *Understanding Police Culture.* Cincinnati, OH: Anderson Publishing Co.

Currant, James (ed.) (1972). *Police and Law Enforcement 1973–1974.* Vol. II. New York: AIMS Press, Inc.

Delattre, Edwin J. (2002). *Character and Cops: Ethics in Policing,* Fourth Edition. Washington, D.C.: American Enterprise Institute.

Frankel, Bruce (1992), Police chiefs worry about job security. *USA Today,* November 19:10A.

Fyfe, James J. (2001).Good Policing. In Roger G. Dunham and Geoffrey P. Alpert (eds.) *Critical Issues in Policing,* Fourth Edition. Prospects Heights, IL: Waveland Press, Inc.

Goldstein, Herman (1977). *Policing a Free Society.* Cambridge, MA: Ballinger Publishing Company.

Goldstein, Herman (1979). Improving policing: A problem-oriented approach to improving police service. *Crime and Delinquency* 25: 236–258.

Goldstein, Herman (1990). *Problem-Oriented Policing.* New York: McGraw-Hill.

Golembiewski, Robert T., Michael Lloyd, Katherine Scherb, and Robert F. Munzenrider (1992). Burnout and mental health among police officers. *Journal of Public Administration Research and Theory* 2(4):424–439.

Greene, Jack R. and Carl B. Klockars (1991). What Police Do. In Carl B. Klockars and Stephen D. Mastrofski (Eds.) *Thinking about police: Contemporary readings,* Second Edition. New York: McGraw-Hill.

Guyot, Dorothy (1979). Bending granite: Attempts to change the rank structure of American police departments. *Journal of Police Science and Administration* 7(3):253–284.

Hatting, Steven H., Alan S. Engel, and Philip A. Russo (1983). Shades of blue: Toward an alternative typology of police. *Journal of Police Science and Administration* 11:54–61.

Hoover, Larry (1992). *Police Management: Issues and Perspectives.* Washington, D.C.: Police Executive Research Forum.

Klockars, Carl B. (1985). *The Idea of Police.* Newbury Park, CA: Sage Publications, Inc.

Law Enforcement Assistance Administration (LEAA) (1976). *Two-Hundred Years of American Criminal Justice.* Washington, D.C.: U.S. Department of Justice.

Lennings, C.J. (1997). Police and occupationally related violence: A review. *Policing: An International Journal of Police Strategies and Management* 20(3):555–566.

Levin, Bernard H. (2007). Human Capital In Policing: What Works, What Doesn't Work, What's Promising? In Schafer, Joseph A. (ed.) *Policing 2020: Exploring the Future of Crime, Communities, and Policing.* U.S. Department of Justice, Federal Bureau of Investigation, Futures Working Group.

Manning, Peter and John Van Maanen (eds.) (1978). *Policing: A View from the Street.* Santa Monica, CA: Goodyear Publishing Company, Inc.

Mastrofski, Stephen D., Roger B. Parks, Albert J. Reiss, Jr., and Robert E. Worden (2003). *How Police Supervisory Styles Influence Patrol Officer Behavior.* Research for Practice, NCJ 194078. Washington, D.C.: U.S. Department of Justice, National Institute of Justice.

Morash, Merry, Robin Haarr and Dae-Hoon Kwak (2006). Multilevel Influences on Police Stress. *Journal of Contemporary Criminal Justice,* 22 (1):26-43.

Muir, William K. (1977). *Police: Streetcorner Politicians.* Chicago: University of Chicago Press.

National Advisory Commission on Criminal Justice Standards and Goals (1973). Report on police. Washington, D.C.: U.S. Government Printing Office.

National Commission on Law Observance and Enforcement (1931). Report on police. Washington, D.C.: U.S Government Printing Office.

Niederhoffer, Arthur and Abraham Blumberg (1976). *The Ambivalent Force: Perspectives on the Police,* Second Edition. Hinsdale, IL: The Dryden Press.

Nowicki, Dennis E. (2003). Human resource management and development. In William A. Geller and Darrel W. Stephens (eds.) *Local Government Police Management.* Washington, D.C.: International City/County Management Association.

O'Neill, Robert J. (2003). Foreword. In William A. Geller and Darrel W. Stephens (eds.) *Local Government Police Management.* Washington, D.C.: International City/County Management Association.

Pollock, Joycelyn M. (2004). *Ethics in Criminal Justice,* Fourth Edition. Belmont, CA: Thomson/Wadsworth.

President's Commission on Law Enforcement and Administration of Justice (1968). *The Challenge of Crime in a Free Society.* New York: Avon Books.

Reuss-Inni, Elizabeth, (1984). *Two Cultures of Policing: Street Cops and Management Cops.* New Brunswick, CT: Transaction Books.

Roberg, Roy, Kenneth Novak, and Cary Cordner (2005). *Police and Society.* Los Angeles: Roxbury Publishing Company.

Selye, Hans (1974). *Stress Without Distress.* New York: Avon Books.

Selznick, Philip (1947). *TVA and the Grass Roots: A Study in the Sociology of Formal Organizations.* Berkeley: University of California Press.

Skolnick, Jerome H., Malcolm M. Feeley, and Candace McCoy (2005). *Criminal Justice: Introductory Cases and Materials,* Sixth Edition. New York: Foundation Press.

Skolnick, Jerome and Thomas C. Gray (eds.) (1975). *Police in America.* Boston: Little, Brown and Company.

Smith, Charles P., Donald E. Pehlke, and Charles D. Weller (1974). *Role Performance and the Criminal Justice System, Volume II: Detailed Performance Objectives, Project STAR.* Cincinnati, OH: Anderson Publishing Company and Santa Cruz, CA: Davis Publishing Company.

Staufenberger, Richard (ed.) (1980). *Progress in Policing: Essays on Change.* Cambridge, MA: Ballinger Publishing Company.

Stephens, Darrel W. (2003). Organization and management. In William A Geller and Darrel W. Stephens (eds.) *Local Government Police Management,* Fourth Edition. Washington, D.C.: International City/County Management Association.

Sweeney, Thomas J. (2003). Patrol. In William A. Geller and Darrel W. Stephens (eds.) *Local Government Police Management,* Fourth Edition. Washington, D.C.: International City/County Management Association.

Sykes, R., J. Fox, and J. Clark (1976). A socio-legal theory of police discretion. In A. Blumberg and E. Niederhoffer (eds.) *The Ambivalent Force: Perspectives on the Police,* Second Edition. Hinsdale, IL: The Dryden Press.

Toch, H., and D. Grant. (2005). *Police as Problem Solvers: How Frontline Workers Can Promote Organizational and Community Change,* 2nd Edition. Washington, D.C.: American Psychological Association.

University of Texas Police Department at Austin (2007). Use of Discretion. Policy Manual, Policy B-25. University of Texas at Austin.

Van Maanen, John (1985). Making rank: Becoming an American police sergeant. *Urban Life* 13:155–176.

Vila, Bryan and Cynthia Morris (eds.) (1999). *The Role Of Police In American Society: A Documentary History*. Westport, Connecticut: Greenwood Press.

Walker, Samuel (1992). *The Police in America: An Introduction*, Second Edition. New York: McGraw-Hill.

Walker, Samuel (1998). *Popular Justice: A History of American Criminal Justice*. New York: Oxford University Press.

Walsh, Willam F. (1984). The analysis of the variation in patrol officer felony arrest rates. Ph.D. dissertation. New York: Fordham University.

White, Susan O. (1972). A perspective on police professionalism. *Law and Society Review*, 61–85.

Wilson, James Q. (1968). *The Varieties of Police Behavior: The Management of Law and Order in Eight Communities*. Cambridge, MA: Harvard University Press.

Wilson, James Q. and George L. Kelling (1982). Broken Windows. *Atlantic Monthly* (March):29-38.

CHAPTER **7**

The Selection, Training, & Education of Personnel

KEY TERMS USED IN THIS CHAPTER

recruitment

active recruitment

passive recruitment

selection process

pre-application conference

ride-along

self-selection

structured interview

unstructured interview

background check

conditional offer of employment

polygraph

psychometric exam

psychological interview

appointing authority

civil service

eligibility list

rule of three

bonus points

assessment center

probationary status

permanent employee status

Civil Rights Act of 1964

protected classes

adverse impact

Equal Employment Opportunity Commission (EEOC)

Griggs v. Duke Power Company

job analysis

remedies

consent decree

affirmative action

reverse discrimination

bona fide occupational qualification (BFOQ)

on-the-job training (OJT)

education

learning

learning domains

mandatory minimum training standards

field training

in-service training

advanced or specialized training

continuing education credit

executive and managerial training

citizen police academy

college academies

THE IMPORTANCE OF HUMAN RESOURCE CONSIDERATIONS

Of all the available resources, people are the greatest asset to the policing function. Granted, the United States is a very advanced technological society, but the services provided by law enforcement agencies are performed by humans. It takes many people working together to carry out the functions performed by policing agencies. Although "robocops" may one day assist in this function, people will continue to be the mainstay for the foreseeable future. (Issues related to technology in policing are discussed in Chapter 11.)

Individuals preparing to enter the criminal justice field are often misinformed or have misinterpreted many aspects of personnel selection, promotion, and career development. It is not difficult to meet someone working in the field that may be bitter, frustrated, or disillusioned about his/her job. Others with a criminal justice education may be frustrated because they have not been successful in obtaining employment. In conversations with those employed in the field, negative statements may be made when asked about job openings and career advancement:

- "It all depends on who you know—it's all politics."
- "Merit has little to do with getting ahead in this department."
- "It doesn't matter how much education or ability you have, you have to play their political games to get ahead."
- "You'll never make it, you're the wrong color (or sex, or religion, or ethnic group)."

Statements such as these may cause some highly-qualified applicants to pursue other careers or agencies. Although there may be some truth to these statements in some agencies, for the most part they are exaggerated and based on emotion rather than fact and understanding of the personnel process. Also, depending on the agency, the hiring process may take a while (up to 2 years for some federal agencies). Furthermore, the motive behind such statements may be suspect. For example, if I am a police officer who knows that the competition for jobs in my agency is very rigorous, might I *discourage* someone from applying if I am trying to support a friend or relative who also is applying (thus reducing the competitive pool)? Or am I upset with my employer and trying to keep highly-qualified persons from applying? Or maybe I do not want a person to join the department because of the potential competition for promotion slots in the future?

The bottom line is: do not believe everything someone tells you about the personnel function of an agency! The personnel function in policing is highly complex and becoming very legalistic. By understanding the legal, political, and social framework of the personnel function, one has a greater likelihood of successfully passing through its stages. One potential outcome is a highly rewarding career in law enforcement.

Personnel and Expenditures

As mentioned in Chapter 4, the policing function in the United States consists of over one million persons employed in about 16,223 agencies. Sworn officers account for about

800,000 of these persons. Annual operating expenditures for local police departments in 2007 amounted to over $55.4 billion; this represents a 14% increase from 2003 after adjusting for inflation (Reaves 2010). When reduced to the local level of policing, police personnel is usually one of the largest, if not the largest, units of employees in a jurisdiction. Generally speaking, the public safety function (police and fire fighting) is the largest expenditure in jurisdictions regarding personnel costs. Within the individual agencies, personnel costs usually consume 75–95% of the budget.

Personnel expenditures include salaries and fringe benefits (health/life/disability/liability insurance, clothing allowances, vacation and holiday pay, etc.). There are also operating costs for agencies, which include furniture, heat, light, communications systems, etc. Beginning salaries for police officers vary widely and are dependent on both the size of the department and the wealth (tax base) of the city or town the department serves. Usually, the smaller the agency, the smaller the starting base salary; this is in part because smaller agencies are cheaper to operate. Departments that serve populations of one million or more cost approximately $365 per officer to operate, whereas departments that serve populations of 25,000 or fewer cost around $216 per officer (Reaves 2010). However, there are always exceptions to the rule. In Massachusetts in 2009, for example, the starting base salary for a police officer in Royalston (serving a population of approximately 1250) was $25,000, compared to $55,000 for a beginning police officer in Boston (serving a residential population of about 600,000). However, police officers in Oak Bluffs, Massachusetts, enjoyed a starting base salary of $59,000 serving a residential population of only 3700. This is because Oak Bluffs is located on Martha's Vineyard (one of the most expensive places to live in Massachusetts), which provides a larger tax base for the police to draw from.

Qualities and Attributes

Although technology is rapidly changing the face of policing, the day-to-day street policing functions have not yet been computerized; it takes thinking people to analyze crime scenes, to interview victims and witnesses, to locate and apprehend suspects, and to prepare cases for prosecution. These aspects of the police function can be assisted by technology, but people are necessary to carry out these tasks associated with bringing offenders to justice. This is no small point. Do we want a machine to do the police function for us? Think of all the ramifications of this question before answering it, because the technology exists today to almost completely "automate" the criminal justice system. Of course, this would mean transforming our society, our Constitution, and our current sense of privacy. Stop reading for just a moment and answer this question: What qualities and attributes do you want in the police officers that protect you and your family? August Vollmer (1969) is credited for making the following statement concerning police officers:

> The citizen expects police officers to have the wisdom of Solomon, the courage of David, the strength of Samson, the patience of Job, the leadership of Moses, the kindness of the Good Samaritan, the strategical training of Alexander, the faith of Daniel, the diplomacy of Lincoln, the tolerance of the Carpenter of Nazareth, and finally, an intimate knowledge of every branch of the natural, biological, and social sciences. If he had all these, he might be a good policeman (222).

As a society and as individuals, we expect a great deal from our law enforcement personnel. We expect integrity, honesty, self-control, tolerance, intelligence, objectiveness, courtesy, courage, concern for others, fairness, maturity, commitment, dedication, a strong character, physical and emotional strength, and insight. Few will argue against such qualities, but take another look at these expectations. How can they be identified in the selection process? How are these measured? How can they be "trained" into an individual? In short, how are such expectations turned into realities? There are no easy solutions to this quest; however, it does take commitment from administrators to strive toward the goal of selecting promising candidates.

THE RECRUITING AND SELECTION PROCESS

Not everyone who wants to become a law enforcement official will become one, just as some who enter law school never become attorneys and some who enter medical school never become doctors. It is important to understand that there are many variables that go into the hiring of law enforcement personnel. Everyone simply cannot be hired; there are not enough positions in agencies for that to occur. Of course, "wanting" to be an agent or officer is usually a prerequisite to selection, but it alone is not sufficient.

Recruitment

Recruitment is the development and maintenance of an adequate supply of qualified persons interested in being employed by a specific agency. In reality, there are two types of recruiting efforts: active and passive. **Active recruitment** occurs when an agency makes a concerted effort to attract candidates. This may entail the deployment of existing personnel, either sworn or civilian, as recruiters and sending them into the community to generate interest among potential applicants. This task can be done by personnel specifically assigned to that function or by personnel as part of their regular assignments. **Passive recruitment** is when the agency has openings and takes applications from those who come to the agency. No outreach or concerted effort is made to attract candidates; it is a "sit back, wait, and see" approach.

Some departments spend considerable resources attempting to attract qualified applicants. Recruiting brochures are printed; officers are sent out of town on recruiting trips to colleges, universities, and job fairs; and public announcements are placed in local public media (newspapers, public service announcements on radio, television, and even the Internet). Recruitment material can contain a generous amount of information about the hiring process and the opportunities within the agency, or may contain only the basics with telephone numbers and an address at which to pick up the application. The Phoenix (Arizona) Police Department's Web site on employment information contains considerable detail about the department, such as the selection process, salary, and fringe benefits. As a recruiting tool, it attempts to answer many basic questions. **Figure 7-1** depicts the salary schedule and **Figure 7-2** lists the fringe benefit package reported on the Web pages of the Phoenix Police Department.

FIGURE 7-1 Police Officer Salary Information- Phoenix Police Department

	Hourly	Monthly	Annually
New Recruit (During 18 week Academy)	20.13	3,489.20	—
Starting Pay (Upon Graduating Academy)	21.68	3,468.8	**$45,094.40**
After 6 Months of Employment	23.12	3,976.27	**$47,715.20**
Maximum Pay	30.50	4,880.00	**$63,440.00**

Source: Phoenix Police Dept., 2010, http://www.phoenix.gov/police/pdjob4.html

The major objective of the recruiting process is to ensure an adequate supply of interested applicants from which selection will occur, with the underlying premise being that the larger the pool of applicants, the greater the likelihood of obtaining enough qualified candidates to process through the selection procedures. Although the recruiting phase is focused on increasing the number of candidates available for hire, it is also important to attract serious and qualified applicants. Sheer numbers alone are not sufficient; some agencies attract thousands of applicants every time they offer the entrance exam, even if there are no current openings! The recruiting phase should present an accurate portrayal of the job and the responsibilities it carries. Being an officer is not all red lights and sirens, and those who are attracted because of that image may be some of the first to be disqualified. Likewise, some potential and needed candidates, such as women and members of minority groups, may have a perception of not being wanted, as these groups have not always been treated well by some law enforcement personnel, or the image of abuse or perceptions and reputations of mistreatment may be prevalent in their immediate environments. If the reputation of an agency is a negative one, attempting to recruit highly-qualified candidates from any segment of the community may be difficult. An active recruitment program is often the best approach to

FIGURE 7-2 Selected Fringe benefit package—Phoenix Police Department*

(Effective 7/12/2010 – 6/30/2012)

SALARY STEP PROGRESSION
9 steps for base class of Police Officer; 6 months at Step 3, then 1 year between steps.

WORKWEEK
Five 8-hour shifts or four 10-hour shifts in seven days.

CALL OUT (CALL BACK) PAY
3 hours at 1½ times regular rate.

CAREER ENHANCEMENT PAY (Officers qualifying for:)
Level Biweekly amount
1 $ 73.20
2 $146.40
3 $219.60
4 $292.80

COMPENSATORY TIME MAXIMUM ACCRUAL
200 hours.

COURT INTERPRETATION & TRANSLATION PAY
$4 per half-day when exceeds 15-minute minimum, for sustained word-for-word oral and written assignments.

LONGEVITY PAY
Qualify: 7 yrs continuous service. 1 year at top step. $80 ($125 for employees at 20 years up to the 22nd year)
semi-annually for each year in excess of 6 years up to 19th year. Semi-annual max = $1,040/$2,000.
Annual max = $2,080/$4,000. Qualify: 6/13/11, Paid: 7/1/11. Qualifications for longevity pay are made in the base class and will
not be affected by movement into or out of assignment positions or positions within the same pay range.

MILEAGE ALLOWANCE
55.5 cents per mile, effective 7/1/2011

OVERTIME PAY
1½ times regular rate for over 8 hours per shift or 40 hours per week if on 4-10s or any hours worked within the 15-hour
minimum (13 for 4-10) that employees are meant to be off between shifts, which certain assignment units can waive.

SHIFT DIFFERENTIAL PAY
$0.60/hour for shifts (or any portion of a shift) ending at or after 10 p.m., plus $0.25/hour for weekend shifts starting between
2:00 pm Friday and 11:59 pm Sunday.

SICK LEAVE PAYOUT AS SALARY FOR PUBLIC SAFETY
Optional monthly conversion of sick leave accrual to pay, for minimum 3 years, if at least 1,714 unused hours, 6-yr maximum.

STANDBY PAY
$40/workday and $60/non-workday

STANDBY PAY FOR COURT
2 hrs at 1½ times base hourly rate if before 1200 hours.
2 hrs at 1½ times base hourly rate if after 1200 hours.
Additional hr at 1½ times if required to remain after 1200 hours.

SWORN POLICE TO INTERPRET & TRANSLATE PAY
$10 per hour in addition to base pay.

TRAINING PAY
5% of regular rate of pay for Canine Unit Training Officers, Field Training
Officers, and officers assigned to train traffic/ DUI enforcement.

UNIFORMS/CLOTHING ALLOWANCE
$1,150 annual allowance; one-time allowance and annual maintenance for designated assignments.

(continued)

FIGURE 7-2 Selected Fringe benefit package—Phoenix Police Department* (*Continued*)

VACATION PAYOUT
Employees who have accrued max vacation carryover, with 17 years of service, can be paid for additional vacation leave for a one-time 3-year period; may receive a one-time 1-year extension to the 3-year period. May elect to invoke this benefit one additional time, provided at least 300 leave hours have accrued at the time of the second election. Also: 80 hours of vacation time can be accumulated above the max carryover into the last 3 years of service. These hours must be used as paid time off prior to retirement.

BEREAVEMENT LEAVE
Up to 3 days for death of immediate family member with additional time for air travel if out-of-state.

Citywide Phoenix Benefits Program Includes**

MEDICAL COVERAGE

DENTAL COVERAGE

LIFE INSURANCE

EMPLOYEE ASSISTANCE PROGRAM (EAP)

RETIREMENT PLAN

DEFERRED COMPENSATION PROGRAM

VACATION

SICK LEAVE

HOLIDAY PAY

FLEXIBLE SPENDING ACCOUNTS

DEPENDENT CARE SUBSIDY

COPPER SUN CHILD DEVELOPMENT CENTER

LEGAL INSURANCE PROGRAM

PRE-TAX BENEFITS

WELLNESS PROGRAM

ELDER CARE SERVICES

LONG TERM DISABILITY PROGRAM

FLEXIBLE SCHEDULES

FREE OR DISCOUNTED BUS AND LIGHT RAIL FARES

EDUCATIONAL ASSISTANCE/REIMBURSEMENT

PROFESSIONAL MEMBERSHIPS

JURY DUTY PAY

EMPLOYEE SUGGESTION PROGRAM

RIDESHARE PROGRAM

CAREER COUNSELING

Source: * Extracted and edited from *http://phoenix.gov/employment/benefits/benefitsprogram/beneindx.html* with contract, state code, and city references removed.

** See: *http://phoenix.gov/employment/benefits/benefitsprogram/index.html*

overcoming negative perceptions. Of course, an agency's administrators must also be responsive to any known negative perceptions on the part of the community and should be investigating the source of them.

The Selection Process

The **selection process** includes the various techniques, devices, and procedures used to identify candidates to whom offers of employment may be made. It is often viewed as a series of events linked together and through which an applicant must pass in order to be hired. Most perceive the application form as the beginning of the process and a job offer as the conclusion; however, that is not completely accurate. The selection process actually begins during the recruiting phase or at the announcement of job openings. Would-be applicants then begin assessing their true desires and aspirations about applying (some would call this "soul-searching"). Some agencies also require a **pre-application conference** with a ranking field officer. This meeting is for the conveyance of information about the job, the required training, and the agency's expectations of its personnel. It may include watching a videotape and obtaining information about the academy training and probationary periods.

The primary objective of the pre-application conference is to supply accurate, realistic information and to clarify any misperceptions for the future applicant. Some departments encourage possible applicants to meet with officers to discuss the realities of police work before applying; some departments even offer **ride-along** opportunities with uniformed patrol officers for any member of the public, but especially for potential applicants. By obtaining accurate information about the position and agency, future applicants can better assess their desire and willingness to work for that jurisdiction. This is sometimes referred to as **self-selection,** in the sense that the applicant is making an informed and more objective decision to continue in the selection process.

Figure 7-3 depicts the typical phases of the selection process at a medium to large agency. The sequence may vary somewhat among agencies, and some agencies may omit certain phases. Smaller agencies may have a slightly shorter process. Each of the phases is described in

this section only briefly, and it must be understood that detailed information about each phase is beyond the scope of this text; the reader should consult the references at the end of this chapter for additional information.

The Application

The application form varies greatly from one agency to the next; there is no universally applied standard form. It may be a single page to a 10-page (or more) document. The information requested may range from basic identification-type inquiries to a complete educational and employment history, coupled with questions about drug use. Usually, those agencies that utilize a longer, more detailed application use it as part of the background investigation, whereas the shorter formats are used to contact the applicant and to identify him/her at the next phase of the process.

Written Exam

Written exams are very common in today's selection process. They have changed somewhat over the years because of certain technical and legal requirements (discussed in the next major section of this chapter). Some exams are developed by the local jurisdiction, while others may be developed by private companies or public entities that specialize in testing. The examination itself usually consists of several sections, which may test a selected number of the following topics:

- English grammar, spelling, punctuation, and sentence structure
- English comprehension, vocabulary, and word usage
- Basic mathematics, percentages, and thought problems
- Essay or writing samples, printing samples
- Memorization of facts, numbers, and/or photos and descriptions
- Reasoning/judgment based on scenarios or situational analyses
- Interpretation/application of law/code sections to situations
- Questions about material distributed before the examination that applicants were told to study

FIGURE 7-3 Typical stages in a selection process

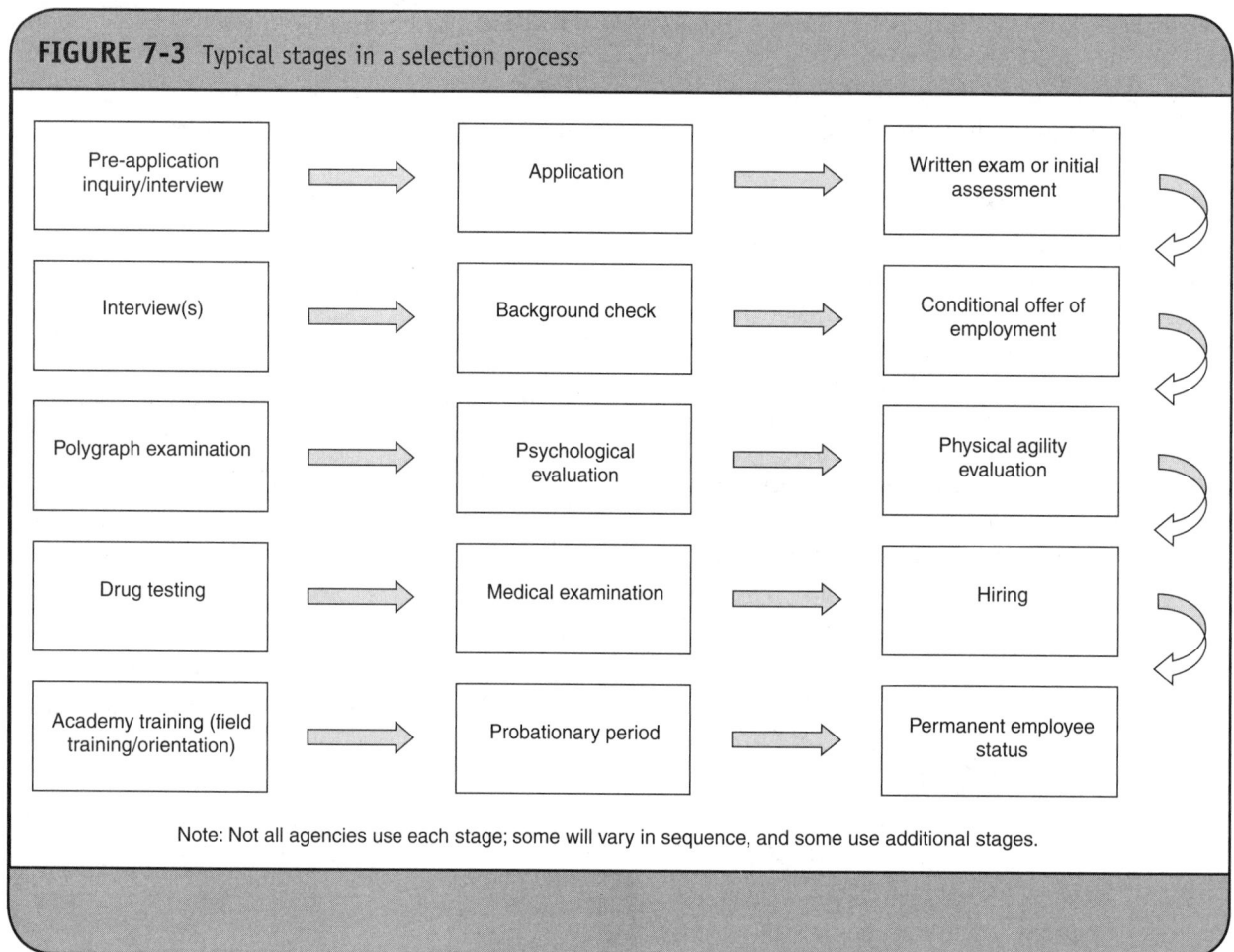

Note: Not all agencies use each stage; some will vary in sequence, and some use additional stages.

Interview(s)

Of all the phases of the selection process, the interview is the most universal regardless of the size of the agency. There may be one, two, or even three interviews, which may be conducted by an individual or by a group (sometimes referred to as an interview or selection board), by civilians (e.g., personnel officials, elected officials), and/or police personnel. They may be conducted at the police department, in the applicant's home, or at another agency location (e.g., personnel office, mayor's office).

There are two types of interviews: structured and unstructured. The **structured interview** usually consists of specifically compiled questions that focus on various aspects of the job or the applicant's abilities and background. Some follow-up questions may also be asked, many of which are also of a structured nature. The **unstructured interview** consists of general areas of focus, but the questions are not specifically spelled out. There is greater potential for the unstructured interview to wander off-course during follow-up questions to initial responses, which could be problematic in legal challenges to the selection process.

Candidates for positions sometimes believe that there are right and wrong responses to the questions asked during the interview. In the majority of interviews, it is less a matter of specific responses than it is the reasoning, directness, and appropriateness of what is said as well as the manner in which statements are made; interviewers often evaluate oral communication skills, poise, composure, responsiveness, and appearance rather than the content or accuracy of the specific responses.

Background Check

As the phrase implies, a **background check** is a formal review and verification of the candidate's formal education, current and previous residences, current and prior employment, traffic and criminal citations and convictions (if any), reported drug history, and credit rating. This usually includes interviews with neighbors, named references, teachers and/or professors, employers, and possibly relatives. In some jurisdictions, background checks are done in person by investigators of the agency to which one has applied; in others they are conducted by mail and over the phone. If an applicant is from another town, the agency may request certain background information from the police in the candidate's local jurisdiction. An applicant will be required to sign certain release forms that grant the background investigators the authority to gain access to records that would otherwise be confidential.

Conditional Offer of Employment

Because of certain potential liabilities and allegations, this phase of the selection process has become an important stage in public agencies. A **conditional offer of employment** means that the candidate is suitable and eligible for hire at that point in the selection process, and it also means that the candidate will be employed if certain other factors related to physical ability and medical and mental conditions are within job-related limits. Ultimately, if physical, mental, and/or medical conditions are identified that are not within the standards for the position, the offer of employment will be withdrawn.

Polygraph Examination

While sometimes considered part of the background check, polygraph testing should be considered a separate phase of the selection process. The **polygraph** is a scientifically-calibrated instrument that records physiological changes in respiration (pneumograph), electrical resistance of the skin (galvanograph), and changes in blood pressure and pulse rate (cardiosphygmograph); these three measurements are recorded independently of each other by three pen-like devices on graph paper in the instrument. It operates by the existence of a direct relationship between a person's state of mind and their physiological condition (Territo 1974). The purpose of polygraph testing is to verify a person's truthfulness or detect deception regarding an area of inquiry. The central premises upon which the polygraph is based are that: (a) lying leads to conflict, (b) conflict causes fear and anxiety, and (c) these mental states are the direct cause of measurable physiological changes (Shattuch 1973, 5–6).

Psychological Evaluation

The Strawbridge (1990) survey of 72 major police departments in 1990 found 66 (91.6%) agencies included either a **psychometric exam** or **psychological interview** as part of the selection process (similarly, a 1994 survey of 59 departments found 91.5% utilizing psychological interviews [Langworthy et al. 1994]). This is in stark contrast to surveys done in 1972 and 1976, where the rates were 39% and 20%, respectively, for the agencies surveyed (Conser and Thompson 1976; Eisenberg et al. 1973). Generally speaking, the larger the department, the greater the likelihood of requiring some form of psychological evaluation for potential employees. Approximately 72% of all departments utilize psychological evaluation in the hiring process, with nearly 100% of departments serving populations of 25,000 or more doing so (Reaves 2010). Some state regulatory commissions require this type of evaluation as a condition for certification and/or employment of officers throughout the state.

Psychometric examinations, as used here, refer to written instruments used to measure various psychological characteristics such as intelligence, interests/preferences, and personality traits/characteristics. There is a wide variety of such instruments, but the most common to the police selection process include the MMPI (Minnesota Multiphasic Personality Inventory), the CPI (California Personality Inventory), the IPI (Inwald Personality Inventory), the Myers-Briggs Type Indicator, Rorschach Psychodiagnostic Inkblots, Human Figure Drawing, and the Wonderlic Personnel Test. Some departments utilize more than one test and may combine the process with exams that measure reading levels, attitudes, opinions, and ethical values. Some of these tests can be machine scored and interpreted, while others may require interpretation by a trained psychologist/psychiatrist. The most appropriate approach and use of these tests is when the results are normed against police officer samples. That is, individual results are compared to averages found in the police population rather than the general population at large. The Law Enforcement Assessment and Development Report (LEADR) and the Minnesota Personnel Interpretive Report (MPIR) are attempts to do just that (Moriarty and Field 1994, 212–215).

Psychological interviews, where utilized, are conducted by trained psychologists or psychiatrists. Such interviews may be conducted privately or in group sessions. While many of the psychometric tests have specific, more objective scoring schemes, the psychological interview is considered more subjective and interpretive and, of course, is dependent on the specialist's ability and experience. Both techniques attempt to accomplish the same objective: to select a psychologically stable person who is free of psychopathic tendencies (mental illnesses).

However, psychological evaluation is not an exact science; the process usually results in "screening-out" candidates with known or suspected unacceptable traits or "selecting-in" candidates with acceptable or predictable traits believed to make a good police officer.

Physical Ability Test

Historically, the physical ability (or agility) test (PAT) in selection processes often consisted of completing a specific number of sit-ups, push-ups, and/or chin-ups and performing certain events that included climbing, pushing, running, or crawling. Today, because of adverse court decisions and law-related expectations, the physical ability testing has undergone considerable change, so such testing must be related to job tasks and functions performed by police officers. The test now often consists of some type of obstacle course that simulates what an officer may experience in the field, a 150–170 lb "dummy drag," and a combination of running and sprinting. It may also include other routines such as dry-firing a service weapon and/or making a simulated arrest. **Figure 7-4** reports the recommendations of a national conference

---

FIGURE 7-4 Recommended Physical Abilities Test

1. The person taking the test must complete a 1/4 mile course consisting of a series of 20–40 yard runs/sprints interspersed with the events listed below.
2. The course includes a 5–6 foot wall climb, 4 foot horizontal jump (may be done while running), a stair climb (six steps up, six steps down), the drag of a 160–170 pound dummy for 50 feet, and another run/sprint in different directions. No specific order or frequency of events was established, but all events should appear at least once.
3. At the conclusion of the course, the applicant must dry fire the service weapon five times with both strong and weak hands.

> **NOTE:** The addition of a 1.5 mile run may be legally defensible for agencies that can demonstrate extended endurance is a needed physical ability that is job-related and consistent with business necessity.

The passing time for completion of this test is to be determined by each agency based on the levels of performance required of its employees. The passing times should not be age or gender adjusted.

Since all physical abilities needed to perform as a law enforcement officer are not tested in this recommended task test, a department may choose to separately test such areas as vision, speech, hearing, reading, writing, manual dexterity, flexibility, sitting, standing, reflexes, and weight/body composition.

Source: Major City Chiefs Association, et.al., (1993), *Physical Fitness Testing in Law Enforcement: An Analysis of the Impact of the Americans with Disabilities Act, The Civil Rights Act of 1991, and the Age Discrimination in Employment Act, A Conference Report, pp. i-ii, 1993, Federal Bureau of Investigation.*

held on the matter of physical fitness testing in law enforcement by the Major City Chiefs Association, the National Executive Institute Associates, and the Federal Bureau of Investigation (Major City Chiefs Association 1993). For up-to-date, specific information, any search of the Web using "physical abilities test" and the name of a law enforcement agency should yield information about a particular agency's requirements.

However, there is still great controversy over physical fitness standards because of the Americans with Disabilities Act (ADA) and the Civil Rights Act of 1991. Litigation continues on these matters and the Supreme Court has yet to rule definitively on physical fitness standards. The issues appear to be whether an agency should establish validated *job-related standards* or *fitness standards*. If they establish job-related standards, the standards must be the same for all ages and for both men and women, but if the agency establishes *fitness standards*, they may be gender-and age-based. The New Hampshire legislature in 1998 enacted statutory law that, effective January 1, 2001, required every full-time police, state, corrections, and probation/parole officer hired by a state, county, or local law enforcement agency in the state to pass the same medical exam and physical fitness test that the state training council prescribed for new recruits, on an ongoing basis at three-year intervals throughout their careers, as a condition of maintaining their police certification. The tests are based on the Cooper Aerobics standards at the 35th percentile for the applicant's age and sex to enter the academy and the 50th percentile as an exit standard (Sweeney 1999). The State of Ohio instituted an exit standard at the 50th percentile for peace officer academy cadets in 2002. Other states have academy exit standards, but the percentile scores for successful completion can vary.

Police academy cadets

Source: Courtesy of the California Department of Corrections and Rehabilitation

Drug Testing

Employers have the right to prohibit all employees from using or being under the influence of alcohol or illegal drugs at the workplace. Of the 72 major law enforcement agencies surveyed by Strawbridge in 1990, 55 (76%) conducted drug tests as part of the selection process (Strawbridge 1990), while another estimate suggests that 95% of departments serving 25,000 or more residents use drug testing as a standard screening method (Reaves 2010). Because law enforcement agencies have the responsibility of enforcing the country's drug laws and because of possible impairment while under the influence of drugs (which constitutes a safety hazard to others), police agencies are justified in conducting such exams. The major precaution that must be taken is to grant appeals and second tests to those who test positive for drug use when they claim the test is inaccurate and has unfairly disqualified them from employment consideration.

Medical Examination

Medical fitness for police officer candidates is an obvious expectation on the part of an employer. The hiring of an unfit/unhealthy candidate could cost the employer (and taxpayer) large sums of money should the person have to retire early on disability or another abnormality that renders them unfit for duty. The focus of concern here is the detection of respiratory, circulatory, or skeletal conditions that are early signs of existing or degenerative diseases or conditions that would interfere with the performance of required tasks and functions. During the late 1980s, some departments began not hiring persons who smoked because of the likelihood of developing respiratory and circulatory diseases (which are covered under some retirement systems). Some agencies still have such restrictions in their hiring process; however, since 1989, at least 29 states and the District of Columbia have enacted legislation prohibiting employers from requiring, as a condition of employment, that employees or prospective employees abstain from the use of tobacco products outside the course of employment (Bureau of National Affairs 1993). In 2003, an officer in Fall River, Massachusetts became the third public safety officer in the state in 10 years to lose his job because of smoking, as a state statute prohibits public

safety workers hired after January 1, 1988 from smoking either on or off duty (*Law Enforcement News* 2003). Virginia Beach (VA) public safety officers also are prohibited from using tobacco products either on or off duty as a condition of employment (City of Virginia Beach 2011). The 2010 civil service announcement for the City of New Britain, Connecticut (population 70,000) states that the "Applicant must submit a 'No-Smoking affidavit' at time of Oral Interview and, if hired, at time of appointment. Police officers are required to maintain no-smoking status as a condition of continued employment" (City of New Britain 2010). Today, departments that emphasize greater health consciousness or physical health maintenance in their personnel processes have the added benefit of reducing or slowing the rising cost of their health insurance premiums.

Hiring

In every jurisdiction there is an **appointing authority** that, according to law, officially hires every successful applicant. The title of the appointing authority may vary according to the type of jurisdiction; it may be the mayor of a city, the sheriff of a county, a board of supervisors or trustees of a township, the department head of a state agency, a personnel official, or some other official granted such authority. It often is believed that the administrative head of the law enforcement agency (the chief, superintendent, commissioner, etc.) is the one who appoints new candidates; however, it is more accurate to say that the chief administrator "recommends" the candidates to the appointing authority.

The hiring process may also involve a central personnel office of a jurisdiction. This office is usually separate from any personnel unit found in the law enforcement agency. For example, some jurisdictions are covered under **civil service** law or regulations. These vary from state to state, so general statements are difficult, but where civil service law exists, strict adherence to the regulations is required. The regulations may relate to written examinations, medical exams, residency, citizenship, bonus points, eligibility lists, appeals, grievances, promotions, layoffs, dismissals, and so on.

A civil service or central personnel agency may actually conduct the initial phases of the selection process and develop a list of qualified candidates; this is known as an **eligibility list** in some jurisdictions. It is from this list of qualified candidates that the law enforcement agency must select its employees. Certain requirements of the law may also apply in considering candidates from such a list. For example, in Ohio, statutory civil service law prior to 1995 required consideration of the top three candidates on a ranked eligibility list for every open entry-level position. This is known in personnel practices as the **rule of three**, which allows the appointing (and recommending) authority some discretion in hiring. In 1995, the statutory law was modified to allow the rule of 10, so now the top 10 candidates can be considered for the open position.

The ranking of candidates on the eligibility list is based on the raw score of written examinations or assessment procedures and any **bonus points** awarded for certain factors or job-related criteria, such as previous police experience, state peace officer certification, college education, military experience (veteran status), and residency.

Utilizing **assessment centers** or an assessment center approach is also becoming a popular choice as a selection method for law enforcement:

> First, *police* administrators must realize the difference between an assessment center and an assessment center approach. An assessment center is a place where a series of events or exercises will occur; however, the assessment center approach is a method that supplements the traditional assessment and *selection procedures* with situational exercises designed to simulate actual *police officer* responsibilities and working conditions. (Decicco 2000, 5)

Approximately 35% of police agencies use the assessment center approach in some form (Decicco 2000). In general, a candidate testing for a department using an assessment center approach could expect to take the police officer exam, and if he/she was one of the top-scoring individuals, would next report for the assessment test, which usually takes place during a day-long session. The assessment testing would be based on policing dimensions such as "a candidate's ability to deal with the public, maintain emotional stability in stressful situations, work in teams, communicate adequately, and demonstrate the proper use of force" (Decicco 2000, 5). The goal in the assessment center approach is to develop a comprehensive process that tests for specific skills thought to be needed in police work.

Any person interested in employment with a particular agency is encouraged to inquire about the details of its selection process. One needs to develop a full understanding of the process in order to know what to expect and to appreciate its complexity. Some agencies are bound by very rigid civil service or merit system procedures, while others offer continuous hiring opportunities.

Academy Training

Once appointed to a law enforcement position, some form of academy training is normally required (unless the person has been a practicing police officer elsewhere, in which case minimal refresher or indoctrination training may be all that is necessary). We will discuss this process

Instructor with cadets—physical training

Source: © JHB Photography / Alamy Images

later in this chapter. The basic training of a new recruit may take from 6 to 36 weeks, and could extend up to a year or more if field training is counted. In medium-sized and larger departments, newly-hired persons are paid a regular salary during the basic training period; in smaller departments, officers may have to attend classes on their own time and at their own cost before being considered for the job.

Probationary Period

At the time candidates are hired, they are placed on **probationary status**, which means that their employment is conditional. Not only must their performance meet acceptable standards, their attitudes toward others, willingness to follow orders, ability to be a team player, and so on are also under evaluation. Probationary periods vary in length, with the norm being between 6 and 24 months; one year is the average length of probation. During the probationary period in most jurisdictions, the new officer may be dismissed without cause or a reason being given. The rights and limitations of probationers are usually controlled by law and department policy. In some agencies, probationers receive lower rates of pay, are not permitted to patrol solo, may not be allowed to join an officer's union, and have limited appeal rights if dismissed.

Permanent Employee Status

Once a candidate has successfully passed through the probationary phase of employment, the officer then achieves **permanent employee status**, which brings with it additional rights and privileges. This status often includes a pay raise; the right to join a union, officer's association, or credit union; additional grievance and appeal rights; and the inclusion of selected personnel benefits such as educational benefits, leave, and certain types of insurance. Once officers reach this phase, the selection process has been completed.

THE LAW AND PERSONNEL PRACTICES

Chapter 3 described the evolution of policing in the United States in broad terms and generalities. It was mentioned that in the early years of policing, particularly in municipalities, the selection of officers and other personnel practices were highly political. Following the passage of

the Pendleton Act in 1883, the concepts and procedures of civil service (or merit system) were introduced and adopted in many states throughout the country. Civil service and other personnel-related statutes became the guiding influence upon personnel practices until the 1970s. However, events occurred in the 1960s that set the stage for a decade that would see great challenges to the personnel practices of agencies at all levels across the United States.

The Civil Rights Legislation of 1964 and 1972

Although two other major civil rights acts had been enacted by Congress in the 1800s (the Civil Rights Acts of 1866 and 1871), neither had focused its attention specifically on the employment process. In 1964, Congress enacted the **Civil Rights Act of 1964** because of its concern over the reported and documented racial discrimination in employment throughout the country. Specifically, Title VII of the act stated, in part:

> It shall be an unlawful employment practice for an employer... to fail or refuse to hire or to discharge any individual, or otherwise to discriminate against any individual with respect to his compensation, terms, conditions, or privileges of employment, because of such individual's race, color, religion, sex, or national origin... (Public Law 92-261, Section 703).

The concept of **protected classes** can be used to describe one of the outcomes of this legislation. Persons who are discriminated against in employment because of their race, color, religion, sex, or national origin are "protected" by law and may have a right to sue that employer. (The list of who is protected has been extended to other "classes" of persons by other federal and state statutes and now includes military veterans, persons over age 40, the handicapped, the disabled, pregnant women, and, in some jurisdictions, homosexuals.) One method that is used to determine violations of Title VII is whether the practice in question has an **adverse impact** (also called disparate impact) on a protected class. A procedure or qualification that appears neutral on its face can actually impact negatively one group more than another. For example, a height requirement of 5'9" may appear reasonable, but it excludes about 95% of the females in the United States;

therefore, it has an adverse impact on women. Unless the requirement can be substantiated as being required to do the job (job relatedness), the requirement is discriminatory. Another problem dealing with job requirements and descriptions becomes apparent when examining the American Disabilities Act (ADA) and the Fair Labor Standards Act (FLSA). For example, a common practice in many departments is to assign light duty to officers who acquire permanent health conditions, which preclude them from performing previously held positions within the department. Risher (2003) uses the hypothetical example of "Sergeant Smith," who suffered a major heart attack and was granted a light duty assignment—answering calls at the switchboard—to illustrate this point. Given that Sergeant Smith no longer fulfills his supervisory job description at the switchboard, he is no longer exempt from the FLSA (which poses issues with payroll). In addition, given that the switchboard position does not require a person to be able to withstand the physical requirements necessary to perform the duties of a police officer, the hypothetical Jones who applies for Smith's job after his retirement, and who is denied employment based on his disability, may file suit for violating the ADA. The most common method used to allege adverse impact is statistical comparison of hiring rates, promotion rates, and passing rates of protected classes to majority rates (Sauls 1991).

The Civil Rights Act of 1964 also created the **Equal Employment Opportunity Commission (EEOC)**, which is authorized to enforce the legislation and to develop guidelines for its implementation. The 1964 Act did not apply to public employers and, therefore, had no immediate impact on their practices. However, some agencies did begin a review of their personnel practices to address possible discrimination.

In 1971, the landmark case of ***Griggs v. Duke Power Company*** (401 U.S. 424) was decided by the U.S. Supreme Court. It was the first interpretation of the Civil Rights Act of 1964 by the court, and as such its decision became precedent and guiding. The court said that "good intent or absence of discriminatory intent does not redeem employment procedures or testing mechanisms that operate as 'built-in headwinds' for minority groups and are unrelated to measuring job capability" (Griggs 1971, 432). The court ruled that Griggs and other employees had been

Martin Luther King in Civil Rights March on Washington, D.C., August 28, 1963.

Source: http://www.archives.gov/exhibits/documented-rights/exhibit/section4/detail/mlk.html

discriminated against because the requirements imposed for promotional opportunities (a high school diploma and passing a standard intelligence test) were not adequate measures to determine suitability for the job. The court concluded: "If an employment practice which operates to exclude Negroes [a protected class] cannot be shown to be related to job performance, the practice is forbidden" (Griggs 1971, 431). The court's decision in *Griggs* essentially established that job qualifications and selection devices must be related to job performance criteria, and that artificial, arbitrary, and unnecessary barriers to employment be removed.

Congress amended the Civil Rights Act of 1964 with the Equal Employment Opportunity (EEO) Act of 1972, which extended the provisions of the 1964 law to public employers with 25 or more employees. The EEO Act also granted authority to the EEOC to sue public agencies when necessary to redress the effects of discrimination in employment. Following the passage of this act, public agencies (especially police and fire departments) were sued by members of protected classes, often because their selection processes were inadequate and sometimes indefensible.

The essence of Title VII, as amended (along with other anti-discrimination policies in employment law), is that employers must determine what job skills, knowledge, and abilities (SKAs) are required for proper performance in a particular position. Determining these SKAs is usually done through a **job analysis** (or task analysis) of the position in question (police officer, supervisor, commander, etc.). The results of the job analysis then are used to develop the criteria that will be used for selection, promotion, transfer, and other personnel actions. The details of conducting job analysis are beyond the scope of this text; however, the intent of it is to determine such things as minimum qualifications for employment, the necessary content for training curriculums, and required criteria for promotion and/or transfer. However, one can observe the outcome of job analysis in the job description and listing of qualifications for an announced opening.

Other Legislative Mandates

Besides the Civil Rights Act of 1964 and the Equal Employment Opportunity Act of 1972, several other pieces of federal legislation have been enacted that impact the personnel practices of law enforcement agencies. The following is a selected listing, with only a brief description of each as to the personnel practices affected.

- Equal Pay Act of 1963—Made applicable to public agencies by 1974 amendments, it provides equal pay for equal positions regardless of one's gender. Bona fide seniority plans are exempt from the act.
- Age Discrimination in Employment Act of 1967—amended in 1974 to apply to the public sector, it protects persons over the age of 40 from discrimination based on age.
- Civil Rights Act of 1968—Provides criminal penalties for interfering with any person applying for or enjoying employment or related privileges, or interfering with a person's use of hiring halls, labor organizations, or employment agencies.

- Rehabilitation Act of 1973—Protects individuals from discrimination based on mental or physical disabilities (originally referred to as "handicapped"). State and local governments are impacted if receiving federal assistance.
- Americans with Disabilities Act of 1990—This legislation modified and extended aspects of the Rehabilitation Act of 1973 and applies to all public employers with 15 or more employees. It states that agencies cannot discriminate against otherwise qualified individuals with a disability.
- Civil Rights Act of 1991—Reestablished and reaffirmed some of the provisions and judicial interpretation of earlier legislation. It also prohibits punitive damages in lawsuits against public agencies.

Other state and local legislation in addition to those listed above may impact the personnel practices of law enforcement agencies. The total picture adds up to a very legalistic quagmire with which police administrators must cope every day.

Remedies, Affirmative Action, and Reverse Discrimination

One segment of the law is referred to as **remedies**, and it is usually defined in terms of making a person who has been wronged "whole again." In grievances and lawsuits regarding personnel practices, the following remedies are commonly sought through the legal system:

Injunction: A court order prohibiting certain actions by an agency or person.

Writ of Mandamus: A petition to a court seeking an order that compels certain actions by an agency or person (orders that it be done).

Back Pay: If a complaint is found to be justified, the court could order back pay (the amount that would have been earned) to the injured party.

Back Seniority: The injured party can receive seniority from the time of the original action that injured him or her.

Attorney Fees: The injured party is awarded monetary fees to cover the expense of the litigation against the party that wronged him or her.

Quotas: The setting of fixed ratios of protected group members to receive preference in certain personnel functions. For example, this may lead to an agency hiring two minority members for every majority member hired or the hiring of one woman for every two males hired.

Goals/Time Tables: Unlike quotas, this is the setting of a percentage or numerical targets to be achieved within certain time limits. It does not require the specific ratios of quotas.

Any one or a combination of these remedies may be ordered by the court or agreed to by the parties to a lawsuit. An out-of-court agreement is called a **consent decree**, and it often includes conditions (such as quotas or revisions of personnel policies and practices) that cause hardships or morale problems for law enforcement agencies. Of course, it can also modernize personnel practices and sometimes bring needed resources to the personnel function of an agency or jurisdiction.

One concept that has become broadly debated is that of **affirmative action**. The concept itself refers to taking a more aggressive position at recruiting and hiring protected classes that are underrepresented in an agency's workforce, though it is sometimes interpreted by many to mean that members of protected classes are given preference in personnel actions. This belief occasionally leads to allegations of **reverse discrimination** by majority members. It is these allegations and beliefs that cause tension and frustration among many officers already employed and many of those who apply for positions and are not hired. The concept of affirmative action is not illegal; however, showing preference during hiring and other personnel practices is. Consider the words of the U.S. Supreme Court:

> In short, the Act does not command that any person be hired simply because he was formerly the subject of discrimination, or because he is a member of a minority group. Discriminatory preference for any group, minority or majority, is precisely and only what Congress has proscribed (Griggs 1971, 430–431).

The Court was referring to Section 703 (j) of the Civil Rights Act of 1964, which reads:

> Nothing contained in this title shall be interpreted to require any employer… subject to this title to grant preferential treatment to any individual or to any group because of the race, color, religion, sex, or national origin of such individual or group on account of an imbalance which may exist with respect to the total number or percentage of persons of any race, color, religion, sex, or national origin employed by any employer… in comparison with the total number or percentage of [such] persons… in any community, state, section, or other area, or in the available work force.

In 2003, the U.S. Supreme Court reviewed two cases involving affirmative action in admissions policies of the University of Michigan. In *Grutter v. Bollinger*, 539 U.S. 306 (2003), the admissions process of the law school of the University of Michigan was upheld because it used race in admissions decisions in a narrowly tailored way; the university was attempting "to further a compelling interest in obtaining the educational benefits that flow from a diverse student body." The court stated that such a policy is not prohibited by the Equal Protection Clause, Title VI, or §1981 (USC). In the second University of Michigan case, *Gratz v. Bollinger*, 539 U.S. 244 (2003), the court ruled that the university's current policy, which automatically distributed 20 points to every "underrepresented minority" applicant solely because of race, was not narrowly tailored to achieve educational diversity, and therefore, violated the Equal Protection Clause, Title VI, and §1981. In short, the court ruled that the concept of affirmative action does not violate the Constitution and discrimination statutes, but race can be considered only when narrowly tailored to achieve diversity.

Other court decisions over the years indicate that anti-discrimination laws apply to all persons, not just minorities. The significance of all this is that agencies must have justifications for their personnel qualifications and practices. They cannot do things simply out of tradition or by intuition and whim. If challenged, they may have to justify their actions to a court or to an investigative agency. In recent years some jurisdictions (most notably California's adoption of Proposition 209) have rescinded or modified state affirmative action statutes that permitted preferential treatment of protected groups. The U.S. Supreme Court refused on November 3, 1997 to interfere with the enforcement of the 1996 ballot initiative prohibiting preferential treatment (Savage 1997). The California Supreme Court ruled in August 2010 that Proposition 209 was proper and valid, and that "the government is not required to allow racial preferences" (Egelko 2010).

Bona Fide Occupational Qualification

The personnel laws enacted to date allow for some discrimination if based on a **bona fide occupational qualification (BFOQ)**. This is a form of "legal discrimination" in that it allows the establishment of certain criteria if they are shown to be necessary for the operation of the business (or agency). There are limitations that restrict BFOQs to religion, sex, or national origin, meaning that they cannot discriminate on the basis of race or color. In 1985, the city of Dallas, Texas successfully defended its college education requirement (45 hours of credit) for police officers by using a BFOQ-based justification (see *Davis v. City of Dallas*, 777 F.2d 205, 1985). Appeal of the case to the U.S. Supreme Court was denied, thus allowing the appellate decision supporting the requirement to stand. The Appellate Court found that the characteristics of professionalism, unusual degree of risk, and unique public responsibility were part of the position of police officer and were not capable of specific identification and quantification (see Carter et al. 1988).

The Recruitment and Retention of Women in Law Enforcement

There are several complex and hotly debated issues when examining women in law enforcement. Lonsway et al. (2002) paint a rather discouraging picture of women's representation in law enforcement:

> In 2001, women accounted for only 12.7% of all sworn law enforcement positions in large agencies (with 100 or more sworn personnel)—a figure that is less than 4% higher than in 1990, when women comprised 9% of sworn officers. In small and rural agencies (fewer than 100 sworn personnel),

women comprise an even smaller percentage (8.1%) of all sworn personnel. When these figures are combined in a weighted estimate, they indicate that women represent only 11.2% of all sworn law enforcement personnel in the United States—dramatically less than the participation of women in the whole of the labor force at 46.5% (2002, 2).

However, while Lonsway et al. observed declining numbers of women in law enforcement in 2000 and 2001, it appears that this grim picture of female representation in policing may be getting a little better, as data suggest women in local law enforcement increased from 11.3% in 2003 to 11.9% in 2007 (Reaves 2010). Why is there such a dramatic underrepresentation of women in law enforcement?

Chief Cathy L. Lanier assumed the leadership position as Chief of Metropolitan Police Department on January 2, 2007; Confirmed by D.C. Council on April 3, 2007

Source: Courtesy of Chief Cathy L. Lanier

Lonsway et al. (2002) argue that, "Despite overwhelming evidence that women and men are equally capable of police work, widespread bias in police hiring, selection practices, and recruitment policies keeps the numbers of women in law enforcement artificially low" (2).

Consent decrees beginning in the 1970s mandated many agencies to hire and promote qualified female applicants. While in place, these decrees have been highly successful in increasing the percentage of female representation in police departments; for example, prior to an imposed court order (from 1975 to 1991), only 1% of Pittsburgh's Police Department was female, but by 1990, female representation on the force was at 27.2% (Lonsway et al. 2003a). However, once these decrees are lifted, the recruitment and retention of female officers can drop dramatically. In 2001, Pittsburgh's Police Department reported that only 22% of their officers were female, and the percentage of women hired dropped from the mandated 50% to 8.5% shortly after the decree expired (Lonsway et al. 2003a). Unfortunately, the Pittsburgh Police Department is not alone in this trend.

Physical entrance exams may also be an impediment to female entry into the field of policing. A recent study funded by the National Center for Women and Policing found that agencies that did not employ physical agility testing employed 45% more sworn female officers than those agencies that did utilize them (Lonsway et al. 2003b). Lonsway and her colleagues suggested possible alternatives for physical agility testing that include no physical testing, health-based screening, job simulation tests, and post-academy training.

Future research into this area is greatly needed. In today's society, such a low representation of women in law enforcement is unacceptable and undesirable. Research suggests that women make excellent police officers and bring with them invaluable skills. Seklecki and Paynich (2004) found that:

> When looking at the dispersion of the data, it appears that for the categories of responding to calls for service, interviewing witnesses and victims, writing reports, investigating crime scenes, gathering evidence, and dispute resolution, a significant percentage (at least 30%) felt that they performed these duties better in

quality than their male counterparts. In fact, 61.8% of female officers felt that they wrote better or far better reports than male officers (28).

Additionally, research suggests that the majority of female police officers love their jobs, feel they are making a difference in the community, and do not intend on leaving their career in law enforcement (Seklecki and Paynich 2007). Therefore, it is important that attention is focused on the recruitment and retention of women in policing.

TRAINING CONCEPTS AND PHILOSOPHY

The thought of putting untrained people in uniform and expecting them to enforce the law is a foreign concept by modern standards. However, some of today's police officers experienced just that when they entered the field of law enforcement! A survey of 4000 police departments, conducted by the International Association of Chiefs of Police in 1956, found that 85% of all officers received no pre-service training (President's Commission 1967, 138). For most of America's history, police officers learned their duties and acquired necessary skills through **on-the-job training (OJT)**. On-the-job training included the lessons taught by co-workers and supervisors and allowed officers to obtain experience through performing the daily tasks of the job. While some of these lessons were formal, most were informal and guided by the individual experience and attitude of the "teacher." Another term used to describe this early form of OJT was "apprenticeship," which is a term commonly used in the trade and vocational fields. Today, a true apprenticeship program would be more structured and formal than what OJT actually was.

Today, it is readily apparent that the tasks and responsibilities of law enforcement officials are so complex and burdened with liability that the need for training is uncontested. However, even though there is unilateral agreement on the need for training, there is little consensus about the amount, type, and format of training that is necessary for the modern officer. A reflection of this lack of consensus is the great diversity in the level and quality of police training across the country. Access to resources is also important. Some academies have access to and utilize the latest technology available, such as interactive computer-assisted learning and virtual reality scenarios, while others are relegated to primarily the lecture and drill format, with little or no integration of technology into the classrooms.

As a concept and philosophy, "training" can mean different things to different people. Some hear the term and immediately think of formal physical exercise and skill development similar to basic military training. Others think of it as a combination of classroom and field-based learning in preparation for a job, while still others perceive it as extensive college preparation followed by an internship and residency, as in medical training. Many discussions of training simply presume that students in criminal justice understand what happens at the police academy and have a common understanding of training concepts.

At the outset of this section, permit us to state our philosophical position on a number of concepts. We define **education** as what one has learned. **Learning** can be defined as a process that changes a person's behavior or attitude, and it specifically refers to changes that are determined primarily by the individual's interaction with his or her environment (Eson 1972, 58). A person's education is

achieved by various means: socialization, experience, academics, training, and so on; it is not limited to the classroom or formal setting. Some in the criminal justice field have insisted on making a distinction between "training" and "education," essentially stating that training inculcates the *how* to do something, while education focuses on the *why*. Traditionalists argue that training emphasizes skill and ability development while education emphasizes concepts, theory, and critical thinking. Such simple distinctions are unfortunate because as Saunders (1970, 115) stated, "the best of each will always contain elements of the other." In lieu of distinctions between the concepts, we believe it is more relevant to focus on matters of process and outcomes. The common link between education and training is the process of teaching or instruction, which includes a broad range of activities (Conser 1981, 42, 64). In this perspective, both training and education are considered outcomes, and the "teaching–instruction" process becomes the critical focal point. Various instructional methods can then be utilized to structure the desired outcome. The relationship of these outcomes to the learning process is illustrated in **Figure 7-5**.

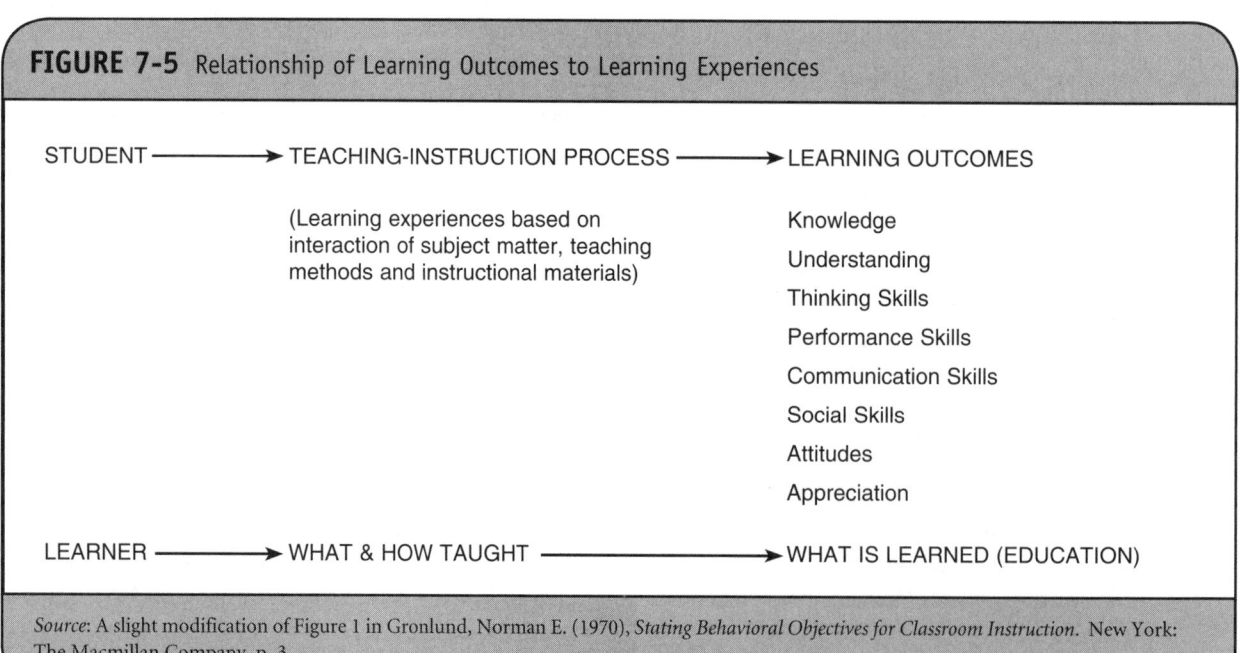

FIGURE 7-5 Relationship of Learning Outcomes to Learning Experiences

STUDENT ───────▶ TEACHING-INSTRUCTION PROCESS ───────▶ LEARNING OUTCOMES

(Learning experiences based on interaction of subject matter, teaching methods and instructional materials)

Knowledge

Understanding

Thinking Skills

Performance Skills

Communication Skills

Social Skills

Attitudes

Appreciation

LEARNER ───────▶ WHAT & HOW TAUGHT ───────────────▶ WHAT IS LEARNED (EDUCATION)

Source: A slight modification of Figure 1 in Gronlund, Norman E. (1970), *Stating Behavioral Objectives for Classroom Instruction.* New York: The Macmillan Company, p. 3.

Major Purposes of Training

Police training serves a number of organizational purposes. First, it orients the person to his or her new job or position. Second, it indoctrinates the person to identify with the organization and believe in its goals and objectives. Third, it transfers the skills and knowledge necessary to do the job. Fourth, it standardizes procedures and increases efficiency. Fifth, it builds confidence in the person since critical tasks can be practiced and mastered in learning situations. Sixth, it improves safety and helps assure survival. Finally, it yields other benefits such as morale and discipline.

It is important to appreciate the complexity of these purposes of training. Often, to a new recruit, it seems that one attends the academy to "learn how to do the job." However, the purposes identified above go beyond that simple notion. Recruits must understand the various objectives of the training experience; otherwise, their focus may be very narrow in terms of what is expected of them. They may miss the "bigger picture" of the learning process.

It also can be argued that training is the foundation for the interrelationship (linking together) of conduct, ethics, and discipline, which is graphically illustrated in **Figure 7-6**.

These concepts should be presented in a very positive fashion. For example, people often think of discipline as a negative process, when the root of the word comes from the Latin and Greek concepts for training and instruction.

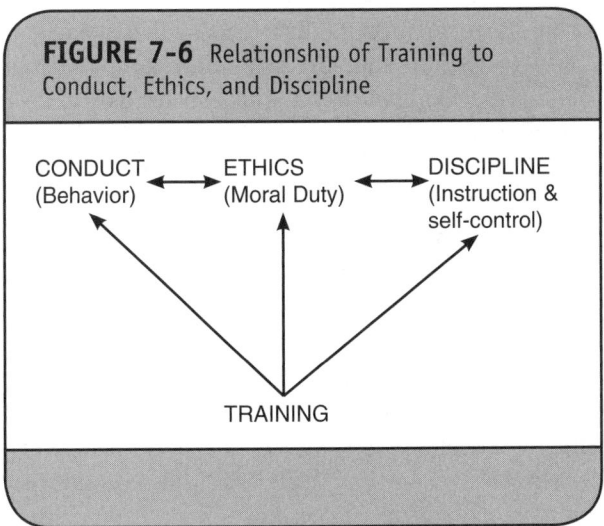

FIGURE 7-6 Relationship of Training to Conduct, Ethics, and Discipline

CONDUCT (Behavior) — ETHICS (Moral Duty) — DISCIPLINE (Instruction & self-control)

TRAINING

We need to think of the term in relation to a "well disciplined" group of officers (or a self-disciplined individual), referring to those who are well trained, know how to conduct themselves properly, and perform well in critical situations. Training provides the standards by which conduct is measured and judged acceptable. Related to the concepts of conduct and discipline are issues of ethics, morality, societal values, democratic values, and the public interest. These must be discussed and presented in a training context because they are related to the standards just mentioned. The point being made here is that there are very complex relationships that exist between these concepts—relationships that are missed or not properly specified when training and education are presented as two distinct processes.

Learning Domains and Styles

There are three generally accepted levels of learning, called the **learning domains** (Bloom, 1956):

Cognitive—refers to acquiring new knowledge, understanding, and thinking skills. Learning in this domain includes remembering the definitions of crimes, translating legal terms so that others can understand them, and evaluating a given situation when given certain facts and making a decision based on those facts and your knowledge of the law. It also would include knowing which methods and techniques to employ in a given situation, such as writing reports or sketching a crime scene.

Psychomotor—relates to motor skills and the ability to physically perform a specific behavior. Simple tasks such as learning to walk or ride a bike are examples; policing examples include properly firing a weapon, conducting a crime scene search, dusting for fingerprints, driving a vehicle at high speeds in a safe manner, and mediating a domestic argument. This domain builds upon the cognitive domain in that one may know theoretically "how" to do something, but may not be able to actually do it. In law enforcement, skills are learned and practiced so that they become almost automatic (performed without much forethought). Some of the more critical skills relate to self-defense, defensive driving, and radio procedure.

It is a general principle of training that during a critical situation, officers revert to the manner in which they learned such skills.

Affective—relates to learning that impacts one's values, emotions, and/or attitudes. In policing it relates to "appreciations" and keeping an open, accepting mind to new knowledge. Persons who are "set in their ways" and are not receptive to new ideas or thinking about things differently are difficult to train. If an officer is to properly benefit from training, he or she must be willing to learn; this is a precondition to learning. Examples of the affective domain include listening attentively, accepting differences in race and culture, demonstrating a belief in democratic principles, accepting responsibility for one's own behavior, maintaining good health habits, displaying safety consciousness, and accepting and practicing ethical standards of the law enforcement profession.

Within each domain are different levels of learning; the higher levels are more difficult and complex. For example, in the cognitive domain, six levels are part of the taxonomy:

1. Knowledge: ability to remember previously learned material.
2. Comprehension: ability to grasp the meaning of words and concepts.
3. Application: ability to use learned material in new situations.
4. Analysis: ability to break down material into its component parts so that its structure can be understood.
5. Synthesis: ability to put parts together to form a new whole.
6. Evaluation: ability to judge the value of material for a given purpose.

Notice that "knowledge" and "comprehension" are the lowest levels of cognitive learning, whereas "synthesis" and "evaluation" are the higher levels. Often academy training (and even some college-level course work) focuses on the lower levels of these domains; not much time is spent on the higher levels. Unfortunately, success on the street and in complex interpersonal situations often requires one to use higher levels of learning in these domains. Learning how to analyze and synthesize the information gathered during incidents and interpersonal contacts is very important in today's society, especially in multicultural and ethnically diverse population centers, which pose new experiences for officers who have different backgrounds.

Another challenge to instructors is determining the learning styles of students. This refers to how one learns or acquires new information and processes it internally. Each person has their own set of ways by which he or she learns best. Some people learn quite well from lectures, some by visually seeing the material in the form of charts and graphs; others learn from actively doing things. There are several categorizations of learning styles and the terminology varies among them. Some of the common categories include (a) visual, (b) auditory, (c) tactile (small motor movements), and (d) kinesthetic (large motor movements) (Xavier University 2004). Each of us has a preferred learning style. For example, a law enforcement trainee may prefer to visualize the activities carried out on patrol rather than just read about them, or she may prefer to actually walk through the activities in order to learn and associate the duties, procedures, and techniques that are being taught. There are several excellent Web sites that discuss learning styles and some offer a free learning style test or inventory; they are provided in the chapter specific internet links.

The significance of understanding learning styles is to develop training and education methods that ensure the person learns the material that is being presented. This is one reason why educators and trainers today attempt to incorporate multiple learning style materials into their presentations.

Methods of Instruction

There are a number of acceptable methods of instruction used in law enforcement training of all types and levels. **Figure 7-7** identifies these methods according to those being taught: a group or an individual.

Of course, this listing of methods does not tell the whole story. We all know that lectures, for example, can be either boring or interesting depending on the instructor's delivery, the content, and the learner's interest. Likewise, computer-aided instruction can be a simple computerized

> **FIGURE 7-7** Methods of Instruction
>
> | For Groups | For Individuals |
> | --- | --- |
> | Lectures | Inquiry |
> | Field Experience | Field Experience/Practice |
> | Field Observation | Field Observation |
> | Case Studies | Case Studies |
> | Field Trips | Field Trips |
> | Demonstrations | Demonstrations |
> | Interviews | Interviews |
> | Role-Playing | Supervised Study |
> | Seminars | Reading Clubs |
> | Conferences | Job Rotation |
> | Discussions | Correspondence Courses |
> | Debates | Computer-Based Instruction |
> | Distance Learning | Distance Learning |
>
> *Source*: Data from A.Z. Gammage, *Police Training in the United States*, p. 206, © 1963, Charles C. Thomas Publishers, Ltd.; and Project STAR, *Police Officer Role Training Program*, p. 75, 1974, National Institute of Justice; with current techniques added.

quiz or tutorial program, or it can consist of multimedia presentations, interactive decision-making, Internet-based assignments, and/or virtual reality scenarios. The method of instruction alone does not ensure successful learning of course objectives. The methods listed in Figure 7-7 are not mutually exclusive and some may involve aspects of others mentioned.

Officers must apply learned concepts to field situations. They must analyze behavior and motives of subjects in evaluating truthfulness of statements. They must gather bits and pieces of information and synthesize them for meaning and development of inferences, probable cause, or other conclusions.

TYPES OF TRAINING

In law enforcement, there are many different forms or types of training. The average person watching TV shows depicting police or their favorite *Police Academy* movie usually is exposed to only one type: the training of recruits. However, training is an on-going process in an officer's career. Laws change: new ones are added, the Supreme Court may modify existing police procedure that does not conform to constitutional standards, and better ways of accomplishing tasks (most often through new technology) are developed—all require that new information be conveyed to current officers.

Let us review some fundamental descriptions of the various types of training. It must first be mentioned that there is no single accepted authority that has defined these different types of training, nor is there consensus on the terminology used to differentiate one type from another. For example, what is "in-service" training in one agency could be "advanced" training in another.

Mandatory/Basic/Recruit/Entry-Level Training

The universal training of recruits is a recent development in the United States. Although police academies date back to the early 1900s (see **Figure 7-8**), it was not until the late 1950s and 1960s that most states adopted **mandatory minimum training standards**. In 1959, California and New York established their commissions on Peace Officer Standards and Training (POST) for the purpose of establishing minimum training and selection criteria, and all but two states now have an office that has legislative authority to establish state minimum standards for law enforcement personnel (Flink 1997, 1). Generally, these offices oversee the certification and/or licensing of peace officers. Although many of these commissions are referred to as POSTs, they may have different agency titles, such as "council" or "board," and they may or may not have the terms "peace officer" and "standards" in their title. For example, in Alaska the agency is known as the Alaska Police Standards Council; in Indiana, it is called the Indiana Law Enforcement Training Board; and in Florida it is the Florida Department of Law Enforcement. Provisions vary from state to state; however, the International Association of Directors of Law Enforcement Standards and Training (IADLEST) has published a "Model Minimum State Standards," which provides recommendations for law enforcement agencies on various issues related to training and recruitment.

FIGURE 7-8 Police Academy Training and College Program Time Line

1895—New York City establishes its School of Pistol practice.

1908—First formal training school established in Berkeley, California by Marshal August Vollmer (initially the program was for in-service training).

1909—New York City instituted its police academy (for in-service and recruits).

1911—City of Detroit's first police training school started.

1916—First university-level police training school created at the University of California at Berkeley.

1918—The first school for policewomen was presented at the University of California at Los Angeles.

1919—Louisville, Kentucky Police School organized.

1924–28—University of Southern California sponsored a series of lectures of LAPD command officers that eventually leads to a full police curriculum in the Department of Public Administration.

1930—San Jose State College initiated its police science program. Students could earn an associate in arts degree and then a bachelor's degree.

1933—The nation's first baccalaureate degree in criminology was approved at the University of California at Berkeley.

1935—The FBI Police Training School, renamed The National Academy, began offering its special course work for state and local officers.

1935—Michigan State College initiated its baccalaureate program and optional 5-year police program.

1936—The Traffic Institute at Northwestern University (Evanston, Illinois) began operation.

1946—The Delinquency Control Institute was established at the University of Southern California.

1951—The Southern Police Institute at the University of Louisville began operation.

1959—The states of New York and California both set up their state minimum standards boards, the Municipal Police Training Council and the Commission on Peace Officer Standards and Training, respectively.

1963—49 two-year institutions in the United States were identified.

1968—The passage of the Omnibus Crime Control and Safe Streets Act authorized the funding of new academic and training programs.

1974—The University of Louisville opened the National Crime Prevention Institute.

Source: Adapted with permission from A.Z. Gammage, *Police Training in the United States*, © 1963, Charles C. Thomas Publishers, Ltd.; and G.D. Eastman, and J.A. McCain, "Education, Professionalism, and Law Enforcement in Historical Perspective," *Journal of Police Science and Administration*, Vol. 9, No. 2, pp. 119-130, © 1981, International Association of Chiefs of Police.

(The URL for this document can be found in the chapter specific internet links section of this chapter.)

The training hours for new recruits also vary from jurisdiction to jurisdiction. The state mandatory minimum hours of training is exactly that—a minimum (see Appendix IV at the end of this text for examples of minimum hours of training for the states of New York, California, and Florida). Many training academies exceed the state minimums, especially academies that service large municipalities and state agencies. Recent data illustrate the variation in the number of "classroom" hours required in selected jurisdictions in the United States (Reaves and Hickman 2004).

According to the 2007 Law Enforcement Management and Administrative Statistics survey (Reaves 2010), the median number of training hours for municipal police was 922, while another study of state and local law enforcement training (Reaves 2009) found requirements to be much higher, with the average number of combined classroom and field training hours for municipal officers to be

1458; for sheriff's departments, 1084; and for state agencies, 1324 (2282 for State POST agencies). Occasionally (and today, more frequently), the question of reciprocity between states and/or municipalities arises because of officers moving to other jurisdictions. This is a difficult question to answer (as is exemplified in **Figure 7-9**) because of the various regulations and rules within and among the various states.

The topics addressed in a basic training academy are numerous, in some schools numbering over 100 (especially when all the "sub-topics" are totaled). Instead of discussing the details of these topics here, see Appendix IV of this text for the condensed listing of subjects and the minimum mandated hours for selected states. Keep in mind that local agency academies may add topics and hours to the state minimums. An interesting note is that at least two-thirds of municipal police departments (and a higher proportion of sheriff's and state agencies) reported

---

FIGURE 7-9 Training Reciprocity Between Jurisdictions

Can the police training received in one jurisdiction be transferred to another if an officer changes departments? The answer to this question varies greatly. In some states, departments will not honor or recognize the training hours a person received while working in another jurisdiction, within the same state. If a current officer decides to change departments, he or she may have to complete the entire academy training at the new agency. On the other hand a person may be able to change departments, go to another state, and only have to take the hours necessary to learn that state's criminal code—usually 40 to 80 hours.

Some states require a certified officer from another state to take their state exam before receiving a new certification. If you plan a career in law enforcement and intend to start in one agency and move to another, you should learn about any possible reciprocity before you join the first agency; you may have to attend the academy a second time. Other factors enter into the equation, such as moving from a local to state agency, or from a local or state agency to a federal agency. In short, portability of training is not consistent.

---

having "training environments they described as predominately stress or more stress than non-stress" (Reaves 2009, 10). This is important because non-completion rates for females in these training environments are higher than in non-stress training environments and contributes to our understanding of low female representation in local and state law enforcement.

Usually, persons attending basic academies have been hired by a law enforcement agency; however, a recent trend in some states allows "students" to pay their own way through the academy whether sponsored by an agency or not. Where this is permitted, the student can attend the academy, graduate, and seek employment with an agency in that state that recognizes the training. Additionally, 23 states permit colleges to conduct some or all of the entry-level law enforcement training (Flink 1997, 113). Although this is a significant number, the training usually must be regulated or meet the specific guidelines and standards of the state office that certifies the training.

Once a person is employed by an agency, even during the attendance of a basic academy, he or she is said to be "on probation," which usually includes one's attendance at the basic academy. The probationary period may extend from 6 to 24 months, but one year is the norm. For most officers, the probationary period represents the only time during which the department can terminate an employee without cause (Gaines and Forester 1983), although this is an overstatement in today's litigious society.

Field Training

Field training consists of formalized, actual on-the-job instruction by specially selected and trained personnel called Field Training Officers (FTOs). Field training (generally combined with periodic evaluation of the recruit's performance) usually occurs immediately after the recruit completes the classroom portion of basic training" (McCampbell 1986, 2). A 1997 survey of state regulatory commissions found that only seven states mandated field training for entry-level personnel as part of state standards (Flink 1997, 89). Of course, local agencies are normally responsible for this type of training. One of the most noted formalized field training programs was established in 1972 in the San Jose, California Police Department and has been a model for many departments.

(See **Figure 7-10** for an overview of the San Jose Program, as originally implemented.)

Most field training programs commence after the recruit has completed the basic academy (which normally is 10–15 weeks in duration). Next, the recruit is assigned to an FTO, or to several of them, for a number of weeks; some field training programs last up to a year. The FTO is responsible for evaluating the recruit during the field training period. The evaluations usually are formal and very detailed and may occur on a daily or weekly basis.

FIGURE 7-10 San Jose Academy and Original Field Training Model

Phase I

Weeks 1–16

Academy and in-agency classroom and range training.

Successful academy performance leads to Phase II. Failure at the Academy leads to dismissal.

Phase II

Weeks 17–18

Assigned to primary FTO. No evaluations.

During Phase II, recruit is assigned to initial FTO, then to two other FTOs on different shifts. Then back to initial FTO. Recruit receives a District Evaluation after completing assignment with each FTO.

Weeks 19–28

Daily observation reports by FTOs with weekly evaluation reports by supervisors.

Weeks 29–30

Daily and weekly reports continue, but primary FTO rides in plain clothes with recruit.

At completion of Phase II, successful recruit goes to Phase III. Otherwise, recruit may receive remedial training or be dismissed.

Phase III

Weeks 31–36

Recruit works a solo beat outside the Training District. Supervisors evaluate biweekly.

Recruit begins solo assignment and initial biweekly evaluations followed by monthly ones.

Weeks 37–40

Recruit continues solo beat. Supervisors evaluate monthly.

At ten month review, recruit is certified to continue in Phase III or is recommended for remedial training.

Weeks 41–44

Recruit continues solo beat. Ten Month Review Board meets to recommend retention, remedial training, or dismissal.

At completion of Phase III, recruit becomes certified as a permanent employee or has Phase III extended. The option of dismissal still exists.

Weeks 45–52

Reserved for remedial training if needed. Special board meets to review the performance of recruits with deficiencies.

Source: Adapted from M.S. McCampbell, Field Training for Police Officers: State of the Art, *Research in Brief,* 1986, National Institute of Justice.

If any weaknesses are found in the recruit's performance, they must undergo remedial training. If successful, the recruit can move on to a solo assignment. The officer must continue to perform successfully during this solo phase or he can be assigned for remedial training. During this intensive evaluation period, the department also determines whether the officer should be terminated. Successful completion of the field training leads to permanent employment status. Of course, variations to this sequence may occur, since not all jurisdictions are alike in their operation of field training programs. Hughes et al. (1996) found that probation officers spent an average of 125 days with an FTO and that the top three typical duties of an FTO were "teaching by example," "mending weaknesses," and "allowing the probationer to take initiative." In California, effective January 1, 1999, every peace officer who is required to complete the regular basic training course must also complete an approved field training program. The FTO program, at a minimum, must include 10 weeks of training; the criteria for structured training, remediation, and evaluation; daily trainee evaluations; and criteria for the selection and training of field training officers and program administrators. As of June 1999, over 400 programs had been approved (O'Brien 1999).

Not all departments have formal FTO programs; however, most departments do have some type of orientation or "break-in" period that involves different types of training to orient the new recruits to the field of policing Some departments are taking a serious look at their FTO programs, realizing that how their recruits are trained on the job (and by whom) has a large impact on how they will perform later on. In the Metro Nashville Police Department, after graduation from the academy, rookie officers are oriented and evaluated by "Master Patrol Officers" for a period of six months. They ride with one MPO for two months, then ride with another MPO, in another area of the city, for another two months. Following a rotation to a third MPO, the MPOs and Patrol Supervisors hold a meeting to decide whether to keep the officer, extend probation, or terminate the rookie's employment. The National Association of Field Training Officers (2011) maintains a page on its Website that lists links to approximately 40 FTO programs in policing.

In-service Training

During a police officer's career, ongoing training is necessary to keep up with changes in the criminal law and procedures. **In-service training** (sometimes called "refresher" training) is the phrase used to refer to training received by officers following their recruit training. It is usually done at the department's facilities, and may be during regular tours of duty (while on-duty). The form of in-service training may vary from "roll-call" training sessions (held just prior to or after a tour of duty) to ones several hours in length. The subject matter of in-service training normally is related to the general assignments of most officers, or officers of a particular unit. Common material covered in such sessions includes legal updates in criminal procedure, new or modifications to standard operating procedures, the proper use of new equipment or weapons, and utilization of new forms or means of incident reporting. Some in-service sessions are used as "refreshers" that include updated material on topics originally covered at recruit school. In the pre-recruit academy years of policing, in-service training served as the primary means of upgrading personnel.

In-service training may be mandated by state law or regulations. By 1997, 33 states required such training for law enforcement personnel (Flink 1997, 77). Such training may include firearms re-qualification, an additional minimum number of hours, or other types of training. The time frame for such training may be annually or up to every 48 months.

Advanced/Specialized

Advanced or **specialized training** refers to those sessions that address specialty topics or material that is an extension or a more enhanced version of what was received at basic academies. Such training allows officers to specialize in selected areas of the field. For example, general recruit training covers traffic accident investigation and crime scene processing, but advanced training is available to allow officers to become traffic accident specialists and crime scene technicians. The length of advanced/specialty courses can range from one day to three weeks, although some courses at special institutes may be from one to nine months in length. The following listing is a portion of the 90 different courses offered at the Ohio Peace Officer Training Academy in London, Ohio, which is the state's advanced training center for local law enforcement.

Infant/Child Death Investigation	Advanced Hostage Negotiations
Dealing with the Suicidal	Death Investigation
Dignitary Protection	Financial Investigative Techniques
Incident Command System	Chemical Agents
Evidence Technician I and II	Surveillance Photography and Videography
Basic Instructor Training	
Bloodstain Evidence	Trip Wires and Explosive Devices
Drug Impaired Detection	
Internet Investigation I and II	Traffic Accident Reconstruction

In addition to specialized institutes and periodic training courses offered by professional associations, most states have some type of advanced training facility that offers specialized course work. Colleges and universities also routinely offer specialized courses for police personnel, and many of the courses carry **continuing education credit**. Such credit may be awarded in the form of hours or units, which usually apply to any state or local requirement where training hours are required each year.

Executive and Managerial Training

Another type of training, sometimes called **executive and managerial training**, focuses on administrative decision-making or supervision issues and skills. Courses in this type of training address subjects such as leadership, motivation, budgeting, first-line supervision, FTO program development and administration, media relations, public speaking, and communication skills. Some states require promoted officers to attend a managerial or supervisor's course as a condition of promotion; however, usually there is no such requirement to do so. **Figure 7-11** is an illustration of a course description of the line supervision course in the state of Florida.

A California-based program is rather unique to the field; it is known as the California Law Enforcement

FIGURE 7-11 Line Supervision Course

Tailored to the new supervisor, this course will assist the student with understanding the transition from operations to management responsibilities. It will also provide the experienced supervisor with the additional knowledge, skills, and attributes to function effectively in this significant role. Topics include: communications and semantics, management theory, elements of supervision, organization theory, reporting and records, human relations, planning practices, staff work requirements, considerations in policy development and enforcement, budgeting practices, performance appraisal techniques, staffing and assignment of personnel, community relations, civil liability, methods of developing personnel and proper use of discipline.

Source: Reprinted from Tallahassee Community College, Florida Public Safety Institute (2011).

Command College. Originally, it was a 24-month program consisting of 10 workshops and independent study projects, though it has evolved into an 18-month, 7-session program. Its faculty consists of university professors and consultants who are recognized for their expertise. The Command College curriculum is designed "to provide a leadership course with a futures perspective to prepare law enforcement leaders of today for the future" (California Commission on POST 2011). Attendees must be employed in a management position in a California law enforcement agency. The objectives of the program are to help these individuals develop strategies and methods for managing the complex issues facing law enforcement today and in the future. A "futures research" orientation is a fundamental component to the program. Each participant must complete an independent study project that will contribute to the body of knowledge of law enforcement through information sharing. **Figure 7-12** identifies the session sequence and content of the Command College Program.

Citizen Police Academy

In recent years, **citizen police academies** have begun appearing in many jurisdictions. This academy usually is a means of establishing a liaison and dialogue with the

FIGURE 7-12 California Command College Program

Sessions
1. Defining the Future
   A conceptual roadmap for studying the future, and the role of law enforcement leadership to help shape it. Using the STEEP futures scanning model (Social, Technological, Environmental, Economic, and Political), the students will learn techniques to identify indistinct signals and emerging issues that may be important to the future of California law enforcement.
2. Social Issues and Futures Research
   Forecasting methods and the importance of scenario writing. Today's vague signals and emerging trends as they relate to social issues, the first element of STEEP, will be discussed. The potential impact of these social issues on the student's agency and his/her role as a leader will be explored.
3. Enhanced Leadership and Politics
   Leadership and ethics theories; innovation and creativity as a function of management, and how they relate to the students as leaders. Self-assessment instruments, facets of self-mastery, and creative decision-making that will be instrumental to identify their role as leaders today and in the future.
4. Economics and Strategic Planning
   Explore multiple forecasts of economic and political issues, including the public policy making process. In-depth discussions will be conducted concerning the impact of these issues on law enforcement. Students will create alternative scenarios and define probable futures.
5. Technology and Change Leadership
   Discussions examining emerging technological issues & change leadership research and practice. Students will research cutting edge technology and environmental issues, share information, and assess their potential impact on law enforcement leadership.
6. Futures Planning Tools
   This "tool box" includes strategic planning, organizational culture, group dynamics, and human-centered innovation skills and concepts. Emphasis is placed on expanding the student's knowledge of resources that enhance leadership roles and strategies for mitigating the impact of change on the agency.
7. Politics of Change
   An overview of the program and research results. Executive panels discuss practical application of change strategies. The session concludes with graduation ceremonies.

Source: Reprinted with permission from Center for Leadership Development, State of California Commission on Peace Officer Standards and Training (2011), The Law Enforcement Command College.

community. The format varies, but such a program can consist of one evening a week for 8–10 weeks. The course is open to residents of the jurisdiction and covers many of the same topics as taught in a regular police academy. The sessions are taught by members of the local police department who speak on their areas of expertise. The course is designed to give an overview of the department's policies and procedures, but the course also can provide a forum for the participants to offer suggestions and provide input regarding the operations of the agency. Some citizens' academies provide simulations so participants can learn what it is like to approach suspects, patrol in a cruiser, and fire a weapon, and firearms training is an option in some academies. One of the objectives of the citizen police academy is to achieve a greater public awareness and understanding of the agency's role in the community through the educational aspects of the program. According to the National Citizen's Police Academy Association (2011), the concept of the Citizen Police Academy actually started in the United Kingdom in 1977. However, it was not until 1985 that the Orlando (FL) Police Department introduced it in the United States.

Citizen Police Academy training

Source: © Rob Byron/ShutterStock, Inc.

THE HIGHER EDUCATION AND TRAINING MERGER

Since the early 1900s, professionals in the field of policing have been advocating college education for officers. However, the standard educational requirement for most local (75%) and state (66%) agencies in the United States is a high school diploma or GED. The 2007 LEMAS survey of local police departments found that about 16% of local agencies required some college and about 9% required a 2-year degree (Reaves 2010). Of the 49 state agencies, approximately 33% required some college, 12% required an associate's degree, and 2% required a baccalaureate degree at the time of appointment (Reaves and Hickman 2004, v). Two states, Minnesota and Wisconsin, reported that law enforcement personnel were required by state standards to possess a minimum of an associate's degree (however, in Wisconsin, an officer has up to 5 years to complete the associate's degree after appointment).

In 1967, the President's Commission on Law Enforcement and Administration of Justice (1967b, 109–110) recommended that "the ultimate aim of all police departments should be that all personnel with general enforcement powers have baccalaureate degrees," and

"police departments should take immediate steps to establish a minimum requirement of a baccalaureate degree for all supervisory and executive positions." Later, in 1973, the National Advisory Commission on Criminal Justice Standards and Goals stated in Standard 15.1 that every police agency should, no later than:

- 1975: require as a condition of initial employment the completion of at least 2 years of college education.
- 1978: require as a condition of initial employment the completion of at least 3 years of college education.
- 1982: require as a condition of initial employment the completion of at least 4 years of college education.

A study published by the Police Executive Research Forum (PERF) in 1989 reported on the state of education in the police field (Carter et al. 1989). It found that 55% of all police officers in the study had completed 2 years of college, as compared to 15% in 1970. The study's recommendations included (Ayers 1990, 17):

- All law enforcement agencies should develop long-range plans for requiring a college degree as a minimum criterion for promotion and employment by 1995.
- Effective immediately, all candidates for promotion to management and command ranks should be required to have baccalaureate degrees.
- Effective immediately, all candidates for promotion to first-line and supervisory positions should have a minimum of 60 college credits.
- The federal government should develop a program to provide financial aid to in-service officers to help further their educations.

Obviously, these time periods have come and gone and the requirement of a college education—even 2 years of college—has not yet become a requirement in most agencies. In 1967, the President's Commission reported that only 70% of the police agencies in the United States minimally required a high school diploma as a condition of employment, although the median educational level for all police officers in the country was 12.4 years. By 1988 (in a survey of 531 law enforcement agencies with 100 or more sworn officers or serving a population of 50,000 or more) the average educational level of officers was 13.6 years (Carter and Sapp 1992). Although the minimum educational requirements for entry into the field are not increasing significantly, the competition for the jobs is. Persons possessing only a high school level education are competing with applicants with baccalaureate and master's degrees. Colleges and universities are graduating thousands of criminal justice majors annually in the United States, and many are seeking employment in the policing field. According to the U.S. Census Bureau, approximately 52% of Americans have had at least some college or more, and about 27% have earned a bachelor's degree. Given these figures about the general population's education level, do citizens want officers whose educational levels are below average?

There are plenty of educational programs at the college level today and there is ample opportunity for interested persons to attend college, though this was not always the case. By the early 1960s, only about 60 educational programs existed nationally. With the creation of the Law Enforcement Education Program (LEEP) as part of the Law Enforcement Assistance Administration of the late 1960s and early 1970s, by 1977 there were over 750 programs (Hoover 1983). Although exact data are not available, it is estimated that there are about 1000 criminal justice education programs in the United States today. There has been ample debate over the type and quality of educational programming in the United States, and little consensus exists on curricular matters. In 1998, the Academy of Criminal Justice Sciences adopted a set of "Standards for Criminal Justice Education Programs," which are voluntary guidelines and recommendations. They generally address content areas, qualification of faculty, facilities, student-to-faculty ratios, and so on.

Tulsa, Oklahoma became the largest city in the nation and the only city in that state to require a baccalaureate degree for new recruits, effective January 1998. Prior to that, in 1981 the agency required 108 semester credit hours of college. Then-Chief Palmer stated that officers with college degrees

> come to you a little bit more mature, they're a little more aware of diversity issues, and they're more prone to use their minds to

problem-solve than one that doesn't have that type of background… What I've seen here is that there's a world of difference between a high school graduate and a college graduate in regard to skill levels and the handling of people" (Men & Women of Letters 1997, 1).

However, Bruns (2010) reports that Tulsa is not the norm regarding departments with degree requirements; most police departments with degree requirements have fewer than 100 sworn officers. Of the 36 respondents in her study, the range of sworn officers was 15 at the smallest department to 844 sworn officers at the largest department (Tulsa—although by January 2011, the agency's sworn strength has dropped to about 730 because of layoffs and attrition).

Rather than mandate college education as a pre-employment requirement, many departments are opting to offer incentives to attract officers with degrees in hand or to entice their existing officers to hit the books. Several incentive options exist, including tuition assistance or reimbursement programs, educational pay incentive programs, shift adjustments or days off, duty pay while attending class, credits or bonus points for promotional exams, and college education requirements for promotions. Reaves (2010) reports approximately 37% of surveyed local departments in 2007 offered tuition reimbursement incentives (64% of agencies serving populations of 10,000 or higher) and 32% of departments offered education pay incentive (58% of agencies serving populations 10,000 or higher) to its officers.

Research on Law Enforcement and Higher Education

Essentially, empirical studies examining education levels of police officers to date can be divided into two broad categories: behavioral measures (arrest rates, citizen complaints, commendations, etc.) and attitudinal measures (job satisfaction, receptivity to innovation, etc.). The research, in general, has shown having a college degree to be a positive in the field of policing. However, research has yielded inconsistent and often conflicting results. For example, when examining education and police management, Withal (1985) argued that "[f]ormal schooling and varied experience offer police chiefs no guarantee of effectiveness." However, Krimmell and Lindenmouth (2001), in contrast to Withal, found that not only was education an important factor in predicting leadership success, but that there were significant differences on 35 different performance and leadership indicators between police chiefs with a background that included some college and those police chiefs who only possessed a high school diploma.

Behaviors

Job Performance. Assumptions of several management reforms suggest that increased education of the police will affect job performance in several ways. Under community- and problem-oriented policing, higher education is assumed to improve problem-solving skills and provide police with a wider range of solutions available to them besides simply responding to a call for service and arresting individuals involved in illegal activity. Under the model of professionalism, higher education, alongside training, is assumed to improve actual skills involved in the daily activities of policing such as communication with the public, diffusing potentially dangerous situations, and skills necessary to effectively solve crimes or prevent them from occurring.

> In sum, it is argued that a college-educated officer has a broader comprehension of civil rights issues from legal, social, historical, and political perspectives. Moreover, these officers have a broader view of policing tasks and a greater professional ethos, thus their actions and decisions tend to be driven by conscience and values, consequently lessening the chance of erroneous decisions. If these arguments are valid, the logical conclusion is that the college-educated officer would be less likely to place the department in a liability situation (Carter and Sapp 1989, 162).

Typical performance measures in empirical studies have included: arrests, tenure, citizen evaluations, and composite performance measures (Hayeslip 1989). Cohen and Chaiken (1973) found that police officers with higher education received fewer complaints and subsequent disciplinary actions. Several studies have concluded that

police officers with higher education have higher corresponding arrest rates (Bozza 1973; Glasgow, Green, and Knowles 1973)—which in the era of community-oriented policing may not necessarily be a positive advancement.

Cascio (1977) found that higher-educated officers had fewer preventable accidents and took less sick time away from work, and Lester (1979) concluded that officers with more education performed better in police training. Rydberg and Terill (2010) in their study of Indianapolis, IN and St. Petersberg, FL police officers found no significant impact of higher education on the decision to arrest or search, but that officers with a college education were significantly less likely to use force in a police–suspect encounter.

Several studies have identified strong positive relationships between education and specific police performance measures (Cohen and Chaiken 1972; Finnegan 1976; Sanderson 1978; Saunders 1970). Others have only reported moderate relationships between education and aggregate performance ratings (Cascio 1977; Roberg 1978; Spencer and Nichols 1971; Weirman 1978), or weak (Hayeslip 1989) to no relationships (Griffin 1980; Kedia 1985; Marsh 1962; Worden 1990). Furthermore, some studies have actually found an inverse relationship between higher education and overall performance (Gottlieb 1974; Smith and Ostrom 1974).

Overall, research suggests more highly-educated officers rate themselves higher in their ability to deal with criticism, change, workload, and stress. In addition, college-educated officers rate themselves higher on knowledge of the law, use of mediation and conflict resolution, investigation and report-writing skills, leadership, responsibility, and problem-solving skills (Kakar 1996; Krimmel 1998). However, it is interesting to note that Kakar found no significant differences in an officer's attitude toward their job, office, or department, and that those officers with higher levels of education reported themselves lower on scores of job satisfaction and fulfillment and indicated more overall frustration.

The inconsistent findings in the research may serve well to point out that higher levels of education may be "relevant to many aspects of police work but should not be assumed to predict all areas of job performance" (Truxillo et al. 1998, 269). For example, Truxillo et al. found that while college education was statistically significant for a variety of performance measures, it was not important in reducing disciplinary problems—a key variable in much of the literature on higher levels of education in policing.

Communication Skills. Education is assumed to improve police officers' communication in two distinct ways. First, under reforms of community-oriented policing, police officers are encouraged to keep open lines of communication between themselves and the communities they patrol. Because community problems do not always involve law violations, police officers must have a greater knowledge base from which they draw available solutions. Second, it is assumed that the process of a college education strengthens the written and oral skills necessary to improve police officers' report writing and communication with a variety of different people throughout the day.

Empirical research suggests overall that education does indeed have a positive impact on communication. Vodicka (1994) concluded that police officers with more education had better communication skills and had a greater openness to change. Both Vodicka and Carter and Sapp (1992) found that college-educated police candidates, for the most part, have better verbal and written communication skills, make better discretionary decisions, and have more empathy and tolerance for people with different attitudes and lifestyles. Worden (1990) concluded that according to citizen reports, police officers who were college graduates were overall better problem-solvers, but were less courteous than their less educated counterparts. In addition, Worden found that there was no relationship between education and citizen evaluations of officer performance in police–citizen encounters. Hooper's (1988) research a few years earlier suggests that college graduates were also better at report writing and received fewer citizen complaints. Other studies have made similar conclusions regarding lower levels of citizen complaints and higher levels of education (Carter and Sapp 1989; Kappeler, Sapp, and Carter 1992; Shernock 1992; and Tyre and Braunstein 1992) and fewer disciplinary problems and college education (Carter and Sapp 1989).

Attitudes/Demeanor

The demeanor in which a police officer conducts his/her job duties and the attitudes he/she holds about policing are important in understanding both job performance and citizen encounters. Because police officers work with a variety of people who differ in their attitudes, culture, and lifestyles, it is important for police officers to have a more tolerant and understanding demeanor, especially in community-oriented policing. Bayley (1986) asserts that "for disturbances, the manner in which contact was initiated had consequences for both processing and exit." He continues by stating that the demeanor of police has "substantial" explanatory usefulness for both disturbances and traffic stops—routine occurrences during daily patrol. Research examining police demeanor and attitudes has also suggested that college-educated officers are less authoritarian, less conservative, less rigid and legalistic, and less likely to invoke the criminal justice process (Dalley 1975; Finckenauer 1975; Smith et al. 1967, 1970; Taylor 1983). In addition, they tend to be less cynical, more open-minded, have a broader conception of the police role, and have more positive attitudes toward legal restrictions on police powers (Niederhoffer 1967; Parker et al. 1976; Powell 1980; Roberg 1978; Worden 1990). Furthermore, college-educated police officers also have a more holistic attitude towards police work, place a higher value on ethical conduct, are more creative, and are more tolerant of people of different lifestyles, races and ethnicities (Carter and Sapp 1989; Lynch 1976; Shernock 1992; Smith et al. 1970; Trojanowicz and Nicholson 1976; Wycoff 1987).

Other studies suggest that there is no relationship between higher education and attitudes, specifically cynicism (Lotz and Regoli 1977; Regoli 1976; Weiner 1976; Wycoff and Susmilch 1979). Smith (1978b) and Sherman and Blumberg (1981), in their respective reviews of the relevant literature, suggest that, overall, findings on the relationship between education and attitude are mixed.

Test-Taking Skills and Job Satisfaction. The link between higher education and test-taking is more important when one also looks at the relationship between education, job satisfaction, and promotion. If reforms giving more autonomy in decision making and making problem solving an important job function coincide with increased levels of education, it can be hypothesized that job satisfaction will also increase, though empirical research on this area indicates that this may not always be the case. Dantzker (1993) identified a curvilinear relationship between job satisfaction and higher education; specifically, he found that job satisfaction for college-educated officers was only evident during the first five years of experience:

> If a hypothesis were to have been offered based on the premise of the research, I would have suggested that college-educated patrol officers become less satisfied with their jobs the longer they remain in patrol while their high-school-only-educated colleagues remain more satisfied. The data appears to support this suggestion (106).

Dantzker suggested that the drop in job satisfaction after five years came from both the realization that education was not a predictive factor for promotion, and that there existed a significant difference between what college-educated officers were capable of doing and what they actually could do when attempting to solve problems in the community (this issue will be further examined in Chapter 13). In another study conducted by Dantzker (1994), he again concluded that "while findings from a national sample have indicated a strong correlation with education and perceived job satisfaction, in this department education had very little impact." In a third study, Dantzker (1998) found the relationship between education and job satisfaction to be dependent upon the amount of education the officer has. Cascio (1977) produced findings inconsistent with Dantzker, in that he found higher-educated officers to be more highly job motivated.

Charles Sherwood (2000) argued that the level of education did not make a significant difference on officer's feelings about job characteristics; in his study, what was more important was the notion of job enrichment. Similarly, in a survey of the Spokane Police Department in Washington State, Zhao, Thurman, and He (1999) found that "skill variety, task identity, and autonomy contribute most to the variation in officers' work satisfaction." Autonomy was especially important, and Worden's (1990) work backs up these findings by suggesting that the dissatisfaction experienced by college-educated officers is most likely due to a rigid work environment and an inability for officers to exercise their ideas.

Job satisfaction is inherently linked to attrition and turnover rates within law enforcement. Numerous studies have found a positive and significant relationship between higher levels of education and higher levels of attrition in policing (Burbeck and Furnham 1985; Daniel 1982; Weirman 1978). However, other studies have found no relationship (Marsh 1962), and still even others have found an inverse relationship (Sanderson 1978).

Promotion. The notion of job satisfaction has been linked not only to police officers' overall satisfaction with their job functions but also to whether or not higher education is a predictive factor in promotion. The literature suggests that higher education is not necessarily a straight shot to job promotion. Education might be a consideration in some promotions, but there are few guarantees.

Penegor and Peak (1992), in their study of hiring practices of police chiefs, concluded that education may be more of a predictive factor when outside hiring is conducted, but not when chiefs are hired from within their own department. Truxillo et al. (1998) found statistical relationships between college education and promotion and college education and supervisory ratings of job knowledge. They suggest that education and promotion could be related in several possible ways. First, the individual "motivation for educational achievement may be the same as for promotions." Second, skills such as studying and test-taking may be more finely-tuned in officers with a college background; these skills are certainly necessary in the process of promotion. Third, perhaps "college education instills a higher degree of professionalism and maturity that is needed and valued at higher organizational levels." When examining law enforcement promotion and education, Polk and Armstrong (2001) suggest that:

> Higher education reduces time required for movement in rank and assignment to specialized positions and was positively correlated to promotion into supervisory and administrative posts. Implications are that higher education will enhance an officer's probability of rising to the top regardless of whether the agency requires a college degree as a precondition of employment (78).

Although the research is inconsistent, significant findings suggest that college-educated officers perform policing tasks better, are better communicators, are more flexible in dealing with difficult situations, are more professional, adapt better to organizational change, and have fewer administrative and personal problems than their less-educated counterparts.

Combining Training and Education

For the most part, police training and college education still operate "separately and distinctly" from each other, and only recently have the two begun to merge in selected programs or areas in the United States. One of the largest mergers occurred in the state of Minnesota in 1977 with the creation of the Peace Officer Standards and Training Board to replace the older Peace Officer Training Board. It was the first state to establish "licensing" requirements. The "Minnesota Model" was initiated to decentralize the training of recruits by making fuller use of the state's college and vocational school system. Also, requirements for continuing education for license renewal were implemented.

In Minnesota, there is an alternative to the traditional route of securing employment with a police agency first and then attending the recruit training. A person can complete a POST-certified law enforcement program at a 2- or 4-year academic institution and then sit for the academic portion of the licensing exam. Upon successful completion of the exam, the person can enroll in a law enforcement skills course (of approximately 8 weeks in length). Then, after passing the skills training, the person takes the skills portion of the licensing exam. If both portions of the licensing exam are successfully completed, the candidate can then seek employment anywhere in the state as a police officer. Following a successful 1-year probationary period, the new officer is granted a license. The academic portion of the program consists of the following subject areas (Minnesota State Statutes, §§ 626.843 and 626.845):

a. Administration of Justice
b. Minnesota Statutes
c. Criminal Law
d. Human Behavior
e. Juvenile Justice
f. Law Enforcement Operation/Procedures

The skills training consists of the following subject areas:

a. Techniques in Criminal Investigation and Testifying
b. Patrol Functions
c. Traffic Law Enforcement
d. Firearms
e. Defensive Tactics
f. Emergency Vehicle Driving
g. CJ Information Systems
h. First Aid

The State of Minnesota remains the only state to require a post-secondary degree for entry-level officers and it is one successful model that can lead to incremental increases in overall education levels of state and local officers (Hilal and Erickson 2010).

Another recent development in the training and education merger is exemplified by the West Virginia State Police Training Program. In conjunction with Marshall University's Community and Technical College, the completion of the 960-hour, 28-week training course leads to an associate's degree in addition to certification as a West Virginia state police officer. This venture began in 1985 and as of this writing is still in effect. Cadets earn up to 72 semester hours of credit and take a number of regular college courses taught by Marshall University professors. Troopers who successfully complete the probationary period are afforded the opportunity to continue their education and obtain their bachelor's degree through Marshall's 2+2 program (West Virginia State Police 2010).

During the late 1980s, developments in Ohio also led to a greater merger of education and training requirements at selected institutions. It is now possible for students to complete the total requirements for peace officer certification at state-approved **college academies** and sit for the mandated state exam. Students attending the college academies essentially complete the requirements for training as they complete their college degree program. Originally, most of the college academies "blended" academic material with training curriculum requirements over a 2-year course of study. Recently, however, most of the college academies in the Ohio system have gone to a "caboose" delivery system—the mandatory training curriculum material is taught at the end of the associate's degree program. Examples such as these are common in many states, especially in California and Florida, but most merger arrangements are associated with community colleges. Much of the debate against such programs has come from baccalaureate-granting institutions/programs that emphasize the traditional differences between education and training and criticize narrow vocationally-oriented programs. However, it is not uncommon for advanced training academies or programs to affiliate themselves with colleges and universities that allow the granting of limited college credit or continuing education units for advanced or specialty courses. Nevertheless, today's trend is toward a greater merger of training and educational endeavors. According to a 2006 Bureau of Justice Statistics (BJS) survey of training academies across the United States, of "648 state and local academies operating during 2006, a total of 292, (45%) were operated by an academic institution, such as a 2-year or 4-year college, a university, or a technical school... Municipal police departments were the primary operating agency for 143 academies, 22% of the total" (Reaves 2009, 1).

Three Major Emerging Factors

There are three emerging factors that will greatly impact current aspects of police training and education: (1) the evolving utilization of technology to enhance the learning process, (2) federal legislation and grants, and (3) problem-oriented training. Greater use of technology, especially computer-based police training, is now used in the training academies at the federal level and in many of the states. Programs for basic, in-service, and advanced training are being developed and becoming cost-effective. The BJS survey of state and local academies found that 75% of the academies had access to firearms simulators and 32% had access to driving simulators (Reaves 2009, 4). Multimedia and virtual reality programs are emerging in course work beyond firearms training, where many such programs were originally applied. The Federal Law Enforcement Training Center (FLETC) in Glynco, Georgia now uses marine simulators and interview avatars in their basic training programs (Gregory 2008) (see Chapter 11 for more about technology in law enforcement).

The future of police training will be closely tied to computerization for several reasons: the sheer volume of information and material that needs to be mastered by police recruits, the individual attention that a computer can give to and demand of the user, the need for documentation on individual police officers relating to their mastery of concepts and material to be maintained, and the realism that will be available through virtual reality and artificial intelligence programming. The BJS survey of state and local training academies found that:

- 98% of the academies provided access to computers (64% had mobile computer access).
- about 75% had access to a media lab or video production facility, and about half of these were on-site facilities.

FLETC Marine Simulator

Source: Courtesy of Department of Homeland Security, Federal Law Enforcement Training Center

- advanced communications technologies were available for online classes (66%), video conference classes (49%), and satellite information services (36%) (Reaves 2009, 4).

The second major factor influencing police training and education relates to federal legislation and grants. One major piece of legislation, the Violent Crime Control and Law Enforcement Act (VCCLEA) of 1994, signed by President Clinton, contained provisions for several programs and cost over $30 billion. The act provided for the establishment of the Office of Community Policing, which approves funding to local communities for the hiring of additional officers for community policing activities. This was part of the initiative to add 100,000 officers to the policing community nationwide during the mid-1990s. Another initiative under the Act has been the establishment of "regional community policing institutes" (RCPIs) around the country. The national network of RCPIs has trained more than 210,000 officers, community members, and government leaders in innovative approaches to community policing. Many, but not all, of the programs funded or initiated under the VCCLEA have been extended and exist today. These institutes have assisted in bringing a wide range of training topics and programs to local and state agencies. These have included state-of-the-art courses that focus on improving training as well as the content of training materials. Today there is a myriad number of funding opportunities for law enforcement agencies either to attend specialized training programs or to develop them. Programs administered through various federal departments such as the Department of Justice (e.g., Edward Byrne Memorial Justice Assistance Grant Program and the Violence Against Women Act funding) and the Department of Homeland Security (e.g., Homeland Security Grants and Preparedness Grants) often provide grants for training, equipment, and new technology. The "federalization" factor influences the direction of training and other initiatives at the state and local levels.

A third emerging force that will greatly impact law enforcement training is the trend toward problem-oriented training. This trend has several names or derivatives. Some describe it as "problem-based" or "scenario-based" training; others refer to it as "facilitated training." Traditional training methods have emphasized the cognitive knowledge and psychomotor skills of policing. Problem-based training attempts to move learning to the higher domains (refer to the previous section on learning domains) of analysis, synthesis, and evaluation. The method generally flows like this: The cadet is expected to learn the cognitive aspects of policing early in the training process. This is followed by a development of psychomotor skills, and then the cadet is immersed in a series of scenarios or problem-based situations where he or she must draw upon learned knowledge and skills and apply them to the situation encountered. Traditionally, this is what has been called role-playing situations; however, instead of just a few role-playing situations, a significant amount of time is spent with these scenarios. Cadets work individually and in groups in responding to these situations. Roles are carefully scripted to achieve maximum education potential and the review and the evaluation process assist the cadets in developing the critical thinking skills necessary to become decision-makers on the street. The problem-based training method has emerged under several so-called "models." The SARA Problem Solving Model (described in Chapter 13) is the foundation for these models.

Why is this approach significant as an emerging force in the training arena? We believe that if this trend continues across the United States, it will enhance the professionalization of the policing function. In part, it will demonstrate the need for recruiting persons who can learn cognitive material quickly and early in the process—this may mean that some college education may become a de facto minimum expectation for entry into the academy environment. The trend is also significant because it will better prepare cadets for the critical thinking necessary in today's society.

SUMMARY

Personnel are the lifeblood of law enforcement agencies. The quality of service rendered by these persons is dependent on the thoroughness of the selection process, the effectiveness of the training process, the commitment to promoting capable people, and the accountability demanded by supervisors and administrators.

Training and education in the law enforcement field have evolved from on-the-job training to a merger of the traditional training academy with an academic curriculum. Variations, of course, do exist because the United States is a very large and diverse country of multiple jurisdictions, and there simply are no nationally-accepted standards. Training and education should be viewed as a compound phrase and not two individual and different terms. Education is the more global learning outcome desired for today's officers who must police a complex world, and training is only one method of acquiring the knowledge and skills necessary for the task.

Although national commissions have recognized the importance of and recommended higher education as a condition of employment for local police officers, few departments require it. The majority of police officers, however, do have some college education, according to various surveys. This trend is an important one, since most officers can remain on the job for 20–30 years, but departments must ensure that continued education and training occur or their officers will begin to lag behind the average educational levels of society.

The formal training process is considered a major aspect of the socialization of the law enforcement officer. This socialization plays a key role in modifying or developing an officer's attitudes, values, and beliefs. Researchers have been investigating the socialization of police and the resulting occupational subculture. Although studies are sometimes contradictory, the findings have brought a greater understanding of the job and those who perform it.

The issues and controversies related to training and education are diverse and complex, and this chapter has addressed only the major ones. Issues related to certification versus licensure, reciprocity of training, the granting of college credit for training (both recruit and advanced), the merger of training and education, mandated continuing education credits/hours, and minimum education requirements as conditions for employment and promotion, have been debated for over 45 years, and no consensus or national standard has been reached yet.

Critical Thinking Questions

1. What are the major stages of the police selection process, and why are they more complex in some departments than in others?

2. Define the concept of "protected class," and describe how it relates to personnel functions such as selection and promotion.

3. What is the significance of the legal concept of "remedies," and what are the typical ones often implemented in cases alleging job discrimination in law enforcement agencies?

4. What is the relationship between learning, learning domains, and teaching to the concept of education?

5. What are the seven reasons for or purposes of training?

6. What are five types of training commonly found in law enforcement? Give examples of each.

7. What did the National Advisory Commission on Criminal Justice Standards and Goals recommend regarding educational levels as conditions of employment for police officers?

8. What are three major emerging influences on police education and training?

CHAPTER SPECIFIC INTERNET LINKS

Phoenix Police Department: http://www.phoenix.gov/ police/pdjob4.html

Learning Style Inventories:

- http://www.ldpride.net/learningstyles.MI.htm
- http://www.engr.ncsu.edu/learningstyles/ilsweb.html
- http://agelesslearner.com/assess/learningstyle.html

Ohio Peace Officer Training Academy: http://www .ohioattorneygeneral.gov/OPOTACourses

National Center for Women and Policing: http://www .womenandpolicing.org/

National Black Police Association: http://www.blackpolice .org/

U.S. Equal Employment Opportunity Commission: http://www.eeoc.gov/

International Association of Directors of Law Enforcement Standards and Training: http://www.iadlest.org/ modelmin.htm

California Law Enforcement Command College: http:// www.post.ca.gov/command-college.aspx.

Georgia Police Officer Standards and Training (POST): http://gapost.org/

Utah Police Officer Standards and Training (POST): http://publicsafety.utah.gov/post/

Police Association for College Education (PACE): http:// www.police-association.org/

CHAPTER GLOSSARY

Advanced or specialized training—educational sessions that address specialty topics or material that is an extension or a more enhanced version of what was taught at basic academies.

Active recruitment—when an agency makes a concerted effort to attract desired candidates to it; includes using existing personnel, either sworn or civilian, as recruiters and sending them into the community to generate interest among potential applicants.

Adverse impact—one form of proving job discrimination, where the procedure or qualification affects a protected class more negatively than the majority group.

Affirmative action—taking a more aggressive position at recruiting and hiring protected classes that are underrepresented in an agency's workforce.

Appointing authority—an official who hires a person for a particular job according to established law and procedures.

Assessment center—a process/procedure involving observation and measurement of a candidate for promotion; it normally includes simulated job situations or scenarios that would be encountered in the promoted position.

Background check—the formal review and verification of the candidate's application information and general suitability for employment; it usually addresses formal education, current and previous residences, current and prior employment, traffic and criminal citations and convictions (if any), reported drug history, and credit rating.

Bona fide occupational qualification (BFOQ)—certain criteria deemed required or necessary for the operation of the business (or agency) and which may have adverse impact on some protected classes.

Bonus points—the awarding of additional credit (beyond written exam scores) for certain factors or job-related criteria, such as previous police experience, state peace officer certification, college education, military experience (veteran status), and residency.

Citizen police academy—an informative program containing many of the subjects taught in a basic police academy, but meant for members of the community so they can learn more about the typical duties, policies, and procedures related to policing in their local communities.

Civil Rights Act of 1964—federal legislation that addressed the equal rights of persons; one part, Title VII, prohibited discrimination in employment in the private sector on grounds of race, color, religion, sex, and national origin.

Civil service—a term referring to non-military government employment or to a specific personnel system established by state or local law.

College academies—state-approved recruit training programs incorporated into the academic curriculum of an institution of higher education.

Conditional offer of employment—an offer made to a candidate that is suitable and eligible for hire at a particular point in the selection process and will be employed if certain other factors related to one's physical ability and medical and mental conditions are within job-related limits.

Consent decree—an out-of-court settlement by parties to a lawsuit where each agrees to do specified things (remedies) under certain conditions.

Continuing education credit—formal recognition of additional training received following recruit training; it may be required by state law to remain in your position.

Education—that which is learned.

Eligibility list—a list of qualified candidates from which the law enforcement agency must select its employees; it is usually associated with state and local civil service systems.

Equal Employment Opportunity Commission (EEOC)—the federal agency authorized to enforce anti-discrimination in employment legislation and to develop guidelines for employers.

Executive and managerial training—training that focuses on administrative decision-making or supervision issues and skills. Courses in this type of training address subjects such as leadership, motivation, budgeting, first line supervision, field training officer program development and administration, media relations, public speaking, and communication skills.

Field training—consists of formalized, on-the-job instruction by specially selected and trained personnel called Field Training Officers (FTOs).

Griggs v. Duke Power Company—the landmark decision by the U.S. Supreme Court in 1971 that interpreted the Civil Rights Act of 1964.

In-service training—refers to training received by officers following their recruit training.

Job analysis—the process of examining and evaluating the required performances of a particular job to determine what job skills, knowledge, and abilities (SKAs) are required.

Lateral entry—the transferring to another agency without any loss of seniority, rank, or salary.

Learning—a process that changes a person's behavior or attitude.

Learning domains—various levels of learning that include the cognitive, motor skills, and affective domains.

Mandatory minimum training standards—the minimum training requirements usually established by statutory or regulatory mandates.

On-the-job training (OJT)—the lessons learned by actually doing the job without any pre-service instruction; it includes methods and techniques taught by co-workers and supervisors.

Passive recruitment—when the agency has openings and takes applications from those who come to the agency; it is a "sit back, wait, and see" approach.

Permanent employee status—achieved after successful completion of probation; it grants additional rights and privileges related to the position.

Polygraph—a scientifically-calibrated instrument that records physiological changes in respiration, electrical resistance of the skin, and changes in blood pressure and pulse rate; sometimes called a lie detector.

Pre-application conference—usually a meeting with a ranking field officer for the conveyance of information about the job, the required training, and the agency's expectations of its personnel.

Probationary status—conditional employment during which time the person's performance must meet acceptable standards, and their attitudes toward others, willingness to follow orders, ability to be a team player, and so on also are under evaluation.

Protected classes—individuals and/or groups against which discrimination in employment is prohibited by federal, state, or local law.

Psychological interview—discussion conducted by trained psychologists or psychiatrists, one-on-one or in group sessions, in an attempt to determine suitability, stability, and any psychopathic diseases or illnesses.

Psychometric exam—written instruments used to measure various psychological characteristics such as intelligence, interests/preferences, and personality traits/characteristics.

Recruitment—the development and maintenance of an adequate supply of qualified persons interested in being employed by a specific agency.

Remedies—that portion of law consisting of various actions or conditions that can be implemented or ordered to make a person "whole" again when wronged.

Reverse discrimination—allegation by majority members claiming that their rights have been violated by an employer who is showing unlawful preferences to minorities or women.

Ride-along—the opportunity to accompany a uniformed patrol officer while on-duty for purposes of observation and learning more about what the job is like.

Rule of three—the practice of considering the top three candidates on a ranked eligibility list for every open entry-level position.

Selection process—includes the various techniques, devices, and procedures used to identify candidates to employ; it is often a series of events linked together and through which an applicant must pass in order to be hired.

Self-selection—the concept of providing accurate, in-depth information to potential applicants so they can make an informed and more objective decision about entering the selection process.

Structured interview—usually consists of specifically-compiled questions that focus on various aspects of the job or of the applicant's abilities and background; some follow-up questions also may be asked.

Unstructured interview—consists of general areas of focus, but the questions are not specifically spelled out.

CHAPTER REFERENCES AND ADDITIONAL READINGS

Ayers, Richard M. (1990). *Preventing Law Enforcement Stress: The Organization's Role*. Alexandria, VA: National Sheriffs' Association.

Bayley, David H. (1994). *Police for the Future*. New York, NY: Oxford University Press, Inc.

Bloom, Benjamin Samuel (ed.) (1956). *Taxonomy of Educational Objectives: Cognitive Domain*. New York: David McKay Company, Inc.

Bozza, C.M. (1973). Motivations Guiding Policemen in the Arrest Process. *Journal of Police Science and Administration*. 1(4):468–476.

Bruns, Diana (2010). Reflections from the One-Percent of Local Police Departments with Mandatory Four-Year Degree Requirements For New Hires: Are They Diamonds in the Rough? *Southwest Journal of Criminal Justice*. 7(1):87–108.

Buckley, Leslie B., James H. McGinnis, and Michael G. Petrunik (1992). Police Perceptions of Education as an Entitlement to Promotion: An Equity Theory Perspective. *American Journal of Police*. 12(2):77–99.

Burbeck, E. and A. Furnham (1985). Police Officer Selection: A Critical Review of the Literature. *Journal of Police Science and Administration*. 13:58–69.

Bureau of National Affairs (1993). *Individual Employment Rights Manual*. Washington, D.C.: Bureau of National Affairs.

Buzawa, E.S. (1984). Determining Patrol Officer Job Satisfaction: The Role of Selected Demographic and Job-Specific Attitudes. *Criminology*. 22:61–81.

Buzawa, Eve, Thomas Austin, and James Bannon (1994). The Role of Selected Sociodemographic and Job-Specific Variables in Predicting Patrol Officer Job Satisfaction: A Reexamination Ten Years Later. *American Journal of Police*. 13(2):51–75.

California, State of, Commission on Peace Officer Standards and Training (May 29, 1998). http://www.post.ca.gov/

Carlan, Philip E. (1999). Occupational Outcomes of Criminal Justice Graduates: Is the Master's Degree a Wise Investment? *Journal of Criminal Justice Education*. 10(1):39–55.

Carter, David L. and Allen D. Sapp (1989). The Effect of Higher Education on Police Liability: Implications for Police Personnel Policy. *American Journal of Police*. 8(1):153–166.

Carter, David L. and Allen D. Sapp (1992). College Education and Policing: Coming of Age. *FBI Law Enforcement Bulletin*. January:11.

Carter, David L. and Allen D. Sapp (1992). College Education and Policing: Coming of Age. *FBI Law Enforcement Bulletin*. January:11.

Carter, David L., Allen D. Sapp, and Darrel W. Stephens (1989). *The State of Police Education: Policy Direction for the 21st Century*. Washington, D.C.: Police Executive Research Forum.

Cascio, W.F. (1977). Formal Education and Police Officer Performance. *Journal of Police Science and Administration*. 5:89–96.

Center for Leadership Development, State of California Commission on Peace Officer Standards and Training (2000). *The Law Enforcement Command College*. Sacramento, CA: Commission on Peace Officer Standards and Training.

City of New Britain (December 2010). Civil Service Commission Announces An Open Competitive Examination To Create an Employment List for Police Officer. Examination No. 1192.

City of Virginia Beach Police Department (2010). Do I Qualify to be a Police Officer? http://www.vbgov.com/vgn.aspx?vgnextoid=e8b722e0a0446110VgnVCM100000190c640aRCRD&vgnextchannel=dc1e54cf18ad9010VgnVCM100000870b640aRCRD&vgnextfmt=default

Cohen, B. and J.M. Chaiken (1972). *Police Background Characteristics and Performance*: Summary. New York: Rand Institute.

Cohen, B. and J.M. Chaiken (1973). *Police Background Characteristics and Performance*. Lexington, MA: Lexington Press.

Colorado, State of, Peace Officers Standards and Training Board (May 29, 1998). http://www.state.co.us/gov_dir/dol/post96mv2/96m/pa.htm.

Commission on Peace Officer Standards and Training (2011). *Command College Program*. Sacramento, CA: State of California.

Conser, James A. (1981). The Training and Education Cosmos. *The Police Chief*. July:42, 64.

Conser, James A. and Roger D. Thompson (1976). *Police Selection Standards and Processes in Ohio: An Assessment*. Youngstown, Ohio: Youngstown State University.

Dalley, A. (1975). University vs. Non-University Graduated Policemen: A Study of Police Attitudes. *Journal of Police Science and Administration*. 3:458–468.

Daniel, E. (1982). The Effects of a College Degree on Police Absenteeism. *The Police Chief*. September:70–71.

Dantzker, M.L. (1993). Issue for Policing: Educational Level and Job Satisfaction: A Research Note. *American Journal of Police.* 12(2):101–119.

Dantzker, M.L. (1994). Measuring Job Satisfaction in Police Departments and Policy Implications: An Examination of a Mid-Size, Southern Police Department. *American Journal of Police.* 13(2):77–101.

Dantzker, M.L. (1998). Police Education and Job Satisfaction: Educational Incentives and Recruit Educational Requirements. *Police Forum.* 8:1–3.

Davis v. City of Dallas, 777 F.2d 205 (1985).

Decicco, David. (2000). Police Officer Candidate Assessment and Selection. *FBI Bulletin.* 69(12):1–6.

Egelko, Bob (August 3, 2010). S.F. loses challenge to affirmative action ban. SFGate.com http://articles.sfgate.com/2010-08-03/bay-area/22010254_1_justices-racial-preferences-women-and-racial-minorities

Eisenberg, Terry, Deborah Kent, and Charles Wall (1973). *Police Personnel Practices in State and Local Government.* Washington, D.C.: Police Foundation.

Eson, Morris E. (1972). *Psychological Foundations of Education,* 2nd Edition. New York: Holt, Rinehart and Winston, Inc.

Fielding, N., and J. Fielding (1987). A Study of Resignation During British Police Training. *Journal of Police Science and Administration.* 15:24–36.

Finckenauer, J.O. (1975). Higher Education and Police Discretion. *Journal of Police Science and Administration.* December:450–457.

Finnegan, J. (1976). A Study of the Relationship Between College Education and Police Performance in Baltimore, Maryland. *The Police Chief.* August: 60–62.

Flink, William L. and the International Association of Directors of Law Enforcement Standards and Training (1997). *Sourcebook: Executive Summary.* Richmond, VA: CJ Data/Flink and Associates.

Gaines, Larry K. and William Forester (1983). Recruit Training Processes and Issues. In Swank, Calvin J. and James A. Conser (Eds.) *The Police Personnel System.* New York: John Wiley and Sons, Inc.

Gammage, Allen Z. (1963). Police Training in the United States. Springfield, IL: Charles C. Thomas and Project STAR, Police Officer Role Training Program (1974). Santa Cruz, CA: Davis Publishing Company, Inc.

Glasgow, E.H., R.R. Green, and L. Knowles (1973). Arrest Performance Among Patrolmen in Relation to Job Satisfaction and Personal Variables. *The Police Chief.* April:28–34.

Gottlieb, M.C. and C.F. Baker (1974). Predicting Police Officer Effectiveness. *Journal of Forensic Psychology.* December:35–46.

Gratz v. Bollinger, 539 U.S. 244 (2003)

Gregory, Alicia (January 1, 2008). FLETC augments training with technology. Marine Tactical. http://www.fletc.gov/news/press-clips/fletc-augments-training-with-technology.html

Griffin, G.R. (1980). *A Study of Relationships Between Level of College Education and Police Patrolmen's Performance.* Saratoga, CA: Century Twenty-One.

Griggs v. Duke Power Company, 401 U.S. 424 (1971).

Gronlund, Norman E. (1970). *Stating Behavioral Objectives for Classroom Instruction.* New York: The Macmillan Company.

Grutter v. Bollinger, 539 U.S. 306 (2003)

Harris, Richard (1973). *The Police Academy: An Inside View.* New York: John Wiley and Sons, Inc.

Hayeslip, David W., Jr. (1989). Higher Education and Police Performance Revisited: The Evidence Examined through Meta-Analysis. *American Journal of Police,* 8(2):49–63.

Hilal, Susan M. and Timothy E. Erickson (2010). The Minnesota Police Education Requirement: A Recent Analysis. *FBI Law Enforcement Bulletin.* 79(6):17–21.

Hooper, M.K. (1988). *The Relationship of College Education to Police Officer Job Performance.* Doctoral Dissertation, Claremont Graduate School.

Hoover, Larry T. (1983). The Educational Criteria: Dilemmas and Debate. In Swank, Calvin and James A. Conser (Eds) *The Police Personnel System.* New York: John Wiley and Sons, Inc.

Hughes, Thomas, Beth Sanders, and Robert Langworthy (1996). Police Officer Training: A Survey of Major Police Departments in the United States. *Police Forum.* (6)2:18–20.

Hunter, J.E., F.L. Schmidt, and G.E. Jackson (1982). *Meta-Analysis: Cumulating Research Findings Across Studies.* Beverly Hills: Sage Publications.

Kakar, Suman (1998). Self-Evaluations of Police Performance: An Analysis of the Relationship between Police Officers' Education Level and Job Performance. *Policing.* 21(4):632.

Kappeler, V.E., A.D. Sapp, and D.L. Carter (1992). Police Officer Higher Education, Citizen Complaints, and Departmental Rule Violations. *American Journal of Police.* 11(2):37–55.

Kedia, P.R. (1985). *Assessing the Effect of College Education on Police Performance.* Doctoral Dissertation, University of Southern Mississippi.

Kenney, Dennis J., and Gary W. Cordner (1996). *Managing Police Personnel.* Cincinnati, OH: Anderson Publishing.

Krimmel, John T. (1996). The Performance of College-Educated Police: A Study of Self-Rated Police Performance Measures. *American Journal of Police.* 15(1):85–95.

Krimmel, John T., and Paul Lindenmouth (2001). Police Chief Performance and Leadership Styles. *Police Quarterly.* 4(4):469–483.

Langworthy, R.H. and L. F. Travis III (1994). *Policing in America: A Balance of Forces.* New York: Macmillan Publishing Co.

Law Enforcement News (2003). Where there's smoke, there's fired. August 31:1, 10.

Lester, D. (1979). Predictors of Graduation From a Police Training Academy. *Psychological Reports.* 44:362–368.

Lotz, R. and R. Regoli (1977). Police Cynicism and Professionalism. *Human Relations.* 30:175–181.

Lynch, G.W. (1976). The Contributions of Higher Education to Ethical Behavior in Law Enforcement. *Journal of Criminal Justice.* 4(4):285–290.

Major City Chiefs Association, National Executive Institute Associates, and Federal Bureau of Investigation (1993). *Physical fitness testing in law enforcement: An analysis of the impact of the Americans with Disabilities Act, The Civil Rights Act of 1991, and the Age Discrimination in Employment Act: A Conference Report.* Washington, D.C.: Federal Bureau of Investigation.

Marsh, S. (1962). Validating the Selection of Deputy Sheriffs. *Public Personnel Review.* January:41–44.

McCampbell, Michael S. (1986). *Field Training for Police Officers: State of the Art.* Research in Brief. Washington, D.C.: National Institute of Justice.

"Men & Women of Letters" (1997). *Law Enforcement News.* November 30:1.

Minnesota, State of, (1978). *Minnesota Code of Agency Rules: Peace Officer Standards and Training Board.* St. Paul, MN: Office of the State Register.

Minnesota State Statutes (1998), §§ 626.843 and 626.845.

Moriarty, Anthony R. and Mark W. Field (1989). Police psychological screening: The third generation. *The Police Chief.* February:36–40.

Moriarty, Anthony R. and Mark W. Field (1994). *Police Officer Selection: A Handbook for Law Enforcement Administrators.* Springfield, IL: Charles C. Thomas.

National Advisory Commission on Criminal Justice Standards and Goals (1973). *Report on Police.* Washington, D.C.: U.S. Government Printing Office.

National Association of Field Training Officers (2011). FTO Program Websites. http://nafto.org.dnnmax.com/Resources/FTOPrograms.aspx

National Citizen's Police Academy Association (2011). Frequently Asked Questions. http://www.nationalcpaa.org/FAQ.html

Niederhoffer, A. (1967). *Behind the Shield: The Police in Urban Society.* New York: Doubleday.

O'Brien, Kenneth (1999). Mini Report. International Association of Directors of Law Enforcement Standards and Training, Conference Manual. Orlando, FL: (June 8):271.

Parker, L. Jr., D. Donnelly, J. Gerwitz, J. Marcus, and V. Kowalewski (1976). Higher Education: Its Impact on Police Attitudes. *The Police Chief.* 43:33–35.

Patterson, D.E. (1991). College Educated Police Officers: Some Impacts on the Internal Organization. *Law and Order.* 39(11):68–71.

Penegor, Janice K., and Ken Peak (1992). Police Chief Acquisitions: A Comparison of Internal and External Selections. *American Journal of Police.* 11(1):17–32.

Polk, O Elmer, and David A. Armstrong (2001). Higher Education and Law Enforcement Career Paths: Is the Road to Success Paved by Degree? *Journal of Criminal Justice Education.* 12(1):77–99.

Powell, D.D. (1980). *A Study of Police Supervisors, Criminal Justice Educators, Non-Criminal Justice Educators, and Citizen's Attitudes in Michigan Concerning the Need for Higher Education in Michigan.* Doctoral Dissertation, Michigan State University.

President's Commission on Law Enforcement and Administration of Justice (1967). *Task Force Report: The Police.* Washington, D.C.: U.S. Government Printing Office.

President's Commission on Law Enforcement and Administration of Justice (1967). *The Challenge of Crime in a Free Society.* Washington, D.C.: U.S. Government Printing Office.

Project STAR (1974). *Police Officer Role Training Program.* Santa Cruz, CA: Davis Publishing Company, Inc.

Public Law 92-261, Section 703(a) (Civil Rights Act of 1964, Title VII).

Public sector unionism—origins and perspective—part I: historical summary (1972). UCLA Law Review 19(6): 893–894, in Richard M. Ayres and Thomas L. Wheelen (eds.).

Reaves, Brian. (2009). *State and Local Law Enforcement Training Academies, 2006.* Washington D.C.: U.S. Department of Justice.

Reaves, Brian. (2010). *Local Police Departments, 2007.* Washington D.C.: U.S. Department of Justice.

Reaves, Brian and Matthew J. Hickman (2004). *Law Enforcement Management and Administrative Statistics, 2000: Data for Individual State and Local Agencies with 100 or More Officers.* Washington, D.C.: U.S. Department of Justice.

Regoli, R. (1976). The Effects of College Education on the Maintenance of Police Cynicism. *Journal of Police Science and Administration.* 4:340–345.

Risher, Julie (2003). A chief's conundrums: Light duty, ADA, FLSA. *The Police Chief.* May:12–13.

Roberg, R.R. (1978). An Analysis of the Relationships Among Higher Education, Belief Systems, and Job Performance of Patrol Officers. *Journal of Police Science and Administration.* 6(3):336–344.

Rydberg, Jason. And William Terrill. (2010). The Effect of Higher Education on Police Behavior. *Police Quarterly,* 13(1):92–120.

Sanderson, B. (1978). Police Officers: The Relationship of College Education to Job Performance. *The Police Chief.* 44 (August):62–63.

Sauls, John Gales (1991). Employment discrimination: A title VII primer. *FBI Law Enforcement Bulletin.* December:8–24.

Saunders, Charles B., Jr. (1970). *Upgrading the American Police: Education and Training for Better Law Enforcement.* Washington, D.C.: The Brookings Institution.

Savage, David G. (1997). High court allows Prop 209's repeal of affirmative action. *Los Angeles Times.* November 4:1.

Seklecki, Richard and Rebecca Paynich. (2004). *A national survey of female police officers: An overview of findings.* Paper presented at the national Academy of Criminal Justice Sciences conference in Las Vegas, March.

Seklecki, R. & R. Paynich, (2007) "A National Survey of Female Police Officers: An Overview of Findings." *Police Practice & Research: An International Journal.* 8(1):17–30.

Shattuch, John (1973). *The Lie Detector as a Surveillance Device.* New York: American Civil Liberties Union.

Sherman, L. and M. Blumberg (1981). Higher Education and Police Use of Deadly Force. *Journal of Criminal Justice.* 9(4):317–331.

Shernock, S. (1992). The Effects of College Education on Professional Attitudes Among Police. *Journal of Criminal Justice Education.* 3 (1): 71–92.

Sherwood, Charles W. (2000). Job Design, Community Policing, and Higher Education: A Tale of Two Cities. *Police Quarterly.* 3(2):191–212.

Skolnick, Jerome (1969). *The Politics of Protest.* New York: Simon and Schuster.

Smith, A.B., B. Locke, and B. Fenster (1970). Authoritarianism in Policemen Who Are College Graduates and Non-College Graduates. *Journal of Criminal Law, Criminology and Police Science.* 61:313–315.

Smith, A.B., B. Locke, and W.F. Walker (1967). Authoritarianism in College and Non-College Oriented Police. *Journal of Criminal Law, Criminology and Police Science.* 58:128–132.

Smith, D.C. (1978a). Dangers of Police Professionalization: An Empirical Analysis. *Journal of Criminal Justice.* 6(3):199–216.

Smith, D.C. (1978b). *Empirical Studies of Higher Education and Police Performance.* Washington, D.C.: Police Foundation.

Smith, D., and E. Ostrom (1974) The Effects of Training and Education on Police Attitudes and Performance: A Preliminary Analysis. In H. Jacob (Ed) *The Potential for Reform in Criminal Justice.* Beverly Hills, CA: Sage Publications.

Spencer, G., and R. Nichols (1971). A Study of Chicago Police Recruits. *The Police Chief.* June:50–55.

Strawbridge, Peter and Deirdre (1990). *A networking guide to recruitment, selection and probationary training of police officers in major police departments of the United States of America.* New York: John Jay College of Criminal Justice.

Sweeney, Earl M. (1999). *New Hampshire's Ongoing Fitness Assessment Program*. Annual Conference Manual, International Association of Directors of Law Enforcement Standards and Training, Orlando, FL: June 8.

Tallahassee Community College, Florida Public Safety Institute (2011). Courses. https://fpsi.tcc.fl.edu/pages/layout_advspec.aspx

Taylor, M. (1983). Police Training: Towards a New Model. *The Police Journal*. 56:124–133.

Territo, Leonard (1974). The use of the polygraph in the pre-employment screening process. *The Police Chief*. July:51.

Trojanowicz, Robert, and T. Nicholson (1976). A Comparison of Behavioral Styles of College Graduate Police Officers v. Non-College Going Police Officers. *The Police Chief*. August:56–59.

Truxillo, Donald M., Suzanne R. Bennett, and Michelle L. Collins (1998). College Education and Police Job Performance: A Ten-Year Study. *Public Personnel Management*. 27(2):269–280.

Tyre, M. and S. Braunstein (1992). Higher Education and Ethical Policing. *FBI Law Enforcement Bulletin*. 61(6):1–5.

Vodicka, A.T. (1994). Educational Requirements for Police Recruits. *Law and Order*. 420:91–94.

Vollmer, August (1969). The Police and Modern Society. Publications of the Bureau of Public Administration, University of California.

Weiner, N. (1976). The Educated Policeman. *Journal of Police Science and Administration*. 4:450–458.

Weirman, C. (1978). Variances of Ability Measurement Scores Obtained by College and Non-College Educated Troopers. *The Police Chief*. August:34–36.

West Virginia State Police (April 2010). Open the Door to a New Career. http://www.wvstatepolice.com/employ/brochure.pdf.

Wilson, James Q. (1983). *Crime and Public Policy*. San Francisco: ICS Press.

Withal, D. (1985). *The American Law Enforcement Chief Executive: A Management Profile*. Washington, D.C.: Police Executive Research Forum.

Worden, R.E. (1990). A Badge and a Baccalaureate: Policies, Hypotheses, and Further Evidence. *Justice Quarterly*. 7(3):565–592.

Wycoff, M. (1987). New 'Yes Person' Managers. *Police Manager: Newsletter of the Police Management Association*. June: 18.

Wycoff, M., and C. Susmilch (1979). The Relevance of College Education for Policing: Continuing the Dialogue. In D. Peterson (ed) *Police Work: Strategies and Outcomes in Law Enforcement*. Beverly Hills, CA: Sage Publications.

Xavier University (2004). Learning Styles. Cincinnati, OH: The Learning Assistance Center. http://www.xu.edu/lac/learning_styles.htm

Zhao, Jihong, Quint Thurman, and Ni He (1999). Sources of Job Satisfaction Among Police Officers: A Test of Demographic and Work Environment Models. *Justice Quarterly*. 16(1):153–173.

CHAPTER 8

Socialization, Advancement, & Professionalism

LEARNING OBJECTIVES

This chapter examines three aspects of the police profession: socialization, advancement, and professionalism. As you will learn, socialization into the culture of law enforcement is a complex process. It is not a single event; socialization is a continuing process that influences advancement and the continued professionalism of law enforcement. By studying the concepts and principles presented here, you will be able to:

- Define the concept of police subculture.
- Explain the negative and positive characteristics of the police subculture.
- Describe the legal prerequisites and limitations of personnel functions.
- Explain at least four different methods utilized in policing for promoting persons to higher rank and responsibility.
- Distinguish between the concepts of "labor relations" and "collective bargaining."
- Describe the purpose of a code of ethics and explain the basic tenets of the police code of conduct.
- Understand the different types of police misconduct and how early warning signs and other efforts attempt to control them.

CHAPTER OUTLINE

KEY TERMS USED IN THIS CHAPTER

socialization process	benevolent associations
police subculture	profession
occupational dimension	craft
psychological dimension	code of ethics
political dimension	morality
social dimension	moral behavior (or right conduct)
symbolic assailant	
detraining syndrome	police crime
promotion	occupational deviance
career development	corruption
lateral entry	abuse of authority
labor relations	civilian review
collective bargaining	decertification

Eric Smith, 32-year veteran police officer

Source: Courtesy of Eric Smith

SOCIALIZATION INTO THE CULTURE OF LAW ENFORCEMENT

Eric Smith is a 32-year veteran police officer for the city of Brockton, Massachusetts. Brockton is located just south of Boston, has a population of just over 96,400 persons, and had an incidence of 1194 violent crimes and 3207 property crimes in 2009. The Brockton Police Department employs approximately 200 personnel—180 sworn and 20 civilian. If you were to ask Eric why he became a police officer, his answer would be similar to many other officers across the nation. First, he had people in his immediate family who were police officers. Both Eric's father and grandfather were Boston police officers and while growing up, although Eric was not always clear his career would be in law enforcement, he knew he wanted to work in an exciting field that allowed him to help people. Second, Eric had prior experience in the military, where he worked overseas in a Helicopter Rescue unit in the early 1970s. He later moved into the corrections field, working as a guard at the Charles Street Jail in Boston and eventually making his way to the Brockton Police Department.

One could argue that, in several important ways, Eric was socialized to be a police officer. First, by watching his father and grandfather and only socializing with other law enforcement families, Eric learned early on many of the values and norms associated with policing. Second, military training taught Eric how to respond quickly to uncertain and dangerous conditions and how to work well in a hierarchical organization. Research suggests that individuals with an interest in law enforcement careers are more likely to come from families with law enforcement and military backgrounds (Caldero and Crank 2004). In Eric's case, both the military and family law enforcement backgrounds played heavily into his decision to make a career of policing.

Socialization is the process whereby individuals learn and internalize the attitudes, values, and behaviors appropriate to persons functioning as social beings and responsive, participating members of their society. Socialization ensures that the individual will develop an identity, or self-concept, and also the motivation and requisite knowledge to perform adequately in the social roles he or she is called upon to enact throughout his or her lifetime (Socialization 1974). As discussed in Chapter 7, some of the purposes of police training include job orientation, indoctrination, safety/survival, and morale. As such, training is a key feature in the **socialization process.**

The Police Culture

Socialization plays a vital role in any culture and prepares its people to function in society according to its norms and values. In an occupational aspect, every employment field has its own unique culture; in law enforcement, it is often referred to as the **police subculture**. Goldstein (1977, 10) describes it as "that intricate web of relationships among peers that shapes and perpetuates the pattern of behavior, values, isolation, and secrecy that distinguish the police." The police subculture has been referred to by numerous terms in the literature, including: police social system, police ethos, occupational personality, the cop personality, and the police mystique (Conser 1980).

In 1968, James Sterling wrote about the relationship of training to the socialization process in these terms:

Socialization for the police recruit includes both the adoption of normative modes of police behavior and the extinction of certain other behaviors, which were appropriate for his previous civilian roles. In learning the new role, the police recruit undertakes a complex process of learning, which includes more than just knowledge and skills. He will also learn a system of attitudes, beliefs, perceptions, and values. The most important learning related to perception concerns the identification of role relevant reference groups and a sensitivity to their expectations and evaluations (112).

Police culture continues to be a topic of lively and vital discussions. Culture, in its broadest sense, is a shared sense of values, goals, and expectations among members about an organization or profession. Police culture, then, is the sum total of the values, goals, and expectations that law enforcement officers share. There are many ways in which police culture has been viewed, and one effort attempted to integrate prior perspectives by searching for common themes that tie police together (Crank 1998). Crank argued that police culture reproduces itself in similar ways in different locations, and that it results from a shared application of practical skills while facing similar problems and environments and engaging in similar daily routines. These similarities produce shared themes that Crank identifies as coercive territorial control, the unknown solidarity with other officers, death, and a collection of "loosely coupled" themes (e.g., deception, outsiders). Crank's view—that the nature of the work in a particular environment produces culture—conflicts with other views of policing organizations as being influenced by external political factors (Zhao 1996), while beat style is influenced by the nature of the beat (Klinger 1997). It has been suggested that cultural differences exist between agencies. Little empirical work has been conducted in this area, partially because of the vagueness of the term "organizational culture," but the notion appears to be an accepted one by many authors (Armacost 2004; Boke and Nalla 2009; Braunstein 2007) and is important for officers and citizens alike to consider.

Conceptually, the police subculture can be viewed as containing four dimensions (Goldsmith and Goldsmith 1974). The **occupational dimension** considers the uniquely job-related factors that affect and condition the police to behave in selected ways. The **psychological dimension** focuses of police self-identity and personality development. The **political dimension** considers the relationship between the police community and the policy-making authorities of the agency and society at large. The **social dimension** addresses the police officers' social organization, subculture norms, and the nature of police solidarity. It must be noted that although these dimensions permit a nontechnical framework for viewing the police subculture, the variables and effects found in each are not isolated to that dimension; the variables are dynamic and can influence the factors or variables in other dimensions.

The Occupational Dimension

Research associated with this dimension focuses on the unique characteristics of the job of policing and how they influence officers. Studies have concluded that policing often leads to collectively-supported secrecy among officers; such secrecy is considered so important that officers may break the law or their ethical code to support it (Westley 1956). Role conflict, development of police styles, isolationism, and negative perceptions of citizens have been issues discussed in much of the research concerning occupational variables (Banton 1964; Bayley 1994; Bittner 1990; Goldstein 1963; Manning 1997; White 1972; and Wilson 1968).

The work of Jerome Skolnick regarding the "working personality" of police officers has become a classic in the scholarship of policing. His findings suggest that the variables of danger and authority, when viewed in the context of a prevailing pressure to be efficient, are fundamental to the development of an officer's occupational personality. This preoccupation with potential violence also fosters the development of a **symbolic assailant**, which is a person who uses "gesture, language, and attire that the police have come to recognize as a prelude to violence" (Skolnick 1994, 44). Police are trained to be suspicious, partly because that suspicion may mean the difference between injury and non-injury, or survival and death. Unfortunately, according to Skolnick (1994), this suspicion may be generalized toward the public at large, which results in increased isolation from citizens and increased police solidarity.

The symbolic assailant concept

Source: © iStockphoto/Thinkstock

The Psychological Dimension

The psychological dimension emphasizes the self-concept and personality development of officers and attempts to answer the question: "Do officers' personalities change because of the job, independently of the job—or not at all?" There is no definitive answer to this question, and studies can be found that are contradictory and inconclusive. The variables that are usually addressed in this dimension have to do with conservatism, authoritarianism, stereotyping, cynicism, aggressiveness, mental strength and toughness (machoism), and sexism.

William Doerner (1985) wrote about his experience going from professor to police officer and the psychological changes he experienced as a result of the transition: "Changes, which I thought were subtle and only partially visible to others, have altered me to such a degree that I am an entirely different person with a completely different set of values, beliefs, and attitudes" (394). Doerner's description of his transition is similar to George Kirkham's,

who completed the same process in the early 1970s. Both reflect the "reality shock" of working the street and how it affected their outlook. Their accounts, and others in the literature, discuss how an officer's personality appears to change. For example, they become somewhat callous, less trusting, more cynical, and sometimes frustrated. Of course these are generalizations; not all officers experience these changes to the same degree, and some may not experience them at all. Other research suggests that people with certain personality traits tend to be attracted to careers in policing and that these traits predate an individual's entrance into the career. Nonetheless, the research is mixed concerning possible personality changes brought on by becoming a police officer.

The Political Dimension

The political dimension attempts to analyze policing in light of community power structures and internal/external influences upon the officer (Skolnick 1969; Wilson 1975).

Louis A. Radelet (1973) pointed out four distinguishable types of police–political relationships:

1. Police–Partisan relationships occur when police engage in politics in a partisan manner. The history of partisan politics in policing generally has been one of the spoils system and corrupt practices (see Chapter 3).
2. Police–Cultural relationships occur when the police enforce local mores and expectations, even though they may not be lawful. In other words, priorities are given to local parochial interests at the expense of "outsiders."
3. Police–Fraternalistic relationships occur within the police organization itself, usually through lobbying and/or union efforts.
4. Police–Administrative relationships pertain to the relationships of the department's chief executive officer to decision-makers in government, such as the mayor, city manager, city councils, and so on. It relates to influencing public opinion, budget decisions, and department goals. It encompasses the leadership role, which is integral to effective public administration.

Radelet stated that the police–administrative relationship is the only legitimate political relationship and that the others are questionable at best, often having resulted in improper, sometimes even illegal, actions by police. However, contemporary developments involving community policing create a new set of problems. Consider these comments from Carter (Carter and Radelet 1999):

> And now community policing adds yet another dimension to the politics and structure of administration. Traditionally, police activities have been dictated by a complete "top-down" approach. That is, police administrators would define programs, the types of crimes that would be addressed, and assorted activities of officers, usually based on a crime analysis that balanced trends with efficiency. Sometimes, this would be even more "top directed" when elected officials asked (or instructed) the police department to focus on specific issues—violent crimes and the illicit drug trade serve as recent examples (426).

Remember, in the ideal community-policing model, it is the community who identifies the types of problems they want to be addressed, the types of activities they would like officers to engage in, and the overall policing goals they would like within their community. In actual practice, however, this has been a very rare development, but progress is being made in many jurisdictions.

The Social Dimension

The social dimension focuses on the role of the police officer, primarily in terms of role conflict, group behavior, and the socialization process. It suggests that loyalty, comradeship, solidarity, and secrecy are critical aspects of police culture and group dynamics strongly influence officer behavior and how they indoctrinate (socialize) and accept new members. For example, according to Harris (1973), the most significant consequence of police training is the cultivation of solidarity—the subjective feeling of belonging, moral support, and depersonalization (toward other non-officers).

Other aspects of the social dimension have focused on such things as rates of divorce, alcoholism, suicide, and stress-related health issues within the police as compared to other groups. The empirical evidence on these matters varies from place to place and from study to study. We cannot conclude that officers suffer from higher rates of divorce, heart disease, ulcers, alcoholism, and so on because the empirical evidence is mixed. However, stress still plays an important role in the police subculture, so we need to address several key findings in the literature. First, while policing can be a physically and emotionally demanding job, research suggests that the majority of the stress that officers face is from politics at work and friction between the line level and administration (see Caldero and Crank 2004 for a more thorough discussion). Second, research suggests that women and men suffer similar rates of stress in policing, although the coping strategies and physical impacts can vary dramatically between them (Bradway 2009). Third, the size of the department may not matter much in terms of the amount of stress an officer may experience, but it does change the dynamics of the causal factors of the stress; for example, Oliver and Meire (2004) found that the 947 officers in their study of 11 West Virginia departments reported stress about several job-related items primarily in the categories of security and working conditions. Fourth, American police are not alone in the stress they experience. Buker and Wiecko (2006) found that Turkish police also experience high levels of stress, and the primary stressor for many officers appears to be organizational stress (similar to U.S. police). Lastly, there is some research that suggests police officers, due to the nature of their work, have biologically different patterns than non-police officers, which impact their health and relationships in important ways. Kevin Gilmartin's work in *Emotional Survival for Law Enforcement* (2002) argues that officers, even in less busy departments, are on a "biological rollercoaster" due to high stress (and moments of perceived high stress) and the more frequent and sporadic release of adrenaline experienced than persons in other occupations. This biological rollercoaster can wreak havoc on an officer's health and personal relationships.

In addition to the mixed research on stress and policing, the research is also inconsistent relative to the police subculture. Some research suggests that different agencies retain their own culture. Regardless, one thing is certain: a police subculture exists, although we may not agree as to its universal characteristics, codes, and behavior. The police themselves perceive it, and as long as they do, it is real to them. Barbara Bennett (1978) referred to it as the "police mystique," "a body of ideas and attitudes that has become associated with a group of people or an institution… often more imagined than real" (46).

Of course, there are also studies that refute the importance of the police subculture and the impact of police socialization on officers. Some of the newer developments, such as community policing and emphasis on crime prevention and social service roles, may reverse or impede some of the negative aspects of the police subculture. In addition, since a more-educated class of individual is being attracted to the field, their backgrounds may modify the traditionally negative impact of some of the socialization process. Moreover, academic and academy programs are placing greater emphasis on some aspects of the negative side of police subculture, coupled with greater emphasis on ethics and integrity as a positive force for change and integrity maintenance in policing. Conser (1980) has suggested the following policy recommendations in order to

reduce or lessen some of the perceived negative aspects of the police subculture and the socialization process:

1. A commitment to a more open system organization that, in part, reduces the secretiveness that often permeates the structure.
2. A greater understanding of the role of the officer in policing the community, particularly regarding norm violations and minor misdemeanors.
3. A greater emphasis at training academies on the police subculture and its positive and negative effects—possibly taught by non-police personnel or in a cooperative effort with selected non-police trainers.
4. A greater care and emphasis on the selection and training of Field Training Officers in order to overcome aspects of the **detraining syndrome**— the process of transforming the highly motivated, idealistic recruit to one that is disillusioned and distrustful.
5. A greater commitment to and recognition of individual integrity and ethical standards in order to reduce conformity pressures.
6. A commitment to excellence in supervision— developing educated, well-trained, and enlightened supervisors who understand principles of leadership, motivation, accountability, and integrity (52–53).

If the police subculture is the result of the learning process, then that process can be utilized to reduce the negative attributes usually associated with the subculture. Greater transparency of police operations and a more educated populace also contributes to a reduction of negative attributes and influences organizational culture (Braunstein 2007).

PROMOTION AND CAREER DEVELOPMENT

Persons entering the law enforcement field look forward to a long and satisfying career, with the majority of officers remaining with the same agency for their entire career. They look forward to promotion and/or career development and growth, which may also include a specialized assignment. **Promotion** generally refers to a positive change in rank status: a patrol officer is promoted to sergeant, a sergeant is promoted to lieutenant, and so on. **Career development** refers to a desired change in work assignment that is accompanied by increased responsibility and may involve additional training and/or education. Career development may include a promotion; however, it is not necessary. For example, officers may prefer to continue working in a particular assignment, such as patrol or investigations, and not seek promotion to positions that may be more supervisory or managerial in nature. In any case, because of the diversity of police work, career development in the form of new skills, training/education, and experiences can take many paths as officers' progress in their careers.

Modern departments recognize the fact that not everyone wants to be promoted in rank and are therefore developing compensation schemes that reward officers who pursue excellence in the critical areas of patrol and investigation. Also, some departments are streamlining their rank structures and eliminating middle management positions. As this movement continues, the opportunities for promotion will decrease, and so the challenge in such departments is how to increase the incentives of career development in those ranks that continue to exist.

Promotion

Promotion for law enforcement officers can be based on a number of variables, which can vary from department to department. The differences are often contingent upon an agency's personnel system and city, county, or state laws governing personnel practices. The most prevalent variables (deciding factors) in promotions include: seniority, past achievements, merit, written testing (under civil service or central personnel office policies), assessment of skills (as discussed in Chapter 7 for the hiring process), or a combination of the above; and in some cases, promotions are based on political connections. Each deciding factor or model is briefly discussed in the following sections.

Political

The least common variable is promotional considerations that fall under the concept of "who you know." This had been a common practice in the early years of policing (see Chapter 3). It is based on influence and power; it

does not consider merit, ability, or experience. Under this concept, power brokers and political leaders influence the promotion of officers. In short, promotion is a reward for devoted and loyal service to those individuals. This variable is uncommon today, but still exists in some areas; however, professional policing rejects this variable as a consideration or an appropriate influence in promotional decisions.

Seniority

Seniority is a common variable in many promotional systems. Specifically, length of service with the agency is one consideration, but it is usually not the sole criterion for promotion.

Experience and Accomplishments

Experience and accomplishments are often variables in promotional decisions. The premise here is that if an individual has performed well in one position and grown professionally because of that experience, they will do well in the next rank level. While this might not always prove correct, it is a strong indicator when other factors are considered. Again, experience is one consideration, but it is usually not the sole criterion for promotion.

Merit

Promotion based on merit, which includes an assessment of the candidate's attributes like ability, talents, skills, and knowledge, are common in most promotional systems. Merit is based on an evaluation of the candidate's strengths (i.e., talents, skills, and knowledge), experiences, and accomplishments. Again, merit is one consideration, but it is usually not the sole criterion for promotion.

Testing

Many jurisdictions administer written exams for promotion. Some agencies use highly- rigid procedures that do not consider other variables (e.g., seniority, experience, merit) and simply use the results of the test to dictate promotional rankings. The rule of one is used often in such systems, meaning that the person with the highest test score is the next person promoted. While there are benefits to this approach, it relies heavily on book knowledge and test-taking ability and does not necessarily measure interpersonal communications and other leadership qualities, nor does it adequately simulate field conditions under which this person must make decisions.

Assessment Center

The assessment center approach to promotion involves observation and measurement of what a candidate does and how well it is done in simulated job situations or scenarios that would be encountered in the promoted position. It may involve interviews, oral presentations, psychological testing, writing memos, and role playing. The "assessors" in this approach may be top-level managers/administrators inside the department and/or individuals (with policing expertise) from outside the department. The objective is to analyze the candidate's ability to perform in situations that are common to the promoted position. Elements of stress and confrontation are usually part of this assessment. The entire process may take several days or be conducted intermittently over several weeks.

Hybrid

A hybrid model of promotion may involve two or more of the above approaches. For example, a civil service promotion system may involve a written exam, a supervisory rating, and seniority points; another example is an appointment system that involves past performance ratings, ratings of supervisors, and an oral board. This is the most common method for promotions in American policing.

Whichever system of promotion is used, one must remember that the law of personnel practices discussed above applies, and therefore, if challenged, the agency must be able to show that the criteria for promotion were job-related and relevant. Just as many agencies found themselves in court over selection procedures, many have had their promotional procedures examined and thrown out.

Career Development

Career development is closely associated with various types of training that are discussed in detail in Chapter 7. However, besides the training component, career development involves increasing levels of responsibility and personal growth. Some departments allow for growth within a given rank by establishing sub-ranks or classifications within ranks such as Police Officer I, II, and III, or Sergeant I, II, and III. This allows an officer to remain within a specific rank or job category and still pursue an increase in responsibility and a change of assignment.

Some departments allow for personal growth and assignment change through **lateral entry**. It usually refers to conditions where an officer at the patrol, investigative, or supervisory level can transfer to another agency without any loss of seniority, rank, and salary. Lateral entry is not as common in municipal departments or state agencies as it is in sheriff's departments. Most seniority systems, central personnel system policies, and/or union contracts protect officers within agencies from the lateral transfer of officers outside the agency (which is a form of protectionism).

LABOR RELATIONS IN LAW ENFORCEMENT

The concept of **labor relations** refers to the sum total of all interactions between the administration of an agency and its employees. One area of concern under the topic of labor relations is the involuntary termination of a sworn police officer. As public safety employees, police officers can be fired for exhibiting inappropriate behavior that might reflect upon the integrity of the department; for example, while all citizens are guaranteed the right to free expression under the First Amendment, officers can be terminated for expressing disparaging remarks (such as stating that the chief is a complete jerk), which are deemed a matter of "private concern," about the department. However, if the remarks expressed are a matter of "public concern" (stating that many of the officers are frequently drunk on duty), the remarks may be protected under the U.S. Constitution. The court utilizes a two-step approach. First, the court determines whether or not the officer's speech was a matter of public concern, and second, whether or not the individual's interests outweigh the employer's "in promoting the efficiency of the public services it performs through its employees" (Newbold 2003, 10).

A second issue of concern involves name-clearing hearings. Essentially, when an employee has a "liberty interest," which is "when his or her good name, reputation, honor, or integrity is at stake because of what the government is doing to that employee" (Unkelbach 2003, 13), they have the right to a predetermination name-clearing hearing. However, there are certain restrictions placed on the eligibility for these hearings:

> The Circuit Court for the Tenth Circuit has set forth a four-part test which must be met before a claim of deprivation of liberty interests is actionable: (1) the statements at issue must impugn the good name, reputation, honor, or integrity of the employee; (2) these statements must be false; (3) these statements must occur in the course of terminating the employee or must foreclose other employment opportunities; and (4) these statements must be published (Unkelbach, 2003, 13).

Some form of labor relations occurs in all law enforcement agencies; some of these are formal, while others are informal. The most formal means of labor relations is referred to as **collective bargaining**, in which a representative of an employee group (often a union) negotiates the terms and conditions of employment with the representative of the employer. The negotiated document that results from this process is usually called "the contract" or "the agreement." In a 1990 survey of 72 major departments in the United States, 56 (77.7%) permitted union membership, 9 (12.5%) compelled it, and 5 (6.9%) forbade it (3 [4%] agencies gave no response to the question) (Strawbridge 1990). In the Local Police Departments (2007) study, 38% of local police departments employing approximately 66% of all sworn officers authorized collective bargaining. In addition, an estimated 62% of departments serving populations of 10,000 or more authorized collective bargaining for their officers. However, formal collective bargaining varies from state to state. For example, in recent testimony before Congress, it was noted that the states of

> Arizona, Arkansas, Georgia, Indiana, Kansas, Kentucky, Mississippi, Missouri, New Mexico, North Dakota, Tennessee, Texas, and West Virginia have consistently considered and rejected state legislation that would grant public safety officers [the] right to collectively bargain. Virginia and... North Carolina have long standing statutes that expressly prohibit collective bargaining in the public sector (Hankins March 10, 2010).

History of the Police Union Movement

The unionization movement in the public sector can be traced to the 1830s, when mechanics, carpenters, and other craftsmen employed by the federal government joined existing unions made up of private sector employees. Some of the early issues addressed by public sector employees at that time included the desire for a shorter (10-hour) workday and better wages, but most of the gains made in the public sector up through the 1880s came after such work conditions were considered a standard in the private sector (Public Sector Unionism 1972).

Police officers, too, in the late 1880s began to organize. Initially, their organizations were **benevolent associations**, which focused on improving the working conditions and providing assistance (in the form of funeral expenses and widows and orphans funds) to its members who suffered losses. These early associations were often controlled by high ranking officers, and they did not generally interfere with the operation of the department. In addition to benevolent purposes, these associations often served the fraternal and social aspects of the officers. Although not unions in the formal sense, these associations were early forms of employee organizations.

By the early 1900s, associations were common in most major cities. Some agencies had even encountered more organized officer groups: Ithaca, New York experienced a walk-out in 1889 because officers' pay had been reduced from $12 to $9 per week, and Cincinnati, Ohio experienced a strike by 450 officers in 1918 over issues of union organization. By 1919, the American Federation of Labor (AFL) had changed its position on granting formal charters to police locals, and it was immediately swamped with 65 applications which, by the end of summer, resulted in 37 locals (with a total of over 4000 officers) being officially recognized (see Gammage and Sachs 1977 and Smith 1975 for details of early police unionism).

The Boston Police Strike of 1919

One of those locals chartered (August 8, 1919) included the Boston Police Social Club. The officers of Boston had been at odds with the city administration over a pay raise and working conditions for almost a year. The pay raise offered by the city had been deemed insufficient by the social club, which had acted as a representative of the officers in conferring with the city. Eventually, the city yielded by granting higher wages; however, with the soaring costs and the delayed increase, the amounts were still inadequate. **Figure 8-1** describes the working conditions found in the Boston Police Department in 1919.

Two days after the Boston Police Social Club received its charter (as the Boston Policemen's Union), Police Commissioner Curtis issued the following order, which in essence prohibited officers from joining a union affiliated with any national organization:

> *No member of the force shall join or belong to any organization, club or body composed of present or present and past members of the force which is affiliated with or a part of any organization, club or body outside the department, except that a post of the Grand Army of the Republic, the United Spanish War Veterans, and the American Legion of World War Veterans may be formed within the department (Spero 1977, 384).*

A "war of words" raged for weeks. On August 26, the commissioner filed charges against eight police officers who had been elected to positions in the union; shortly thereafter, 11 more were charged. Although discussions between the union and members of a select citizens' committee (appointed by Mayor Peters) attempted to resolve the conflict and were making progress, the commissioner insisted on pursuing the charges against the officers. On September 8, after refusing a settlement proposed by the citizen's committee, the commissioner found the officers guilty and suspended them from service.

The reaction of the stunned union came quickly. Later that same day, the union membership voted 1134 to 2 to strike at 5:45 pm on September 9, 1919. For days, Mayor Peters attempted to engage the assistance of Governor Calvin Coolidge, but he refused to become involved; even a meeting of the citizen's committee with the Governor on the night of September 8th proved fruitless. At noon on the 9th, the Governor issued a letter explaining why he would not interfere in the developments in the department. At 5:45 pm, 1117 of 1544 patrol officers left their posts.

Although the commissioner had promised the mayor and the governor that he had planned for continued protection of the city, general rioting, looting, disorder, and individual robberies occurred. By morning, the commissioner said his resources were inadequate and asked the mayor to activate the troops stationed in the city. The mayor did this, but also assumed command of the department under statutory authority and restored order to the city. Then, not to be outdone, Governor Coolidge activated the state militia throughout the state and sent it to Boston; he then assumed control of the department. It appeared as though every politician was going to make political points out of the situation. Some reports indicate that 100 people were injured, 7 were killed, and over one million dollars' worth of property damage was done during the four-day strike.

Overnight the opinion of the public had turned against the officers; where sympathy for their cause had once existed, condemnation was universal. Over 1100 striking officers were dismissed from the Boston police force and the AFL dissolved all charters to police organizations. For the next 20–30 years, the police unionization movement reverted back to local fraternal associations.

Governor Coolidge became nationally recognized because of the Boston police strike and his famous statement, "There is no right to strike against the public safety, by anyone, anywhere, anytime." It helped propel him to the vice presidency and then, following the death of President Harding, to the presidency in 1923. Did the

---

FIGURE 8-1 Working Conditions in the Boston Police Department in 1919

— 78–90 hour work week, depending on assignment

— $21 a week salary

— Officers had to purchase own uniforms

— Political promotion

— Graft at command levels

— Unsanitary, rodent infested station houses

— Unanswered grievances

Source: Adapted with permission from J.D. Smith, Police Unions: An Historical Perspective of Causes and Organizations, *Police Chief*, November 1975, p.24, © 1975, International Association of Chiefs of Police.

strike have any benefits for the Boston police officers? Yes, working conditions improved after the strike, not only in Boston but in other cities as well, but none of the striking officers were rehired.

Labor Legislation and Growth of Public Sector Unionization

From the early 1900s through the 1950s, police associations at the local level increased significantly in number. While the law in many states did not permit formal collective bargaining, it was not prohibited in most. Municipalities at the local level began to recognize local associations as representing the local department's rank and file. This led to formal dialogue (but not necessarily binding, negotiated contracts) between the association and the administration of agencies.

The efforts of national associations such as the Fraternal Order of Police; the International Conference of Police Associations; the American Federation of State, County, and Municipal Employees; and other groups kept the issue of formal labor relations and the rights of employees in the forefront of personnel discussions. In 1959, Wisconsin enacted a collective bargaining statute for the public sector; President Kennedy issued Executive Order 10988 in 1962, granting bargaining rights to federal employees; and in 1967, New York State enacted the Taylor Law, which permitted collective bargaining in the public sector. By 1974, there were 35 states with legislation granting collective bargaining rights to public employees (only 27 of these allowed it for police officers, however). By 1985, 40 states had passed some form of legislation dealing with public employees (Gaines et al. 1991, 313).

It was the 1960s that experienced the largest growth in formal unionization efforts. Four general factors have been identified as contributing to that growth during those chaotic years: (1) the perception of increased public hostility, (2) rising crime rates and public demand for law and order, (3) salaries and benefits that were lower than those for other public employees and the private sector, and (4) poor personnel practices of police agencies (Juris and Feuille 1974). These factors and the conditions related to them brought about a police militancy never experienced before in the United States. Work stoppages, slow downs, sick-outs (known as the "blue flu"), ticket blitzes,

and strikes occurred frequently during labor disputes in the late 1960s and through the mid-1970s. However, because of major strikes in the cities of Albuquerque, New Mexico; Oklahoma City, Oklahoma; and San Francisco, California, in 1975 unions came under heavy criticism by the public, press, and politicians (Ayres 1977, 431).

Contemporary Unionism

Police unions today are more organized and sophisticated than they have ever been. They have access to excellent legal representation, and they are powerful forces in political lobbying. They have matured greatly in the last three decades. There are many more unionized forces than before, and many departments have to negotiate with more than one union because state laws often allow different unions to represent officers in supervisory ranks. Unions and formal collective bargaining are the norm, which means that personnel practices for the most part are controlled through negotiated agreements. In essence, if an officer believes that he or she has been mistreated by management, the contract is the first document consulted. In many departments, this document (the contract) is as important to the officers as the state criminal code book. Lately, the focus of collective bargaining issues has centered on fringe benefits, especially health insurance and premium co-pays. On average, starting salaries for police officers who are employed with departments with collective bargaining agreements are 38% higher (which translates to about $10,900 in increased pay) (Reaves 2010).

Today, about 38% of public safety (police and fire) personnel are represented by unions nationally. As indicated above, this varies from state to state. On the national level, in 2009, 7.9 million public sector employees belonged to a union, compared with 7.4 million union workers in the private sector. The union membership rate for public sector workers, 37.4%, was substantially higher than the rate for private industry workers, 7.2% (Bureau of Labor Statistics 2010).

PROFESSIONALISM AND ETHICS

Ethics is the philosophical study of moral values and rules. Applied ethics is the branch of ethics that examines questions concerning what is morally right and wrong arising in specific areas of practical concern—for example, in medicine, business, or law enforcement. In a democracy, a major component of the covenant between "the people" and their government is the understanding that government employees are moral and exercise their professional duties as moral agents. Consequently, a law enforcement officer cannot be considered a professional unless he or she is ethical.

Benefits and Characteristics of Profession Status

Since the late 1800s, various police reform movements in the United States have been identified by practitioners and researchers (see Fogelson 1977; Kelling and Moore 1988; and Walker 1977). Some of the reform efforts were directed toward reducing corruption in agencies, some were focused on improved working conditions and economic benefits for officers, some targeted personnel improvement through education and training, and others centered on different models of delivering police services. Whether one agrees with the various classifications and categorizations of reform efforts is not the issue—what should be understood is that the motivations for most of the reform efforts included the underlying beliefs that the police occupation should receive higher public status, should not be controlled by politicians, should be more efficient and effective, and should be worthy of the public trust.

Our discussion here focuses on the quest for **profession** status. In order to understand several of the terms and concepts usually associated with this discussion, we present the following definitions:

(a) Occupation: any activity or endeavor by which one provides or obtains the means to survive (i.e., "earns a living").

(b) Profession: an occupational type based on a special competence with a high degree of intellectual content; a specialty heavily based on or involved with knowledge (see Clark, 1966).

(c) Professional: the person who possesses the characteristics of a profession as defined by colleagues in the profession; aspects associated with a profession.

(d) Professionalism: the character trait of affirming the characteristics or standards of a profession; it is a state of mind exhibited through one's conduct.

(e) Professionalization: the process of achieving or striving toward the goal of professionalism.

The idea or concept of professionalism evolves from a sense of pride in one's work and altruism (a devotion to others and to humanity), as opposed to the underlying selfishness or greed often associated with corruption. As such, any discussion about professionalism must include aspects of values, morality, ethics, what should be done, what is right, standards, and criteria. These terms and concepts often are difficult to define or appreciate because of a lack of consensus among those in the occupation and the various groups and individuals that make up society. The following presentation will not center on the highly philosophical or intellectual aspects of professionalism, but rather on the basic premises underlying the traditional perspective of the search for profession status.

Benefits of Profession Status

Several benefits can be identified for the policing field in pursuing profession status. First, there is greater likelihood of public support and cooperation. If citizens perceive the police as professional, they are more apt to interact positively with them, have less fear of them, and assist in local policing efforts. Second, the quality of applicants and recruits will improve. Persons seeking employment in the police field usually do not seek employment with departments with negative reputations and internal problems (unless they intend on playing a part in changing that reputation for the better). Agencies with good reputations and public support have little problem hiring highly qualified applicants, as they are attracted to such agencies.

Third, professional departments often enjoy higher compensation. Of course, this is relative to the economic ability of the local community and comparisons should be made between the agency and local private and public employment, not necessarily between agencies elsewhere. Four, personnel in professional agencies tend to have higher morale and *esprit de corps*. Such agencies generally have better working conditions and internal relationships among officers. Fifth, and maybe foremost, the citizens of the community of professional departments should receive efficient and effective police protection and service. In other words, the community benefits from the professionalism of the agency and the officers it employs.

By reviewing these benefits, it should be understood that there is interaction among those identified. It could be argued that money alone could achieve most of these benefits. It could improve morale, it could attract qualified candidates, and it could ensure higher salaries, all of which could result in good police service that could assure public support and confidence. Money alone could do these things, and it may in some places, at least in the short term, but money alone is no guarantee to professionalism. If it were, there would be no doubt about how to achieve professional status. But first let us review the traditional characteristics of a profession.

What are the Characteristics of a Profession?

The traditionally recognized fields having "profession" status have included medicine and law, with theology and teaching sometimes in the listing. But what made these occupations different from others? What characteristics today are needed to be recognized as a profession? The traditional characteristics of a profession help guide us in understanding the answers to these questions. The following are the typical characteristics identified in most discussions of traditional criteria of professions:

1. A specific and specialized body of knowledge
2. Extensive preparation through education and training
3. A code of ethics
4. Licensing and regulation boards, associations, or councils
5. A commitment and obligation to a clientele
6. Relative autonomy of its members
7. Public acknowledgment of profession status

Often, the debate over the inclusion of policing as a profession centers on the above criteria and whether the police "measure up" to them. **Figure 8-2** outlines the points and counterpoints of the debate.

FIGURE 8-2 The Debate Over Profession Designation of Policing

Point

1. Policing has a specific body of knowledge associated with crime theory and techniques of handling people.
2. The police field has education and training standards that are rigorous and necessary before one can do the job.
3. The police field has a code of ethics describing the expectation of behavior.
4. Every state has some type of regulating board regarding the certification and/or licensing of officers.
5. The police serve the public and are committed to law, order, and public service. Their obligation is to uphold the law.
6. Officers have considerable discretion and often work alone and make independent decisions.
7. The public recognizes the police field as unique, it understands and appreciates the complexity of public safety services.

Counterpoint

1. The knowledge of policing is not grounded on extensive research and intellectual exploration.
2. Educational standards are rarely beyond high school diplomas and training is counted in hours, not years, as in recognized professions.
3. A single code of ethics is not recognized across the field of law enforcement and there are questions about its enforcement and commitment to it.
4. Many of the boards and licensing agencies lack enforcement powers, are weak, and merely set minimum standards.
5. Are the police truly committed to the public or to themselves? Are they obligated to a clientele or to the law? Are their motivations service-oriented?
6. Police officers do not work independently of others, they have supervisors and are employees of agencies; their autonomy is very limited.
7. The public at large still has many concerns about the integrity and honesty of those in policing, albeit it varies greatly from jurisdiction to jurisdiction. The field as a whole does not have public recognition as a profession.

Policing: Craft or Profession

One of the major debates in the quest for profession status is whether policing is a **craft** or an endeavor that is truly based on scientific principles, research (a specific body of knowledge), and rational analysis (see Bayley and Bittner, 1993 and Roberg and Kuykendall, 1993). A craft usually involves the development of skills that are generally learned through experience, not in a classroom. This debate may appear to be a superficial one at first, but it raises several questions. Why do many working police officers downgrade academy training and state that real policing can only be learned by doing it (which makes it more like a craft)? Some of these same officers then turn around and want profession designation because their tasks are so complex and difficult. Likewise, if it is a craft, why worry about entrance standards when one must experience the job in order to learn it? This kind of belief would negate the need for much of the current entrance testing, screening, or ranking of candidates. Sometimes in the quest for profession status, police officers are their own worst enemies!

If the field is a true profession, then it should be guided by specific principles based on research and analysis, and yet, time and time again major research studies have found that police practices did not yield their intended results (see Chapter 13 regarding research into various police strategies). A major challenge to policing, if it is a profession, is to engage in systemic analysis of all that it does for the purpose of discovering truths about its practices and desired outcomes. It then follows that those practices that are not effective are changed or discontinued.

R.M. Pavalko (1971) once stated that the distinctions between professions and non-professions are differences of degree and not differences of kinds. He asserted that as work becomes more complex and technical, claims of profession status are heard with increasing frequency. In the field of law enforcement, such assertions are frequently made. The individual exhibiting professionalism in an occupation not yet considered a profession is actively engaged in the process of professionalization. Without this process, the non-profession would not become a profession. On the other hand, once the profession status has been "granted" to an occupational field by the public, the individual can hurt or erode the status via nonprofessional behavior. As such, one can argue that professionalism begins and ends with the individual. **Figure 8-3** illustrates the process of professionalization and maintenance of profession status once it is achieved.

An occupation will not achieve profession status (which must be earned from the public) without its individual members exhibiting professional behavior. Likewise, if an occupation achieves profession status, it cannot maintain it unless the individual exhibits continued professional conduct. This, in part, explains why the traditional professions of law, medicine, and theology have seen a slight decline in their professional ratings and

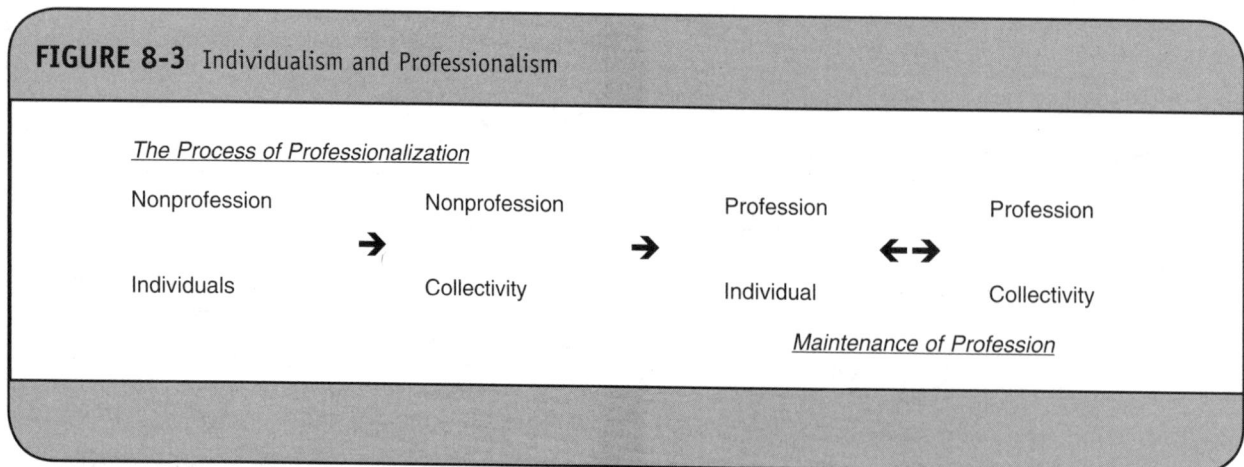

FIGURE 8-3 Individualism and Professionalism

The Process of Professionalization

Nonprofession	Nonprofession	Profession	Profession
Individuals	Collectivity	Individual	Collectivity

Maintenance of Profession

public acceptance in recent years—because of perceived inappropriate behavior by some members of those professions and the widespread publicity that accompanies it. Public perceptions about the professions and about institutions can be measured to some degree by the Gallup organization's annual Honesty and Ethics survey. For the years 2008, 2009, and 2010, when asked about how different fields would be rated for honesty and ethical standards, the percentage of respondents who ranked police officers as "very high or high" was 56%, 63%, and 57%, respectively. Although dropping 6% from 2009, police officers were still ranked as the sixth highest occupation, behind nurses, military officers, pharmacists, grade school teachers, and medical doctors (Jones 2010). Regarding confidence in institutions, according to Gallup surveys for 2009 and 2010, the police (as an institution) has ranked third behind the military and small business (Saad 2010).

We believe that there is another perspective that influences the rise and decline of profession designation, and it refers to the *availability* and *access* to specialized and uncommon knowledge and skill. It was mentioned above that a specific and specialized body of knowledge was the first prerequisite for traditional professions. This characteristic of a profession may be more related to the availability of and access to that knowledge than to the actual possession of it. Historically, doctors, attorneys, clergy, and teachers were perceived as professionals because they possessed knowledge that the common person did not. Today, medical information, legal information, theological documents/sacred writings, and information about teaching techniques are all readily available to the masses. Medical databases and books are consulted by individuals today who possess no special training. Standard legal documents can be purchased in printed or electronic form so the average citizen can write a will or use common legal agreements without engaging an attorney. As the masses have greater access to technical, scientific, legal, and "how to" information, the mystique and aura of those fields tend to wane and employment in said fields is considered less impressive. Some police officers have expressed that, "Everybody thinks they know how our job should be done, so we get no respect and much second-guessing." Our contention is that as long as the public thinks that way, policing will not achieve profession status.

Ethical Codes

The law enforcement community of the United States does have an established and published **code of ethics**; in fact, it has more than one. The International Association of Chiefs of Police (IACP), at its 64th Annual Conference in 1957, adopted a code of ethics for the occupation, along with The Canons of Police Ethics, containing 11 articles. In 1989, a new code of ethics was adopted by the Executive Committee of the IACP during its 96th Annual Conference. At the 98th Annual Conference (1989), the code of ethics was renamed "The Police Code of Conduct" and the 1957 version of the code of ethics was resurrected, revised, and adopted as the (1991) Law Enforcement Code of Ethics. In 1998, at the 105th Annual Conference, IACP adopted the Law Enforcement Oath of Honor, which states:

> On my honor, I will never betray my badge, my integrity, my character, or the public trust. I will always have the courage to hold myself and others accountable for our actions. I will always uphold the Constitution and community I serve (Higginbotham 1999).

Internationally, countries may substitute the word "Constitution" with a monarchy or person or ideal. The IACP, as well as other professional associations, has been very concerned about ethics and integrity in the field. Several key documents such as the IACP's *Law Enforcement Code of Ethics* (**Figure 8-4**), *The Police Code of Conduct* (**Figure 8-5**), and the *Canons of Police Ethics* (**Figure 8-6**) are reprinted here, as well as the *National Sheriffs' Association's Code of Ethics for the Office of the Sheriff* (**Figure 8-7**).

But what is a code of ethics and why is it important have one? A code of ethics is a basic set of guidelines, or set of standards of behavior, to which one should conform in the performance of his or her duty. The word "ethics" has several connotations, including the study of human conduct in light of **morality**; the science dealing with moral duty; and the science of doing the right thing, at the right time, in the right way. Morality refers to the conformity to rules of **right conduct** and **moral behavior** and can be described as representing actions prescribed by society for the welfare of the people and society as a whole. The interconnectedness of ethics, morality, and right conduct becomes evident upon review of these terms and their

---

FIGURE 8-4 The Law Enforcement Code of Ethics

As a law enforcement officer, my fundamental duty is to serve the community; to safeguard lives and property; to protect the innocent against deception, the weak against oppression or intimidation, and the peaceful against violence or disorder; and to respect the Constitutional rights of all to liberty, equality, and justice.

I will keep my private life unsullied as an example to all and will behave in a manner which does not bring discredit to me or my agency. I will maintain courageous calm in the face of danger, scorn, or ridicule; develop self-restraint; and be constantly mindful of the welfare of others. Honest in thought and deed in both my personal and official life, I will be exemplary in obeying the law and the regulations of my department. Whatever I see or hear of a confidential nature or that is confided to me in my official capacity will be kept ever secret unless revelation is necessary in the performance of my duty.

I will never act officiously or permit personal feelings, prejudices, political beliefs, aspirations, animosities, or friendships to influence my decisions. With no compromise for crime and with relentless prosecution of criminals, I will enforce the law courteously and appropriately without fear or favor, malice or ill will, never employing unnecessary force or violence and never accepting gratuities.

I recognize the badge of my office as a symbol of public faith, and I accept it as a public trust to be held so long as I am true to the ethics of police service. I will never engage in acts of bribery nor will I condone such acts by other police officers. I will cooperate with all legally authorized agencies and their representatives in the pursuit of justice.

I know that I alone am responsible for my own standard of professional performance and will take every opportunity to enhance and improve my level of knowledge and competence. I will constantly strive to achieve these objectives and ideals, dedicating myself before God to my chosen profession . . . law enforcement.

Source: International Association of Chiefs of Police. Adopted by resolution at the 98th Conference, October 1991. Modified version of the original Code of 1957, © 1991. International Association of Chiefs of Police.

FIGURE 8-5 The Police Code of Conduct

All law enforcement officers must be fully aware of the ethical responsibilities of their position and must strive constantly to live up to the highest possible standards of professional policing.
The International Association of Chiefs of Police believes it is important that police officers have clear advice and counsel available to assist them in performing their duties consistent with their standards, and has adopted the following ethical mandates as guidelines to meet these ends.

Primary Responsibilities of a Police Officer
A police officer acts as an official representative of government who is required and trusted to work within the law. The officer's powers and duties are conferred by statute. The fundamental duties of a police officer include serving the community; safeguarding lives and property; protecting the innocent; keeping the peace; and ensuring the rights of all to liberty, equality, and justice.

Performance of the Duties of a Police Officer
A police officer shall perform all duties impartially, without favor of affection or ill will and without regard to status, sex, race, religion, political belief or aspiration. All citizens will be treated equally with courtesy, consideration, and dignity.

Officers will never allow personal feelings, animosities, or friendships to influence official conduct. Laws will be enforced appropriately and courteously and, in carrying out their responsibilities, officers will strive to obtain maximum cooperation from the public. They will conduct themselves in appearance and deportment in such a manner as to inspire confidence and respect for the position of public trust they hold.

(continued)

FIGURE 8-5 The Police Code of Conduct (*Continued*)

Discretion

A police officer will use responsibly the discretion vested in the position and exercise it within the law. The principle of reasonableness will guide the officer's determinations and the officer will consider all surrounding circumstances in determining whether any legal action shall be taken.

Consistent and wise use of discretion, based on professional policing competence, will do much to preserve good relationships and to retain the confidence of the public. There can be difficulty in choosing between conflicting courses of action. It is important to remember that a timely word of advice rather than arrest—which may be correct in appropriate circumstances—can be a more effective means of achieving a desired end.

Use of Force

A police officer will never employ unnecessary force or violence and will use only such force in the discharge of duty as is reasonable in all circumstances. Force should be used only with the greatest restraint and only after discussion, negotiation and persuasion have been found to be inappropriate or ineffective. While the use of force is occasionally unavoidable, every police officer will refrain from applying the unnecessary infliction of pain or suffering and will never engage in cruel, degrading, or inhuman treatment of any person.

Confidentiality

Whatever a police officer sees, hears, or learns of, which is of a confidential nature, will be kept secret unless the performance of duty or legal provision requires otherwise. Members of the public have a right to security and privacy, and information obtained about them must not be improperly divulged.

Integrity

A police officer will not engage in acts of corruption or bribery, nor will an officer condone such acts by other police officers. The public demands that the integrity of police officers be above reproach. Police officers must, therefore, avoid any conduct that might compromise integrity and thus undercut the public confidence in a law enforcement agency. Officers will refuse to accept any gifts, presents, subscriptions, favors, gratuities, or promises that could be interpreted as seeking to cause the officer to refrain from performing official responsibilities honestly and within the law. Police officers must not receive private or special advantage from their official status. Respect from the public cannot be bought; it can only be earned and cultivated.

Cooperation with Other Officers and Agencies

Police officers will cooperate with all legally authorized agencies and their representatives in the pursuit of justice. An officer or agency may be one among many organizations that may provide law enforcement services to a jurisdiction. It is imperative that a police officer assist colleagues fully and completely with respect and consideration at all times.

Personal/Professional Capabilities

Police officers will be responsible for their own standard of professional performance and will take every reasonable opportunity to enhance and improve their level of knowledge and competence. Through study and experience, a police officer can acquire the high level of knowledge and competence that is essential for efficient and effective performance of duty. The acquisition of knowledge is a never-ending process of personal and professional development that should be pursued constantly.

Private Life

Police officers will behave in a manner that does not bring discredit to their agencies or themselves. A police officer's character and conduct while off duty must always be exemplary, thus maintaining a position of respect in the community in which he or she lives and serves. The officer's personal behavior must be beyond reproach.

Source: International Association of Chiefs of Police. Adopted by resolution at the 98th Conference, October 1991. Modified version of the original Code of 1957, © 1991. International Association of Chiefs of Police.

FIGURE 8-6 Canons of Police Ethics

ARTICLE I. PRIMARY RESPONSIBILITY OF JOB
The primary responsibility of the police service, and of the individual officer, is the protection of the people of the United States through the upholding of their laws; chief among these is the Constitution of the United States and its amendments. The law enforcement officer always represents the whole of the community and its legally expressed will and is never the arm of any political party or clique.

ARTICLE II. LIMITATIONS OF AUTHORITY
The first duty of a law enforcement officer, as upholder of the law, is to know its bounds upon him in enforcing it. Because he represents the legal will of the community, be it local, state, or federal, he must be aware of the limitations and proscriptions which the people, through the law, have placed upon him. He must recognize the genius of the American system of government which gives to no man, groups of men, or institution, absolute power, and he must insure that he, as a prime defender of that system, does not pervert its character.

ARTICLE III. DUTY TO BE FAMILIAR WITH THE LAW AND WITH RESPONSIBILITIES OF SELF AND OTHER PUBLIC OFFICIALS
The law enforcement officer shall assiduously apply himself to the study of the principles of the laws which he is sworn to uphold. He will make certain of his responsibilities in the particulars of their enforcement, seeking aid from his superiors in matters of technicality or principle when these are not clear to him; he will make special effort to fully understand his relationship to other public officials, including other law enforcement agencies, particularly on matters of jurisdiction, both geographically and substantively.

ARTICLE IV. UTILIZATION OF PROPER MEANS TO GAIN PROPER ENDS
The law enforcement officer shall be mindful of his responsibility to pay strict heed to selection of means in discharging the duties of his office. Violations of law or disregard for public safety and property on the part of an officer are intrinsically wrong; they are self-defeating in that they instill in the public mind a like disposition. The employment of illegal means, no matter how worthy the end, is certain to encourage disrespect for the law and its officers. If the law is honored, it must be honored by those who enforce it.

ARTICLE V. COOPERATION WITH PUBLIC OFFICIALS IN THE DISCHARGE OF THEIR AUTHORIZED DUTIES
The law enforcement officer shall cooperate fully with other public officials in the discharge of authorized duties, regardless of party affiliation or personal prejudice. He shall be meticulous, however, in assuring himself of the propriety, under the law, of such actions and shall guard against the use of his office or person, whether knowingly or unknowingly, in any improper action. In any situation open to question, he shall seek authority from his superior officer, giving him a full report of the proposed service or action.

ARTICLE VI. PRIVATE CONDUCT
The law enforcement officer shall be mindful of his special identification by the public as an upholder of the law. Laxity of conduct or manner in private life, expressing either disrespect for the law or seeking to gain special privilege, cannot but reflect upon the police officer ant the police service. The community and the service require that the law enforcement officer lead the life of a decent and honorable man. Following the career of a policeman gives no man special privileges. It does give the satisfaction and pride of following and furthering an unbroken tradition of safeguarding the American republic. The officer who reflects upon this tradition will not degrade it. Rather, he will so conduct his private life that the public will regard him as an example of stability, fidelity, and morality.

ARTICLE VII. CONDUCT TOWARD THE PUBLIC
The law enforcement officer, mindful of his responsibility to the whole community, shall deal with individuals of the community in a manner calculated to instill respect for its laws and its police service. The law enforcement officer shall conduct his official life in a manner such as will inspire confidence and trust. Thus, he will be neither overbearing nor subservient, as no individual citizen has an obligation to stand in awe of him nor a right to command him. The officer will give service where he can, and require compliance with the law. He will do neither from personal preference or prejudice but rather as a duly appointed officer of the law discharging his sworn obligation.

(continued)

FIGURE 8-6 Canons of Police Ethics (*Continued*)

ARTICLE VIII. CONDUCT IN ARRESTING AND DEALING WITH LAW VIOLATORS

The law enforcement officer shall use his power of arrest strictly in accordance with the law and with due regard to the rights of the citizen concerned. His office gives him no right to prosecute the violator nor to mete out punishment for the offense. He shall at all times, have a clear appreciation of his responsibilities and limitations regarding detention of the violator; he shall conduct himself in such a manner as will minimize the possibility of having to use force. To this end he shall cultivate a dedication to the service of the people and the equitable upholding of their laws whether in the handling of law violators or in dealing with the law-abiding.

ARTICLE IX. GIFTS AND FAVORS

The law enforcement officer, representing government, bears the heavy responsibility of maintaining, in his conduct, the honor and integrity of all government institutions. He shall, therefore, guard against placing himself in a position in which any person can expect special consideration or in which the public can reasonably assume that special consideration is being given. Thus, he should be firm in refusing gifts, favors, or gratuities, large or small, which can, in the public mind, be interpreted as capable of influencing his judgment in the discharge of his duties.

ARTICLE X. PRESENTATION OF EVIDENCE

The law enforcement officer shall be concerned equally in the prosecution of the wrong-doer and the defense of the innocent. He shall ascertain what constitutes evidence and shall present such evidence impartially and without malice. In so doing, he will ignore social, political, and all other distinctions among the persons involved, strengthening the tradition of the reliability and integrity of an officer's word.

The law enforcement officer shall take special pains to increase his perception and skill of observation, mindful that in many situations his is the sole impartial testimony to the facts of a case.

ARTICLE XI. ATTITUDE TOWARD PROFESSION

The law enforcement officer shall regard the discharge of his duties as a public trust and recognize his responsibility as a public servant. By diligent study and sincere attention to self-improvement he shall strive to make the best possible application of science to the solution of crime and, in the field of human relationships, strive for effective leadership and public influence in matters affecting public safety. He shall appreciate the importance and responsibility of his office, hold police work to be an honorable profession rendering valuable service to his community and his country.

Source: Copyright © International Association of Chiefs of Police.

meanings. Thus, to act ethically is to act according to certain agreed-upon expectations of proper (right) conduct. The purpose of a code of ethics, then, is to guide the behavior of persons in that particular occupation (or profession). The code becomes the standards against which others will judge the actions of those in the occupation.

Developing a code designed to regulate behavior, however, does not make decision making in law enforcement any easier. Police officers are value-based decision makers. In any given situation, officers must make decisions based on competing values such as equality versus efficiency, security versus liberty, and the individual good versus the collective good. Codes of ethics are simply guidelines for law enforcement to reflect upon when making difficult decisions. These codes do not, however, tell an officer which value to choose over another equally important and respected value. For example, some would argue that the overarching value in law enforcement is what is termed the "noble cause" (Caldero and Crank 2004). The noble cause is a moral commitment to make the world a safer place to live; put simply, it is getting bad guys off the street. People are trained and armed to protect the innocent and

[T]hink about that goal in terms of "keeping the scum off the streets." It is not simply a verbal commitment, recited at graduation at the local Peace Officer Standards and Training (POST) academy. Nor is it something police have to learn. It's something

FIGURE 8-7 Code of Ethics for the Office of the Sheriff

As a constitutionally elected Sheriff, I recognize and accept that I am given a special trust and confidence by the citizens and employees whom I have been elected to serve, represent and manage. This trust and confidence is my bond to ensure that I shall behave and act according to the highest personal and professional standards. In furtherance of this pledge, I will abide by the following Code of Ethics.

I SHALL ENSURE that I and my employees, in the performance of our duties, will enforce and administer the law according to the standards of the U.S. Constitution and applicable State Constitutions and statutes so that equal protection of the law is guaranteed to everyone. To that end I shall not permit personal opinions, party affiliations, or consideration of the status of others to alter or lessen this standard of treatment of others.

I SHALL ESTABLISH, PROMULGATE AND ENFORCE a set of standards of behavior of my employees which will govern the overall management and operation of the law enforcement functions, court related activities, and corrections operations of my agency.

I SHALL NOT TOLERATE NOR CONDONE brutal or inhumane treatment of others by my employees nor shall I permit or condone inhumane or brutal treatment of inmates in my care and custody.

I STRICTLY ADHERE to standards of fairness and integrity in the conduct of campaigns for election and I shall conform to all applicable statutory standards of election financing and reporting that the Office of the Sheriff is not harmed by the actions of myself or others.

I SHALL ROUTINELY CONDUCT or have conducted an internal and external audit of the public funds entrusted to my care and publish this information so that citizens can be informed about my stewardship of these funds.

I SHALL FOLLOW the accepted principles of efficient and effective administration and management as the principle criteria for my judgments and decisions in the allocation of resources and services in law enforcement, court related and corrections functions of my Office.

I SHALL HIRE AND PROMOTE only those employees or others who are the very best candidates for a position according to accepted standards of objectivity and merit. I shall not permit other factors to influence hiring or promotion practices.

I SHALL ENSURE that all employees are granted and receive relevant training supervision in the performance of their duties so that competent and excellent service is provided by the Office of the Sheriff.

I SHALL ENSURE that during my tenure as Sheriff, I shall not use the Office or Sheriff for private gain.

I ACCEPT AND WILL ADHERE TO THIS CODE OF ETHICS. In so doing, I accept responsibility for encouraging others in my profession to abide by this Code.

Source: Copyright © National Sheriffs' Association.

to which they are morally committed. Those who don't feel it are not destined for police work and will be quickly liberated from the hazards of a career in blue (Caldero and Crank 2004, 29).

At face value, if the noble cause is indeed the overarching value of law enforcement, police officers then must simply make those decisions that make our streets safer. However, when taking a deeper look into the elements of daily police work, seemingly simple tenants of the noble cause become blurred. For example, "bad guys" are often victims themselves; victims often precipitate their own victimization. Arresting the "bad guy" is not always possible,

nor is it always the most desirable or effective response. The "bad guy" is not always a criminal and "crime" in and of itself is not always the biggest problem in a community. In addition, value-based decisions in law enforcement are further complicated when looking at means and ends. Decisions made regarding the ends of policing (getting the bad guy off the street) may be ethical until one looks at the means of doing so (planting evidence or lying in a report). Furthermore, the ethical standards society holds police to are also situational. For example, society is much more accepting of unethical behavior by law enforcement if it results in the life of a child being saved versus if police acted unethically in investigating a tax fraud case.

Methods for Policing to Achieve Profession Status

There have been several commissions and national studies over the last 40 years that have identified weaknesses or areas in policing that need improvement. It is difficult to achieve profession status until most publicly-acknowledged weaknesses are corrected. To that end we can identify seven areas that the occupation of policing needs to address in its quest for profession status:

1. <u>Improved Selection Standards</u>: Chapter 7 discussed the need for job-related standards, but these criteria must also take into account the intellectual and mental aspects of policing. Improving educational and psychological standards should become priorities for the entire field.

2. <u>Improved and More Demanding Training Standards</u>: In many states, the minimum level of training to become a police officer is less than it is to become a barber. Chapter 7 addressed the issues of training; its importance cannot be over-stated. With society becoming so complex, the importance of better training is obvious.

3. <u>Intensive Evaluation of Performance During Probation</u>: Too many departments treat the probationary period as superficial and automatic. It should contain specific performance criteria and intensive/extensive evaluation of the new officer to determine fitness for the job.

4. <u>Mandatory and More Rigorous In-service Training/ Education</u>: Changes in the law, procedures, and technology demand continuous updating of skills and knowledge, and yet many states and departments still do not mandate in-service training or provide incentives for officers to obtain advanced education. Some departments actually make it difficult, if not impossible, for a patrol officer to attend college while off-duty because of rotating schedules or schedules not being synchronized with local colleges and universities.

5. <u>Acceptance of and Commitment to the Practice of a Code of Ethics</u>: While most officers are persons of high integrity and honesty, some appear to have never read the code of ethics or never heard of it (see the next section). Having a code of ethics or calling oneself professional does not make it so. Ethics are exhibited through one's behavior and professional status is awarded by the persons served.

6. <u>Providing Effective, Efficient, and Courteous Service</u>: The emphasis here is on service and the manner in which it is rendered. All too often the impression left with those served is not a professional one; it can breed distrust and does not move the occupation toward profession status.

7. <u>Systematic Analysis and Research, Which Guides the Above Activities</u>: While some will recognize that this should be possibly first in this list, other research and commission reports have identified most of these items as deficient or needing attention in the field. A greater amount and more sophisticated levels of research are needed to guide the law enforcement community in effective directions.

POLICE MISCONDUCT AND DEPARTMENTAL RESPONSES

Maintaining discipline and high morale in law enforcement agencies is not an easy task. As discussed in other chapters, the use of discretion often opens an officer or agent to criticism. Officers who use force, including deadly force, are placed under scrutiny not only by the department, but also by the news media and public. While the use of this discretion and force may have been appropriate and proper, the department must investigate alleged misconduct in order to assure the public that the integrity of the force is intact.

Traditional Terms and Newer Categories

Police misconduct is used here as a general phrase to describe various forms of behavior that the public and the police themselves consider inappropriate for officers of the law. In 1999, the Gallup News Service released its findings of a poll related to the public's perception of police brutality:

The poll, conducted March 5–7, shows that 38% of Americans believe there have been incidents of police brutality in their area, while 57% disagree. That compares with a similar Gallup poll conducted in March 1991, in which roughly the same number, 35%, said police brutality existed in their area. The poll also underscores perceptions that minorities feel unfairly targeted by police officers. Fifty-eight percent of non-whites believe police brutality takes place in their area, compared to only 35% of whites. When asked, "Have you personally ever felt treated unfairly by the police or by a police officer?" 27% of Americans said yes. Again, the answers differ along racial lines, with 39% of non-whites saying yes, compared to just 24% of whites. Police brutality is also more likely to be reported in urban areas (57%, compared to 35% in rural areas) and in the West and the South (43% and 41% respectively) (Gillespie 1999).

Unfortunately, there has not been an updated survey of perceptions of police brutality for comparative purposes. A Gallup poll in 2005 suggests that public perception of police has furthered declined. Gallup's annual "Crime Poll" found that 53% of Americans feel "a great deal" or "quite a lot" of confidence in the police to protect them from violent crime; in 2004, 61% expressed the same level of confidence. Confidence in this regard had been near or above 60% since 1998 (Jones 2005, 1). This low level had not been seen since 1995.

An extensive study of law enforcement nationwide found seemingly widespread appearance of intentional use of excessive force (Skolnick and Fyfe 1993). According to a special report by Human Rights Watch (1998),

Police abuse remains one of the most serious and divisive human rights violations in the United States. The excessive use of force by police officers, including unjustified shootings, severe beatings, fatal chokings, and rough treatment, persists because overwhelming barriers to accountability make it possible for officers who commit human rights violations to escape due punishment and often to repeat their offenses.

It is beyond the scope of this section, however, to examine this problem in detail. Many scholarly sources have reported on the typical types of behavior associated with police misconduct. **Figure 8-8** contains a listing of some of the more common terms associated with the various forms of police misconduct.

Research into police misconduct by Kappeler, Sluder, and Alpert is reported in their text, *Forces of Deviance* (1998), which examines this issue in detail. They categorize deviant police behaviors into four types: **police crime, occupational deviance, corruption**, and **abuse of authority.** Police crime includes those acts where the officer's authority and powers as a police officer assisted or facilitated the commission of crime(s). Occupational deviance is akin to police crime, but in these situations the acts (ticket fixing, strip searching females in custody, abusing a prisoner) probably could not have been committed by anyone not employed in the police occupation. Corruption, as defined in this categorization, "involves the potential for personal gain and the use of police power and authority to further that gain." The emphasis and distinction here is the element of personal gain, and it is usually tied to economic gain. Abuse of authority refers to the mistreatment and/or violation of human and legal rights, regardless of motive or intention, by officials possessing police authority. Such abuse may be physical, psychological, or legal (Kappeler et al. 1998, 20–25). **Figure 8-9** identifies sample behavior of each of the above-mentioned categories of police misconduct.

Major Scandals of the Last Decades

The evolution and history of policing in the United States is fraught with incidents of police misconduct. Media attention to the subject appears to have reached an all-time high. The early 1990s were not very favorable to the police occupation. Some of the nation's largest police departments were spotlighted because of police misconduct. In March 1991, the Rodney King incident occurred; it resulted in over 3 years of litigation, disturbances at the end of the criminal trial on state charges where officers were found not guilty, two officers being sentenced to prison for violating the civil rights of King, and a civil suit award of $6 million to King. Only a portion of the videotape that captured the incident was shown (over and over again) on all major television networks, but it left an indelible impression in the minds of all who saw it. The findings of the Christopher Commission, which was appointed to investigate the conditions within the LA Police Department following the King incident, led some to conclude that, "[w]hat emerges from such statistics is a department where the use of force

---

FIGURE 8-8 Terms and Phrases Associated with Police Misconduct

Booming doors—the practice of confiscating from drug dealers keys of apartments where drugs and guns are hidden and then going there to steal drugs, guns, and money.

Bribery—payments of cash or gifts for past or future assistance to avoid prosecution; usually higher in value than in "mooching."

Chiseling / badging in—police demands for discounts or free admission to entertainment whether on duty or not.

Extortion—demands by officers for advertisements in police magazines or for the purchase of tickets to police sponsored events through the use of compulsion, force, or fear. Also could involve sums of cash to avoid arrest or for "protection."

Favoritism—granting immunity from traffic arrest or citation or from a summons for minor offenses because of relationship to officer or because of display of window sticker or license plate emblem.

Grass-eaters—officers who take advantage of opportunities for graft that might arise but do not aggressively initiate them.

Meat-eaters—officers who aggressively seek opportunities for graft and other forms of misconduct.

Mooching—receiving free coffee, cigarettes, liquor, food, or other items either as a consequence of being in an underpaid occupation or for future acts of favoritism which might be expected or received by the donor.

Pad—refers to a shadow organization (group) within the department that receives shares of regular bribe payments from citizens; amounts of share depend on rank.

Shakedown—practice of appropriating expensive items for personal use from crime scenes (and may include money, gifts, or favors from citizens).

Shopping—practice of picking up small items (candy, food, etc.) at a store where the door has been accidentally left unlocked after business hours.

Testilying—the making of false arrests, tampering with evidence, and then committing perjury on the witness stand.

Source: Adapted from: Stoddard, E. "Organizational norms and police discretion: An observational study of police work with traffic violators," *Criminology*, Vol. 17, No. 2, pp. 159–71; Langworthy, R.H., F. Travis III (1994), *Policing in America: A Balance of Forces*. New York: Macmillan Publishing Co.: 341; and "NYPD corruption woes bring more bad news" (May 15, 1994), *Law Enforcement News*: 13.

---

against citizens is not considered a matter of great concern" (Alpert et al. 1992, 476).

At the other end of the country, a major drug-related scandal that took years of persistent investigation by a determined internal affairs investigator (Sgt. Joseph Trimboli) began to surface in 1992. "The Loser's Club" was a group of rogue cops led by Michael Dowd that engaged in wholesale drug racketeering. By the end of 1992, there were 101 police officers of the NYPD who had been arrested for misconduct in that year alone.

The Mollen Commission was established to hear testimony and to investigate corruption within the NYPD. (The scandal brought back memories of the Knapp Commission of the early 1970s and the testimony of Detective Frank Serpico.) The Mollen Commission heard testimony about robberies, thefts, on-duty drug abuse, excessive use of force, and scams. In 1994 a series of arrests and internal actions occurred:

- March 15: While off duty, an officer was arrested and charged with beating a man in a convenience store. He pled guilty, and he and two other officers who were with him (all had been drinking heavily) were suspended from the department.

- March 18: Three officers were arrested after a police sting videotaped them breaking into an apartment, ransacking it, and beating an undercover officer.

FIGURE 8-9 Examples of Police Misconduct by Category

Police Crime	Occupational Deviance	Corruption	Abuse of Authority
Off-duty burglary	Theft of evidence	Accepting bribes	Perjury
Off-duty robbery	Tampering with evidence	Selling drugs	Illegal wire taps
Domestic Abuse	Prisoner abuse	Selling "protection"	Forced confessions
Child Abuse	Ticket fixing	Accepting sexual favors	Physically beating suspects/prisoners
Prostitution	Improper strip searches	Extortion	Humiliating witnesses
Gambling	Driving impounded vehicles		

Source: Compiled from Kappeler, Victor E., Richard D. Sluder, and Geoffrey P. Alpert (1998), *Forces of Deviance: Understanding the Dark Side of Policing, Second Edition*. Prospect Heights, IL: Waveland Press, Inc., All rights reserved.

- March 30: A community police officer was arraigned on 14 counts of grand larceny ("shake downs" of several local merchants).
- April 14: Fourteen officers (from the 30th Precinct) were arrested on charges of stealing drugs, money, and guns from narcotics dealers and criminals.
- April 15: Twelve more officers were arrested on similar charges from the same precinct.
- May 4: Eleven more officers at the 30th Precinct had service weapons and badges confiscated and were assigned to "administrative duty." (*Law Enforcement News* 1994b; *Law Enforcement News* 1994c).

New York and Los Angeles were not alone in the problem of controlling police misconduct. Washington, D.C., as of December 1993, had 113 officers under indictment or with charges pending. A group of 12 officers was arrested in mid-December 1993 after "bragging" about misdeeds to an undercover FBI agent posing as a drug dealer. The chief of the department was quoted as saying that during 1989 and 1990, "mistakes" were made in an intensive recruiting effort; most of the officers arrested had been hired during that time (Fields 1993, 3A). In July 1995, the City's Civilian Complaint Review Board closed its doors because of a budget cut, and the backlog of 770 pending cases of police misconduct was transferred to the Police Department for further action. By the middle of 1998, it was reported that 500 officers were under charges of wrongdoing in the Washington, D.C. Police Department (*Law Enforcement News* 1998a).

In November 1992, Malice Green was reportedly pulled from his car and beaten by two officers with their hands and flashlights. A total of seven officers were present before the incident ended. Two of the officers were convicted of second degree murder, initially, but after appeals and new trials, convictions for involuntary manslaughter were rendered in 2000 (Brand-Williams 2000). In the Atlanta area, three officers were arrested in 1993 for murder, two others for robbery. All were thought to be part of a burglary and robbery ring (Edmonds 1993, 2A; Kappeler et al. 1998, 276). In New Orleans, between 1992 and 1996, 40 officers were arrested on charges including auto theft, robbery, rape, aggravated assault, and even murder (Kappeler et al. 1998, 57). One female officer killed three people as she attempted to rob a restaurant; she's now on death row in Louisiana.

The allegations and revelations of the O.J. Simpson trial of 1995 prompted a number of internal investigations and created an atmosphere of great suspicion toward the police in that city and elsewhere. Also during 1995, it was revealed that over 20 officers in the city of Philadelphia were charged with various counts of perjury, civil rights violations, and engaging in drug trafficking. Many of the cases handled by those officers were reopened, and wrongfully convicted subjects were released from prison. The FBI came under great scrutiny during 1995 as well because of its involvement in the Waco incident, the shooting of a wife and daughter of a Montana fugitive (several years earlier), and allegations that the forensics experts from the crime lab routinely doctored evidence and lied in court.

As the 1990s came to an end, the problem of police misconduct and allegations of abuse continued to plague the law enforcement community. Such issues also received much media attention. New York City again was the site of controversy when, on February 4, 1999, an African immigrant, Amadou Diallo, was shot 19 times by four officers who fired 41 rounds at the 22-year-old man. The man was apparently unarmed and the four officers were indicted (*Law Enforcement News* 1999). As this matter was being investigated, another high profile allegation of police abuse from August 1997 was going to trial in New York City. The broomstick torture case of Haitian immigrant Abner Louima went to trial in May 1999. Five officers were indicted for the alleged station house bathroom beating of Louima; two were charged with using a broom handle to sodomize him (Hays 1999). During the trial, one officer changed his plea to guilty. Of the other four, one was found guilty and three not guilty. Also in May 1999, the survivors of Tyisha Miller, 19, filed a federal civil rights lawsuit against five officers and the city of Riverside, California. In December 1998, officers found Miller in a locked car. She appeared unconscious but a handgun was seen on her lap. The officers broke the window and tried to remove the handgun. When they did, Ms. Miller reached for the weapon and the officers shot her 12 times. The District Attorney's investigation cleared the officers of criminal charges, although he criticized their judgment (*USA Today* 1999). In each of these incidents, the subject involved was a person of color and most of the officers were white, which heightened the tensions and allegations of racial unrest. In 1999, Attorney General Janet Reno called for a national commission to investigate police integrity in light of several incidents involving allegations of police abuse and the high levels of public mistrust of the police, especially among minority segments of the nation (Johnson 1999).

Corruption and scandal do not just hit the large cities. For example, during 1998:

- The entire command structure of two departments in Cicero, IL and West New York, NJ, was replaced because of systematic corruption.
- A sheriff in Starr County, Texas was indicted for kickbacks.
- A three-year corruption scandal in North Carolina resulted in the firing of two highway patrol supervisors and the demotion of another.
- Fifty-five officers in Suffolk County, NY faced dismissal related to fraudulent actions in a hiring entrance exam scandal.
- Officers in Dallas; Philadelphia; Erie County, NY; and Pioneer Village, KY face charges in shootings or deaths of others, not related to on-duty incidents.
- Federal authorities charged 44 persons in a corruption probe, many of them police and corrections officers in the Cleveland, Ohio area.
- In Mahoning County, Ohio, six officers from local departments and the sheriff's office were indicted on charges ranging from felony theft in office and complicity to commit theft to dereliction of duty; other law enforcement officials were under investigation in a large corrupt-practices probe in northeast Ohio; by early 1999, the Mahoning County Sheriff had been indicted, and three former officers, including the retired chief of police of Campbell, Ohio, were imprisoned.
- A former police captain in Akron, Ohio was sentenced to life for the killing of his ex-wife outside her medical office. (*Law Enforcement News* 1998a; *Law Enforcement News* 1998b; Meade and Niquette 1998; Associated Press 1998.)

Police abuse and corruption has continued in the new millennium. The city of Los Angeles is still suffering the aftermath of the Rampart scandal that began in 1999. By March 2003, the city had paid out over $40 million in settlements and had approximately 100 cases where either convictions were overturned or charges canceled. Of the 70 officers investigated, 9 have gone to prison (Associated Press 2003). Chief of Police William J. Bratton called for an independent Blue Ribbon Rampart Review Panel, which was convened in July 2003 to investigate and review the response by the city and others to the Rampart Area scandal in order to determine the extent to which the underlying causes for the scandal have been identified and addressed. In November 2004, an assistant police chief was disciplined for her supervisory role in the 2001 scandal, "in which dozens of people, mostly Mexican immigrants, were wrongly jailed on drug charges based on fake evidence" (Associated Press 2004); a deputy chief announced his retirement, as well. In April 2004, three Miami police officers were convicted for their part in a scheme in which guns were planted near the bodies of two fleeing robbers shot to death by police. The incidents occurred between 1995 and 1997, and a total of 11 officers were tried on various charges. Three had been convicted earlier, four were acquitted, and juries were deadlocked on four others. Of the three convicted in 2004, one officer was convicted for planting the weapon; two others were convicted for conspiracy, perjury and obstructing justice (Wilson 2004).

Another example in the news is the federal criminal case of several New Orleans Police Officers in the death of Henry Glover. Glover's burnt remains were discovered in the aftermath of Hurricane Katrina in 2005. According to a witness involved in the case, William Tanner, Glover was shot by an unknown assailant shortly after the hurricane struck New Orleans. Tanner transported Glover to a school where New Orleans Police Officers "had set up camp" but the officers:

> Refused to treat Glover or call for an ambulance, allowing him to bleed to death in the back seat of the vehicle… Police, according to Tanner, then seized both the auto and Glover's body. The car, a Chevrolet Malibu, was eventually discovered in an isolated spot along the Mississippi River. Inside was Glover's severely burnt corpse, which had been reduced to little more than ashes and bone fragments, autopsy records and photos show. No witness has yet come forward to describe how the car caught fire (Thompson 2009).

Federal prosecutors won their first convictions in this case in December 2010, but the Glover case is not the only incident of misconduct stemming from the aftermath of Katrina.

> The Glover case is one of nine civil rights investigations into the New Orleans Police Department started by the FBI and Justice Department in recent years, most of which involve police conduct in the chaotic post-Katrina period. Ten New Orleans police officers face pending charges in three separate cases, including the well-publicized Danziger Bridge shooting two days after Glover was shot. Five former New Orleans police officers have pleaded guilty in a cover-up of that incident, in which two men were killed and four people injured (Maggi 2010).

In August of 2011, five additional New Orleans officers were convicted of 25 federal charges related to the Danziger Bridge incident (U.S. Department of Justice 2011). Unfortunately, we could list even more examples of law enforcement officer misconduct. There is an excellent source of additional material regarding police corruption and integrity maintained by the Michigan State University Library. The site contains links to over 40 Web sites. You are encouraged to visit this site and review the related material.

Early Warning Signs and Efforts to Control Misconduct

It must be understood that misconduct is not controlled with one simple technique or program. Establishing an internal affairs unit does not ensure control. Control of misconduct (the goal) is achieved through the use of multifaceted control mechanisms (the means); these include professional selection standards, in-depth background investigations, training, corporate values, codes of ethics, written policies and expectations, managerial/supervisory training, citizen complaint procedures, internal investigations systems, complaint monitoring, and civilian review processes. Administrative and elected officials and the public also need to demand accountability. Police errors and intentional wrongdoing can and do lead to substantial penalties from civil litigation. These errors can include everything from the handling of an accident scene to intentional infliction of physical injury (Kappeler 1997). The costs can add another burden to the taxpayers and to government budgets.

A.C. Germann once stated the following regarding traditional policing. The words have a unique relevance to this discussion of misconduct:

There are far too many police whose values are selfish and individualistic, and who make the position work for them in many ways—free coffee, newspapers, foods, liquor, unnecessary overtime—a plethora of freebies that can lead all the way to theft of property, resale of drugs... Unprofessional police misuse their power and authority against anyone they choose to and, particularly against anyone who does not show deference... Traditional internal discipline is more harsh and punitive with respect to violations of policy and procedure involving facilities and equipment than it is with respect to violations of human rights... The traditional police academy seems to have as its goal the preparation of brutal hit-squad members, rather than community helpers and non-violent conflict resolvers... The traditional police union or employee organization resists any and all attempts to eliminate unsavory customs and traditions... The majority of traditional officers support their colleagues with a code of silence, cover-up, and sophisticated political pressure that often results in the dismissal or resignation of professionally-oriented administrators (1994, 6, 10).

On the other side of the coin, Germann recognizes that there are:

police administrators, supervisors and officers who are very professional, very honorable, very truthful, and who are truly the unsung heroes of our age... People like these—professional, well-educated, highly motivated, with keen minds, social sensitivity, strength of character, and the courage to tell the king that he is naked—are the pride of the American police service. They need to be encouraged, supported, and given the access to the authority and power that are needed for immediate implementation of necessary changes of policy and procedure (1994, 6).

While it is recognized that the negative aspects of the police subculture are prevalent, it has been argued that the subculture itself can be an agent for change in agencies. Not only can enlightened administrators and supervisors encourage proper behavior, but the subculture can be used by professional officers to support and maintain a highly professional atmosphere (Conser 1980). Good, honest, dedicated officers need to take a stand and tell recalcitrant officers that misconduct isn't tolerated here!

Because of the attention given to police misconduct in recent years, many jurisdictions have turned to **civilian review** of police misconduct complaints and allegations. In a 1991 study of the nation's 50 largest city police departments, Walker and Bumphus found that 30 had some form of civilian review procedures. (Ten of these had been established in just three years, indicating an upward trend.) They categorized the review procedures into three types:

Class I—(a) Initial investigation and fact-finding by non-sworn personnel; (b) Review of investigative report and recommendation for action by non-sworn personnel or board consisting of a majority of non-sworn persons.

Class II—(a) Initial investigation and fact-finding by sworn police officers; (b) Review of investigative report and recommendation for action by non-sworn personnel or board which consists of a majority of non-sworn persons.

Class III—(a) Initial investigation and fact-finding by sworn officers; (b) Review of investigative report and recommendation for action by sworn officers; (c) Opportunity for the citizen who is dissatisfied with the final disposition of the complaint to appeal to a board which includes non-sworn persons (Walker and Bumphus 1991, 3).

Of the 30 civilian review programs, 12 were Class I, 14 were Class II, and 4 were Class III. Historically, police officer unions and employee associations have resisted the establishment and operation of civilian review boards because they do not believe that civilians can adequately judge their actions. Officers often have demonstrated over such proposals. In August 1992, New York City officers demonstrated at City Hall to protest the proposal of an all-civilian review board. It polarized the various groups of police officers, with the Grand Council of Guardians (a Black officers' group) denouncing the protest (*USA Today* 1992). By 1991, over

66% of the 50 largest cities in the United States had created some form of civilian review (Walker and Bumphus 1992). Kappeler, Sluder, and Alpert summarize this trend by stating, "The boards are viewed by many as important vehicles for making the police more democratic and accountable. Although some boards have achieved a measure of success, many of the efforts at civilian oversight have met with failure" (1998, 250).

Efforts to identify early warning signs for officers at risk for misconduct are nothing new. In 1992, the Los Angeles Sheriff's Department became the first to begin developing a computerized system designed to collect and store information on problem officers (Kanable 2010). The system, Police Personnel Index (PPI) is designed to track officers with the goal of identifying problem officers utilizing early warning signs. Lt. Judy Gerhardt, LASD Discovery Unit supervisor and PPI administrator, says, "PPI was designed as an early warning system to identify trends in employee performance." The PPI catalogs employee administrative investigations, operational vehicle investigations, civil claims, lawsuits, use of force, use of lethal force (officer-involved shootings), public commendations and complaints, and internal commendations. Managers (commanders and above) have access to different parts of the system at different security levels. They can look at use of force, citizen complaints, and lawsuits relating to one officer or across an entire unit. Looking at trends individually or collectively, Gerhardt says the LASD can then use the data to address specific needs in training and redirect resources, if necessary (Kanable 2010).

Analysis of the PPI data suggests that identifying problem officers early is possible and doing so can reduce a department's civil liability. In addition, key relationships among behaviors can be identified and used to predict future problems. Specifically:

- Misuse of force allegations in administrative investigations are associated with a higher average number of shootings, lawsuits and civil claims.
- Citizen's complaints alleging "unreasonable force" are associated with higher levels of "founded" administrative investigations.

- The likelihood of finding officers whose truthfulness and candor has been or will be questioned grows as the number of "unresolved" findings rise.
- Allegations in administrative investigations including "performance to standards," "derogatory language," "absence," "false statements," and "Policy of Equality" allegations had particularly noteworthy relationships to higher levels of other potentially problematic behavior (Kanable 2010).

In many states today, the state certification or licensing boards are attempting to address possible future unprofessional conduct by officers by reviewing and enforcing standards at the state level. This process is sometimes referred to **decertification** and, in essence, removes the officers from their law enforcement position. One very transparent example of such state action is the Arizona Peace Officer Standards and Training Board. The Board investigates and decides on appropriate actions at regularly scheduled meetings (see **Figure 8-10** for examples).

SUMMARY

This chapter has examined three overlapping aspects of the police profession: socialization, advancement, and professionalism. You have learned that socialization into the culture of policing is a complex and imperfectly understood process. Moreover, it is not a single event, but a continuing process that influences an officer's advancement within an agency and his or her professional development throughout a career. Additionally, you have learned that the police culture has both a positive and negative component and the outgrowth of the negative component is often evident in police deviance. You have also learned that the institution of policing has undergone a process of organizational development, including, among other things, a move toward collective bargaining and unionization. Finally, you have learned that the institution of policing has steadily advanced toward professionalization, a process that reached maturity in 1990s. Unfortunately, you also have learned that some current officers act unprofessionally and bring discredit upon the profession.

FIGURE 8-10 Arizona Officers Must Maintain Standards

The Arizona Peace Officer Standards and Training Board (AZ POST) is mandated by the legislature to establish and enforce the physical, mental, and moral fitness standards for all peace officers in the state. The Board meets the charge to protect the public by overseeing the integrity of Arizona's law enforcement officers by reviewing cases and taking action against the certification of individuals who violate the AZ POST Rules. The following is a summary of some of the actions taken by the Arizona Peace Officer Standards and Training Board.

Case of Theft
Officer F shoplifted a ten dollar item from a sporting goods store. He was observed and videotaped carrying a packaged item through the store, pausing in one area and leaving that area without the package. The package was found in that area without the item in it. The officer's fingerprint was inside the package. The Board revoked his certification for committing an offense involving dishonesty. (Integrity Bulletin—Volume 51 January 2011)

Case of ACJIS Violations
Officer E used ACJIS and other restricted databases to collect information on women he was dating. One of the women found information about her past, her former husband, her daughter and another woman in Officer E's home. He was indicted on six felony counts of computer tampering and he pled guilty to one count, an undesignated Class 6 felony that may or may not be classified a misdemeanor following probation. The Board revoked his peace officer certification for committing a felony and malfeasance in office. (Integrity Bulletin—Volume 51 January 2011)

Consent Agreements
The Board adopted consent agreements calling for a voluntary relinquishment of certification in the following fact situations. The scenarios stated here reflect the allegations giving rise to the POST case, but the facts were not proven before the Board.

- An officer committed computer tampering and identity theft.
- A deputy conducted an unlawful search and seized money with no legal justification and failed to impound the money.
- An officer transported a female he had in custody to a secluded location and inappropriately touched her.
- An officer made a traffic stop and escalated the situation to a use of force for no reason.
- A lieutenant had sex on duty and sent threatening text messages to the subordinate employee with whom he was involved.
- An officer was untruthful to his supervisor regarding a vehicle pursuit.
- A deputy assaulted his wife and caused her injury.

(Integrity Bulletin—Volume 50 October 2010)

Case of Dishonesty
Officer A provided false information in connection with obtaining employment and certification as a peace officer on at least ten occasions. He also used excessive force during an arrest when he tripped a handcuffed suspect and lied during the internal investigation about the arrest. The Board revoked his peace officer certification for willfully providing false information in connection with obtaining certification and committing offenses involving dishonesty and physical violence. (Integrity Bulletin—Volume 48 June 2010)

Source: Courtesy of the Arizona Peace Officer Standards and Training Board. Additional incidents can be found at: http://www.azpost.state.az.us/Integrity.htm .

Critical Thinking Questions

1. What is meant by the police subculture?

2. What are the negative and positive characteristics of the police subculture, as summarized in this chapter?

3. How does training impact the socialization of law enforcement officers?

4. What are the seven different methods by which an officer can be promoted to higher rank and responsibility?

5. What are the differences between the concepts of "labor relations" and "collective bargaining"?

6. What was the significance of the Boston Police Strike of 1919 in terms of its impact on police unionism?

7. What are four types of police misconduct? Describe each.

CHAPTER SPECIFIC INTERNET LINKS

PoliceCrimes.com: http://www.policecrimes.com/police_code.html

Institute for Criminal Justice Ethics: http://www.lib.jjay.cuny.edu/cje/html/policeethics.html

Michigan State University Library: http://staff.lib.msu.edu/harris23/crimjust/polcorr.htm

U.S. Department of Justice, Division of Civil Rights, Official Misconduct Cases: http://www.justice.gov/crt/about/crm/selcases.php#conduct

CHAPTER GLOSSARY

Abuse of authority—the mistreatment and/or violation of human and legal rights, regardless of motive or intention, by officials possessing police authority; may be physical, psychological, or legal.

Benevolent associations—one form of employee association; early associations attempted to provide employees with benefits that employers did not, and were also fraternal and social in nature. Today, a police benevolent association (PBA) may also be a union for purposes of collective bargaining.

Career development—a desired change in work assignment that is accompanied by increased responsibility and may involve additional training and/or education; career development may, but not always, include a promotion.

Civilian review—the review of police misconduct complaints and allegations by non-police persons.

Code of ethics—a basic set of guidelines or set of standards of behavior.

Collective bargaining—the most formal means of labor relations, in which a representative of an employee group (often a union) negotiates the terms and conditions of employment with the representative of the employer.

Corruption—actions that involve the potential for personal gain and the use of police power and authority to further that gain.

Craft—an occupation that involves the development of skills that are generally learned through experience and not in a classroom.

Decertification—the process of removing an officer's state authority, certificate of training, or license because of infractions of law or unprofessional conduct. This action is usually taken by a state licensing or training certification board.

Detraining syndrome—the process of transforming the highly-motivated, idealistic recruit to one that is disillusioned and distrustful.

Labor relations—the sum total of all interaction between the administration of an agency and its employees.

Lateral entry—the transferring to another agency without any loss of seniority, rank, and salary.

Moral behavior or right conduct—actions prescribed by society for the welfare of the people and society as a whole.

Morality—conformity to rules of right conduct.

Occupational deviance—akin to police crime, but are acts which probably could not have been committed by anyone unless employed in the police occupation.

Occupational dimension—the uniquely job-related factors that affect and condition the police to behave in selected ways.

Police crime—those acts where the officer's authority and powers as a police officer assisted or facilitated the commission of crime(s).

Police subculture—an intricate web of relationships among peers that shapes and perpetuates the pattern of behavior, values, isolation, and secrecy that distinguish the police.

Political dimension—the relationship between the police community and the policy-making authorities of the agency and society at large.

Profession—an occupational type based on a special competence with a high degree of intellectual content; a specialty heavily based on or involved with knowledge.

Promotion—usually refers to a positive change in rank status.

Psychological dimension—the self-identity and personality development aspects of the police subculture.

Social dimension—the police officers' social organization, subculture norms, and the nature of police solidarity.

Socialization process—the process whereby individuals learn and internalize the attitudes, values, and behaviors appropriate to persons functioning as social beings and responsive, participating members of their society.

Symbolic assailant—a person who uses gesture, language, and attire that the police have come to recognize as a prelude to violence.

CHAPTER REFERENCES AND ADDITIONAL READINGS

Alpert, Geoffrey, W.C. Smith, and D. Watters (1992). Implications of the Rodney King beating. *Criminal Law Bulletin.* 28(5):476.

Armacost, Barbara E. (2004). Organizational Culture and Police Misconduct. *The George Washington Law Review.* 72:453–546.

Associated Press (1998). Cop gets life in ex-wife's killing. *The Vindicator* (24 August):B4.

Associated Press (2003). Los Angeles police review big scandal. March 1, *NY Times* on the Web, as reported at http://www.truthinjustice.org/rampart-redux.htm.

Associated Press (2004). Dallas police shake-up continues. November 23, http://www.chron.com/cs/CDA/ssistory.mpl/metropolitan/2916435.

Ayres, Richard M. and Thomas L. Wheelen, (eds.) (1977). *Collective bargaining in the public sector: selected readings in law enforcement.* International Association of Chiefs of Police.

Banton, Michael (1964). *The Policeman and the Community.* London: Taviatock.

Bayley, David H. (1986). The Tactical Choices of Police Patrol Officers. *Journal of Criminal Justice.* 14.

Bayley, David H. (1994). *Police for the Future.* New York, NY: Oxford University Press, Inc.

Bayley, David H. and Egon Bittner (1993). Learning the Skills of Policing. In R.G. Dunham and G.P. Alpert (Eds.) *Critical Issues in Policing: Contemporary Readings, 2nd Edition* (pp. 106–129) Prospect Heights, IL: Waveland Press, Inc.

Bennett, Barbara (1978). The Police Mystique. *The Police Chief.* April:46.

Bittner, Egon (1990). *Aspects of Police Work.* Boston, MA: Northeastern University Press.

Boke, Kaan and Mahesh K. Nalla (2009). Police Organizational Culture and Job Satisfaction: A Comparison of Law Enforcement Officers' Perceptions in Two Midwestern States in the U.S. *Journal of Criminal Justice and Security,* 11(1):55–73.

Bradway, Jacquelyn (2009). Gender Stress: Differences in Critical Life Events among Law Enforcement Officers. *International Journal of Criminal Justice Sciences.* 4(1):1–12.

Brand-Williams, Oralandar (2000). Nevers gets no break in 2nd Green sentence. *The Detroit News.* May 17, http://www.detnews.com/2000/metro/0005/17/c01-57902.htm.

Braunstein, Susan (2007). The Future of Law Enforcement Communications. In Joseph A. Schafer (Ed.). *Policing 2020: Exploring the Future of Crime, Communities, and Policing* (pp. 133-172). Futures Working Group. Washington, D.C.: U.S. Department of Justice.

Buker, Husan. and Filip Wiecko. (2007). Are Causes of Police Stress Global? Testing the effects of common police stressors on the Turkish National Police. *Policing: An International Journal of Police Strategies & Management,* 30(2): 291–309.

Bureau of Labor Statistics (2010). *Economic News Release: Union Members Summary – 2009.* Washington, D.C.: Bureau of Labor Statistics. http://www.bls.gov/news.release/union2.nr0.htm

Caldero, Michael A. and John P. Crank (2004). *Police ethics: The corruption of noble cause.* Dayton, OH: LexisNexis/Anderson Publishing.

Carter, David L. and Louis A. Radelet (1999). *The Police and the Community,* 6th Ed. Upper Saddle River, NJ: Prentice-Hall, Inc.

Clark, B.R. (1966), Organizational adaptation to professionals. In H.M. Vollmer and D.L. Mills (Eds.) *Professionalization* (pp. 282–291). Englewood Cliffs, NJ: Prentice-Hall.

Conser, James A. (1980). A literary review of the police subculture: Its characteristics, impact, and policy implications. *Police Studies.* 2(4):46–54.

Crank, John P. (1998). *Understanding Police Culture.* Cincinnati: Anderson Publishing Co.

Doerner, William G. (1985). I'm Not the Man I Used to Be: Reflection on the Transition from Prof to Cop in Blumberg, In Abraham and Elaine Niederhoffer (eds.), *The Ambivalent Force.* Hinsdale, IL: Dryden Press.

Edmonds, Patricia (1993). Detroit calm for officers' beating trial. *USA Today,* June 2:2A.

Fields, Gary (1993). Indictment: D.C. cops bragged about crimes. *USA Today,* December 16:3A.

Fogelson, Robert M. (1977). *Big-City Police.* Cambridge, MA: Harvard University Press.

Gaines, Larry K., Mittie D. Southerland, and John E. Angell (1991). *Police Administration.* New York: McGraw-Hill, Inc.

Gammage, Allen Z. and Stanley L. Sachs (1977). Development of public employee/police unions. In Ayres, Richard M. and Thomas L. Wheelen, (eds.). *Collective bargaining in the public sector: selected readings in law enforcement.* International Association of Chiefs of Police.

Germann, A.C. (1994). Changing the police: An impossible dream? *Law Enforcement News,* June 30:6, 10.

Gillespie, Mark (1999). *One third of Americans believe police brutality exists in their area.* The Gallup News Service, March 22. Princeton, NJ: The Gallup Organization.

Gilmartin, Kevin M. (2002). *Emotional Survival for Law Enforcement: A guide for officers and their families.* Tucson, AZ: E-S Press.

Goldsmith, Jack and Sharon Goldsmith (eds.) (1974). *The Police Community.* Pacific Palisades, CA: Palisades Publishing Company.

Goldstein, Herman (1963). Police Discretion: The Ideal vs. the Real. *Public Administration Review.* 23:140–148.

Goldstein, Herman (1977). *Policing a Free Society.* Cambridge, MA: Ballinger Publishing Company.

Hankins, Ellis (March 10, 2010). Testimony Before the House Subcommittee on Health, Employment, Labor, and Pensions regarding H.R. 413, Public Safety-Employer-Employee Cooperation Act of 2009.

Harris, Richard (1973). *The Police Academy: An Inside View.* New York: John Wiley and Sons, Inc.

Hays, Tom (1999). Brutality case testimony: Officer showed off stick used in torture. *USA Today,* May 21:5A.

Higginbotham, Charles (1999). Law enforcement oath of honor. Resolution adopted 21 October.1998. Correspondence regarding action taken at the 105th Annual Conference of the International Association of Chiefs of Police, June 3, at Salt Lake City, Utah.

Human Rights Watch (1998). Shielded from Justice: Police Brutality and Accountability in the United States. http://www.hrw.org/press98/july/polic707.htm.

International Association of Chiefs of Police (1991). The law enforcement code of ethics. Adopted by resolution at the 1998 Conference, October (modified version of the original Code of 1957).

International Association of Chiefs of Police (1991). The police code of conduct. Adopted by resolution at the 98 Conference, October (modified version of the original Code of 1957).

Johnson, Kevin (1999). Too many believe they can't trust police, Reno says. *USA Today*. April 16:8A.

Jones, Jeffrey M. (Nov. 10, 2005). Confidence in Local Police Drops to 10-Year Low, *Gallup News Service*. Available On-Line. http://www.gallup.com/poll/19783/Confidence-Local-Police-Drops-10Year-Low.aspx. [accessed January 2011].

Jones, Jeffrey M (2010). Nurses Top Honesty and Ethics List for 11th Year. *Gallup.com*. http://www.gallup.com/poll/145043/Nurses-Top-Honesty-Ethics-List-11-Year.aspx

Juris, Henry A. and Peter Feuille (1974). Employee Organizations. In O. Glenn Stahl and Richard A. Staufenberger (eds.). *Police Personnel Administration*. Washington, D.C.: Police Foundation.

Kanable, Rebecca. (2010). Early Warning. *Law Enforcement Technology*. 37(9):68,70–74.

Kappeler, Victor E. (1997). *Critical issues in police civil liability*. Prospect Heights, IL: Waveland Press.

Kappeler, Victor E., Richard D. Sluder, and Geoffrey P. Alpert (1998). *Forces of deviance: Understanding the dark side of policing*, Second Edition. Prospect Heights, IL: Waveland Press, Inc.

Kelling, George L. and Mark H. Moore (November 1988), The Evolving Strategy of Policing. *Perspectives on Policing*. Washington, D.C.: U.S. Department of Justice and John F. Kennedy School of Government, Harvard University.

Klinger, David A. (1997). Negotiating Order in Patrol Work: An Ecological Theory of Police Response to Deviance. *Criminology*. 35(2):277–306.

Langworthy, R.H. and L. F. Travis III (1994). *Policing in America: A balance of forces*. New York: Macmillan Publishing Co.

Law Enforcement News (1994a). Around the Nation. June 15:2.

Law Enforcement News (1994b). NY corruption woes bring more bad news. May 15:13.

Law Enforcement News (1994c). Bountiful harvest of bad apples. March 31:4.

Law Enforcement News (1998a). Justice by the numbers. XXIV (501, 502) December 15/31:19.

Law Enforcement News (1998b). On the side of the law—or are they? XXIV (501, 502) December 15/31:17.

Law Enforcement News (1999). NYPD under fire over killing of unarmed man. XXV (507) March 15:1, 10.

Los Angeles Police Department (2003). The blue ribbon Rampart review panel moves forward in its quest. Press Release, November 18, http://www.lapdonline.org/portal/generic.php?page=/press_releases/press_releases.htm.

Maggi, Laura (2010). Henry Glover guilty verdicts are first in sprawling federal probe of New Orleans police misconduct. Nola.com, December 9, http://www.nola.com/crime/index.ssf/2010/12/henry_glover_guilty_verdicts_a.html .

Manning, Peter K. (1997). *Police Work: The Social Organization of Policing*, 2nd Edition. Prospects Heights, IL: Waveland Press, Inc.

Meade, Patricia and Mark Niquette (1998). Six charged with taking cash, drugs., September 2:A1.

Niederhoffer, A. (1967). *Behind the Shield: The Police in Urban Society*. New York: Doubleday.

Newbold, Mark (2003). Free expression and the public safety employees. *The Police Chief*. March:10–11.

Oliver, William M., and Cecil A. Meier. (2004). Stress in Small Town and Rural Law Enforcement: Testing the assumptions. *American Journal of Criminal Justice*. 29(1) 37–58.

Pavalko, Ronald M. (1971). Sociology of Occupations and Professions. Itasca, Illinois: F E Peacock.

Public sector unionism. (1972). Origins and perspective—part I: historical summary. UCLA Law Review 19(6): 893–894. Quoted in Ayres, Richard M. and Thomas L. Wheelen (eds.) (1977). *Collective bargaining in the public sector: selected readings in law enforcement*. International Association of Chiefs of Police.

Radelet, Louis A. (1973). *The Police and the Community*. Beverly Hills, CA: Glencoe Press.

Reaves, Brian. (2010). *Local Police Departments, 2007*. Washington D.C.: U.S. Department of Justice.

Roberg, R.R. and J. Kuykendall (1993). *Police and Society*. Belmont, CA: Wadsworth Publishing Co.

Saad, Lydia (July 22, 2010). Congress Ranks Last in Confidence in Institutions. Gallup.com http://www.gallup.com/poll/141512/Congress-Ranks-Last-Confidence-Institutions.aspx

Skolnick, Jerome (1969). The Politics of Protest. New York: Simon and Schuster.

Skolnick, Jerome (1994). *Justice Without Trail: Law Enforcement in Democratic Society*, 3rd Edition. New York: Macmillan College Publishing Company, Inc.

Skolnick, Jerome H. and James J. Fyfe (1993). *Above the law: Police and the excessive use of force*. New York: Free Press.

Smith, D.C. (1978). Dangers of Police Professionalization: An Empirical Analysis. *Journal of Criminal Justice*. 6(3):199–216.

Smith, Joseph D. (1975). Police unions: An historical perspective of causes and organizations. *The Police Chief*. November:24.

Socialization (1974). *Encyclopedia of Sociology*. Guilford, CT: The Dushkin Publishing Group.

Spero, Sterling D. (1977). The Boston police strike. In Ayres, Richard M. and Thomas L. Wheelen, (eds.) *Collective bargaining in the public sector: selected readings in law enforcement*. International Association of Chiefs of Police.

Sterling, James (1968). *Changes in Role Concepts of Police Officers during Recruit Training*. Gaithersburg, MD: International Association of Chiefs of Police as cited in Louis A. Radelet (1973). *The Police and the Community*. Beverly Hills, CA: Glencoe Press.

Stoddard, E. (1979). Organizational norms and police discretion: An observational study of police work with traffic violators. *Criminology*. 17(2):159–171.

Thompson, A.C. (March 28, 2009). FBI Opens Inquiry into Death of Henry Glover. *ProPublica.* Available On-line. http://www .propublica.org/article/fbi-open-inquiry-into-death-of-henry- glover-090328. [January 2011].

USA Today (1992). Police protest, August 21:3A.

USA Today (1999). Suit filed against California officers in fatal shooting, July 1.

Unkelbach, L. Cary (2003). Name-clearing hearings. *The Police Chief.* July:13–16.

U.S. Department of Justice (2011). New Orleans Police Officers Convicted of Civil Rights Violations in Danziger Bridge Case. Washington, D.C.: Office of Public Affairs, Department of Justice, August 5. http://www.justice.gov/opa/pr/2011/August/11-crt-1021.html.

Walker, Samuel (1977). *A Critical History of Police Reform: The Emergence of Professionalism.* Lexington, MA: Lexington Books.

Walker, Samuel and Vic W. Bumphus (1991). *Civilian review of the police: A national survey of the 50 largest cities.* Omaha, NE: University of Nebraska at Omaha.

Walker, Samuel and Vic W. Bumphus (1992). The effectiveness of civilian review: Observations on recent trends and new issues regarding the civilian review of the police. *American Journal of Police.* XI(4):1–21.

Westley, William A. (1956). Secrecy and the Police. *Social Forces.* 34:254–257.

White, Susan (1972). A Perspective on Police Professionalization. *Law and Society Review.* 7:61–85.

Wilson, Catherine (2004). 3 Miami officers convicted in gun cover-up. Associated Press. http://www.montereyherald.com/mld/monterey- herald/8330467.htm.

Wilson, James Q. (1968). *Varieties of Police Behavior.* Cambridge, MA: Harvard University Press.

Wilson, James Q. (1975). *Thinking About Crime.* New York: Basic Books.

Zhao, Jihong (1996). *Why Police Organizations Change.* Washington, D.C.: Police Executive Research Forum.

CHAPTER 9

Legal Restrictions and Challenges

LEARNING OBJECTIVES

Law enforcement is obviously involved with the law and the courts, but the degree of that involvement and the resulting limitations placed on law enforcement are not so obvious. In order to briefly examine those limitations, this chapter starts with where law comes from, how it affects law enforcement, and why it matters to law enforcement officials. After studying this chapter, you will be able to:

- Describe the major sources of law in the United States.
- Summarize the structure of the system of justice in the United States and explain the relationship between state and federal courts.
- State the basic principles of the criminal law.
- Identify the major procedural legal restrictions on law enforcement personnel in the United States and explain why these restrictions exist.
- Understand the rule of law and how it both restricts and protects officers.
- Identify the basic sources of legal threats to the officer on a personal and professional basis.

CHAPTER OUTLINE

I. Sources of Law in the United States
   A. Common Law
   B. Criminal and Civil Law
   C. Statutory and Code Law
   D. The Constitution
   E. Administrative Law
II. The U.S. System of Justice
   A. Federal Courts
   B. Federal Courts and State Crimes
   C. State Courts
III. Procedural Limitations on Law Enforcement
   A. Searches and Seizures
   B. Arrest of the Person
IV. Consequences of Unlawfully Obtained Evidence
   A. The Exclusionary Rule
   B. Interrogation
   C. Fruit of the Poisonous Tree
V. Liability
   A. Tort Law
   B. Civil Rights
VI. Summary

KEY TERMS USED IN THIS CHAPTER

common law	preliminary hearing
precedent	probable cause
stare decisis	suppression
civil law	search
criminal law	seizure
felony	warrant requirement
misdemeanor	stop and frisk
statutory law	plain view doctrine
model penal code	exigent circumstances
rap sheet	exclusionary rule
constitutional law	custodial interrogation
administrative law	fruit of the poisonous tree
delegation of authority	inevitable discovery
minimum administrative due process	negligent acts
	respondeat superior
writ of *certiorari*	principal
writ of *habeas corpus*	

SOURCES OF LAW IN THE UNITED STATES

Law in the United States is derived from several sources. These sources have become more numerous as the nation has grown and become more complex, both socially and economically. Law enforcement personnel must understand the sources of law because they are also the sources of authority for their decisions and actions. The first part of this chapter provides an overview of these sources.

Common Law

The first source of law that traditionally involved law enforcement was the **common law**. Derived from England, this body of legal rules developed over a period of several hundred years. English judges were frequently faced with problems, or cases, for which there were no legal guidelines. Nevertheless, courts needed to reach decisions in an attempt to resolve these problems. Acting under the authority of the king, courts developed legal rules to settle these cases.

These decisions, over time, were relied upon by other judges with similar problems and came to be called **precedent**. Courts would draw upon these older cases to help decide new ones; in effect, the old cases gave the judges guidance. The act of applying and relying upon precedent was called *stare decisis*, meaning that prior decisions should be followed if the facts of the case at issue were similar to the prior case. The courts could construct new rules only if the case to be decided was unlike prior cases. Gradually, this body of law developed and was called the common law.

Criminal and Civil Law

The common law included two distinct legal concepts, called **civil law** and **criminal law**. Generally speaking, crimes are offenses against the public (or the state), and civil violations are violations against individuals (while individuals are frequently victims in criminal offenses such as assault, rape, or murder, the law considers the public at large to be the victim). The theory is that a society must have order and must protect its members, so if the rules of that order are violated and a crime is committed, it is society that is offended. This perspective has governed American law for over 200 years, but

as we see elsewhere in this book, emerging theories of victims' rights and restorative justice are challenging this long-held assumption, thus recognizing the harm done to individuals.

In criminal cases, the state is represented by the prosecutor (or district attorney) who initiates the criminal charge (a process described below). In civil cases, each side is represented by private counsel, and the complaining party (or counsel) must file a complaint alleging a civil violation. A violation of a criminal statute can result in jail or prison time, while civil cases can only result in monetary damages or orders compelling parties to do or not do something. One does not go to jail or prison for a civil violation (generally speaking); however, if a court order is ignored or violated, one could be jailed for contempt of court, which technically is not a crime. Similarly, those who are ordered to pay child support and fail to do so despite the ability to pay may similarly be jailed. In both cases, civil actions could result in being jailed, but only because a court order was ignored or violated.

Civil law includes contracts, torts, property, and civil procedure. A tort is a civil injury to a person or a person's property. Examples of a tort include cutting down a tree belonging to another or damaging a person's car by reckless driving. Torts may be intentional or negligent (described below). It is important to understand, however, that an action by someone may create both a criminal act and a tort. For example, suppose two people get into an argument and one strikes the other. The person who struck the victim committed an assault and battery (discussed below) for which they could be charged and, if convicted, be sent to jail. That would be a criminal charge.

Additionally, the person who was struck could file a civil complaint alleging the tort of assault and battery, an intentional tort, and seek damages from the assailant. In the O.J. Simpson case, the family of Ronald Goldman, one of the two victims Simpson is alleged to have killed, sued O.J. Simpson. While Simpson was tried for murder when the State of California brought criminal charges and was found innocent by a jury, he nevertheless was required to defend a civil action alleging a wrongful death. Eventually, he lost that tort litigation and owed the family of Ronald Goldman millions of dollars in damages awarded in the lawsuit. Essentially, a wrongful death alleges that a person (i.e., Ronald Goldman) was killed due to the unlawful actions of the defendant (i.e., O.J. Simpson) and that the defendant is liable for damages resulting from the death. Thus, the same act resulted in criminal charges and civil complaints.

Another famous example of a criminal and civil incident is a white-collar offense that extended over several decades. In December 2008, Bernard Madoff was arrested and charged with securities fraud. By March 2009, 10 additional felonies were added: investment advisor fraud, mail fraud, wire fraud, international money laundering to support specified unlawful activity, international money laundering to conceal and disguise the proceeds of specified unlawful activity, money laundering, false statements, perjury, making a false filing with the U.S. Securities and Exchange Commission, and theft form an employee benefit plan (*United States of America v. Bernard L. Madoff*). Madoff's activities may be the largest financial fraud in history, amounting between $13 and $50 billion from over 100 investors. He was sentenced in June 2009 to 150 years in prison (Frank 2009). Since the fraud was uncovered, numerous civil suits have been filed by individuals and governments against Madoff's investment firm, business associates, and banks allegedly connected to the fraud (Bernstein 2010).

Photo of Bernie Madoff

Source: © Louis Lanzano/AP Photos

Common law courts created the **felonies** of murder, suicide, manslaughter, burglary, arson, robbery, larceny, rape, sodomy, and mayhem. These offenses generally carried a possible sentence of more than a year in prison. These same courts gradually developed a set of **misdemeanor** crimes including assault, battery, false imprisonment, libel, perjury, corrupting morals, and disturbing the peace. These offenses were generally punishable by a sentence of less than a year in prison. Many states in the United States, particularly on the East Coast, relied and continue to rely heavily on the common law definitions of these crimes.

Statutory and Code Law

As the nation grew, the complexity of life and changing social norms outstripped the ability of the courts to respond. The creation of common law took centuries and required centuries to evolve, but the changes that came with expansion and industrialization required a more rapid adjustment, so reformers used legislative efforts to create new laws. Legislative bodies such as the Congress of the United States and state legislatures passed formal laws that adopted common law definitions of some crimes, but these legislatures also created new crimes. Laws that are passed by a legislative body are called statutes and are compiled into a coded (numbered) collection of laws (often referred to as the "state code"). When a law is passed by a legislative body, it becomes **statutory law**. It is assigned a number and placed into the state's code. The process of numbering statutes is called codification. All laws of a given type are placed in one section of the code, making it easy to find. For example, each state has a Penal Code or Criminal Code, and all crimes in that state are organized in that section of the code, usually called a "Title" (e.g., Title 29). Also, statutes can be related to one another and cross-referenced by the numbering system. This process of adding new social rules to the criminal law greatly increased the number and kinds of things for which a person could be punished. Today, with state and federal jurisdictions included, every person in the United States is subject to thousands of laws for which they can be criminally prosecuted. It is important to locate statutes and cases for research and reference purposes. **Figure 9-1** will assist in an initial understanding of how to read statutory and case references.

FIGURE 9-1 Reading Code and Case Citations

Criminal justice students are frequently confronted with footnotes that refer to a case or a statute. How would you find these cases or statutes if you wanted to see the original? The citation attached to each case or statute is the key to finding the original. But what do they mean?

Looking up a Statute   42 USC 1981
The statute noted here is described later in this chapter. Where would you find the original? In citing a statute, common practice requires the *first* number to be the volume or *title* of the code in which this section is found. The second number is the number given to that section of the title. Sections are always in consecutive order (e.g., 1981, 1982, 1983, etc.). The letters in the middle are an abbreviation for the name of the code. The way to read this statute citation is **Title 42, United States Code, section 1981**. Once you know that, all you need to do is find a copy of the Federal Code in the library. Locate the volume labeled 42 (this title may be split into several volumes due to its size). Flip through the pages to section 1981. You will notice that after a code section, there is long list of what are called *annotations*. These are brief (usually short paragraphs) summaries of cases which interpreted that section. This is a good way to see what this section means.

State Codes
The various state codes vary considerably in format and numbering. For example, 13-1105 ARS is the shorthand citation for the Arizona Revised Statute, Title 13, Section 1105 which is the criminal code section for first-degree murder.

In Ohio, RC § 2907.04 is the Ohio Revised Code section for unlawful sexual conduct with minor. RCW 9A.40.020 refers to the Revised Code of Washington for its statute on kidnapping in the first degree. One can find all the state codes by searching the Wide World Web, especially at http://www.findlaw.com/11stategov/indexcode.html.

Looking up a Case   Rizzo v. Goode 423 U.S. 362, (1976)
The case name is that assigned by the court issuing the opinion. Case names carry the name of *two* of the parties to the case. There may be more, but this is the official title of the case. The *first* number is the volume of the *reporter* in which the case is found. Reporters literally report cases. In this case, U.S. is read as United States Reports, which is the official reporter for the United States Supreme Court. Volumes are in consecutive order. Every time a case is decided by the Supreme Court, it is placed in the reporter. Cases are placed in consecutive order based upon the date they are decided. Cases appearing in Volume 422, therefore, were merely announced before this case. The second number is the *page* number of the volume in question. Hence, this case citation is read as **Rizzo versus Goode, volume 423 of the United States Reports, at page 362**. The date, 1976, is used as a reference point only. The volume and page numbers are critical. One set of reference books, called Shepard's Citations, permits you to take the volume and page number of this case (or any case) and look up *the citations of every case that cited this case*. This is how legal research is done. The same process works for statutes and code sections.

The Model Penal Code

Many crimes have been standardized into the **model penal code** (MPC), which was adopted by many states. The MPC was written by the American Law Institute, which is supported by the legal community and sought to bring consistency to issues of law common in all states. If each state adopted the same code and each used the same definitions for each crime, confusion and inequity would decrease. Despite these efforts, however, even states adopting the MPC have changed major portions of that code. What is either legal or a minor offense in one state may well be illegal or a very serious offense in another. For example, in Georgia, breaking into an unattached garage is felony burglary; in Ohio, it is criminal trespass, a misdemeanor. Similarly, possession of a small amount of marijuana may be trivial in one state such as Ohio or California, but very serious in Mississippi. While "common law" crimes are basically illegal in all states, the punishment for any one of them may not be the same in all states. This causes confusion for law enforcement, and it also makes it very difficult to keep records that communicate useable information on offenders. A computerized **rap sheet**, which is a record of an individual's offenses, will usually not describe in detail the nature of a crime in the state from which the conviction was noted. This can cause a problem if the defendant can be charged with enhanced penalties or a higher level of offense based upon a prior offense. For example, in many states a conviction for petty theft (misdemeanor theft) may elevate a subsequent petty theft to the felony level of grand theft merely on the basis of a prior theft offense, but if the title of the prior crime is unclear, it could be overlooked. The same is true for registered sex offenders, or morals offenses. In some states, people accused of urinating in public were frequently charged with indecent exposure, but that offense is now seen as a "sex" offense, requiring offenders to register as sex offenders, a result that surely was not intended.

The Constitution

Another source of law that significantly influences law enforcement is the Constitution of the United States (see Appendix I). The body of law that has evolved around the Constitution is called, quite simply, **constitutional law**. The Constitution is the "supreme law of the land" (*Marbury v. Madison*, 1 Cranch 137, 1803), meaning that no state law may contradict the U.S. Constitution. The Constitution plays a specific role in our system of law and politics. Theoretically, it is a grant of power from the people to the government, which means that the power of government is limited by the terms of the grant (the Constitution).

The Constitution is a contract. Political theorists describe it as a social contract. If you buy a car and you obtain a loan, you agree to pay a certain amount of money each month. The loan company cannot change the terms of that agreement and make you pay more. In the same way, the Constitution is a limited grant of authority. However, the government (both state and federal) can use every bit of that authority until it is revoked or altered by amending the Constitution.

The first portion of the U.S. Constitution sets out, in very broad terms, the powers of Congress, the president, and the federal judiciary. The Constitution specifically

created a Supreme Court, but it left the size of the court to be determined by Congress. The size of the Supreme Court has varied from four members to its current size of nine.

The Bill of Rights

While the Constitution itself is a limited grant of authority, there are also specific limitations on the use of that authority. We call these the Bill of Rights. Generally, people think of these as the first 10 amendments to the Constitution, but in fact, only the first eight are truly rights; the ninth and tenth amendments attempt to clarify the meaning of limited federal authority and the retention of state roles. The actual meaning of these last two amendments remains the subject of great debate among scholars in constitutional law, and today several controversial issues such as immigration enforcement, mandatory purchase of health insurance, marriage, and gun rights are working their way through the court systems across the United States.

The federal constitution, specifically the Bill of Rights, tends to play more of a restrictive role on law enforcement. The amendments we call the Bill of Rights have been repeatedly interpreted by the Supreme Court of the United States. It is these amendments that are the trickiest for law enforcement, since theoretically officers must follow the court's pronouncements or risk losing a case, being sued, or both (see Appendix I for the Bill of Rights). We will see later in this chapter, however, that the assumption that officers in fact heed the law is not always accurate.

Originally, the Bill of Rights did not apply to the states. When the Constitution was reported out from the Constitutional Convention in 1787 for ratification by the 13 former colonies, there was no Bill of Rights. During the debate over approval (ratification) of the Constitution, concern was expressed in many states over the potential power of a centralized government. This concern resulted in the adoption of a Bill of Rights, which was attached to the Constitution in 1791. These amendments sought to limit the power of the federal government and were not intended to apply to the states. The Supreme Court held in 1833 that the Bill of Rights was only a limitation upon the power of the national government (*Barron v. Mayor and City Council of Baltimore*, 7 Pet. 243, 1833), and until the Civil War, this was the understanding of the role of the Bill of Rights.

The 14th Amendment

The 14th Amendment was adopted in 1868, after the Civil War, and was forced on the secessionist states (the southern states that tried to leave the union) as part of the terms to end the war. This amendment was designed to restrict the states in their operations and power, an action that seemed necessary after the Civil War. However, it was nearly 80 years before the 14th Amendment was interpreted by the Supreme Court as protecting individual rights from encroachment by the states. Beginning in the mid-1940s, the Supreme Court held that portions of the Bill of Rights were incorporated into the 14th Amendment (see **Figure 9-2**). This meant certain rights found in the Bill of Rights were considered to be part of that amendment and, therefore, applicable to the states.

Many restrictions of state power in the area of criminal procedure have resulted from this incorporation approach. For example, a search of one's belongings and a seizure of evidence are restricted by the Fourth Amendment. The Constitution governs the daily activities of law enforcement because it directly limits how officers perform their duties.

Administrative Law

Another source of law that affects law enforcement comes from what is known as **administrative law**. This body

FIGURE 9-3 Examples of Administrative Law Affecting Policing

State Training Curriculum	State Labor Relation Procedures
Mandated Selection Criteria	OSHA-type Safety Regulations
Civil Service Testing Procedures	Personnel Appeals Boards
Police Insignia and Uniform Standards	Vehicle/Equipment Bidding Procedures
Promotion Procedures and Criteria	Licensing/Certification Provisions

of law is relatively recent and includes court-made law, agency rules, and statutory law. It had its beginnings with the creation of the civil service and state regulation of the economy in the 1880s. The purpose of administrative law is to guide the process of administrative officers in government agencies and guard against arbitrary decisions. Essentially, administrative law flows from one central principle—the rule of law—which seeks to remove arbitrariness from decision making (Carter and Harrington 1991). An arbitrary decision is one that has no clear objective criteria from which to judge each event. If a decision is made without clear criteria, the possibility is very high that the decision rule will differ from case to case; different standards could be used for different people, which is obviously unfair. This means that decisions of administrative officers must meet, and be based upon, criteria or standards that are applied to each case in the same manner. This area of law impacts law enforcement because, among many other things, it deals with the procedures for hiring, promoting, and disciplining law enforcement officers (see **Figure 9-3**).

Actions of an administrative officer (such as a chief of police) must be based upon statutory authority, which is delegated to that administrative officer. This is called **delegation of authority**, which means that a legislative body gave authority to make laws or administrative rules

FIGURE 9-2 Section 1 of Amendment XIV to The Constitution of The United States

Section 1. All persons born or naturalized in the United States and subject to the jurisdiction thereof, are citizens of the United States and of the State wherein they reside. No State shall make or enforce any law which shall abridge the privileges or immunities of citizens of the United States; nor shall any State deprive any person of life, liberty, or property, without due process of law; nor deny to any person within its jurisdiction the equal protection of the laws.

Source: U.S. Constitution, Amendment XIV

in a certain area to a specific administrative officer or agency. The reasons for the need for administrative law are twofold: (1) legislatures cannot plan all possible situations within a given law, and (2) administrative agencies must have some freedom to make rules based upon their experience, but guided by the law. This is guided discretion. Rules must be adopted in a public manner and generally must be supported with facts: not only must decisions be free of arbitrariness, but so must rules. For example, a state statute may give chiefs of police authority to make "all necessary rules and regulations for the orderly management" of their department. Relying upon standards of the profession and known training standards, a chief might promulgate (or write) rules that govern procedures for citizen complaints, review of disciplinary actions, job functions, and the like. These are known as the Policy and Procedures Manual, but they are not the same from department to department; that is because the chief was given discretion to draw rules that are merely guided by some standard principles. Hence, the rules are not arbitrary, nor are their application. The rule-making process must produce written regulations (as oral regulations are not enforceable).

Additionally, rules must be applied to everyone in the same manner. Exceptions cannot be made. If there are "exceptions," they are based on the rules and, therefore, are not really exceptions. In fact, many administrators make exceptions, but it is important to understand that once exceptions are made, it is difficult to argue that everyone is treated the same. More importantly, because true "exceptions" are outside of the rules, you cannot distinguish between one exception and another. For example, suppose a chief of police has three rookie police officers, each of whom has violated similar, but minor, rules during their field training. Assuming the violations are similar, the chief generally would be required to treat all three similarly.

A decision must be based upon standards or criteria found in the rules, and facts must support the decision. This is the process designed to prevent biased decisions from being made and ensures due process, that people with similar facts or problems will be treated in the same manner. Law enforcement officers should also know that this process protects them. If you follow policy, you generally will be safe.

Parties that are affected by a rule or its potential enforcement must be given an opportunity to challenge any potential adverse decision before it is made. This is usually called an opportunity for an administrative hearing coupled with "notice." Notice means simply being informed of what the substance of the claim involves and the time and place set for the hearing. An administrative hearing does not mean a trial, or even face-to-face discussion; it simply means that an administrative officer is preparing to make a decision, and that the time and place of the decision is given to the affected parties. It also means the affected parties are entitled to know the position of the administrative officer and may respond before a decision is reached on the merits of the issue. Finally, some process of appeal is essential.

Together, all of these requirements are generally called **minimum administrative due process**. Due process essentially requires fundamental fairness. In the area of administrative law, this usually means notice of the nature of a pending administrative action, an opportunity to respond, and the basis of the proposed action. This is a constitutional standard applied to ensure that the government does not treat people unfairly or arbitrarily. **Figure 9-4** contains a section from the Federal Administrative Procedures Act that describes certain rights of individuals who suffer legal wrong because of federal agency actions.

Other examples of administrative law are those which comprise the process of hiring, training, promoting, deploying, and disciplining personnel. These are sometimes called personnel policies, and some of these issues are covered in detail in Chapters 7 and 8 of this text. For example, what authority does a chief of police have in prohibiting officers under her command from speaking to the press or city council? What limitations are there for assigning personnel to various duties? What actions are required in order to fairly terminate someone's employment? These and other similar matters are the subject of administrative law.

It is clear that each of these sources of law affects law enforcement in many ways. Because law enforcement must respond to all of these areas of law, the environment for law enforcement is growing more and more complex. Law enforcement officers prior to the 1960s rarely had to worry about such matters. United States law continues

FIGURE 9-4 Review of Federal Agency Actions

§ 702. *Right of Review*

A person suffering legal wrong because of agency action, or adversely affected or aggrieved by agency action within the meaning of a relevant statute, is entitled to judicial review thereof. An action in a court of the United States seeking relief other than money damages and stating in a claim that an agency or an officer or employee thereof acted or failed to act in an official capacity or under color of legal authority shall not be dismissed nor relief therein be denied on the ground that it is against the United States or that the United States is an indispensable party. The United States may be named as a defendant in such action and a judgment or decree may be entered against the United States: *Provided,* That any manda-tory or injunctive decree shall specify the Federal officer or officers (by name or by title), and their successors in office, personally responsible for compliance. Nothing herein (1) affects other limitations on judicial review or the power or duty of the court to dismiss any action or deny relief on any other appropriate legal or equitable ground; or (2) confers authority to grant relief if any other statute that grants consent to suit expressly or impliedly forbids the relief which is sought.

§ 703. *Form and Venue of Proceedings*

The form of proceeding for judicial review is the special statutory review proceeding relevant to the subject matter in a court specified by statute or, in the absence of inadequacy thereof, any applicable form of legal action, including actions for declaratory judgments or writs or prohibitory or mandatory injunction or habeas corpus, in a court of competent jurisdiction. If no special statutory review proceeding in applicable , the action for judicial review may be brought against the United States, the agency by its official title, or the appropriate officer. Except to the extent that prior, adequate, and exclusive opportunity for judicial review is provided by law, agency action is subject to judicial review in civil or criminal proceedings for judicial enforcement.

Source: Federal Administrative Procedures Act, 5 U.S.C. §702 and 703, 2004.

to evolve, and law enforcement must be alert to these developments.

THE U.S. SYSTEM OF JUSTICE

The U.S. system of justice is frequently called a "dual system of justice" because there are two parallel systems of courts. The state court system is typically made up of three levels of courts: trial, appellate, and supreme, and the federal system is generally designed along the same pattern (see **Figure 9-5**). Both systems have special types of trial courts, but these courts differ in their jurisdic-tions (the types of cases a court can hear). Geographical jurisdiction (also called venue) means the courts can hear only cases occurring in their city, county, state, or district. Some federal courts, such as the U.S. Supreme Court, have no geographical limits and theoretically may hear a case originating anywhere in the United States or its territories, so long as it is on appeal (the original jurisdiction of the

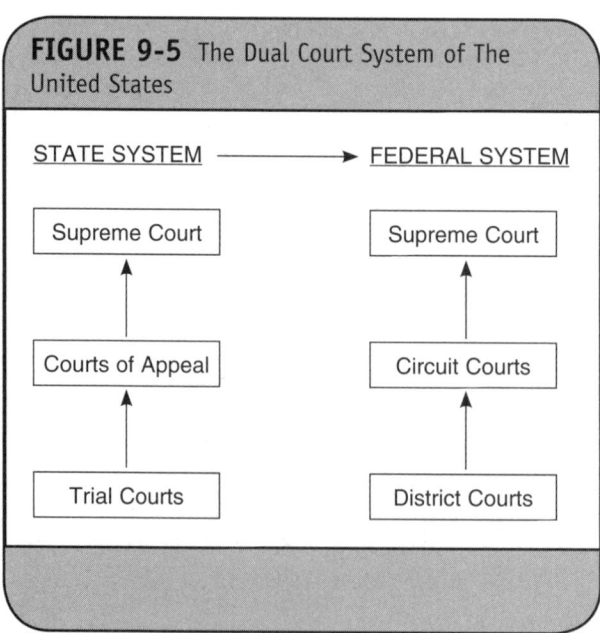

FIGURE 9-5 The Dual Court System of The United States

STATE SYSTEM ⟶ FEDERAL SYSTEM

Supreme Court ← Courts of Appeal ← Trial Courts

Supreme Court ← Circuit Courts ← District Courts

Supreme Court is very limited). Other jurisdictional factors involve the seriousness of the case; if a case is civil but involves only a small amount of money, jurisdiction may be restricted to a municipal court. The same is frequently true for misdemeanor offenses in criminal codes, which is an example of jurisdiction based upon the substance of the case. This provides the difference between subject matter jurisdiction (the type of case) and geographical jurisdiction (an area such as a county or city). Municipal courts, for example, rarely have subject matter jurisdiction to try felony cases, but a county trial court such as the Superior Court in California does have subject matter jurisdiction of felony trials. Similarly, the courts in Columbiana County, Ohio do not usually have jurisdiction over crimes that occurred in Franklin County, Ohio (unless venue is moved for reasons of fairness to the defendant).

Federal Courts

Generally speaking, federal courts cannot hear cases based upon state law, and state courts cannot hear cases based upon federal law. For example, the federal system employs bankruptcy courts for the special function of trying cases of economic bankruptcy, and no state court can hear a bankruptcy claim. In the same manner, a federal trial court such as the Federal District Court cannot hear a case based upon a state's criminal law. State courts can interpret the United States Constitution, but the federal judiciary has the final word on this interpretation, while state supreme courts have the final say in the interpretation of state law so long as it does not involve a federal constitutional question. Law enforcement officers at the state and local government level rarely have contact with federal criminal courts, unless they are working on cases involving federal agents that go to trial (this occurs today with some of the cases developed by federal task forces that include state and local law enforcement personnel).

Sometimes a federal court will hear a case that could have been tried in a state court, but which was removed to federal court because the parties live in different states. This is called diversity of jurisdiction and is provided for in the federal code (28 U.S. C. § 1332), which sets out the jurisdiction of the federal courts in civil controversies exceeding $75,000.

Federal Courts and State Crimes

There are only two ways that a state criminal case can be heard by a federal court. First, a defendant might appeal an issue, such as the constitutionality of an ordinance or state law. Initially, a state trial court adjudicates such a claim. Regardless of the results of such a ruling, the losing side has the right to appeal. Appeals go to the state court of appeals. Similarly, the court of appeals has the authority to rule on the issue. Again, the losing side may then seek an appeal to that state's highest court. (In most states the highest court is called the Supreme Court. However, in New York the Supreme Court is the trial court and the Court of Appeals is the highest court. The names of courts usually indicate their level, but not always.)

In most states, the Supreme Court of that state can refuse an appeal at its discretion. Whether refused or heard, however, the losing side may still ask the Supreme Court of the United States to hear the case when it involves a federal question that has already been heard by the highest court in that state. This is done by petitioning the Supreme Court to issue a **writ of *certiorari***, which is an order requiring the lower court to give the Supreme Court the record for review. Taking a case to the U.S. Supreme Court is rare, however. Millions of cases, both criminal and civil, are filed in the United States each year, yet only about 7000 appeals are filed with the Supreme Court each year, and, in a given year, the Supreme Court generally hears only about 90 of those cases. Because state courts are usually bound by *stare decisis* on constitutional issues, they will rarely contradict a rule that the Supreme Court of the United States previously announced.

A second method by which a state criminal case can be heard in a federal court is less rare, but still not very frequent. If a prisoner exhausts all traditional appeals after conviction (as discussed above), there is usually little that can be done. However, if the law upon which he or she was convicted is later challenged or if there is new evidence that was not known at the time of trial, the prisoner may seek a federal **writ of *habeas corpus***. This is an order requiring the person who is holding the prisoner, such as a warden or sheriff, to show cause why the prisoner should not be released. It is not truly a criminal case at this stage, but rather a civil case based upon federal law. If the court issues the writ, the prisoner must be released. The state may appeal to the U.S. Court of Appeals or, if need be, the Supreme Court of the United States.

Efforts to secure writs of habeas corpus are not very successful and have generated a good deal of dispute. There is a growing debate over the use of such methods to stall death penalty executions, for example. Still, courts are reluctant to see innocent people punished, and the justice system must assume that errors can be made in any human decision process.

State Courts

States divide trial responsibility between courts of general jurisdiction and those of limited jurisdiction. The former are generally organized along county boundaries, and are sometimes called common pleas or superior courts. These courts typically hear serious misdemeanors and all felonies, as well as large civil lawsuits. Lower state trial courts, such as district, municipal or county courts, generally have jurisdiction over traffic cases and misdemeanors as well as uncomplicated civil lawsuits, such as small claims. Boundaries of courts with limited jurisdiction are usually within one county, but they encompass only a portion of that county. Some of these lower courts also have the power to hear the beginning of a felony case, called a **preliminary hearing**. This is a hearing to determine if there is sufficient evidence (probable cause) to send the case to the district attorney or grand jury for further prosecution.

Trial Courts

Law enforcement officers who go to court will spend most of their time in state trial courts. When an officer makes an arrest, contact with the local court is initiated. Arrests may be the result of either officer discretion or a warrant for arrest previously issued by a court. Officer discretion arrests occur when an officer determines that **probable cause** exists to arrest. Probable cause is not always easy to define, but one U.S. Supreme Court decision described it this way:

> Probable cause exists where the facts and circumstances within the [arresting officers'] knowledge and of which they had reasonably trustworthy information [are] sufficient in themselves to warrant a [person] of reasonable caution in the belief

that an offense has been or is being committed [by the person to be arrested] (*Brinegar v. United States*, 338 U.S. 160, 175–176, 1949).

A determination to arrest may be subject to review first by the officer's supervisor. After the officer submits a report justifying the action, a formal approval or disapproval is noted by the supervisor. In practice, many who are arrested are released at the discretion of the officer and his or her supervisor. Written reports reflect the justification for the action.

Those who study the relationship between law enforcement and the courts notice certain behaviors, which reflect the experience of working with one another. For example, even though probable cause may exist, an experienced officer, detective, or supervisor may know that there is insufficient evidence to satisfy the judge or district attorney likely to handle the case, and so the officers may decide to dispose of the matter at their level. Sometimes officers release a suspect because of assistance the suspect gave on a co-suspect or on another case. It is also possible that, on further investigation, the case looked different or another suspect emerged. Finally, officers could "look the other way" in order to develop a confidential informant for future use, though typically superiors must be informed if this is the case.

In many cases, officer discretion will prevail. However, it is also possible that an assistant district attorney (ADA) or assistant prosecutor will review the reports and initial charges and make an independent determination whether or not to proceed with the charge. Frequently, officers confer with an ADA in order to get advice on cases. Once a charge is made, it may also be reviewed by a court in a probable cause hearing (for misdemeanors) or a preliminary hearing (for felonies). In each case, the purpose of the hearing is to determine whether there is probable cause to proceed with the charge. At any stage of the proceedings, a court has the authority to dismiss a case with or without prejudice. If it is dismissed with prejudice, the charge cannot be re-filed at a later date regardless of the evidence then available. If it is dismissed without prejudice, the charge may be re-filed.

Arrest warrants are issued by an officer of the court after a probable cause hearing as the result of an indictment by a grand jury, or by the issuance of a prosecutor's information. In each case, the investigating officers must present testimony to justify issuance. The process varies slightly from state to state. If a charge is formally approved and moves to the warrant stage, the next step is a dismissal, a plea, or a trial. If there is a plea to the charges, it may involve what is called a plea bargain. Typically, this involves a discussion involving defense counsel, the prosecutor, and a judge. Law enforcement officers are frequently involved in plea discussions and should be prepared to make their case. It is possible that other participants in plea discussions will include victims, probation officers, psychologists, and social workers.

The object of plea bargaining is to obtain a guilty plea. One way to obtain that is to either agree to the potential sentence of a defendant or reduce the charge to a lesser-included offense. In either case, the potential sentence of a defendant appears to be reduced. This induces defendants to plead guilty, avoid a trial, and presumably avoid a tougher sentence. The actual sentence may be determined by statute so that the only real "bargaining" concerns the level of offense, but a sentence discussion may also include a fine, restitution to be paid to a victim, probation terms, and time to be served.

The process of plea bargaining produces heated debate in the public. Some argue that it saves time and money because it eliminates trials. If the incentive were eliminated, defendants might decide to try their case since they could not receive a worse sentence for doing so. In effect, there would be nothing to lose by going to trial. Since only 5% or fewer of all cases go to trial, even a slight increase in trials would overwhelm the already overburdened justice system. Not only would more officers spend their time waiting in courthouse hallways to testify, we would need to add more clerk and court personnel, and more citizens would have their lives disrupted for jury service. The cost in additional judges and prosecutors (who would not be available for other duties) would be tremendous. Others argue that deals should not be made with criminals, and the cost should be absorbed by the current system, while still others argue there is really no plea bargain process at all. Some who have studied several courts across the United States suggest that sentencing outcomes do not differ much regardless of the use of plea bargaining. Rather, each courthouse seems to have

a "going rate" for each kind of offense, considering the record of the defendant. In this view, the "bargaining" is really a process of further identifying what the correct charge should be (Eisenstein, Flemming, and Nardulli 1988; Nardulli, Flemming, and Eisenstien 1988).

If there is no plea in the case or if it is not dismissed, the case will go to trial. Before a trial begins, and in some states during trial, hearings may occur that determine the admissibility of evidence. These are called **suppression** hearings. Evidence may be suppressed because of the manner in which it was seized, because it was not presented to the other side during pre-trial discovery, or because of some legal restriction on its use (such as forcing a priest to testify about a parishioner).

Appellate Courts

While lower trial courts may rule on matters such as the admission of evidence or the constitutionality of a law, it is the state courts of appeals that settle disputes of law by interpreting state law or the state and federal constitutions. Consequently, these courts have a large impact on law enforcement, though officers rarely attend the oral arguments before such courts. These courts hear criminal and civil appeals, as well as appeals from lower courts involving civil service cases and related disputes, including law enforcement hiring and discipline. Because lower courts are required to follow the precedents of the appeals courts, appellate decisions shape behavior in the courts below.

PROCEDURAL LIMITATIONS ON LAW ENFORCEMENT

The substantive criminal law is carefully defined by statute. Unfortunately, the procedural restrictions on law enforcement are not so clear. They are unclear because they are based upon relatively vague constitutional provisions such as due process and unreasonable searches and seizures. We will consider only an overview of procedural limitations here, along with some recent U.S. Supreme Court decisions, and as 600-page textbooks are published on the topic of criminal procedure, we cannot devote space to every aspect of the issue. The legal restrictions on law enforcement personnel are considerable, and among the most significant are without question those applying to searches and seizures.

Searches and Seizures

Law enforcement personnel are bound by the Fourth Amendment to the Constitution of the United States and the interpretations that have been made of its language:

The right of the people to be secure in their persons, houses, papers, and effects, against unreasonable searches and seizures, shall not be violated, and no warrants shall issue, but upon probable cause, supported by oath or affirmation, and particularly describing the place to be searched, and the persons or things to be seized.

A **search** is generally defined as the invasion, by an agent of the state, of an area that a person believes is protected or private; an area in which it is reasonable for a person to have an expectation of privacy, and those expectations change depending upon where you are. You obviously have a higher expectation of privacy in your own home than you do walking down a public street, even though you have some expectation of privacy there (e.g., the expectation that you will be left alone if you are doing nothing wrong). That belief will be upheld and a search negated by a court if the "person exhibited an actual (subjective) expectation of privacy, and… the expectation is one that society is prepared to recognize as 'reasonable'," (*Katz v. United States*, 389 U.S. 347, 361, 1967). It should be noted here that there are exceptions to this generalization—in other words, the courts (on behalf of society) may recognize actions by law enforcement personnel as being reasonable. Many of these exceptions are discussed below, and they are often the controversial issues that are decided in U.S. Supreme Court decisions.

A **seizure** is generally defined as a "meaningful interference with the possessory interests of the suspect," (*United States v. Jacobsen*, 466 U.S. 109, 113, 1984). The Fourth Amendment applies to searches and seizures of evidence in the same way it applies to arrests. The general **warrant requirement** means that a search or seizure of evidence or persons without a warrant is presumed to be unreasonable. **Figure 9-6** depicts a sample form for a search warrant affidavit and the warrant itself. An officer seeking a search warrant must produce facts in the affidavit which is sworn to in the presence of a judge. The facts must support a conclusion that there is probable cause to

believe that evidence of a crime, or a person, will be found in the location named. The affidavit and the warrant, pursuant to constitutional requirements, must "specifically" identify the things or persons to be searched or seized. That specification is the limit of the warrant. Once the items or persons are found the search must end. If evidence turned up in the process of executing the warrant, additional warrant authority must be sought to continue the search. A search can be of a person or a person's property, just as a seizure may be of property, but it may also be of a person; the latter are called arrests. After arrest, suspects are questioned, and this behavior is limited by the Fifth and Sixth Amendments. Arrests are discussed in more detail below this section on searches.

The general rule of searches and seizures holds that without a warrant, any search or seizure is presumed to be unconstitutional (see *Payton v. New York*, 445 U.S. 573, 1980 and *Chimel v. California*, 395 U.S. 752, 1969). The Fourth Amendment does not require a warrant; it only prohibits a search or seizure that is "unreasonable." The Supreme Court of the United States firmly established the doctrine that absence of a warrant raises the presumption that the search or seizure in question is unreasonable and, therefore, unconstitutional. It is also generally required that before serving a warrant, officers must "knock and announce" their intentions of serving a search or arrest warrant at a premises (Cerullo and Means 2004). The court also created many exceptions to this doctrine, which serve to rebut the presumption of unreasonableness. In effect, the court made these exceptions statements of reasonableness. If any of the recognized exceptional circumstances apply, the search or seizure is considered reasonable. The ability to understand search and seizure limits on law enforcement, therefore, depends upon one's knowledge of the exceptions to the warrant rule.

One way to think of these exceptions to the warrant rule is to imagine the expectation of privacy as a cave. The deeper law enforcement seeks to go into the cave, the greater the justification it needs. The exceptions to the warrant rule focus on the question of how reasonable the claimed expectation of privacy may be in the particular circumstances of that search. Some of the most important of these exceptions we address next.

FIGURE 9-6 Sample Search Warrant and Affidavit

(DISTRICT) (COUNTY) COURT, EL PASO COUNTY, STATE OF COLORADO CRIMINAL
ACTION NUMBER _____

APPLICATION AND AFFIDAVIT FOR SEARCH WARRANT

The undersigned, a peace officer as defined in 18-1-901 (3) (1), C.R.S.1973 as amended, being first duly sworn on oath moves the Court to issue a Warrant to search those person (s) and/or premised known as:

_____
_____
_____
_____

The undersigned states that there exists probable cause to believe that the following person, property or thing (s) to be searched for, and if found, seized will be found on the aforementioned person (s) and or premises and are described as follows: _____

_____
_____
_____
_____
_____
_____
_____

The grounds for the seizure of said person(s), property or thing(s) are that probable cause exists to believe that it: ( ) Is stolen or embezzled, or ( ) Is designed or intended for use as means of committing a criminal offense, or ( ) Is or has been used as a means of committing a criminal offense, or ( ) Is illegal to possess, or ( ) Would be material evidence in a subsequent criminal prosecution, Or ( ) Is a person, property or thing the seizure of which is expressly required, authorized or permitted by a statute of the State of Colorado, or ( ) Is kept, stored, transported, sold, dispensed, or possessed in violation of a statute of the State of Colorado, or ( ) Is kept, stored, transported, sold, dispensed, or possessed in violation of a statute of the State of Colorado under circumstances involving a serious threat to the public safety, or order, or to the public health, (mark x according to fact):

The facts submitted in support of this application are set forth in the accompanying attachment designated as Attachment "_____" which is attached hereto and made a part hereof.

Applicant: _____

Law enforcement agency: _____

Position: _____

Sworn and subscribed before me this _____ day of _____ 20 _____

Judge: _____

S 209-86 REV 7/01

Source: Courtesy of Chief Richard Myers, Colorado Springs, CO, 2010

Stop and Frisk

Most of us would expect to have some privacy as we walk along a public street. But our behavior, even if not criminal per se, may lead others to conclude that we may be preparing to commit a crime. In *Terry v. Ohio* (392 U.S. 1, 1968), Chief Justice Earl Warren of the United States Supreme Court contemplated a case in which an off-duty Cleveland, Ohio police detective saw such activity (**Figure 9-7**). In the holding, the court announced the rule for **stop and frisk** cases; while the court permitted a pat-down of the outer clothing for weapons, a full search of the person was not reasonable in the circumstances. In 1993, the court revis-

ited this issue and focused on a pat-down that found not weapons, but crack cocaine. The court found that while an officer could seize something other than a weapon after a stop and frisk pat down, the nature of the item would need to be clear after a mere pat down. In reversing the conviction in this case, the court found that the officer had to manipulate the item through the outer clothing to determine what it might be. That, the court held, was going too far (*Minnesota v. Dickerson*, 506 U.S. 366, 1993). In other words, the item being felt had to be identifiable immediately. Moreover, a *Terry* search cannot be conducted on a hunch, but only upon facts that can be articulated and produce reasonable suspicion that crime may be afoot, thus justifying a brief stop and inquiry. The pat-down is merely for safety of the officers and others, including the subject of the inquiry.

In 2009, the U.S. Supreme Court ruled that a *Terry* search could be extended to passengers in a legally stopped vehicle. The initial traffic stop occurred in April 2002 when officers pulled over an automobile at night after a license plate check revealed that the vehicle's registration had been suspended for an insurance-related violation. The vehicle had three occupants, and while one officer dealt with driver outside the car, another officer engaged one of the passengers in conversation, asking his name and requesting identification. She noticed he wore clothing indicative of gang membership and that he was holding a police scanner. Based on her concerns regarding possible gang affiliation and suspicion he may be armed, the officer conducted a limited search for a weapon by patting down his waistband area, where she discovered a gun. The defendant was convicted of a gun-possession charge at trial, but the Arizona appeals court reversed the decision and the state's supreme court denied review of the case. The U.S. Supreme Court reversed the state appellate court ruling, remanding the case for further proceedings as the lower court had not addressed whether the officer had reasonable suspicion that the defendant was armed at the time of the stop (*Arizona v. Johnson*, 555 U.S. 135, 2009; Baker 2009).

Search Incident to Arrest

Another exception, rarely commented upon but the subject of many Supreme Court cases, is the limit of a search incident to arrest. When a person is lawfully

---

FIGURE 9-7 Stop and Frisk

"We merely hold today that where a police officer observes unusual conduct which leads him reasonably to conclude in light of his experience that criminal activity may be afoot and that the persons with whom he is dealing may be armed and presently dangerous, where in the course of investigating this behavior he identifies himself as a policeman and makes reasonable inquiries, and where nothing in the initial stages of the encounter serves to dispel his reasonable fear for his own or others' safety, he is entitled for the protection of himself and others in the area to conduct a carefully limited search of the outer clothing of such persons in an attempt to discover weapons which might be used to assault him." *Terry v. Ohio*, 392 U.S. 1, (1968).

"It remains unclear how many different types of non-arrest detentions might usefully or perhaps must be distinguished for Fourth Amendment purposes. Those detentions of major concern are what is often called 'investigatory stops,' 'investigatory detentions,' 'field stops,' or—memorializing *Terry v. Ohio*—'*Terry* stops.' They are widely assumed to be detentions made in the field for the purposes of gathering further information upon which to base a decision as to whether or not to arrest the suspect. It is similarly assumed that they are and should be effected in situations presenting inadequate grounds for arrest and that they cannot involve either prolonged detention of the suspect or substantial movement of the suspect during the detention."

Source: Miller, Frank W., Robert O. Dawson, George E. Dix, Raymond I. Parnas, (1991), *The Police Function, 5th Edition*. Westbury, NY: The Foundation Press, Inc., p. 210.

arrested (by warrant or otherwise), law enforcement officers may search the immediate vicinity of the person in order to secure any weapons or prevent the destruction of evidence within the suspect's reach (*Chimel v. California*, 395 U.S. 752, 1969). This does not include an entire house, or even an entire car or locked baggage in a car. However, officers may conduct a "protective sweep" of a house to search very briefly for more victims or potential assailants who may pose a threat to the officers, if the officers might reasonably expect to find such persons (*Maryland v. Buie*, 494 U.S. 325, 1990). Obviously, people do not hide in cupboards or in drawers, so this is a limited exception.

Police making an arrest

Source: © Corbis

Automobile Search Exception

Officers may conduct a full search of a vehicle at the time of an arrest or stop if there is probable cause to believe the vehicle contains evidence of the offense for which the person was arrested or stopped. In 2009, the U.S. Supreme Court decided *Arizona v. Gant* (129 S. Ct. 1710), which clarified the procedural guidelines for searching a vehicle incidental to an arrest. The Court concluded:

> *Police may search a vehicle incident to a recent occupant's arrest only if the arrestee is within reaching distance of the passenger compartment at the time of the search or it is reasonable to believe the vehicle contains evidence of the offense of arrest. When these justifications are absent, a search of an arrestee's vehicle will be unreasonable unless police obtain a warrant or show that another exception to the warrant requirement applies.*

In *Gant*, the defendant was arrested outside his vehicle for driving under a suspended license and placed in a police cruiser. Officers then searched his vehicle and found cocaine in a jacket. He was convicted on drug charges and appealed, claiming that the search was unconstitutional. The Arizona Supreme Court ruled the search unconstitutional and U.S. Supreme Court affirmed.

The theory behind the automobile exception is, first, that cars are mobile and can carry away the evidence they contain. Secondly, automobiles are highly regulated and, therefore, offer a low expectation of privacy. Since 1981, law enforcement officers have followed the general guideline established in *New York v. Belton* (453 U.S. 454) that allowed the search of the passenger compartment of the vehicle when the officer had made a lawful custodial arrest of the occupant. The *Gant* decision now restricts the scope of such searches. The case raised several concerns about convictions under the *Belton* standard, but one concern was decided in 2011 when the U.S. Supreme Court in *Davis v. United States* refused to apply the exclusionary rule to evidence obtained under pre-*Gant* precedence. Willie Davis had been convicted of possession of a firearm by a convicted felon. The weapon had been discovered in his jacket in a vehicle in which he was a passenger following a traffic stop. The discovery of the weapon was lawful under the search and seizure precedents at the time of the arrest in 2007.

Davis appealed the conviction because the evidence would be inadmissible under the guidelines established in Gant in 2009. The Court held that "searches conducted in objectively reasonable reliance on binding appellate precedent are not subject to the exclusionary rule" (*Davis v. United States*, 564 U.S. ____, slip opinion, p.1). **Figure 9-8** illustrates the complexity involved in legal issues surrounding automobile searches.

FIGURE 9-8 California v. Acevedo, 500 U.S. 565 (1991)

BLACKMUN, J., delivered the opinion of the Court,

Although we have recognized firmly that *the doctrine of stare decisis serves profoundly important purposes* in our legal system, *this Court has overruled a prior case on the comparatively rare occasion when it has bred confusion or been a derelict or led to anomalous results.*

In the case before us, *the police had probable cause to believe that the paper bag in the automobile's trunk contained marijuana.* That probable cause now allows a warrantless search of the paper bag. The facts in the record reveal that *the police did not have probable cause to believe that contraband was hidden in any other part of the automobile and a search of the entire vehicle would have been without probable cause and unreasonable under the Fourth Amendment.*

Our holding today neither extends the Carroll doctrine nor broadens the scope of the permissible automobile search delineated in Carroll, Chambers, and Ross. *It remains a cardinal principle that "searches conducted outside the judicial process, without prior approval by judge or magistrate, are per se unreasonable under the Fourth Amendment subject only to a few specifically established and well-delineated exceptions."* Mincey v. Arizona, 437 U.S. 385, 390 (1978), quoting Katz v. United States, 389 U.S. 347, 357 (1967)

Until today, this Court has drawn a curious line between the search of an automobile that coincidentally turns up a container and the search of a container that coincidentally turns up in an automobile. The protections of the Fourth Amendment must not turn on such coincidences. We therefore interpret Carroll as providing one rule to govern all automobile searches. The police may search an automobile and the containers within it where they have probable cause to believe contraband or evidence is contained. (Emphasis Added).

Source: California v. Acevedo, 500 U.S. 565 (1991).

In April 1999, the U.S. Supreme Court ruled in *Wyoming v. Houghton* (526 U.S. 295) that when law enforcement officers have probable cause to search a car, they may inspect passengers' belongings found in the car that are capable of concealing the object of the search.

Global Positioning System Tracking

Areas involving "searches" of vehicles using technological devices are less clear. Currently, it is unclear, for example, if global positioning system (GPS) sensors can be attached to vehicles without a warrant. This would enable law enforcement to track a vehicle wherever it went, an important investigative tool. At the moment, the law is unclear, since different state supreme courts have rendered different answers. In August 2010, two federal courts (one in California and the other in Washington, D.C.) reached different opinions, so it is just a matter of time until the U.S. Supreme Court will have to decide the issue. In those cases allowing the use of GPS tracking devices on vehicle, the argument has been that no search of the vehicle occurred—the device was put on the vehicle when it was in plain view or on public streets—while the argument against the warrantless use of GPS tracking is that it is an invasion of privacy. Ultimately, the U.S. Supreme Court will be asked to "decide the privacy impact of the new surveillance technology in products such as cellphones and vehicle-navigation systems" (Hsu 2010). In December 2009, the Ohio Supreme Court ruled that "The warrantless search of data within a cell phone seized incident to a lawful arrest is prohibited by the Fourth Amendment when the search is unnecessary for the safety of law-enforcement officers and there are no exigent circumstances" (*State v. Smith*, 124 Ohio St.3d 116). It was a precedent-setting case and limits the warrantless searches of cellphones (and maybe similar devices).

In 2001, the U.S. Supreme Court did address the use of advanced technology by striking down a conviction in Oregon for drug cultivation where the police employed a thermal imaging device on a home to literally see through the house—including into the bathroom—in order to gather evidence to obtain search and arrest warrants. Based on this device, it was obvious that the residents of the house were growing large numbers of marijuana plants. The court found that the use of such a device "not generally in use in the public" violated the expectation of privacy and effectively suppressed all of the evidence (*Kyllo v. United States*, 533 U.S. 27, 2001).

Administrative or Inventory Searches of Vehicles

Officers may seize a vehicle when the driver is arrested or the automobile is evidence in a crime, and they may conduct an impoundment (or inventory) search. If personal belongings or automobiles are routinely seized at arrest as a matter of departmental policy, these may be fully searched in order to protect the property of the defendant and to protect officers from claims of property theft, loss, or damage. However, there must be some departmental rule or standard practice that supports an impoundment (*South Dakota v. Opperman*, 428 U.S. 364, 1976 and *Chambers v. Maloney*, 399 U.S. 42, 1970). Any evidence or contraband found in the process of such an inventory search may be seized and can lead to additional charges against the person arrested.

Stop and Identify

It is also important to keep in mind that police cannot randomly stop you on the street and demand that you identify yourself. In order for them to do this, there must be some reasonable suspicion that you are engaging in some sort of crime or that you may be a witness to a criminal offense that the officer is investigating. In 2004, the U.S. Supreme Court ruled that under such circumstances, failure to give your name when asked can constitutionally lead to an arrest (*Hiibal v. Sixth Judicial District Court of Nevada*, 542 U.S. 177, 124 S. Ct. 2451, 2004). The *Hiibal* decision upheld the Nevada law that required individuals to identify themselves to law enforcement officers who are investigating incidents; the law does not require the production of identification, just a verbal response identifying them by name. Some statutes, such as the one in Ohio, requires the disclosure of the person's name, address, or date of birth when requested by a law enforcement officer under certain circumstances (see **Figure 9-9**). Today, there are approximately 12 states that have "stop and identify" statutes.

Check Points

Another type of exception is the checkpoint. Checkpoints may be employed in a number of limited circumstances.

FIGURE 9-9 Failure to disclose personal information

(A) No person who is in a public place shall refuse to disclose the person's name, address, or date of birth, when requested by a law enforcement officer who reasonably suspects either of the following:

(1) The person is committing, has committed, or is about to commit a criminal offense.
(2) The person witnessed any of the following:
   (a) An offense of violence that would constitute a felony under the laws of this state;
   (b) A felony offense that causes or results in, or creates a substantial risk of, serious physical harm to another person or to property;
   (c) Any attempt or conspiracy to commit, or complicity in committing, any offense identified in division (A)(2)(a) or (b) of this section;
   (d) Any conduct reasonably indicating that any offense identified in division (A)(2)(a) or (b) of this section or any attempt, conspiracy, or complicity described in division (A)(2)(c) of this section has been, is being, or is about to be committed.

(B) Whoever violates this section is guilty of failure to disclose one's personal information, a misdemeanor of the fourth degree.
(C) Nothing in this section requires a person to answer any questions beyond that person's name, address, or date of birth. Nothing in this section authorizes a law enforcement officer to arrest a person for not providing any information beyond that person's name, address, or date of birth or for refusing to describe the offense observed.
(D) It is not a violation of this section to refuse to answer a question that would reveal a person's age or date of birth if age is an element of the crime that the person is suspected of committing.

Effective Date: 04-14-2006

Source: Extracted from Ohio Revised Code, § 2921.29.

One example is the sobriety checkpoint. Automobiles may be stopped and the driver directed to answer questions if certain conditions are met. First, the initial stop at a checkpoint must be directed at all vehicles passing the point. Second, the intrusion must be minimal in order to remain "reasonable" under the standards of the Fourth Amendment; merely stopping each car briefly in order to make limited inquiries is reasonable. Further inquiries, such as field sobriety testing, can be done if and only if the initial contact produced reasonable suspicion to proceed further (*Michigan Department of State Police v. Sitz*, 496 U.S. 444, 1990). This type of stop is considered reasonable because the expectation of privacy on public highways is very low, and automobiles are highly regulated. Although the U.S. Supreme Court ruled that checkpoints are reasonable in many situations, 11 states do not permit them, either by state law or interpretation of their state constitutions (National Highway Traffic Safety Administration 2006, 1–14).

Generally, random stops are not permissible (*United States v. Martinez-Fuerte*, 428 U.S. 543, 1976), but an investigative or informational checkpoint is valid. If officers stop vehicles coming through an area where a crime has been committed (in this case a vehicular homicide), then a simple inquiry as to whether the driver or passengers saw anything is a reasonable reason to stop vehicles, so long as all are stopped at that point (*Illinois v. Lidster*, 540 U.S. 419, 2004). Crime control checkpoints with drug-sniffing dogs and visual examination of the interior of the vehicle are not constitutionally permissible (*City of Indianapolis v. Edmond*, 531 U.S. 32, 2000), though greater latitude has been upheld at border patrol checkpoints for citizenship papers (*U.S. v. Martinez-Fuerte*, 428 U.S. 543, 1976) and searches of vehicles crossing the U.S. border. The issue of border searches of electronic devices (such as laptops and cell phones) may become the next legal battle. In 2010, the American Civil Liberties Union and others sued the Department of Homeland Security, claiming that the search of such devices without reasonable suspicion is a Constitutional violation of the Fourth Amendment (Bray).

Airports and Public Transit

Since the events of September 11, 2001, airport security, and the security concerns regarding ports and other public conveyances, has escalated significantly. However, search and seizure law has, for a considerable time, reflected the dual concerns of privacy expectations and security needs in these locations. The law regarding airports, and, by implication, other public conveyances, has developed into three different types of possible exceptions to the warrant rule. First, administrative searches (based upon the same

principles as general administrative searches) may be carried out for passenger screening, so long as it is employed as a regulatory scheme to deter hijackers and not for the purpose of criminal investigation (e.g., narcotics trafficking) (*United States v. Davis*, 482 F.2d 893, 9th Circuit, 1973). Second, *Terry* searches may be conducted so long as the conditions warrant. In the leading case, the search was conducted in the lounge at the boarding gate and the bulge in the passenger's pocket and his nervous demeanor suggested further inquiry was in order. However, the courts have distinguished between passengers about to board and other people in the air terminal (*United States v. Moreno,* 475 F.2d 44, 5th Circuit, 1973 and *United States v. Skipwith*, 482 F.2d 1272, 5th Circuit, 1973). Finally, there are issues of implied and express consent. Generally, passengers must be given the opportunity to avoid a search by refusing to fly. However, if they place their luggage on the conveyer for boarding, the implication is that they have consented (*United States v. Pulido-Baquerizo*, 800 F.2d 899, 9th Circuit, 1986).

Schools

The rules generally followed in schools regarding the search of students and their property were established by the U.S. Supreme Court in the *New Jersey v. T.L.O.* decision of 1985. (See **Figure 9-10** for the Court's key statements concerning school searches and a general rule regarding searches on public school grounds.) In 2009, the Court ruled that a 13-year-old student's Fourth Amendment right was violated when she was subjected to a search of her bra and underpants; the Court ruled the search was constitutionally unreasonable (*Safford Unified School District #1 et al. v. Redding*, 557 U.S. ____, 2009)

Plain View

Another very important exception is the **plain view doctrine**. Essentially, this holds that an officer may seize evidence of a crime or contraband that falls into the plain view of the officer when the officer otherwise has a right to be at that location. If in the process of investigating one crime, an officer sees what is clearly evidence of another crime, it may be seized (*Coolidge v. New Hampshire*, 403 U.S. 443, 1971). However, the officer may not take any action to "discover" additional evidence beyond those

FIGURE 9-10 School Searches

To hold that the Fourth Amendment applies to searches conducted by school authorities is only to begin the inquiry into the standards governing such searches. Although the underlying command of the Fourth Amendment is always that searches and seizures be reasonable, what is reasonable depends on the context within which a search takes place .... Of course, the Fourth Amendment does not protect subjective expectations of privacy that are unreasonable or otherwise "illegitimate ...." To receive the protection of the Fourth Amendment, an expectation of privacy must be one that society is "prepared to recognize as legitimate ...."

Although this Court may take notice of the difficulty of maintaining discipline in the public schools today, the situation is not so dire that students in the schools may claim no legitimate expectations of privacy. We have recently recognized that the need to maintain order in a prison is such that prisoners retain no legitimate expectations of privacy in their cells, but it goes almost without saying that "[t]he prisoner and the schoolchild stand in wholly different circumstances, separated by the harsh facts of criminal conviction and incarceration ...." Against the child's interest in privacy must be set the substantial interest of teachers and administrators in maintaining discipline in the classroom and on school grounds. Maintaining order in the classroom has never been easy, but in recent years, school disorder has often taken particularly ugly forms: drug use and violent crime in the schools have become major social problems.

How, then, should we strike the balance between the schoolchild's legitimate expectations of privacy and the school's equally legitimate need to maintain an environment in which learning can take place?

The warrant requirement, in particular, is unsuited to the school environment: requiring a teacher to obtain a warrant before searching a child suspected of an infraction of school rules (or of the criminal law) would unduly interfere with the maintenance of the swift and informal disciplinary procedures needed in the schools. Just as we have in other cases dispensed with the warrant requirement when "the burden of obtaining a warrant is likely to frustrate the governmental purpose behind the search," we hold today that school officials need not obtain a warrant before searching a student who is under their authority.

The fundamental command of the Fourth Amendment is that searches and seizures be reasonable, and although "both the concept of probable cause and the requirement of a warrant bear on the reasonableness of a search, ... in certain limited circumstances neither is required."

Under ordinary circumstances, *a search of a student by a teacher or other school official will be "justified at its inception" when there are reasonable grounds for suspecting that the search will turn up evidence that the student has violated or is violating either the law or the rules of the school. Such a search will be permissible in its scope when the measures adopted are reasonably related to the objectives of the search and not excessively intrusive in light of the age and sex of the student and the nature of the infraction* (emphasis added).

Source: New Jersey v. T. L. O., 469 U.S. 325 (1985).

actions necessary to carry out the tasks that originally called the officer there (*Arizona v. Hicks*, 480 U.S. 321, 1987). Plain view means plain view, literally right out there for everyone to see (Hunsucker 2003).

Exigent Circumstances

Exigent circumstances refer to the conditions that create a need for immediate action to prevent the destruction of evidence. Sometimes referred to as emergency conditions, such circumstances may include (1) entries of residences and buildings during hot pursuit, (2) the warrantless search of an automobile, (3) searches incidental to arrest (Zalman 2008, 266), (4) the prevention of destruction of evidence, (5) immediate threats to public safety, and (6) the need to assist an individual in peril (Lippman 2011, 138). The need to take action without delay, coupled with probable cause, is prerequisite to any subsequent determination of reasonableness. In *Brigham City, Utah v. Stuart,* (547 U.S. 398 2006), officers responding to an early morning loud party complaint observed violence inside a residence, announced their presence, and entered to prevent any additional violence or injury. The U.S. Supreme

Court held that their warrantless entry was reasonable and justified.

Consent

Another exception to the warrant requirement, which is more a waiver of rights than a true exception, is that of consent. If a person permits a search to occur without a warrant, assuming the consent was freely and intelligently given, he or she cannot later contest the results of the search. The person who gives consent must have actual or apparent authority to do so, otherwise an officer's search will be unreasonable (*Illinois v. Rodriguez*, 497 U.S. 177, 1990). The legal issues that arise under consent searches involve review of the voluntariness of the consent, the scope of consent, and whether the situation involved third party consent.

Arrest of the Person

The U.S. Supreme Court traditionally interpreted arrest to mean any substantial limit upon the ability of a person to freely come and go, though that same court later revised that principle: "An arrest requires either physical force... or, where that is absent, submission to the assertion of authority" (*California v. Hodari D.*, 499 U.S. 621, 1991). When is a warrantless arrest an "unreasonable" seizure under the Fourth Amendment? Generally speaking, the following rules have emerged. An arrest is reasonable if one of the following is true:

1. The offense was committed in the presence of an officer.
2. The offense is a felony, and the officer has probable cause to believe the defendant committed it.
3. The offense, though a misdemeanor, is one of violence, and the officer has probable cause to believe that the defendant committed the offense (the test is most applicable to domestic violence cases, for example). This applies whether or not the offense was committed in the presence of the officer.

Each of these exceptions relies upon the establishment of probable cause. It is certainly easier to establish probable cause if the officer sees the defendant assault someone or commit some other offense; otherwise, law enforcement officers must rely upon their training, education, and experience to determine if probable cause is present and sufficient to justify a warrantless arrest.

If the case falls outside these exceptions, then law enforcement officials must seek the issuance of an arrest warrant based upon the evidence available. This typically requires a "neutral magistrate" (typically a judge or in some states a clerk of courts) to determine whether sufficient evidence exists for a warrant to issue. The same standard of probable cause used for warrantless arrests applies for the issuance of a warrant.

The reason for the general warrant requirement is to reduce the likelihood of arbitrary arrests. The reason for the exceptions to the warrant requirement is the belief that in those circumstances set forth above, arrest without a warrant is "reasonable" within the meaning of the Fourth Amendment. For example, it makes sense that if a crime is committed in front of an officer, it would frustrate the meaning of justice in a civil society to delay arrest. Similar rationales are used by courts in the other circumstances. However, it is still good practice to obtain a warrant if there is time to do so; the risk of being wrong is not worth mere convenience.

CONSEQUENCES OF UNLAWFULLY OBTAINED EVIDENCE

The above exceptions (and some others, such as abandoned property, open fields, inevitable discovery, etc.) play a particular role in the administration of the Fourth Amendment relative to searches and seizures. However, if no applicable exception exists and no valid warrant was obtained, the search is unreasonable and is therefore unconstitutional.

The Exclusionary Rule

The punishment for conducting an unreasonable search is suppression of the evidence. This generally means the evidence may not be used against the defendant. Suppression of evidence is one of the technicalities that can derail a prosecution. The notion of suppression comes from the **exclusionary rule** at the federal level, which dates back to 1914. The rule was extended to the states as a result of flagrant abuse of authority by police officers in Cleveland, Ohio in the case of *Mapp v. Ohio* (367 U.S. 643, 1961). Officers fabricated a story of a fleeing fugitive to burst into a woman's home. When she demanded a warrant and was shown a piece of paper, she grabbed the paper, placing it inside an article of her clothing. The officers wrestled her to the ground and removed the paper from her blouse. It was not a warrant. Based upon such outrageous conduct the U.S. Supreme Court had little trouble suppressing the evidence officers seized from her home (pornography, which today would look like a famous mail order catalogue) and applying the exclusionary rule to the states, hence ending the prosecution of Ms. Mapp.

Interrogation

The rules that restrict police questioning of a suspect are, in at least one sense, fairly clear, though in another, they are not at all. However, there are a few basic notions that we can accept. First, a voluntary statement made by a suspect without any questions being asked is always admissible (*Colorado v. Connelly*, 479 U.S. 157, 1986). However, it is much more likely that an officer will ask questions. In order for any responses to be admissible in a court (generally speaking), the suspect must be warned not to say anything. These are the famous *Miranda* (*Miranda v. Arizona*, 384 U.S. 436 1966) warnings (**Figure 9-11**).

FIGURE 9-11 The Miranda Warnings

"(W)e hold that when an individual is taken into custody or otherwise deprived of his freedom by the authorities in any significant way and is subjected to questioning, the privilege against self-incrimination is jeopardized. Procedural safeguards must be employed to protect the privilege, and unless other fully effective means are adopted to notify the person of his right of silence and to assure that the exercise of the right will be scrupulously honored, the following measures are required. *He must be warned prior to any questioning that he has the right to remain silent, that anything he says can be used against him in a court of law, that he has the right to the presence of an attorney, and that if he cannot afford an attorney one will be appointed for him prior to any questioning if he so desires. Opportunity to exercise these rights must be afforded to him throughout the interrogation...* (T)he individual may knowingly and intelligently waive these rights and agree to answer questions or make a statement."

Source: *Miranda v. Arizona*, 384 U.S. 436, (1966) (emphasis added).

It is important to remember that these are warnings, not rights in and of themselves. The warnings were developed by the U.S. Supreme Court because of a long history of abuses by governments using torture to obtain confessions. The history of the Fifth Amendment and its prohibition against self-incrimination is based upon historical lessons. Whenever government has the power to compel confessions, it will use it. If there are no limits, then when is one confession valid and another not? In one case, *Brown v. Mississippi* (297 U.S. 278, 1936), the defendants were beaten and whipped until they confessed. The deputies who presided over the beatings openly admitted their acts (see **Figure 9-12**). It is difficult to imagine how a confession obtained in such a manner can be acceptable in a democracy. Most law enforcement officers today have never seen such behavior. But, at one time it was all too common a practice.

On first reading the *Brown* case, most students cannot believe it happened in the United States, and yet it did. If our system is designed to seek justice, coerced confessions work against the system. How can a confession which results from threats or intimidation be trustworthy? If a person confesses but is not guilty, it will permit the truly guilty person to continue victimizing society. We must be certain those whom we punish are the guilty parties; the convenience of law enforcement is not the most important concern. The *Miranda* warnings, therefore, seek to restrain government's power and ensure justice. Many in law enforcement do not agree with the warnings, but the truth is that the mandatory use of the warnings did not cause any loss of effectiveness. Indeed, it is now generally and widely recognized that these and other procedural restrictions on law enforcement forced better training, better procedure, and more professional behavior. As you read in the previous chapters regarding training, education, and professionalization, the push for standardized policies and procedures has in fact produced much improved and more effective law enforcement.

The warnings themselves are basic and, while the U.S. Supreme Court has permitted some deviation from the written warnings, they should be remembered by all law enforcement officers. It would be a mistake to assume that they are no longer important, and indeed, the court has recently reaffirmed its support of their importance.

FIGURE 9-12 The Privilege Against Self-Incrimination

MR. CHIEF JUSTICE HUGHES delivered the opinion of the Court.

The question in this case is whether convictions, which rest solely upon confessions shown to have been extorted by officers of the State by brutality and violence, are consistent with the due process of law required by the Fourteenth Amendment of the Constitution of the United States.

Petitioners were indicted for the murder of one Raymond Stewart, whose death occurred on March 30, 1934. They were indicted on April 4, 1934, and were then arraigned and pleaded not guilty. Counsel were appointed by the court to defend them. Trial was begun the next morning and was concluded on the following day, when they were found guilty and sentenced to death.

Quoting the lower federal court: The crime with which these defendants, all ignorant negroes, are charged, was discovered about one o'clock p.m. on Friday, March 30, 1934. On that night one Dial, a deputy sheriff, accompanied by others, came to the home of Ellington, one of the defendants, and requested him to accompany them to the house of the deceased, and there a number of white men were gathered, who began to accuse the defendant of the crime. Upon his denial they seized him, and with the participation of the deputy they hanged him by a rope to the limb of a tree, and having let him down, they hung him again, and when he was let down the second time, and he still protested his innocence, he was tied to a tree and whipped, and still declining to accede to the demands that he confess, he was finally released and he returned with some difficulty to his home, suffering intense pain and agony. The record of the testimony shows that the signs of the rope on his neck were plainly visible during the so-called trial. A day or two thereafter the said deputy, accompanied by another, returned to the home of the said defendant and arrested him, and departed with the prisoner towards the jail in an adjoining county, but went by a route which led into the State of Alabama; and while on the way, in that State, the deputy stopped and again severely whipped the defendant, declaring that he would continue the whipping until he confessed, and the defendant then agreed to confess to such a statement as the deputy would dictate, and he did so, after which he was delivered to jail.

Further details of the brutal treatment to which these helpless prisoners were subjected need not be pursued. It is sufficient to say that in pertinent respects the transcript reads more like pages torn from some medieval account, than a record made within the confines of a modern civilization which aspires to an enlightened constitutional government.... But the freedom of the State in establishing its policy is the freedom of constitutional government and is limited by the requirement of due process of law. Because a State may dispense with a jury trial, it does not follow that it be substituted for the witness stand. The State may not permit an accused to be hurried to conviction under mob domination.... And the trial equally is a mere pretense where the state authorities have contrived a conviction resting solely upon confessions obtained by violence. The due process clause requires "that state action, whether through one agency or another, shall be consistent with the fundamental principles of liberty and justice which lie at the base of all our civil and political institutions" (*Hebert v. Louisiana*, 272 U.S. 312, 316). It would be difficult to conceive of methods more revolting to the sense of justice than those taken to procure the confessions of these petitioners, and the use of the confessions thus obtained as the basis for conviction and sentence was a clear denial of due process.

Source: Brown v. Mississippi, 297 U.S. 278 (1936)

In a 2004 case, a man was indicted by a federal grand jury. When the officers went to his home to serve the warrant and arrest him, they did not advise him of his *Miranda* rights, despite the attachment of the formal charge which begins the process in which *Miranda* attaches. Instead, they questioned him, eliciting incriminating statements. Later, at the jail house, they read him his rights but used the prior statements to elicit more incriminating statements. The court held that all of his statements must be suppressed and could not be used at trial (*Fellers v. United States*, U.S. 124 S Ct 1019, 2004). In short, once the "rights attach," by custody or formal charge, the *Miranda* rights must be given. But that is different than the general right to counsel, which may not be interfered with once invoked; once requested, questioning must stop and none can occur absent the participation and agreement of counsel (Means 2003).

The exact wording of the *Miranda* warnings as used on a standard form in Tampa, Florida was ruled upon by the U.S. Supreme Court in early 2010. The form stated, "You have the right to talk to a lawyer before answering any of our questions" instead of "You have the right to the presence of an attorney during questioning." The defendant was convicted because of admissions made after signing the form and answering questions. On appeal the Florida Appellate Court suppressed the admissions and the state Supreme Court agreed. The U.S. Supreme Court reversed and remanded the case back to Florida stating:

> Nothing in the words used indicated that counsel's presence would be restricted after the questioning commenced. Instead, the warning communicated that the right to counsel carried forward to and through the interrogation: Powell could seek his attorney's advice before responding to "any of the officers' questions" and "at any time… during the interview." Although the warnings were not the *clearest possible* formulation of *Miranda*'s right-to-counsel advisement, they were sufficiently comprehensive and comprehensible when given a commonsense reading" (*Florida v. Powell*, 559 U.S. ____, 2010)

What is interrogation? It is important to understand that failure to administer *Miranda* warnings does not necessarily invalidate statements made by a suspect. The theory of Miranda is based upon possible coercion from **custodial interrogation**. Custodial interrogation occurs (1) if words or actions which call for some verbal response are (2) made by someone acting on behalf of the state (3) while the suspect is in custody (*Pennsylvania v. Muniz*, 496 U.S. 582, 1990). The person asking questions could be an officer or an informant such as a cell mate.

In order for custody to exist, the suspect must (1) know she is in custody or (2) believe her freedom is significantly curtailed. These rules apply at the point that someone *reasonably* becomes a suspect (*Oregon v. Mathiason*, 429 U.S. 492, 1977). Moreover, whether or not *Miranda* warnings are given, a fully voluntary statement, not in response to questions, is admissible. The courts generally presume a statement is involuntary without *Miranda* warnings.

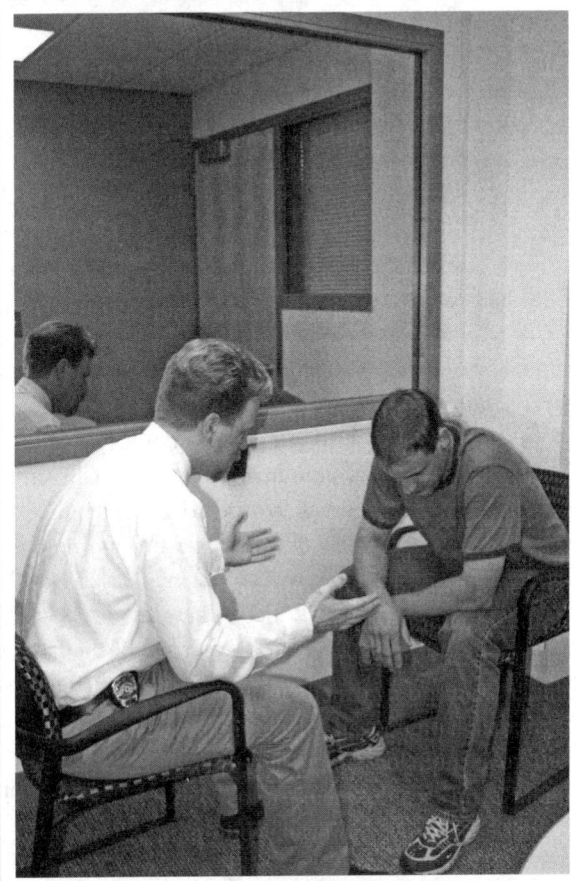

Officer conducting an interview or interrogation

Source: © Jones & Bartlett Learning

However, this can be rebutted based on circumstances surrounding the statement. The best practice, of course, is to give *Miranda* warnings when a person becomes a suspect. But, those warnings do not prevent questions or inducements to give statements, nor do they prevent the suspect from waiving the right against self-incrimination. However, if counsel is requested, questioning must stop.

Fruit of the Poisonous Tree

Sometimes, an officer may make an error and obtain evidence or testimony improperly. What happens if that evidence or testimony leads investigators to other testimony or evidence? Usually, it means that the testimony or evidence is poisoned or tainted because of the initial error (e.g., unlawful search or arrest). In such a case, all the evidence obtained is poisoned and inadmissible. However, in the case of *Wong Sun v. United States* (371 U.S. 471, 1963), the U.S. Supreme Court ruled that not all evidence (fruit) may be tainted. The test was whether or not conditions intervened to "cut" the connection to the "poisonous tree" of the original invasion. In Wong Sun's case, his home was invaded as a result of evidence obtained at an earlier bad search. Although he was taken into custody, he was later released without charges. He later returned voluntarily and made a statement which resulted in his charges and conviction.

In a 1984 case, a suspect kidnapped and murdered a 10-year-old girl from a community gathering on Christmas Eve. When he was arrested, he was Mirandized, and he requested counsel. While officers were transporting the suspect, one of the officers (without asking questions) told the defendant he should tell them where the body could be found. The officer alluded to the sorrow of the family, the time of year, an approaching snow storm, and the need for a Christian burial. The defendant relented and showed them the body. That, of course, was compelling evidence against him. It was also taken from a poisonous tree in that the interrogation was unlawful due to the defendant's request for counsel. However, the court reasoned that since the body was found in the search zone of a search team, the evidence was going to be discovered inevitably. Hence, the **inevitable discovery** exception to the fruit of the poisonous tree rule was established (*Nix v. Williams*, 467 U.S. 431, 1984; also, see *Oregon v. Elstad*, 470 U.S. 298, 1985).

LIABILITY

Liability law is a body of civil law that really is a subtheme of tort law. Tort law is the body of civil law that defines behaviors for which someone can be held legally and financially responsible. It also defines the methods by which the injured parties are made "whole." Usually, this means monetary damages, but a verdict or court order may also force or command policy changes in an organization or agency.

Tort Law

Tort law is a very large area of the law. For our purposes, we are interested in a brief discussion of two major areas of tort law. The first is in the area of so-called "common law torts," while the second is federal civil rights law. Of the common law torts, those which pose the largest threat to law enforcement, particularly patrol officers, are clearly assault and battery or, in the event an assault goes too far, wrongful death. These usually are described in the law enforcement literature as training and use of excessive force issues. First, we will briefly discuss assault and battery.

The common law tort of assault was the threat to do harm to someone without a privilege to do so, and battery was a non-permitted touching of another resulting in physical harm without privilege to do so. In modern usage, assault is merged with battery so that one term is applied to both. Privilege is a defense to both. Law enforcement officers have a privilege to commit what would otherwise be an assault if force is used to detain or arrest a person. However, excessive force would negate the privilege.

The well known case of the Rodney King arrest in Los Angeles involves this issue. Criminal charges against several officers resulted from the beating they inflicted upon King in a traffic stop. However, tort claims also arose from that incident. If the use of force is more than necessary to affect an arrest, the privilege to commit an assault ends. More problematic for law enforcement officers is the reality that community standards determine when force is too much. Effectively, juries make this decision. While guidelines exist in each state's law, they are merely words. Images and witnesses impact juries in different ways.

Departments have tried to protect themselves by developing rules on excessive force and they have tried to train officers in the appropriate use of force. It is important to know that if departmental operations or training standards are violated resulting in the injury of someone, liability follows. This is true because departmental rules and training, as well as state law and constitutional law decisions, set the appropriate standards of behavior. If standards are violated, liability follows. This can be very costly for the individual officer (who is individually liable), as well as for that officer's department and governmental subdivision (e.g., city, township, county). Conduct an Internet search using the phrase "excessive force case" and review some of the incidents; you will notice numerous cases and some large dollar settlements.

Since the 1980s, many departments adopted some type of use-of-force continuum. In 1990, the Federal Law Enforcement Training Center's (FLETC) Use-of-Force Oversight Committee developed a use-of-force model (or continuum) that was consistent with Department of Treasury policies (**see Figure 9-13**). That model was used to train federal officers until 2005, when it was discontinued and replaced with "increasing legal instruction (focusing on *Graham v. Connor*), dispelling common myths about use of force, enhancing mental preparation training, and most important, enhancing use of force report writing and articulation skills" (Bostain 2009). FLETC now believes that a

major benefit of teaching use of force without a continuum is the reduction of unnecessary hesitation by officers in determining which force option to employ in critical incidents. Hesitation is often caused by trying to apply a structured, unyielding, cognitive tool such as a continuum, to a stressful, continually changing, emotional situation like a use of force incident. Even the most ardent supporter of continuums can agree that use of force incidents do not occur in the nice, neat, structured way that continuums and models imply" (Bostain).

Civil Rights

The most significant liability concern for law enforcement, for both patrol and supervision, is undoubtedly that which springs from section 1983 of Title 42 of the United States Federal Code (see **Figure 9-14**). Originally part of

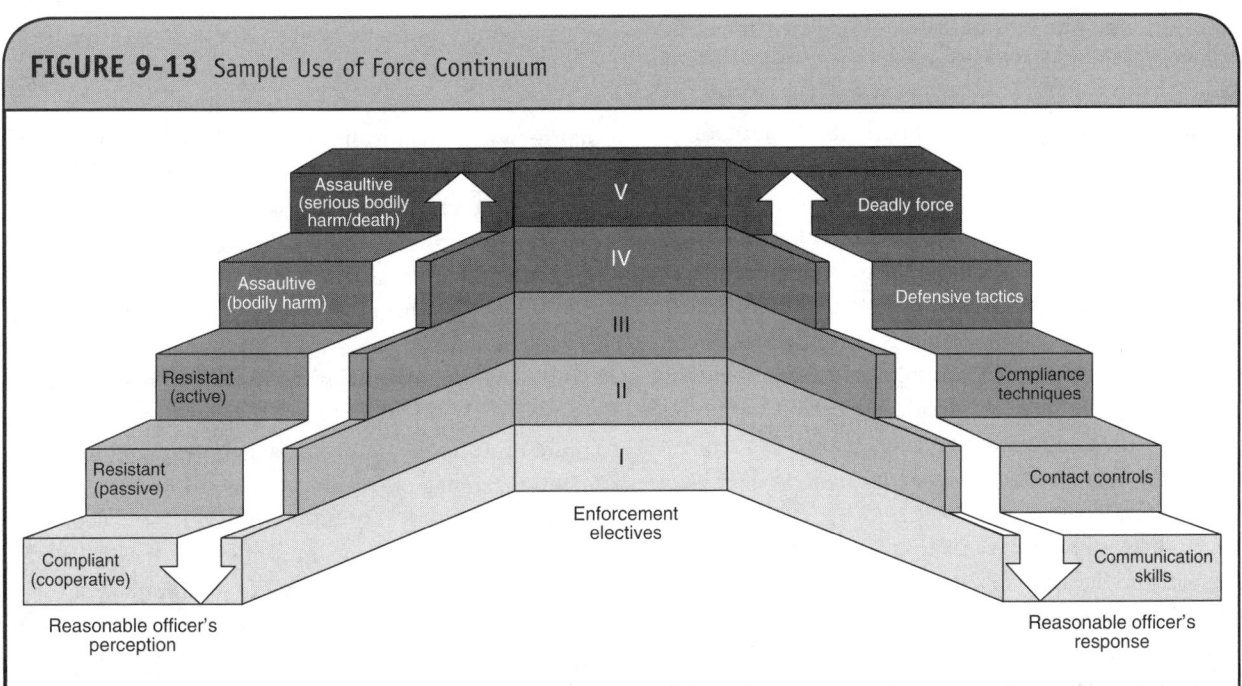

FIGURE 9-13 Sample Use of Force Continuum

Assaultive (serious bodily harm/death)	V — Deadly force
Assaultive (bodily harm)	IV — Defensive tactics
Resistant (active)	III — Compliance techniques
Resistant (passive)	II — Contact controls
Compliant (cooperative)	I — Communication skills

Enforcement electives

Reasonable officer's perception   Reasonable officer's response

Source: Federal Law Enforcement Training Center cited in United States General Accounting Office (1996), "Use of Force," ATF Policy, Training and Review Process are Comparable to the DEA's and FBI's, March, p. 39. Model discontinued in 2005; continuums can be more restrictive than law requires.

FIGURE 9-14 Federal Civil Rights Statute

42 U.S.C. § 1983. Civil action for deprivation of rights.
Every person who, under color of any statute, ordinance, regulation, custom, or usage, of any State or Territory or the District of Columbia, subjects, or causes to be subjected, any citizen of the United States or other person within the jurisdiction thereof to the deprivation of any rights, privileges, or immunities secured by the Constitution and laws, shall be liable to the party injured in an action at law, suit in equity, or other proper proceeding for redress. For the purposes of this section, any Act of Congress applicable exclusively to the District of Columbia shall be considered to be a statute of the District of Columbia.

Source: 42 U.S.C. § 1983. Civil action for deprivation of rights.

the post-Civil War reconstruction acts, this section is the basis for large numbers of lawsuits. Whether or not one agrees with the policy of the statute, it is a reality that has been on the books for over 100 years and is not likely to be changed. We will consider briefly the implications of this statute.

Basically, the act provides that anyone acting under the "color of any statute, ordinance, regulation, custom, or usage" and who subjects someone to the deprivation of their constitutional rights is liable to that person for damages. False arrest, false imprisonment, use of excessive force, conduct which fails to meet training standards, failure to obtain medical aid for a suspect, and a hundred other specific events will trigger this statute. The deprivation of any known constitutional right will produce liability (Antieau 1998).

If there is probable cause to arrest or search someone, there is a privilege to violate certain rights; in other words, citizens are free from unreasonable searches and seizures, but not from those that are reasonable. Probable cause gives us reasonableness, but the arrest, detention, seizure, or search must be accomplished in a reasonable manner.

Law enforcement officers are limited in the amount of force they may use to effectuate an arrest or search. The amount of force may only be the force reasonably

necessary to place a person into custody. In examining any claim of unreasonable use of force, the U.S. Supreme Court has ruled that:

> [the] test of reasonableness under the Fourth Amendment… requires careful attention to the facts and circumstances of each particular case, including (1) the severity of the crime at issue, (2) whether the suspect poses an immediate threat to the safety of the officers or others, and (3) whether he is actively resisting arrest or attempting to evade arrest by flight [numerals added] *Graham v. Connor,* 490 U.S. at 396).

In summary, the totality of circumstances must be reviewed.

Deadly force may be used only if the suspect is threatening the safety of the officer or another person. Any law, custom, or rule to the contrary cannot be relied upon by law enforcement officers. In *Tennessee v. Garner* (471 U.S. 1, 1985) the Supreme Court struck down a state statute that permitted the use of deadly force on any fleeing felon. In doing so, it permitted the parents of a dead teenager to sue a police officer and his department despite the fact that he was trained to fire upon unarmed fleeing felons. Improper use of force will result in personal liability.

Of concern to supervisors and managers is the fact that they can be held liable for the civil rights violations of their subordinates. Essentially, liability may be established if it can be shown that a supervisor or manager "knew or should have known" that the event might happen. Liability of superiors for the actions of subordinates has been based upon poor hiring practices, poor training, failure to discipline, improper assignment, and improper retention, among other things (Russell 1994).

In most cases, insurance will not cover an officer's losses resulting from violations of either the Civil Rights Acts generally or those resulting from an unlawful use of force specifically. Officers who violate these rules do so at their own financial peril. These are not negligent events; rather, they are intentional acts. Because most insurance polices will not pay claims for intentional acts, officers risk their own property. Worse, these kinds of debts are not generally subject to bankruptcy proceedings. If law enforcement officers lose, they lose big. Officers are held to a high standard, since they are expected to know the Constitution to which they take a pledge (see a sample oath of office in **Figure 9-15**).

Most insurance policies covering law enforcement will cover only **negligent acts**, which were not intended. Negligent acts happen when a law enforcement officer owes a duty to someone but violates that duty, causing an injury. For example, if an officer drives his or her patrol car at excessive speed without emergency display (lights or siren), in most circumstances it would be negligent, and any traffic accident caused would result in liability. The failure to obtain medical treatment for someone in custody where clear signs of illness were ignored could be another source of negligence. In virtually every contact with the public, whether handling people or information, officers have duties set out by law, training, or departmental rules. Failure to perform any such duty is negligence.

We noted before that supervisors and managers may be held liable for civil rights violations of subordinates as well as intentional acts. They may also be held liable for negligent actions of subordinates. The legal theory of *respondeat superior* holds that a **principal** (supervisor or manager) is liable for the actions of his or her agent (subordinate) when those actions are taken in the course of employment. Usually, what an officer does in off-duty time will not create liability for the agency or superiors.

Some commentators suggest that *respondeat superior* is the theory of liability used in civil rights cases. However, it is not, and it is important to know the difference. In negligence law, *respondeat superior* makes a superior liable for every act by a subordinate done in the course of employment. In civil rights law, a superior can be liable only if he or she knew or should have known that the act would occur, and the act must be the result of some law, rule, or custom (departmental or individual patterns of behavior). Obviously, this can cover actions which are outside the scope of employment. Most officers drive vehicles too fast from time to time, but no one is hired with the intention of doing acts which violate civil rights by, for example, beating a prisoner. Therefore, civil rights liabilities beyond the offending officer are harder to establish, but have a broader reach. In general, the defense to a civil rights claim is that of "qualified immunity." To establish this, the officer sued must show either that (1) the facts alleged do not show a constitutional right was violated or (2) this right was not clearly established prior to the event in question, so that the officer could not "know or should have known" that his or her actions would violate a right. The test is similar for supervisors, including chiefs and sheriffs. If a deputy or officer has a known history of violence, and management took no action to ameliorate the problem or end employment, the agency executives, too, may be found liable because they "knew or should have known" that someone under their supervision was a "walking time bomb" (Spector 2002).

Other areas of tort law that we did not examine are destruction or damage to the property of another, slander, libel, false arrest or imprisonment, and conversion of property, all of which arise from common law and state statutes that have codified the common law. These and a number of other torts are important, and deserve discussion at a later date in a separate course. A good policy is to act conservatively, since officers have no way of knowing what interpretation a court may place on his or her behavior. For example, a court ruled in 1992 that not only may testimony of a suspect not be used if the suspect is not Mirandized, the officer may be liable under section 1983 for the failure to do so (*Cooper v. Dupnick*, 963 F.2d 1220; 113 S Ct 407, 1992; see also Ronzio 1993), though the Supreme Court of the United States overturned that principle (*Chavez v. Martinez*, 538 U.S. 760, 2003). The point is that it took 10 years for the rule to be changed, and in that

---

FIGURE 9-15 Typical Oath of Office

I, do solemnly swear, that I will support and defend the Constitution of the United States, and the Constitution of the State of California against all enemies, foreign and domestic; that I will bear true faith and allegiance, to the Constitution of the State of California; that I take this obligation freely, without any mental reservations or purpose of evasion; and that I will well and faithfully discharge the duties, of the office of Police Officer of the City of Anaheim, acting to the best of my ability.

Source: Anaheim Police Department (2004), "Police Officer Oath of Office," http://www.anaheim.net/article.asp?id=639

period of time countless officers were subjected to litigation under the Cooper rule.

Another area of great public concern, as well as police executive concern, is the problem of the high-speed chase to apprehend a suspect. In 2007, the U.S. Supreme Court ruled that a "police officer's attempt to terminate a dangerous high-speed car chase that threatens the lives of innocent bystanders does not violate the Fourth Amendment, even when it places the fleeing motorist at risk of serious injury or death" (*Scott v. Harris*, 550 U.S. 372). Harris, the driver of the vehicle that Deputy Scott was trying to stop, filed suit under 42 U. S. C. §1983, alleging the use of excessive force resulting in an unreasonable seizure under the Fourth Amendment. Deputy Scott used the Precision Intervention Technique (PIT) maneuver, which caused Harris' vehicle to leave the roadway, run down an embankment, and overturn. Harris was rendered a quadriplegic from the crash.

High speed pursuits may endanger others

Source: © iStockphoto/Thinkstock

Regardless of the Scott decision, many departments have revisited their policies on pursuit, since they are not only a threat to innocent civilians, but to the officers as well. Injury to officers, damage to equipment, the possibility of legal action, and the loss of public confidence all are costly to departments. See **Figure 9-16** for an example

---

FIGURE 9-16 Sample vehicle pursuit order

41.5.1 EVALUATING THE CIRCUMSTANCES

A. Preservation of life.
    One of the primary objectives of the Naperville Police Department is to arrest violators of the law while preserving life. When a pursuit is necessary, the Department will make use of all available resources such as air support, telecommunications, and computer networks to reduce the threat to the public, Department employee(s), and violator(s).

B. Limitations on pursuits.
    Motor vehicle pursuits are inherently dangerous. Naperville officers will engage in vehicle pursuits only as outlined below.

    1. The Department will make every effort to ensure the safety of the public, as well as employees, at all times and authorize emergency use of Department vehicles when the necessity of immediate response or apprehension of offenders outweighs the level of inherent danger.

    2. The objective of motor vehicle pursuit is to maintain contact with a fleeing driver without unnecessary endangerment to life and property until the individual can be apprehended. Officers and their supervisors will continually evaluate the pursuit with respect to its danger and determine when and if it should be terminated.

    3. Officers will not initiate or become involved in pursuits for traffic offenses, property crimes, whether felony or misdemeanor, or when the suspect flees for unknown reasons except as outlined below in #4, or section 41.5.8.A.

    4. A motor vehicle pursuit will be initiated only when an officer has an articulable reason to believe the occupant(s) of the fleeing vehicle has committed or attempted a forcible felony which involves the infliction or threatened infliction of great bodily harm or is attempting to escape by use of a deadly weapon, or otherwise indicates they will endanger human life or inflict great bodily harm unless arrested without delay. All officers involved in a pursuit must, at all times, be able to justify the continuation of the pursuit.

Source: Courtesy of Chief David Dial, Naperville, PD, 2010 (the entire general order is 11 pages which includes definitions, procedures, and report forms).

of General Order 41.5, Motor Vehicle Pursuit, of the Naperville (Illinois) Police Department.

Finally, the entire area of use of force has come under scrutiny regarding use of less-than-lethal (LTL) weapons, or weapons designed to disable, but not likely kill, suspects. These include 37 mm guns that fire projectiles, including bean bags and rubber bullets, approximately 70 feet, all with the intention of disabling a suspect. Electro-Shock weapons like Tasers are also at issue. According to a 2009 article, there are more than 375,000 stun guns being used at 13,400 law enforcement and military organizations in 44 countries (Richey). The U.S. Supreme Court in 2009 declined to take up Florida case where a motorist was Tasered three times because he disobeyed a deputy sheriff's command to stand up and walk to a patrol car. The lower court ruling that the force was reasonable was allowed to stand (Richey 2009).

The questions of liability were brought to a new level in October 2004 when a 21-year-old college student was killed by a Boston police officer with a pepper-pellet projectile. She was among more than 50,000 people celebrating a Red Sox victory around Fenway Park when she was struck directly in the eye and died a short time later. There is no evidence that she was engaging in criminal behavior; the point is that she was killed with an LTL weapon. After the police investigation on the incident, the officer who accidently killed the student was identified and on May 2, 2005, the city of Boston announced a $5.1 million settlement for her family's lawsuit (Associated Press 2005).

SUMMARY

This chapter illustrated how law enforcement is limited in a number of major and distinct ways by legal restraints. First, it is limited by how the criminal laws are drawn by legislative authority and interpreted by a multitude of other actors. Second, while arrests may be made, a prosecutor, grand jury, jury, judge, or appeals court may disagree as to the guilt or culpability of the suspect. Third, law enforcement is impacted by constitutional procedural limitations. This covers search and seizure, warrants, arrest, interrogation, and a host of other day-to-day activities. Fourth, agencies are limited by administrative law, which orders and restricts the manner in which agencies may manage their own business. Finally, law enforcement is limited by its potential liability in damages for torts and civil rights violations. For these reasons, aspiring law enforcement officers must take to heart their training and education, which, if followed, will generally protect them.

Critical Thinking Questions

1. Regarding the various sources of law in the United States, which do you think places the most restrictions on law enforcement officials? List those restrictions.

2. Why is the "model penal code" significant?

3. Of all the subjects prosecuted for felonies, only a very few are reviewed by the U.S. Supreme Court; what are the ramifications or implications when the top court rules on law enforcement procedures or practices?

4. What appears to be the most complicated exceptions to the warrant preference for conducting a search?

5. Explain the "exclusionary rule" and how it differs from the "fruit of the poisonous tree" doctrine.

6. In a short essay, explain the role that liability and civil rights play in effecting the performance of law enforcement personnel.

CHAPTER SPECIFIC INTERNET LINKS

U.S. Constitution (online): http://www.usconstitution .net/const.html

Paul M. Rashkind. United States Supreme Court, Review: Preview–Overview: Criminal Cases Decided and Granted Review For The October 2009–2010 Terms Thru August 12, 2010: http://www.rashkind.com/ supct.pdf

United States Supreme Court. "Chief Justice's Year-End Reports on the Federal Judiciary": http://www .supremecourt.gov/publicinfo/year-end/2009year-endreport.pdf.

Search Incident to Arrest Doctrine: http://legaltalknetwork .com/podcasts/suffolk-law/2010/07/search-incident-to-arrest-doctrine/

Supreme Court video: *Scott v. Harris*: http://video.google .com/videoplay?docid=2920973987216904078#

Tulsa police pursuit video: http://www.youtube.com/ watch?v=po5DOTYWv2Y

Milwaukee, Wisconsin Report of the Fire and Police Commission on vehicle pursuits: http://city .milwaukee.gov/ImageLibrary/Groups/cityFPC/ Reports/Report_Vehicle_Pursuits.pdf

CHAPTER GLOSSARY

Administrative law—rules and regulations established by government agencies pursuant to statutory law which prevent arbitrary decisions by those agencies, and which act as a guide for those persons or entities regulated.

Civil law—violations against individuals.

Common law—body of legal rules developed over a period of several hundred years by judges acting under the authority of the king.

Constitutional law—the body of law that grew around the Constitution.

Criminal law—a body of legal rules dealing with offenses against the public (or the state).

Custodial interrogation—a line of questioning that occurs (1) if words or actions which call for some verbal response by a suspect are (2) made by someone acting on behalf of the state (3) while the suspect is in custody.

Delegation of authority—the process of a legislative body permitting an administrative agency some authority to make rules to carry out law and to operate the agency, which have the effect of law; in effect, the legislature permits administrators to make law on behalf of the legislative body.

Exclusionary rule—the doctrine that prohibits the use of illegally seized evidence in court.

Exigent circumstances—conditions that create a need for immediate action to protect the general safety of the public, to prevent the destruction of evidence, or to prevent injury to others.

Felony—generally, a serious crime carrying a penalty of more than one year of incarceration.

Fruit of the poisonous tree—evidence that was found solely as a result of a prior illegal search or seizure.

Inevitable discovery—evidentiary doctrine that accepts the argument that the evidence would have eventually been discovered by proper and legal means.

Minimum administrative due process—the idea that, when someone's rights are affected by an administrative decision, that person must be at least accorded certain procedural rights.

Misdemeanor—generally, a less serious crime carrying a penalty of less than one year of incarceration.

Model penal code—a "model" criminal code created by the American Law Institute and adopted by many states.

Negligent acts—those which were not intended but violate a duty owed to another, causing an injury or harm.

Plain view doctrine—the idea that an officer may seize evidence of a crime or contraband that falls into the plain view of the officer, when the officer otherwise has a right to be at that location.

Precedent—decisions, over time, relied upon by other judges with similar issues.

Preliminary hearing—a hearing to determine if there is sufficient probable cause to send the case to the district attorney or grand jury for further prosecution.

Principal—a superior, supervisor, or employer relative to another who serves in a subordinate position.

Probable cause—the standards by which an arrest can be made, which exist where "the facts and circumstances within their [arresting officers'] knowledge and of which they had reasonably trustworthy information [are] sufficient in themselves to warrant a man of reasonable caution in the belief that an offense has been or is being committed [by the person to be arrested]."

Rap sheet—slang term used to describe the list of offenses in a defendant's background, a list usually generated by computer such as the National Crime Information Center.

Respondeat superior—a legal theory that makes a superior or principal liable for any damages caused by a subordinate or agent as a result of any actions taken in the normal course of employment.

Search—the invasion, by the state, of an area which a person believes is protected or private. That belief will be upheld by a court if the "person exhibited an actual (subjective) expectation of privacy, and the expectation is one that society is prepared to recognize as 'reasonable'."

Seizure—a "meaningful interference with the possessory interests of the suspect."

Stare decisis—the legal concept that prior decisions should stand if the facts are similar.

Statutory law—laws created by legislative authority.

Stop and frisk—the situation in which a police officer, in the course of investigating suspicious behavior, is entitled for the protection of himself and others in the area to conduct a carefully limited search of the outer clothing of such persons in an attempt to discover weapons which might be used to assault him.

Suppression—a court order ruling that certain evidence may not be used.

Warrant requirement—the general rule of searches and seizures which holds that, without a warrant, the search or seizure is presumed to be unconstitutional.

Writ of *certiorari*—an order requiring a lower court to give the Supreme Court the record of a case for review.

Writ of *habeas corpus*—an order requiring the person holding a prisoner to show cause why the prisoner should not be released.

CHAPTER REFERENCES AND ADDITIONAL READINGS

Antieau, Chester J. (1998). *Federal Civil Rights Acts: Civil Practice*, 2nd Edition. New York: Lawyers Co-operative Publishing.

Associated Press (2005). Boston Pays $5.1M to Dead Sox Fan's Family, May 3.

Baker, Lisa A. (2009). Supreme Court Cases, 2008–2009 Term. *FBI Law Enforcement Bulletin*. October:21–32.

Bernstein, Jake (2010). Who knew what in Madoff fraud? http://www.msnbc.msn.com/id/37474851/ns/business-small_business/.

Bostain, John (2009). Training without force continuums: Learn to love the law. *PoliceOne.com News*, March 19. http://www.policeone.com/law-enforcement-newsletter/Calibre-Press-Newsline-03-19-09.

Bray, Chad (2010). ACLU Sues Homeland Security Over Search Policies. *Wall Street Journal Online*. http://online.wsj.com/article/SB10001424052748704358904575477740845375312.html, September 7.

Carter, Lief H. and Christine B. Harrington (1991). *Administrative Law and Politics: Cases and Comments*. New York: Harper Collins.

Castro, Hector (2004). Tacoma city manager says no heads to roll over Brame slaying-suicide. *Seattle Post-Intelligencer Reporter*, October 13, http://seattlepi.nwsource.com/local/194994_brame13.html.

Cerullo, Rob and Randy Means (2004). U.S. Supreme Court Sharpens Police Drug-Fighting Tools. *The Police Chief*. 710(2, Feb.):10–12.

Eisenstein, James, Roy B. Flemming, and Peter F. Nardulli (1988). *The Contours of Justice: Communities and Their Courts*. Boston: Little, Brown, and Co.

Frank, Robert and Amir Efrati (2009). 'Evil' Madoff Gets 150 Years in Epic Fraud. *The Wall Street Journal*, June 30: A1. http://online.wsj.com/article/NA_WSJ_PUB:SB124604151653862301.html.

Gould, Jon B. and Stephen D. Mastrofski (2004). Suspect Searches: Assessing Police Behavior under the U.S. Constitution. *Criminology and Public Policy*. 3(3):315–362.

Hsu, Spencer S. (2010). Appeals court limits use of GPS to track suspects. *Washington Post*, Saturday, August 7. http://www.washingtonpost.com/wp-dyn/content/article/2010/08/06/AR2010080604946.html.

Hunsucker, Keith (2003). Right to Be, Right to See: Practical Fourth Amendment Application for Law Enforcement Officers. *The Police Chief*. 70 (9, Sept.):10–14.

Kappelman, Kristin (2010). An Analysis of Vehicle Pursuits in the Milwaukee Police Department, 2002 to 2009. City of Milwaukee, Report of the Fire and Police Commission, July 7. http://city.milwaukee.gov/ImageLibrary/Groups/cityFPC/Reports/Report_Vehicle_Pursuits.pdf.

KOMO Staff (2004). More Fallout From David Brame Tragedy. October 12, http://komotv.com/news/story_m.asp?ID=33480.

Lippman, Matthew (2011). *Criminal Procedure*. Thousand Oaks, CA: SAGE.

Mauro, Tony (2010). Summary rulings spike at the high court. June 30. http://www.law.com/jsp/nlj/PubArticleNLJ.jsp?id=1202463161398&slreturn=1&hbxlogin=1.

Means, Randolph B. (2003). Interrogation Law...Reloaded: Two Rights to Counsel. *The Police Chief*. 70(12, Dec.):11–12.

Miller, Frank W., Robert O. Dawson, George E. Dix, Raymond I. Parnas (1991). *The Police Function*. 5th Edition. Westbury, NY: The Foundation Press, Inc.

Nardulli, Peter F., Roy B. Flemming, and James Eisenstein (1988). *The Tenor of Justice: Criminal Courts and the Guilty Plea Process.* Urbana, IL: University of Illinois Press.

National Highway Traffic Safety Administration (2006). *Countermeasures That Work: A Highway Safety Countermeasure Guide For State Highway Safety Offices.* Washington, D.C.: NHTSA, Office of Research and Technology (January). NTI-130, p. 1–14.

Newbold, Mark H. (2002). Conducted Energy Weapons and Police Liability. *The Police Chief.* 69(5, May):11–12.

Ohio Revised Code §2921.29.

Richey, Warren (2009). Police Tasers: Excessive Force or Necessary Tool? *Christian Science Monitor.* May 28. http://www.csmonitor.com/2009/0528/p02s05-usju.html

Ronzio, Judith A. (1993). Upping the Ante on Miranda. *The Police Chief.* 60(5, May):10–11.

Russell, Gregory D. (1994). Liability and Criminal Justice Management: Resolving Dilemmas and Meeting Future Challenges. *American Journal of Criminal Justice.* 18(2, Spring):177–198.

Smith, Michael R. (1999). Police Pursuits: The Legal and Policy Implications of County of *Sacramento v. Lewis. Police Quarterly.* 2(3, Sept.):261–282.

Spector, Elliot B. (2002). The Confusing State of "Clearly Established Law." *The Police Chief.* 69(12, Dec.):11.

Tulsa Police Department (2003). Vehicle Pursuits. Procedure, August 15.

United States Congress. 28 U.S.C. §1332.

United States General Accountability Office (1996). *Use of Force: ATF Policy, Training and Review Process are Comparable to the DEA's and FBI's.* Washington, D.C.: General Accountability Office, March, p. 39.

Zalman, Marvin (2008). *Criminal Procedure: Constitution and Society.* 5th Ed. Upper Saddle River, NJ: Pearson.

CASES CITED

Adams v. Williams, 407 U.S. 143, 1972

Arizona v. Gant, 556 U.S. ___, 129 S. Ct. 1710 (2009)

Arizona v. Hicks, 480 U.S. 321, 1987

Arizona v. Johnson, 555 U.S. 135, 2009

Barron v. Mayor and City Council of Baltimore, 7 Pet. 243, 1833

Brendlin v. California, 551 U.S. 249, 2007

Brinegar v. United States, 338 U.S. 160, 175–176, 1949

Brigham City, Utah v. Stuart, 547 U.S. 398 2006

Brown v. Mississippi, 297 U.S. 278, 1936

California v. Acevedo, 500 U.S. 565, 1991

California v. Hodari D., 499 U.S. 621, 1991

Carroll v. United States, 267 U.S. 132, 1925

Chambers v. Maloney, 399 U.S. 42, 1970

Chavez v. Martinez, 538 U.S. 760, 2003

Chimel v. California, 395 U.S. 752, 1969

Colorado v. Connelly, 479 U.S. 157, 1986

Coolidge v. New Hampshire, 403 U.S. 443, 1971

Cooper v. Dupnick, 963 F.2d 1220; 113 S Ct 407, 1992

County of Sacramento v. Lewis, 523 U.S. 833, 118 S Ct 118, 1998

Davis v. United States, 564 U.S. ____, 2011.

Fellers v. United States, 540 U.S. 519, 124 S Ct 1019, 2004

Florida v. Powell, 559 U. S. ____, 130 S. Ct. 1195, 2010

Graham v. Connor, 490 U.S. 386 1989

Hiibal v. Sixth Judicial District Court of Nevada, 542 U.S. 177, 124 S Ct 2451, 2004

Illinois v. Lidster, 540 U.S. 419, 2004

Illinois v. Rodriguez, 497 U.S. 177, 1990

Indianapolis v. Edmond, 531 U.S. 32, 2000

Katz v. United States, 389 U.S. 347, 361; 1967

Kyllo v. United States, 533 U.S. 27, 2001

Mapp v. Ohio, 367 U.S. 643, 1961

Marbury v. Madison, 1 Cranch 137, 1803

Maryland v. Buie, 494 U.S. 325, 1990

Michigan Department of State Police v. Sitz, 496 U.S. 444, 1990

Minnesota v. Dickerson, 506 U.S. 366, 1993

Miranda v. Arizona, 384 U.S. 436, 1966

Nix v. Williams, 467 U.S. 431, 1984

Oregon v. Elstad, 470 U.S. 298, 1985

Oregon v. Mathiason, 429 U.S. 492, 1977

Payton v. New York, 445 U.S. 573, 1980

Pennsylvania v. Muniz, 496 U.S. 582, 1990

Safford Unified School District #1 et al. v. Redding, 557 U.S. ___, 129 S. Ct. 2633, 2009

Scott v. Harris, 550 U.S. 372 2007

South Dakota v. Opperman, 428 U.S. 364, 1976

State v. Smith, 124 Ohio St.3d 116, 2009

Tennessee v. Garner, 471 U.S. 1, 1985

Terry v. Ohio, 392 U.S. 1, 1968

United States v. Bernard L. Madoff (2010). Information, Case 1:09-cr-00213 DC Document 38, Filed 03/10/2009

United States v. Davis, 482 F. 2d 893, 9th Circuit, 1973

United States v. Martinez-Fuerte, 428 U.S. 543, 1976

United States v. Morena, 475 F.2d 44, 5th Circuit, 1973

United States v. Pulido-Baquerizo, 800 F.2d 899, 9th Circuit, 1986

United States v. Jacobsen, 466 U.S. 109, 1984

United States v. Skipwith, 482 F.2d 1272, 5th Circuit, 1973

Wong Sun v. United States, 371 U.S. 471, 1963

Wyoming v. Houghton, 526 U.S. 295, 1999

CHAPTER 10

Crime and Theory:
Applying Values and Strategies

LEARNING OBJECTIVES

Policing officials need to understand the basic aspects of crime causation and victimization, as strategies to reduce crime are more effective when root causes of crime and victimization are understood and considered in the process. Police officers need to also understand how crime impacts the local community, as well as state and national policy. This chapter's focus is on crime in the United States. After studying this chapter, you should be able to:

- Describe the role of patrol officers in gathering and interpreting information.
- Identify the major methods by which we count and track crime.
- Describe the impacts of crime on communities and policy making.
- Define the major theories of crime causation.
- Identify the trends in five major areas of crime that may impact future discussions of crime causation theory.

CHAPTER OUTLINE

KEY TERMS USED IN THIS CHAPTER

Uniform Crime Report (UCR)

Part 1 Offenses

Index Crimes

victimless crime

National Incident Based Reporting System (NIBRS)

National Crime Victimization Survey (NCVS)

lost opportunity costs

Drug Abuse Resistance Education (DARE)

public policy

street level bureaucrats

cause of crime

utilitarian principle

pleasure–pain principle

rationalism

deterrence

hot spot

hot dot

associate

learn

differential association

Chicago School

Ecological School

subculture

labeling

social control

socialization

crime prevention through environmental design (CPTED)

defensible space

Routine Activities Theory

Crime Pattern Theory

Lifestyle Exposure Theory

hackers

recidivism

THE NEED TO UNDERSTAND CRIME

Why must a patrol officer or field agent understand the causes of crime or how it is measured? Why should these same officers concern themselves with emerging trends in crime? It is because patrol officers are the front line in the continuing struggle to control antisocial activity, and because they are the eyes and ears of law enforcement management. Patrol officers are the primary sources of community information, and they also have the most frequent and direct interactions with citizens. In order for managers to properly plan, they need to understand developing trends. Contemporary law enforcement management techniques require patrol officers to gather information and assist in its interpretation. In addition, patrol officers are often tasked to implement new crime control strategies or policies. Having an understanding of crime causation can help officers implement these strategies and policies in the most effective ways. Information on individual offenders is also important for sentencing, probation, parole, and corrections assessment. Finally, policymakers in legislative and administrative agencies rely upon data and information collected by officers to project trends and to develop policy. (See Chapter 13 for more discussion of policing strategies.)

Understanding crime and developing solutions are not easy, but police officers, policymakers, researchers, and the public now have access to a new and very informative research-based website at CrimeSolutions.gov (http://www.crimesolutions.gov/). We urge you to explore the website as you study this and other chapters.

Often, patrol officers do not even realize they perform an information-gathering role outside of investigations. They may give statements in court or write various reports (e.g., investigative reports, supplemental reports, administrative reports, or offense reports), but they usually do not think of themselves as "researchers." Officers may also be the subject of opinion surveys or observation by academic researchers, and they may give policy testimony before legislative, policymaking, or other investigative boards. Finally, they may serve on a departmental team or task force reporting to the command staff on community problems and likely solutions. In each of these cases, information either gathered by officers or interpreted by officers goes beyond investigations of an individual case and can be of the utmost importance to the department and other policymakers.

Understanding the various theories of crime causation is one task of the professional law enforcement official. Understanding crime trends is another important task. Data on crime may not match the personal experience of each officer in a given jurisdiction, nor may crime in that jurisdiction fully reflect accepted explanations on the causes of crime. General theories and approaches are just that—general. They give us a view of how things seem overall. We expect individual locations to differ slightly, or even in major ways, from the general trends of data. But that, too, is important for patrol officers to know. If other jurisdictions seem to have one general sort of experience, why, based upon their own experience, is their jurisdiction different? Do trends in criminal behavior in that jurisdiction differ in ways that might give officers a better understanding of the causes of criminality in their community, and therefore an ability to find at least partial solutions? These questions are important and set the tone for emerging expectations of the contemporary law enforcement officer.

Amount and Impact of Crime

There are three primary sources of data on the amount of crime in the United States: self-reported crime by offenders, reported crime, and victim studies.

Self-Reported Crime

The first source of crime data is self-reporting of criminal activity by offenders. This is obviously problematic and not very reliable in many instances, though it may be useful for academic research. It is also limited in scope, as it captures only a picture of one type of offense, some characteristics of some types of offenders, or types of offenders in one area. An example is data that is collected on drug use by offenders in some cities (see **Table 10-1**). This sort of data is important for theory building, but it has less significance for community problem solving. Therefore, we tend to rely upon other sources for major crime data.

Reported Crime

The second and most commonly-known data source is taken from offenses reported to police and is counted at the level of the local law enforcement agency. Collected

TABLE 10-1 Percent of Offenders' Self-Reported Drug Use,* 2009

Primary City	Marijuana	Crack Cocaine	Powder Cocaine	Heroin	Methamphetamine
Atlanta, GA	44.5	18.8	6.4	0.5	0.4
	(3.3)	(2.5)	(1.5)	(0.4)	(0.3)
Charlotte, NC	34.5	9.1	7.3	0.8	0.0
	(3.1)	(1.7)	(1.6)	(0.4)	NA
Chicago, IL	44.3	13.5	8.2	13.1	0.0
	(4.8)	(3.3)	(2.7)	(3.0)	NA
Denver, CO	47.6	14.9	10.2	4.2	4.0
	(2.7)	(1.9)	(1.6)	(1.1)	(1.2)
Indianapolis, IN	4.7	8.5	4.6	2.7	1.2
	(2.7)	(1.4)	(1.1)	(0.8)	(0.6)
Minneapolis, MN	35.2	9.1	3.9	2.4	1.8
	(2.6)	(1.5)	(1.0)	(0.7)	(0.7)
New York, NY	44.3	10.4	9.3	7.1	0.4
	(2.4)	(1.4)	(1.4)	(1.1)	(0.4)
Portland, OR	43.4	10.7	6.9	11.3	13.4
	(2.8)	(1.7)	(1.4)	(1.8)	(1.9)
Sacramento, CA	46.7	5.3	3.7	2.6	25.3
	(2.9)	(1.2)	(1.0)	(0.8)	(2.5)
Washington, D.C.	39.6	10.1	1.5	5.6	NA
	(7.9)	(3.9)	(1.2)	(3.1)	

Source: Adam II Annual Report (2009) Adapted from Table 3.6 Self-Reported Drug Use for past 30 days, 2007 to 2009 http://www
.whitehousedrugpolicy.gov/publications/pdf/adam2009.pdf

*Numbers shown in parentheses ( ) represent the standard error of the estimate presented.

and presented in the **Uniform Crime Report,** or **UCR**, it is published annually by the Federal Bureau of Investigation (FBI) under the title *Crime in the United States*. Participating law enforcement agencies keep monthly records of offenses reported to or discovered by police, and the monthly totals are then forwarded to the Federal Bureau of Investigation. Monthly reports have two parts. **Part 1 Offenses** are also called **Index Crimes,** and are those from which the FBI tracks the "Crime Index," which it reports to the nation through the media (see **Figure 10-1**). If you read or hear a story in the media that crime was reported as going up or down, it is likely based upon this data. These offenses are used to gauge the crime "index," or its rate of decrease or increase.

Table 10-2 shows the total reported numbers of Index offenses for the past two decades. In 2009 there were 10,639,639 (Part 1) offenses reported to law enforcement agencies (and remember, Part 1 offenses only include reported crimes of murder and non-negligent manslaughter, forcible rape, robbery, aggravated assault, burglary, larceny-theft, and motor vehicle theft). Of that, only 1,318,398 (approximately 12%) were violent offenses. This is usually expressed, however, as the rate of offenses per 100,000 people. We express it as a rate in order to compare

FIGURE 10-1 Part 1 Offenses/Index Crimes

- Arson
- Assault
- Burglary
- Forcible rape
- Larceny-theft
- Motor vehicle theft
- Murder and non-negligent manslaughter
- Robbery

Source: Federal Bureau of Investigation (2002).

different time periods and take into consideration population growth. The rates for violent and property crime are shown for the past two decades in **Table 10-3** (Sourcebook of Criminal Justice Statistics Online 2010). Overall crime saw an increase in 1989 that continued until 1992, when it began to decrease. The 1993 crime rate fell 3% from 1992, with similar drops up through 1995. The crime rate fell between 1991 and 2000, and then a slight increase occurred in 2001. In 2002, the crime rate again slightly decreased and has been in a slow and steady decreasing pattern since then overall. However, while overall crime and property crime numbers have continued to fall, slight increases in the violent crime appeared in both 2005 and 2006.

There are some problems with the UCR method of counting crimes, however. First, the UCR covers only crime reported to law enforcement, and much of the crime committed in the United States is not reported because some victims do not trust police or the criminal justice system, or fear retaliation or humiliation, or they believe the police simply cannot do anything about their victimization. Second, the definitions of crimes are not the same from state to state and, in some cases, from year to year. For example, an offense such as entering an outbuilding (storage shed) might be a criminal trespass in Ohio, but a burglary in Georgia; one is a minor offense, while the other is more serious. A third problem with the UCR is that it does not account for **victimless crime**, which is behavior defined as criminal but engaged in by many who think it should not be. Generally, this includes

prostitution, gambling, drug abuse, pornography, and others. A fourth problem with the UCR is that it only counts the most serious offense occurring during an incident. For example, if during the course of a robbery, someone is shot and killed, only the murder is counted in UCR statistics. For all of these reasons and more, the UCR alone is not sufficient for us to grasp the true rate of crime. **Figure 10-2** summarizes the problems with the UCR discussed here.

The **National Incident Based Reporting System** (**NIBRS**), a component of the UCR, was developed because the law enforcement community recognized a need for more detailed information about crime. It provides incident level data and breaks the data down into specific subcategories. NIBRS collects information at the incident level for 22 different offense categories (Group A offenses) and records incident and arrest data, including victim and offender characteristics and types and value of property stolen and recovered. In addition, NIBRS collects arrest data (only) on 11 other offense categories (Group B offenses) (see **Figure 10-3**).

The NIBRS program has several advantages to the UCR. First, it does not have the hierarchy rule and thus will provide information for all crimes that are committed during an incident. Furthermore, NIBRS includes updated definitions for crimes such as rape (the UCR does not count male victims of rape) and differentiates between "attempted" and "completed" crimes (the UCR Summary system does not). Lastly, NIBRS accounts for many "victimless" crimes (e.g., drug offenses), whereas the UCR Summary reporting system only counts crimes against persons and property; NIBRS includes a third category, "crimes against society," in its reporting structure. NIBRS is relatively new in the crime counting game (the South Carolina Law Enforcement Division conducted a pilot demonstration in 1987) and not every state reports NIBRS data. However, the number of agencies participating in the NIBRS is steadily increasing. The FBI reports that as of 2007, approximately 6444 law enforcement agencies reported NIBRS data to the UCR program and that there are 31 state programs certified for NIBRS participation. "The data from those agencies represent 20% of the U.S. population and 16% of the crime statistics collected by the UCR program" (Federal Bureau of Investigation 2010d).

TABLE 10-2 Estimated Number of Offenses Known to Police, 1989–2009

Year	Violent Crime	Property Crime	Murder & Non-negligent Manslaughter	Forcible Rape	Robbery	Aggravated Assault	Burglary	Larceny-Theft	Motor Vehicle Theft
1989	1,646,037	12,605,412	21,500	94,504	578,326	951,707	3,168,170	7,872,442	1,564,800
1990	1,820,127	12,655,486	23,438	102,555	639,271	1,054,863	3,073,909	7,945,670	1,635,907
1991	1,911,767	12,961,116	24,703	106,593	687,732	1,092,739	3,157,150	8,142,228	1,661,738
1992	1,932,274	12,505,917	23,760	109,062	672,478	1,126,974	2,979,884	7,915,199	1,610,834
1993	1,926,017	12,218,777	24,526	106,014	659,870	1,135,607	2,834,808	7,820,909	1,563,060
1994	1,857,670	12,131,873	23,326	102,216	618,949	1,113,179	2,712,774	7,879,812	1,539,287
1995	1,798,792	12,063,935	21,606	97,470	580,509	1,099,207	2,593,784	7,997,710	1,472,441
1996	1,688,540	11,805,323	19,645	96,252	535,594	1,037,049	2,506,400	7,904,685	1,394,238
1997	1,636,096	11,558,475	18,208	96,153	498,534	1,023,201	2,460,526	7,743,760	1,354,189
1998	1,533,887	10,951,827	16,974	93,144	447,186	976,583	2,332,735	7,376,311	1,242,781
1999	1,426,044	10,208,334	15,522	89,411	409,371	911,740	2,100,739	6,955,520	1,152,075
2000	1,425,486	10,182,584	15,586	90,178	408,016	911,706	2,050,992	6,971,590	1,160,002
2001	1,439,480	10,437,189	16,037c	90,863	423,557	909,023	2,116,531	7,092,267	1,228,391
2002	1,423,677	10,455,277	16,229	95,235	420,806	891,407	2,151,252	7,057,379	1,246,646
2003	1,383,676	10,442,862	16,528	93,883	414,235	859,030	2,154,834	7,026,802	1,261,226
2004	1,360,088	10,319,386	16,148	95,089	401,470	847,381	2,144,446	6,937,089	1,237,851
2005	1,390,745	10,174,754	16,740	94,347	417,438	862,220	2,155,448	6,783,447	1,235,859
2006	1,435,951	10,031,359	17,318	94,782	449,803	874,048	2,196,304	6,636,615	1,198,440
2007	1,421,990	9,872,815	17,157	91,874	447,155	865,804	2,187,277	6,587,040	1,098,498
2008	1,392,629	9,775,149	16,442	90,479	443,574	842,134	2,228,474	6,588,046	958,629
2009	1,318,398	9,320,971	15,241	88,097	408,217	806,843	2,199,125	6,327,230	794,616

a. Because of rounding, the offenses may not add to totals. Due to various reporting problems, complete data for a small number of states were not available for some years.

b. Violent crimes are offenses of murder and non-negligent manslaughter, forcible rape, robbery, and aggravated assault. Property crimes are offenses of burglary, larceny-theft, and motor vehicle theft. Data are not included for the property crime of arson.

c. The murders and non-negligent manslaughters that occurred as a result of the events of September 11, 2001 are not included in this table.

Source: Sickmund, Melissa, Sladky, T.J., and Kang, Wei. (2008) "Census of Juveniles in Residential Placement Databook." Online. Available: http://www.ojjdp.gov/ojstatbb/ezacjrp/

Victim Studies

A third means of measuring crime derives from the **National Crime Victimization Survey** (**NCVS**). This is a survey of thousands of households conducted for the Bureau of Justice Statistics (U.S. Department of Justice) by the U.S. Census Bureau. Essentially, this survey measures crimes that were committed against households, residents, and businesses. In conducting the survey, people

TABLE 10-3 Estimated Rate Per 100,000 Inhabitants of Offenses Known to Police, 1989–2009

Year	Violent Crime	Property Crime	Murder & Non-negligent manslaughter	Forcible Rape	Robbery	Aggravated Assault	Burglary	Larceny-Theft	Motor vehicle theft
1989	669.9	5107.1	8.7	38.3	234.3	385.6	1283.6	3189.6	634.0
1990	729.6	5073.1	9.4	41.1	256.3	422.9	1232.2	3185.1	655.8
1991	758.2	5140.2	9.8	42.3	272.7	433.4	1252.1	3229.1	659.0
1992	757.7	4903.7	9.3	42.8	263.7	441.9	1168.4	3103.6	631.6
1993	747.1	4740.0	9.5	41.1	256.0	440.5	1099.7	3033.9	606.3
1994	713.6	4660.2	9.0	39.3	237.8	427.6	1042.1	3026.9	591.3
1995	684.5	4590.5	8.2	37.1	220.9	418.3	987.0	3043.2	560.3
1996	636.6	4451.0	7.4	36.6	201.9	391.0	945.0	2980.3	525.7
1997	611.0	4316.3	6.8	35.9	186.2	382.1	918.8	2891.8	505.7
1998	567.6	4052.5	6.3	34.5	165.5	361.4	863.2	2729.5	459.9
1999	523.0	3743.6	5.7	32.8	150.1	334.3	770.4	2550.7	422.5
2000	506.5	3618.3	5.5	32.0	145.0	324.0	728.8	2477.3	412.2
2001	504.5	3658.1	5.6c	31.8	148.5	318.6	741.8	2485.7	430.5
2002	494.4	3630.6	5.6	33.1	146.1	309.5	747.0	2450.7	432.9
2003	475.8	3591.2	5.7	32.3	142.5	295.4	741.0	2416.5	433.7
2004	463.2	3514.1	5.5	32.4	136.7	288.6	730.0	2362.3	421.5
2005	469.0	3431.5	5.6	31.8	140.8	290.8	726.9	2287.8	416.8
2006	480.6	3357.7	5.8	31.7	150.6	292.6	735.2	2221.4	401.1
2007	472.0	3276.8	5.7	30.5	148.4	287.4	726.0	2186.3	364.6
2008	457.5	3211.5	5.4	29.7	145.7	276.7	732.1	2164.5	315.0
2009	429.4	3036.1	5.0	28.7	133.0	262.8	716.3	2060.9	258.8

a. Because of rounding, the offenses may not add to totals. Due to various reporting problems, complete data for a small number of states were not available for some years.

b. Violent crimes are offenses of murder and non-negligent manslaughter, forcible rape, robbery, and aggravated assault. Property crimes are offenses of burglary, larceny-theft, and motor-vehicle theft. Data are not included for the property crime of arson.

c. The murders and non-negligent manslaughters that occurred as a result of the events of September 11, 2001 are not included in this table.

Note: All rates were calculated on the number of offenses before rounding.

Source: Sickmund, Melissa, Sladky, T.J., and Kang, Wei. (2008) "Census of Juveniles in Residential Placement Databook." Online. Available: http://www.ojjdp.gov/ojstatbb/ezacjrp/

FIGURE 10-2 Problems with UCR Data

- Crime increases may reflect changed enforcement, not crime itself
- Only includes crimes actually reported to (or discovered by) law enforcement agencies
- Voluntary system of reporting; not all law enforcement agencies provide information to the UCR
- Same criminal actions are given different titles in different states
- Cannot provide accurate count for victimless crimes
- Depends largely upon victim reporting behavior

are asked if they have been the victim of a crime in the past year and, if so, to describe it. Detailed information is acquired for each victimization. On the basis of this broad survey, estimates are generated for the nation as a whole. The NCVS provides interesting information, such as the fact that the rate of victimization is generally going down, not up. However, as much as 65% of all crime is not reported, and the rate differs depending on the crime. Very few auto thefts go unreported, as victims need police reports to file insurance claims against the lost property. Some violent crimes, however, have a much higher non-report rate. For example, of the 167,550 rapes that were estimated to have occurred in 1994, only 102,100 were reported to police. This means that an estimated 40% of rapes were not reported during that year.

Still, victimization surveys are limited. Self-reported recollections, as noted above, are not reliable, in part because each respondent interprets events from his or her own perspective. She or he may see a situation as an assault when it was not. Another limitation of the NCVS, like that of the UCR, is its inability to capture information regarding white-collar crime and fraud, or information about crimes in which the respondent may have been involved. Respondents must be relied upon to report offender characteristics, and frequently this information

is not known to the victim at all. Information from the NCVS is important, but it is limited as well, and we need to keep that in mind while interpreting it.

Impact of Crime

The rate of crime and the impression it leaves have very clear effects in society. First, this can affect policy decisions in major ways. In late 1993, Congress passed a crime bill that, among other things, provided for the addition of 100,000 police officers on the streets of the United States. This major policy shift resulted from the perception of increased crime. But was crime increasing? As **Figure 10-4** graphically illustrates, general victimization rates were falling overall, and, while violent crime increased in the period from 1990 to 1994, it decreased in 1995 and continued falling through 2007 (with the exception of slight increases in 2003 and 2005). Violence, of course, is what most people fear, and many people believe violence is increasing, but Figure 10-4 depicts a downward trend. **Figure 10-5** illustrates the Part I index crime percentages in a pie chart. Note that the overwhelming majority of Part I index crimes are considered "nonviolent."

The important thing for law enforcement departments to make clear is the status of offending in their own communities. Use of national data can cause erroneous perceptions. For example, preliminary reports for 2010 suggest that crime for all Part I index crimes are down for the nation as a whole. However, the Northeast experienced a 5.7% increase in murder, a 1.1% increase in forcible rape, a 2.4% increase in aggravated assault, and a 3.9% increase in burglary (Federal Bureau of Investigation, 2010a).

Police officials in the Northeast should be aware of national, regional, and local statistics and patterns of crime to aid their efforts at developing effective solutions. **Table 10-4** presents offenses known to police by community type in 2009. Note the differences in rates across community types.

The sense of increasing crime produced demands, beginning in the 1980s, for stiffer penalties and longer sentences, and for a greater portion of the sentence to actually be served. Hence, while victimization studies consistently showed a general decrease in offenses against persons and households between 1980 and 1995, the rate

FIGURE 10-3 NIBRS Group A & B Offenses

Group A Offenses

1. Arson
2. Assault Offenses—Aggravated Assault, Simple Assault, Intimidation
3. Bribery
4. Burglary/Breaking and Entering
5. Counterfeiting/Forgery
6. Destruction/Damage/Vandalism of Property
7. Drug/Narcotic Offenses—Drug/Narcotic Violations, Drug Equipment Violations
8. Embezzlement
9. Extortion/Blackmail
10. Fraud Offenses
11. Gambling Offenses
12. Homicide Offenses
13. Kidnapping/Abduction
14. Larceny/Theft Offenses
15. Motor Vehicle Theft
16. Pornography/Obscene Material
17. Prostitution Offenses
18. Robbery
19. Sex Offenses, Forcible—Forcible Rape, Forcible Sodomy, Sexual Assault with an Object, Forcible Fondling
20. Sex Offenses, Nonforcible—Incest, Statutory Rape
21. Stolen Property Offenses (Receiving, etc.)
22. Weapon Law Violations

Group B Offenses

1. Bad Checks
2. Curfew/Loitering/Vagrancy Violations
3. Disorderly Conduct
4. Driving Under the Influence
5. Drunkenness
6. Family Offenses, Nonviolent
7. Liquor Law Violations
8. Peeping Tom
9. Runaway
10. Trespass of Real Property
11. All other Offenses

Source: Federal Bureau of Investigation (2010d).

of imprisonment increased dramatically. As **Figure 10-6** demonstrates, the rate with which people were placed in prison escalated quickly between 1980 and 2008—a rate of increase far greater than the drop in the crime rate over the same period. Only very recently have trends suggested a decline in our correctional population, and only a slight decline at that. A census of the 2009 U.S.

Corrections populations indicates that both probationers and parolees are recently declining (Glaze 2010). In addition, while the number of federal inmates increased slightly (3.4%) in 2009, state inmates decreased by 0.2% (its first measured decline since 1977). Furthermore, the growth in the prison population during 2009 was noted as the "slowest annual increase in the current decade and

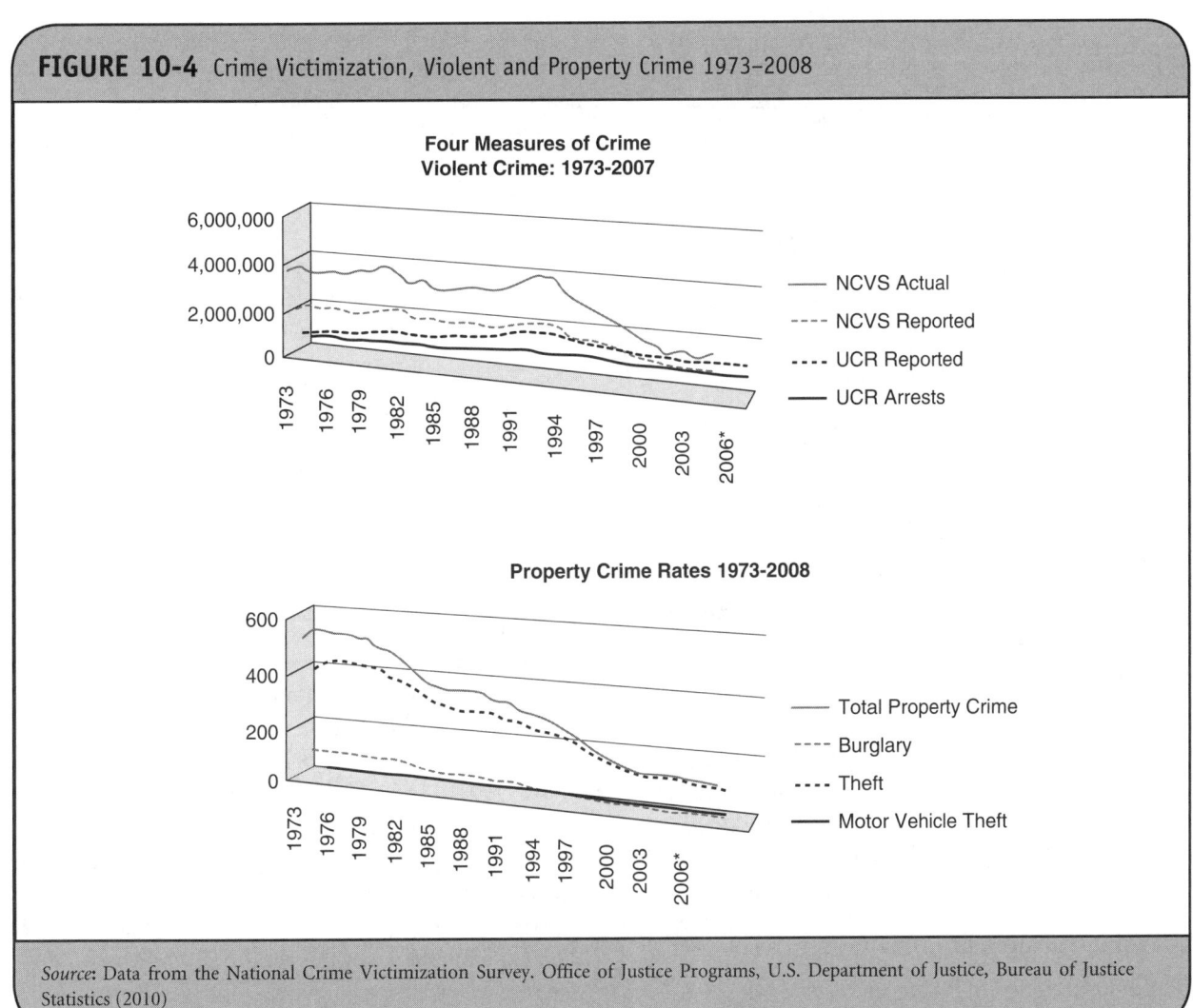

FIGURE 10-4 Crime Victimization, Violent and Property Crime 1973–2008

Four Measures of Crime
Violent Crime: 1973-2007

- NCVS Actual
- NCVS Reported
- UCR Reported
- UCR Arrests

Property Crime Rates 1973-2008

- Total Property Crime
- Burglary
- Theft
- Motor Vehicle Theft

Source: Data from the National Crime Victimization Survey. Office of Justice Programs, U.S. Department of Justice, Bureau of Justice Statistics (2010)

marked the third consecutive year of a declining rate of growth" (Bureau of Justice Statistics, 2010).

Other impacts can be less immediate, but no less clear. There are social and economic costs associated with each offense, including loss of income and property, as well as increased medical costs and insurance. Families of both victim and perpetrator are damaged, and there are costs to society as well (see **Figure 10-7**). Policing, prosecution, and incarceration costs; loss of productivity; and distribution of medical costs by way of insurance premiums or taxes are only some of these costs. **Lost opportunity costs** are also tangible. These losses represent the things that society and victims could have done with the money otherwise wasted on crime. Other losses are community pride and attractiveness. For example, in the wake of the riots associated with the Rodney King case, community groups tried to rebuild South Central Los Angeles, but they found few investors who wanted to risk their money in an area that was thought to be crime- and gang-ridden. The net result is a general and steady decline in the standard of living in the area. This affects the social fabric of the community, the schools, and overall patterns

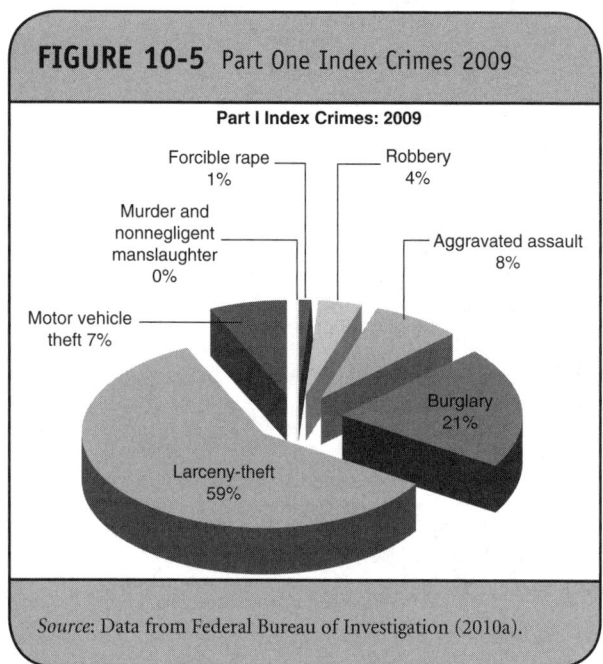

FIGURE 10-5 Part One Index Crimes 2009

Part I Index Crimes: 2009

- Forcible rape 1%
- Robbery 4%
- Murder and nonnegligent manslaughter 0%
- Aggravated assault 8%
- Motor vehicle theft 7%
- Burglary 21%
- Larceny-theft 59%

Source: Data from Federal Bureau of Investigation (2010a).

of crime. In effect, it is a spiral of decline. Research has consistently demonstrated that if people in an area feel safe, they behave differently. Investing, spending, and communication increase, even if the crime rate is stable. Therefore, one of the major impacts of crime prevention and community policing programs has been the elevation of a sense of community security (Skogan 1990).

Changing Patterns of Crime

In the fourth edition of his book *Sense and Nonsense about Crime and Drugs*, Samuel Walker (1998) argues that the patterns of crime have changed in the past decade for several reasons. First, he argues that the "get tough" policies of the 1980s generally failed. Not that they failed in getting tough—rather, the whole idea of getting tougher did not produce an expected dramatic reduction in crime. Second, the appearance of crack cocaine altered the crime problem by changing the manner in which drugs were marketed. Crack was cheaper, more easily transported, and offered a higher profit potential than other drugs, including other forms of cocaine. The latter fact invited widespread violence, as gangs fought over "turf" and market share. In behavior reminiscent of the bootleg days of the 1920s, murder escalated in the major cities of the United States.

A third change was also the result of drugs. In the 1980s, a new war on drugs emerged as middle-class white America brought political pressure to do something about drug use in the country. The result was a rapid tripling of the prison population nationwide, much of this coming in the form of drug convictions (Walker 1998; 2010). As prisons became overcrowded, conditions deteriorated and rehabilitation took a back seat. The crush of cases also inundated the criminal justice system generally. Law enforcement allocated tremendous resources to this crime type, and the courts were overwhelmed by the increased case loads. This left less prison space for violent offenders and fewer law enforcement resources for other areas such as violent crime investigation and patrol activities. Coupled with budget cuts, law enforcement was left more overworked than before. Limited community services that might have helped many who could turn themselves around were further reduced. Despite clear evidence that most offenders can be directed away from crime without the potentially-harmful effects of incarceration, incarceration rates increased. Those convicted of nonviolent offenses (e.g., drug offenses) were given priority, thereby pushing more violent offenders into probation and parole (Irwin 1994). During the late 1980s and continuing through the 1990s, we also experienced a serious increase in the violence of juveniles, despite an overall decline in violent crime in the late 1990s.

Recent data suggest overall juvenile crime, at least at the national level, is on the decline (Puzzanchera 2009). Arrests for juvenile crime were 3% lower than in 2007, and arrests for violent juvenile crime fell about 2%. In comparing the percentage change in juvenile arrests from 1999 to 2008, the change in arrests was –9% for the violent crime index and –20% for the property crime index—a significant decrease for the 10-year span. However, not every region or city has enjoyed the decrease in juvenile crime, and not all juvenile crime is on the decline; robbery committed by juveniles, for example, has been steadily increasing since its low in 2002.

For patrol officers in major cities, these changes (budget cuts, limited community resources, changes in local crime patterns) meant an increased level of danger associated with the job. While the number of American police officers killed each year declined between 1980

TABLE 10-4 Crime in the United States by Community Type, 2009

Area	Population[1]	Violent crime	Murder and nonnegligent manslaughter	Forcible rape	Robbery	Aggravated assault	Burglary	Larceny-theft	Motor vehicle theft
United States									
Total	**307,006,550**	**1,318,398**	**15,241**	**88,097**	**408,217**	**806,843**	**2,199,125**	**6,327,230**	**794,616**
Rate per 100,000 inhabitants		429.4	5.0	28.7	133.0	262.8	716.3	2,060.9	258.8
Metropolitan Statistical Area	**256,734,191**								
Area actually reporting[2] 97.1%		1,109,526	12,616	67,096	366,691	663,123	1,784,613	5,247,592	705,192
Estimated total 100.0%		1,177,758	13,408	72,413	390,483	701,454	1,867,157	5,511,868	734,208
Rate per 100,000 inhabitants		458.7	5.2	28.2	152.1	273.2	727.3	2,146.9	286.0
Cities outside metropolitan areas	**20,040,075**								
Area actually reporting[2] 90.9%		73,338	741	7,394	11,542	53,661	149,740	489,037	26,592
Estimated total 100.0%		79,446	798	8,259	12,639	57,750	164,859	539,720	28,582
Rate per 100,000 inhabitants		396.4	4.0	41.2	63.1	288.2	822.6	2,693.2	142.6
Nonmetropolitan Counties	**30,232,284**								
Area actually reporting[2] 93.0%		57,997	961	6,665	4,794	45,577	156,246	259,148	30,247
Estimated total 100.0%		61,194	1,035	7,425	5,095	47,639	167,109	275,642	31,826
Rate per 100,000 inhabitants		202.4	3.4	24.6	16.9	157.6	552.8	911.7	105.3

[1] Population figures are U.S. Census Bureau provisional estimates as of July 1, 2009.

[2] The percentage reported under "Area actually reporting" is based on the population covered by agencies providing 3 months or more of crime reports to the FBI.

NOTE: Although arson data are included in the trend and clearance tables, sufficient data are not available to estimate totals for this offense. Therefore, no arson data are published in this table.

Source: Federal Bureau of Investigation (2010a: Table 2).

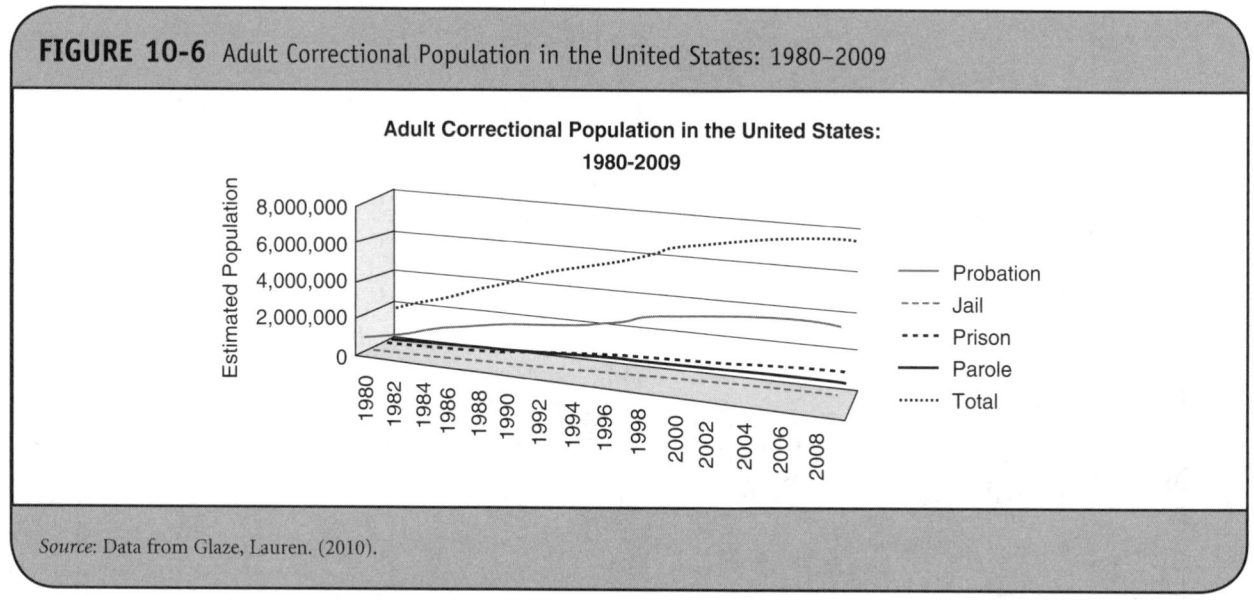

FIGURE 10-6 Adult Correctional Population in the United States: 1980–2009

Adult Correctional Population in the United States: 1980-2009

- Probation
- Jail
- Prison
- Parole
- Total

Source: Data from Glaze, Lauren. (2010).

and 2002 (104 to 56), the number assaulted remained relatively stable (57,847 to 58,066), despite a jump to more than 81,000 in 1992. While the last decade shows some ups and downs in police officer deaths and injuries (see **Tables 10-5** through **10-7**), reports for 2010 suggest a significant increase (up nearly 40% from 2009) for the

FIGURE 10-7 The costs of crime

- Community pride and attractiveness
- Families damaged
- Incarceration costs
- Increased medical costs
- Increased insurance costs
- Loss and damage to property
- Loss of income
- Loss of productivity
- Lost opportunity costs
- Policing
- Prosecution
- Tax revenue loss

number officers killed in the line of duty: 162 (National Law Enforcement Memorial Fund 2011). These conditions are bad enough to keep the level of stress for patrol officers high and reduce the degree of positive interaction with citizens, thereby hampering efforts to reduce crime.

These conditions also significantly altered the social conditions in cities. Earlier, we noted that crime was decreasing rather than increasing. Based upon victimization studies (as opposed to crime indexes), this trend was relatively consistent for the 15 years preceding 1995. However, violent crime increased in some major cities in that same period. Drug arrests, which also dramatically increased, tended to cluster in the major cities. Hence, while the average American was less likely to be a victim of crime in 1995 than in 1978, the average poor citizen and the average African-American citizen were more likely to be a crime victim than had been the case only a decade earlier. The decreased level of safety felt by citizens, mixed with law enforcement's increased sense of community hostility and the clustering of arrests in particular areas in the cities, resulted in increased community resentment and fear. Patrol officers became less connected to the population, more reactive, more aggressive, and more hostile. These pervasive feelings contributed to the Rodney King

TABLE 10-5 Assaults on Law Enforcement Officers and Percent Receiving Personal Injury—By Type of Weapon Used, 2000–2009

Law Enforcement Officers Assaulted
Type of Weapon and Percent Injured, 2000–2009

Year	Total	Firearm Total	Firearm Percent injured	Knife or other cutting instrument Total	Knife or other cutting instrument Percent injured	Other dangerous weapon Total	Other dangerous weapon Percent injured	Personal weapons Total	Personal weapons Percent injured	Number of reporting agencies	Population covered	Number of officers employed
Number of victim officers	590,507	20,459	9.6	10,431	13.3	83,665	24.6	475,952	28.8	103,979	2,257,175,258	5,033,381
2000	58,398	1,749	11.4	1,015	15.2	8,132	26.9	47,502	29.2	8,940	204,598,589	452,531
2001	57,463	1,841	10.3	1,168	15.3	8,233	26.1	46,221	29.7	9,773	213,645,308	471,096
2002	59,526	1,927	11.4	1,061	15.1	8,526	25.7	48,012	29.7	10,164	219,424,713	491,009
2003	58,600	1,879	10.7	1,084	13.4	8,180	25.4	47,457	29.7	10,539	225,769,768	501,738
2004	59,692	2,114	9.0	1,123	12.8	8,645	25.6	47,810	29.4	10,589	226,273,199	501,462
2005	57,820	2,157	8.7	1,059	11.5	8,379	24.6	46,225	29.1	10,119	222,873,755	489,393
2006	59,396	2,290	9.5	1,055	12.7	8,611	23.6	47,440	28.4	10,596	227,360,586	504,147
2007	61,257	2,216	8.7	1,028	10.5	8,692	22.2	49,321	27.6	10,973	234,734,286	523,944
2008	61,087	2,292	8.3	958	13.0	8,466	22.8	49,371	27.7	10,835	238,730,830	541,906
2009	57,268	1,994	8.8	880	13.3	7,801	23.5	46,593	27.6	11,451	243,764,224	556,155

Percent injured (Total column): 27.3, 28.1, 28.3, 28.2, 28.2, 27.8, 27.4, 26.7, 25.9, 26.0, 26.2

NOTE: Assault figures published in prior years' editions of *Law Enforcement Officers Killed and Assaulted* have been updated for inclusion in this table.

Source: Federal Bureau of Investigation (2010c:Table 70).

TABLE 10-6 Law Enforcement Officers Feloniously Killed: 2000–2009

Law Enforcement Officers Feloniously Killed

Type of Weapon, 2000–2009

Type of weapon	Total	2000	2001[1]	2002	2003	2004	2005	2006	2007	2008	2009
Number of victim officers	536	51	70	56	52	57	55	48	58	41	48
Total firearms	490	47	61	51	45	54	50	46	56	35	45
Handgun	357	33	46	38	34	36	42	36	39	25	28
Rifle	94	10	11	10	10	13	3	8	8	6	15
Shotgun	38	4	4	3	1	5	5	2	8	4	2
Type of firearm not reported	1	0	0	0	0	0	0	0	1	0	0
Knife or other cutting instrument	3	1	0	1	0	1	0	0	0	0	0
Bomb	2	0	0	0	0	0	0	0	0	2	0
Blunt instrument	2	0	1	0	1	0	0	0	0	0	0
Personal weapons	1	0	1	0	0	0	0	0	0	0	0
Vehicle	38	3	7	4	6	2	5	2	2	4	3
Other	0	0	0	0	0	0	0	0	0	0	0

[1]The deaths of the 72 law enforcement officers that resulted from the events of September 11, 2001 are not included in this table.

Source: Federal Bureau of Investigation (2010c:Table 27).

incident, and these same conditions ushered in the advent of Community Policing as a major initiative in law enforcement to reconnect law enforcement to the community it served. In many ways, changing crime patterns produced changes in community responses toward law enforcement and in law enforcement's approach to communities.

The lessons for patrol offiers are clear. They must learn to see past the immediate incident, avoid stereotyping, and look for larger trends revealed by the big picture. Many of the problems encountered by patrol officers in cities are the result of a bad mix of poverty, drugs, and despair. Intervention in and interaction with the community are necessary, both to reduce opportunities for crime and reduce tensions. Crime prevention approaches are as important as arrests. In order to make **Drug Abuse Resistance Education** (**DARE**), Neighborhood Watch, or other community involvement approaches work, patrol officers must know the community and become connected to it. They are the eyes and the ears of policy creation and implementation.

CAUSES OF CRIME—OVERVIEW

Public policy is the sum total of what the government decides to do. It is made by elected officials in a democracy and is carried out by administrative agents in executive agencies, such as law enforcement agencies. Patrol officers are, in effect, administrative agents or **street level bureaucrats** with a tremendous amount of discretion (Lipsky 1980). Though they cannot decide what the law is, they can and do decide when to use the law. Policymakers identify problems in society and create public policy (law) in an attempt to respond to observed problems. In the

TABLE 10-7 Law Enforcement Officers Accidentally Killed: 2000–2009

Law Enforcement Officers Accidentally Killed

Circumstance at Scene of Incident, 2000–2009

Circumstance		Total	2000	2001	2002	2003	2004	2005	2006	2007	2008	2009
Number of victim officers	Total	728	83	76	75	81	82	67	66	83	68	47
Automobile accident	Total	415	42	36	40	50	48	39	38	49	39	34
Motorcycle accident	Total	67	6	7	7	10	10	4	8	6	6	3
Aircraft accident	Total	33	7	5	6	1	3	2	3	3	2	1
Struck by vehicle	Total	120	14	19	12	10	10	11	13	12	13	6
	Traffic stop, roadblock, etc.	47	7	7	4	6	3	5	4	7	1	3
	Directing traffic, assisting motorist, etc.	73	7	12	8	4	7	6	9	5	12	3
Accidental shooting	Total	33	3	5	3	2	4	4	4	4	2	2
	Crossfire, mistaken for subject, firearm mishap	21	1	2	2	1	2	2	3	4	2	2
	Training session	5	1	2	0	0	1	1	0	0	0	0
	Self-inflicted, cleaning mishap (not apparent or confirmed suicide)	7	1	1	1	1	1	1	1	0	0	0
Drowning	Total	19	3	1	3	4	3	2	0	2	1	0
Fall	Total	13	3	2	1	2	1	3	0	1	0	0
Other accidental (electrocution, explosion, etc.)	Total	28	5	1	3	2	3	2	0	6	5	1

Source: Federal Bureau of Investigation (2010c:Table 61).

area of crime and criminal justice, public policy initiatives are usually a response to the believed causes of crime.

Religious-based assumptions of crime (sin in church law) date to the dawn of civilized society. Typically, the rules based upon such principles sought to punish evil or influence from the devil. More recently, theorists and researchers focused rigorously on finding a **cause of crime** rooted in human behavior and environment. Modern efforts in this direction can be traced to at least the late 1700s, when Jeremy Bentham (1748–1832), an English philosopher, suggested that the **utilitarian principle** of seeking pleasure and avoiding pain should guide policy responses to crime. Similarly, Cesare Beccaria (1738–1794) held that people will always seek to maximize their pleasure and minimize their pain. In their view, legal institutions could control conduct by increasing one or the other, with pain discouraging crime. These theorists believed that if an act is deemed illegal by society, then the society should only increase the "pain" of committing the act in order to prevent its occurrence. This **pleasure–pain principle** lies at the heart of early crime control ideas (Williams and McShane 1988).

The age in which these theories developed was very much caught up in **rationalism**, and this period produced another rational theory: capitalism. Bentham's early model of **deterrence** reasoning formed a basic set of theoretical principles around which much of our early criminal justice system evolved. However, despite the fact that England used the death penalty for nearly 200 offenses, including picking pockets, crime did not decrease. The simplicity of the pleasure–pain principle did not fully explain the causes of crime. Others tried different techniques, thought to be scientific approaches, to finding causes of crime. These included notions such as counting the bumps on the heads of those convicted of offenses (Williams and McShane 1988). Obviously, this, and other similar methods, left much to be desired in terms of science.

In the 20th century, social sciences including criminology, sociology, psychology, and anthropology, improved society's ability to both accumulate and analyze evidence concerning crime causation, and in the past 40 years, the social sciences have compiled an impressive array of partial explanations for the causes of crime. They are categorized here for discussion purposes into two groups. Some theories focus on the individual offender, while others focus on society as a whole. This is an important distinction for the patrol officer and policymaker to consider.

Persons associated with law enforcement frequently ask why a given defendant committed a particular crime. Usually, in any such discussion, several theories are commonly advanced. These theories tend to focus on background, family, and prior life experiences (drug use, child abuse, etc.). When a defendant is found guilty and a court contemplates the level of punishment, these same issues surface in the sentencing process. In both cases, the focus is on individual actions and history. Policymakers, however, look at large numbers of offenders in a given period of time and determine whether there are events in the society-at-large that explain some crime. Without debating the point, assume that drugs cause crime. If this were true, then a policy directed at limiting the availability of drugs would seem prudent if it could be achieved. Here we are not concerned with the individual; rather, our focus is on social causes of crime. We assume that certain social conditions produce increased or decreased risks of crime. Both individual-focused theory and societal level explanations are useful for patrol officers to know and understand.

A discussion of criminological theories in a policing textbook may seem at first glance unnecessary and more appropriate in a criminology textbook. However, we feel that not addressing theory produces a gap in understanding why police employ the strategies that they do. For example, resting on the assumption that criminals function to seek pleasure and avoid pain, as discussed above, an appropriate police strategy to reduce crime would be to patrol city streets, thus increasing the risk of arrest. Of course, we know from the Kansas City patrol experiment in the 1970s that mere random patrol (e.g., the number of officers randomly driving around a city) is not associated with deterrence or crime prevention. However, we also know that in most cities, a few addresses or locations generate the largest number of calls for service (**hot spots** or **hot dots**), and so targeted patrol is a strategy that employs theories of human behavior and problem solving to structure a focused response to observed problems. Individual-based theories may assist officers in solving a crime or in structuring a plausible motive, while social theories of crime call upon officers to be alert to changes in their environment that may signal changes in the nature and kind of crime they might expect. Some aspects of the theory of community policing address exactly these issues. If officers are alert, proper community intervention may actually prevent crime from occurring.

INDIVIDUAL LEVEL THEORIES OF CRIME

While early theorists focused on offender physical attributes (by counting bumps on the head or measuring body types, for example), others took note of obvious profiles of offenders. They found that offenders tended to be young males with relatively poor intellectual skills. This did not mean, of course, that youth, gender, or lack of intellect caused crime, but rather, it suggested that there might be things about society that influenced young, poorly educated males to commit crimes. Specifically, gender roles might influence males to become more aggressive, young people tend be less cautious and are more easily influenced by peers, and poor educational experiences may cause a person to believe that legal approaches to success are not possible (or will not produce benefits). Poor education also precludes the skills development necessary to see future value to lawful pursuits. In a complex theory reminiscent of the pleasure–pain theory, James Q. Wilson and Richard J. Hernstein argued that much of the explanation for crime lies in the relationship between (1) human needs, (2) the anticipation that these needs will be fulfilled by lawful conduct, and (3) internalized prohibitions against unlawful conduct to fulfill needs (1985). In this view, criminals typically fail to learn internal controls that would prevent needs satisfaction by illegal conduct. Wilson and Hernstein maintain that offenders cannot see how lawful conduct will fulfill those needs.

Similarly, the idea of internalization of norms or values suggests that those who experience a very dysfunctional childhood will either internalize the wrong norms, or no norms at all. On the one hand, if children are exposed to alcohol, drug abuse, or violence, their norms may be very abnormal and at odds with those of society. Children may **associate** or **learn** approaches to satisfying their needs that are wholly illegal. **Differential association**, originally proposed by Edwin Sutherland in 1939, suggests that criminal behavior results when one is exposed to the "patterns" or "definitions" of others that are favorable to, or supportive of, antisocial behavior (Akers 1997, 61). This theory was expanded by Akers and others to include the notion of rewarding or punishing those definitions. This is frequently referred to as learning theory (Akers 1997; Braithwaite 1989; Gorman and White 1995). This may seem like deterrence theory combined with "hanging around with the wrong crowd," but it is not. These theories are complex suggestions about how we respond to examples in our environment and, as a general theory of deviance, apply to us all and to all forms of deviance, even police deviance. If neighborhoods and families present "definitions" to children that are contrary to social standards of lawfulness, and these children are rewarded for accepting those definitions, we should not be surprised that they adopt those behaviors. Hence, interventions with families of offenders may well produce a net reduction in the potential for future crime. On the other hand, if families, neighborhoods, and peers assist in internalizing proper values (including supporting educational performance) and teaching the value of future lawful rewards, crime as a path of conduct will be less likely for that person.

Both of these observations offer value for patrol officers. In one sense, officers can assume there is a good probability that offenders are young and male. It is not a good assumption, however, that all young males are likely offenders (see **Table 10-8**). A small number commit most

TABLE 10-8 Estimated Percent Distribution of U.S. Resident Population and Persons Arrested For All Offenses By Age Group, United States, 2009

Age Group	U.S. resident population	Persons arrested
14 years and younger	20.2%	3.8%
15 to 19	7.0	20.2
20 to 24	7.0	19.6
25 to 29	7.1	14.5
30 to 34	6.5	10.3
35 to 39	6.7	8.6
40 to 44	6.8	7.8
45 to 49	7.4	7.0
50 to 54	7.1	4.4
55 to 59	6.2	2.2
60 to 64	5.2	1.0
Age 65 and older	12.9	0.8

Source: Sickmund, Melissa, Sladky, T.J., and Kang, Wei. (2008) "Census of Juveniles in Residential Placement Databook." Online. Available: http://www.ojjdp.gov/ojstatbb/ezacjrp/

Index offenses. While 30% to 40% of all males will be arrested once before their 18th birthday, only 6% of all young males account for 50% of the arrests (Greenwood 1995). However, this information also suggests a focus of patrol information gathering and departmental intervention. Most juvenile offenders can clearly be pointed in positive directions. For example, pursuing the possibility that a child has been abused or neglected, an officer may have a hand in preventing, possibly even reversing, damaging lessons. Participation in school activities such as sports programs, tutoring, DARE, police athletic leagues, and camp sponsorships can provide positive role models and experiences. In part, officers become role models as a big brother/big sister for children at risk.

SOCIAL LEVEL THEORIES OF CRIME

While some theories focus on the specific attributes of individual offenders, learning environments to which they were exposed, and personal experiences they have had, social level theories choose a much broader perspective. These theories suggest that social structure impacts the prevention or creation of crime. Some of these theories attempt to bridge the distance between individual and social explanations. These theories examine how individuals are exposed to the process of a social system, with the belief that individual behavior is more or less directly influenced by social conditions. Not all people respond in the same way to the same social conditions, but overall, we can predict that many will. Hence, alteration of social conditions will also predictably have an effect, according to these theories.

Chicago School

The **Chicago** or **Ecological School** examined the conditions in which people grow, live, and develop for an explanation of crime. These theorists argued that as an area of a city deteriorates, certain processes take place: a new culture develops with its own norms and values, and these may and probably will differ from the norms of the larger society. For example, gangs may form as social support mechanisms. Gangs represent a local cultural response to conditions of conflict with other cultures. While gangs may turn to the manufacture and sale of drugs, or fencing stolen property, the reason for gang emergence is a sense

of belonging, replacing structures that are missing in their lives (such as a stable family or strong scholastic support). In this respect, the law society seeks to enforce is not theirs because it is not from their culture. If law enforcement officers have difficulty accepting this interpretation, it is understandable, but studies of gangs and the Mafia substantiate the claim that conflict over culture plays a large role in crime creation. Cultures are based upon values that are transmitted to members of that culture. The idea of **subculture** (discussed in Chapter 8 as it applied to police officers and their work) is based upon this theory. Conflict between the main culture, which creates the law, and the culture of a given group or neighborhood (subculture) generates violations of norms from the main culture.

In many cultures, bribing and gambling are accepted, lawful behaviors. In ours, they are illegal. Some Native American tribes claim the right to use some parts of natural plants in their religious ceremonies, but society calls them drugs and bans them. In the 1800s, fist-fighting in streets and bars rarely led to arrest and prosecution. In short, crime is very value laden. Of course, as we will discuss later, some actions strike us as patently wrong (robbery, murder, assault, and rape, to name a few) and it is difficult to imagine a culture in which such conduct would be accepted.

Differential Association

Closely related to the idea of subculture is the theory of differential association. This theory holds that crime is learned from close personal contacts with others, and accordingly, it bridges individual and social level theories. Hence, close contact with a given cultural perspective would lead one to learn those cultural values and act on them, even though these actions were contrary to established law. Because this theory focuses on the process of "learning," it can be thought of as social theory as well as an individually focused theory.

For law enforcement, these theories suggest that mere reaction to criminal events is insufficient to stop crime and that breaking down cultural barriers seems to be a more responsive strategy. Reactive behavior assumes that crime is generated by a rational actor; that is, someone who thinks about the consequences of criminal acts. As discussed earlier, that rational model holds that if offenders know they will get caught and punished, they will not commit the crime. However, if crime is partially created by culture, then rational models do not apply. For example, when Prohibition came into being, very honest, dedicated citizens found themselves on the other side of the law because, in their culture, drinking was not only permitted, it was part of everyday life. This was particularly true for those of European descent.

In the same respect, today's problems of drugs, gambling, sex, gang-related violence, and theft suggest that some of the problem is more cultural than individual. To curb crime, then, law enforcement would need to address community concerns, listen to community interests, and develop a more positive, less conflict-oriented image in the community. These results are achieved by intervention in the culture and neighborhoods, not by traditional enforcement methods alone. Such intervention approaches do not mean lower levels of law enforcement. but instead mean more complex methods with enforcement and prevention mixed together. Law enforcement becomes not merely the response to criminal actions. It must involve the whole environment of the community, including schools, community services, citizen organizations, and alternative outlets. In this respect, modern policing is partially concerned with introducing and positively reinforcing new values. This, in essence, is what community policing means.

Labeling

Other explanations for crime attempted to bridge the gap between theories that focused on the individual and those that focused on the social structure by focusing on the processes by which people were exposed to different forces in society. **Labeling** theory was one prominent notion. There are a number of different perspectives in this approach, but essentially they argue that when an individual is "labeled" deviant, that person is more likely to continue being deviant. For some, this might seem either obvious or not very informative. However, this theory is supported by evidence that juveniles who are subjected to high levels of labeling (that is, repeatedly labeled from one event) are more likely to continue deviant patterns (Braithwaite 1989). **Table 10-9** reveals the formal reasons for which many juveniles are institutionalized.

TABLE 10-9 Detailed Offense Profile in Public and Private Facilities for United States, 2006

Most serious offense	All Facilities	Public	Private
Total	**92,854**	**64,163**	**28,558**
Delinquency	88,137	62,859	25,163
Person	**31,704**	**22,961**	**8,713**
Criminal homicide	988	903	84
Sexual assault	6,792	4,561	2,224
Robbery	6,707	5,624	1,080
Aggravated assault	7,289	5,725	1,558
Simple assault	7,308	4,431	2,869
Other person	2,620	1,717	898
Property	**23,177**	**16,758**	**6,394**
Burglary	9,037	6,484	2,541
Theft	4,648	3,293	1,354
Auto theft	4,650	3,390	1,254
Arson	651	509	139
Other property	4,191	3,082	1,106
Drug	**7,996**	**5,059**	**2,926**
Trafficking	1,758	1,216	542
Other drug	6,238	3,843	2,384
Public order	**9,944**	**6,690**	**3,241**
Weapons	3,669	2,810	855
Alcohol	317	159	157
Other public order	5,958	3,721	2,229
Technical violation	**15,316**	**11,391**	**3,889**
Violent Crime Index*	**21,776**	**16,813**	**4,946**
Property Crime Index**	**18,986**	**13,676**	**5,288**
Status offense	**4,717**	**1,304**	**3,395**
Running away	894	340	547
Truancy	863	201	662
Incorrigibility	1,917	290	1,626
Curfew violation	96	36	59
Underage drinking	524	179	338
Other status offense	423	258	163

*Includes criminal homicide, violent sexual assault, robbery, and aggravated assault.
**Includes burglary, theft, auto theft, and arson.

Source: Sickmund, Melissa, Sladky, T.J., and Kang, Wei. (2008) "Census of Juveniles in Residential Placement Databook." Online. Available: http://www.ojjdp.gov/ojstatbb/ezacjrp/

Evidence from a number of perspectives and studies suggests that non-index crime offenders, particularly juveniles, who pass through the criminal justice system display an increased rate of offending as a result of formal charge processing. In other words, for many offenders, arresting, charging, and formally pursuing a charge caused them to become more likely to offend, not less likely (Ludman 1993). This discovery led to the creation of large diversion programs for first offenders who committed relatively minor offenses. While recent research has called labeling theory into question, prior evidence of this effect has not been fully refuted.

For law enforcement, labeling theory suggests that the use of guided discretion in making arrests is effective in crime prevention. This system cannot work like that of the early days of this century, however, where unlimited discretion was typical. This approach requires departments to develop (in consultation with the prosecution function) a set of policy guidelines on the appropriate use of such methods. It also suggests that crime prevention will result from the application of carefully-defined procedures for diversion. Patrol officers need to understand the theory behind this approach.

Social Control

A final social level theoretical approach attempts to pull all of these diverse perspectives together. **Social control** theory suggests that internal controls (learned values) and restraining controls from other significant influences (family, peers, etc.) dramatically influence behavior. A breakdown of the appropriate controls is caused by, among other things, surrounding culture and life experiences.

Socialization is the process by which we learn the norms of society. The family, as the primary socializing agent of good effect, is central to developing internal restraints in individuals (also see social control discussions in Chapter 1). The breakdown of families makes this more difficult to achieve, though not impossible. Similarly, the breakdown of traditional neighborhoods reduces the reinforcing effects of other socializing agents such as extended families, schools, neighbors, and social organizations. Gangs play a role in replacing all of these missing agents of socialization.

This approach was echoed in one effort to create a general theory of crime (Gottfredson and Hirschi 1990). The authors of this theory argue that the absence of self-control (internal control) and the presence of opportunity account for most criminal behavior that is either violent or theft-related. In this view, people with low self-control are likely to commit antisocial behavior given the opportunity. Self-control, in this theory, is developed early in childhood from all of the contacts with which children interact. This theory may seem abstract and unrelated to the day-to-day activities on the streets and in the station houses, but closer examination may yield some benefits for law enforcement organizations. Other similar efforts to develop a general theory of crime attempt to integrate multiple theories, but are complex enough to justify exploration in a course devoted to criminology (Braithwaite 1989; Tittle 1995).

Because young males produce much of the serious crime in the United States, a focus on youth is important. Preschool care for children, schools in general, sports (both scholastic and community organized), and family units are important socializing agents. In a similar fashion, the neighborhood is a powerful influence. By looking at these particular socializing agents, some general approaches for addressing the problem of crime can be sketched. For law enforcement officers specifically, this theory offers some obvious strategies that deviate from the reactive response model typical to law enforcement until recently.

Volatile patterns of youth crime make crime predictions difficult. For example, Cook and Laub (1998) note that homicide arrests for youth in the 10–17-year age range peaked in 1993, but by 1995 they had declined by 23%. Still, they argue, it is generally true that youth arrests in 1994 for violent crime were about the average for the previous 30 years (Cook and Laub 1998), and so the notion that there has been an epidemic of youth crime is not borne out by the evidence. Still, it is true that violent and property crime is committed disproportionately by young males, and this pattern is one that continues (see **Figure 10-8**) (Miethe and McCorkle 1998).

The evidence is clear that most juvenile offenders will stop offending relatively early in their lives; therefore, law enforcement officers should not look at youthful offenders

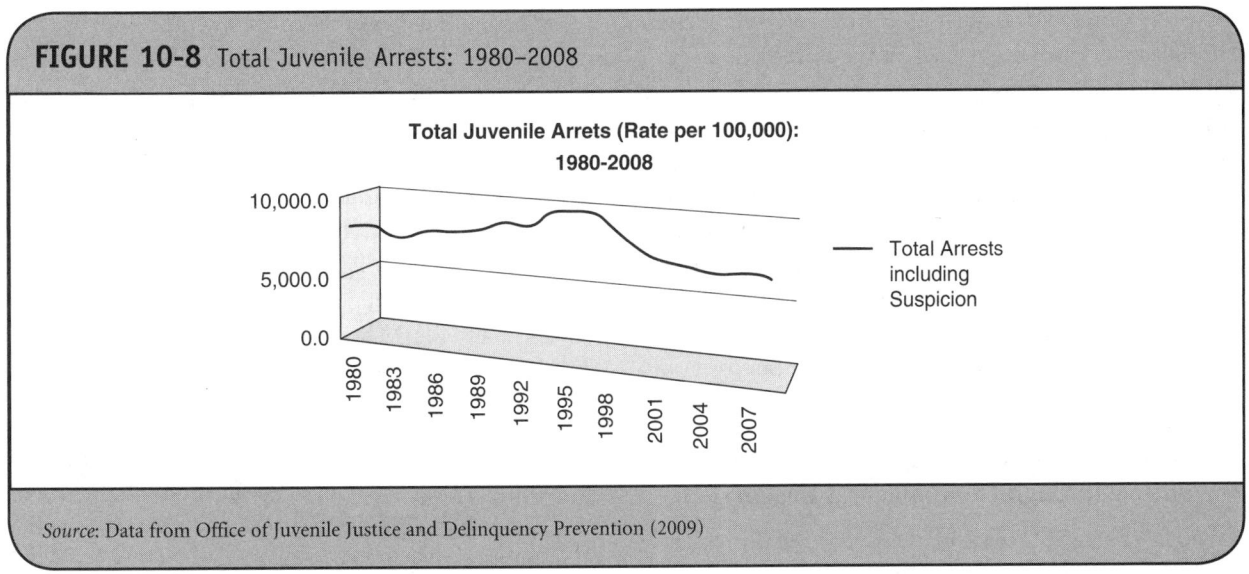

FIGURE 10-8 Total Juvenile Arrests: 1980–2008

Total Juvenile Arrets (Rate per 100,000):
1980-2008

Total Arrests including Suspicion

Source: Data from Office of Juvenile Justice and Delinquency Prevention (2009)

as lifetime troublemakers. Rather, officers should see them as people who are capable of being properly directed. This does not mean going easy on offenders. On the contrary, it means paying close attention, but with the approach that help is being offered. Officers must show offenders that they do care about them as people. No one says this is easy or enjoyable, but one can be tough with offenders and still offer the human touch that may be, and most likely is, missing in their lives. Stopping by their homes, talking to friends and families, going out of the way to find work, or assisting programs to redirect the energies of offenders are all means to the same end: crime prevention. These approaches are also part of community policing. The community is not merely juveniles who are in school, or citizens who have not violated the law; the community is everyone.

Patrol officers must understand that they are the closest and most important law enforcement contacts with the community. They represent, in most respects, not just law enforcement, but the government and society in general. Messages sent by patrol officers are sent on behalf of the whole society. Patrol officers, therefore, are central to the prevention of crime by finding ways to draw young offenders away from offending patterns. This may be by arrest, patrol, and inquiry, or intervention in the schools,

neighborhoods, or families. Patrol officers are the key to successful crime prevention and law enforcement. As Robert Sampson and John Laub argue in their life course theory, youth lives follow certain trajectories, and during that path experience good and bad events. The support of their environment, family, neighborhood, and peers will dictate how they respond and in what direction they may travel next. In short, how we assist youth who experience negative events is associated with future offending patterns (1993).

ENVIRONMENTAL, SITUATIONAL, OPPORTUNITY, AND ROUTINE ACTIVITIES APPROACHES

The first environmental approach we should examine is part theory and part strategy. **Crime prevention through environmental design** (**CPTED**) submits that the physical environment is important in understanding criminal behavior. C. Ray Jeffrey (1971) and Oscar Newman (1972) are both credited with outlining the foundational work in this arena (although the notion of physical design and human behavior is by no means a new concept, nor was it pioneered by Newman or Jeffrey). Look around your world. How many physical design aspects do you think exist to intentionally manipulate your behavior?

In grocery stores, why is the milk (a frequently-purchased item) always located at the back of the store? Is it so you will have to walk through the store and pass lots of other items that might look tempting to you? Even the classrooms at the college campus you attend are designed with behavior in mind. How are they similar? How are they different? How are the seats arranged? Are they arranged around a focal point (where the professor stands to deliver a lecture) or in a circle (where students and the professor face one another at eye level and have an academic conversation)? The design of physical space can foster or impede desirable (or undesirable) behaviors.

Newman's Defensible Space and Crime Prevention Through Environmental Design

Newman's **defensible space** model, developed through his research on public housing projects, argues that physical space can be structured in a way that fosters and reinforces a social structure that defends itself. Newman proposed that crime could be reduced in public housing projects if tenants assumed greater responsibility for public areas, thereby increasing "natural surveillance" (which in theory increased the risks of being observed or caught during the commission of a crime). Newman identified four key elements to defensible space, including territoriality, natural surveillance, image, and milieu. *Territoriality* refers to the ability of residents and other legitimate users of an area to frequently use and to protect the space from nonlegitimate (and possibly criminal) users. *Natural surveillance* is the ability for legitimate users to observe the behaviors of people utilizing a space. In theory, this allows residents to assist law enforcement by being the "eyes and ears" of police and by possibly intervening (calling police, assisting victims, etc.) when necessary. *Image* refers to not just the appearance of the neighborhood (giving cues that the neighborhood is well-cared for), but also the underlying notion that the neighborhood is connected and cohesive. Last, *milieu* involves placing an area within a larger community or physical space that remains free of criminal activity and is a "defensible space."

Newman concluded that defensible space could be achieved (and thus crime reduced) in public housing projects by increasing observation via installing doors and windows in key places, installing better lighting, and creating common areas that residents could both use and control. Subsequent research of Newman's work has been mixed, with some research supporting the relationship between increased defensible space and reduced crime (Repetto 1974; Wilson 1978) and other research suggesting the relationship is weak or spurious (Taylor et al. 1985) or that other variables are more important (Merry 1981) than physical design.

Crowe (2000) outlines the assessment of CPTED with what he calls the "Three-D approach." Essentially, the Three-D approach is based on the notion that human space is designed to fulfill three functions (Crowe, 2000, p. 39):

1. All human space has some designated purpose.
2. All human space has social, cultural, legal, or physical definitions that prescribe the desired and accepted behaviors.
3. All human space is designed to support and control the desired behaviors.

Crowe's Three-D approach argues that spaces that are *designated* with a specific goal in mind, well *defined*, and *designed* appropriately for the purposes for which they were intended are least likely to experience crime or other socially undesirable behaviors.

The Environment, Opportunity, and Rational Choice

One could argue the cornerstone for all criminal behavior is opportunity. Opportunity is a key concept in understanding crime and in developing strategies to reduce crime and prevent victimization. Opportunities are highly specific, tend to cluster in time and space, and are dependent on individual patterns. They are also impacted by social and technological changes and the good news is that they can often be easily interrupted. Felson and Clarke (1998) describe 10 principles of crime opportunity theory, which are paraphrased as the following:

1. The opportunity itself is the initial reason for a crime to take place.
2. These opportunities are very specific.
3. Crime opportunities are very much related to its time and space.
4. Everyday movement presents opportunity for crime.

5. Crime produces further opportunities for more crime.

6. Opportunities are enhanced by valuable products, making them more tempting to have.

7. Social and technological changes provide new opportunities for crime.

8. It is believed that if we reduce these opportunities, we can reduce crime.

9. Reducing opportunity does not displace crime.

10. Focused opportunity reduction reduces crime on a bigger scale.

The theoretical approaches framing these 10 principles of opportunity include the rational choice, routine activities, and crime pattern theories.

Rational Choice

The roots of rational choice perspectives can be traced back to the classical school of criminology (discussed earlier in this chapter). The major premise of rational choice theory is that offenders choose to commit crime based on their perceptions of risk and reward. Essentially, criminals make decisions based on what is best for them at the time, seeking pleasure and avoiding pain.

Recent rational choice approaches include perceived effort and rewards and likely consequences (such as both the likelihood and severity of punishment) in offender decision-making models. (Cornish & Clarke, 1986; 2003) In addition, modern rational choice theorists identify multiple factors in offender decision-making including time constraints, cognitive ability, and available information. These theorists argue that decision-making must be examined from a crime-specific focus. Cao (2004) suggests that opportunity, provocation, varying levels of rationality, variable motives, differing analysis abilities, and different skill levels (among other variables) all need to be accounted for in understanding offender decision-making.

Routine Activities Theory suggests that much violence and property crime is the result of an interaction between motivated offenders, attractive targets, and levels of guardianship (Cohen and Felson 1979). Implications of this theory for law enforcement are significant. Guardianship can be conceived of in many ways; however, in its most broad conception, it would involve neighborhood groups providing surveillance, target-hardening efforts to make property less attractive (e.g., window locks), and police–community interactions to provide other means to increase guardianship and reduce target availability. In theory, community interventions should be able to succeed in reducing some patterns of crime. This theory has many critics (including your authors) and has not successfully been supported by research (Miethe and McCorkle 1998). Like all theories, however, it is important to test the theory against the real world in order to improve our understanding of human behavior as it relates to crime and, in doing so, revise our theories to give policy better direction. Law enforcement is essential in this effort. At the same time, situational crime prevention, which suggests focusing on particular conditions or environments, does seem to work, if by working we mean reducing offending without displacing offending to another location (Felson 2002; Rosenbaum et al. 1998). On the other hand, research has called into question the viability of community policing as a one-size-fits-all answer to crime prevention (Skogan 2004).

Crime Pattern Theory

Crime pattern theory combines rational choice perspectives, routine activities theory, and environmental factors to provide a comprehensive explanation of crime that includes victims, offenders, and location (Brantingham & Brantingham 1981; 1984; 1993). In crime pattern theory, individuals have both activity spaces and awareness spaces. A person's *awareness space* is comprised of those areas he is familiar with, which is usually derived from the individual's activity space. An individual's *activity space* is comprised of various *nodes* of activity, or locations that represent where people live, work, and play. The routes people (victims and offenders) take to travel back and forth from these nodes are called *paths*. *Edges* are those areas on the periphery (both physical and perceptual) of an activity space. These edge areas are excellent places for criminals to offend because the level of "diversity" encountered here (in people from both sides of the edge and their activities) limits the surveillance capabilities of potential guardians. This is an important concept for patrol officers to understand as they patrol different communities that border one another within their larger jurisdictions.

Lifestyle Exposure Approaches

Lifestyle exposure theory approaches emphasize victim behavior as an important variable in a criminal event. As such, victims play a role in their victimization in their own decisions and behaviors that make opportunities more attractive for motivated offenders. Along these lines, lifestyle approaches suggest that the reason that victimization risks are higher for some and not others is because of the movements and activities associated with various factors. One's gender, age, race, profession, hobbies, and generally speaking, lifestyle, can put them at higher risk for different types of victimization. Engaging in non-legitimate activities can also place some persons at higher risks of victimization; for example, prostitutes, drug addicts, and gang members have very high rates of victimization compared to the rest of the population.

Lifestyle approaches help us understand why some people are victimized at greater frequency than others. They also provide valuable cues about which people are at highest risk of being victimized, allowing law enforcement officials to implement proactive measures aimed at reducing and preventing crime.

Understanding the causes of crime—individual, social, and environmental—helps policymakers develop more effective strategies and solutions to reduce crime and prevent victimization. Law enforcement officials need to be aware of the many causal factors involved in order to solve crime related problems. Crime is a complex problem, requiring complicated solutions. The various environmental, situational, and opportunity perspectives to crime causation also infer crime prevention activities—which many officers will be questioned about by their community members.

EMERGING ISSUES IN CRIME CAUSATION

Drugs

Surely one of the most significant changes in crime in the United States during the past few decades has been related to the use, importation, sale, and manufacture of drugs. While general discussion in the nation focused on the relationship between drugs and crime, those either working in the field or studying the subject examined the complex impact that drugs seemed to have on society. It must be noted that there are several different kinds of drugs in ready supply, each of which differs in physical effects, profit potential, ease of transport, sources, and demand. Complicating this is the way in which a legal drug, alcohol, impacts crime and general drug use.

A good place to start is by looking at the usage of drugs. By far the most widely used drugs are alcohol, marijuana, and cocaine (crack form or crystal powder form). Data consistently show that drug use is high among those arrested for criminal offenses, running as high as 50% on average (see **Table 10-10**). The rate of drug use depends on the age and gender of the offender, as well as location and nature of the offense. A study indicates that between 56% and 82% of booked arrestees test positive for one or more illicit drugs (Office of National Drug Control Policy 2010b). Incidence of drug use is closely linked with incidence of violent crime, although drugs are not necessarily a cause of that violence (U.S. Department of Justice 1992). It is just as likely that both violence and drug use are related to a set of conditions that are the core causative agents for both.

Interestingly, drug use rates have declined in the 1990s, except for marijuana use, which increased from 1992 to 1996 after a sharp decline from high levels of usage in the mid-1980s (Walker 1998). Recent research suggests drug use, in general, for young people have continued to decline (Sourcebook of Criminal Justice Statistics Online 2010). The rates among the young are particularly important, as early use is generally highly related to their likelihood to be involved in crime. Because the rate of drug use among youth seems to be declining and young people commit the most offenses, it is no surprise that crime rates are declining slightly (see **Table 10-11**). However, as was noted earlier, violent crime increased during the same time period that drug use was declining, thereby suggesting that overall drug use is not a primary cause of most violent crime (if by "cause" we mean doing drugs produces criminals). It is more reasonable to observe that doing drugs conditionally adds to the probability of criminal activity. Over the long term, drug use has remained relatively stable, as has that of alcohol, and has not fluctuated as widely as crime rates. This suggests a more conditional relationship.

Still, the increase in the rate of violent crime in the 1980s more or less coincides with the appearance of crack cocaine (see **Table 10-12**). This drug is easy to manufacture and transport and offers a large profit margin.

TABLE 10-10 Reported Drug Use by Convicted Prison and Jail Inmates, 1997 and 2004

Percent of State Prisoners who used drugs				
	In the month before offense		At the time of offense	
Type of drug	2004	1997	2004	1997
Any drug	56.0%	56.5%	32.1%	32.6%
Marijuana/hashish	40.3	39.2	15.4	15.1
Cocaine/crack	21.4	25.0	11.8	14.8
Heroin/opiates	8.2	9.2	4.4	5.6
Depressants	5.4	5.1	2.0	1.8
Stimulants	12.2	9.0	6.7	4.2
Methamphetamine	10.8	6.9	6.1	3.5
Hallucinogens	5.9	4.0	2.0	1.8
Inhalants	1.0	1.0	—	—
Percent of Federal Prisoners who used drugs				
	In the month before offense		At the time of offense	
Type of drug	2004	1997	2004	1997
Any Drug	50.2%	44.8%	26.4%	22.4%
Marijuana/hashish	36.2	30.4	14.0	10.8
Cocaine/crack	18.0	20.0	7.4	9.3
Heroin/opiates	5.8	5.4	3.2	3.0
Depressants	4.4	3.2	1.4	1.0
Stimulants	10.8	7.6	7.4	4.1
Methamphetamine	10.1	6.5	7.2	3.7
Hallucinogens	5.8	1.7	1.9	0.8
Inhalants	0.8	0.5	—	—

Source: Mumola and Karberg. (2006).

However, there seems to be a declining market for this and other drugs. The result appears to be a concentrated market in which violence is both a product of the use of the drug and of competition over "turf" to sell the drug. While general use declines, use and sales become more concentrated in the central city. Much of the increase in violence may therefore be specifically related to the crack market, and while there is widespread belief about this, there is insufficient evidence to be certain. Citing an Office of National Drug Control Policy (ONDCP) Fact Sheet (2010b), drug trends of concern to law enforcement include (but by no means is this an exhaustive list):

- Compared to other causes of preventable deaths, drug-induced causes exceeded the 31,224 deaths from injuries due to firearms and the 23,199 alcohol-induced deaths recorded in 2007. In the same year, 34,598 deaths were classified as suicides and 18,361 deaths as homicides.

TABLE 10-11 Percent of Inmates Who Committed Their Offenses for Money to Buy Drugs

Percent of Prisoners Who Committed Offense to Get Money for Drugs, 2004

Most Serious Offense	State	Federal
Total*	16.6%	18.4%
Violent	9.8	14.8
Property	30.3	10.6
Drug	26.4	25.3
Public Order	6.9	6.8

*Includes Offenses not Shown

Source: Mumola and Karberg. (2006).

- Data from a national roadside survey in 2007 indicate that one in eight (12.4%) of weekend nighttime drivers tested positive for at least one illicit drug.
- Based on a self-report survey in 2009, approximately 10.5 million Americans reported driving under the influence of an illicit drug during the past year.
- In 2009, one in three drivers killed in motor vehicle crashes, who were tested for drugs and the results known, tested positive for at least one medication or illicit drug.
- Among high school seniors in 2008, one in 10 (10.4%) reported that in the two weeks prior to their interview, they had driven a vehicle after smoking marijuana.
- The economic cost of drug abuse in the United States was estimated at $180.9 billion in 2002, the last available estimate. This value represents both the use of resources to address health and crime consequences, as well as the loss of potential productivity from disability, premature death, and withdrawal from the legitimate workforce.
- In 2009, 23.5 million persons aged 12 or older needed treatment for an illicit drug or alcohol use problem (9.3% of persons in that age group).

Of these, 7.1 million persons needed treatment for illicit drug problems, with or without alcohol.

- There are significant environmental impacts from clandestine methamphetamine drug labs, including chemical toxicity, risk of fire and explosion, lingering effects of toxic waste, and potential injuries. The number of domestic meth lab incidents, which includes dumpsites, active labs, and chemical/glassware set-ups, dropped dramatically in response to the Combat Meth Epidemic Act (CMEA) of 2005, from nearly 13,000 in 2005 to just over 6000 in 2007. However, traffickers are devising methods to avoid the CMEA restrictions and domestic meth lab incidents are rising again, reaching 9800 in 2009.
- Mexican drug trafficking organizations have been operating on public lands in the United States to cultivate marijuana, with serious consequences for the environment and public safety.

During the last two decades, some proposals for decriminalizing certain drugs and ending the "war on drugs" have been suggested for the United States. We have seen an increase in the number of states adopting medical marijuana laws, but California did vote down a proposal in 2010 to legalize marijuana (and to tax and regulate it). It is unlikely that the current illegal drugs will be made legal soon, but there are more voices calling for transferring the addition problems to the health and rehabilitation arenas. The country of Portugal did this in the early 2000s and evaluations of this program have indicated some success. Drugs were kept illegal, but users are sent to counseling or treatment centers instead of criminal courts and prison. Some of the results since the law was changed include the following (Hatton and Mendoza 2010):

- Drug-related court cases dropped 66%;
- The number of people treated for drug addiction rose 20% from 2001 to 2008;
- There were small increases in illicit drug use among adults, but decreases for adolescents and problem users, such as drug addicts and prisoners; and
- The number of regular users held steady at less than 3% of the population for marijuana and less than 0.3% for heroin and cocaine—figures which show decriminalization brought no surge in drug use.

TABLE 10-12 Drug-Related Homicides

Year	Number of homicides	Percent drug-related
1986	19,257	3.9%
1987	17,963	4.9
1988	17,971	5.6
1989	18,954	7.4
1990	20,273	6.7
1991	21,676	6.2
1992	22,716	5.7
1993	23,180	5.5
1994	22,084	5.6
1995	20,232	5.1
1996	16,967	5.0
1997	15,837	5.1
1998	14,276	4.8
1999	13,011	4.5
2000	13,230	4.5
2001	14,061	4.1
2002	14,263	4.7
2003	14,408	4.6

Source: Reprinted from Bureau of Justice Statistics. Drugs and Crime Facts (2004), Washington, D.C.: U.S. Department of Justice. Available online: http://www.ojp.usdoj.gov/bjs/dcf/duc/htm.

As you can see, the relationship between crime and drugs, with all its complexity, is not going anywhere anytime soon.

Hate Crimes

Because it is difficult to determine if a crime was motivated by racial, religious, ethnic, or gender status hatred, there is very little data on the subject of hate crimes. However, the impression of most people in law enforcement is that crimes motivated by such attitudes are, in fact, on the increase. Hate crimes pose a particular problem for law enforcement since they tend to be random and spontaneous crimes, thereby leaving few traces of evidence from which to proceed.

Enforcement is made more difficult by the fact that merely saying hateful things or making hateful signs is insufficient to overcome the constitutional protection of free speech. In 1992, the United States Supreme Court declared a municipal ordinance, which made it a crime to convey hateful messages, unconstitutional (see **Figure 10-9**). The ordinance in question made the content of the message illegal, and the court refused to permit this infringement of what it called "protected speech" (*RAV v. St. Paul*, 505 U.S. 377). This leaves very little room for the prosecution of hate crimes by other than traditional means: prosecuting the action (assault, arson, criminal damaging, etc.). This issue will no doubt occupy a good deal of litigation as we define what the limits might be for language that is not protected, but rather, "fighting words" that can be prosecuted. In April 1990, Congress passed the Hate Crime Statistics Act and mandated the collection of data on crimes motivated by religious, ethnic, racial, or sexual-orientation prejudices.

In September 1994, the Hate Crime Statistics Act was amended to include bias against persons with disabilities (through the passing of the Violent Crime Control and Law Enforcement Act of 1994). The first publication on the subject (by the Uniform Crime Reporting Program) was *Hate Crime Statistics, 1990: A Resource Book.* In 2009, Congress passed the Matthew Shepard and James Bird, Jr. Hate Crime Prevention Act (named for two victims of hate crimes: Matthew Shepard, a gay college student murdered in Wyoming and James Byrd, an African-American man murdered in Texas) amending the Hate Crime Statistics Act to include the collection of data for crimes motivated by bias against a particular gender/gender identity and crimes against juveniles.

In 2009, Hate Crime Statistics indicate approximately 6604 hate crime incidents involving 7789 offenses (with 2034 law enforcement agencies reporting). Of these:

- 49.1 % of the offenses were motivated by racial bias
- 18.5% stemmed from sexual-orientation bias
- 17.7% were linked to religious bias
- 13.5% involved ethnicity/national origin bias
- 1.2% were motivated by disability bias

Of these offenses, 61.5% were crimes against persons and 38.1% were crimes against property. The majority of the

FIGURE 10-9 RAV v. St. Paul, 505 U.S. 377 (1992)

Decided June 22, 1992

JUSTICE SCALIA delivered the opinion of the Court.

In the predawn hours of June 21, 1990, petitioner and several other teenagers allegedly assembled a crudely made cross by taping together broken chair legs. They then allegedly burned the cross inside the fenced yard of a black family that lived across the street from the house where petitioner was staying. Although this conduct could have been punished under any of a number of laws, [fn1] one of the two provisions under which respondent city of St. Paul chose to charge petitioner (then a juvenile) was the St. Paul Bias-Motivated Crime Ordinance, St. Paul, Minn. Legis.Code § 292.02 (1990), which provides:

Whoever places on public or private property a symbol, object, appellation, characterization or graffiti, including, but not limited to, a burning cross or Nazi swastika, which one knows or has reasonable grounds to know arouses anger, alarm or resentment in others on the basis of race, color, creed, religion or gender commits disorderly conduct and shall be guilty of a misdemeanor.

...(W)e conclude that, even as narrowly construed by the Minnesota Supreme Court, the ordinance is facially unconstitutional. Although the phrase in the ordinance, "arouses anger, alarm or resentment in others," has been limited by the Minnesota Supreme Court's construction to reach only those symbols or displays that amount to "fighting words," the remaining, unmodified terms make clear that the ordinance applies only to "fighting words" that insult, or provoke violence, "on the basis of race, color, creed, religion or gender." Displays containing abusive invective, no matter how vicious or severe, are permissible unless they are addressed to one of the specified disfavored topics. Those who wish to use "fighting words" in connection with other idea— to express hostility, for example, on the basis of political affiliation, union membership, or homosexuality— are not covered. The First Amendment does not permit St. Paul to impose special prohibitions on those speakers who express views on disfavored subjects.

In its practical operation, moreover, the ordinance goes even beyond mere content discrimination to actual viewpoint discrimination. Displays containing some words—odious racial epithets, for example—would be prohibited to proponents of all views. But "fighting words" that do not themselves invoke race, color, creed, religion, or gender—aspersions upon a person's mother, for example—would seemingly be usable ad libitum in the placards of those arguing in favor of racial, color, etc. tolerance and equality, but could not be used by that speaker's opponents. One could hold up a sign saying, for example, that all "anti-Catholic bigots" are misbegotten; but not that all "papists" are, for that would insult and provoke violence "on the basis of religion." St. Paul has no such authority to license one side of a debate to fight freestyle, while requiring the other to follow Marquis of Queensbury Rules.

One must wholeheartedly agree with the Minnesota Supreme Court that "[i]t is the responsibility, even the obligation, of diverse communities to confront such notions in whatever form they appear," ibid., but the manner of that confrontation cannot consist of selective limitations upon speech. St. Paul's brief asserts that a general "fighting words" law would not meet the city's needs, because only a content-specific measure can communicate to minority groups that the "group hatred" aspect of such speech "is not condoned by the majority." The point of the First Amendment is that majority preferences must be expressed in some fashion other than silencing speech on the basis of its content.

. . . (T)he reason why fighting words are categorically excluded from the protection of the First Amendment is not that their content communicates any particular idea, but that their content embodies a particularly intolerable (and socially unnecessary) mode of expressing whatever idea the speaker wishes to convey. St. Paul has not singled out an especially offensive mode of expression. Rather, it has proscribed fighting words of whatever manner that communicate messages of racial, gender, or religious intolerance. Selectivity of this sort creates the possibility that the city is seeking to handicap the expression of particular ideas.

Let there be no mistake about our belief that burning a cross in someone's front yard is reprehensible. But St. Paul has sufficient means at its disposal to prevent such behavior without adding the First Amendment to the fire.

The judgment of the Minnesota Supreme Court is reversed, and the case is remanded for proceedings not inconsistent with this opinion.

It is so ordered.

Source: U.S. Supreme Court

crimes against persons were intimidation crimes (45%) followed by assaults (35.3%) and aggravated assaults (19.1%). Eight murders and nine forcible rapes were reported as hate crimes in 2009. When examining bias-motivated property crimes (which were primarily acts of destruction, damage, or vandalism), 48.5% were committed against individuals, 11.5% against businesses, 9.8% against the government, and 8.0% were directed towards religious organizations (Federal Bureau of Investigation 2010c).

In most respects, the causes of these sorts of crimes are also found in the socialization of the perpetrators and vary across jurisdictions. For example, New York City saw a 14% increase in hate crimes for 2009 increasing, from 599 in 2008 to 683. Religious attacks, primarily on Jewish and Muslim persons and institutions, saw an increase, as did anti-gay hate crimes. Anti-black crimes were down slightly (Dicker 2010). It is important for police officers to be aware of what the trends are for their own communities. This type of crime can be reduced by proper education and socialization of children in the community. Law enforcement can play a key role in educating the community about these crimes and the damage they do to not only individuals, but communities as well.

Computer Crime

One area of crime for which data are virtually nonexistent is computer crime. Once the domain of only federal law enforcement concerns, this complex and virtually transparent crime is now the concern of local enforcement. Computer crime is discussed in depth in Chapter 11 (especially technology-enhanced and high-tech crimes) so we won't spend a lot of time here on the subject, but a review of some headlines illustrates the magnitude and range of the problem:

- Computer Specialist Pleads Guilty to Securities Fraud Committed through Hacking, Botnets, Spam and Market Manipulation (October 20, 2010)
- Nigerian National Sentenced to 102 Months in Prison for Role in Airline Ticket Scam (October 22, 2010)
- Virginia Information Technology Director Sentenced to 27 Months in Prison for Hacking Former Employer's Website (October 29, 2010)

- Tennessee Man Sentenced for Illegally Accessing Former Governor Sarah Palin's E-mail Account and Obstruction of Justice (November 12, 2010)
- Former Students Indicted for Computer Hacking at University of Central Missouri (November 22, 2010)
- Federal Courts Order Seizure of 82 Website Domains Involved in Selling Counterfeit Goods As Part of DOJ and ICE Cyber Monday Crackdown (November 29, 2010)
- Russian Man Charged with Sending Thousands of Spam Emails (December 3, 2010)
- Georgia Man Pleads Guilty to Participating in International Child Pornography Ring Dismantled by International Law Enforcement Effort: Five of 16 Defendants Charged in United States Have Now Pleaded Guilty for Roles in "Lost Boy" Child Pornography Ring (December 14, 2010)
- Blaine Man Stops Trial to Plead Guilty to Hacking into Neighbor's Internet System to Email Threats against the Vice President (December 17, 2010)

The proliferation of thousands of Web sites has opened avenues for illegal distribution of pornography, anonymous messages related to drug deals, and theft of software and other intellectual property (including company trade secrets). These crimes are in addition to embezzlement, illegal fund transfers, data alteration, and simple extensions of existing crime syndicates.

There is limited national accounting of such crime, and the number of unreported (and undiscovered) events is no doubt very large. Accurate figures are difficult to obtain, as businesses choose not to report them. The National Computer Security Survey (NCSS), developed by the Department of Justice, is the nation's first serious attempt to collect more information about cybercrime (Bureau of Justice Statistics 2008). While many might think that law enforcement agencies must react by creating special units to deal with such computer crime, for most departments this is not an option. Instead, it is clear that law enforcement as a whole must become computer literate quickly. There are already substantial resources at the command of law enforcement for information retrieval about suspects, criminal histories, and fingerprints (see Chapter 11).

The causes of this form of crime seem to be rooted in two areas. The traditional causes, such as greed or anger (related to the social control models and socialization), are certainly one realm. However, there is also a new characteristic not common in any crime committing group. Some computer-based crime is committed by highly-capable specialists who commit the offenses solely as a test of their skills. Those who engage in such criminal invasions of computers via phone lines or Internet connections are commonly referred to in the media as **hackers**, and they commit computer crimes as a means to prove their abilities.

Between the years 2000 and 2004, the number of viral attacks on the Web increased by an astounding 300%. In 2005, 7818 businesses responding to a National Computer Security Survey reported over 22 million incidents of cybercrime. The overwhelming majority of these incidents (20 million) were classified as computer security incidents including spyware, adware, phishing, and spoofing (Bureau of Justice Statistics 2008). The appearance of other forms of malicious software, often called malware, also increased in that period of time. Malware comes in many forms. Unlike most viral infections on computers, which seek to destroy data or render your system inoperable, these are small programs that may be tracking cookies that report your Web behavior to another Web site, report your email address book contents to someone else, or prevent some programs from working properly. A number of free solutions to these sorts of parasites are available on the Web. Another form of computer crime has been the appearance of denial of service, or DOS, attacks. This occurs when a Web site is flooded with computer-generated "hits," causing the Web server to crash. Another computer crime involves cyber bullying and cyber-stalking. Cyber bullying is typically perpetrated by school-aged people, but this is not always the case. Finally, another emerging problem is child pornography on the Web, and adults luring children into meeting them someplace through Internet chat rooms. Small law enforcement agencies are not equipped to handle these and related problems, but state police, the FBI, and groups of agencies pooling their resources can reduce the problem. For example, setting up dummy Web sites to lure perpetrators, or pretending to be a teenager in Web chats to lure offenders into capture, have been effective.

Gangs

An area of increasing concern to law enforcement is the continuing influence of youth and street gangs. The impression of most people in and out of law enforcement is that gangs are becoming more prevalent, more violent, and more involved in drugs. Research on gangs is relatively substantial, but one major problem that hampers good policy research is the definition of a gang: There is no generally accepted definition from which research, whether government or private, has proceeded. The result is a wide variation in definitions (Ball and Curry 1995; Winfree et al. 1992).

However, we can say that gangs seem to operate in the manner suggested earlier, as a social mechanism that replaces lost or dysfunctional family and community structures. As such, there is a long history, because we can find references to gang activity in England as early as the 1600s, or earlier, should we choose to include the legend of Robin Hood. A reading of the Charles Dickens classic *Oliver Twist,* for example, details the exploits of Oliver Twist as a member of a young gang of orphaned thieves in 19th-century London.

This evidence of a long-term presence of gangs is useful because it seems that gangs appear to grow more active during times of social upheavals and instability. The evidence suggests that there is a wide variation of gang activity in the United States over the past 30 years; it has not been constant and seems to vary according to the year and the region. Overall, there is no real evidence of an increase in gang size or participation. In many specific areas, however, gang activity has reached the critical stage. These suggestions contradict the commonly held view that gangs are rampant everywhere; part of this seeming contradiction is the difference between the highly-organized gang and mere delinquent groups (so-called "wannabe" groups).

We do know that those who engage in gang membership tend to have a much higher rate of offending and much higher rates of violence than do non-gang members (Esbensen and Huizinga 1993). As a general rule, it is clear that gang member crime patterns are more violent now than at any time in the past, but they are not consistent. However, this behavior does not persist if the member leaves a gang, which suggests the strong social influence of the group (Spergel 1990). For example, in Los Angeles, 25.2% of the murders in 1987 were gang-related, but in Chicago in the same year, only 6.9% were related to gangs. Moreover, despite contrary public views, there is no strong, clear relationship between gangs, drug use, drug sales, and the commission of violent crimes (Klein, Maxson, and Cunningham 1991).

While the growth of crack sales in the 1980s was quite significant, street gang member involvement was low both in New York and Los Angeles. Gang members did not play a predominant role in crack distribution, nor did they seem to elevate the level of violence and organization related to distribution (Thornberry et al. 1993). The sharp rise in 1993 of crack-related shootings in cities altered this perception, but there is no reason to believe that this level of violence will persist or that it is related to gang activity, as opposed to temporary groups of delinquents. Key findings from the most recent National Gang Threat Assessment report (National Gang Intelligence Center 2009, iii) include the following:

- Approximately 1 million gang members belonging to more than 20,000 gangs were criminally active within all 50 states and the District of Columbia as of September 2008.
- Local street gangs, or neighborhood-based street gangs, remain a significant threat because they continue to account for the largest number of gangs nationwide. Most engage in violence in conjunction with a variety of crimes, including retail-level drug distribution.
- According to National Drug Threat Survey data, 58% of state and local law enforcement agencies reported that criminal gangs were active in their jurisdictions in 2008, compared with 45% of state and local agencies in 2004.
- Gang members are migrating from urban areas to suburban and rural communities, expanding the gangs' influence in most regions; they are doing so for a variety of reasons, including expanding drug distribution territories, increasing illicit revenue,

recruiting new members, hiding from law enforcement, and escaping other gangs. Many suburban and rural communities are experiencing increasing gang-related crime and violence because of expanding gang influence.
- Criminal gangs commit as much as 80% of the crime in many communities, according to law enforcement officials throughout the nation. Typical gang-related crimes include alien smuggling, armed robbery, assault, auto theft, drug trafficking, extortion, fraud, home invasions, identity theft, murder, and weapons trafficking.
- Gang members are the primary retail-level distributors of most illicit drugs. They also are increasingly distributing wholesale-level quantities of marijuana and cocaine in most urban and suburban communities.
- Some gangs traffic illicit drugs at the regional and national levels; several are capable of competing with U.S.-based Mexican Drug Trafficking Organizations.
- U.S.-based gang members illegally cross the United States–Mexico border for the express purpose of smuggling illicit drugs and illegal aliens from Mexico into the United States.
- Many gangs actively use the Internet to recruit new members and to communicate with members in other areas of the United States and in foreign countries.
- Street gangs and outlaw motorcycle gangs pose a growing threat to law enforcement along the United States–Canada border. They frequently associate with Canada-based gangs and criminal organizations.

For patrol officers, this evidence provides both useful and disturbing information. The increase in drive-by shootings suggests that extreme caution is needed regarding occupied vehicles. It also suggests that understanding the role of gang-related activity in a neighborhood is essential to understanding the community. In a way, gang activity becomes a barometer of the condition of the community; a perceived increase should send signals that the community itself is suffering. Community involvement and intervention plays a large role in controlling and reducing gang influence in a community that is declining and destabilizing. The fact that members of gangs who leave gangs will return to low levels of criminality offers incentive for officer involvement in community programs to reduce gang influence and provide alternatives for juveniles. The evidence is strong that gangs form when there are insufficient community and family structures to properly socialize young people.

Domestic Violence

While juvenile problems frequently relate to family problems, another family-centered problem of concern to law enforcement is the area of domestic violence. Sometimes referred to as spousal abuse, this arena has taken on a larger meaning as the number of households involving unmarried couples has grown. Moreover, because of the levels of violence surrounding couples who are separated or divorced, the concept must include even those loosely connected to another person in a way that suggests a spousal type of relationship. One effect of the O.J. Simpson trial was to refocus attention on spousal abuse between separated or divorced adults.

Estimates of spousal abuse range greatly, from 2.1 million to more than 8 million per year, and there is a lifetime probability, according to some studies, that 25–30% of all couples will experience a violent incident (Hirschel et al. 1992a). Women make up about 85% of victims, and men 15% (Bureau of Justice Statistics, 2006). Approximately 22% of the non-fatal violence against women involves intimate partner violence, compared to only 3% for men. In 2005, intimate partner violence accounted for 1181 female murder victims and 239 male murder victims nationwide. It is a generally accepted estimate that only about half of those who are abused will report an incident to the police, but for patrol officers it is important to understand that events that are likely to be reported are not typical of the events that occur. Victimization surveys demonstrated that those who do report events of violence are more likely to be poor and uneducated. Nonwhite, lower-income females are almost twice as likely to report an incident than other females. Moreover, the calls are more likely to involve more severe violence. As such, calls that are

made are not representative of all offenses that do occur (Hirschel et al. 1992a).

The traditional law enforcement response to such calls was to attempt to separate the parties and restore order; that approach changed when an experiment addressed alternate approaches. The Minneapolis experiment seemed to suggest that the arrest of the alleged offender was the most effective means of deterring subsequent events. The National Institute of Justice sought to conduct more controlled experiments of this approach to assess the effectiveness of arrest as a deterrent. The first two of these studies found that arrest may not be the most effective. Generally, three possible results were (1) arrest, (2) citation by the officer, or (3) separation and advice. In fact, there was no difference in the rate of **recidivism** (re-offending) regardless of which approach was used. Even more significant were findings from follow-up surveys that the true rates of re-offending were very high, though most subsequent violent events were not reported. Repeat incidents were the rule, not the exception, but were no less frequent for those arrested the first time (Hirschel et al. 1992b). Therefore, the actions of responding officers were not related to subsequent violence.

There could be many reasons for these results. In the one study, most of the offenders had criminal records and came from relationships in which abuse was common. Hence, it was likely to happen again, and a few hours in jail was not very significant to the outcome. Some studies suggest that as few as 10% of calls for domestic violence result in arrest despite the fact that as many as 50% of such cases have sufficient evidence for making arrests (Hirschel et al. 1992b). Because of the shortage of available jail and prison space, it is unlikely that priorities on incarceration will change in the near future. This may help explain, but not justify, the low arrest rate. Even if arrest does occur, past experience suggests few will be convicted unless the criminal justice system as a whole alters the manner in which domestic violence is addressed. In one study, only 35% of the cases produced a finding of guilty, and in only 1% of the cases was any jail time actually served (Gondolf and McFerron 1989). Clearly, research must continue in order to assist law enforcement and the courts in controlling and preventing domestic violence. Still, while there is no evidence that arrest prevents future events of violence, it may be inferred that arrest prevents escalation of current violence.

The evidence to date suggests some approaches for the patrol officer. First, it is likely that a domestic violence incident event is not the first such event in the household. Second, it is more likely to be a serious violent event. Third, a records check is in order where independent evidence of violence seems clear. Fourth, officers should assume that the likelihood of a subsequent offense is great and should endeavor to build trust with the victim in order to establish bridges rather than destroy communications. Fifth, examine the event in light of the neighborhood, and determine if there are any approaches that might be used to involve other services to interdict the situation. Last, a determination to arrest or not should be based upon the question of probable cause and legal authority to arrest, since there is no social science evidence that arrest does harm to the situation.

SUMMARY

Given the above discussion of theory and current crime trends, it is important to discuss how both theory and an understanding of crime influence the strategy employed by an agency and the overall approach implemented to reduce crime.

The challenge for police managers appears to be: How can the police respond effectively to the crime problem and calls for service within their jurisdiction and do it in such a way that they are sensitive to everyone's needs, responsive to victims, and protective of constitutional rights; that they instill trust, reduce fear, and encourage self-defense and community vigilance; and do it all cost-efficiently and without partisan-political interference? We do not mean to imply that this challenge is an impossible one. We merely are pointing out that policing does not occur in a vacuum and that many pressures and issues interact in the selection of an agency's role and the implementation of a policing strategy. Only when the public and all police officers fully understand these issues can a true dialogue and partnership in policing begin to blossom in a community.

An excellent example of innovative police strategy incorporating an understanding of crime statistics, theory, and partnerships between law enforcement and the

community is the High Point Intervention. Summarized by Kennedy (2009):

> A particular drug market is identified; violent dealers are arrested; and nonviolent dealers are brought to a "call-in" where they face a roomful of law enforcement officers, social service providers and "influentials"—parents, relatives and others with close, important relationships with particular dealers. The drug dealers are told that (1) they are valuable to the community, and (2) the dealing must stop. They are offered social services. They are informed that local law enforcement has worked up cases on them, but that these cases will be "banked" (temporarily suspended). Then they are given an ultimatum. If you continue to deal, the banked cases against you will be activated. (12–13)

According to Kennedy, the High Point Intervention has been replicated in at least 25 other cities, and the strategy has been successful in breaking up many drug markets which in most cases have not made a comeback. In High Point, both drug crimes and violent crimes have been drastically reduced in several areas of the city where the strategy was employed, areas that were previously characterized as "hot spots" of crime (Kennedy & Wong, 2009).

In this chapter, we examined many suggested causes of crime (**Figure 10-10** summarizes these). In nearly each case, the theories are based upon the conditions of the community (or environment) in which people live, grow, learn, and work. People's families (or lack thereof), relationships, and experiences all influence behavior, both criminal and noncriminal. Understanding the behavior of people is the key. It is related to determining who has committed an offense, as well as who might commit an offense, and what might be done to prevent future crime. Understanding begins by identifying the underlying causal forces of crime. This very cursory view is intended only as an introduction to the more detailed aspects of criminological theory.

Similarly, this chapter addressed several emerging areas in which particular types of crime pose significant challenges for law enforcement and for patrol officers in particular. Because we are only now learning about many of these kinds of problems in sufficient detail to

FIGURE 10-10 Causes of Crime—Summary

Individual causes
- Pleasure-pain principle
- Internal control deficiency
- Poor education
- Dysfunctional childhood

Social causes
- Ecological conditions
- Differential association and learning labeling
- Social control and socialization

Environmental and Opportunity Approaches
- Crime Prevention Through Environmental Design
- Environmental Opportunity and Rational Choice

Emerging possible causes
- Drugs
- Technological ease
- Discriminatory attitudes
- Gang organization
- Domestic dysfunction

address corrective approaches, the new patrol officer must commit himself or herself to learning about these as knowledge develops. They will form some of the most significant crime challenges of the next decade.

The relationship of role to the selection of a department's policing strategy was mentioned as an important factor in understanding the complexities of these issues.

Finally, the challenge for police appears on three fronts: providing effective service, responding to emerging crime problems, and improving ethical decision making within the ranks. What policing personnel must understand is that their responses to these challenges will determine the likelihood of acquiring respect and satisfaction from the communities they serve.

Critical Thinking Questions

1. What are the underlying problems with UCR data?

2. What are the advantages of NCVS and NIBRS data over UCR data?

3. Compare individual theories of crime to social theories of crime. Which theories offer us more direction in what law enforcement should do? Why?

4. What factors are included in offender decision-making models, according to modern day rational choice theorists? What environmental factors do offenders account for in their decision making?

5. According to routing activities theory, crime is most likely to occur when three criteria exist. Briefly explain these three criteria and provide an example of a crime that happened in your city/town where these three criteria converged.

6. Define, in one or two sentences, each of the major theories of crime.

7. What are the two primary motives of those who commit computer-based crime?

8. What is meant by "lost opportunity costs" of crime?

CHAPTER SPECIFIC INTERNET LINKS

CrimeSolutions.gov: http://www.crimesolutions.gov/

Bureau of Justice Statistics: http://bjs.ojp.usdoj.gov/

Sourcebook of Criminal Justice Statistics Online: http://www.albany.edu/sourcebook/

Federal Bureau of Investigation, Crime Statistics: http://www.fbi.gov/stats-services/crimestats

Crimetheory.com: http://www.crimetheory.com/

Department of Justice: Computer Crime and Intellectual Property Section: http://www.cybercrime.gov/ccpolicy.html

CHAPTER GLOSSARY

Associate—certain traits, norms, or behaviors are learned by close connections with others who act the same way.

Cause of crime—if one thing happens another will follow; in this sense, each theory of the cause of crime states that if the conditions outlined in the theory occur, crime will follow.

Chicago School—the group of theorists who believed that one's surroundings account for subsequent behavior.

Crime Pattern Theory—theory that argues that opportunities for crime exist within routine movements of both victims and offenders. Rational choice and routine activities theories are combined to explain that offenders, through the course of their daily routines, notice opportunities to commit crime (such as unguarded targets).

Crime prevention through environmental design (CPTED)—Crime prevention through environmental design examines the environment as a stimulus that potential offenders and victims respond to. Essentially, CPTED argues that we can reduce crime opportunities by changing the physical environment.

Defensible space—Areas characterized as having high levels of territoriality, natural surveillance, image, and milieu, and according to Newman (1972) are less likely to suffer from high crime rates.

Deterrence—a theory that suggests that people are rational and, if threatened with potential punishment for doing certain things, they will not commit the acts.

Differential association—a theory that holds that close contact with another culture will cause the subject to adopt that culture.

Drug Abuse Resistance Education (DARE)—a national educational program that places police officers in the elementary classrooms to teach children about drugs and the negative aspects of drug use.

Ecological School—see Chicago School.

Hackers—common title used by the media to refer to computer specialists who seek ways to get into other computers and bypass the security systems to test their skills.

Hot dot—(on a map) refers to an address that is responsible for several calls for service within a given time period.

Hot spot—a small geographic area that experiences higher-than-average levels of crime for a consistent period of time.

Index Crimes or **Crime Index**—the number of index crimes committed in each year per 100,000 population; the eight major crimes counted by the UCR.

Labeling—a theory that suggests that juveniles who are repeatedly described as delinquent will come to act in exactly that manner.

Learn—acquire norms or attitudes by observing others with whom there is some close connection.

Lifestyle Exposure Theory—a theoretical approach that suggests that a person's characteristics and lifestyle (age, gender, hobbies, profession, etc.) put them at varying risk for victimization.

Lost opportunity costs—money lost due to crime and which cannot be used for other, more beneficial things in society or individually.

National Crime Victimization Survey (NCVS)—a survey of thousands of households and businesses regarding victimization during the previous year; conducted for the Bureau of Justice Statistics (U.S. Department of Justice) by the Bureau of the Census.

National Incident Based Reporting System (NIBRS)—A component of the UCR, this reporting system collects incident level information on 22 different offense categories and arrest information on 11 different arrest categories.

Part 1 Offenses—see Index crimes.

Pleasure–pain principle—the central aspect of the utilitarian theory, which suggests that people act in ways that increase their pleasure and limit their pain.

Public policy—anything that the government chooses to do or to not do.

Rationalism—the school of thought associated with utilitarianism, which held that people make decisions after weighing the costs and benefits, choosing the course of action most likely to benefit them.

Recidivism—committing crimes after once being punished.

Routine Activities Theory—theory that suggests that the opportunity for crime is much greater when a motivated offender, suitable target, and lack of guardianship exist within the same time and space.

Social control—a theory which contends that family and other similar groups teach people internal controls (self-control) and exercise direct control over their behavior, thereby preventing antisocial actions.

Socialization—the process of learning one's culture.

Street level bureaucrats—term used to apply to government employees, including police, who make street level decisions that affect people's lives.

Subculture—a set of norms and beliefs that are separate from the main culture and represent the beliefs of a small number of people.

Uniform Crime Report or UCR—reports made by participating law enforcement agencies, which keep exact monthly records of offenses reported to them. Monthly totals are given to the FBI.

Utilitarian principle—people attempt to maximize their self-interest (seek pleasure) and will avoid penalties (pain). If the cost of doing something exceeds the value of doing it, then the action will be avoided.

Victimless crime—behavior defined as criminal but engaged in by many who think it should not be.

CHAPTER REFERENCES AND ADDITIONAL READINGS

Akers, Ronald L. (1997). *Criminological theories: Introduction and evaluation.* Los Angeles, CA: Roxbury Publishing.

Ball, Richard A. and G. David Curry (1995). The logic of definition in criminology: Purposes and methods for defining 'gangs.' *Criminology.* 33(2):225–245.

Braithwaite, John (1989). *Crime, shame and reintegration.* Cambridge, UK: Cambridge University Press.

Brantingham, P.J, and Brantingham, P.L. (Eds.) (1981). *Environmental criminology.* Beverly Hills, CA: Sage.

Brantingham, P.J. and Brantingham, P.L. (1984). *Patterns in crime.* New York: Macmillan Publishing.

Brantingham, P.L., and Brantigham, P.J. (1993). Environment, routine and situation: Toward a pattern theory of crime. In R.V. Clarke & M. Felson (Eds.) *Routine activity and rational choice* (pp. 259–294). New Brunswick, NJ: Transaction.

Bureau of Justice Statistics (1994). *Drugs and crime facts.* Washington, D.C.: U.S. Department of Justice.

Bureau of Justice Statistics (1998). *Profile of jail inmates, 1996.* Washington, D.C.: U.S. Department of Justice.

Bureau of Justice Statistics (1999). *Substance abuse and treatment, state and federal prisoners, 1997.* Washington, D.C.: U.S. Department of Justice.

Bureau of Justice Statistics (2002). *Criminal victimization, 2001.* Washington, D.C.: U.S. Department of Justice.

Bureau of Justice Statistics (2002). *National Crime Victimization Survey.* U.S. Department of Justice, Office of Justice Programs. Available online: http://www.ojp.usdoj.gov/bjs/pubalp2.htm#cv.

Bureau of Justice Statistics (2004). *Drugs and crime facts.* Washington, D.C.: U.S. Department of Justice.

Bureau of Justice Statistics (2006) *Intimate Partner Violence in the United States, 1993–2004.* Washington, D.C.: U.S. Department of Justice.

Bureau of Justice Statistics (2010). *Correctional Populations in the United States, 2009.* Washington, D.C.: U.S. Department of Justice, Press Release. http://bjs.ojp.usdoj.gov/content/pub/press/corrections09pr.cfm

Cao, L. (2004). *Major criminological theories: Concepts and measurements.* Belmont, CA: Wadsworth.

Cohen, Lawrence E. and Marcus Felson (1979). Social change and crime rate trends: A routine activity approach. *American Sociological Review.* 44:588–608.

Cook, Philip J. and John H. Laub (1998). The unprecedented epidemic in youth violence. In Youth Violence, Michael Tonry and Mark H. Moore (eds.). Volume 24 of *Crime and Justice: A Review of Research.* Chicago, IL: University of Chicago Press.

Cornish, D.B., and Clarke, R. (Eds.). (1986). *The reasoning criminal: Rational choice perspectives on offending.* New York: Springer-Verlag.

Cornish, D.B., & Clarke, R.V. (2003). Opportunities, precipitators, and criminal decisions: A reply to Wortley's critique of situational crime prevention. In M.J. Smith & D.B. Cornish (Eds.), *Theory for practice in situational crime prevention* (pp. 41–96). Monsey, NY: Criminal Justice Press.

Crowe, T.D. (2000). *Crime prevention through environmental design: Applications of architectural design and space management concepts, 2nd Edition.* Boston, MA: Butterworth-Henemann.

Dicker, Fredric. (Dec 30. 2010). "Hate crimes across the state see 14 percent spike in 2009." *New York Post.* Available On-line. http://www.nypost.com/p/news/local/hate_crimes_across_the_state_see_aTb-2p0FLRXbubYqUUlM3zO [January 2011].

Esbensen, Finn-Aage and David Huizinga (1993). Gangs, drugs, and delinquency in a survey of urban youth. *Criminology.* 31(4): 565–586.

Federal Bureau of Investigation (2002). *Crime in the United States, 2002.* U.S. Department of Justice, Washington, D.C.: U.S. Government Printing Office.

Federal Bureau of Investigation (2010a). Preliminary Semiannual Uniform Crime Report, January-June, 2010.

Federal Bureau of Investigation (2010b). Crime in the United States, 2009. Available On-line: http://www2.fbi.gov/ucr/cius2009/index.html [December 2010]

Federal Bureau of Investigation (2010c). Hate Crime Statistics, 2009. Available On-line. http://www2.fbi.gov/ucr/hc2009/index.html. [December 2010]

Federal Bureau of Investigation. (2010d). Law Enforcement Officers Killed and Assaulted, 2009. Available On-line. http://www2.fbi.gov/ucr/killed/2009/index.html. [December 2010]

Federal Bureau of Investigation (2010e). National Incident-Based Reporting System. http://www2.fbi.gov/ucr/faqs.htm

Felson, Marcus (2002). *Crime and everyday life*, 3rd Edition. Thousand Oaks, CA: Sage Press.

Felson, M. and Clarke, R. (1998). *Opportunity makes the thief: Practical theory for crime prevention*. London, UK: Home Office Police and Reducing Crime Unit.

Glaze, Lauren. (2010). Correctional Populations in the United States, 2009. Available On-line: http://bjs.ojp.usdoj.gov/index.cfm?ty=pbdetail&iid=2316 [December 28, 2010].

Goldstein, Herman (1990). *Problem-oriented policing*. New York: McGraw-Hill.

Gondolf, Edward W. and J. Richard McFerron (1989). Handling battering men: Police action in wife abuse cases. *Criminal Justice and Behavior*. 16(4):429–439.

Gorman, Dennis M. and White, H.R. (1995). You can choose your friends, but do they choose your crime? Implications of differential association theories for crime prevention policy. In H.D. Barlow (ed.), *Crime and public policy: Putting theory to work* (pp. 131–155). Boulder, CO: Westview Press.

Gottfredson, Michael and Travis Hirschi (1990). *A general theory of crime*. Palo Alto, CA: Stanford University Press.

Greenwood, Peter (1995). Juvenile crime and juvenile justice. In James Q. Wilson and Joan Petersilia (eds.), *Crime* (pp. 91–117). San Francisco: ICS Press.

Hatton, Barry and Martha Mendoza (December 27, 2010). Portugal's drug policy pays off; U.S. eyes lessons. The Associated Press. https://www.washingtonpost.com/wp-dyn/content/article/2010/12/26/AR2010122600610.html.

Hirschel, J. David, Ira W. Hutchinson, Charles W. Dean, and Anne-Marie Mills (1992a). Review essay on the law enforcement response to spouse abuse: Past, present and future. *Justice Quarterly*. 9(2):247–283.

Hirschel, J. David, Ira W. Hutchison, Charles W. Dean, and Anne-Marie Mills (1992b). The failure of arrest to deter spouse abuse. *Journal of Research in Crime and Delinquency*. 29(1):7–33.

Irwin, John (1994). *It's about time: America's imprisonment binge*. Belmont, CA: Wadsworth Publishing.

Jefferey, C. R. (1971). *Crime prevention through environmental design*. Beverly Hills, CA: Sage.

Kennedy, David. (2009). Drugs, Race and Common Ground: Reflections on the High Point Intervention. *National Institute of Justice Journal*. 262. Available OnLine. http://www.ojp.usdoj.gov/nij/journals/262/welcome.htm.

Kennedy, David M. and Sue-Lin Wong. (2009). *The High Point Drug Market Intervention Strategy*. U.S. Department of Justice, Office of Community Orient Policing Services.

Klein, Malcolm W., Cheryl L. Maxson, and Lea C. Cunningham (1991). Crack, street gangs and violence. *Criminology*. 29(4):623–650.

Klockars, Carl B. and Stephen D. Matrofski (eds.) (1991). *Thinking about police: Contemporary readings*, 2nd Edition. New York: McGraw-Hill.

Lipsky, Michael (1980). *Street-level bureaucracy: Dilemmas of the individual in public service*. Newbury, CA: Russell Sage Foundation.

Ludman, R.J. (1993), Prevention and Control of Juvenile Delinquency. New York: Oxford University Press.

Maguire, Kathleen, Ann L. Pastore, and Timothy J. Flanagan (1993). *Sourcebook of criminal justice statistics, 1992*. Washington, D.C.: U.S. Department of Justice.

Maguire, Kathleen and Ann L. Pastore (eds.) (2003). *Sourcebook of criminal justice statistics 2002* [Online]. Available: http://www.albany.edu/sourcebook/ [12/14/04].

Merry, S.E. (1981). *Urban danger: Life in a neighborhood of strangers*. Springfield, IL: Mombiosse.

Miethe, Terance D., and Richard McCorkle (1998). *Crime profiles: The anatomy of dangerous persons, places and situations*. Los Angeles, CA: Roxbury Publishing.

Mumola, C. & J. Karberg. (2006). *Drug Use and Dependence, State and Federal Prisoners, 2004*. U.S. Department of Justice, Office of Justice Programs, Bureau of Justice Statistics. Available On-line. http://bjs.ojp.usdoj.gov/content/pub/pdf/dudsfp04.pdf.

National Crime Victimization Survey. Office of Justice Programs, U.S. Department of Justice, Bureau of Justice Statistics. Available online: http://bjs.ojp.usdoj.gov/content/glance/cv2.cfm

National Gang Intelligence Center (2009). National Gang Threat Assessment 2009. Washington, D.C.: U.S. Department of Justice. 2009-M0335-001 http://www.justice.gov/ndic/pubs32/32146/32146p.pdf.

National Institute of Justice (2003). *Annual report 2000: Arrestee drug abuse monitoring*. Washington, D.C.: U.S. Department of Justice.

National Law Enforcement Memorial Fund (January 3, 2011). Law Enforcement Officer Deaths: Preliminary 2010 Report. Research Bulletin. http://www.nleomf.org/assets/pdfs/reports/2010_Law_Enforcement_Fatalities_Report.pdf.

National Sheriffs' Association (nd). Code of ethics for the office of the sheriff. Alexandria, VA.

Newman, O. (1972). *Defensible space: people and design in the violent city*. New York: Macmillan.

Office of Juvenile Justice and Delinquency Prevention. Census of Juveniles in Residential Placement DataBook. Available On-line http://www.ojjdp.gov/ojstatbb/cjrp/asp/Offense_Facility.asp [December 2010].

Office of Juvenile Justice and Delinquency Prevention (2009). Statistical Briefing Book, Law Enforcement and Juvenile Crime, 2008. Available On-line. http://www.ojjdp.gov/ojstatbb/crime/JAR.asp [December 2010].

Office of National Drug Control Policy. 2010a. Adam II Annual Report (2009) http://www.whitehousedrugpolicy.gov/publications/pdf/adam2009.pdf

Office of National Drug Control Policy. 2010b. Fact Sheet. Consequences of Illicit Drug Use in America. Available On-line. http://www.whitehousedrugpolicy.gov/publications/pdf/consdrug_fs.pdf.

Petersilia, Joan (1993). The influence of research on policing. In Dunham, Roger G. and Geoffrey P. Alpert (eds.), *Critical issues in policing: Contemporary readings*. Prospect Heights, IL: Waveland Press, Inc.

Puzzanchera, C. (2009). Juvenile Arrests, 2008. U.S. Department of Justice, Office of Justice Programs, Office of Juvenile Justice and Delinquency Prevention. Available On-line http://www.ncjrs.gov/pdffiles1/ojjdp/228479.pdf. [December 2008].

Rantala, Ramona. (2008). Cybercrime Against Businesses, 2005. Available On-line. http://bjs.ojp.usdoj.gov/content/pub/pdf/cb05.pdf [January 2011].

RAV v. St. Paul, 505 U.S. 377 (1992).

Reppetto, T. (1974). *Residential crime.* Cambridge, MA: Ballinger.

Reppetto, T. (1976). Crime prevention and displacement phenomenon. *Crime and Delinquency.* 22: 166–177.

Rosenbaum, Dennis P., Arthur J. Lurigio, and Robert C. Davis (1998). *The Prevention of crime: Social and situational strategies.* Belmont, CA: Wadsworth Publishing.

Sampson, Robert J. and John H. Laub (1993). *Crime in the making: Pathways and turning points through life.* Cambridge, MA: Harvard University Press.

Sickmund, Melissa, Sladky, T.J., and Kang, Wei. (2008). Census of Juveniles in Residential Placement Databook. Online. Available: http://www.ojjdp.ncjrs.gov/ojstatbb/cjrp/.

Skogan, Wesley G. (1990). *Disorder and decline: Crime and the spiral of decay in American neighborhoods.* New York: Free Press.

Skogan, Wesley G. (2004). *Community policing: Can it work?* Belmont, CA: Thompson/Wadsworth Publishing, Sourcebook of Criminal Justice Statistics Online (2010). Accessed December 2010. http://www.albany.edu/sourcebook/.

Spergel, Irving A. (1990). Youth gangs: Continuity and change. In Michael Tonry and Norval Morris (eds.), *Crime and justice: A review of the research, volume 12.* Chicago: University of Chicago Press.

Taylor, R.B., Shumaker, S.A., & Gottfredson, S.D. (1985). Neighborhood links between physical features and local sentiments: Deterioration, fear of crime, and confidence. *Journal of Architectural and Planning Research.*

Thornberry, Terence P., Marvin D. Krohn, Alan J. Lizotte, and Deborah Chard-Wierschem. (1993). The role of juvenile gangs in facilitating delinquent behavior. *Journal of Research in Crime and Delinquency.* 30:55–87.

Tittle, Charles R. (1995). *Control balance: Toward a general theory of deviance.* Boulder, CO: Westview Press.

U.S. Department of Justice (1992). National center for the analysis of violent crime: Annual report, 1991. Washington, D.C.: Federal Bureau of Investigation.

Walker, Samuel (1998). *Sense and nonsense about crime and drugs,* 4th edition. Belmont, CA: Wadsworth Publishing.

Walker, Samuel (1998). *Sense and nonsense about crime, drugs, and communities: A policy guide,* 7th edition. Cengage Learning.

Williams, A. Kevin (1995). Community mobilization against urban crime: Guiding orientations and strategic choices in grassroots politics. *Urban Affairs Review.* 30(3):407–431.

Williams, Emma Jean (1996). Enforcing social responsibility and the expanding domain of the police. *Crime & Delinquency.* 42(2):309–323.

Williams, Franklin P. and Marilyn D. McShane (1988). *Criminological theory.* Englewood Cliffs, NJ: Prentice Hall.

Wilson, S. (1978). Vandalism and defensible space on London housing estates. In R.V. Clarke (Ed.), *Tackling vandalism* (pp. 14–26). London: Her Majesty's Stationary Office.

Wilson, James Q. and Richard J. Hernstein (1985). *Crime and human nature: The definitive study of the causes of crime.* New York: Touchstone/Simon and Schuster.

Winfree, L. Thomas, Jr., Kathy Fuller, Teresa Vigil, and G. Larry Mays (1992). The definitions and measurement of 'gang status': Policy implications for juvenile justice. *Juvenile and Family Court Journal.* 43(1):29–38.

Wolfgang, M., Robert M. Figlio, and Thorsten Sellin (1972). *Delinquency in a birth cohort.* Chicago: University of Chicago Press.

CHAPTER 11

Technology and Law Enforcement

LEARNING OBJECTIVES

This chapter addresses the impact of technology on crime and the use and application of technology in law enforcement. The average person uses the term technology in many ways. To many, it is limited to the fields of the physical sciences, such as physics and engineering; some include the natural sciences (e.g., biology and chemistry) in the discussion of technology, while still others include the methods and techniques developed from the social sciences (e.g., sociology and psychology). We think of technology as the practical application of any science or tool to common endeavors. As such, this chapter's focus is threefold: it presents (1) the challenges posed by technologically-enhanced criminal behavior, (2) the uses of technology in law enforcement operations, and (3) the future implications of technology on privacy rights. Upon completion of this chapter, you should be able to:

- Describe technology's general impact on criminal behavior by identifying two categories of technologically-enhanced crime and give examples of each.

- Identify the three influencing factors since the early 1900s that led to establishing filing systems and the need for more documentation of law enforcement operations.

- Briefly describe the evolution and importance of the National Crime Information Center (NCIC) and other large databases to law enforcement's mission and operation at the different levels of government.

- Explain the concept of data mining and how it relates to the multiple databases used in law enforcement.

- Identify several reasons for the need of communications interoperability and information sharing among law enforcement agencies and how these concerns are being addressed.

- Identify at least five major applications of technology in the field of law enforcement.

- Identify the major concerns related to the potential abuses of technology in the law enforcement field.

CHAPTER OUTLINE

KEY TERMS USED IN THIS CHAPTER

technologically-enhanced crime

spyware

National Crime Information Center (NCIC)

NCIC 2000

CODIS

Secure Flight

FinCEN

US-VISIT

data mining

data warehouse

interoperability

regional information sharing systems (RISS)

computer-aided dispatch systems

automated vehicle locator system (AVLS)

global positioning system (GPS)

geographic information systems (GIS), or computer mapping, or geocoding

crime analysis

CompStat/ComStat

social networking media

less-than-lethal technologies

biometrics

Integrated Automated
    Fingerprint Identification
    Systems (IAFIS)

teleforensics

personal video surveillance
    systems

gunshot detection devices

personal vertical takeoff and
    landing aircraft (VTOL)

unmanned aerial vehicles
    (UAVs)

augmented reality

privacy rights paradigm

TECHNOLOGY AND CRIME

Americans have a love affair with technology! A major part of our economy is based on goods and services related to technology. Just look around. People everywhere are walking or driving with cellular phones up to their ears, some even wearing handless headset varieties. We observe people using their modern cell phones as personal data assistants (accessing appointment and address books), listening to music, and even accessing the Internet. Digital cameras and camcorders have become commonplace and allow users to immediately view captured images, and, of course, to post those images or video clips directly to the Internet. The most modern and expensive cell phones combine all of these functions into one device. Wearable computers are emerging on the scene, and they will probably be one of the next waves of technological devices to capture the desires of the consuming public (see **Figure 11-1**).

Technologically-Enhanced Crime

We use technology for a variety of purposes: entertainment and leisure, business and commerce, public safety and order, and unfortunately, in criminal endeavors. As technology evolves, so do the methods of operation of criminal perpetrators. **Technologically-enhanced crime** can be classified into two categories: "traditional crimes" and "high-tech crimes." Traditional crimes include those that are committed with the use or aid of technology, such as counterfeiting, money laundering, forgery, theft of trade secrets, identity theft, credit card theft, the distribution of child pornography, the sale of illegal drugs, Internet fraud and scams, illegal gambling, and hate propaganda. Technology enhances the ability of perpetrators to lessen the time to commit such offenses, to enhance obtaining personal information from potential victims, to make detection more difficult, or to enhance the quality of materials or documents used in such offenses. High-tech

FIGURE 11-1 Sci-Fi Becomes Reality

The Dick Tracy wristwatch: For decades the talk has been "when will the Dick Tracy wristwatch get here?" The question referred to a cartoon strip where the key character, beginning in 1946, wore a wristwatch that served as a transmitting and receiving device. In January of 2004, *USA Today* ran an article about the availability of a wristwatch that could also display temperature, wind chill, humidity, stock quotes, news headlines, personal messages, and act as a calendar. The watch cost about $129 plus $59 per year for data service (Baig 2004). Today there are 3G watch phones available from $175 - $400 (3GWatches.com 2010).

George Jetson's Car: *The Jetson's*, a primetime TV cartoon series, ran from 1962-1963 and again from 1985-1987. The futuristic family flew in a small car. When will we all be able to fly our personal vehicles? Some companies have been trying for decades, and the one that produces the first flying car to lift off vertically may capture the market (see FutureCars.com for reviews and videos).

Star Trek's Phaser: The phaser gun has yet to be perfected, but research on lasers and various forms of electrical energy continues. Some of the less-than-lethal weapons described in this chapter may be part of the evolution to the ultimate phaser weapon.

crimes employ new technologies to shield, store, or communicate criminal activities. Such offenses and abuses also include crimes directed against a computer itself or a computer network, including unauthorized use of computer systems (e.g., criminal hacking), denial of service attacks, and virus transmission.

One of the most common traditional crimes in the United States is fraud (a form of theft). In 2004, the Federal Trade Commission (FTC) estimated that 10% of Americans were victims of fraud (Federal Trade Commission 2004a), and the figure rose to 13.5% in 2007 (Federal Trade Commission 2007). Of those victimized, 27% were lured into the fraud by printed media (newspapers, direct mail, posters, etc.), 22% by the Internet or email, 21% by television or radio, and 9%

by telemarketing (Federal Trade Commission 2007). All of these methods are related to technology. In 2010, the Consumer Sentinel Network (CSN), an online database of millions of consumer complaints available only to law enforcement, received over 1.3 million complaints. Of those, 54% were fraud complaints, 19% were identity theft-related, and 27% were other types of complaints (Federal Trade Commission 2011, 3). **Table 11-1** charts the 10-year trend of CSN complaints.

The FTC reports that the median loss for victims of fraud was $594, but totaled over $1.7 billion for all victims (Federal Trade Commission 2010, 3). Those victims identifying the type of initial contact indicated that email was used 45% of the time, with Internet websites accounting for another 11%. The telephone was used in only 10% of the initial contacts (3). Of all the CSN complaints filed in 2010, identity theft (19%) was the largest category, followed by (6):

- Third Party and Creditor Debt Collection (11%);
- Internet Services (5%);
- Prizes, Sweepstakes, and Lotteries (5%);

- Shop-at-Home and Catalog Sales (4%);
- Imposter Scams (4%);
- Internet Auction (4%);
- Foreign Money Offers and Counterfeit Check Scams (3%); and
- Telephone and Mobile Services (3%).

Identity theft is one of the fastest growing crimes in the United States. As mentioned above, it is the largest single category of complaints. In 2007, nearly 8 million households had at least one of its members fall victim to identity theft, according to a Bureau of Justice Statistics report (Langton and Baum 2010, 1), a 23% increase from 2005 data. Over half of the victimized households experienced the unauthorized use or attempted use of a credit card account, while the second-most-common type of identity theft involved the unauthorized use or attempted use of existing accounts, such as a bank, checking, or debit, or cellular phone account (Langton and Baum 2010, 2). Of those victims experiencing a financial loss, the average was $1830, which projects to about a total loss of $10 billion for all victim households.

TABLE 11-1 Consumer Sentinel Network – Complaint Type Count* Calendar Years 2001–2010

| Calendar Year | Consumer Sentinel Network Complaint Count | | | |
	Fraud	Identity Theft	Other	Total Complaints
2001	137,306	86,250	101,963	325,519
2002	242,783	161,977	146,862	551,622
2003	331,366	215,240	167,051	713,657
2004	410,298	246,909	203,176	860,383
2005	437,585	255,687	216,042	909,314
2006	428,398	246,214	215,500	890,112
2007	577,902	259,314	213,167	1,050,383
2008	644,356	314,484	266,155	1,224,995
2009	721,418	278,078	330,930	1,330,426
2010	725,087	250,854	363,324	1339,265

* Counts from CY-2001 to CY-2004 represent historic figures as per the Consumer Sentinel Network's five-year data retention policy; counts exclude Do Not Call Registry complaints.

Source: Reprinted from Federal Trade Commission (2011, 5).

Other costs and statistics related to technologically-enhanced crime are difficult to estimate because of reporting deficiencies; however, various groups have provided estimates from time to time based on surveys and estimated losses:

- In 2009, credit card fraud affected 6.5 million victims and debit card fraud 3.5 million; victims on average paid $314 out of pocket for credit card fraud and $243 for debit card fraud (Bell 2010).
- Actual check fraud losses to banks totaled $1.024 billion in 2008 and industry losses from debit card fraud—POS signature, POS PIN, and ATM transactions combined—reached an estimated $788 million in 2008 (American Bankers Association 2009)
- During the summer of 2010, a Michigan couple was charged with allegedly walking off with an estimated $40 million in General Motors hybrid-related trade secrets, hoping to sell them to a Chinese competitor (Federal Bureau of Investigation, September 24, 2010).
- The International Intellectual Property Alliance (2010) estimated that 2009 trade losses due to copyright piracy was nearly $14 billion in business software for U.S. software publishers, and nearly $1.3 billion in music and record trade losses due to software piracy.

High-Tech Crimes

High-tech crimes employ new technologies to shield, store, or communicate criminal activities. As mentioned above, such offenses and abuses include crimes directed against a computer itself or a computer network, including unauthorized use of computer systems (e.g., criminal hacking), denial of service attacks, and virus transmission. The offender needs to have a very high level of technology understanding and ability to program, interrupt, or manipulate existing operations. For example, identity theft can occur by several methods, from the simple theft of a wallet containing documents and credit cards to the sophisticated planting of **spyware** on one's computer to remotely capture and obtain personal information, bank account numbers, and passwords. Although identity theft

may be considered a traditional crime, obtaining the personal information of victims using spyware is considered high-tech criminal activity. Spyware is the general term used to describe a computer program that is surreptitiously downloaded to one's computer that permits others to obtain information from that computer when it is online (see **Figure 11-2**). Some have referred to the technique as the "virtual peeping Tom."

High-tech criminal activities and diagnosing software vulnerabilities require computer specialists and sophisticated analytical capabilities on the part of government and law enforcement. One such entity is the Computer Emergency Response Team Coordination Center (CERT/CC) of the Software Engineering Institute (SEI) at Carnegie Mellon University (Pittsburgh, PA). CERT/CC tracks computer vulnerabilities reported by public and private sector organizations. In late 1988, the Morris worm incident brought to a halt 10% of Internet systems. The Defense Advanced Research Projects Agency (DARPA) of the federal government then charged the SEI with setting up a center to coordinate communication among experts during security emergencies and to help prevent future incidents (CERT.org, 2010), creating the CERT/CC. The mission of CERT/CC is contained in its Charter:

- Provide a reliable, trusted, 24-hour, single point of contact for emergencies.
- Facilitate communication among experts working to solve security problems.
- Serve as a central point for identifying and correcting vulnerabilities in computer systems.
- Maintain close ties with research activities and conduct research to improve the security of existing systems.
- Initiate proactive measures to increase awareness and understanding of information security and computer security issues throughout the community of network users and service providers (CERT.org, 2010).

CERT/CC works closely with the federal government, especially the United States Computer Emergency Readiness Team (US-CERT), the operational arm of the National Cyber Security Division (NCSD) at the Department of

---

FIGURE 11-2 Forms of Spyware

Cookies: Small pieces of data stored on individual clients' Web browsers on behalf of Web servers that can be retrieved by the Web site that initially stored them. They can potentially track the behavior of users across many Web sites; a passive form of spyware.

Web bugs: Invisible images embedded on pages; a passive forms of spyware; they contain no code of their own, relying instead on existing Web browser functions.

Browser hijackers: Software that changes web browser settings to modify home pages.

Tracks: A generic name for the recording of selected information by an operating system. Recently visited website lists are maintained by most browsers. Malicious programs can mine tracks.

Keyloggers: Software that records all keystrokes in order to capture passwords and account and credit card numbers.

Malware: A variety of malicious software, such as viruses, worms, and Trojan horses that can freeze computers or destroy files.

Spybots: Software that monitors user's behavior, collects logs of activity, and then transmits them to third parties without the user's knowledge.

Adware: A more benign variety of spybot; a program that displays advertisements tuned to the user's current activity, potentially reporting aggregate or anonymized browsing behavior to a third party.

Source: Stefan Saroiu, Steven D. Gribble, and Henry M. Levy (2004), Measurement and Analysis of Spyware in a University Environment, http://www.cs.washington.edu/homes/tzoompy/publications/nsdi/2004/spyware.html.

Homeland Security (DHS). The primary goal is to prevent cyber attacks, protect systems, and respond to the effects of cyber attacks. The US-CERT is charged with providing response support and defense against cyber attacks for the Federal Civil Executive Branch (.gov) and information sharing and collaboration with state and local government, industry, and international partners (US-CERT, 2010). Cybercrime resources are becoming extensive across the United States and several agencies and groups share information on vulnerabilities and forensic investigations (see **Figure 11-3** for some interesting sites online).

Only a portion of technologically-enhanced criminal activity can be presented here. Further examples emerge weekly and the future will undoubtedly reveal new ones. Law enforcement agencies are attempting to address such high-tech crime and some successes are noteworthy. For example, the Department of Justice announced on Cyber Monday (November 29, 2010) that, because of "Operation In Our Sites v. 2.0," seizure orders had been executed against 82 domain names of commercial websites engaged in the illegal sale and distribution of counterfeit goods and copyrighted works. The seizures involved U.S. Attorney

FIGURE 11-3 Cybercrime and Forensic Investigation Links

American Society of Digital Forensics & eDiscovery: http://asdfed.com/
Computer Crime & Intellectual Property Section (DOJ): http://www.cybercrime.gov/index.html
Electronic Crimes Task Forces and Working Groups: http://www.secretservice.gov/ectf.shtml
Electronic Evidence and Search & Seizure: http://www.cybercrime.gov/tecpa.html
High Technology Crime Investigation Association: http://www.htcia.org/
International Association of Computer Investigative Specialists: http://www.iacis.com/
International Society of Forensic Computer Examiners: http://www.isfce.com/
Insider Threat Research and Links and e-Crime Watch Survey: http://www.cert.org/insider_threat/
Internet Crime Complaint Center (IC3): http://www.ic3.gov/default.aspx
National Threat Assessment Center - Insider Threat Study: http://www.secretservice.gov/ntac_its.shtml

Offices and law enforcement agencies in California, Colorado, District of Columbia, Florida, New Jersey, New York, Ohio, Texas, and Washington (U.S. Department of Justice 2010).

Seized counterfeit goods

Source: Courtesy of U.S. Immigration and Customs Enforcement

Another large case involved the first joint cyber investigation between Egyptian law enforcement authorities and U.S. officials, which included the Federal Bureau of Investigation (FBI), the U.S. Attorney's Office, and the Electronic Crimes Task Force in Los Angeles. Labeled "Operation Phish Phry," the investigation led to 53 persons being charged with 51 counts of conspiracy to commit wire fraud and bank fraud; another 47 suspects were identified in Egypt. The operation required extensive cooperation and support from many agencies according to the FBI press release (October 9, 2009):

> The investigation in the United States was… supported by the Electronic Crimes Task Force in Los Angeles and the FBI's Legal Attaché in Cairo, Egypt. Several agencies provided considerable assistance to this investigation, including the Los Angeles Police Department, the Los Angeles District Attorney, the United States Secret Service, the Culver City Police Department, the El Segundo Police Department, and the United States Social Security Administration. U.S. Customs

and Border Protection, the Drug Enforcement Administration, the Department of Water and Power, and local law enforcement departments in various counties assisted during today's arrests.

Another multi-agency investigation, "Operation Web Snare," ran from June 1 to August 26, 2004 and consisted of more than 160 investigations. The focus of the operation was a variety of online economic crimes including identity theft, fraud, counterfeit software, computer intrusions, and other intellectual property crimes. Investigators identified more than 150,000 victims with estimated losses of more than $215 million. More than 140 search and seizure warrants were executed as part of the operation, and prosecutors obtained 117 criminal complaints, informations, and indictments. The charges led to more than 150 arrests or convictions. Operation Web Snare involved coordination among 36 U.S. Attorneys' offices nationwide, the Criminal Division of the Department of Justice, 37 of the FBI's 56 field divisions, 13 of the Postal Inspection Service's 18 field divisions, and the FTC, along with a variety of other federal, state, local, and foreign law enforcement agencies (U.S. Department of Justice 2004).

In summary, as technology changes, so do the methods of committing crime, and investigations often become very complex and multi-jurisdictional. Traditional crimes still occur, but with greater ease and a higher volume because of the assistance the technical advances provide. With some technology, especially computer technology, new types of crime emerge. The new and exciting technologies bring both positive benefits and negative consequences for society, as well as significant challenges for law enforcement.

INFORMATION TECHNOLOGY

When the criminal justice system is officially invoked, one element of the process is universal: information has been the basis for action. Today, officers' observations and actions are recorded and may become the foundation for any subsequent initiation of arrest and prosecution. Historically, these actions took place with little documentation. In early years, an officer's word and testimony were sufficient, and little was done in maintaining a record base or filing system. Incidents were not that frequent, so one's memory was not cluttered with other cases and field notes. The court system was not backed up, and jails were not overcrowded. "Justice" was often swift and definite with few appeals. Extensive documentation simply was not necessary.

Those days are long gone!

By the turn of the twentieth century, three influencing factors led to the establishment of filing systems and the need for more documentation. The first was the increasing level of crime (primarily in urban areas) and the need to keep information about each case in an accurate and detailed manner. One's memory simply could not keep all details readily available. The second influencing factor was the professionalization of policing, which emphasized the increased use of scientific tools and processes (such as fingerprinting, photography, and analysis of crime incidents) and extensive record-keeping systems to help identify suspects. The third influencing factor was the evolving legal requirements related to the rules of evidence and judicial review of cases. All of these factors led to greater emphasis on processing, storing, and retrieving information.

Today, there probably is not a law enforcement officer alive who goes to work without carrying a pen or pencil and some kind of notepad (unless working undercover). Of course, some carry handheld, notebook, or netbook computers, and many carry sophisticated cell phones. Information gathering and storage also includes the use of mobile digital terminals (MDTs) in patrol cars, audio recording devices, and video technology. The reason for much of this emphasis on information is obvious—it is the basis of operation for the criminal justice process. Another reason for the importance of technology is that society and the criminal justice system itself demand accountability—that information is accurate, detailed, verifiable, and readily accessible. The system has become so complex today that information technology is more important than ever.

General History of Information Technology

One can argue that the history of information technology began with the evolution of language and writing. The first recordings of pictographic signs and symbols date back to the Sumerian clay tablets of 4000–3500 BC. Early

Mobile Digital Terminal in cruiser

Source: © Comstock/Thinkstock

uses of papyrus and inks have been dated to 2500 BC. The abacus, a device to assist in the computing of numbers, dates to 3000 BC. Although scrolls began to be replaced by an early form of "books" around 360 AD, and the use of lamp-black ink by Chinese artists about 650 AD led to the introduction of wood blocks for printing, the printing press was not perfected until Johann Gutenberg in the 1450s, and black-lead pencils were first used in England in 1500. Consequently, modern societies have been recording information routinely for only about 500 years (see Augarten 1984 and Grun 1991 for additional historical information about this evolution).

The use of mechanical devices to process information is a more recent endeavor. Appendix 11-A identifies the most significant developments from the years 1600 to 2010 in the ideas and devices related to the evolution of computerized information technology. Understanding this evolution leads to an appreciation of where society has been and how rapidly new advancements are occurring. In fact, there are so many significant changes and applications occurring today that one cannot do justice to the timeline in our Appendices. Just as our grandparents and great-grandparents witnessed the transition from the horse and buggy to the automobile and then to space travel, today's generations are witnessing the transition from playing PacMan on TVs to simulating real situations through virtual reality on wearable computers (including the Wii, Xbox 360, Natal, and PlayStation Move). The question that remains is, "What will be our capabilities in the next 5 to 20 years?" Are *Star Trek*, *Stargate SG-1*, and *Avatar* really far-fetched, or will many of us living today actually witness those possibilities?

The majority of adults today were born before computers became commercially available. Personal computers entered the school system only after the mid-1980s, so today's grade school, high school, and college students have grown up with personal computers, cellular phones, CD/DVD players, MP3 players, iPods, and/or other computerized devices at home and school. While young people today may take computing and digital video in stride (and for granted), some adults are still hesitant to learn about and use them. This situation also exists, to a lesser extent, in law enforcement agencies: older personnel may resist the increased use of technology while younger officers take it in stride, although some older officers are reportedly more adept at incorporating technology than younger officers. The reality is that no generalized comment can be made about generational acceptance of new technology—there is such diversity among agencies and personnel that it would be an error to generalize. One thing is certain, however: Acquisition of new technology requires resources, and most times the differences among agencies are differences in economic resources available for new technology.

Information Technology in Law Enforcement

The evolution of information technology in law enforcement activities is a very interesting one and needs to be placed in context. Today in policing we take many things for granted, such as cell phones and portable radios. It must be remembered that it has been less than 100 years since officers had the means of communicating with headquarters and other officers. Appendix 11-B presents a timeline in order to appreciate the evolution of major applications in law enforcement from the mid-1800s to the 2000s. Persons entering the law enforcement field today may witness as much change, or more, during their careers as those who preceded them.

One of the most important milestones for U.S. law enforcement regarding the application of information technology occurred in 1967 with the establishment of the FBI's **National Crime Information Center (NCIC),** the national repository for crime-related information on wanted persons and stolen property. Originally located in Washington, D.C. at FBI headquarters, the center's new national headquarters opened in July 1999 at Clarksburg, West Virginia. It provides computerized information to thousands of criminal justice agencies in the 50 states, the District of Columbia, Puerto Rico, the U.S. Virgin Islands, and Canada on a 24-hour, 7-days-a-week basis.

Initially established on January 27, 1967 following lobbying efforts from the law enforcement community at all levels of government, it had 16 terminals, 15 participating agencies, and a database of 23,000 records in five file categories: wanted persons, stolen vehicles, stolen plates, stolen firearms, and identifiable stolen items (FBI 1984; FBI 1996–1997). Over the years, other file categories have been added. Of the automated files, the major ones now include FBI (2010b):

1. Stolen vehicle
2. Stolen license plate
3. Stolen boat
4. Stolen gun
5. Stolen article file
6. Stolen securities
7. Stolen parts
8. Supervised release
9. National Sex Offender Registry
10. Foreign fugitives
11. Unidentified persons
12. Protection orders
13. Wanted persons
14. Missing persons
15. U.S. Secret Service protective
16. Gang members
17. Known or suspected terrorists
18. Identity theft files
19. Immigration violators

NCIC responds to over 7.5 million inquiries daily (over 2 billion yearly). It provides access to over 80,000 criminal justice users through more than 110,000 terminals and maintains over 15 million active records (FBI 2010b, Pilant 1996, and Sessions 1993). Any record entered into NCIC must be associated with a document and must contain the identity of the agency entering the record, as well as other specific data, depending on the file. Some files can be updated only by specifically-authorized agencies. Local agency users must furnish the network system with a specific request and a special NCIC-assigned code that identifies the agency. A standard code for various types of requests is entered and then processed. A response is transmitted back to the initiating agency, and when an inquiry about a person or property matches data contained in one of the files, it is referred to as a "hit."

In 1992, the center became part of the newly structured Criminal Justice Information Service Division within the FBI. Artificial intelligence software capabilities have been incorporated into the system in an effort to detect related (linked) criminal activity in its early stages, and to detect misuse of information by helping to ensure accuracy and reliability of the data. Image technology has been incorporated in order to permit the improved transmission of mug shots and fingerprint images in response to inquiries. In all, over 60 planned upgrades have been incorporated into the revamped system called **NCIC 2000** (Buckler 1998 and Federation of American Scientists 2004).

The NCIC is only one of several major databases available to law enforcement agencies (or other selected agencies). In recent years, because of greater computerization, networking, and the need to share information, a number of databases have been developed. Four examples of such databases include the following:

(a) **CODIS**—a database containing the DNA signatures of convicted offenders; CODIS refers to COmbined DNA Indexing System. It enables federal, state, and local crime labs to exchange and compare DNA profiles electronically, thereby linking crimes to each other and to convicted offenders. As of November 2010, over 9,110,000 offender profiles and 346,613 forensic profiles were on file. At least 200 local crime labs across the country can run DNA samples through the database and find matches (Federal Bureau of Investigation 2010c).

(b) **Secure Flight**—a program of the Transportation Security Administration (TSA). It is a behind-the-scenes watch list-matching program that screens airline passengers and is designed to identify known or suspected terrorists.

(c) **FinCEN**—the U.S. Treasury Department's Financial Crimes Enforcement Network database identifies possible money laundering transactions. It is a neural network used to scan huge volumes of financial information for suspicious patterns in money movement. The FinCEN organizations employs over 300 experts and analysts that focus on financial crimes, including terrorist financing, money laundering, and other illicit activity. Today, over 20 law enforcement agencies are involved in FinCEN (U.S. Department of Treasury 2010).

(d) **US-VISIT**—operational since January of 2004, the database contains scanned fingerprints of the index fingers and a photograph of most foreign visitors traveling to the United States on a visa. This information is made available only to authorized officials and selected law enforcement agencies responsible for ensuring the safety and security of U.S. citizens and foreign visitors (U.S. Department of Homeland Security 2010a).

See **Figure 11-4** for more examples of law enforcement databases.

Since the 9/11 attacks in 2001, there has been a growing concern and a need among law enforcement agencies not only to share information, but also to provide more effective means for searching that information. As databases grow in size and number, there is a need to tie them together in order to optimize their potential. However, databases are not always compatible with one another because of their internal programming code and structure. Because of this, sophisticated software that permits "super searches" of multiple databases has been and is being developed. **Data mining** is the technique that uses such software to search database(s) for hidden patterns in a group of data, which can then be used to predict future behavior or to link related data. This is just one technique in attempting to connect the dots among the mountains of information available today. The term **data warehouse** is sometimes used to describe large computer networks utilized for storing, retrieving, and managing large amounts of data.

Several such programs exist in the law enforcement field today and more are on the way. One source (Yaukey, 2007) stated that at least 52 different federal agencies use

---

FIGURE 11-4 Other Law Enforcement Databases

National Sex Offenders Registry (NSOR)—Accessed through NCIC, the NSOR is a national database at the FBI that tracks the whereabouts and movements of each person who has been convicted of a criminal offense against a victim who is a minor, or has been convicted of a sexually violent offense, or is a sexually violent predator; it also registers and verifies the addresses of sex offenders who reside in states that do not have a "minimally sufficient" sex offender registry (SOR) program. (The public can access the The National Sex Offender Public Website which acts as a portal to state sex offender registries: http://www.fbi.gov/scams-safety/registry.)

National Integrated Ballistic Information Network (NIBIN)—An ATFE program that provides for the nationwide installation and networking of automated ballistic imaging equipment in partnership with state and local law enforcement agencies. Currently, about 190 law enforcement locations are making use of this valuable technology. Since its inception, NIBIN equipment assisted law enforcement agencies in finding more than 34,700 links, or "hits." In each of these instances, evidence from two or more crime scenes was identified as being potentially linked.

Bomb and Arson Tracking System (BATS)—Allows state, local, and other federal law enforcement agencies to share information about bomb and arson cases and incidents. Participants receive a user ID and password from ATFE and then can capture, store, and exchange information such as the type of incident, target, date, and location.

National Virtual Pointer System (NVPS)—Proposed to expand the information sharing with the National Drug Pointer Index (NDPIX). The NVPS would reach state and local law enforcement agencies through linkages with High Intensity Drug Trafficking Area (HIDTA) Systems, the National Law Enforcement Telecommunications System (NLETS), and the Regional Information Sharing Systems (RISS). The NVPS will allow existing target deconfliction systems to exchange information concerning targets under investigation for all types of criminal activity.

National Child Victim Identification System—In a partnership with the National Center for Missing and Exploited Children, Immigration and Customs Enforcement (ICE), the FBI, the U.S. Postal Inspection Service, the U.S. Secret Service, and the Department of Justice are developing the National Child Victim Identification Card Program. Together with its partners in this important effort, ICE's CyberSmuggling Center is hosting the nation's only comprehensive, searchable system for identifying digital child pornography images. With its capacity to search and identify known images, the system is designed to help law enforcement agencies throughout the world identify and rescue children featured in the images. The system is also designed to facilitate prosecution of those who possess or distribute digital child pornography images in the wake of a 2002 Supreme Court decision (*Ashcroft v. Free Speech Coalition*) requiring proof that such images depict an actual child.

Student and Exchange Visitor Information System (SEVIS)—A database that the Department of Homeland Security uses to track international students and scholars studying or researching in the United States. SEVIS will allow the United States to ensure that foreign students and exchange visitors who have entered our nation to study in our schools actually enroll in those schools. As of September 2010, SEVIS contained records for 1,164,691 active nonimmigrant students, exchange visitors, and their dependents associated with over 10,000 schools. SEVIS implements section 641 of the Illegal Immigration Reform and Immigrant Responsibility Act (IIRIRA) of 1996.

Sources: Federal Bureau of Investigation, Bureau of Alcohol, Tobacco, Firearms and Explosives, Drug Enforcement Agency, Bureau of Immigration and Customs Enforcement, and Department of Homeland Security.

---

data mining technology, and there are at least 199 different data mining programs in use. We will identify only a few of the programs in use today. The Department of Homeland Security has three programs recently described in a report to Congress:

- *Automated Targeting System (ATS)*: an intranet-based enforcement and decision support tool that

is the cornerstone for all Customs and Border Patrol targeting efforts. It compares traveler, cargo, and conveyance information against intelligence and other enforcement data by incorporating risk-based targeting scenarios and assessments. Its primary purpose is targeting, identifying, and preventing potential terrorists and terrorist weapons from entering the United States. ATS data mines three modules of the system: ATS-P (passengers), ATS-Inbound (inbound cargo), and ATS-Outbound (exports) (U.S. Department of Homeland Security 2008, 10-13).

- *Data Analysis and Research for Trade Transparency System (DARTTS)*: administered by Immigration and Customs Enforcement (ICE), it generates leads for and otherwise supports ICE investigations of trade-based money laundering, contraband smuggling, trade fraud, and other import–export crimes. DARTTS analyzes trade and financial data to identify statistically-anomalous transactions that may warrant investigation. ICE investigators and analysts must understand the relationships among importers, exporters, and the financing for a set of trade transactions to determine which transactions are suspicious. DARTTS is designed specifically to make this investigative process more efficient by automating the analysis and identification of anomalies for the investigator (U.S. Department of Homeland Security 2008, 20-21).

- *Freight Assessment System* (FAS): administered by the TSA, it is a risk-assessment tool that can be used to identify cargo that may pose a heightened risk to passenger aircraft. To reduce the current reliance on random inspections, FAS uses a rules-based model developed by security subject-matter experts that is software-based and incorporates machine-derived rules and predictive indicators to identify and assess high-risk cargo. Cargo identified as high-risk is flagged and set aside for further inspection by air carriers (U.S. Department of Homeland Security 2008, 27).

Data mining and warehousing is controversial in the United States because of privacy and freedom issues. Law enforcement agencies do not publish much about such capabilities for security reasons. For example, the FBI's website describes the National Security Branch (NSB) as consisting of the "FBI's Counterterrorism Division (CTD), Counterintelligence Division (CD), Directorate of Intelligence (DI), and the new Weapons of Mass Destruction Directorate (WMDD) and combines the missions, capabilities, and resources of each" (Federal Bureau of Investigation 2010d). The additional information about NSB explains the mission of each division and outlines the needs of securing the nation. However, a 2009 exposé of the NSB describes it as containing a hodgepodge of data sets packed with more than 1.5 billion government and private-sector records about citizens and foreigners: records from hotel chains, rental car agencies, federal prisoner phone call logs, credit card transactions, reverse White Pages with 696 million names and addresses tied to U.S. phone numbers, listings of all active pilots, and 500,000 names of suspected terrorists from the Unified Terrorist Watch List (Singel 2009). The article claims that data mining occurs on all this information.

The significance of the wide variety of databases and information available to law enforcement lies not in the fact that the data is stored somewhere, but most importantly that it shared and available. One of the challenges in today's technological world is the issues of compatibility and **interoperability**. Communications interoperability is the ability of public safety agencies to talk across disciplines and jurisdictions via radio communications systems, exchanging voice and/or data with one another on demand, in real time, when authorized (see **Figure 11-5**).

The sharing of data has been less of a problem than radio communication interoperability. There are a number of **regional information sharing systems (RISS)** that have emerged over the last several decades, which consist of a network of computers linked together on a regional basis that are designed to serve multiple agencies by providing access to databases, analysis, and other services. The national RISS Program is composed of six regional intelligence centers operating in mutually-exclusive geographic regions that include all 50 states, the District of Columbia, U.S. territories, Australia, Canada, and England. The centers have the following names: The Middle Atlantic-Great Lakes Organized Crime Law Enforcement Network (MAGLOCLEN), the Mid-States Organized Crime Information Center (MOCIC), the New England State Police Information Network (NESPIN), the Regional Organized Crime Information Center (ROCIC), the Rocky Mountain Information Network (RMIN), and the Western States Information Network (WSIN). The six

---

FIGURE 11-5 Nationwide Interoperable Communications

The National Commission on Terrorist Attacks Upon the United States determined that the inability to communicate was a critical element during the 9/11 incidents where multiple agencies and multiple jurisdictions responded. One of the Commission's recommendations addressed this problem:

> *Congress should support pending legislation which provides for the expedited and increased assignment of radio spectrum for public safety purposes. Furthermore, high-risk urban areas ...should establish signal corps units to ensure communications connectivity between and among civilian authorities, local first responders, and the National Guard. Federal funding of such units should be given high priority by Congress (National Commission on Terrorist Attacks Upon the United States, 2004: 397).*

The Federal Communications Commission administers the nation's telecommunications policy and assigns frequencies to public safety agencies. There is considerable debate over these issues and the result is often the lack of interoperability among agencies at the federal, state, and local levels. The debate includes the assigning of sufficient radio spectrum bandwidth, funding, and cooperation across jurisdictions. Communications systems are extremely expensive and require considerable planning. The Department of Homeland Security initiated the SAFECOM program in August of 2004 to serve as the umbrella program within the Federal Government to help local, tribal, state, and federal public safety agencies improve public safety response through more effective and efficient interoperable wireless communications. In July of 2004, the Department announced another project, RapidCom 9/30, to ensure that ten high-threat urban areas have incident-level, interoperable emergency communications capability by September 30, 2004. The areas include: New York, NY; Chicago, IL; Washington, D.C. and the surrounding Capital Region; Los Angeles, CA; San Francisco, CA; Philadelphia, PA; Houston, TX; Jersey City, NJ; Miami, FL; and Boston, MA. However, this capability is not true interoperability since it uses existing equipment that is made interoperable by a patch-panel device, interconnecting various models of equipment that would otherwise not be compatible. See the following sources for additional information about this important topic.

Sources: National Commission on Terrorist Attacks Upon the United States (2004), "The 9/11 Commission Report." Authorized Edition, New York: W.W. Norton & Co.; Raymond E. Foster (2005), *Police Technology*, Upper Saddle River: New Jersey, Pearson Education, Inc.; http://www.safecomprogram.gov/; and http://www.dhs.gov/dhspublic/display?content=3869.

---

centers combined serve nearly 8500 local, state, federal, and tribal law enforcement and criminal justice member agencies by facilitating and encouraging information sharing and communications. Typical targets of RISS activities are terrorism, drug trafficking, violent crime, cybercrime, gang activity, and organized criminal activities. The range of services varies among the centers. However, since September 11, 2001, increased emphasis has been placed on anti-terrorism activity, in addition to traditional law enforcement activities. RISS also operates RISSNET—the RISS nationwide secure criminal intelligence network for communications and information sharing by law enforcement member agencies. An important service provided on RISSNET is the availability of secure email among participants. It also provides access to the Investigative Leads Bulletin Board (RISSLeads), the RISS Criminal Intelligence Databases (RISSIntel), the RISS National Gang Database (RISSGang—which now includes a national gang intelligence database, website, bulletin board, secure e-mail, and numerous tools and resources regarding gangs and gang activities.), Officer Safety Event Deconfliction System (RISSafe), the RISS training website (RISSTraining), as well as access to each center's website for additional information and services, such as criminal activity bulletins and publications (Regional Information Sharing Systems 2010, U.S. Department of Justice, Office of Justice Programs, Global Justice Information Sharing Initiative, Security Working Group 2004).

Emergency and Non-Emergency Telephone Numbers

Today, most people living in the United States take 911 for granted, using it as the local number to dial for emergency services of all kinds: police, fire, or medical. It is estimated that more than 240 million 911 calls are made annually (National Emergency Number Association 2010). Many of these calls are received by what are referred to as **computer-aided dispatch systems,** which assist with determining locations and transmitting addresses and phone numbers to responding emergency personnel. However, even in our highly technical and modern world, the 911 number does not work everywhere in the United States. It is estimated that about 100 counties in the United States covering one percent of the population do not have 911 emergency number services (National Emergency Number Association 2010).

Dialing a three-digit number to request assistance was first implemented in England in 1937, but did not appear in the United States until January 1968, when AT&T announced the creation of 911 (following Congressional support of the concept in 1967). The first actual 911 phone call was placed on February 16, 1968 in Haleyville, Alabama through the independent Alabama Telephone Company system (Allen 2010). "Within a relatively few years, 911 systems were established in many urban areas. Within 10 years, police chiefs of large departments were beginning to complain that ever-increasing 911-generated calls for service were starting to distort and even overwhelm the balanced deployment of police resources" (Seaskate, Inc. 1998). The 911 systems are of two types: Basic 911 and Enhanced 911. The differences are that enhanced 911 has greater automated features, such as the ability to display and record the address and phone number of the caller, which allows for proper routing of the call and the dispatching of the proper jurisdictional personnel. Cellular phones have complicated the delivery of emergency services because the signals have not been

Nashville, Tennessee emergency communications center

Sources: © Jones & Bartlett Learning. Photographed by Glen E. Ellman compatible with the land-based systems. By May 2004, cellular phone companies were required to have in place the necessary technology to permit the location tracking of a 911 call made from a cell phone; that deadline was not met and, at publication, still has not been met, and so the deadline has been moved September 2012 for cellular carriers to provide emergency responders with the latitude and longitude of the caller's location. Some law enforcement agencies advise cell phone users not to call 911 if reporting a crime, because their calls usually go to the state police or state patrol instead of the local police of the jurisdiction they are calling from. Other technical problems also exist with tying Voice over Internet Protocol (VoIP) to the enhanced 911 systems. It appears that some callers using VoIP don't fall under the Federal Communications Commission's definitions regarding 911 services. Another future initiative being discussed is how to access local 911 systems through texting—the challenges of future technology are on-going!

Because of the overwhelming use (and abuse) of the 911 system, many large urban areas have overhauled, or are overhauling, their systems (see **Figure 11-6**). New York City in 2004, for example, received about 12 million 911 calls a year—that translates to 23 calls per minute! New York City has been undergoing a massive $2 billion revamping of the 911 system to improve efficiency and reduce redundancy, but as of late 2010, it was experiencing call drops during quality reviews (Gonzalez, September 1, 2010).

Because of the overwhelming number of 911 calls in urban areas, many of which were not emergency service calls, cities have undertaken the establishment of a simple non-emergency number: 311. The first 311 system was established in Baltimore, MD in 1997 (U.S. Department of Justice, COPS 2004), following approval by the FCC in February 1997, designating 311 as a national, non-toll, and voluntary non-emergency phone number. Other cities with 311 systems in operation or soon to be in operation include San José Police Department, CA; Birmingham Police Department, AL; Houston Police Department, TX; Los Angeles City Police Department, CA; Dukes County Sheriff's Office, MA; Miami City Police Department, FL; Rochester City Police Department, NY; New York City, NY (see **Figure 11-7**); Austin Police Department, TX;

FIGURE 11-6 Chicago's 911 upgrade

By 1993, Chicago's 911 system consisted of three independent dispatch centers. Emergency calls to the centers were recorded by hand on cards and then keypunched into time-clock systems. The city undertook a massive consolidation of the system and in September of 1995, a new five-story emergency call center opened for police, fire, and EMS. Caller information could be located in 1.2 seconds of making the call. The consolidation effort cost $214 million over all phases, including construction, training, and working with multiple vendors.

The center today serves as a model for other cities contemplating upgrades to their emergency call systems. The system can send voice messages to 2500 mobile police terminals and 490 fire stations. It tracks every fire vehicle by plotting coordinates on a geographical positioning system (GPS) map. The system is constantly being improved and is on its third evolutionary upgrade. In 2009, improvements linked operators to police surveillance cameras around the city.

Source: Based on McKay (2004a) and Meincke, (February 19, 2009).

FIGURE 11-7 Dial 311 in New York City

In the last decade years, New York City established a 311 system that consolidated over 40 call centers and 14 pages of telephone numbers. It has over 300 operators and sometimes handles more than 30,000 calls daily. Calls to the 311 system are routed through the regular phone system and do not require the data collection that the 911 system does. The 311 call center provides assistance in over 170 languages. In 2009, the city launched 311Online to serve requests via the Internet in addition to the phone system; and it issues some assistance updates using Twitter, iPhone, and Skype.

Source: Based on McKay (2004a) and New York City (2010).

Framingham Police Department, MA; and Orange County Sheriff's Office, FL (U.S. Department of Justice, COPS 2004). As of September 2008, approximately 55.8 million residents have access to the 311 number, or about 18% of the population (Dispatch Magazine On-Line 2010).

Other Information Technologies

During the last two decades, advancements in computer technology have led to great interest in and implementation of systems beyond 911 and 311. The **automated vehicle locator system** (**AVLS**) permits electronic map displays of the location of agency vehicles. It has recently been incorporated into some 911 systems (see **Figure 11-8**). Vehicles equipped with **global positioning system** (**GPS**) transmitters can be identified by dispatchers as being the

closest ones to respond to emergencies. Such technology permits dispatchers to know the direction of vehicle pursuits without the driver having to constantly verbalize a change. The AVLS system also improves officer safety by indicating exact locations in need of assistance. Of course GPS technology can be used to track other vehicles (and objects) as well, including suspect vehicles or ones carrying special cargo or hazardous materials through a jurisdiction. GPS vehicle technology has become commercially available through the OnStar system marketed through some automobile manufacturers, and millions of units of personal vehicle navigation systems and handheld units have been sold to the public. GPS is now part of cellular phone technology and is becoming standard equipment on some new cars.

Many progressive law enforcement agencies have placed their records of criminal incidents and calls for service online for quick access and retrieval. Such databases, when properly configured, can be utilized in conjunction with **geographic information systems** (**GIS**) to perform **computer mapping** and other types of analyses. Such systems permit the displaying of jurisdictional maps along with any number of selected types of key structures (e.g., schools, hospitals, bridges, museums) and features (e.g., parks, rivers, closed roads). Crime-related incidents can be **geocoded** onto these maps in order to conduct **crime analysis**. The International Association of Crime Analysts (IACA) defines crime analysis as "a type of law enforcement analysis that is focused on the study of criminal incidents; the identification and analysis of patterns, trends, and problems; and the dissemination of information that helps a police agency develop tactics and strategies to solve patterns, trends, and problems." There are several different types of crime analysis, including tactical crime analysis, strategic crime analysis, and administrative crime analysis. In addition, other types of analyses include criminal intelligence analysis, criminal investigative analysis, and geographic profiling (see Boba 2005; Bruce 2004).

There are many different types of maps that might be constructed, depending on the type of analysis that is being performed (Paynich and Hill 2009). An analyst might map a simple, single incident, or show the distribution of crime across a particular area such as a police beat or district. A crime map might also show multiple "hot

---

FIGURE 11-8 Use of AVLS in Law Enforcement Agencies

The purpose of using automatic vehicle locator systems (AVLS) is to track the position of active duty vehicles on a mapped computer screen. Digital displays permit commanding officers to observe locations of vehicles, and officers in their cars can see the same display as well. The system tracks speed, location, direction, and time of day—information that can improve responses to calls for service, officer safety when assistance is needed, and agency review incidents (such as high-speed pursuits or allegations of officer misconduct). AVLS is often a part of a larger technology installation that also gives officers the ability to file reports directly to the system, look up criminal histories, and watch live dispatch entries in their cars. Some departments using AVLS today include:

- Houston (TX) Police Department
- Dallas (TX) Police Department
- San Diego (CA) Police Department
- Charlotte-Mecklenburg (NC) Police Department
- East Orange (NJ) Police Department
- Virginia Beach (VA) Police Department
- Escandido (CA) Police Department
- West Haven (CT) Police Department
- Ft. Lauderdale (FL) Police Department

spots" located across a jurisdiction or related to multiple criminal events, or it may focus on a single offender or group of offenders in a series of connected criminal events (such as a child molester or serial murderer). Mapping capabilities are also being combined with sophisticated statistics in prediction efforts to identify an offender's next target or areas where offenders might live, work, play, or retreat to after performing a criminal event. Figures 11-9 through 11-11 are examples of different types of maps that might be utilized for law enforcement purposes. All of these maps were created by Bryan Hill, Crime Analyst for Glendale, AZ Police Department. **Figure 11-9** depicts a simple map of a protest march identifying not only the planned path of the protesters, but also the police resources needed at various points along the march. In **Figure 11-10**, a journey-to-crime map identifies areas

most likely to house an offender's anchor point (where he/she starts his "journey to crime," often thought to be the offender's residence but could be a work address or a significant other's address, such as a girlfriend or mother's house). Finally, in **Figure 11-11**, an indecent exposure series is analyzed in efforts to predict the area most likely to be hit next.

An example of GIS technology being applied to crime analysis appears on popular television shows, where often the chief and his or her top commanders are shown in a small auditorium viewing graphical displays of recent crimes or trends. This recent combining of crime analysis, computerization, GIS, and managerial accountability is called **CompStat/ComStat**. The name is derived from "computer" and "statistics." Most of the literature on CompStat traces its development to a program

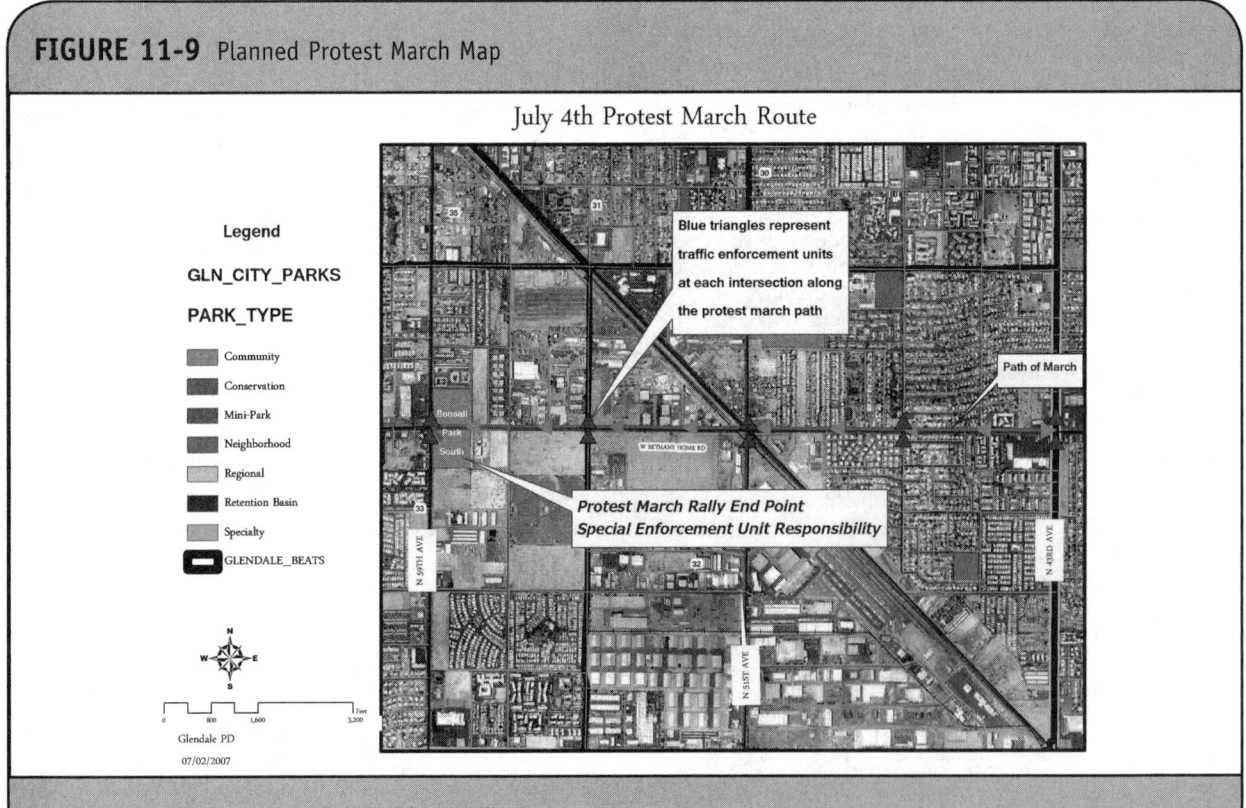

FIGURE 11-9 Planned Protest March Map

Source: Bryan Hill, Crime Analyst for Glendale, AZ Police Department.

FIGURE 11-10 "Journey to Crime" Map

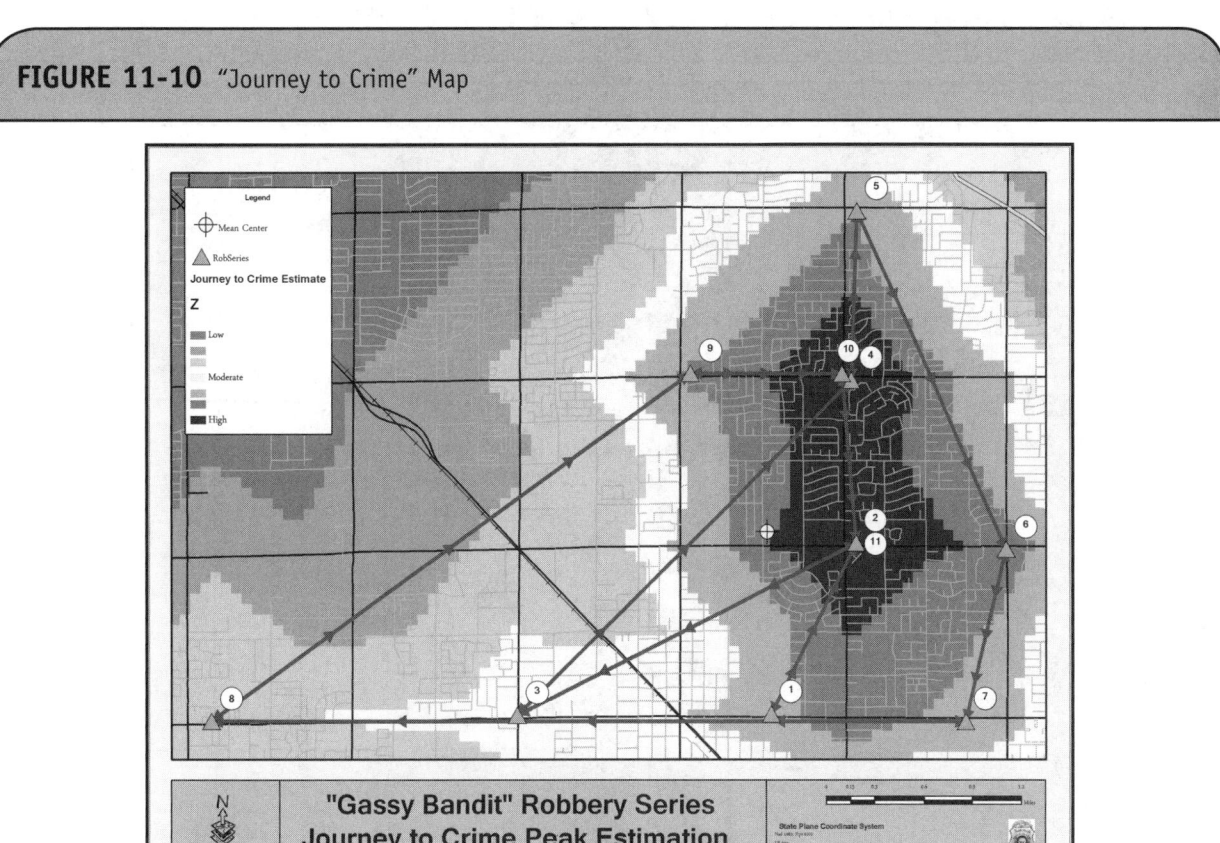

"Gassy Bandit" Robbery Series
Journey to Crime Peak Estimation

Source: Bryan Hill, Crime Analyst for Glendale, AZ Police Department.

developed in New York City in the 1990s, where commanders and bureau chiefs were held accountable for crime and clearance rates in their respective precincts or areas of responsibility. The NYC model was based on four crime-reduction principles: accurate and timely intelligence, effective tactics, rapid deployment of personnel and resources, and relentless follow-up and assessment (Shane 2004). CompStat is a strategic management concept that spread across the country during the last two decades. As more and more cities utilize these principles successfully, others take notice and seek the same results. However, few evaluation studies have been conducted on CompStat practices; some officers have complained that weekly meetings are often "stale" and "laborious," and some believe it creates intense pressure to manipulate crime figures (Fenton 2010). See **Figure 11-12** for more information on CompStat trends.

The possibilities for GIS and Crime analysis are seemingly endless, especially as technology has rapidly advanced in recent years and continues to progress at an exhausting pace. As discussed earlier in Chapter 5, our ability to utilize information effectively is directly tied to technology. We now have the capability to collect, store, and analyze massive amounts of information in a very short period of time. In fact, the current technology allows for many types of crime maps and analyses to be

FIGURE 11-11 Indecent Exposure Series

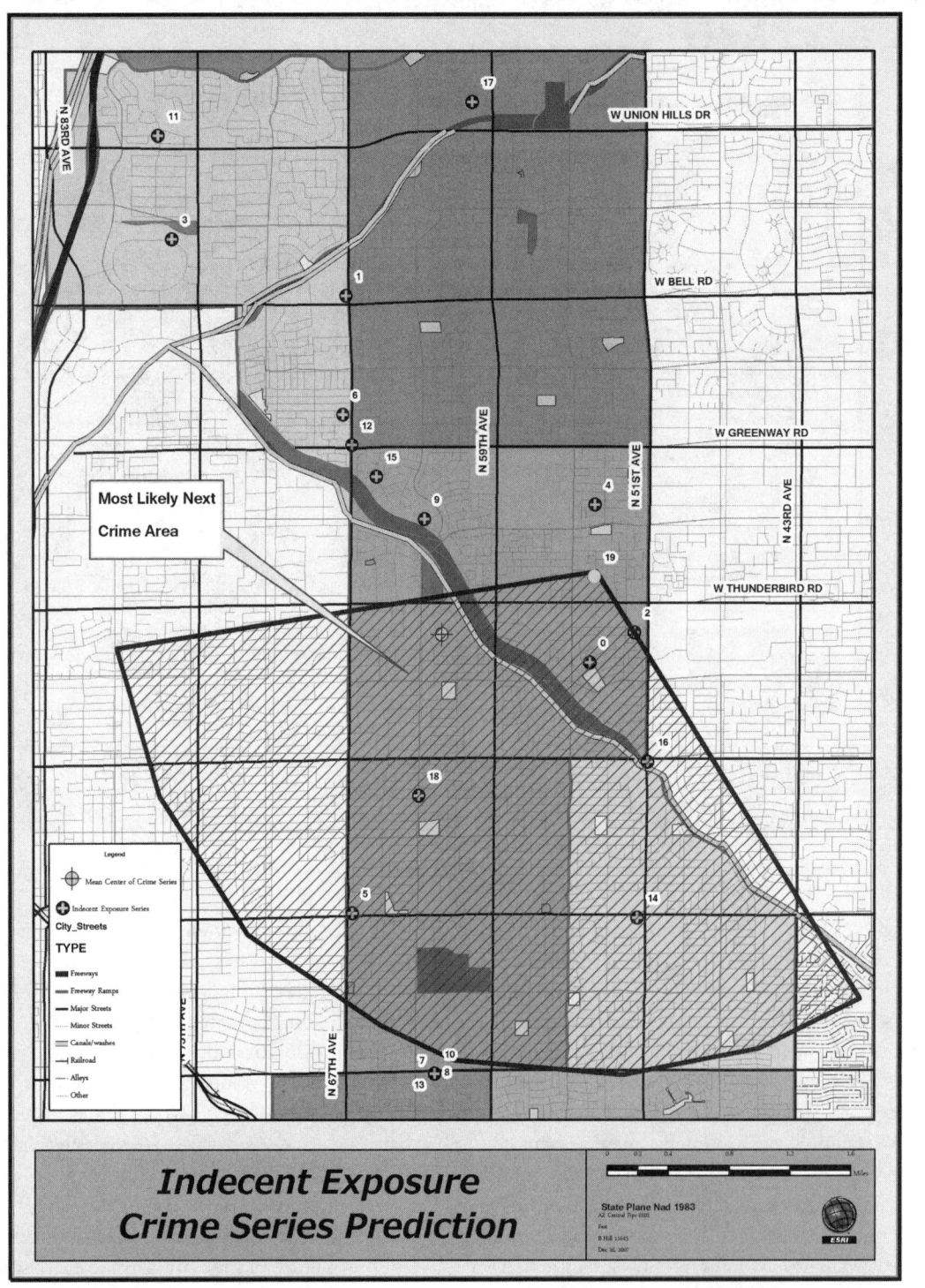

Source: Bryan Hill, Crime Analyst for Glendale, AZ Police Department.

FIGURE 11-12 Compstat—Emerging Trends

During a recent town hall meeting held in Orlando, Florida by the Police Executive Research Forum, police executives discussed the "Future of Compstat." Many indicated that CompStat meeting in agencies today are less contentious and more focused on crime patterns, hot spots, and accomplishments. Some quotes from the meeting include the following:

"I think it's important to understand that Compstat is not the answer to crime. It is a vehicle to figure out how to come up with solutions and ways to address crime. If you look at Compstat as the answer, it's going to fail. The bottom line is it's a vehicle to get there."

—Newark Police Director Garry McCarthy

"...the lion's share of our staff sees it [meetings] as an opportunity to showcase what they're doing great—and to give the Commissioner and the rest of command staff an opportunity to see who needs to be elevated."

—Philadelphia Deputy Commissioner Richard Ross

"We've evolved to where we're doing a lot more predictive analysis. We look at what happened in the last week, but we're also asking each of them to do something about patterns we'll likely see in the coming week. We also make sure that investigations evolve, so that they're being held accountable in terms of what they're doing."

—Minneapolis Chief Tim Dolan

"One of the primary things I've found from our Compstat is that it helps you make sure that all your resources are being coordinated. Often, especially in large departments, the more specialty units that you have, the cops may be doing good work but it's not necessarily what you need them to do, or what the district captain needs them to be doing."

—Philadelphia Commissioner Chuck Ramsey

"We're using Intelligence-Led Policing, crime analysis, and problem oriented policing to address crime. We're trying to attack crime where it is happening and trying to predict where it may happen next.... Compstat is alive and well and I don't see it going away anytime soon."

—Topeka, KS Chief Ronald Miller

"Compstat is our version of a staff meeting. When I'm with the officers, the officers attribute most of the guidance that they get to things that occurred in Compstat. We don't need to yell at Compstat meetings; I hardly ever raise my voice. But there is peer pressure."

—Nashville Chief Steve Anderson

Source: Extracted from Police Executive Research Forum (October 2010).

fully automated. Agencies can set up their GIS and other computer and information systems to create, print, and distribute maps and analyses to officers at regular intervals on a daily basis (at roll call, for example). GIS software also offers law enforcement the opportunity to easily utilize different sources of data from other agencies (health department, census bureau, social welfare agencies) in their analyses of crime problems and problem solving efforts.

Social networking media is another form of information technology available to law enforcement agencies. A 2010 survey of 728 law enforcement agencies from 48 states and the District of Columbia revealed the following (IACP, Center for Social Media 2010, 1):

- 81.1% of agencies surveyed use social media;
- 66.8% of agencies surveyed have a Facebook page;
- 35.2% of agencies surveyed have a social media policy, with an additional 23.2% in the process of crafting a policy;
- The top activities for which social media was used included criminal investigations, notifying the public of crime or emergencies, crime prevention, community outreach, and soliciting crime tips; and
- Resource constraints (time and personnel) were the most cited barrier to social media use by surveyed agencies.

Another survey by the Canadian Association of Police on Social Media found 800 accounts on social media sites belong to police officers or agencies in the United States. American police were strongest of the three countries surveyed at tweeting (posting messages on Twitter.com) missing and wanted person information, but were least likely to tweet community and police volunteer activities (Madison, Miller, and Worden 2010).

MAJOR APPLICATIONS OF TECHNOLOGY IN LAW ENFORCEMENT TODAY

The previous section focused primarily on information technology and how it has evolved and affected law enforcement. Suffice it to say, any form of administrative and management processes (e.g., fiscal control/payroll, training records, personnel records, incident reports) can be automated with various kinds of information technology. While some agencies still use paper-based reporting and processing systems, most of the larger and progressive ones have incorporated field-based tablet computers or mobile digital technology that permits officers to file electronic reports. These are then processed through internal networks and databases. In this section, we move to other applications of technology that are being utilized in operational and investigational aspects of policing.

The uses and applications of technology in law enforcement are as broad as one's imagination and creativity. (See **Figure 11-13** regarding the application of

> **FIGURE 11-13** Applied Technology—Project Lifesaver
>
> Technology can be used in many ways, but one way that has helped save considerable time and effort in locating and returning wandering adults and children to their families and caregivers is called Project Lifesaver. It is an innovative program that aids victims and families suffering from Alzheimer's disease and related disorders such as Down Syndrome and autism. The program forms partnerships with local law enforcement and public safety organizations in order to acquire equipment and train officers. A personalized radio transmitter worn by vulnerable individuals can be used to track them should they become lost or disoriented. The technology used by the public safety organization is capable of tracking a signal up to a mile by ground and five to nine miles by air. These devices work by giving an audible signal that leads law enforcement to the victims. The devices transmit over special radio frequency equipment that is considered the most reliable and practical technology available in locating the missing and wandering. It is considered more reliable than GPS technology at this time. Project Lifesaver is being adopted by law enforcement agencies across the country.
>
> *Source*: Adapted from Project Lifesaver (2010).

technology to the very time-consuming task of locating lost individuals). Today, individual officers are developing new applications—the process is no longer one limited to the research and planning of communications sections of an agency. The advent of the personal computer in the 1980s has brought computing power to the individual level and has opened a new realm of applications. Greater interest in science and electronics has expanded the potential of applications to the law enforcement field. A detailed examination of the emerging applications of technology in law enforcement is not possible here because it is expanding so rapidly. However, we do recommend that online searches be conducted and professional periodicals such as *The Police Chief, Law and Order, Law Enforcement Technology, Public Safety IT, Police and Security News,* and *Government Technology* be reviewed for ever-changing technology and its applications (and remember to read the advertisements related to the latest technology).

Besides information technology, what other areas of policing have been impacted by improved technology? With regard to weapons, the days of the simple pistol and rifle have given way to automatic weapons, laser-scoped rifles, and Tasers. Nighttime (low-light) vision devises, thermal imaging cameras, and high-tech surveillance equipment are now less costly and more readily available. Of course, the automobile has continued to be refined, streamlined, and equipped with low-profile light emitting diode (LED) lights and electronic sirens. Hand tools such as flashlights, batons, PR-24s, and even handcuffs have undergone redesign and improvements. Radar systems for detecting speeders on the highways have begun using lasers.

Since the terrorist attacks of 9/11, there has been greater interest in improving the technology transfer from military research and development to civilian law enforcement applications. In the 2000s, the Pentagon spent about $35 billion a year on research and development, and the U.S. Department of Justice spent only about $5 million (Komarow 1994). In a 1994 "Memorandum of Understanding," the Department of Defense and the Department of Justice agreed to work more closely in developing and sharing technology that could be applied to civilian law enforcement. The National Law Enforcement and Corrections Technology Center (NLECTC) was established within the Justice Department to coordinate and facilitate technological transfer to the civilian law enforcement sector. The Office of Law Enforcement Technology Commercialization (OLETC) is the primary unit in the NLECTC working on this effort. The Center is heavily involved in high-technology research to enhance the law enforcement function and to protect officers. One of the center's publications is called *TechBeat* and is available online (see the links at the end of this chapter). The next sections of this chapter will review some of the other technologies emerging from laboratories and being used in many (but not all) law enforcement agencies.

Less-than-Lethal Technologies

In the last twenty years, greater scientific inquiry and research have been conducted into **less-than-lethal technologies**— those that subdue individuals in ways that would lessen the chance of serious injury or death. Besides protecting officers from hostile individuals, a major impetus for such research

Radio controlled robot

Source: © TFoxFoto/ShutterStock, Inc.

has been an attempt to avoid lawsuits for wrongful death filed against police departments or allegations of excessive force. The major categories of less-than-lethal technologies, according to the National Institute of Justice, include the following (National Institute of Justice 2010; Taser.com 2010; Rowe 2010; Foster 2004; Hambling 2004; Pilant 1998; Boyd 1995):

- *Conducted Energy Devices* (CEDs) *or Electroshock Weapons*: Some CEDs can induce involuntary muscle contractions that temporarily incapacitate people; such a device (often referred to as a Taser, which is actually the company name of the leading producer of the device) is used by over 4000 police departments in the United States. It is an electric shock gun that fires small darts that trail current-carrying wires; when the darts hit the intended target, the current causes involuntary muscle contractions, momentarily stunning and incapacitating the target. The latest version of this technology permits multiple firings of the device, and there is also a self-contained cartridge that can be fired from a 12-gauge shotgun at a range up to 100 feet. Other CEDs deter an individual from a course of action, and these include stun guns and stun belts. One stun gun under development utilizes electrically-conductive fibers shot through the air in a stream toward the target; it utilizes no wires. The TASER Shockwave barrier is designed to fire a bank of six electrified probes at the same time in a single direction. Another CED device is the Close Quarters Shock Rifle, which projects an ionized gas, or plasma, toward the target that receives an electrical shock; it is reported to also interfere with electronic ignition systems of vehicles. Still another uses solid-state lasers that ionize the air, producing long, thread-like filaments of glowing plasma that deliver a shock to the target. Stun belts can be used by remote control to restrain prisoners in transport and in disruptive courtroom appearances.

- *Directed energy devices.* This new technology uses radiated energy to achieve the same effect as blunt force, but has a lower probability of injury. Laser devices and weapons have disruptive (visual) and destructive (primarily thermal) effects upon their targets. The Personnel Halting and Stimulation Response (PHaSR) is a rifle-sized laser weapon system that uses two nonlethal laser wavelengths to deter, prevent, or mitigate an adversary's effectiveness. The laser light generated by this weapon illuminates or "dazzles" aggressors, temporarily impairing individuals and their ability to see the laser source. Another directed energy device is the military's Active Denial System (ADS), which uses a focused beam of 3.2mm-wave electromagnetic radiation toward a human target. This heats the water and fat molecules on the skin, causing the target's temperature to rise; such discomfort usually causes the target to flee. Another directed energy device includes the Long Range Acoustic Device. It transmits narrow beams of sound waves that can be heard clearly from 300 meters (about 1000 feet) away. If the power is increased, it can emit a warning tone so loud that anyone in its path would have no choice but to cover their ears and run.

- *Chemicals.* These chemicals include pepper spray (also known as OC—oleoresin capsicum), tear gas, and stink bombs. These have been used by law enforcement for years, but a research question about chemicals has been raised: could drugs be used successfully as a less-than-lethal weapon?

- *Distraction.* This equipment temporarily incapacitates people while causing little harm. Examples include the laser dazzler, bright lights, and noise devices. One device, called Strobe-and-Goggle Technology, is designed to disorient subjects during raids or assaults on barricaded structures. It uses bright flashing light to blind subjects while officers wearing special goggles enter to apprehend subjects.

- *Vehicle-stopping technology.* This equipment can stop cars during high-speed chases. It includes remote-controlled barrier strips that would pop-up and puncture the tires of a vehicle. The use of these is an attempt to limit the dangers of setting up spike strips during high-speed vehicular pursuits, as these remote-controlled strips would be activated by police as the vehicle being pursued approaches them. Another vehicle-stopping technology on the "wish list" is the fleeing vehicle tagging system, where officers might one day be able to "tag" a vehicle with a miniature radio transmitter or GPS device that would allow them to track the vehicle at a safe distance without giving immediate chase and endangering the lives of others. Vehicle disablers are another technological application being researched; it would be a device that police could aim at a vehicle and disable its internal computer system, which would cause the engine to shut down. The vehicle would be useless, and the occupants could be trapped inside. Currently, similar technology is used in stolen car stakeouts as seen on the TruTV show *Bait Car*.

- *Barriers.* These include nets, foams, and physical barriers. Sometimes called "people netting" (as with fishnets), nets could be used to control unruly persons or crowds. This netting would entangle the subjects, making movement difficult. Sticky Foam is a taffy-colored, gel-like substance that turns into a glue that sticks on contact. It can be dispensed from a shoulder-slung apparatus that contains the material under pressure. When applied, it expands, becomes sticky, and trips-up subjects. At the present time, it takes a large amount of material to be effective, and clean-up is a problem. One type of barrier is the backseat airbag, which can be deployed to control unruly subjects who attempt to kick out windows or to damage partitioning screens.

- *Blunt force.* Projectiles used in crowd-control deter people from a course of action. These devices include the beanbag shotgun capable of firing bags of several different shapes and forms, but usually containing rubber pellets. If not properly used, the ammunition can cause serious injury (blunt force trauma) and even death. The tactical 37mm launcher is a special less-lethal control device that expels wooden or rubber bullets or chemical agents toward large crowds; they have a psychological effect as well because of the amount of smoke, noise, and flash that is produced.

Some manufacturers integrate multiple effects into one device. For example, a multisensory stun grenade combines noise, light, chemicals, and blunt force. Stun grenades disorient people, giving police officers the opportunity to arrest a suspect without harming them unnecessarily.

In 1997, the Pentagon created the Non-Lethal Weapons Program to research and develop new technologies, similar to a National Institute of Justice (NIJ) program that began in 1986. In 1994, the NIJ created a working partnership with the Department of Defense, with the goals of the NIJ program being the "identification and development of new or improved weapons and other technology that will minimize the risk of death and injury to officers, suspects, prisoners, and the public, and contribute to the reduction of civil and criminal liability suits against police, sheriff, and corrections departments" (Pilant 1998, 55). An example of NIJ's involvement in developing safety products for law enforcement is described in **Figure 11-14.**

Investigative Tools

The ongoing search for better detection equipment and identification technologies continues in both the research lab and the field. The FBI's Biometric Center of Excellence (BCOE) was created as a one-stop shop for biometric collaboration and expertise (Federal Bureau of Investigation 2010e). **Biometrics** are the measurable biological (anatomical and physiological) or behavioral characteristics used for identification of an individual. Fingerprints are a common biometric modality, but others include things like DNA, irises, voice patterns, palmprints, and facial patterns. The BCOE is a collaborative initiative of the

---

FIGURE 11-14 How Did Soft Body Armor Originate?

The technology used for soft body armor worn by police officers was initially developed for heavy-duty military truck tires that were bullet-resistant. In 1972, a researcher from the U.S. Department of Justice's National Institute of Justice (NIJ) stumbled upon the fiber used in the tires, better known by its trade name Kevlar. Vests were subsequently developed, and NIJ conducted field tests in 15 cities. Since 1975, it is estimated that soft body armor has saved the lives of thousands of police officers.

Development continues today on vests and helmets that would offer greater protection to officers. In the near future, inserts made of titanium and ceramic may be available that offer greater bullet protection. The vests are designed to be more concealable and offer greater freedom of movement. Research is underway on a liquid body armor that becomes rigid when suddenly hit. The military and other agencies test new products using prototypes.

Sources: David G. Boyd (July 1995), John J. Pennella and Peter L Nacci (February 1997), and Christina M. Miller (2004).

Laboratory Division, the Operational Technology Division, the Criminal Justice Information Services Division, and the Special Technologies and Applications Office.

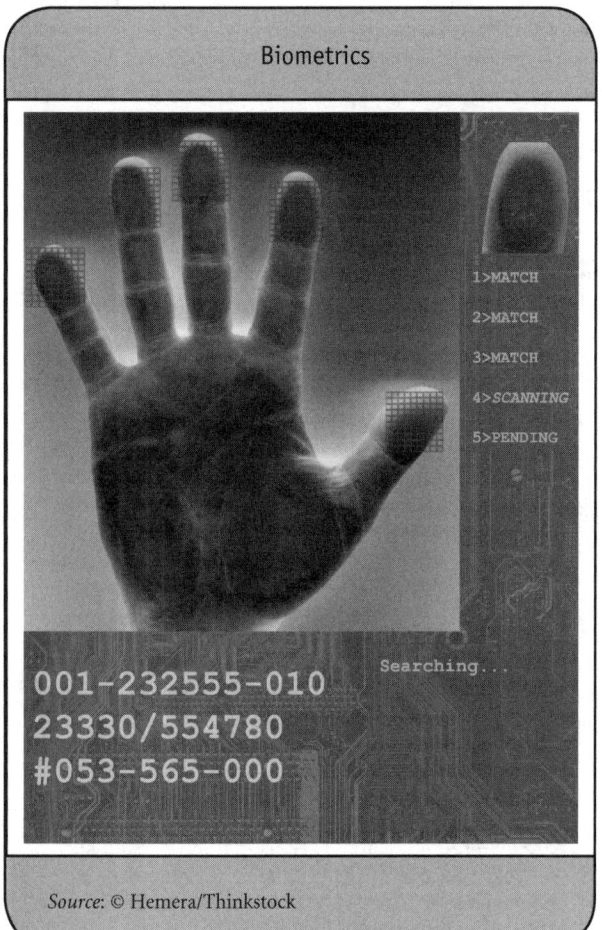

Biometrics

1>MATCH
2>MATCH
3>MATCH
4>SCANNING
5>PENDING

Searching...

001-232555-010
23330/554780
#053-565-000

Source: © Hemera/Thinkstock

The **Integrated Automated Fingerprint Identification Systems** (IAFIS) allows access to the National Criminal History Record File of the national Criminal Justice Information System, where the fingerprints of over 62 million persons can be searched. Such technology increases the chances of identifying suspects and reduces the time to do so—the average response time is less than eight minutes (Federal Bureau of Investigation, Biometric Services Section 2010). As its name implies, IAFIS systems use computer technology for the imaging, transmission, comparison, and storage of fingerprints. Systems are now in operation in many jurisdictions across the nation and some

can be accessed even from patrol cars equipped with fingerprint scanners. In October 2010, the City of Brockton (MA) Police Department became the first agency in the country to use the Mobile Offender Recognition and Identification System (MORIS), an iPhone application that takes iris images, fingerprints, and photos of subjects on the street. This biometric data can then be uploaded on a secure network for the purpose of identifying the individual in seconds. As the system is refined and upgraded, more agencies in Massachusetts are expected to use the technology (Siuru 2010). This is but a sample of things to come regarding smart phone applications. Some existing applications that are very useful for law enforcement include Photo Map (which captures not only the date and time of a picture taken, but the location as well) and QuickVoice2TextE-mail (Pro Recorder—takes a recorded message and creates a texted e-mail with the click of a button).

Some envision other devices to assist police in detecting weapons on subjects, something like a hand-held magnetometer but could be used some distance from the subject. It may be possible one day to stand outside a building and detect the person or persons inside through infrared technology. Some "smart-guns" are used today that cannot be fired unless being held by an authorized person. Subjects who steal such weapons or take guns from officers during a struggle would find them useless if attempting to fire them. They have been available for years, but are expensive and controversial.

The body scanning equipment used today at airports to detect weapons and the equipment used to detect explosives is just the most visible of recent technologies used in law enforcement. Concealed weapons detection equipment is under development that may be able to prevent random firearm violence and protect criminal justice and military personnel as they perform their tasks. Programs initiated in 1995 are pursuing five technological approaches to detect concealed weapons on individuals: passive millimeter wave (MMW) sensors and infrared (IF) cameras, X-ray sensors, active low-frequency magnetic sensors, magnetometers, and a sensor system combining ultrasound and radar sensors. The hope is to create a portable system that can detect concealed weapons from up to 30 feet (Pennella and Nacci 1997). Such devices could be used in airports, prisons, courts, police stations, schools, and at large public gatherings. As the devices become more portable, they could become standard equipment on the uniform of officers.

Ballistics analysis technology also has evolved in recent years. At the federal level, the Bureau of Alcohol, Tobacco, Firearms, and Explosives (ATFE) and FBI have integrated their systems into the National Integrated Ballistic Information Network (NIBIN). The network utilizes Integrated Ballistics Identification System (IBIS) units to obtain firearm information from state and local law enforcement agencies for comparisons. These units allow technicians to acquire, digitize, and compare markings made by a firearm on bullets and cartridge casings. The network also permits the analysis to link offenses related to those bullets or casings. See Figure 11-5 for additional information regarding NIBIN and **Figure 11-15** for two "Hits of the Week" press releases.

Digital imaging systems coupled with wireless technology now permit the sending of crime scene videos, street photos, mug shots, etc. to and from central police stations. Video and digital imaging technology is revolutionizing crime scene investigation. One strategy, called **teleforensics,** permits the recording of crime scenes using a camcorder fitted with a wireless transmitter that sends images to remote monitors in real time. Several companies now market three-dimensional laser scanning equipment utilizing special software "to measure, photograph, reconstruct, analyze and present crime scenes," and dozens of law enforcement agencies are using such technology (DeltaSphere.com 2010). The equipment and software creates a panoramic view of the crime scene, which can be used to reduce possible contamination of the scene and can even be extended into a scene on a pole or by a robot. Investigators can add notations directly to the recorded model of the crime scene and some models can transmit the information anywhere in the world, if necessary.

Other investigative technologies include automated versions of the composite sketch devices and software that has been available for years. One vendor now has a version that is Web-based, allowing access to five billion different facial composites (Smith & Wesson Advanced Technologies 2003).

A number of other electronic devices are making crime detection and investigation more technical. Ohio

---

FIGURE 11-15 NIBIN—Examples from "Hits of the Week."

Week of May 3, 2010

On June 23, 2009, Campbell (OH) Police Department responded to a non-fatal shooting where the victim had been shot on a public sidewalk sustaining eight gunshot wounds to the chest and head. On September 18, 2009, Youngstown (OH) Police Department responded to a shooting where the suspect chased the victim on foot up and fired up at the victim up to the victim's residential driveway. Officers arrested the suspected shooter. Using NIBIN, Ohio Bureau of Criminal Identification - Northeast Laboratory was able to match the firearm to both shootings. On December 15, 2009, the defendant was convicted of Attempted Murder with a Firearm Specification and was sentenced to a period of ten years and three years imprisonment, to be served consecutively.

Week of May 10, 2010

On December 13, 2008, Columbus (OH) Division of Police responded to a drive-by shooting where the shooter had fired at a passing vehicle striking one of the occupants twice in the back. On March 2, 2009, Columbus Division of Police responded to a home invasion in an apartment complex, arrested one suspect, and recovered a 9mm pistol. Using NIBIN, Columbus Division of Police's Crime Laboratory was able to match the firearm to the shooting incident. On June 30, 2009, the defendant pled guilty to burglary and improper handling-of a firearm and was sentenced to three years imprisonment.

Source: Extracted from ATFE (2010).

---

added license plate recognition equipment to selected locations on the Ohio Turnpike in 2004. The system scans vehicle license plates and processes them electronically through NCIC's stolen license plate file. If there is a match, dispatchers are alerted; they verify the information and then notify troopers to intercept the vehicle (Meade 2004). These recognition systems can capture up to 3600 license plates per minute and are now utilized in hundreds of agencies across the country. One Virginia agency found a stolen vehicle in the first 10 minutes of use and another agency found one in the first 30 minutes of using the equipment (Wilson 2010).

Cruisers also have been outfitted in many departments with in-car video cameras. About 72% of all state police and highway patrol vehicles have been equipped with video systems that record officer actions and serve as evidence of offenses committed by subjects. In one survey of 3000 respondents, officers accused of wrongdoing were exonerated 96.2% of the time because of video evidence captured by in-car camera systems (Westphal 2004). The technology supporting in-car video systems is continuing to advance; the latest equipment is now digital and can record two cameras simultaneously. Although not common yet, **personal video surveillance systems** consisting of a small camera and microphone attached to the shirt of an officer and a transmitter attached to the duty belt, which sends images and sounds to a receiver/recorder subsystem located in the officer's vehicle, could become standard equipment for officers in the near future. Wearable video cameras are now in use or being tested in departments across the country. The TV reality show, *Police POV*, uses headset-style cameras to show the viewer what officers are actually seeing on the job. We expect this type of technology to become common in the next decade.

Global positioning system (GPS) technology can now be applied to crime scene processing to aid in measuring the location of evidence and enhancing crime scene sketching. This technology is used for surveillance purposes, especially in tracking suspect vehicles or tracing valuable cargo or property shipments. For example, police used GPS technology to track the whereabouts of a suspect before he was charged in the death of his wife and their unborn son (McKay 2004b).

Some urban departments are now employing **gunshot detection devices** (or gunshot location system— GLS) to locate the source of gunfire in their jurisdictions. Also called instant gunfire recognition systems, microphones pick up the sound of gunfire and then a camera zooms in on the area. Another system uses acoustic sensors "deployed over areas from one square mile up to hundreds of linear miles to locate gunfire and other violent threats within seconds" that pinpoint the location onto a map image and cross-reference to the nearest street address, allowing the appropriate law enforcement response (ShotSpotter.com 2010).

Another advancement in technology includes the **personal vertical takeoff and landing aircraft (VTOL)**. The VTOLs of the future will be staffed with a single person and will be potentially less costly to maintain and more maneuverable than helicopters. Prototypes are already being tested and some are envisioning their application to law enforcement situations (Cowper 2004a). **Unmanned aerial vehicles (UAVs)**—also referred to as drones—have proven to be very effective in military operations. The Customs and Border Patrol began using drones for border surveillance and protection in June 2010 (Homeland Security Newswire 2010).

Drone similar to those used by the U.S. Border Patrol

Source: © REUTERS/DOD /Landov

There simply is no end to the advancement and application of technology to the various law enforcement functions. As we contemplate what the future holds for this topic, one can only imagine how things might be. As we reflect on the changing world around us, we see subtle changes being made. Sometimes we don't realize how fast things are changing. Artificial intelligence in computing was quite new two decades ago, and now there are many software developments that utilize it. Virtual reality has been employed in training systems and its continued applications will spread as the technology becomes less expensive; however, its applications beyond training may be limited. The movie *Avatar* is an example of where some of this technology is heading. Recently, the trainers at the Federal Law Enforcement Training Center (FLETC) began using ABIS (Avatar-Based Interview Simulator) to teach trainees interviewing skills. The Avatar responds to questions related to a number of scenarios; all questions and responses are recorded for student review and instructor critiques (Kuykendall 2010).

Augmented reality, however, is being discussed today in the law enforcement arena and it may be upon us before we know it. It is a technological application that combines the real and the virtual, displaying information in real time in a way that enhances the individual abilities of people operating in the real world (Cowper 2004b). The helmet technologies displayed in the movie *Robocop* may best illustrate this concept. Various types of information—pictures, diagrams, and instructions—were received by the helmet's sensors to augment the situation that Robocop experienced. This additional information assisted him in carrying out his mission. We may soon have that same ability (see **Figure 11-16** for a more detailed explanation).

Law Enforcement and Privacy

Since technology is at the heart of many privacy issue debates, and the use and abuse of that technology is often the focal point of debate in policing, it is appropriate to review some of the issues related to technology that reduce privacy and enhance possible detection. Included in this category are technologies that reduce privacy (liberty) rights of an individual by increasing the ability of others to identify, locate, and follow an individual. Examples are geographic information systems (GIS), global positioning systems (GPS), satellite imagery (SI), remote sensing, telephony interception (including wiretapping, pen registers, and dialed number recorders), concealed weapons detectors, electronic license plate readers, surveillance cameras, and listening devices (Conser 1997). Radio Frequency Identification (RFID) technology today is used for inventorying commercial products, tracking animals, tracking selected drugs, hazardous materials, and even automobile tires (Page 2004). RFID tags can be extremely small and barely visible. Their use has sparked a debate regarding potential privacy issues.

FIGURE 11-16 What Is Augmented Reality?

According to one policing technology expert, augmented reality (AR) "uses wearable components to overlay virtual (computer-generated) information onto individuals' real-world view or into their real-world experiences in a way that improves and enhances their abilities to accomplish a wide variety of tasks and missions." It combines the real and the virtual, displaying information in real time, in a way that enhances the individual abilities of people operating in the real world.

Although still in its early stages of development and applications, it is being utilized in football broadcasting (the yellow first down line superimposed on the football field), race car broadcasting (the driver and speed information tagged to race cars), and in military operations (aircraft systems data superimposed on cockpit monitors along with enemy targets).

A fully interactive AR system may derive information from a multitude of sources. Data can be transmitted wirelessly from a computer network, accessed from the wearable computer carried by the AR user. By using virtual graphics, three-dimensional maps, textual annotations, auditory information, and haptic (touch) sensations in a coordinated real-time presentation, AR brings together a variety of technologies to display information to individuals in a way that instantly applies to a given task or situation. Future law enforcement applications could include real-time language translations coupled with data on cultural customs and traditions; real-time display of intelligence information or crime analysis information about a neighborhood situation; facial and biometric recognition data about known criminal offenders and wanted persons; integration of chemical, biological, and explosive sensors to improve officer safety; and accessibility to maps and building plans to enhance hostage negotiations and SWAT situations; enhanced surveillance operation by coordinating use of robots, unmanned aerial vehicles (UAVs), and satellite images.

Source: Thomas Cowper (2004), "Improving the View of the World: Law Enforcement and Augmented Reality Technology," FBI Law Enforcement Bulletin, January, pp. 12–18.

Michael G. Curry (1997) authored an excellent article that examines the potential invasion of privacy capabilities of GIS, GPS, SI, and remote sensing technologies when coupled with geodemographics. The combination of satellite surveillance technology and personal demographic information (age, occupation, income, race, education, etc.) can be utilized to track and locate an individual. The inappropriate use of this technology, which has little or no regulation restricting its use, is of concern. These same technologies, however, also can provide valuable services to consumers such as assisting lost motorists, locating stolen vehicles, or locating a desired destination.

Telephony interception capabilities include wiretaps, pen registers, and dialed number recorders. The differences among these are: wiretaps refers to the interception of telecommunications conversations, verbal or digital, wire or wireless; pen registers record the phone numbers of incoming phone calls to a target phone; and dialed number recorders (DNRs) capture all numbers dialed from a target phone. Of course, this technology is not just for phone calls. Since computer networks and modems operate on phone lines, the same technology is used to monitor and trace those types of communications as well. Congress enacted the Communications Assistance for Law Enforcement Act (CALEA) in 1994, which requires telecommunications companies to protect the privacy and security of communications and call-identifying information unless a court order authorizes interception. It also requires that the companies ensure that law enforcement has the capability to conduct court-ordered surveillance (Anderson 1997). The Electronic Surveillance Technology Section (ESTS) of the FBI today serves as the agency that coordinates that capability. It works with the telecommunications industry to assure that lawful electronic surveillance by law enforcement agencies can be carried out efficiently and effectively (Clifford 2003).

Concealed weapons detectors, electronic license plate readers, surveillance cameras, and listening devices all reduce privacy and liberty in that they are used in the detection of criminal behavior. However, they are used usually to screen or observe all individuals in a particular area, which means they reduce the privacy of all who are in that area. As early as 1996, cities such as Redwood City (CA), Baltimore (MD), Camden (NJ), Philadelphia (PA),

and Washington, D.C. have experimented with or are using surveillance cameras and hidden listening devices to "patrol high-crime areas" (Lewis 1996). In Britain, over 400 city centers have used cameras to monitor public streets where crime was expected, resulting in a 60% decrease in crime in some areas (Scanning 1997). In the workplace, it is common practice for employers to monitor email, voice mail, and phone calls and to log Internet transactions to detect improper employee behavior. Such monitoring has been upheld by the courts, especially when accompanied by prior stated policy (Levin 1995; Sahlberg 1991; Wallace et al. 1995).

Conser (2000) proposed what he called the **privacy rights paradigm**. It is premised upon the principles found in the Preamble to the Constitution and the concepts of ordered liberty, citizenship, and responsibility. It has a guiding philosophy of a social compact that attempts to balance individual rights with the rights of society and an embodiment of the idea of "for the greater good." The proposed paradigm (see **Figure 11-17** is designed to provide greater privacy rights to the individual at the personal and intimate relationship levels. As interactions increase with a larger society and begin to involve the type of relationships that are of governmental concerns, privacy rights are more limited and subject to government control and determination (when government has a substantial interest).

The paradigm is not a panacea for the current privacy controversies and dilemmas facing society, but it is one approach to discussing the limits and parameters of proper government intrusion into our lives. It does require the recognition that the government has the right and authority to regulate morality to certain degrees, the right to protect national security interests, and the right to determine civil rights. The paradigm is a start; it is not meant to be a finished product. Some will not like it.

The paradigm does adhere to the basic principles of communitarianism as presented by Amitai Etzioni. Etzioni's (1999) communitarianism is based on a social philosophy that a good society seeks a carefully-crafted balance between individual rights and social responsibilities, between liberty and the common good. He states "responsive communitarians seek to balance individual rights with social responsibilities, and individuality with

FIGURE 11-17 Relationship of Privacy Rights to Government Interests Depending on the Context of Social Interaction

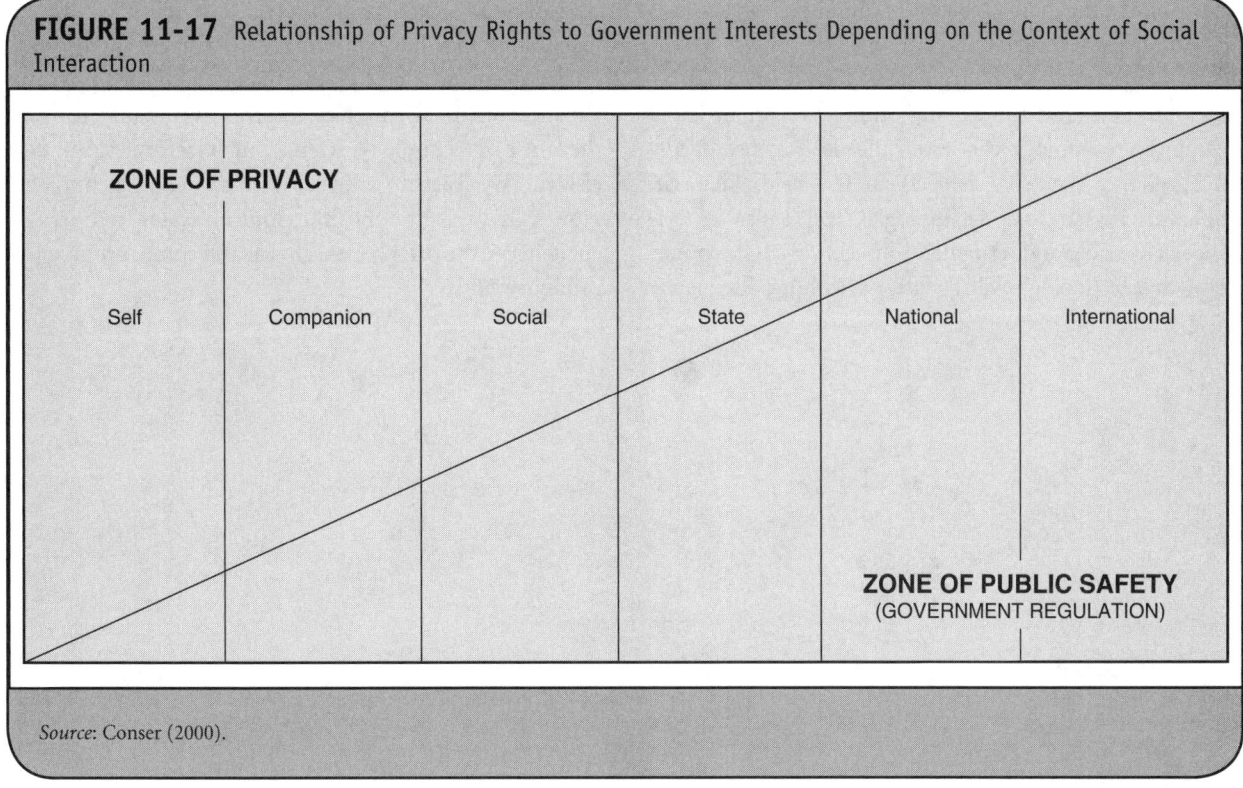

Source: Conser (2000).

community" (198). The approach advocated by Etzioni recognizes that rights and liberties are contingent on socio-historical contexts and that the balancing of individual and societal rights is necessary for the common good, which supports the social contract advocated in the Constitution's Preamble.

SUMMARY

This chapter has reviewed the tremendous impact that technology is having on law enforcement today. Information and other technology may be one of law enforcement's most important tools in detecting and investigating crime. Information is the greatest asset to the law enforcement function—whether it is gained from incident reports, crime lab analysis findings, informants, intelligence operations, crime analysis matrices, or modus operandi files. Like any other tool, information technology systems can be used to streamline law enforcement processing of copious amounts of data and factual information. Resources can be better utilized, and the sharing of information should assist in detecting conspiracies, serial incidents, and trends. Since the terrorist attacks of 9/11, much emphasis and resources have been placed on intelligence gathering and sharing. Technology is at the heart of such efforts.

With the proper planning, organizing, and control, technology can become one of the most valuable tools used in law enforcement. As with any tool, abuses are possible, and one of the most controversial aspects of the use of information technology in policing today is the issue of privacy and the accuracy of information in the databases and systems used by law enforcement. Information is power in an information-based society, but power can be abused, and with abuses come oversight and restrictions. The greater the restrictions, the less effective the information system becomes, so it is incumbent upon the law enforcement community to ensure that progress in information technology does not restrict or impinge on the civil liberties of citizens unlawfully and unreasonably.

This is one of the major debates surrounding civil liberties and homeland security.

Other technologies hold great promise for law enforcement. In the not-too-distant future, less-than-lethal restraining technology will lessen the need to use deadly force against aggressive subjects in the field. Likewise, improved investigative technologies will assist in evidence gathering and criminal prosecutions. Of course, all of this technology will be useless without adequately qualified and trained personnel to use it. In many respects, technology may have an impact on increasing the hiring qualifications needed to enter the field. Future applicants should prepare themselves for this eventuality through the study of technology, science, and electronics. But how else can we learn to adjust to the changing technology? How can we better position ourselves for tomorrow's challenges? We offer a little advice and some resource tips in **Figure 11-18**.

FIGURE 11-18 How to Keep Up with Changing Technology Trends

Think about this for a few minutes: From the time you were a freshman in high school to the time you graduated from high school (normally a four-year period), what has changed in technology? How many different personal computers did you use? How many times did you upgrade software? Did you change cell phones? Did you purchase a new MP3 player? Did you give up film cameras to make the move to digital? Did you upload a video clip directly to Youtube? Did you buy an e-book reader? Many of you in just four short years did all of these things and some of you did some of these more than once! Some of you did only a few of these things and some did none of these! Such is the diversity in the use of technology on the personal level. But the point here is that there will be significant changes in technology during the next four years! By the time you graduate from college, there will be faster and smaller computers, more people with smart cell phones, and more sophisticated digital video cameras. Some technology will become faster and smaller, while some technology will be completely new. How can we keep abreast of the changing technology trends and their applications to policing and public safety? The answer is to read technology-related magazines, browse selected Web sites using key terms in search engines, review specific technology-related URLs, and read the professional literature. A few suggestions appear below:

Technology/professional periodicals:
Scientific American
Government Technology
Law Enforcement Technology
Police Chief Magazine
Police and Security News
Law and Order
SC Magazine
TechBeat

Key terms for search engines:
"police technology"
"GIS"
"GPS tracking"
"surveillance"
"law enforcement technology"
"comstat"
"compstat"
"crime analysis"; "crime mapping"

Specific technology-related URLs:
www.justnet.org/Pages/About.aspx
www.ncjrs.org
www.iacptechnology.org/
www.nist.gov/programs-projects.cfm
www.ojp.usdoj.gov/nij/maps/
www.foresight.org/
www.cert.org
www.fcw.com
www.scmagazineus.com
www.antiphishing.org
www.fas.org/programs/index.html
www.kurzweilai.net/
www.law.com/jsp/lawtechnologynews/index.jsp
www.techweb.com/
www.centerdigitalgov.com/
www.sciencedaily.com/

Critical Thinking Questions

1. Do you think that technologically-enhanced crime could overwhelm local law enforcement agencies because of a lack of expertise and resources to competently investigate such crime?

2. What is the significance of information to the police function, and why is information technology important to the law enforcement community?

3. Why are national databases and data mining becoming so important to national security today?

4. What are your thoughts about less-than-lethal technology? Is the investment in such devices worth it, and could their use actually lead to greater incidents of the use of force?

5. What are other technological innovations that could be applied to policing and crime investigation?

6. Do you think that future technologies will make privacy impossible in the United States?

CHAPTER SPECIFIC INTERNET LINKS

Watch phones and videos: http://www.3gwatches.com/index.html

Federal Trade Commission: http://www.ftc.gov/opa/index.shtml

Regional Information Sharing System: http://www.riss.net/

Listen to Chicago Police, Zone 12 Radio Live: http://www.chicagofd.org/oemc/cpdzone12radio.html

National Emergency Number Association (2010b). United States E9-1-1 Deployment Map (as of October 28, 2010): http://nena.ddti.net/Documents/NENA%20Wireless%20E911%20deployment%20map.pdf

Various videos related to law enforcement technologies: http://www.policemag.com/Videos/Channel/Technology/List.aspx

Police iPhone Apps: http://www.policeiphoneapps.com/

Michigan Vehicle Tests: 2012 Ford Police Interceptor: http://www.policemag.com/Videos/Channel/Vehicles/2010/12/2011-Michigan-Tests-Ford-Police-Interceptor.aspx

National Law Enforcement and Corrections Technology Center's publication, *TechBeat*: http://www.justnet.org/Pages/TechBeatAbout.aspx

Less-Than-Lethal Weapon Video: http://wn.com/Future_Weapons_Beretta_LTL_7000_Less_Than_Lethal

Taser International videos: http://www2.taser.com/pages/videos.aspx

Combined Tactical Systems, Incorporated (examples of less lethal ammunition and launchers): http://www.less-lethal.com/

National Institute of Justice, less lethal technologies website: http://www.ojp.usdoj.gov/nij/topics/technology/less-lethal/types.htm

FBI's Biometric Center of Excellence: http://www.biometriccoe.gov/About.htm

NASA's Puffin Vertical Takeoff and Landing Personal Aerial Vehicle Video: http://www.youtube.com/watch?v=GV0qBU_u3tQ

ScanStation 2—Forensic 3D Crime Scene Scanner Video, Albuquerque (NM) Police Department: http://www.youtube.com/watch?v=Xc9VZkCr3v8&feature=related

International Association of Crime Analysts: http://www.iaca.net/

Mapping and Analysis for Public Safety (MAPS): http://www.ojp.usdoj.gov/nij/maps

CHAPTER GLOSSARY

Augmented reality—a technological application that combines the real and the virtual, displaying information in real time, in a way that enhances the individual abilities of people operating in the real world.

Automated vehicle locator system (AVLS)—a system used to locate vehicles outfitted with a receiver/transmitter that picks up positioning signals from satellites. The information can be transmitted to a computer-aided dispatch system capable of displaying a map showing the location.

Biometrics—the measurable biological (anatomical and physiological) or behavioral characteristics used for identification of an individual, including fingerprints, DNA, irises, voice patterns, palmprints, and facial patterns.

CODIS—acronym for COmbined DNA Indexing System; a database containing the DNA signatures of convicted offenders.

CompStat/ComStat—a strategy and technique that combines crime analysis, computerization, GIS, and managerial accountability to crime investigation and solvability. The name is derived from the two words "computer" and "statistics."

Computer-aided dispatch systems—an automated system that assists in prioritizing emergency situations and locating and guiding public safety personnel to incidents in the shortest time possible.

Crime analysis—a type of law enforcement analysis that is focused on the study of criminal incidents; the identification and analysis of patterns, trends, and problems; and the dissemination of information that helps a police agency develop tactics and strategies to solve patterns, trends, and problems.

Data mining—the process of conducting "super searches" of multiple databases using sophisticated software that detects patterns in a group of data.

Data warehouse—phrase used to describe large computer networks utilized for storing, retrieving, and managing large amounts of any type of data.

FinCEN—The U.S. Treasury Department's Financial Crimes Enforcement Network database that identifies possible money laundering transactions.

Geographic information systems (GIS)—also known as **computer mapping** or **geocoding,** it is a system for displaying and analyzing data. It can be used to display location, find patterns, and model scenarios.

Global positioning system (GPS)—a system that utilizes satellite technology that receives signals from ground transmitters and then converts the exact longitude and latitude into locations on Earth.

Gunshot detection devices—a system that uses microphones or acoustic sensors to detect firearms discharge locations, which can then be recorded and transmitted to dispatch centers for appropriate law enforcement response.

Integrated Automated Fingerprint Identification System (IAFIS)—a computerized process that scans a fingerprint and converts it into a digital image that is then analyzed and compared to other known images for matching purposes.

Interoperability—the ability of communications systems and computer networks to exchange voice/data across agencies and jurisdictions on demand, in real time.

Less-than-lethal technologies—scientific inquiry and research that focuses on the subduing of individuals or controlling of crowds in ways that would lessen the chance of serious injury or death.

National Crime Information Center (NCIC)—The national database maintained by the FBI that contains the names of missing and wanted persons and various stolen items. It is accessible to officers throughout the country through a system of computer networks.

NCIC 2000—the planning and strategic effort underway by the FBI since the late 1990s to upgrade the National Crime Information Center.

Personal vertical takeoff and landing aircraft (VTOL)—a type of aircraft that permits individuals to take off and land in a vertical position.

Personal video surveillance systems—a system consisting of a small camera and microphone attached to the shirt of an officer and a transmitter attached to the duty belt, which sends images and sounds to a receiver/recorder subsystem located in the officer's vehicle.

Privacy rights paradigm—a proposed perspective based on the concepts of ordered liberty, citizenship, and responsibility; it is designed to provide the greater privacy rights to the individual at the personal and intimate relationship levels and fewer privacy rights when the type of relationships are of governmental concern.

Regional information sharing system (RISS)—large computer systems servicing a regional geographical area and which usually serves as a gateway to the NCIC.

Secure Flight—a program of the Transportation Security Administration (TSA) intended for the screening of airline passengers and will only look for known or suspected terrorists, not other law enforcement violators.

Social networking media—online platforms or internet-based resources that allow users to create profiles, post information, and/or socialize with others using various technologies.

Spyware—the general term used to describe a computer program that is surreptitiously downloaded to one's computer, which permits others to obtain information from that computer when it is online.

Technologically-enhanced crime—offenses in which scientific advances permit less time to commit offenses, make personal information from potential victims more readily available, make detection more difficult, or improve the quality of materials or documents used in offenses; can be classified into two categories: traditional crimes and high-tech crimes.

Teleforensics—a strategy that permits the recording of crime scenes using a camcorder fitted with a wireless transmitter that sends images to remote monitors in real time.

Unmanned aerial vehicles (UAVs)—remotely-controlled small aircraft that are usually equipped with surveillance technology.

US-VISIT—The U.S. Department of Homeland Security's database that contains scanned fingerprints of the index fingers and a photograph of most foreign visitors traveling to the United States on a visa.

APPENDIX 11-A THE EVOLUTION OF INFORMATION TECHNOLOGY

1600s Galileo Galilei, the Italian mathematician, astronomer, physicist, and inventor who assisted in the renaissance of mathematics as a scientific language. His early work in applied science and technology fostered the emergence of modern science.

1614 The first publication of the discovery of logarithms (the exponent of a base number indicating to what power that base must be raised to produce another given number) by John Napier of Scotland.

1620s The slide rule was developed by William Oughtred and others to assist in the rapid calculation of numbers.

1640 Blaise Pascal developed an "adding machine" device, called the Pascaline, which remembered information and executed calculations by the use of wheels and interlocking gears. Its basic principle was used in adding machines for the next 300 years.

1673 Gottfried Wilhelm von Leibniz designed a machine, the Leibnitz Calculator, that could process numbers beyond just addition. Leibniz is better known, however, for his co-development or discovery of calculus along with Isaac Newton.

1800s Charles Babbage, an English mathematician, proposed the "Difference Engine," and later the "Analytic Engine," which would have been a true computing device. Neither was ever perfected, and the latter was not completed because of problems in manufacturing the necessary parts. Augusta Ada Byron (daughter of Lord Byron, the poet) later assisted in translating and explaining Babbage's principles and theories.

1804 The first fully-automated loom was developed by Joseph Marie Jacquard. It was made possible by a memory device controlled by punched holes on a card and could weave very complicated patterns.

1840s George Boole devised a form of algebra (Boolean Algebra) that included the basic operators of AND, OR, and NOT. In 1867, Charles Sanders Pierce brought Boolean Algebra to the United States and continued to modify and extend it.

1890 Building on the punched card principle, Herman Hollerith devised a system of tabulating census forms (the machine counted the holes on the card). Hollerith went on to form the Tabulating Machine Company, which after several mergers and name changes came to be known as the International Business Machines Corporation (IBM).

1930s Vannevar Bush, an MIT professor, built a pioneering machine capable of solving differential equations. Bush thought it could be improved. Ultimately, this led to one of his graduate students, Claude Shannon, applying Boolean Algebra to the design of electrical circuits. His work lies at the foundation of modern telephone systems. Other researchers such as John Atanasoff of Iowa State College, George Stibitz of Bell Telephone Laboratories, and Konrad Zuse of Germany were also independently advancing the "computer evolution" with their work in electronics.

1941 Konrad Zuse designed and built (in Germany) the first operational computer that was program-controlled and based on the binary system.

1943 IBM and Howard Aiken succeeded in building the Mark I, a machine using punched paper tape that could "crunch" numbers up to 23 digits long. It was used by the navy to solve difficult ballistic problems.

The British built an electro-mechanical machine called COLOSSUS, which was used to decipher German codes and messages. It used vacuum tubes, which was a breakthrough in the development of the computer.

1945 John W. Mauchly and J. Presper Echert successfully tested the first all-electric digital computer. This Electronic Numerical Integrator And Calculator (ENIAC) was introduced in 1944 at the University of Pennsylvania. It filled an entire room (occupying 3000 cubic feet), weighed 30 tons, had 17,468 vacuum tubes, and consumed 200 kilowatts of electricity (enough to light 70–80 homes).

1947 Howard Aiken advised officials of the National Bureau of Standards that "there will never be enough problems, enough work for more than one or two of these computers."

The transistor was invented at Bell Telephone Laboratories, but did not appear economically in computer components until 1959. It was initially applied to radio technology.

1940s　The first magnetic tape recorders are available commercially.

1948　The Cathode Ray Tube (CRT) was applied to the Mark I by F.C. Williams.

1950s　The cold war with the Soviet Union fueled the government's willingness to invest large sums of money into the development of larger and faster computers.

1951　The first commercial computer, UNIVAC (UNIVersal Automatic Computer), was built by Echert and Mauchly. UNIVAC could process words as well as numbers, and was placed on the market by the Remington Rand (Sperry) Corporation. UNIVAC and other subsequent computers were made practical because of two innovations advocated during the mid- to late-1940s by the collective work of John W. Mauchly, J. Presper Echert, and John von Neumann, who recommended use of (a) a binary number system—1s and 0s, coupled with Boolean algebra, and (b) a stored program concept of instructions.

1953　Jay W. Forrester conceived and first used magnetic core memory successfully in the WHIRLWIND Computer at MIT, which was part of a massive federally-funded project. This project led to others, such as SAGE.

1954　The IBM 650 Computer was placed on the market as the first mass-produced computer. During the '50s and '60s, there were many advances in the computer industry, such as the development and refinement of various programming languages including FORTRAN, COBOL, ALGO, and BASIC.

1958　Texas Instrument engineer Jack Kilby created the first bona fide integrated circuit, which led to the miniaturization of computer parts.

1960s　Many computers were built with integrated instead of transistor circuitry. This opened the era of the minicomputer as well.

1961　The first commercially produced electronic chips (silicon chips) containing integrated circuits became available, but were very expensive.

1967　The first digital tape recorder invented.

1968　The first 256-bit chip was introduced, followed by the 1024-bit chip a few months later.

1970　The first microprocessor chip, the Intel 4004 (4-bit chip), was manufactured after being invented by Ted Hoff.

1972　The first 8-bit microprocessor, the Intel 8008, was introduced, which opened the microcomputer era.

1974　The Intel 8080 became commercially available.

1975　The first personal computer, the Altair 8800, was sold through Micro Instrumentation and Telemetry Systems of Albuquerque, New Mexico, thus launching the personal computer industry.

1976　A microcomputer on a "board" 50 3 80 could outperform the ENIAC.

The Z-80 microprocessor (an 8-bit chip) was introduced by Zilog Company.

The Intel 8086 (16-bit) chip was introduced.

1977　The Commodore PET, TRS-80 Model I, and Apple I personal computers, as well as 28 other brands, became commercially available.

1978　Zilog Z8000 (16-bit) microprocessor was introduced.

1979　Motorola 68000 (16-bit) microprocessor was introduced.

The Osborne I portable, with built-in 5 1/4-inch diskette drive, was introduced with a 5.5 inch CRT.

1981　IBM enters the personal computer field with the production of the IBM PC.

The 32-bit microprocessor chip was introduced by Hewlett-Packard.

1983　The 80286 microprocessor chip became commercially available.

The Tandy Model 100 laptop was introduced.

1984　The first laptops with a built-in disk drive were marketed.

1985　Handheld and laptop computers begin to become economically attractive.

1986　The 80386 microprocessor became commercially available.

1989　The 80486-based microcomputers are marketed.

1990　The World Wide Web, built by Tim Berners-Lee, becomes a reality.

1993　The first Pentium (80586) microcomputers become available.

1995　The first Digital Video Disc (DVD) was introduced.

1996 The first MP3 player, Listen Up, was introduced by Audio Highway.

1997 The first Pentium II microcomputers become available.

1998 The first e-book reader was introduced.

1999 The Pentium III processor was introduced into personal computers.

2000 The microprocessors move into the Gigihertz speed range and move from 32 bit toward 64 bit microprocessors.

New recording and storage devices such as DVDs appeared.

2000 Ericsson introduced the touchscreen smartphone R380.

Intel Pentium 4 processor is marketed.

2001 Digital satellite radio became available.

2002 The first BlackBerry hit the market.

First social networking websites appear.

2003 The social network website MySpace becomes functional.

2004 The social network service Facebook was launched.

2006 Twitter was introduced to the public.

2007 The iPhone was introduced, along with the Android phone.

First Kindle (e-book reader) was introduced by Amazon.

2008 iPhone 3G introduced by Apple.

Intel microprocessors Core i7-920 and Core Extreme Processor X9100 were introduced.

2010 The iPad was launched by Apple in January; iPhone 4 debuted in June.

Intel Core i5-650 Processor is released.

APPENDIX 11-B THE EVOLUTION OF INFORMATION TECHNOLOGY IN POLICING

1845 All precinct stations of the New York City Police Department were connected by telegraph.

1867 Telegraph police call boxes were first installed.

1878 The Washington, D.C. Police Department installed its first telephone.

1880 Chicago installed telephones in call boxes on officer's beats.

1881 Chicago installed the first emergency police telephone booths.

1900s Telephotography was employed by several departments, which permitted the sending of photos from one city to another.

1902 An electric police alarm box system was installed in Kansas City, Missouri.

1920s The teletypewriter became a workhorse for communication between departments.

1926 Radio-equipped patrol cars with "receive only" capability were introduced in Berkeley, California.

1928 The Detroit Police Department initiated mobile radio receivers after several years of development.

1929 The Police Department of Cleveland, Ohio adds mobile radio receivers.

1929 The first state-wide teletypewriter system was installed by the Pennsylvania State Police.

1933 Two-way police radio communications were initiated in Bayonne, New Jersey, followed by Indianapolis, Indiana.

1940s Three-way communications capability was introduced.

1960s Portable radios became less expensive and more popular.

1964 The St. Louis Police Department was the first and only in the United States to have a computer system. Also, none were in use at the state or national levels.

1967 The FBI's National Crime Information Center (NCIC) began operation in January.

1968 AT&T announced the creation of 911 in January.

At least 10 states and 50 cities had acquired computerized systems.

Kansas City, Missouri began operation of ALERT I (Automated Law Enforcement Response Team).

The Ohio Law Enforcement Automated Data System (LEADS) became operational after 2.5 years of planning; as a statewide system, it linked Ohio to the Criminal Justice Information System (CJIS), which tied into NCIC and was later connected to National Law Enforcement Telecommunications System (NLETS).

1970s A big push through Law Enforcement Assistance Administration grants allowed many other departments to computerize information systems.

1970 New York City's Special Police Radio Inquiry Network (SPRINT) was implemented.

1972 NLETS became operational, linking all states except Alaska and Hawaii.

Over 400 systems were in use in criminal justice agencies nationally, 46% of which were at the state level and 54% at the local level. An LEAA survey identified 39 functions being performed by computer—mostly record keeping related to police calls, personnel, and fiscal accounting.

ALERT II in Kansas City, Missouri expanded and included mobile digital terminals (MDTs) in cruisers.

1976 Computer Aided Dispatch systems were added to several agencies, such as Virginia Beach, Virginia, also with mobile digital terminals.

1978 The first Automated Fingerprint and Identification Systems (AFIS) were developed. The large expense for these systems resulted in only a few sales.

1983 Over 800 systems were in use in criminal justice agencies nationally, not counting microcomputer systems.

Renewed interests in AFIS surfaced among larger departments. By 1987, at least 15 states and 20 cities and counties had or were about to acquire AFIS systems.

1984 Notebook-size computers were incorporated into the daily routine of St. Petersburg, Florida police officers.

1985 The use of microcomputers expanded into every aspect of law enforcement imaginable. Officers began purchasing their own for home and department use.

1986 Cellular telephones were incorporated into the police vehicles in St. Petersburg, Florida.

1987 Optical disk technology is coupled with microcomputers to offer several advantages and new applications.

1990s Handheld computers appeared in agencies for traffic ticket enforcement; pen-based systems appeared for report-taking tasks; "paperless" and "near-paperless" police departments begin to emerge; vehicle-mounted video cameras document traffic stops; personal video surveillance systems used to record officer actions.

1993 The first red light camera ticketing system was put in use in New York City.

1995 Law Enforcement OnLine (LEO), the national interactive computer communications system and information service, was initiated in the FBI.

1997 FCC approved and designated 311 as a national, non-toll, voluntary non-emergency phone number in February.

The first 311 non-emergency number system becomes operational in Baltimore, Maryland.

The National Drug Pointer Index system became operational in the United States in October.

1999 NCIC is relocated to Clarksburg, West Virginia.

The Integrated Automated Fingerprint Identification System goes online at the FBI.

2000 NIBIN integrated ballistics identification system merges the existing systems of the FBI and the ATFE and becomes part of the Firearms Programs Division of the ATFE.

2004 US-VISIT becomes operational in the Department of Homeland Security

2006 3-D scanning technology to record and document crime scenes is in use.

2007 Whole-body imaging (scanning) machines were first used at an airport.

2009 FLETC develops Avatar-based Interview Simulator.

Wearable video cameras tested and used by several departments.

2010 Drones first used for surveillance and protection along the Mexican–U.S. border by Customs and Border Patrol

iPhone apps begin to appear for law enforcement applications

CHAPTER REFERENCES AND ADDITIONAL READINGS

3GWatches.com (2011). Cell Phone Wristwatch: All-In-One Mobile Multimedia Device. http://www.3gwatches.com/products.html.

Allen, Gary (2010). History of 911. Dispatch Magazine On-line http://www.911dispatch.com/911/history/.

American Bankers Association (November 2009). 2009 Deposit Account Fraud Survey Report. http://www.aba.com/Surveys+and+Statistics/2009_Deposit_Fraud.htm.

Anderson, Teresa (1997). Legal Reporter. *Security Management*, May:86.

ATFE (2010). NIBIN Hits of the Week, May 3, 2010 and May 10, 2010. http://www.nibin.gov/press/releases/2010/050310-051710-hits-of-the-week.html.

Augarten, Stan (1984). *Bit by Bit: An Illustrated History of Computers.* New York: Ticknor & Fields.

Baig, Edward C. (2004). A forearm forecast, and more. *USA Today*, January 8:5B.

Bell, Stephanie (October 2010). In Accepting Mobile Payment, Merchants Face Higher Fraud Risk. *American Banker*, http://www.americanbanker.com/issues/175_196/merchants-face-higher-fraud-risk-1026965-1.html.

Boba, R. (2001). *Introductory guide to crime analysis and mapping*. Washington, D.C.: COPS, USDOJ.

Boba, R. (2005). *Crime analysis and crime mapping*. Thousand Oaks, CA: Sage Publications.

Boyd, David G. (1995). On the Cutting Edge: Law Enforcement Technology. *FBI Law Enforcement Bulletin*, July:1–6.

Bruce, C. (2004). Fundamentals of crime analysis. In C. W. Bruce, S.R. Hick, & J.P. Cooper (Eds.). *Exploring crime analysis: Reading on essential skills*. Overland Park, KS: IACA Press.

Buckler, Marilyn (1998). NCIC 2000: More Than Just Images. *The Police Chief*, April 16:18–19.

Bulwa, Demian (July 27, 2010). Many police use cameras to record interactions. SFGate.com. http://articles.sfgate.com/2010-07-27/news/21999160_1_cameras-officers-police-watchdogs

CERT.org (2010). Meet CERT. http://www.cert.org/meet_cert/

Clifford, Michael P. (2003). Electronic Surveillance Technology. *The Police Chief*, July:31–35.

Communications Assistance for Law Enforcement Act (1994). PL: 103–414.

Conser, James A. (1997). The Right to Privacy in Digital America. Paper presented at the Annual Meeting of the Academy of Criminal Justice Sciences, Louisville, Kentucky, March 13.

Conser, James A. (2000). Privacy Rights and Public Safety in a Digital World. Futuristics and Law Enforcement: The Millennium Conference. Quantico, VA: FBI Academy, July 11.

Cowper, Thomas (2004a). Vertical takeoff & landing aircraft for 21st century policing. *Law Enforcement Technology*, September:36–41.

Cowper, Thomas (2004b). Improving the view of the world: Law enforcement and augmented reality technology. *FBI Law Enforcement Bulletin*, January, 12–18.

Curry, Michael G. (1997). The Digital Individual and Private Realm. *Annals of the Association of American Geographers*, 87 (4):681–699.

DeltaSphere.com (2010). Capture crime scenes quickly and accurately in 3D and color with the DeltaSphere-3000. http://www.deltasphere.com/.

Dispatch Magazine On-Line (2010). 311 Non-Emergency Systems http://www.911dispatch.com/info/311_page.html.

Etzioni, Amitai (1999). *The Limits Of Privacy*. New York: Basic Books.

Federal Agency Data Mining Reporting Act of 2007, Pub. L. No. 110-53, 121 Stat. 266.

Federal Bureau of Investigation (1984). National Crime Information Center: An Investigative Tool. Washington, D.C.: U.S. Department of Justice.

Federal Bureau of Investigation (1996–1997). National Crime Information Center: 30 Years on The Beat. *The Investigator*, December/January.

Federal Bureau of Investigation (October 7, 2009). One Hundred Linked to International Computer Hacking Ring Charged by United States and Egypt in Operation Phish Phry. U.S. Department of Justice, Press Release. http://losangeles.fbi.gov/pressrel/2009/la100709.htm.

Federal Bureau of Investigation (September 24, 2010). Trade Secret Theft Couple Conspires to Steal Hybrid Technology. http://www.fbi.gov/news/stories/2010/september/steal-hybrid-technology/border-gang-threat.

Federal Bureau of Investigation (2010b). National Crime Information Center. http://www.fbi.gov/about-us/cjis/ncic/ncic.

Federal Bureau of Investigation (2010c). CODIS—NDIS Statistics. http://www.fbi.gov/about-us/lab/codis/ndis-statistics.

Federal Bureau of Investigation (2010d). National Security Branch. http://www.fbi.gov/about-us/nsb.

Federal Bureau of Investigation (2010e). About the Biometric Center of Excellence. http://www.biometriccoe.gov/About.htm.

Federal Bureau of Investigation, Biometric Services Section (2010). Integrated Automated Fingerprint Identification System, Fact Sheet. Statistical Trending, Analysis & Reporting Group, August 11. http://www.fbi.gov/about-us/cjis/fingerprints_biometrics/iafis/iafis_facts.

Federal Trade Commission (2004a). FTC Releases Consumer Fraud Report. August 5, http://www.ftc.gov/opa/2004/08/fraudsurvey.htm.

Federal Trade Commission (October 29, 2007). FTC Releases Consumer Fraud Survey, http://www.ftc.gov/opa/2007/10/fraud.shtm.

Federal Trade Commission (2011). Consumer Sentinel Network, Data Book for January–December 2010, http://www.ftc.gov/sentinel/reports/sentinel-annual-reports/sentinel-cy2010.pdf.

Federation of American Scientists (2004). NCIC, http://www.fas.org/irp/agency/doj/fbi/is/ncic.htm.

Fenton, Justin (April 9, 2010). Baltimore police idle Comstat meetings. Baltsun.com.http://articles.baltimoresun.com/2010-04-09/news/bal-md.ci.comstat08apr09_1_comstat-police-department-s-operations-anthony-guglielmi.

Finnie, Toby, Tom Petee, and John Jarvis (eds.)(2010). *The Future Challenges of Cybercrime: Volume 5 Proceedings of the Futures Working Group*. Federal Bureau of Investigation: Quantico, VA.

Foster, Raymond E. (2004). *Police Technology*. New York: Prentice Hall.

FutureCars.com (2010). Flying Cars: Reviews. http://www.futurecars.com/flying-cars-reviews.html.

Gonzalez, Juan (September 1, 2010). Setback for city's 911 system overhaul: Officials ready to cancel contract with failed system. NYDailyNews.com. http://www.nydailynews.com/ny_local/2010/09/01/2010-09-01_call_911_for_big_fix_new_emergency_system_melts_down_under_stress_fails_test.html.

Grun, Bernard (ed.) (1991). *The Timetables of History*, 3rd Revised Edition. New York: Simon and Schuster.

Hambling, David (2004). Sweeping stun guns to target crowds. *New Scientist*, June 16, http://www.newscientist.com/news/news.jsp?id=ns99996014.

Heibutzki, Ralph (October 13, 2010). Impacts of Credit Card Fraud on Issuers. http://www.ehow.com/list_7325210_impacts-credit-card-fraud-issuers.html#ixzz18Ffrc9E4.

Homeland Security Newswire (June 25, 2010). More UAVs, personnel, money for U.S.-Mexico border protection. http://homelandsecuritynewswire.com/more-uavs-personnel-money-us-mexico-border-protection.

IACP, Center for Social Media (2010). Survey Results, IACP Social Media Document. http://www.iacpsocialmedia.org/Portals/1/documents/Survey%20Results%20Document.pdf.

International Association of Crime Analysts, "Frequently Asked Questions", http://www.iaca.net/FAQ.asp.

International Intellectual Property Alliance (2010). 2010 USTR Decisions Special 301, Table of Estimated Trade Losses and Piracy Levels. http://www.iipa.com/pdf/IIPA2010USTRDecisionsSpecial301TableofEstimatedTradeLossesandPiracyLevels061110.pdf.

Komarow, Steve (1994). Technology could tip scales in crime war. *USA Today*, March 23.

Kuykendall, Jason (2010). Future Training Innovations: Introducing the FLETC Avatar-Based Interview Simulator. *FLETC Journal*, Fall:8-11, 34.

Langton, Lynn and Katrina Baum (June 2010). *Identity Theft Reported by Households, 2007–Statistical Tables*. NCJ 230742. Washington, D.C.: U.S. Department of Justice, Bureau of Justice Statistics.

Levin, Robert B. (1995). The Virtual Fourth Amendment: Searches and Seizures in Cyberspace. *Maryland Bar Journal*, May/June11 VIII(3):2–5.

Lewis, Claude (1996). Will residents trade privacy for security? *The Vindicator*, February 15:A15.

Madison, Laura, Christa M. Miller, and Chris Worden (2010). A Survey of Official and Unofficial Law Enforcement Twitter Accounts in Canada, the United Kingdom, and the United States. Canadian Association of Police on Social Media, http://www.scribd.com/doc/36761664/ Survey-of-Official-Unofficial-Law-Enforcement-Twitter-Accounts-in-Canada-the-United-Kingdom-the-United-States.

Mayer, Allison (January 2009). Geospatial Technology Helps East Orange Crack Down on Crime. *Geography & Public Safety*. Vol. 1. No. 4:7–9.

McKay, Jim (2004a). Fixing 911. *Government Technology*, August:19–24.

McKay, Jim (2004b). Nowhere to Hide. *Mobile Government*, June:6–9.

Meade, Patricia (2004). Scanners target stolen cars. *The Vindicator*, August 11:A1.

Meincke, Paul (February 19, 2009). Improvements made to 911 center. abc7chicago.com. http://abclocal.go.com/wls/story?section=news/ local&id=6667981.

Miller, Christina M. (2004). Body Armor Update: 2004. *Police and Security News*, July/August:31–36.

National Commission on Terrorist Attacks Upon the United States (2004). *The 9/11 Commission Report, Authorized Edition*. New York: W.W. Norton & Co.

National Institute of Justice (2010). Types of Less-Lethal Devices. Department of Justice, Office of Justice Programs. http://www.ojp .usdoj.gov/nij/topics/technology/less-lethal/types.htm.

National Emergency Number Association (2010). 9-1-1 Statistics. http:// www.nena.org/911-statistics.

Page, Douglas (2004). RFID tags: Big brother is a small device. *Law Enforcement Technology*, August:128–133.

Paynich, R. & B. Hill. (2009). *Fundamentals of Crime Mapping*. Sudbury, MA: Jones & Bartlett Publishers.

Pennella, John J. and Peter L. Nacci (1997). Department of Justice and Department of Defense Joint Technology Program: Second Anniversary Report, February, Washington D.C.: U.S. Department of Justice.

Pilant, Lois (1996). Imaging & Identification Systems. *The Police Chief*, August:63–68.

Pilant, Lois (1998). Crime & War: An Analysis of Non-lethal Technologies and Weapons Development. *The Police Chief*, June:55–68.

Police Executive Research Forum (October 2010). The Future of Compstat. *Subject to Debate* (Newsletter) Vol. 24, No. 9:4-5.

Project Lifesaver (2010). http://projectlifesaver.org/Lifesaver/about/.

Regional Information Sharing Systems (2010). Regional Information Sharing Systems – Overview. U.S. Department of Justice, Bureau of Justice Assistance. http://www.riss.net/overview.aspx.

Rowe, Aaron (January 4, 2010). 10 Sci-Fi Weapons That Actually Exist. Wired.com. http://www.wired.com/dangerroom/2010/01/sci-fi-weapons/3/.

Sahlberg, John (1991). Employee Privacy and Investigations. Paper presented at American Society for Industrial Security Annual Seminar, September 16.

Saroiu, Stefan, Steven D. Gribble, and Henry M. Levy (2004). Measurement and Analysis of Spyware in a University Environment. Paper presented at the First Symposium on Networked Systems Design and Implementation. March 29–31, http://www.cs.washington.edu/ homes/tzoompy/publications/nsdi/2004/spyware.html.

Scanning (1997). *Police Futurist*, Winter:9.

Seaskate, Inc. (1998). The Evolution and Development Of Police Technology. Excerpts From A Technical Report prepared for The National Committee on Criminal Justice Technology National Institute of Justice, July 1, http://www.911dispatch.com/911_file/ history/911history.html.

Sessions, William S. (1993). Criminal Justice Information Services: Gearing Up For the Future. *FBI Law Enforcement Bulletin*, February:1–3.

Shane, Jon M. (2004). Compstat Process. *FBI Law Enforcement Bulletin*, April:12–21.

ShotSpotter.com (2010). ShotSpotter Gunshot Location System. http:// www.shotspotter.com/solutions/index.html.

Silverstein, Ed (October 13, 2010). FCC Takes Steps to Improve Responses to Wireless 911 Callers. http://www.tmcnet.com/ channels/e911-hosted-solutions/articles/108570-fcc-takes-steps-improve-responses-wireless-911-callers.htm.

Singel, Ryan (2009). Newly Declassified Files Detail Massive FBI Data-Mining Project. Wired.com http://www.wired.com/ threatlevel/2009/09/fbi-nsac/.

Siuru, Bill (2010). MORIS – The Future of Perp Identification. *Police and Security News*, 26(5): 22, 25.

Smith & Wesson Advanced Technologies (2003). https://swat .smithandwesson.com.

Taser.com (2010). Products for Law Enforcement & Corrections. TASER International Corporation, http://www.taser.com/products/law/ Pages/default.aspx.

TSA (2010). Secure Flight Program. http://www.tsa.gov/what_we_do/ layers/secureflight/index.shtm.

U.S. Department of Homeland Security (2004a). Fact Sheet: RapidCom 9/30 and Interoperability Progress, http://www.dhs.gov/dhspublic/ display?content=3869.

U.S. Department of Homeland Security (2008). 2008 Report to Congress, Data Mining: Technology and Policy. Washington, D.C.: DHS Privacy Office.

U.S. Department of Homeland Security (2010a). US-VISIT, http://www .dhs.gov/files/programs/usv.shtm.

U.S. Department of Homeland Security (2010b). About SAFECOM http://www.safecomprogram.gov/SAFECOM/about/default.htm.

U.S. Department of Justice (2010). Federal Courts Order Seizure of 82 Website Domains Involved in Selling Counterfeit Goods as Part of DOJ and ICE Cyber Monday Crackdown. Press Release. http:// www.cybercrime.gov/OperationInOurSites.pdf.

U.S. Department of Justice (2004). Justice Department Announces Operation Web Snare Targeting Online Fraud and Crime. August 26, http://www.usdoj.gov/opa/pr/2004/August/04_crm_583.htm.

U.S. Department of Justice, COPS (2004). 311 Initiative Timeline. Office of Community Oriented Policing Services, http://www.cops.usdoj.gov/default.asp?Item=509.

U.S. Department of Justice, Office of Justice Programs, Global Justice Information Sharing Initiative, Security Working Group (2004). Applying Security Practices to Justice Information Sharing. March, http://it.ojp.gov/documents/asp/introduction/index.htm.

U.S. Department of Treasury (2010). FinCEN Organization.http://www.fincen.gov/about_fincen/wwd/organization.html.

Video Privacy Protection Act of 1988, 102 Statute 3195.

Wallace, Donald H. and Everett K. Woods (1995). Surveillance, Eavesdropping and Citizens' Rights. *Journal of Security Administration*, December:10–17.

Westphal, Lonnie J. (2004).The In-Car Camera: Value and Impact. *The Police Chief*, August:59–65.

Wilson, Patrick (2010). VA cops getting (and liking) LPRs. *The Virginian-Pilot*. PoliceOne.com, June 5, http://74.217.207.167/police-technology/articles/2077422-Va-cops-getting-and-liking-LPRs/.

Yaukey, John (March 7, 2007). Feds test new data mining program. http://www.usatoday.com/news/washington/2007-03-07-datatools_N.htm.

CHAPTER **12**

National Security, Homeland Security, and Private Sector Protection

KEY TERMS USED IN THIS CHAPTER

al-Qaeda

Central Intelligence Agency

Foreign Intelligence Surveillance Act (FISA)

USA Patriot Act

Homeland Security Act of 2002

National Response Framework (NRF)

National Incident Management System (NIMS)

Fragmented system

Interagency task forces

National Security Agency (NSA)

Defense Intelligence Agency

National Security Council (NSC)

Intelligence-led policing

Fusion centers

High Intensity Drug Trafficking Area (HIDTA)

private police/security

proprietary security personnel

contract security personnel

private military security companies

9/11 Commission Report

critical infrastructure

Atlanta City WorkSite

LAW ENFORCEMENT'S ROLE IN NATIONAL SECURITY AND HOMELAND SECURITY

While local law enforcement has always had a role in first response and critical incident management, the terrorist attacks of September 11, 2001 forever changed the way law enforcement officers view their responsibilities in defense of their communities. Immediately after the attack, law enforcement officials around the country began assessing their new role and restructuring their resources in response to terrorism. While a very small number of agencies were involved in multijurisdictional anti-terrorist task forces before the attacks, most agencies across the country did not have anti-terrorist or intelligence units. Prior to 9/11, the consensus in law enforcement circles was that international terrorism (e.g. the hijacking of airplanes, the bombing of the Marine Barracks in Beirut, the bombing of the American Embassies in Kenya and Tanzania, the bombing of the USS Cole, etc.) was a federal problem. Domestic terrorism, on the other hand (e.g. the Unabomber, Timothy McVeigh and the bombing of the Murrah Building in Oklahoma City, the 1993 World Trade Center bombing, acts of eco-terrorism, etc.), while problematic, was an infrequent and isolated problem and thus did not become a major focus of limited agency resources. The attacks of 9/11 changed these perceptions.

As the nation recoiled from the devastation of the attacks, we began to question the philosophy and structure of our defenses. International terrorists had lived in our communities, had attended our schools, and had traveled freely in and out of the country as they planned their acts of terrorism. Intelligence and law enforcement officials knew that **al Qaeda** was responsible for many terrorist acts prior to 9/11. In fact, the **Central Intelligence Agency** (CIA) had shared critical information about some of the 9/11 conspirators with the Federal Bureau of Investigation (FBI) in the summer of 2001. However, FBI officials were restricted in using the information because the two agencies worked under different legal standards. There was a "wall of separation" between the agencies; information supplied by the CIA had not been secured in compliance with the **Foreign Intelligence Surveillance Act** (**FISA**) or with ordinary criminal warrant procedures.

Consequently, officials in the Justice Department were concerned that the civil liberties of the suspects in question might be violated. The rules for foreign intelligence collection—as opposed to domestic criminal intelligence and investigations—are very different. The problem of sharing intelligence between the two agencies was addressed with passage of the **USA Patriot Act** in October 2001. However, passage of the law was controversial itself. You can examine the documents that define these differences and the controversy surrounding the issue, including a short editorial article that explains the "wall of separation" controversy, by visiting the websites listed in **Figure 12-1**. You can also visit the FBI's Ten Most Wanted website (see Chapter Specific Internet Links at the end of the chapter).

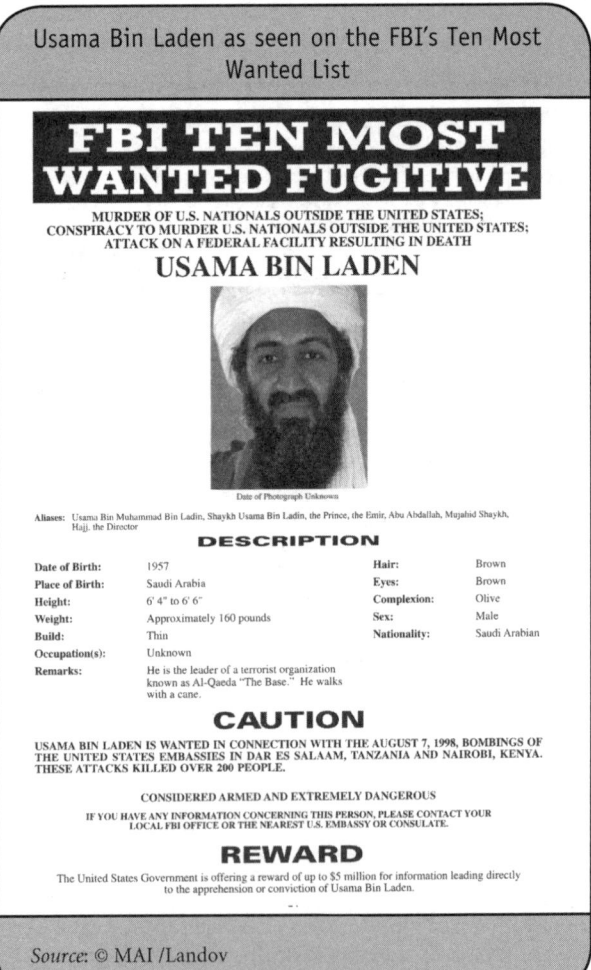

Usama Bin Laden as seen on the FBI's Ten Most Wanted List

Source: © MAI /Landov

FIGURE 12-1 American Intelligence References & Sources

For additional information on American intelligence, counterintelligence, and law enforcement, visit the following websites:

"An Overview of the United States Intelligence Community" (2007): http://www.dni.gov/overview.pdf

A report by the Congressional Research Service (2004) "The Foreign Intelligence Surveillance Act: An Overview of the Statutory Framework and Recent Judicial Decisions": http://www.fas.org/irp/crs/RL30465.pdf

The 9/11 Commission Report (2004): http://govinfo.library.unt.edu/911/report/index.htm

Baker, Stewart (2003), "Wall Nuts: The wall between intelligence and law enforcement is killing us," posted on Slate: http://www.slate.com/id/2093344/

USA Patriot Act, 2001: http://epic.org/privacy/terrorism/hr3162.html

"Attorney General Guidelines for FBI Foreign Intelligence Collection and Foreign Counterintelligence Investigations" (1989) (redacted): http://www.cnss.org/forintelguide1995.pdf

The American Presidency Project, Presidential Executive Orders, Ronald W. Reagan, 1982 Executive Order 12333, "United States Intelligence Activities": http://www.presidency.ucsb.edu/executive_orders.php?year=1981

The events of 9/11 had made it clear that state and local agencies "needed more information and training on the nature, dynamics and operations of international" and domestic terrorism. Moreover, state and local agencies needed help with "intelligence gathering capabilities; acquiring and using equipment or technology; and accessing external funds;" in short, they needed federal help (Murphy, Plotkin, and Edelson, 2001).

Local Policing and National Preparedness

The post-9/11 problem facing every law enforcement officer in America was daunting. The International Association of Chiefs of Police (IACP) captured the problem succinctly when they observed:

In the aftermath of these attacks, as the nation struggled to comprehend the new menace confronting our society, our nation's law enforcement agencies realized that they now had a new and critically important mission. No longer could they focus their energies solely on traditional crime fighting efforts. Now they would be asked to confront a new threat to their communities, perpetrated by individuals and organizations that had vastly different motivations and means of attack from that of traditional criminals. Accepting this challenge required law enforcement agencies to reassess their operations and reevaluate their priorities. At the same time, realizing that confronting international and domestic terrorism required a national effort, these agencies also looked to the federal government for both leadership and resources (International Association of Chiefs of Police 2005).

Responding to the challenge, law enforcement officials at the federal, state, and local levels began developing coordinated strategies to prevent and prepare for terrorism. As they began their task, they encountered the reality of the situation: While federal agencies were well positioned to work from a national and international perspective, state and local level agencies simply did not have the resources to work effectively. On the other hand, while state and local agencies were well positioned to work within their jurisdictions, they were ill prepared to counter the array of activities that supported terrorism. To help address this problem, President George W. Bush established the Office of Homeland Security (OHS) on October 8, 2001. A year later, the **Homeland Security Act of 2002** consolidated OHS operations, and that of 22 other federal agencies, into the Department of Homeland Security (DHS) (see **Figure 12-2**). The DHS mission was to "leverage resources within federal, state, and local governments, coordinating the transition of multiple agencies and programs into a single, integrated agency focused on protecting the American people and their homeland" (Department of Homeland Security 2011).

World Trade Center, 9/11

Source: © kentannenbaum/Fotolia.com

Issues and Challenges

As the federal government organized under the DHS, the International Association of Chiefs of Police began a campaign to define the role of state and local law enforcement agencies. They suggested that, while important progress had been made, much of what had been developed by the DHS was done "without sufficiently seeking or incorporating the advice, expertise or consent of public safety organizations at the state, tribal, or local level" (International Association of Chiefs of Police 2005). To correct this weakness, the IACP suggested a "new homeland security strategy" that embraced five principles:

1. <u>All terrorism is local</u>. While terrorism may spring from foreign sources, the act (crime) is local, requiring the immediate response of local agencies. Therefore, "as homeland security proposals are designed, they must be developed in an environment that fully acknowledges and accepts the reality that local authorities, not federal, have the primary responsibility for preventing, responding to and recovering from terrorist attacks" (International Association of Chiefs of Police 2005, 3).

2. <u>Prevention is paramount</u>. While response and recovery are important, the "need to build our capacity to prevent terrorist attacks from happening" should be our first priority (International Association of Chiefs of Police 2005, 4). This can be accomplished by enhancing the ability of state and local law enforcement agencies in their efforts to identify, investigate, and apprehend terrorist suspects before they can strike.

3. <u>Hometown security is homeland security</u>. Simply stated, the intimate knowledge that law enforcement officers have about their communities, and the close relationships they hold with the citizens they serve, is a cost-effective asset in attempts to prevent terrorism. Consequently, federal funding in support of local law enforcement (i.e., Law Enforcement Block Grant Program, the Edward Byrne Memorial Grant Program, and the Community Oriented Policing Services Programs) should not be reduced or eliminated, which the IACP complained was occurring under the Bush administration (International Association of Chiefs of Police 2005).

4. <u>Homeland security strategies must be coordinated nationally, not federally</u>. In other words, the IACP

FIGURE 12-2 DHS Organizational Chart

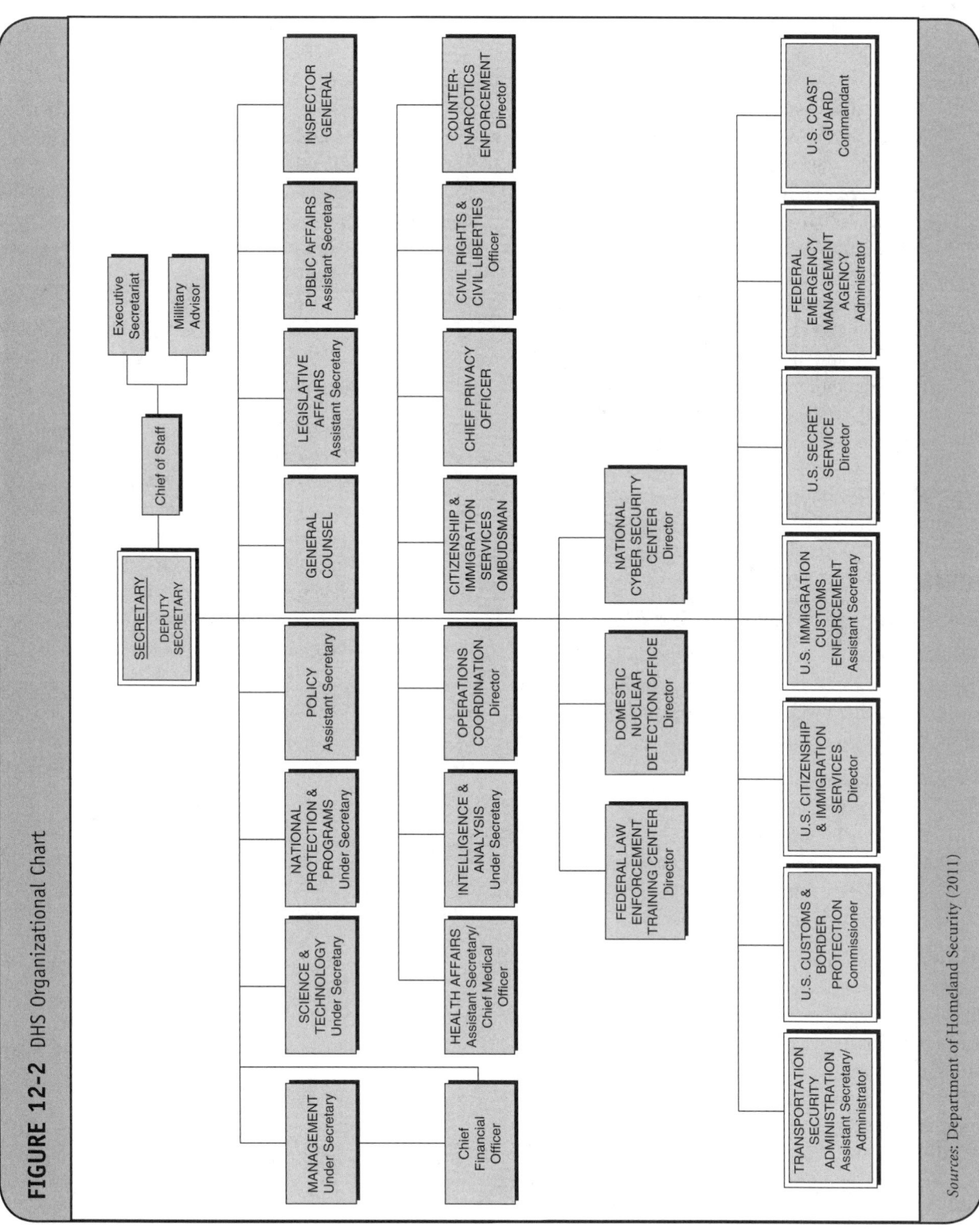

Sources: Department of Homeland Security (2011)

complained, just participating "in advisory panels and working groups" after a policy is developed minimizes the experiences and expertise of state and local law enforcement officials. Subsequently, "policies promulgated by federal agencies are often viewed by state, tribal, or local law enforcement as overly prescriptive, burdensome, and sometimes impractical" (International Association of Chiefs of Police 2005, 6).

5. Bottom-up engineering. Locally-designed homeland security strategies offer the best model for developing strategies because they reflect the great diversity and needs of American policing. The IACP reminded the DHS that, "A truly successful national strategy must recognize, embrace, and value the vast diversity that exists among state, tribal, and local law enforcement and public safety agencies" (International Association of Chiefs of Police 2005, 6).

HOMELAND SECURITY

The Department of Homeland Security

Amid considerable political discussion, including that offered by the IACP, the DHS began its tasks of directing and coordinating a wide array of programs that center on five main areas of responsibility:

1. Guarding against terrorism
2. Securing the nation's borders
3. Enforcing immigration laws
4. Improving the nation's readiness for, response to, and recovery from disasters
5. Maturing and unifying the DHS

As they implemented their mandate, a few DHS programs and strategies have proven controversial (e.g. the inability to secure our southern border, or the policy of screening all passengers, regardless of age or circumstance, at airport security checkpoints). One program above all others has generated great concern: the airline passenger-screening program used by the Transportation Security Administration (TSA) that employs non-ionizing radio frequency energy to produce a body image has raised privacy concerns (see the body image scan on this page).

Despite these challenges, the DHS has developed a number of successful programs, two of which warrant special mention. Each entity is designed to prevent, mitigate (if possible), and ultimately prepare citizens in the event of natural and manmade disasters. The first entity is the **National Response Framework** (**NRF**, which replaced The National Response Plan in 2008). The NRF offers guiding principles that enable all response partners to prepare for, and provide a unified national response to, disasters and emergencies. It includes a coordinated and comprehensive plan for first-responders in the event of a terrorist attack, natural disaster, or other large-scale emergency. The second entity is the **National Incident Management System** (**NIMS**). It

> provides a systematic, proactive approach to guide departments and agencies at all levels of government, nongovernmental organizations, and the private sector to work seamlessly to prevent, protect against, respond to, recover from, and mitigate the effects of incidents, regardless of cause, size, location, or complexity, in order to reduce the loss of life and property and harm to the environment (Federal Emergency Management Agency 2011).

Both of these entities are featured on the Federal Emergency Management Agency (FEMA) website (see Chapter Specific Internet Links at the end of this chapter). We urge you to visit the FEMA website and spend some time perusing its many valuable resources.

Federal and State Framework

There are over 16,000 law enforcement agencies in the United States, which vary significantly in size, scope of responsibility, and authority (see Chapter 4 for more detailed data and discussion). The model of law enforcement that has evolved in the United States can be referred to as a **fragmented system** (see Chapter 4) since we do not have a national police force. By design, the country's approximately 11,218 local police departments, 3067 sheriff's departments, 49 state police/patrol agencies, and 1889 special jurisdiction agencies are decentralized and independently organized. Since 9/11 and the creation of the Department of Homeland Security at the national level, many states have attempted to prepare and coordinate their fragmented law enforcement agencies by establishing Homeland Security Departments or assigning such responsibilities to existing agencies. For example, 27 states now have Homeland Security Departments or Offices at the state level; 9 have combined those responsibilities by adding the "Homeland Security" title to their Emergency Management Agencies; and the balance have assigned the responsibilities to existing agencies (such the Department of Public Safety, Emergency Services, Domestic Security, or State Civil Defense). A complete listing of the states and their respective homeland security and emergency management offices is available online (see Chapter Specific Internet Links, p. 373).

Because crime and homeland security issues are not confined to political boundaries, national, state and local law enforcement agencies have developed communications networks and protocols to facilitate interstate and intrastate cooperation. The National Crime Information Center (NCIC) is an excellent example of a national computerized database and communications network that connects state, local, and federal agencies. It is supported (agencies feed information into the system) and used by every law enforcement agency in the country. The NCIC database, which is maintained and operated by the FBI, provides extensive criminal record history information, information on fugitives, stolen property, and missing persons. Another example of the interconnection between federal, state, and local law enforcement is the Integrated Automated Fingerprint Identification System (IAFIS), which also is maintained by the FBI. The IAFIS provides law enforcement agencies access to a database that contains millions of fingerprints, mug shots, and scars and tattoo photos (see picture on this page). As with the NCIC, law enforcement agencies across the country voluntarily contribute to the databases. States have also developed their own communications networks and these often are tied into the national systems just described and to the National Law Enforcement Telecommunications System (see Chapter 11 for more discussion of communication systems).

Additionally, many cooperative arrangements and protocols to facilitate interstate investigations have been established. For example, extradition warrants are a common practice that states use to bring fugitives from

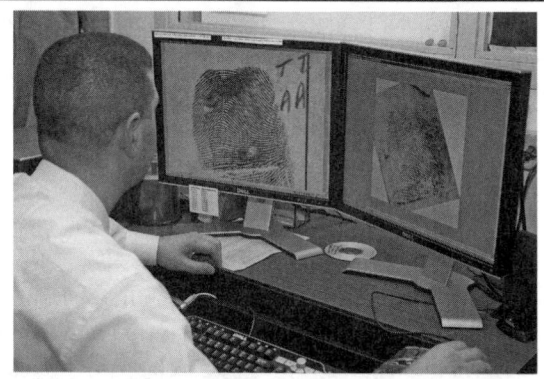

NY State Police employee working with IAFIS

Source: Courtesy of Public Information Office, New York State Police

one state (where they have been arrested) back to the state where they are wanted. National, state, and local law enforcement agencies also form **interagency task forces** (based on memorandums of understanding) to address crime problems that span multiple jurisdictions. California offers an excellent example of the development and use of interagency task forces. To review the scope of one state's interagency development, visit the California Office of Attorney General interactive website (see Chapter Specific Internet Links, p. 373). A review of this website demonstrates just how extensive interagency cooperation has become in efforts to prevent and address crime that crosses political boundaries.

While we have a fragmented system of law enforcement, it is also a system interconnected by technology, ingenuity, established standards, and practical cooperation. Two entities have been at the forefront of this movement: the National Institute of Justice (NIJ) and the International Association of Chiefs of Police. Since 1968, the NIJ has been responsible for evaluating the outcome and cost–benefit of criminal justice programs and technologies. They have promoted collaborative research that aims to make the field more efficient and effective by bring current research knowledge to criminal justice practitioners and policymakers. The IACP has an even longer history of promoting professionalism and innovative policies and standards for policing. Beginning in 1893, the IACP has pressed for standardized police operations and management practices (review Chapter 3 for more discussion of the IACP). Today, the efforts of the IACP, the NIJ, and other agencies like the Police Executive Research Forum (PERF), the National Organization of Black Law Enforcement Executives (NOBLE), and the Commission on Accreditation for Law Enforcement Agencies (CALEA) have brought the nation's law enforcement agencies under one philosophical umbrella that promotes professional service. Consequently, while agencies gain their authority from different political subdivisions in a fragment system, they are also very connected from a practical working perspective.

National Intelligence Framework

Our nation has a vast Intelligence Community (IC) consisting of 16 agencies and organizations, plus the Office of the Director of National Intelligence. The sixteen members of the IC include:

- Air Force Intelligence
- Army Intelligence
- Central Intelligence Agency
- Coast Guard Intelligence
- Defense Intelligence Agency
- Department of Energy
- Department of Homeland Security
- Department of State
- Department of the Treasury
- Drug Enforcement Administration
- Federal Bureau of Investigation
- Marine Corps Intelligence
- National Geospatial-Intelligence Agency
- National Reconnaissance Office
- National Security Agency
- Navy Intelligence

The Intelligence Community has three general areas of responsibility: Foreign intelligence (e.g., the Central Intelligence Agency and the **National Security Agency**), military intelligence (e.g., the **Defense Intelligence Agency**), and domestic intelligence (e.g., the Federal Bureau of Investigation). All of the intelligence collected by these agencies is eventually synthesized and funneled to the **National Security Council (NSC)**, which is responsible for providing the President and his advisors with accurate information upon which to develop national security and foreign policy. One person, the Director of National Intelligence (DNI), oversees and directs the national intelligence program. He is the principal advisor to the President, the National Security Council, and the Homeland Security Council. His responsibilities are included in a document entitled *Mission and Support Activities for the IC* (see **Figure 12-3**). A review of this list gives us some insight into the complexity of foreign, military, and domestic intelligence operations allied in defense of the homeland and of U.S. interests abroad.

Intelligence-led Policing, Fusion Centers, and Interagency Task Forces

One of the lessons learned as a consequence of the 9/11 attacks, is that

> *the functions of intelligence gathering and information sharing must be woven into the daily fabric of state, local, and tribal (SLT) law enforcement. This fabric should encompass not only the efforts of police officers, state troopers, tribal police, and sheriffs, but the fusion centers and the other resources dedicated to the collection and analysis of information (International Association of Chiefs of Police 2010).*

Consequently, **intelligence-led policing** and **fusion centers** have gained wide acceptance in contemporary policing. These initiatives also dovetailed with the ongoing and successful strategy of interagency task forces.

Intelligence-led policing, as we have explained, is a relatively new philosophy in policing. It "is about managing information; specifically, the information that is needed to identify threats of concern to a community, and having sufficient information about the threat to develop operational responses to prevent or mitigate the threat" (Carter 2009, 99). We have become an information-driven society; intelligence-led policing simply capitalizes on the diversity and availability of information (raw intelligence), synthesizes and analyzes it, and then develops law enforcement strategies based on this knowledge. In practice, intelligence-led

FIGURE 12-3 Duties of the Director of National Intelligence (DCI)

The Director of National Intelligence (DNI) serves as the head of the Intelligence Community (IC), overseeing and directing the implementation of the National Intelligence Program and acting as the principal advisor to the President, the National Security Council, and the Homeland Security Council for intelligence matters related to the national security. Working together with the Principal Deputy DNI (PDDNI) and with the assistance of Mission Managers and four Deputy Directors, the Office of the DNI's goal is to effectively integrate foreign, military, and domestic intelligence in defense of the homeland and of United States interests abroad.

With this goal in mind, Congress provided the DNI with a number of authorities and duties, as outlined in the Intelligence Reform and Terrorism Prevention Act (IRTPA) of 2004. These charge the DNI to:

- Ensure that timely and objective national intelligence is provided to the President, the heads of departments and agencies of the executive branch; the Chairman of the Joint Chiefs of Staff and senior military commanders; and the Congress;
- Establish objectives and priorities for collection, analysis, production, and dissemination of national intelligence;
- Ensure maximum availability of and access to intelligence information within the Intelligence Community;
- Develop and ensure the execution of an annual budget for the National Intelligence program (NIP) based on budget proposals provided by IC component organizations;
- Oversee coordination of relationships with the intelligence or security services of foreign governments and international organizations;
- Ensure the most accurate analysis of intelligence is derived from all sources to support national security needs;
- Develop personnel policies and programs to enhance the capacity for joint operations and to facilitate staffing of community management functions; and
- Oversee the development and implementation of a program management plan for acquisition of major systems, doing so jointly with the Secretary of Defense for DoD programs, that includes cost, schedule, and performance goals and program milestone criteria.

Source: Office of the Director of National Intelligence (2011), http://www.dni.gov/who.htm

policing requires managing and sharing information based on a deductive seven-step process (Carter 2009, 100):

1. Strategic priority: What problem is important (remember that law enforcement executives are presented with many challenges, but have limited resources to deal with them)?

2. Intelligence requirements: What information do I have and what additional information do I need to better understand the problem, its causes, and its effects?

3. Collection plan: Where (sources) and how (methods) will I get the additional information that I need to better understand the problem?

4. Analysis: Collectively, what does the new information mean and what new insights does it provide about the problem?

5. Intelligence product: What actionable information do I need to tell other people in order to prevent or control the problem?

6. Operational response: What explicit operational activities may be implemented to prevent or mitigate the priority problems? What resources are needed?

7. Review process: Was the information accurate and useful? Could the problem be altered as a result of the information? What will make the process better?

Fusion centers support intelligence-led policing. They are geographically-located facilities funded by various local, state, and federal funds. They are intended to be "an effective and efficient mechanism to exchange information and intelligence, maximize resources, streamline operations, and improve the ability to fight crime and terrorism by analyzing data from a variety of sources" (Department of Justice 2006, 2). To accomplish this integrated mission, fusion centers are staffed by representatives from federal (e.g. FBI, DEA, ATF, DHS), state (e.g. state police, district attorneys), and local law enforcement (e.g., police and sheriffs) agencies. Working in concert, these representatives marshal, coordinate, and employ the resources and expertise of their individual agencies in a collective and focused effort (they "fuse" it) to identify, prevent, and respond to criminal threats to the community. Simply stated, they turn information into actionable knowledge by collecting, analyzing, and disseminating information to concerned agencies in response to specific requests and/or in support of intelligence-led policing initiatives.

The intelligence fusion process is a new evolution in law enforcement, one that recognizes that, prior to 9/11, information sharing between law enforcement agencies and the intelligence community was very poor. It also recognizes the complexity of modern cross-jurisdictional crime patterns, including international threats to local or regional communities. This includes white-collar crime, drug trafficking, and terrorism.

Today, many of the country's 72 fusion centers are collocated with **High Intensity Drug Trafficking Area (HIDTA)** intelligence centers, which were formed in the 1980s and became successful as counterdrug initiatives (for more information about HIDTAs, see the Office of National Drug Policy website listed in the Chapter Specific Internet Links). While not every fusion center functions in exactly the same way (understand that different regions have somewhat different needs), they all operate on four basic assumptions (Carter 2009, 171; Masse and Rollins 2007):

1. Intelligence and the intelligence process play a vital role in preventing terrorist attacks.
2. It is essential to fuse a broader range of data, including nontraditional source data, to create a more comprehensive threat picture.
3. State, local, and tribal law enforcement and public-sector agencies are in a unique position to make observations and collect information that may be central to the type of threat assessment referenced above.
4. Having fusion activities take place at the sub-federal level can benefit state and local communities, and possibly have national benefits, as well.

Interagency task forces have existed for many years within the law enforcement community. In fact, their success led to the creation of HIDTA teams. While most interagency task forces are not located within fusion centers (their sheer numbers make this impractical), they use fusion centers for research and information. Conversely, because of their great diversity and expertise, interagency task forces contribute vital information to the fusion process. For example, interagency task forces include regional auto theft teams, criminal apprehension/fugitive teams, narcotics enforcement teams, animal cruelty teams, alcohol/drunk driving enforcement teams, anti-graffiti and anti-gang teams, child abuse and exploitation teams, burglary apprehension teams, etc. Consequently, interagency task forces remain an effective tool in the prevention and suppression of crime, and an efficient mechanism to exchange information and intelligence in the fight against crime, including terrorism.

PRIVATE SECTOR PROTECTION IN THE UNITED STATES

An interesting and often overlooked police-related field is the **private police/security** profession. It does not have a single title—it has been referred to as "private security," "private policing," "loss prevention," "loss control," "assets protection," and even "risk management." The field encompasses dozens of job titles extending from the uniformed officer at financial and retail establishments to corporate security directors of international companies. It includes private detectives, hospital security personnel, railroad police, nuclear power plant SWAT team members, armored car officers, computer security specialists, access control specialists, electronic technicians, occupational health/safety personnel, fire safety experts, contingency/disaster management planners, and security and crime prevention consultants. Regardless of titles and terms, the field consists primarily of proprietary and contract security personnel. **Proprietary security personnel** are those who are employed directly by the entity they serve and protect, while **contract security personnel** are those who are employed by a security services company that contracts security services to others. During the Iraq war, considerable attention and notice was given to security companies (also called private military companies) providing various functions to the U.S. Military, usually in overseas theaters.

Officer monitoring surveillance cameras, Operation Shield, Atlanta, GA

Source: © Digital Vision/age fotostock

The 9/11 Commission Report (National Commission on Terrorist Attacks 2004) emphasized the importance of private sector preparedness in responding to terrorist incidents in the United States:

> The mandate of the Department of Homeland Security does not end with government; the department is also responsible for working with the private sector to ensure preparedness. This is entirely appropriate, for the private sector controls 85 percent of the critical infrastructure in the nation. Indeed, unless a terrorist's target is a military or other secure government facility, the "first" first responders will almost certainly be civilians. Homeland security and national preparedness therefore often begins with the private sector.

According to Coleman (2010), "the term '**critical infrastructure**' is often defined as systems and assets, whether physical or virtual, so vital to the United States that the incapacity or destruction of such systems and assets would have a debilitating impact on the security, national economic security, national health or safety,

or any combination of those matters." In the United States, this infrastructure includes many physical facilities and information-based assets that if interrupted or destroyed, "would cause a serious effects on the health, safety, security and overall well-being of people or the ability of industries or the government to effectively function" (Coleman 2010). In essence, the critical infrastructure of the country includes the following sectors of our economy or facilities and the personnel who operate them (Coleman 2010):

- Agriculture
- Banking and finance
- Chemical
- Commercial facilities
- Dams
- Defense manufacturing
- Drinking water facilities
- Wastewater treatment facilities
- Emergency services
- Energy
- Government facilities
- Information technology
- National monuments and icons
- Nuclear reactors and nuclear waste
- Postal and shipping facilities
- Public health and health care
- Telecommunications
- Transportation systems

Based on this information, it is clear that private sector police, loss prevention personnel, uniformed guards, crime prevention experts, consultants and safety engineers all have a major role in protecting the United States.

Associations and Personnel

The private security/loss prevention field has many professional associations, the largest one (in terms of individual memberships) being ASIS International (formerly known as the American Society for Industrial Security, but it now encompasses all aspects of the security/loss prevention/assets protection arena). Founded in 1955, ASIS International has a worldwide membership of over 37,000 and has a staff of 82 employees. It is headquartered in Alexandria, Virginia and has an extensive website (see Chapter Specific Internet Links, p. 373). Another influential association is the National Association of Security Companies (NASCO), which is also based in Alexandria, Virginia. NASCO members employ nearly 250,000 trained security guards throughout the government and commercial sectors in the United States (National Association of Security Companies 2010). The International Foundation for Protection Officers (IFPO) was established in 1988 and its primary purpose is to facilitate "the training and certification needs of protection officers and security supervisors from both the commercial and proprietary sectors" (International Foundation for Protection Officers 2010a). The National Council of Investigation and Security Services (NCISS), founded in 1975, is an association for investigation and security services companies. It has more than 1100 member firms "representing nearly 15,000 investigators and security services professionals and encourages the exchange of information and best practices to improve performance and raise ethical standards" (National Council of Investigation and Security Services 2010a). Another association of interest is the International Peace Operations Association (IPOA), also known as the International Stability Operations Association (ISOA), which is a trade association of private companies that are utilized in conflict and post-conflict environments (International Peace Operations Association 2010). The IPOA's membership includes many of the larger corporations that some call **private military security companies** (Mayer 2010). These companies often conduct security-related functions in war zones such as Iraq and Afghanistan (usually under government contracts). Other major associations include: Information Systems Security Association (ISSA), Security Industry Association (SIA), International Association for Healthcare Security & Safety (IAHSS), World Association of Detectives (WAD), Private Investigators Association of America (PIA), and Association of Certified Fraud Examiners (ACFE).

The exact number of security personnel in the United States is difficult to determine because there is no central reporting mechanism to collect such data. According to industry trends over the last decades, some general estimates indicate that the private sector outspends public law

enforcement by 73% and employs twice the workforce. If that is true today, the private security/loss prevention field would be a $173 billion industry employing about 1.6 million to 2 million persons. Since 9/11, segments of the private security industry have grown annually at rates ranging from 8% to 15% per year. One of the fastest growing components is the manufacture, distribution, and installation of security equipment and technology. Historically, the growth rate for private security services is double that of the public sector (Cunningham et al. 1991) and that was prior to the 9/11 attacks. The uniformed private security component alone is a $13 billion industry and, according to the U.S. Bureau of Labor Statistics, employment of security guards and gaming (casino) surveillance officers is expected to grow by 14% from 2008 to 2014 because of concern for crime, fraud, vandalism, and terrorism (Bureau of Labor Statistics 2009). The security field, however, is much broader than the uniformed officers, alarm systems, locks, and security equipment areas. There are numerous types of supervisory positions on the local, regional and national levels. Think about it: How do multinational corporations, such as IBM, Citicorp, General Motors, Microsoft, Toyota, and Wal-Mart, protect their personnel, facilities, and other assets? There is significant opportunity in the private sector. Consider the following career areas that utilize protection personnel and services (ASIS International n.d.):

Construction
Corporate
Credit Card
Educational Institutions
Entertainment
Executive Protection
Financial Institutions
Gaming/Wagering
Government Operations
Healthcare
Hi-Tech Industry
Information Systems
Insurance
Lodging
Manufacturing
Nuclear

Pharmaceutical
Retail
Security Consulting
Security Training
Special Event
Anti-Terrorism
Transportation
Utilities

What is the earning power of positions in the private policing field? Annual salaries range from $18,000 to over $100,000 depending on the position and type of business in which one is employed. Obviously, the higher salaries are for the "directors" or "chiefs" of security or loss prevention, and the lowest is for uniformed positions.

Authority and Regulation of Private Police

The authority of private police is primarily dependent upon the law of the state in which the person is employed. Generally, they have no more authority than private citizens, although even that varies from state to state. Many states have enacted specific statutes regulating and delimiting the authority of private persons employed in a security or protective capacity. States may permit the carrying of weapons, the right to detain and arrest, and the right to search persons. State law may address actions ranging from the arrest of shoplifters (in mercantile statutes) to the use of deadly force. The focus of most state regulation is to license certain types of security-related activity such as carrying a firearm, private detective services, security guard services, and alarm installation services.

There are no U.S. federal requirements for training of critical infrastructure guards other than airport screeners and nuclear guards. Twenty-two states do require basic training for licensed security guards, but few specifically require counter-terrorism training. State regulations regarding criminal background checks for security guards vary. Sixteen states have no background check regulations (Parfomak 2004). Currently, 40 states license and regulate private security companies and security guards (Ricci 2007). In Ohio, only armed, licensed officers must successfully complete a minimum of 20 hours of firearms-related training; if not armed and/or working in a proprietary (as opposed to a contract—for hire—officer) capacity, there is

no state requirement of any training. In some states such as California, Florida, and Oklahoma, unarmed security officers must complete 40 hours of training, while in 30 other states there are no specific training requirements. Approximately 22 states require officers to pass a federal background check (Sutherland 2003). In 22 states they do not have to be licensed and in 16 states there are no state background checks required (Hall 2003). Therefore, private businesses with their own security force and private security companies that provide contract officer services often take it upon themselves to train their own officers. Many establish education and training requirements for employment and even provide annual training to officers. Historically, most regulation of the field by states has focused on contract security officers and not proprietary officers, but that may be changing. The state of California in 2005 enacted legislation (Senate Bill 194) requiring a person who meets the definition of a proprietary private security officer to register with the Department of Consumer Affairs, Bureau of Security and Investigative Services (Bureau of Security and Investigative Services 2010). The law does not mandate training for such officers, but it does require fingerprints and background checks. In the state of Connecticut, as of October 1, 2004, a new state law requires all security officers, contract or proprietary, to pass an eight-hour certification course, register with the state, and undergo a nationwide criminal background check (Connecticut 2007). There is a trend toward greater state regulation, certification, and identification of security officers, but federal legislation has been minimal. (See **Figure 12-4** for selected state agencies that regulate security officers.)

Because of the variations among the states, and the reluctance of Congress to set any national standards, professional associations like NASCO and ASIS International are placing greater efforts on influencing state legislatures (Sutherland 2003). ASIS International has a standing Commission on Guidelines which has recommended several for the field, one of which is the Private Security Officer Selection and Training Guideline (see **Figure 12-5** for other guidelines). Other guideline projects are being planned with the intent of advancing the profession. In 2004, however, Congress did enact the Intelligence Reform and Terrorism Prevention Act of

---

FIGURE 12-4 Links to Selected State Agencies that Regulate Security Officers

Arizona: http://licensing.azdps.gov/Licensesecurityguard.asp

Connecticut: http://www.ct.gov/dps/cwp/view.asp?a=2158&q=294506

Florida: http://licgweb.doacs.state.fl.us/security/index.html

Indiana: http://www.in.gov/pla/pisg.htm

Montana: http://bsd.dli.mt.gov/license/bsd_boards/psp_board/board_page.asp

Ohio: http://homelandsecurity.ohio.gov/ohs_pisg.stm

Oklahoma: http://www.ok.gov/cleet/Licensing/Security_Guards/index.html

Texas: http://www.txdps.state.tx.us/psb/

2004 (Public Law No.108-458) which included the Private Security Officer Employment Act of 2004. The provisions provided private security officer employers with access to the FBI's criminal history records. Congress required that the employers always go through their state identification bureaus in order to get that access, however, which has been a criticism of the Act. According to Floyd Clarke (2007), "states have generally not exercised this authority and private security officer employers still cannot regularly screen prospective employees against the national database."

Case law (the court's previous decisions) is extremely important within states as to how the law applies to private police or security personnel. For example, in *Bowman v. State* (1983), an Indiana court ruled that Miranda warnings (informing those arrested of their rights) did not have to be given by private police, since they were not involved in "state action" (Hess and Wrobleski 1992, 100). Generally, U.S. constitutional protections only apply to governmental actions, not those of private citizens. In 1921, the U.S. Supreme Court clearly stated in *Burdeau v. McDowell* (1921) that the Fourth Amendment gives protection against unlawful searches and seizures conducted by governmental agencies. The court held

that the Constitution does not protect persons against arrests, searches, and seizures conducted by private parties (including private security personnel). However, the courts also have indicated that if there is a close relationship or a state connection to the actions of the security officer, a review based upon constitutional considerations may be required. In other words, if private security personnel are acting at the request of governmental agents, their actions may be governed by constitutional restrictions (see: *Romanski v. Detroit Entertainment* 2005; *Johnson v. Larabida Children's Hospital* 2004; *United States v. Shahid* 1997; *Wade v. Byles* 1996; *Euller* 1980; and *People v. Selinski* 1979).

Certifications and Professionalism

We noted above that there is very limited regulation of the security industry. Since the 1970s, the security field has been attempting to improve its image and overall professionalism, and one effort that has achieved some success and national recognition is the certification efforts of various national organizations. ASIS International awarded its first Certified Protection Professional (CPP) designation in Fall 1977. Recently, the organization added two other certifications: the Physical Security Professional (PSP) and

FIGURE 12-5 ASIS International—Standards and Guidelines

The ASIS Commission on Standards and Guidelines Policy and Procedures has developed or is developing standards and guidelines for the security industry. The following is a listing of published documents available from ASIS. There are several standards in progress, and additional guidelines may be developed in the future as well. You are encouraged to check on their current status at the website: http://www.asisonline.org/guidelines/guidelines.htm.

Published Standards Topics
Chief Security Officer Organizational Standard
Organizational Resilience: Security, Preparedness, and Continuity Management Systems

Standards In Progress
Auditing Management Systems for Security, Preparedness, and Continuity Management with Guidance for Application Standard
Business Continuity Management Standard
Organizational Resilience Maturity Model - Phased Implementation Standard
Physical Asset Protection Standard (formerly *Facilities Physical Security Management*)
Resilience in the Supply Chain Standard
Risk Assessment Standard
Workplace Violence Prevention and Intervention Standard

Published Guideline Topics
Business Continuity: A Practical Approach for Emergency Preparedness, Crisis Management, and Disaster Recovery
Chief Security Officer
Facilities Physical Security Measures
General Security Risk Assessment
Information Asset Protection
Preemployment Background Screening
Private Security Officer Selection and Training
Threat Advisory System Response
Workplace Violence Prevention and Response

Guidelines In Progress
None (As of December 2010)

Source: Adapted from ASIS International (2010) http://www.asisonline.org/guidelines/guidelines.htm

the Professional Security Investigator (PSI). The eligibility criteria for each certification are displayed in **Table 12-1** (ASIS International 2010a). The IFPO has established several professional certifications as well. They include the Certified Protection Officer Program (CPO), the Certified in Security Supervision and Management Program (CSSM), and the Certified Protection Officer Instructor (CPOI) (International Foundation for Protection Officers 2010b). The Loss Prevention Foundation was founded in 2006 and recently has developed Loss Prevention Qualified (LPQualified) and Loss Prevention Certified (LPCcertified) designations geared primarily toward the retail sector. The Qualified designation is more for novice personnel, while the Certified designation is for more experienced personnel (Loss Prevention Foundation 2010). Generally speaking, obtaining these recognized certifications can assist one's advancement in the security field.

Generally speaking, the security/loss prevention/private policing field does not have a high public recognition for professionalism. This varies, of course, because of the

TABLE 12-1 ASIS International Certifications

| | Criteria for Eligibility | | | |
Certification	Experience*	Education*	National Exam	Other
Certified Protection Professional (CPP)	9 years of security experience, at least 3 years of which shall have been in responsible charge of a security function; OR	An earned Bachelor's Degree or higher from an accredited institution of higher education and 7 years of security experience, at least 3 years of which shall have been in responsible charge of a security function.	Yes	No convictions for any criminal offense that would reflect negatively on the security profession, ASIS, or the certification program
Physical Security Professional (PSP)	4 years of progressive experience in the physical security field and an earned Bachelor's Degree OR 6 years of progressive experience and a high school diploma or GED	An earned Bachelor's Degree or higher from an accredited institution of higher education and 4 years of progressive physical security experience OR A high school diploma or GED equivalent	Yes	No convictions for any criminal offense that would reflect negatively on the security profession, ASIS, or the certification program
Professional Certified Investigator (PCI)	5 years of investigations experience, with at least two (2) years in case management	A high school diploma or GED equivalent	Yes	No convictions for any criminal offense that would reflect negatively on the security profession, ASIS, or the certification program

Source: Adapted from ASIS International, http://www.asisonline.org/certification/index.xml

*For exact definitions of terms see: http://www.asisonline.org/certification/eligibility.xml.

vast extent of the field. A security director at a Fortune 500 company is hardly perceived the same as a contract security officer at a local fast food restaurant. But perceptions can be deceiving, because both of these individuals could be very professional in their demeanor and actions. There are efforts across the industry to improve the status and perception of security-related personnel. One aspect of professionalism is to abide by a code of ethics. There are actually several Codes of Ethics in the field representing different constituents. ASIS International supports a code

of ethics for its members (ASIS International 2010c). The National Council of Investigation and Security Services (National Council of Investigation and Security Services 2010b) has its own code, as does The Information Systems Security Association (National Council of Investigation and Security Services 2010).

Public and Private Police Relationships

Both the public and private police fields exist for specific purposes or reasons. Public law enforcement is usually responsible for the enforcement of criminal behavior by investigating crime and apprehending offenders. As such, it is reactive in nature and usually responds upon receiving a complaint from a citizen or company. Private policing, on the other hand, has traditionally been focused on the prevention of crime, accidents, injuries, and loss of resources, as well as the detection of crime or emergency situations. Private security extends beyond crime and policing and into areas of loss reduction, safety, hygiene, and risk management.

There are areas of obvious conflict and concern in which it appears that public and private police are responsible for the same thing, such as protecting areas open to the public (e.g., supermarkets, banks, bus terminals). When uniformed private officers are involved, they are supplementing the public agency's responsibility. Public agencies do not have enough personnel to permanently assign officers to private establishments to provide protection. Private officers also complement public agency responsibility, in that the public officers have limited authority on private property and may not even provide the services that the private officers perform. These services include private employment background checks, armored car services, private detective work, alarm installation and monitoring, initial investigation of suspected financial crimes, and protection of trade secrets or sensitive corporate information and data.

The general relationship between private and public officers varies from place to place. Some communities have worked hard to promote a clear understanding of the roles of each entity. In other places, visible conflict may exist. This may be the case even though some estimates categorize 20% of the security personnel in the United States as off-duty public officers working a second job. In fact, both groups are needed. The public cannot afford to employ all the security personnel at its expense, and clearly much of what private security involves is not a public responsibility.

Since the terrorist attacks of 9/11, greater emphasis and concern regarding the relationships between public law enforcement and private policing entities has arisen. Several cities are including local private security and loss prevention personnel in their overall emergency planning strategies. One unique program, in operation since 1990,

is a technique used by the Atlanta Police Department called Communications Network (COMNET); it is a continuous link between private sector security providers and the department. It is a two-way, VHF radio network, established to provide quick and efficient communications between the security providers and the department. In 2007, COMNET partnered with the Atlanta Police Foundation in establishing Operation Shield. The program has three major components: COMNET, Atlanta CityWorkSite (a secure web-based platform channel), and Surveillance Camera Integration (surveillance cameras fed live to the Atlanta Police Department and uploaded to Atlanta CityWorkSite). The city recognizes that private security officers can often serve as the first line of notification for the police department since they are visible, trained, and strategically posted on property throughout the city. Today, Operation Shield links member sites that include campus police departments, federal agencies, the downtown improvement district, corporate and hotel security departments, retail loss prevention departments, and property management companies (Atlanta Police Foundation 2010).

The city of Dallas partnered with the non-profit group Downtown Dallas, Inc. in 2001 to establish the Downtown Emergency Response Team (DERT). In 2004, the Downtown Safety Patrol (DSP) was added, in which about 50 officers patrol the central business area on foot and bicycle (Anderson 2010, 66). The details of any major crisis or event can be announced over a local AM radio station dedicated to emergency announcements. Key groups are updated throughout the incident. Once an incident is reported, other groups such as the Downtown Improvement District (DID) can put an emergency call on the organization's email-based text-messaging system that can reach DERT's members via emails and by text message to mobile devices—cell phones, PDAs, and pagers. Property managers, security directors, and engineers in all of the downtown buildings are kept informed of the incident, which helps coordinate resources in both the public and private sectors. DERT was actually envisioned prior to 9/11, but the attacks brought greater interest and cooperation from the downtown community to get organized for major incidents or catastrophes. Dallas has had a history of public police and security cooperation.

For example, the Law Enforcement and Private Security (LEAPS) program, which began in 1995 and has been operated by the Dallas Police Department, has over 125 local law enforcement and corporate members and holds monthly meetings to share information. One major function of the LEAPS is to coordinate issues and problems related to law enforcement and security (Anderson 2004). Other major cities have similar programs; for example, New York City's program is called Area Police–Private Security Liaison Program (APPL) and has 1300 members, consisting of business leaders, who work in cooperation with the NYPD to prevent crime (Kelly 2005).

With approximately 85% of the nation's infrastructure protected by private security personnel, there needs to be greater cooperation between public and private policing efforts. In 2004, a national policy summit was undertaken through the cooperative efforts of the International Association of Chiefs of Police and the Office of Community Oriented Policing Services (COPS) of the Department of Justice (International Association of Chiefs of Police and the Office of Community Oriented Policing Services 2004). The summit participants undertook their tasks in six working groups and produced five policy recommendations. According to the report of the proceedings of the summit, the first four recommendations are national-level and long-term in scope. The fifth recommendation relates to local and regional efforts that could begin immediately. The policy recommendations are:

1. Leaders of the major law enforcement and private security organizations should make a formal commitment to cooperation.
2. The Department of Homeland Security and/or Department of Justice should fund research and training on relevant legislation, private security, and law enforcement–private security cooperation.
3. The Department of Homeland Security and/or Department of Justice should create an advisory council composed of nationally prominent law enforcement and private security professionals to oversee the day-to-day implementation issues of law enforcement–private security partnerships.
4. The Department of Homeland Security and/or Department of Justice, along with relevant

membership organizations, should convene key practitioners to move this agenda forward in the future.
5. Local partnerships should set priorities and address key problems as identified by the summit. Examples of local and regional activities that can and should be undertaken immediately include the following:

- Improve joint response to critical incidents
- Coordinate infrastructure protection
- Improve communications and data interoperability
- Bolster information and intelligence sharing
- Prevent and investigate high-tech crime
- Devise responses to workplace violence

A dedicated national initiative, the Law Enforcement–Private Security Consortium, has a website dedicated to numerous sources documenting professional cooperative programs across the United States. It is an excellent source for additional information on law enforcement and private sector partnerships. (To visit this site, see Chapter Specific Internet Links, p. 373) If the United States is going to be a safe nation, secure in its infrastructure and institutions, the public law enforcement sector must initiate cooperative initiatives with private security and assets protection agencies and their personnel, who work diligently every day to prevent crime and to protect property, visitors, and employees.

SUMMARY

Since the attacks of 9/11, our nation's law enforcement agencies have restructured their role in defending the nation. Beyond defending the public against common criminals, law enforcement agencies have adopted an enhanced role of helping to defend the nation against terrorism. This has required that federal agencies like the CIA and the FBI share information with the DHS and ultimately with state and local law enforcement agencies in a coordinated effort. Additionally, federal, state, and local law enforcement agencies have joined hands in fusion centers around the country to collect, analyze, and share information about a wide range criminal activity.

Private security agencies have been called to increase protection for private property that cannot be provided by local public police. The major focus of private policing is on the prevention and detection of crime rather than the investigation of crime and the apprehension of offenders. The events of September 11, 2001 have had a significant effect on both the public and private sectors of law enforcement and security. Greater focus has been placed on prevention, intelligence sharing, and public-private partnerships.

Critical Thinking Questions

1. In light of national security and homeland security issues, do you think our fragmented system of law enforcement is preferable to a national law enforcement system (i.e. a system under one command with standardized policies and procedures that spans all 50 states)? As you answer the question, describe what you believe are the strengths and weakness of each model, including political considerations.

2. The Department of Homeland Security was created in response to the terrorist attacks of 9/11. In your opinion, was it a good idea from a policy perspective, or simply an act of political expediency? Why did national leaders not create a similar entity following the attack on the World Trade Center in 1993? To answer these questions, you may want to search the archives of news organizations like the *Wall Street Journal*, the *New York Times*, or your local newspaper. Remember to review their editorial pages, too.

3. Explain why passage of the *USA Patriot Act* was controversial to some citizens and an essential tool in defense of our nation to others. To answer this question you may want to search the archives of news organizations like the *Wall Street Journal*, the *New York Times*, or your local newspaper. Remember to review their editorial pages, too.

CHAPTER SPECIFIC INTERNET LINKS

ASIS International: http://www.asisonline.org/

California Office of Attorney General: http://ag.ca.gov/cbi/index.php

Central Intelligence Agency (CIA): https://www.cia.gov/

Defense Intelligence Agency (DIA): http://www.dia.mil/

Department of Homeland Security (DHS): http://www.dhs.gov/index.shtm

Federal Bureau of Investigation (FBI): http://www.fbi.gov/

Federal Bureau of Investigation's Ten Most Wanted List: http://www.fbi.gov/wanted/wanted_terrorists.

Federal Emergency Management Agency (FEMA): http://www.fema.gov/index.shtm

Homeland security and emergency management websites: http://www.dhs.gov/files/resources/editorial_0306.shtm

Fusion Center Guidelines (DOJ) document: http://it.ojp.gov/documents/fusion_center_guidelines_law_enforcement.pdf

High Intensity Drug Trafficking Areas (HIDTA), visit the Office of National Drug Policy: http://www.whitehousedrugpolicy.gov/hidta/

International Association of Chiefs of Police (IACP): http://theiacp.org/

National Crime Information Center (NCIC): http://www.fas.org/irp/agency/doj/fbi/is/ncic.htm

National Incident Management System (NIMS): http://www.fema.gov/emergency/nims/

National Response Framework (NRF): http://www.fema.gov/pdf/emergency/nrf/nrf-core.pdf

National Security Agency (NSA): http://www.nsa.gov/

National Security Council (NSC): http://www.whitehouse.gov/administration/eop/nsc)

Private Security Consortium: http://www.lepsc.org/

State Regulation of Security Guards in the State of Oklahoma: http://www.ok.gov/cleet/Licensing/Training/

CHAPTER GLOSSARY

The 9/11 Commission Report—an extensive report of the findings of the National Commission on Terrorist Attacks Upon the United States following the attacks of 9/11/01. The Report investigated the shortcomings of the U.S. intelligence and national security systems and made multiple recommendations to improve them.

Al-Qaeda (translation: the base)—"is an international terrorist network led by Usama bin Laden [the "Osama" spelling is deprecated, because there is no letter "O" in Arabic]. Established around 1988 by bin Laden, al-Qaeda helped finance, recruit, transport, and train thousands of fighters from dozens of countries to be part of an Afghan resistance to defeat the Soviet Union. To continue the holy war beyond Afghanistan, al-Qaeda's current goal is to establish a pan-Islamic Caliphate throughout the world by working with allied Islamic extremist groups to overthrow regimes it deems 'non-Islamic' and expelling" Westerners (Global Security Organization 2010).

Central Intelligence Agency (CIA)—an independent agency responsible for providing national security intelligence to senior U.S. policymakers. The agency is divided into four basic components: the National Clandestine Service, the Directorate of Intelligence, the Directorate of Science and Technology, and the Directorate of Support. It collects, analyzes, and disseminates intelligence information to senior U.S. government officials.

Contract security personnel—individuals working in the security field who are employed by a company that contracts their services to others; the security company utilizing such persons are often regulated by the state.

Critical infrastructure—defined as systems and assets, whether physical or virtual, so vital to the United States that the incapacity or destruction of such systems and assets would have a debilitating impact on the security, national economic security, national health, or safety.

Defense Intelligence Agency (DIA)—a component of the Department of Defense. The DIA collects and manages foreign military intelligence and provides that information to the branches of the military and national defense policymakers.

Foreign Intelligence Surveillance Act (FISA)—passed by Congress in 1978, it prescribes procedures for requesting judicial authorization for electronic surveillance and physical search of persons engaged in espionage or international terrorism against the United States on behalf of a foreign power. Requests are adjudicated by a special 11-member court called the Foreign Intelligence Surveillance Court.

Fragmented system—a system law enforcement where the law enforcement community is decentralized and independently organized in line with political boundaries, divided by federal, state, local, and tribal authority. In the United States, it reflects our federalist system of government.

Fusion centers—geographically-located facilities funded by various local, state, and federal funds that are staffed by a representative collection of law enforcement officials. Fusion centers are intended to be an effective and efficient mechanism to exchange information and intelligence, maximize resources, streamline operations, and improve the ability to fight crime and terrorism by analyzing data from a variety of sources.

High Intensity Drug Trafficking Area (HIDTA)—multiagency task forces teamed to prevent and suppress major drug trafficking operations in specific geographical areas.

Homeland Security Act of 2002—established the Department of Homeland Security, an executive department of the United States. Its primary mission is to prevent terrorist attacks within the United States, to reduce the vulnerability of the United States to terrorism, to minimize the damage of a terrorist attack, and to assist in the recovery from terrorist attacks that do occur within the United States.

Intelligence-led policing—a relatively new proactive philosophy (model) of policing that seeks to manage (collect and analyze) information in a deductive seven-step process, in order to identify threats to a community and then develop operational responses to prevent or mitigate the threat.

Interagency task forces—cooperative entities comprised of selected representatives from various law enforcement agencies that band together (usually under a memorandum of understanding) to address a specific crime problem, generally a problem that crosses political boundaries (i.e., city, county, or state). Interagency task forces vary in size, composition, and mission. They have traditionally been directed at common criminals or crimes. However, since 9/11, interagency task forces have also been formed or redirected to fight terrorism.

National Incident Management System (NIMS)—"provides a systematic, proactive approach to guide departments and agencies at all levels of government, nongovernmental organizations, and the private sector to work seamlessly to prevent, protect against, respond to, recover from, and mitigate the effects of incidents, regardless of cause, size, location, or complexity, in order to reduce the loss of life and property and harm to the environment" (Federal Emergency Management Adminstration 2010).

National Response Framework (NRF)—"a guide to how the Nation conducts all-hazards response. It is built upon scalable, flexible, and adaptable coordinating structures to align key roles and responsibilities across the Nation, linking all levels of government, nongovernmental organizations, and the private sector. It is intended to capture specific authorities and best practices for managing incidents that range from the serious but purely local, to large-scale terrorist attacks or catastrophic natural disasters" (Department of Homeland Security 2008, 1).

National Security Agency (NSA)—a governmental agency whose core missions are to protect U.S. national security systems and to produce foreign signals intelligence information.

National Security Council (NSC)—the President's principal forum for considering national security and foreign policy matters with his senior national security advisors and cabinet officials. The NCS correlates, synthesizes, and analysis intelligence received from the CIA, NSA, DIA, FBI, and other sources.

Private military security companies—companies conducting security-related functions in war zones of other areas of the world where there is strife and conflict; they are often under contract to a governmental authority.

Private police/security—a policing-related field found in the private sector that is referred to as "private security," "private policing," "loss prevention," "loss control," "assets protection," or "risk management;" the field emphasizes prevention and detection of crime and safety hazards.

Proprietary security personnel—those individuals working in the private security field for private or non-public employers and are supervised and directed by those employers; they act as an agent of those employers, usually serving on the employer's premises. **USA Patriot Act**—short for "Uniting and Strengthening America by Providing Appropriate Tools Required to Intercept and Obstruct Terrorism;" passed by Congress on October 11, 2001. Among other things, it establishes a counterterrorism fund, condemns discrimination against Arab and Muslim Americans, and increases funding for a variety of programs related to homeland defense. It grants the President authority to confiscate any property of any foreign person, country, or organization involved with an attack on or armed hostilities with the United States. It amends Federal criminal law to provide for authority to intercept wire, oral, and electronic communications relating to computer fraud and abuse offenses. It permits disclosure to specified Federal personnel of Federal grand jury matters pertaining to intelligence or counterintelligence. It also allows sharing of electronic, wire, and oral interception information by Federal law enforcement and other specified Federal officials. In addition, it permits the similar sharing of foreign intelligence information.

CHAPTER REFERENCES AND ADDITIONAL READINGS

Anderson, Teresa (2004). Dallas Gets DERT on Downtown. Retrieved November 17, 2010. http://www.securitymanagement.com/article/dallas-gets-dert-downtown

Anderson, Teresa (October 2010). Downtown Dallas. Security Management, 62–66.

ASIS International (n.d.). Career Opportunities in Security, Alexandria, VA: ASIS International.

ASIS International (2010a). Board Certifications in Security. http://www.asisonline.org/certification/index.xml.

ASIS International (2010b). Standards and Guidelines. http://www.asisonline.org/guidelines/guidelines.htm

ASIS International (2010c). Code of Ethics. http://www.asisonline.org/membership/resources/codeofethics.pdf.

Atlanta Police Foundation (2010). Operation Shield. http://www.atlantapolicefoundation.org/OperationShield-10.

Burdeau v. Mcdowell, 256 U.S. 465 (1921).

Bureau of Labor Statistics (2009). Occupational Outlook Handbook, 2010-11 Edition, Security Guards and Gaming Surveillance Officers. http://www.bls.gov/oco/ocos159.htm

Bureau of Security and Investigative Services (2010). Did You Know? - Proprietary Private Security Officer. http://www.bsis.ca.gov/forms_pubs/dyk_ppso.shtml.

Carter, David L. (2009). Law Enforcement Intelligence: A Guide of State, Local, and Tribal Law Enforcement Agencies (Second edition), U.S. Department of Justice, Office of Community Oriented Policing Services, Washington, D.C.

Clarke, Floyd I. (2007). Statement Before the United States House of Representatives, Committee on the Judiciary, Subcommittee on Crime, Terrorism, and Homeland Security. April 26.

Coleman, Kevin (2010). Protecting our critical infrastructure. http://www.defensesystems.com/Articles/2010/06/07/Digital-Conflict-Protecting-Critical-Infrastructure.aspx.

Connecticut (2010). Department of Public Safety, Special Licensing and Firearms, Private Security Companies. http://www.ct.gov/dps/cwp/view.asp?a=2158&q=294506.

Cunningham, William C., John J. Struchs, and Clifford W. Van Meter (1991), Private Security: Patterns and Trends. Washington, D.C.: National Institute of Justice.

Department of Homeland Security (2008). National Response Framework, Retrieved November 18, 2010, http://www.fema.gov/pdf/emergency/nrf/nrf-core.pdf.

Department of Homeland Security (2011). http://www.dhs.gov/index.shtm.

Department of Justice (2006). Fusion Center Guidelines: Developing and Sharing Intelligence in a New Era. Bureau of Justice Assistance, Office of Justice Programs, U.S. Department of Justice, Washington, D.C.

Euller, Stephen (1980). Private Security in the Courtroom: The Exclusionary Rule Applies. Security Management, 24(3):38–40.

Federal Emergency Management Administration (2010), National Incident Management System (NIMS), Retrieved November 18, 2010, http://www.fema.gov/emergency/nims/AboutNIMS.shtm.

Global Security Organization (2010). Definitions. Retrieved November 19, 2010, http://www.globalsecurity.org/

Hall, Mimi (2003). Private Security Guards: Homeland defense's weak link. USA Today, January 23, pp. 1A and 6A.

Hess, Karen M. and Henry M. Wrobleski (1992). Introduction to Private Security, Third Edition. St. Paul, Minnesota: West Publishing Co.

International Association of Chiefs of Police (2005), White Paper, "From Hometown Security to Homeland Security: IACPs Principles for a Locally Designed and Nationally Coordinated Homeland Security Strategy," IACP, Arlington, VA.

International Association of Chiefs of Police and the Office of Community Oriented Policing Services (2004). National Policy Summit: Building Private Security/Public Policing Partnerships to Prevent and Respond to Terrorism and Public Disorder. Ohlhausen Research, Inc., http://www.cops.usdoj.gov/mime/open.pdf?Item=1355.

International Association of Chiefs of Police (2010), "Enhancing the Law Enforcement Intelligence Capacity: Recommendations from the IACP's Strategic Planning Session," IACP, Arlington, VA.

International Foundation for Protection Officers (2010a). IFPO – Objectives. International Foundation for Protection Officers. http://www.ifpo.org/objectives.html.

International Foundation for Protection Officers (2010b). IFPO Professional Development Opportunities. http://www.ifpo.org/products/index.html.

International Peace Operations Association (2010). About ISOA. http://ipoaworld.org/eng/aboutisoa.html

Information Systems Security Association (2010). ISSA Code of Ethics. http://www.issa.org/page/?p=17.

Johnson v. Larabida Children's Hospital (2004). 372 F.3d 894, 896-97 (7th Cir.).

Kelly, Raymond W. (2005). The NYPD Strategic Approach to Stopping Graffiti Vandalism. *The Police Chief*, 72(8).

Law Enforcement–Private Security Consortium (2010). http://www.lepsc.org/.

Loss Prevention Foundation (2010). Loss Prevention Certification. http://www.losspreventionfoundation.org/certification.html

Masse, Todd and John Rollins (2007). A Summary of Fusion Centers: Core Issues and Options for Congress. CRS Report for Congress, Congressional Research Service, United States Congress, Washington, D.C.

Mayer, Don (2010). Peaceful Warriors: Private Military Security Companies and the Quest for Stable Societies. *Journal of Business Ethics* 89:387–401.

Murphy, Gerard, Martha Plotkin, and David Edelson (2001). *Discussion Draft: Local Law Enforcement's Role in Preventing and responding to Terrorism*. Police Executive Research Forum, (PERF): Washington, D.C.

National Commission on Terrorist Attacks (2004). *The 9/11 Commission Report*. http://govinfo.library.unt.edu/911/report/index.htm.

National Association of Security Companies (2004). Mission Statement. Retrieved November 17, 2010, http://www.nasco.org/nasco/mission-summary.asp.

National Association of Security Companies (2010). About NASCO. http://www.nasco.org/about-nasco.

National Council of Investigation & Secuirty Services (2010a). http://www.nciss.com/.

National Council of Investigation & Secuirty Services (2010b). Code of Ethics. http://www.nciss.com/about_nciss/code_of_ethics.htm.

Parfomak, Paul W. (2004). *Guarding America: Security Guards and U.S. Critical Infrastructure Protection*. Washington, D.C.: Congressional Research Service, The Library of Congress.

People v. Zelinski (1979). 594 P.2d 1000.

Public Law 108-458 (2004). http://www.nctc.gov/docs/pl108_458.pdf.

Ricci, Joseph (2007). The Direction And Viability Of The Federal Protective Service. Testimony Before the House Committee On Homeland Security Hearing, May 1.

Romanski v. Detroit Entertainment, et al. (2005). 428 F.3d 629 (6th Cir.).

Sutherland, Randy (2003). Pushing for Better Private Security Officers. Retrieved November 17, 2010, http://securitysolutions.com/mag/security_pushing_better_private/.

United States v. Shahid (1997). 117 F.3d 322, 324 (7th Cir.).

U.S. Census Bureau (2006). General Purpose Law Enforcement Agencies –Number, Employment, and Expenditures. Retrieved November 15, 2010, http://www.allcountries.org/uscensus/354_general_purpose_law_enforcement_agencies_number.html.

Wade v. Byles (1996). 83 F.3d 902, 905-906 (7th Cir.).

CHAPTER **13**

Policing Models, Strategies, and Tactics

LEARNING OBJECTIVES

In this chapter, you will learn about the models, strategies, and tactics of American law enforcement. It builds on much of the material you have reviewed in previous chapters, but ties many of these concepts and ideas to the complex operations of contemporary policing. The chapter begins with an introduction to the various models that have been used by scholars to describe the institution of policing and/or an agency's service style; we use the term model here as a conceptual way to label or describe an agency's service outlook and approach. However, because the institution of policing has evolved over the course of its development, scholars have conceptualized different model types to describe an agency's general service outlook during a particular timeframe. Here we will give particular attention to the professional, the standard, and the community policing models of policing. We will also discuss several popular operational strategies associated with contemporary policing, including strategic policing and problem-oriented policing. After studying this chapter, you should be able to:

- Identify the major models of policing.
- Describe how and why these models evolved.
- Describe some of the more common strategies of policing.
- Explain why there can never be a "perfect" policing strategy.
- Identify some of the criticisms of the Professional Model of Policing.
- Identify some of the challenges facing the Community-policing Model of Policing.

CHAPTER OUTLINE

I. Setting the Stage: Definitions and Terms
II. The Professional Model of Police Practices
    A. Criticisms of the Professional Model
    B. Research Findings
III. The Standard Model of Police Practices
    A. *Report on Police* and National Standards of Police Practices
    B. The Patrol Function: Random Patrol and Calls of Service
    C. Where All Police Works Begins
IV. The Community Policing Model of Police Practices
    A. Challenges facing the Community Policing Model
 V. Common Operational Policing Strategies
    A. Strategic Policing
    B. Problem-oriented Policing
VI. Summary

KEY TERMS USED IN THIS CHAPTER

model of policing

strategies of policing

operational plans

professional model
  (professional crime-
  fighting model)

traditional model of policing

bureaucratic model of policing

reactive policing

proactive policing

preventive patrol

standard model of policing

call of service

patrol function

philosophy of community
  policing

coproduction of order

strategic policing

intelligence-led policing

problem-oriented policing

SARA model

SETTING THE STAGE: DEFINITIONS AND TERMS

The phrase **model of policing** is a general statement that refers to an agency's service outlook and approach. Models represent an agency's general philosophy of service and are evident in their values, traditions, and organizational cultures. On the other hand, the phrase **strategies of policing** refers to an agency's definition of what the organization proposes to do and how. Strategies represent an agency's methods and are evident in their plans, technologies, products, and approaches to achieving goals and objectives. Additionally, because strategies of policing provide the outline for **operational plans**, they help managers evaluate performance.

We should note that the following models and strategies of policing are not mutually exclusive or exhaustive— elements of more than one model or strategy may exist in an agency at the same time, and other formal strategies might emerge in the future. We should also note that the strategies discussed here coexist throughout the policing community—no one strategy necessarily dominates the others, and it is not necessarily accurate to claim that one is "better" or "worse" when compared to another.

Before we begin our study of the models, strategies, and tactics of American policing, we should also point out an important fact that underlies and influences the subject of this chapter. Law enforcement agencies are tasked with a seemingly impossible mandate: they must provide public safety services, maintain order, respond to incidents of crime and disorder, prevent them when possible, control traffic, investigate crimes, locate and arrest suspects, and collect, process, and disseminate information (Skogan and Frydl 2004). Most importantly, they must accomplish these tasks efficiently, professionally, and lawfully with limited budgets. To bring this point into perspective, in 2007 the average police department spent $116,500 to employ an officer for one year; this includes salary, training, and benefits, including health insurance (Reaves 2010). Notwithstanding the costs, and even under the best of circumstances, it would be difficult for law enforcement agencies to satisfy every requirement of their mandate. The best they can do is to design and adopt policies that move them closest to these elusive goals. In view of these circumstances, the best models, strategies, and tactics of a law enforcement agency are imperfect in the sense they cannot completely reach their goals. This creates a perpetual search for better and more efficient methods and strategies to conduct the business of policing.

THE PROFESSIONAL MODEL OF POLICE PRACTICES

The **professional model**, or the **professional crime-fighting model** of policing, as it is sometimes known, became the dominant approach to policing as a result of reforms championed by concerned citizens associated with the progressive reform movements of the 1920s and 1930s (see Chapter 3). Its early manifestation, according to historian Robert Fogelson (1977, 155), was based on the idea that "policemen were professionals and policing was a profession. Like doctors, lawyers, teachers, and engineers, policemen were expected to meet high admission standards, undergo extensive training, serve their clients, devote themselves to the public interest, subscribe to a code of ethics, and possess a wide range of extraordinary skills." As a reform strategy, the professional model was meant to raise the status of policing, and it succeeded. Its introduction also succeeded in uniting members of the police profession (from patrol officer to chief) behind a common ideal: professionalism. Equally important, it was widely accepted by "upper-middle and upper-class Americans outside the law enforcement community" as a way to remove partisan political interference in department matters (Fogelson 1977, 158). While its definition was left purposely vague to attract a wide audience, the concept that professional status is gained, and then maintained, through the legal exercise of police authority free of partisan political interference for the specific purpose of achieving crime control through expert service was easily understood. George Kelling and Mark Moore (1988) observed that the professional crime-fighting model carried policing from a world of amateurism, lawlessness, and political vulnerability to a world of professionalism, integrity, and political independence. It remains the foundational concept of policing.

The professional model was instrumental in bringing the institution of policing into its own during the 50 years that it dominated policing philosophy. Consequently, it is sometimes referred to as the **traditional model of policing**. Under its banner, from the early 1930s to the 1970s,

Speed enforcement responsibilities

Source: © Igor Karon/ShutterStock, Inc.

policing slowly evolved from an amateurish and incompetent institution to a bureaucratic, disciplined, technically-sophisticated, quasi-military, well-trained crime-fighting force. It helped free the institution of policing from the corrupting political and criminal influence that had once consumed it (see Chapter 3). It introduced and refined many of the technologies and tactics still in use today: radio-equipped patrol vehicles, random preventive patrol, the strategy of responding quickly to calls for service, and expert follow-up investigations utilizing modern criminalistic technologies and techniques. It also introduced modern management concepts, including an emphasis on officer accountability, centralized operations, written policies and procedures, and close supervision. Consequently, it is sometimes referred to as the **bureaucratic model of policing**. As we have noted, the professional model also embodied the quest for professional status advocated by early and mid-twentieth-century reformers like Reverend Charles Parkhurst, Theodore Roosevelt, August Vollmer, and others. Its principles, doctrines, and values were instrumental in building the highly-competent forces we enjoy today.

Criticisms of the Professional Model

While it succeeded in greatly reforming the institution of policing, some of the operational practices of the professional model have been criticized by some scholars for

perceived weaknesses. While we do not necessarily agree with all of the criticism, we list selected items for your consideration. For example:

- It is primarily **reactive policing**, as opposed to **proactive policing**.
- It is tradition bound, inflexible, and captured by a rigid and closed police culture.
- Crime prevention is premised primarily on **preventive patrol** (the highly-visible and random presence of the police).
- It assumes the police are experts at fighting crime and, therefore, should be allowed to solve problems with little interaction with or involvement of the community.
- It removes officers from close proximity of citizens in the sense that a highly-mobilized force runs from one call to the next, not having time to interact with the normal, law-abiding citizen, thus leaving the perception that officers are more bureaucratic and less accessible.
- In many respects, it fails to control crime, the fear of crime, or the underlying social causes of criminal and anti-social behavior.

Research Findings

During the 1970s and 1980s, a number of research studies were conducted that tested the effectiveness and perceived benefits of several of the methods and operational tactics utilized in the professional crime-fighting approach. The concept of preventive patrol, with its objectives of deterring crime and intercepting crimes in progress, were some of the first tactics scrutinized. Preventive patrol tactics are associated with the uniformed officer's use of "uncommitted time" during a shift (or time between calls for service and other specific assignments). The options available to an officer during this time are varied, as summarized by Cordner and Trojanowicz (1992):

Patrolling can be stationary or mobile; slow-, medium- or high-speed; and oriented toward residential, commercial, recreational or other kinds of areas. Some patrol officers intervene frequently in peoples' lives by stopping cars and checking out suspicious circumstances; other officers seem more interested in inanimate matters such as parked cars and the security of closed businesses; still other officers rarely interrupt their continuous patrolling. Some officers devote all of their uncommitted time to police-related business, while others devote substantial time to loafing or personal affairs (5).

While the amount of uncommitted time varies greatly from department to department, and from beat to beat within departments, until the 1970s departments rarely questioned the effectiveness of preventive patrol. In the early 1970s, a one-year study of the effects of preventive patrol was undertaken in the Kansas City, Missouri Police Department. A portion of the city was divided into 15 beats, and these beats were grouped according to similar characteristics and demographics. One of three patrolling tactics was used in each beat: (1) no preventive patrol activities: squad cars entered the area only to respond to specific calls for service; (2) customary patrol, including normal preventive patrol tactics; and (3) increased preventive patrol, using additional cars to double and triple the normal levels of preventive patrol. Citizen surveys and interviews were conducted before, during, and after the experiment concerning a number of factors, including

Patrol officer responds to accident scene

Source: © steve estvanik/ShutterStock, Inc.

reported crime, arrests, fear of crime, citizen satisfaction, and traffic accidents. An analysis of the findings yielded the following:

- The practice of having marked police cars conduct random patrol on pre-assigned beats does not necessarily prevent crime or reassure the citizens, even if the police strength is increased significantly.
- Police can stop routinely patrolling beats for up to a year without necessarily being missed by the residents and without a rise in crime rates in the patrol area (Petersilia 1993).

The Kansas City Preventive Patrol Experiment neither went unnoticed nor without criticism; however, it was a landmark study because of its findings and because it ushered in an era of other major studies and experiments that focused on the widely-held beliefs in police operations. It is not our purpose here to examine these in depth, but a listing of the major studies demonstrates the research efforts directed at police operations since the early 1970s and the various police practices that have been scrutinized:

Response Time Studies—From 1977 through 1982, beginning with Kansas City, Missouri and including the cities of Jacksonville, Florida; San Diego, California; Peoria, Illinois; and Rochester, New York; studies have concluded that police response time was unrelated to the probability of making an arrest or locating a witness. Also, neither dispatch nor travel time were strongly associated with citizen satisfaction. These studies concluded that because of the delay in reporting incidents by citizens, police response time has a negligible impact on crime outcomes (Klockars and Mastrofski 1991; Petersilia 1993).

Alternative Patrol Strategies—Following the preventive patrol and response time studies, several projects were undertaken during the mid-1970s to modify the traditional model of patrol. In San Diego, community-oriented policing (described in greater detail below) was initiated and allowed patrol officers greater flexibility to analyze police-related problems and to develop and implement measures to cope with them. In New Haven, Connecticut, the uses of directed deterrent runs (D-runs) were initiated.

The patrol activity was directed by detailed crime analysis of the times and places of criminal activity. Tactics such as saturation patrol (increased aggressive patrol of selected areas) were implemented to address the identified problems. In Wilmington, Delaware, the split patrol program was developed, which allowed about one-third of the patrol force to engage in directed (or structured) patrol activities designed to increase criminal apprehensions. These various alternatives to traditional preventive patrol clearly demonstrated that other patrol utilization tactics could produce equal or better results (Gay et al. 1977; Petersilia 1993; Schell et al. 1976).

Investigations Research—During the mid-1970s, two major studies were undertaken regarding the criminal investigation process in policing. The RAND Corporation study was national in scope while the other, by the Stanford Research Institute, focused on Alameda County, California (Greenberg et al. 1975). Both studies, plus the follow-up projects that followed, yielded several conclusions:

- Many serious crimes are not and often cannot be solved.
- Patrol officers are responsible for most arrests because of either on-scene apprehensions or obtaining identifications from victims or witnesses that lead to apprehensions.
- Only a small percentage of all Part I arrests result from detective investigations that require special organization, training, or skill.
- Investigators play a critical role in the post-arrest process, particularly in collecting evidence that will enable the prosecutor to file formal criminal charges (Petersilia 1993, 228).

THE STANDARD MODEL OF POLICE PRACTICES

As we explained in the previous section, during its evolution the institution of policing was characterized by scholars under three conceptual models: *traditional, bureaucratic,* and *professional.* What is important to remember is that none of these models is exclusive; in fact, elements of each overlap and blend with the others in a continuing process of innovation, trial-and-error, reform/adoption, and innovation. Today the process continues;

however, its practices are now based on professional standards and model policies established by the International Association of Chiefs of Police. Consequently, the strategies and tactics of policing are common practices in agencies across America. Collectively, they have come to represent the standard model of police practices.

The standard model of policing has evolved from the professional model to fulfill a complex mandate. Today, the public expects the police to be an omnipresent protective force; preventing crime when possible; aggressively ferreting out crime and criminals; disciplined, decisive, and lawful when in action; yet non-obtrusive or officious without cause. In an attempt to meet these high expectations, the standard model of policing is characterized by six interconnected practices: random preventive patrol, calls for service, traffic enforcement, initial investigations, follow-up investigations, and administrative activities that support these functions. Two philosophies underlie these functions: a commitment to professional public service and intensive enforcement/arrest policies. Contemporary scholars have labeled it the **standard model of policing** because it relies "on the uniform provision of police resources intended to prevent crime and disorder across a wide array of crimes and across all parts of the jurisdiction that" an agency serves (Skogan and Frydl 2004, 223). It rests on the tenants of the professional model and serves as the foundation for all contemporary strategies of policing, specifically community policing, strategic policing, and problem-oriented policing.

The standard model of policing is supported by a hierarchical command and control system, in an environment where authority, responsibility, and accountability are explicitly defined in department directives, yet where officers are given a great deal of discretionary authority in making service and enforcement decisions. It is traditional (and in fact it is sometimes referred to as the traditional model) in the sense that its applications have evolved over the years through trial and error. Today, virtually all police and sheriff's departments are professionally organized, managed, and staffed under this model (thus, it is sometimes referred as the professional model of policing). In fact, nationally, 7 in 10 municipal police officers are assigned to the patrol function in support of the standard model of policing, and in agencies serving fewer the 10,000 residences, 9 in 10 officers are assigned to the patrol function in support of the standard model of policing (Reaves 2010, 6).

Report on Police and National Standards of Police Practices

The institution of policing received a great deal of attention in the early 1970s, which confirmed many aspects of the professional model and moved it toward national standards. Specifically, in 1973, the National Advisory Commission on Criminal Justice Standards and Goals published six detailed reports (in six volumes) regarding the criminal justice system. The reports contained a comprehensive set of service standards covering each component of the criminal justice system—police, courts, correction, prosecution, and defense. Collectively, the reports were intended to help practitioners improve the delivery of criminal justice services in a coordinated and systemic effort to reduce crime. One of the volumes, *Report on Police* (1973), greatly influenced key aspects of what was then called the professional model of policing. Commission members concluded that patrol officers were the primary force responsible for reducing and preventing crime, and so consequently, their 120 recommendations centered on increasing police effectiveness at the patrol level. This meant that they were primarily concerned with procedural matters and offered a comprehensive set of priorities, recommendations, and standards that officers could use in their day-to-day work. The report became a reference book for officers of all ranks, from patrol officers all the way up to the police chief or sheriff, and would lead to the establishment of national standards for policing.

The recommendations were specific and offered systematic advice on how a police executive might implement each standard. For example, each standard was accompanied by a commentary section that placed the standard in context with its role and relationship to a democratic society, and, consequently, its subsequent value as a police management tool. In time, the commission's suggestions would have a profound impact on the day-to-day operations and continued professionalization of American policing. This included suggestions for improving the police function in areas like "community

[relations], planning and organization, technology and support services, fiscal management, and coordination with other criminal justice agencies" (*Report on Police*, 1973, 1). The report also recommended that, in order to improve cooperation between the police and the community, law enforcement agencies should:

- Establish a specialized unit for maintaining communication with citizens
- Encourage and participate in neighborhood security programs
- Establish procedures to facilitate processing of complaints
- Adopt stricter personnel requirements
- Increase employee benefits
- Employ more women, minorities, and civilians in police work (*Report on Police*, 1973)

We should note that, today, each of these suggestions have been incorporated into every police and sheriff's department in the country. (You can see this if you visit the 2007 *Local Police Report* through Bureau of Justice Statistics.)

The Patrol Function: Random Patrol and Calls for Service

While the core mandate of American policing has changed very little since the first police departments were established in the late 1830s, the strategies and tactics of policing have continued to evolve, as have the methods and technologies for providing service. In fact, four technologies have combined since the early 1940s and today define contemporary policing: the automobile, telephone, two-way radio, and, most recently, the computer.

Two strategies grew out of these technologies—random preventive patrol and coordinated responds to **calls of service**. Here we describe them as if they were separate entities, but, in fact, the two strategies are so closely connected that officers move back and forth between them many times each shift. To explain this from an operational perspective, patrol officers are considered to be "in service" and available for assignments when they are not actively engaged in a "call for service" or some other detail. Moreover, as soon as they have completed or "cleared the call," they return to patrol or "in service" status and are ready to receive additional calls for service, as needed. On many occasions during peak service hours (approximately 1800 to 0300), patrol units may be assigned multiple calls for service before they have cleared prior calls. Consequently, patrol duty can be a very hectic and fast-paced environment, where conditions change in seconds and coordination between other patrol units and their dispatch center is critical. Moving in a carefully choreographed dance, these tandem strategies form what is commonly referred to as the **patrol function**, the heart of policing in America.

While it has been criticized by some scholars, the importance of random preventive patrol cannot be overstated. It allows patrol officers to move about their assigned areas based on an officer's intuitions, experiences, and training. Random patrol, with its tradition of unencumbered patrol time, is an essential element of contemporary police service and can trace its roots to the earliest traditions of urban policing, a time when officers walked their beats providing rudimentary services, a visible presence, and a tenuous deterrent to crime. Today, it provides at least the illusion of an omnipresent protective force. Yet, the term "random" should not be confused with aimless. During unencumbered patrol time, officers conduct a great deal of police business. For example, they may patrol an area where citizens have recently complained about speeding vehicles; they may return to visit an elderly victim, simply to check on her welfare; or they may stop to visit a new business and distribute public safety literature. In many areas, unencumbered patrol time is a luxury for patrol officers, a time when they can patrol their assigned areas looking for potential problems or violations of the law based on their own experiences, department directives, or public requests. These periods of activity are critical to the mission of policing, public service, order maintenance, and law enforcement. Patrol officers will tell you that random patrol provides a physical police presence and deterrence to some criminal activities (despite what the Kansas City Preventative Patrol Experiment found), it promotes a sense of community security, and it helps build positive relationships between community residences and their public servants. These factors are difficult to measure but are serious issues.

One very unglamorous activity is also conducted during periods of unencumbered patrol time: report writing.

Officers must document almost everything they do; consequently, many hours are spent writing (or inputting) criminal and non-criminal incident reports, traffic accident reports, arrest reports, and a wide variety of supplemental reports documenting their actions and investigations. Officers in most police and sheriff's departments do not have the luxury of going out-of-service to write reports, so most report writing occurs while officers are in-service on patrol status. To aid officers, over 90% of departments serving populations greater than 25,000 residents provide in-field computers or mobile digital terminals (MDTs) and 52% provide laptop computers to write field reports (Reaves 2010, 23, 39). While officers continue to monitor radio traffic for their own calls for service, they must also remain alert to calls assigned to other units.

While not on random patrol, much of a patrol officer's time is spent handling calls for service, which are dispatched in 91% of all departments via 911 systems (Reaves 2010, 15). Most of these calls are noncriminal in nature, as only a small percentage regard criminal matters. Collectively, random preventive patrol and requests for service bring officers into contact with the public as service providers, problem solvers, counselors, authority figures, and ultimately the gatekeepers of the criminal justice system.

Where All Police Work Begins

Generations of uniformed officers have been educated and socialized into the traditions, culture, and art and craft of policing in the course of conducting random patrols or responding to calls for service. Under the guidance of a field training officer (FTO), rookies learn to prudently apply their authority in discretionary circumstances ranging from the mundane to the extraordinary (see Chapter 7 on training and Chapter 8 on socialization). They learn to recognize and appreciate the social patterns and norms of a community, its problems and potential problems, the suspicious and the criminal. It is a gradual and sometimes harsh education, but it leads to the essential knowledge they need as gatekeepers of the criminal justice system. In the end, new officers learn that police work is a balancing act of discretionary decisions hinged between legislative intent, department policy, and community values and expectations. Based on their actions, it is a time when the public either affirms or rejects the legitimacy of police authority.

THE COMMUNITY POLICING MODEL OF POLICE PRACTICES

Community policing is the leading edge of a reform strategy that can trace its contemporary roots to the community relations movement of the late 1960s and early 1970s (Earl 1972). It is a movement, according to John Eck and William Spelman (2000, 188), that grew out of the "riots of the 1960s," a time when police across the country "began to examine their ties to the communities they served." It was an examination, according to Greene and Mastrofski, (1988, *xi*) that revealed weaknesses in the professional model of policing, weaknesses that were blamed for making the police "indifferent to their clientele" as they became more "encumbered by administrative rules" and isolated from the "policy-making process."

The solution to this indifference and isolation, according to Greene and Mastrofski (1988), rested in the tenets of community policing. It affords line officers a more liberalized and legitimate role in problem solving. Under the new **philosophy of community policing**, officers are given wider latitude in social order decision-making. In fact, they are encouraged and expected to work with members of the community in designing and implementing strategies to correct a wide spectrum of social/crime problems. In many ways, this was a refinement of traditional police practices, practices undertaken on an informal and individual basis. In other words, the subtle strategies considered to be "good policing" in years past were now given a formal title and expanded into a coordinated plan of action. However, the new plan was different in one important way: it rested on the concept of a **coproduction of order** (Zhao 1996, 30).

At its philosophical core, the new concept proposed that a great deal of police work really involves social service activities in support of, or in addition to, order maintenance. Moreover, addressing social problems in partnership with affected community members would help to alleviate some of the demands for order maintenance. In this way, community policing calls for a more balanced philosophical position. Police officers are expected to assume a prominent role as social agents and/or problem solvers working in harmony with the citizens they serve, while still maintaining a law enforcement posture. Consequently, according to Wilkinson and Rosenbaum (1994, 110), "community policing represents

a fundamental change in the basic role of the police officer, including changes in his or her skills, motivations, and opportunity" to serve the public. Moreover, it has become a very popular model of police service. (For evidence of the popularity of community policing, see **Figure 13-1**).

If we accept the proposition that community policing is the new orthodoxy of policing, it is certainly a model with many hats. Therefore, a definition of community policing would have to account for a number of dimensions. Below, we list five dimensions for consideration:

- First, it is an "ideology, an organizing framework for many police activities, and a set of individual programs" (Greene and Mastrofski 1988, *xiii*).
- Second, a definition must account for a broad collection of crime prevention strategies, programs, and tactics (Eck, et al. 1996; Mastrofski 1988).
- Third, it must explain that community policing is a philosophy of service (defined in a specific set of service values), which is evidenced in the attitudes and behaviors of officers as they collaborate, design, execute, and implement a broad collection

FIGURE 13-1 The Continuing Popularity of Community Policing

- From 2003 to 2007, the percentage of local police officers employed by a department that trained all new recruits in community policing increased from 73% to 81%.
- A majority of local police departments serving 50,000 or more residents operated a full-time specialized unit dedicated to community policing during 2007.
- During 2007, a majority of local police departments serving 50,000 or more residents supported community policing efforts by partnering with citizen groups, upgrading technology, and conducting a citizen police academy.
- An estimated 47,000 full-time local police officers were designated as community policing officers in 2007, about 8,000 fewer than in 2003. Most of this decline occurred among departments serving fewer than 50,000 residents.

Source: Selections from Reaves (2010)

of crime prevention strategies in cooperation with the citizens they serve (Trojanowicz and Bucqueroux 1990).

- Fourth, a definition must account for community policing's intent to reform the police (in practice, in philosophy, and in organizational structure), making them more responsive to community needs (Cordner and Trojanowicz 1992; Goldstein 1979).

- Finally, a definition of community policing must include a statement concerning its supplemental role in supporting a police department's traditional responsibility to address random community problems, as well as persistent problems, which are associated with social disorder, crime, and the fear of crime (Eck and Rosenbaum 1994; Green and Mastrofski 1988).

A precise definition of this model is elusive. Definitions found in the literature range from prescriptions of what an author hopes community policing could be, to descriptions of specific or very limited programs (Eck et al. 1996). In any event, it is a popular and elastic concept that finds its definition in two interrelated concepts: problem solving and community engagement (Lurigio and Rosenbaum 1994, 147). Notwithstanding these insights, "there is no single operational definition of community policing" (Eck et al. 1966, 4), because there is, as Weisel and Eck (1994, 53) observe, "no single articulated form of community policing."

Despite the fact that community policing is a diverse collection of operational practices and programs (see **Figure 13-2** for a sample of the most common community policy practices), there is wide agreement in the literature that community policing is premised on a single philosophy (Trojanowicz, et al 1998, 6):

Community policing is a philosophy and an organizational strategy that promotes a new partnership between people and their police. It is based on the premise that both the police and the community must work together as equal partners to identify, prioritize, and solve contemporary problems such as crime, drugs, fear of crime, social and physical disorder, and overall neighborhood decay, with the goal of improving the overall quality of life in the area.

Community policing has assumed a prominent place in contemporary police. To appreciate its promise, it might be helpful to review Trojanowicz and Bucqueroux's (1990) ten principles of community policing. A slightly condensed version of the principles are listed below:

1. Community policing is both a philosophy and an organizational strategy that allows the police and community residents to work closely together in new ways to solve the problems of crime, fear of crime, physical and social disorder, and neighborhood decay.

2. Community policing's organizational strategy first demands that everyone in the department, including both civilian and sworn personnel, must investigate ways to translate the philosophy into practice.

3. To implement true community policing, police departments must also create and develop a new breed of line officer, the Community Police Officer (CPO), who acts as the direct link between the police and people in the community.

4. The CPO's broad role demands continuous, sustained contact with the law-abiding people in the community, so that together they can explore creative new solutions to local concerns involving crime, fear of crime, disorder, and decay, with private citizens serving as unpaid volunteers.

5. Community policing implies a new contract between the police and the citizens they serve, one that offers the hope of overcoming widespread apathy, and at the same time restrains any impulse to vigilantism.

6. Community policing adds a vital proactive element to the traditional reactive role of the police, resulting in full-spectrum police service.

7. Community policing stresses exploring new ways to protect and enhance the lives of those who are most vulnerable—juveniles, the elderly, minorities, the poor, the disabled, and the homeless.

8. Community policing promotes the judicious use of technology, but it also rests on the belief that nothing surpasses what dedicated human beings, talking and working together, can achieve.

9. Community policing must be a fully integrated approach that involves everyone in the department,

FIGURE 13-2 The 25 Most Common Community Policing Activities and Strategies

This list represents a consolidated sample of the 25 most common community policing activities and strategies currently employed in the United States. This list was culled from four data sets collected between 1993 and 1997 by the Police Foundation and the Office of Community Oriented Policing (Maguire and Mastrofski, 2000). The data sets were original collected to determine the national extent of community policing activities and strategies. Consequently, they represent a broad cross section of programs and strategies that are currently (or have recently been) employed within American police departments.

Activities or Strategies	Cumulative %
Patrol officers work with citizens to identify and resolve area problems.	86.4%
Patrol officers regularly work with detectives on cases in assigned beat areas.	81.7%
Officers participate in drug education programs in schools.	86.1%
Patrol officers develop familiarity with community leaders in area of assignment.	81.1%
Department employs directed-patrol strategies.	76.4%
Supervisors elicit input from officers about solutions to community problems.	75.5%
Patrol officers teach residents how to identify and address community problems.	72.2%
Patrol officers organizing community actions/activities against crime and disorder.	69.7%
First line supervisors are responsible for establishing interagency relationships.	69.1%
Patrol officers make door-to-door contacts in neighborhoods.	67.6%
Citizens participate in Neighborhood Watch Programs.	67.5%
Department has developed partnerships with other government agencies.	67.0%
Patrol officers work in schools or other public agencies to teach crime prevention.	65.6%
Patrol officers develop partnerships with civic groups to combat crime.	65.3%
Department participates in anti-drug programs.	64.4%
Department employs a specialized crime prevention unit.	62.7%
Department participates in a Drug Tip Hotline or Crime Stoppers program.	62.2%
Citizens work with police to identify and resolve neighborhood problems.	61.6%
Officers have regularly scheduled meetings with community groups.	60.1%
Computer systems are used to analyze information on repeat calls for service.	59.8%
Supervisors are required to maintain regular contact with community leaders.	58.0%
Department participates in or supports a victim assistance program.	55.8%
Officers participate in youth athletic leagues or other youth programs.	55.4%
Supervisors make final decisions about crime prevention programs.	54.5%
Department has developed a partnership with business groups to combat crime.	54.2%

Source: Compiled and extracted from Maguire, E.R. and S.D. Mastrofski (2000).

with the CPOs as specialists in bridging the gap between the police and the people they serve.

10. Community policing provides decentralized, personalized police service to the community. It recognizes that the police cannot impose order on the community from outside, but that people must be encouraged to think of the police as a resource they can use in helping to solve contemporary community concerns (xiii–xv).

Rape Aggression Defense Training Team

Source: Printed with the permission of the Randolph Herald, a GateHouse Meda publication.

Challenges Facing the Community Policing Model

In the preceding definition of community policing, we see an optimistic wish for better government and safer communities. Yet, underlying this hopefulness and desire for change, we recognize the magnitude of our social problems, the complexity of our institutions, the natural reluctance to change and, therefore, the limitations of its promise. Based on these challenges, Wesley Skogan (1994, 167) notes that many scholars are "professionally skeptical" of community policing's claims. They do not believe it is a panacea to resolve all the problems of crime, inadequate social services, or prevent deviant behavior. In fact, Eck and Rosenbaum (1994, 6) suggest "exaggerated claims" of its potential may even undermine its "legitimate claims."

These cautionary words are abundantly apparent in a simple observation: The introduction of community policing has not substantially changed the basic bureaucratic structures of American policing, which, according to Greene, et al. (1994, 93) "is more or less organized and implemented as it was at the turn of the century." One reason there has been so little change in the structure of policing is offered by Mark Moore (1994, 286), who observes that American police departments "were founded and have long operated on wholly different premises," specifically, the idea that police are the experts and do not need outside help.

Whether Moore's (1994) observation is correct or not, the indisputable fact remains that police agencies are structured to respond to a diverse spectrum of criminal and non-criminal calls for service. They operate in an environment where the public demands and expects a predictable, professional, and efficient response to these diverse and random calls for service. Moreover, as John Crank (1998, 45) points out, it is an environment where "random preventive patrol" is widely practiced and has become "highly institutionalized," where "effectiveness" and the need for random patrol is "unquestioned in most police organization." Consequently, responding to random complaints or engaging in observational enforcement of the law remains a fundamental police responsibility, a task currently defined by the standard model of policing (also referred to as the professional model) and its crime-fighting emphasis.

Importantly, "Research over the past 20 years has underscored the limitations of the 'professional law enforcement' model of policing that continues to dominate the practice of most police departments" (Rosenbaum 1994, xi). During this period, there has been an "increased realization" that the traditional forms of policing were not always "effective, equitable, and efficient" in providing communities with police services (Eck and Rosenbaum 1994, 5-7). Other scholars (Cordner and Trojanowicz 1992; Mastrofski 1988) agree. They suggest that the current enthusiasm for community policing is an acknowledgment that the professional model of policing, with its emphasis on preventive patrol, has not been particularly effective in preventing crime (a goal that is

Bomb squad robot

Source: © iStockphoto/Thinkstock

never truly achievable)[1]. Despite major methodological flaws in the experiment, the Kansas City Preventive Patrol Experiments has provided some scholars with reason to criticize traditional forms of policing (Kelling et al. 1974).

The historical emphasis by police on efficiency and effectiveness—means over ends—was, in the opinion of Eck and Rosenbaum (1994, 10), what led Herman Goldstein (1979) to review the strategies of traditional policing and to develop the concept of problem-oriented policing. In fact, there has been a steady cry for reform and greater police "interaction with the community toward the resolution of persistent community problems supposed to lead to crime and social disorder" (Greene and Mastrofski 1988, *xi*). Yet, other scholars, including ourselves, suggest that problem-oriented policing and "community policing [are] not intended to completely substitute for motor patrol," but are intended to "supplement and complement motor patrol's reactive efforts"

(Cordner and Trojanowicz 1992, 12). Consequently, advocates of community policing are not discarding traditional police functions (i.e., the standard model, with its foundations resting on aspects of the professional model)—they are attempting to reform policing by adding proactive strategies and calling for a restructuring of policing priorities. Under its larger umbrella of solving community problems, advocates of community policing are calling for a "new philosophy" of police service, a philosophy that pervasively informs and directs the strategies and methods of policing. Consequently, the true promise of community policing rests in an agency's philosophical restructuring (as opposed to an organizational restructuring) that will lead to "closer and more productive contact between officers and area residents" as they work together to resolve persistent community problems (Cordner and Trojanowicz, 1992, 12).

COMMON OPERATIONAL POLICING PRACTICES

At this point, then, what are the most common operational practices of policing agencies today at the local levels? Please note that we are primarily describing the practices of uniformed agencies of the state and local jurisdictions.

Strategic Policing

Strategic policing refers to attempts to expand the operational strategies of law enforcement through more sophisticated, analytical, and targeted crime control applications. This approach employs a variety of operational strategies, including: directed patrol operations, decoy and sting operations, drug task forces, violent crimes task forces, and special teams to address specific problems (ranging from street crime to sophisticated computer and white-collar offenses). These strategies are quite popular; the 2007 *LEMAS Report* found that 35% of all local agencies assigned officers to a special unit for drug enforcement on a part time basis, and 24% of all local agencies assigned officers on a full-time basis (Reaves 2010).

Strategic policing maintains centralized control of operations and problem identification. It hinges on greater intelligence gathering and information analysis. Consequently, it is sometime referred to as **intelligence-led policing**. It is also coupled with sophisticated forensic

---

[1] For an excellent discussion and review of the evolution in strategies of American policing between 1930 and 1970, see George L. Kelling and Mark H. Moore (1988), "From Political to Reform to Community: The Evolving Strategy of Policing." In, Jack R. Greens and Stephen D. Mastrofski, *Community Policing Rhetoric or Reality*, pg. 3–25.

science methods. The principal value of strategic policing is improved crime control through proactive directed methods and data gathering. An excellent example of strategic policing are "crackdowns," which Lawrence Sherman (1990, 2), describes as a "sudden, usually proactive change in activity… intended to drastically increase either the communicated threat or actual certainty of apprehension." Crackdown targets have included drug trafficking locations, gang enforcement operations, loitering and disorder problems, subway station crimes, prostitution, and DUI enforcement operations.

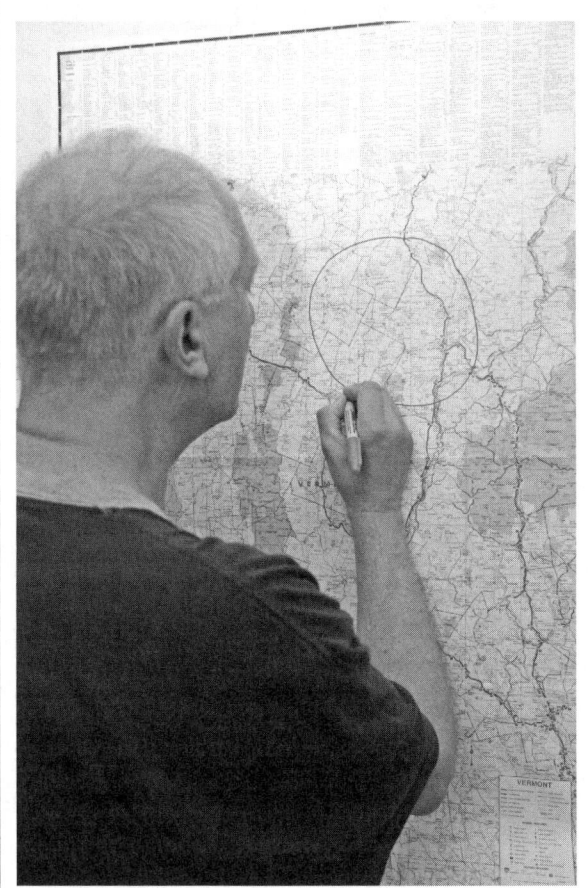

Officer emphasizing area of concern

Source: © Jones & Bartlett Learning. Photographed by Sarah Cebulski.

Problem-oriented Policing

Problem-oriented policing (POP) is a strategy based on the assumption that crime is successfully controlled by discovering the underlying reasons or causes for offenses and targeting that aspect of the problem. Instead of treating criminal activity by simply responding to individual "incidents," the police respond to the underlying causes of community problems. To accomplish this, police are trained to engage in systemic problem solving by utilizing a four-step process referred to as the **SARA model**, which is an acronym for Scanning, Analysis, Response, and Assessment (Goldstein 1990):

- Scanning—The identifying and clarifying of what the problem is: its specific location, who is involved, what behavior is occurring, and when it occurs.
- Analysis —Obtaining detailed information specifically about the perceived problem. It is an attempt to answer the appropriate who, what, where, when, how, and especially why questions that surface regarding the particular problem.
- Response—The development of alternative approaches to resolve the problem and selecting from among those alternatives the ones that are likely to significantly impact the problem.
- Assessment—The evaluation of the response(s) used in order to determine whether it (or they) worked.

Problem identification in problem-oriented policing often involves more interaction with the community than does strategic policing. Additionally, data and information gathering takes a broader perspective, since the range of agency responses is not limited to the traditional arrest and prosecution tactics. Since the ideas about the causes of crime and methods for controlling it are substantially widened, the data gathering and response to crime or disorder must be broadened as well. According to Goldstein (1990), the "level of analysis" varies according to the problem being addressed. Some problems require a "top-level analysis," some "street-level analysis," while others require some "intermediate level of analysis" within the police organizational structure. For example, if a problem exists throughout the city, a top-level analysis would be appropriate. If the problem were localized to a particular part of the jurisdiction or just a few neighborhoods, a street-level analysis would be appropriate. Goldstein (1990) adds that problems ought to be explored as close to the operating (local) level as possible.

SUMMARY

In this chapter, you learned that scholars have described the institution of policing and/or an agency's service style as conforming to one or more models of policing. You also learned that the term *model* is simply a conceptual way to label or describe an agency's service outlook and approach. Moreover, because the institution of policing has evolved over the course of its development, scholars have conceptualized different model types (e.g., the traditional, the bureaucratic, the professional, the standard, and the community policing model) to describe an

agency's general service outlook during particular stages of development. What is important to remember is that none of these models is exclusive; in fact, elements of each overlap and blend with the others in a continuing process of innovation, trial-and-error, reform/adoption, and innovation. You have learned that agencies choose various *strategies of policing*, which represent an agency's methods and are evident in their plans, technologies, products, and approaches to achieving goals and objectives. Finally, you have learned that the models and strategies of policing are not mutually exclusive or exhaustive—elements of more than one model or strategy may exist in an agency at the same time. Moreover, models and strategies coexist throughout the policing community—no one strategy necessarily dominates the others, and it is not necessarily accurate to claim that one is "better" or "worse" when compared to another.

Critical Thinking Questions

1. Explain why there can never be a "perfect" policing strategy.

2. Explain how the philosophy of community policing led to policing strategies that are much different from strategies associated with the professional model of policing.

3. Explain why the strategy commonly referred to as "random patrol" has been so criticized, but remains central to contemporary policing.

CHAPTER SPECIFIC INTERNET LINKS

Center for Problem Oriented Policing: http://www.popcenter.org/

Community Oriented Policing Series: http://www.cops.usdoj.gov/

International Association of Chiefs of Police: http://theiacp.org/

Law Enforcement Management & Administrative Statistics (LEMAS) report: http://bjs.ojp.usdoj.gov/content/pub/pdf/lpd07.pdf

CHAPTER GLOSSARY

Bureaucratic model of policing—a form of policing characterized by an hierarchical organizational structure, authoritarian style command, close supervision, semi-military bearing, and strong internal discipline.

Call of service—a term used to by law enforcement agencies to describe police activity wherein a patrol unit is dispatched to a location at the request of a citizen.

Coproduction of order—phrase used to describe a mutual arrangement where law enforcement officers work in partnership with concerned citizens to resolve a community problem.

Model of policing—an academic construct that attempts to characterize an agency's general service outlook and approach. It is a philosophy of service and is evident in an agency's values, traditions, and organizational cultures.

Operational plans—an agency's methods and tactics.

Patrol function—a phrase used to describe a diverse collection of activities conducted by field units as they patrol and respond to calls for service. The vast major of a police department's resources are devoted to the patrol function or in support of the patrol function.

Philosophy of community policing—a concept that promotes organizational strategies, which support the systematic use of partnerships and problem-solving techniques, to proactively address the immediate conditions that give rise to public safety issues such as crime, social disorder, and fear of crime.

Preventive patrol—also referred to as random preventive patrol, this is when officers walk (travel) their beats providing rudimentary services, a visible presence, and a tenuous deterrent to crime. Today, it provides at least the illusion of an omnipresent protective force and is an essential component of the patrol function.

Proactive policing—any police strategy that is designed to prevent, deter, or dissuade criminal activity.

Problem-oriented policing (POP)—the use of analysis and assessment to address crime and disorder problems. The origins of the POP approach can be found in the work conducted by police scholar Herman Goldstein, and its application has led to promising practices in crime reduction strategies among police agencies across the nation and around the world.

Professional model—sometimes referred to the **professional crime-fighting model** of policing, it is based on the idea that policing is a profession and like other professionals, police officers should meet high admission standards, undergo extensive training, serve their clients, devote themselves to the public interest, subscribe to a code of ethics, and possess a wide range of extraordinary skills. As a reform strategy, the professional model raised the status of policing to a profession.

Reactive policing—refers to the simple fact that due to the nature of crime and social disorder, the police are forced into a reactive mode. Since most crimes and incidents of social disorder cannot be prevented, the police are forced to act after the fact.

SARA model—Scanning, Analysis, Response, and Assessment, which are central components of problem-oriented policing.

Standard model of policing—the evolutionary product of the professional model of policing. It relies on the uniform provision of police resources intended to prevent crime and disorder across a wide array of crimes and across all parts of the jurisdiction that an agency serves. Today all police and sheriff's departments are organized under this model.

Strategic policing—attempts to expand the operational strategies of law enforcement through more sophisticated, analytical, and targeted crime control applications; sometimes referred to as **intelligence-led policing**.

Strategies of policing—an agency's definition of what the organization proposes to do and how. They represent an agency's methods and are evident in plans, technologies, products, and approaches to achieving goals and objectives.

Traditional model of policing—a phrase sometimes used to describe the practice of policing between the early 1930s and the 1970s. In a more contemporary and general sense, it refers to long held practices and customs within the institution of policing, some of which remain today.

CHAPTER REFERENCES AND ADDITIONAL READINGS

Cordner, Gary and Robert C. Trojanowicz (1992). Patrol. In Cordner, Gary W. and Donna C. Hale (eds.), *What works in policing?* Cincinnati, OH: Anderson Publishing Co.

Cordner, G.W. and G.L. Williams (1996). *Community policing and accreditation: A content analysis of CALEA*. Washington, D.C.: Police Executive Research Forum.

Crank, John P. (1998). *Understanding police culture*. Cincinnati, OH: Anderson Publishing Co.

Earl, Howard H. (1972). *Police-Community Relations: Crisis In Our Time*. Springfield, IL: Charles Thomas, Publisher.

Eck, John and William Spelman (1987). *Problem solving: Problem-oriented policing in Newport News*. Washington, D.C: Police Executive Research Forum.

Eck, John E. and Dennis P. Rosenbaum (1994). The new police order: Effectiveness, equity, and efficiency in community policing. In Dennis P. Rosenbaum (ed.), *The challenge of community policing: Testing the promises*. Thousand Oaks, CA: Sage Press, 3–23.

Eck, John E., Karin Schmerler, Amy Schapiro, and Deborah Lamm Weisel (1996). *Themes and variations in community policing: Case studies in community policing*. Washington, D.C.: Police Executive Research Forum (PERF).

Fogelson, Robert M. (1977). *Big-City Police*. Cambridge, MA: Harvard University Press.

Gay, William G., Theodore H. Schell, and Stephen Schack (1977). *Improving patrol productivity, Volume I, Routine patrol*, and *Improving patrol productivity, Volume II, Specialized Patrol*. Washington, D.C.: Law Enforcement Assistance Administration, pp. 220–226.

Goldstein, Herman (1979). "Improving policing: A problem-oriented approach to improving police service." *Crime and Delinquency*, 25:236–258.

Goldstein, Herman (1990). *Problem-oriented policing*. New York: McGraw-Hill.

Greenberg, Bernard, et al. (1975). *Felony investigation decision model: An analysis of investigative elements of information*. Menlo Park, CA: Stanford Research Institute.

Greene, Jack R. and Stephen D. Mastrofski (1988). *Community policing: rhetoric or reality*. New York, NY: Praeger Publishers.

Greene, Jack R., William T. Bergman, and Edward J. McLaughlin (1994). "Implementing community policing: Cultural and structural changes in police organizations." In Dennis P. Rosenbaum (Editor.), *The challenge of community policing: testing the promises* (pp. 92–109). Thousand Oaks, CA: Sage Publications.

Kelling, George L. and Mark H. Moore (1988). *The evolving strategy of policing*, Washington, D.C.: National Institute of Justice and Cambridge, MA: Harvard University.

Kelling George L. and Mark H. Moore, (1988). From political to reform to community: The evolving strategy of policing. In Jack R. Greens and Stephen D. Mastrofski, *Community policing: Rhetoric or reality* (pp. 3–25). New York, NY: Praeger Publishers.

Kelling, George L., Tony Pate, Duane Dieckman, and Charles E. Brown (1974). *The Kansas City preventive patrol experiment: A summary report*. Washington, D.C.: Police Foundation.

Klockars, Carl B. and Stephen D. Matrofski (eds.) (1991). *Thinking about police: Contemporary readings*, 2nd Edition. New York: McGraw-Hill.

Lurigio, Arthur J. and Dennis P. Rosenbaum (1994). The impact of community policing on police personnel. In Dennis P. Rosenbaum (ed.), *The challenge of community policing: Testing the promises* (pp. 147–163). Thousand Oaks, CA: Sage Publications.

Maguire, E.R. and S.D. Mastrofski (2000). Patterns of Community Policing in the United States. *Police Quarterly*, 3(1): 4–45.

Mastrofski, Stephan D., (1988). Community policing as reform: A cautionary tale. In Jack R Greene and Stephen D. Mastrofski (eds), *Community policing: rhetoric or reality?* (pp. 47–68). New York, NY: Praeger Publishers.

Moore, Mark H. (1994). "Research synthesis and policy mplications." In Dennis P. Rosenbaum (ed.), *The challenge of community policing: Testing the promises* (pp. 285–299). Thousand Oaks, CA: Sage Publications.

National Advisory Commission on Criminal Justice Standards and Goals (1973). *Report on Police*. U.S. Department of Justice, Office of Justice Programs, Bureau of Justice Statics: Washington, D.C.

Petersilia, Joan (1993). The influence of research on policing. In Dunham, Roger G. and Geoffrey P. Alpert (eds.), *Critical issues in policing: Contemporary readings*. Prospect Heights, IL: Waveland Press, Inc.

Reaves, Brian. (2010). Local Police Departments, 2007. Washington D.C.: U.S. Department of Justice, Bureau of Justice Statistics. http://bjs.ojp.usdoj.gov/index.cfm?ty=pbdetail&iid=1750.

Rosenbaum, Dennis P. (ed) (1994). *The challenge of community policing: Testing the promises*. Thousand Oaks, CA: Sage Publications.

Schell, Theodore H., et al. (1976). *Traditional preventive patrol*. Washington, D.C.: Law Enforcement Assistance Administration.

Sherman, Lawrence W. (1990). *Police crackdowns*. NIJ Reports. Washington, D.C.: U.S. Department of Justice.

Skogan, Wesley G. (1994). The impact of community policing on neighborhood residents: A cross-site analysis. In, Dennis P. Rosenbaum (Ed.), *The challenge of community policing: Testing the promises* (pp. 167–181). Thousand Oaks, CA: Sage Publications.

Skogan, Wesley and Kathleen Frydl (2004). *Fairness and effectiveness in policing: The evidence*. Washington, D.C.: The National Academies Press.

Trojanowicz, Robert and Bonnie Bucqueroux (1990). *Community policing: A contemporary perspective*. Cincinnati, OH: Anderson Publishing.

Trojanowicz, Robert, Victor E. Kappeler, Larry K. Gaines, and Bonnie Bucqueroux (1998). *Community policing: A contemporary perspective, 2nd Ed.*. Cincinnati, OH: Anderson Publishing.

Weisel, Deborah L. and John E. Eck (1994). Toward a practical approach to organizational change: Community policing initiatives in six cities. In Dennis P. Rosenbaum (Ed.), *The challenge of community policing: testing the promises* (pp. 27–52). Thousand Oaks, CA: Sage Publication.

Wilkinson, Deanna L., and Dennis P. Rosenbaum (1994). The effects of organizational structures on community policing: A comparison of two cities. In Dennis P. Rosenbaum (Ed.), *The challenge of community policing: testing the promises* (pp. 110–126). Thousand Oaks, CA: Sage Publications.

Zhao, Jihong (1996). *Why police organizations change: A study of community-oriented policing.* Washington, D.C.: Police Executive Research Forum (PERF).

CHAPTER **14**

Future Issues in Law Enforcement and Recommendations

LEARNING OBJECTIVES

The future—that which lies ahead. How well can you foresee the future? How predictable are events such as the terrorist attacks of September 11, 2001? Did those attacks affect law enforcement operations in the United States? Of course they did; they changed the focus of several key functions, many of which were discussed in previous chapters. This chapter's focus is twofold: (1) to identify many of the future issues that will affect law enforcement in the United States by reviewing past events and current trends, and (2) to make recommendations about improving law enforcement agencies and personnel. After studying this chapter, you will be able to:

- Identify the global challenges affecting the law enforcement community today and in the near future.
- Recite several recommendations to improve policing in the United States.
- Describe the cultural, societal, and demographic trends affecting the United States.
- Discuss several legal issues that will continue to affect law enforcement operations.
- State the challenges to law enforcement agencies in maintaining a competent workforce.
- Summarize several methods to research and envision future issues affecting law enforcement in the United States.

CHAPTER OUTLINE

I. Future Problems Affecting Law Enforcement
   A. Why Study the Future?
   B. How Does One Anticipate the Future?
II. Global Challenges and Social Changes
   A. Foreign Terrorist Threats
   B. Free Trade and Border Protection
   C. Immigration Patterns
   D. World Trade and Economic Patterns
III. National Changes and Challenges
   A. Domestic Terror and Hate Advocates
   B. Demographic and Workforce Changes
   C. Disasters and Civil Unrest
   D. Medical Issues
   E. Neighborhood Decay and Gangs
IV. Legal Issues
   A. Interrogation
   B. Criminal Law
   C. Evidence
   D. Administrative Law and Liability
V. Agency Management Issues
VI. Local Law Enforcement Trends and Preferable Futures
VII. Summary

KEY TERMS USED IN THIS CHAPTER

foresight

North American Free Trade Agreement (NAFTA)

reductions in force (RIF)

local militias

mass murder

serial killing

hate crime

penalty enhancement

baby boom generation

generation X

generation Y/Millennials

blood borne pathogens

encryption

Nominal Group Technique (NGT)

Delphi Technique

FUTURE PROBLEMS AFFECTING LAW ENFORCEMENT

Law enforcement faces the same changes impacting the economic, social, and governmental structures of our nation. Law enforcement also must respond to the call for changes from the justice system and advocacy groups. In order to assess the nature of those changes, each organization must look to its own environment. This chapter is intended to stimulate the curiosity of the reader and to encourage exploration of emerging forces of change, which may be global, national, or local in character. In previous chapters, we mentioned the systems approach to viewing environmental forces. Future challenges peculiar to law enforcement, and what they may mean for patrol officers, supervisors, and managers, are examined in this chapter. We review the means by which all law enforcement personnel may scan for information, identify issues, and help develop solutions (or at least strategies) to these various challenges.

It is obvious that the problems and challenges on the horizon are important to managers in law enforcement. Indeed, the nationally-acclaimed Command College of the California Commission on Peace Officer Standards and Training and other leadership institutes in other states are specifically-designed as a futures and strategic planning program for managers. But, why should front line personnel (patrol officers, agents, and investigators) or supervisors pay attention to such issues? As noted earlier in this text, line officers and their supervisors are the eyes and ears of law enforcement. They are frequently the first to notice changes in neighborhoods with which they interact, as they are closer to said changes in the environment and, accordingly, they will be aware of information sooner and in greater depth than analysts sitting in either headquarters or in some distant agency or university. It is not that these analysts are not important, because they certainly are; rather, both types of law enforcement personnel are important. Field and supervisory personnel must learn to analyze changes within their environment and then interact with other types of analysts and planners in order to discuss the implications of such change. Only then can successful adjustment strategies or countermeasures be developed and implemented.

Why Study the Future?

The answer to this question may appear obvious, but there are actually several reasons. An article in *The Futurist* (Wagner 2002) magazine described 10 reasons to watch for trends. The ones most applicable to our purpose in this chapter can be summarized and paraphrased as follows: To prepare yourself for the future, to be informed of the forces affecting your field, to be informed about forces affecting other fields, to understand the differences between a trend and a fad, to obtain confidence in decision making, and to be forewarned of possible crises. These are basic reasons to give serious attention to what is going on in the world, and specifically to what is happening in your chosen career field.

Foresight is the ability to think and envision what may happen in the future. We are not talking about taking a wild guess, or trying to predict the date of an event; we are referring to the ability to first identify possibilities, develop evidence of probabilities, and evaluate what options are preferable. The "Possible–Probable–Preferable" approach to studying and evaluating environmental forces assists in understanding the future. In other words: What are the possible outcomes related to the problem being considered, what are the probable courses of action based on the current environment and resources, and what are the preferred and most desirable outcomes? Often in criminal justice courses, the preferable futures are not seriously dealt with, as described by Joseph Schafer in *Policing 2020* (2007:22–23):

> Even in the academic community, the study of policing and criminal justice futures is not always taken seriously. Most policing texts address futures issues in a few pages, if at all. In reality, discussions tend to be more focused on contemporary issues (drugs, gangs, community relations, extremist groups, and, more recently, terrorism) rather than actual future concerns. When true futures considerations are seen, they typically are relegated to a few pages and deal very generally with very predictable topics (technology, population shifts, and personnel changes). In effect, authors focus on probable/possible futures, ignoring preferable futures. This is a critical failure of the academic

study of policing. Introductory policing and police administration texts have the opportunity to plant the seed of alternative visions of the police in the minds of the leaders of tomorrow; by and large, this opportunity is squandered.

Another reason for developing the skill of foresight is that it can help overcome "fear of the future." Cornish (2010) addresses this in an article of *The Futurist* periodical, stating that a key challenge faced by many young people today may be "their inability to think realistically, creatively, and hopefully about the future" and that they suffer from "futurephobia." Young people "lacking foresight are prone to act recklessly—drive too fast, use drugs, play with guns, commit crimes, and even kill themselves (or others)" (Cornish 2010:51). He argues that foresight should be recognized as a life skill and should be nurtured and developed in our schools and colleges.

How Does One Anticipate the Future?

There are a number of techniques available that can be utilized to improve foresight. **Figure 14-1** identifies 12 techniques for anticipating the future proposed by the World Future Society, an international association whose members are interested in future trends and developments. The association publishes a number of books, a research journal, and a professional magazine, which you can learn more about at its Web site (see Chapter Specific Links). Other organizations interested in the future can be found on the Internet by using search terms such as "futures research," "futurists," "foresight," and "trend analysis." The Society of Police Futurists International (PFI) is a professional association dedicated to studying and discussing issues affecting policing and criminal justice in general; information about PFI can be accessed via their website (see Chapter Specific Links). Members of these and other organizations believe that, by studying the future, they can have a role in shaping it.

One important aspect of the future is that it is built on the past. For that reason, much of this text has included an historical perspective of where law enforcement has been and where it is currently. We continue that theme by reviewing a number of international, national, legal, and managerial issues facing the law enforcement community. We have not included all the issues affecting the law enforcement environment, but we believe that you will be able to pursue others on your own.

FIGURE 14-1 Techniques for Anticipating The Future

Scanning—a systematic survey of newspapers, magazines, Web sites, and other media for indications of changes with future implications.

Trend Analysis—examinations that identify the nature, causes, and direction of developments and their impacts.

Trend Monitoring—watching key trends and reporting to key decision makers.

Trend Projections—the plotting of data related to identified trends in order to project future direction and impact.

Scenario Development and Analysis—descriptions based on perceived and projected possibilities; usually depicts one or more plausible ways in which the future may unfold.

Consulting Others (Polling)/Delphi—asking others, including experts, what they think about specific issues.

Modeling—an imitation or static representation of real events or possible future events.

Simulations or Gaming—role playing and using simulated situations to determine possibilities or to experience life-like events.

Computer Simulations—automated simulations including complex data and numerical analyses and projections.

Historical Analysis—an analysis of past events and situations in order to detect trends and forecast possible future directions of selected factors.

Brainstorming—articulating new ideas through small groups assembled for creative thinking and problem solving.

Visioning—the systematic creation of visions of a desirable future.

GLOBAL CHALLENGES AND SOCIAL CHANGES

In 1985, then-Senator and later Vice President Albert Gore Jr. introduced a bill in the U.S. Senate that would require the U.S. government to create a group whose special function would be to focus on world trends and events and to project changes in the future in order to address them (Gore 1990). It is difficult to assess how such a group, if started in 1985, might have helped the nation deal with the changes of the past 25 years. One thing is certain: We were not prepared to deal with these changes (such as terrorism, homeland protection, and economic recessions) and they have had profound effects on law enforcement, not to mention all other aspects of society in the United States.

Foreign Terrorist Threats

While problems in international relations were once a subject far removed from the day-to-day concerns of local law enforcement, that luxury has now passed. Over the past decade, the United States has been recovering from the devastating attacks of September 11, 2001, the military operations in Iraq and Afghanistan, recessions, and high unemployment rates. Additionally, the collapse and fragmentation of the Soviet Union into various entities, the continuing disputes in the Middle East between the Palestinians and Israelis, open trade with Central and South America, and even increasing illegal immigration rates are all issues affecting the global economy and international security. Local governments must now recognize the threat of international terrorists, not because the next attack will necessarily occur in small-town USA, but because of the residual effects of such incidents. Those residual effects included diverting much needed resources to homeland security activities and the protection of infrastructures such as the power grid, transportation systems, shipping ports, railroads, schools, and so on.

On the matter of homeland security, communities must now consider themselves more vulnerable as a result of the 2001 terrorist attacks and their aftermath. Those attacks occurred at three sites and killed nearly 3000 people, but it was not the first terrorist attack on our soil, and others have occurred since. The "underwear bomber" of 2009 has heightened airport security and recent debates over airport screenings and pat downs may continue for

some time. The causes of terrorism and the failures or successes of the intelligence community will be topics of debate for years, but what is known is that terrorists are willing to use violence and even die in order to make a political statement of the most profound sort.

Training for terror attacks

Source: Courtesy of Mass Communications Specialist Kirk Worley/U.S. Navy

Use of released U.S. Navy imagery does not constitute product or organizational endorsement of any kind by the U.S. Navy.

While few localities expect to witness events of the magnitude of September 11, all should anticipate the possibility of something happening and should prepare for it. Events in one part of the country now affect other parts because of our mobility and interconnectedness. The September 11 incidents grounded all aircraft throughout the United States and other parts of the world. It led to an economic recession and transformed security functions at airports, ports, and other modes of transportation. There have been dozens of books and articles written since these attacks, but international terrorism is not a new phenomenon. It is, however, the current prevailing justification for much of what national and state law enforcement agencies are doing. According to the U.S. State Department, in 2009 there were about 11,000 acts of international terrorism in 83 countries, resulting in 58,000 victims including 15,000 fatalities (U.S. Department of State 2010:293). The Worldwide Incident Tracking System (WITS) of the National CounterTerrorism Center (NCTC) listed 5305 attacks for 2010 (National CounterTerrorism Center 2010). **Table 14-1** shows the number of terrorist incidents worldwide from 2005–2009, while **Figure 14-2** contains a portion of a Worldwide Caution statement of the U.S. State Department advising Americans who travel overseas

to be aware that certain facilities and activities tend to be targets for travelers.

Obviously, international terrorism can be classified as an ongoing future issue for local law enforcement; the difficulties this creates are immense. The language barriers involved where incidents are international in character are significant and often prevent adequate intelligence gathering. Furthermore, the nature of the threat demands multi-agency involvement and increased liaisons between state and federal law enforcement. Managing a relationship between multiple agencies at two levels of government in the midst of serious threats or disasters requires substantial prior planning and attention *at all levels*. The involvement of foreign nationals makes information-gathering difficult, but patrol officers who know the community can

TABLE 14-1 Incidents of Terrorism Worldwide 2005–2009

	2005	2006	2007	2008	2009
Attacks worldwide	11,023	14,443	14,435	11,725	10,999
Attacks resulting in at least 1 death, injury, or kidnapping	7,963	11,278	11,097	8,411	7,875
Attacks resulting in the death of at least 1 individual	5,083	7,412	7,235	5,045	4,764
Attacks resulting in the death of 0 individuals	5,940	7,031	7,200	6,680	6,235
Attacks resulting in the death of only 1 individual	2,853	4,127	3,984	2,870	2,694
Attacks resulting in the death of at least 10 individuals	226	295	353	234	234
Attacks resulting in the injury of at least 1 individual	3,805	5,774	6,243	4,869	4,536
Attacks resulting in the kidnapping of at least 1 individual	1,156	1,343	1,156	961	877
People killed, injured, or kidnapped as a result of terrorism	74,327	74,616	71,856	54,653	58,142
People worldwide killed as a result of terrorism	14,482	20,515	22,736	15,727	14,971
People worldwide injured as a result of terrorism	24,795	38,314	44,139	34,057	34,057
People worldwide kidnapped as a result of terrorism	35,050	15,787	4,981	4,869	4,869

* "Terrorism" defined as premeditated, politically motivated violence perpetrated against non-combatant targets by subnational groups or clandestine agents. Includes attacks within Iraq and Afghanistan.

Source: Reprinted from U.S. Department of State (2010:292–293).

FIGURE 14-2 Worldwide Caution Statement, U.S. State Department

The Department of State has issued this Worldwide Caution to update information on the continuing threat of terrorist actions and violence against U.S. citizens and interests throughout the world. U.S. citizens are reminded to maintain a high level of vigilance and to take appropriate steps to increase their security awareness. This replaces the Worldwide Caution dated February 12, 2010, to provide updated information on security threats and terrorist activities worldwide.

The Department of State remains concerned about the continued threat of terrorist attacks, demonstrations, and other violent actions against U.S. citizens and interests overseas. U.S. citizens are reminded that demonstrations and rioting can occur with little or no warning. Current information suggests that al-Qaida and affiliated organizations continue to plan terrorist attacks against U.S. interests in multiple regions, including Europe, Asia, Africa, and the Middle East. These attacks may employ a wide variety of tactics including suicide operations, assassinations, kidnappings, hijackings, and bombings.

Extremists may elect to use conventional or non-conventional weapons, and target both official and private interests. Examples of such targets include high-profile sporting events, residential areas, business offices, hotels, clubs, restaurants, places of worship, schools, public areas, and locales where U.S. citizens gather in large numbers, including during holidays.

U.S. citizens are reminded of the potential for terrorists to attack public transportation systems and other tourist infrastructure. Extremists have targeted and attacked subway and rail systems, as well as aviation and maritime services. In the past several years, attacks have occurred in cities such as London, Madrid, Glasgow, and Moscow.

Issued: August 12, 2010; information was current as of January 2011.

Source: Extracted from U.S. Department of State, Bureau of Consular Affairs (2011).

large amount of information over a long period of time before patterns emerge.

While the attacks of September 11 were, in part, the result of Middle East tensions and disdain for U.S. foreign policy, there are many places in the world equally volatile. Afghanistan, Bosnia, Pakistan, Indonesia, parts of Latin America and Africa, and certain areas of the former Soviet Union are only a few of the world regions with internal turmoil that have the potential to spread to the United States and to selected communities within our borders. Officers should be aware of world and national trends and events. Recent terrorist events have increased the heightened awareness of what could happen on U.S. soil and to our way of life. Various scenarios are now examined regarding what could happen and how we should be better prepared for such incidents. One insightful author, Joseph Coates, has written about potential disasters and their policy implications. **Figure 14-3** lists some the key issues that Coates identifies.

FIGURE 14-3 Potential Terrorist Disasters and Policy Implications

Ten Specific Impending Terrorist Disasters

1. Disrupt Global Business
2. Initiate Deadly Panic
3. Deploy Radioactive Dust
4. Deploy Dangerous Chemicals
5. Poison the Air
6. Silence Telecommunications Capabilities of Washington, D.C.
7. Put Computer Servers Out of Service
8. Infect Pets
9. Target Cruise Ships
10. Miscellaneous

Seven Policy Implications

1. Understand why they hate us
2. Abjure the use of "war"
3. Think like terrorists
4. Prepare the public to expect terrorist acts
5. Terrorist acts by good people
6. Understand Islamic cultures
7. Don't demonize

Source: Coates, Joseph F. (2002), *The Futurist*, "What's Next? Foreseeable Terrorist Acts," September–October, pp. 23–26; and "Were I Bin Laden," World Future Society website, www .wfs.org, 2002.

interpret patterns of neighborhood events or individual behavior that are out of the norm. Such events are a cause for inquiry and are worthy of note. No officer can assume that information is unimportant merely because they are not aware of a crime. Well-kept notes are very important in such conditions, since you may need to accumulate a

What is the future of foreign terrorism? If we knew the definitive answer, we'd be working for the U.S. Government. Our purpose here is to engage your thought process and increase your awareness of the issues. There are dozens of books published on this topic and also a major study published in 2008 listing 55 trends shaping terrorism (see Cetron and Davies 2008a). Another study by Cetron and Davies (2008b) addresses 55 trends shaping the future of policing; with regards to terrorism, several of their observations include the following:

- Terrorism will be a continuing problem long into the future, particularly in European nations with large, poorly-integrated Muslim immigrant populations. Security concerns, therefore, will take up more time and resources in the future, especially for big-city police departments (8).
- Cities with large, concentrated Arab-American Muslim populations, such as Detroit and New York City, could witness low level acts of terrorism such as suicide bombings (9).
- Concentrating the poor and powerless in cities produces conditions ideal for the spread of petty crime, violence, and the kind of religious extremism that lends itself to terror-prone political ideologies (10).
- The West, and particularly the United States, must expect more—and more violent—acts of terrorism for at least the next 20 years. Europe faces a significant homegrown Muslim extremist movement, and the United States may also face this same threat in the near future. Thanks largely to waves of immigration since the 1980s, Islam is the fastest-growing religion in both regions (26).
- In a country still suffering from shock after the 9/11 attacks, but also faced with the real threat of future terrorism, the spread of Islam—the fastest growing religion in the United States—will require police to build close ties with unfamiliar, and even suspect, communities. This will be an uncommonly delicate task for a profession that has not always been known for delicacy (67).

Free Trade and Border Protection

Other international concerns are those regarding free trade and open borders. The notion of free trade will most likely help the general economy in the long run, which can only be good for law enforcement at all levels. However, it also poses interesting and complex problems (Cornish 1990). The increase in truck and other vehicular traffic that followed the **North American Free Trade Agreement** (**NAFTA**) has increased smuggling dramatically (Burnett 2010, Rowlands 2010, and Immigration and Customs Enforcement 2010). Freedom of travel across borders offers commercial opportunities for transport. Of course, it will not only be illegal narcotics and marijuana; illegal alcohol, medicinal drugs (which have not yet been approved by the Federal Food and Drug Administration for the treatment of illnesses), counterfeit products, and even banned items, such as ivory, Rhinoceros horn, and other products related to endangered species, potentially will have new entry points. Paradoxically, the desire by some to have increased trade contradicts the desire by others to tighten the borders for purposes of homeland security.

Burnett (2010) states that,

In Nuevo Laredo, Mexico, the Gulf Cartel is battling the Zetas for control of the plaza, whose prize is the World Trade Bridge, the biggest commercial port on the southwest border. Each day, 4800 trucks cross the bridge. That's one truck every 15 seconds. From there, via Interstate 35, it's a straight shot to America's drug-loving heartland.

There are dedicated lanes at several border-crossing bridges for the pre-approved container trucks. Approximately 4.7 million commercial trucks cross into the United States from Mexico annually, and at best only one out five are thoroughly inspected. The drug cartels know the math and take the risks by including contraband in many trucks realizing that some may get caught, but the others will go through the checkpoints. According to U.S. federal law enforcement and Mexican security sources, drug mafias have thoroughly infiltrated Mexican export and trucking companies (Burnett 2010).

Law enforcement problems are most likely to appear in locations with close proximity to seaports or international highway access. Unfortunately, that includes most of the continental United States. Even the states along the Great Lakes have international seaports. Examine the map

U.S.-Mexico Border Crossing near Tijuana, Mexico

Source: © iStockphoto/Thinkstock

of the United States in **Figure 14-4** that shows the 317 of the 327 official ports of entry in the country. A port of entry is an officially-designated location (seaports, airports, and/or land border locations) where federal officers or employees are assigned to accept entries of merchandise, clear passengers, collect duties, and enforce the various provisions of related laws. If you are within 500 miles (a one-day drive) from such an entry point, consider your location to be impacted. Obviously, very little of the nation is excluded. Recently, a number of incidents of violence have border states worried about criminal activity in Mexico crossing over into the United States. Criminal activity, plus the ongoing national issue of border protection and illegal immigration, are common news stories:

- December 14, 2010: A U.S. Border Patrol Agent was killed on patrol while trying to catch "bandits" who prey on illegal entrants (Stout 2010).

- A Department of Homeland Security Inspector General's report indicates that Customs and Border Patrol officers are not enforcing the law requiring all travelers to have a passport or other secure identification before entering the United States; an estimated 2.3 million travelers who failed to provide proper paperwork at U.S. land ports of entry had been allowed to enter the United States anyway during the eight-month evaluation period (Corsi 2010).

- In July 2010, the U.S. Department of Justice filed an injunction to permanently enjoin the State of Arizona from enforcing a controversial illegal immigrant law that had been signed into law earlier in the year (U.S. Department of Justice July 6, 2010).

- March 27, 2010: Rancher Robert Krentz was murdered on his property near the Arizona–Mexico

FIGURE 14-4 U.S. ports of entry

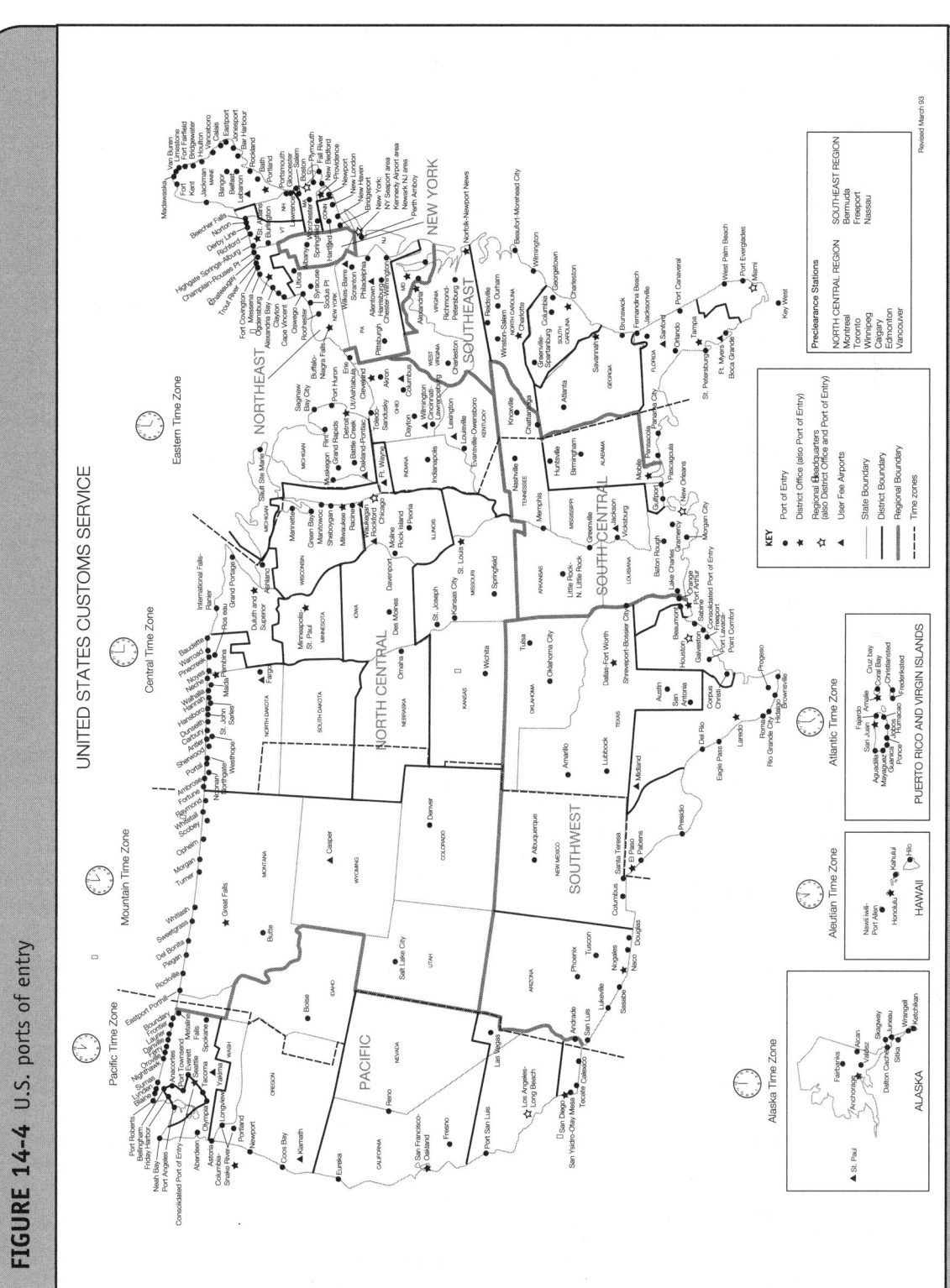

Source: Reprinted from Importing into the United States, U.S. Customs Service Publication 5D4A, pp. 48–49, 1994, U.S. Customs Service

border; after tracking a suspect's shoe prints south to the border, the search was called off (Nunez 2010).

- From 2006 through 2010, more than 30,000 people were killed in drug violence in Mexico; the killings are typically attributed to rival drug gangs, but civilians, police, and recovering drug addicts have also been targeted (Associated Press 2010).

Illegal immigration was believed to be a major political issue in the 2010 national and state elections. The change in leadership in the House of Representatives from the Democrats to the Republicans signals a change from "comprehensive immigration reform" to one focused on "border enforcement, immigration law enforcement and strengthening visa security;" there's also indications of reviewing the interpretation of the 14th Amendment on matters of so-called "anchor baby" citizenship (Marczak 2010).

Immigration Patterns

Changes in immigration patterns may impact many things other than just contraband importation or culture conflict. Accelerated immigration (legal and illegal) can be anticipated from a number of sources in the future, including Haiti, Mexico, Cuba, Eastern Europe, Russia, the Middle East, China, and Singapore, to name only a few. As these populations immigrate to the United States, they present challenges similar to those presented by the Irish and Italians when they settled in the nineteenth century. One example is the explosion of the "Russian Mafia" and its activities in the United States:

> In fact, the FBI [Federal Bureau of Investigation] has indicated that roughly 60% of FBI cases targeting Russian organized crime involve fraud. The types of fraud and scams that Russian criminals participate in cross industries from health care and strategic commodities (e.g., precious metals) fraud to credit card, insurance, securities, and investment fraud. They are also involved in scams in domains such as tax evasion and energy price rigging. Many Russian organized crime groups operate in New York, New Jersey, Boston, Philadelphia, Chicago, Los Angeles, San Francisco, and Miami, among other cities (Finklea 2010:17, footnotes omitted).

The top organized crime threats as identified by the FBI have the following backgrounds: Russian/Eurasian, Asian, Italian, Balkan, Middle Eastern, and African. There is concern that the fraudulent activities of organized crime in the United Sates could weaken the already fragile economy and that some of its activities are linked to terrorist groups, since both are tied to large sums of money and forged documents. The National Intelligence Council has estimated that, by 2025, some organized crime networks may be strong enough to take over and run certain countries (Finklea 2010:15–24).

According to government and other sources, there are between 820,000 and 1,131,500 legal immigrants per year to the United States, with another 800,000 to 1 million entering and staying without documentation. The Population Reference Bureau states that as:

> U.S. fertility fell from a peak of 3.7 children per woman in the late 1950s to 2.0 today, the contribution of immigration to U.S. population growth increased. Between 1990 and 2010, the number of foreign-born U.S. residents almost doubled from 20 million to 40 million, while the U.S. population rose from almost 250 million to 310 million. Thus, immigration directly contributed one-third of the U.S. population growth and, with the U.S.-born children and grandchildren of immigrants, immigration contributed half of U.S. population growth (Martin and Midgley 2010:1–2).

The same source indicates that the United States has the most foreign-born residents of any country—three times more than number two (Russia), and more unauthorized residents than any other country in the world.

This trend will change the "face of America" over the coming decades. In terms of the country or area of origin for these immigrants, approximately 41% will be from Latin America, 34% will be from Asia, 15% will come from Europe and Canada, and 10% will be from other areas (Martin and Midgley 2010:3). **Table 14-2** shows the percentage of the population by race and ethnic background from 2000 through projections for 2050. Note that for the year 2050, the non-Hispanic white category drops to about 50% of the population.

Immigration patterns will have other impacts. Tightly-knit families with their own language will be less open to

TABLE 14-2 Projected Population of the United States, by Race and Hispanic Origin: 2000 to 2050

(In thousands except as indicated. As of July 1. Resident population.)

Population or percent and race or Hispanic origin	2000	2010	2020	2030	2040	2050
POPULATION						
TOTAL	282,125	308,936	335,805	363,584	391,946	419,854
White alone	228,548	244,995	260,629	275,731	289,690	302,626
Black alone	35,818	40,454	45,365	50,442	55,876	61,361
Asian Alone	10,684	14,241	17,988	22,580	27,992	33,430
All other races 1/	7,075	9,246	11,822	14,831	18,388	22,437
Hispanic (of any race)	35,622	47,756	59,756	73,055	87,585	102,560
White alone, not Hispanic	195,729	201,112	205,936	209,176	210,331	210,283
PERCENT OF TOTAL POPULATION						
TOTAL	100.0	100.0	100.0	100.0	100.0	100.0
White alone	81.0	79.3	77.6	75.8	73.9	72.1
Black alone	12.7	13.1	13.5	13.9	14.3	14.6
Asian Alone	3.8	4.6	5.4	6.2	7.1	8.0
All other races 1/	2.5	3.0	3.5	4.1	4.7	5.3
Hispanic (of any race)	12.6	15.5	17.8	20.1	22.3	24.4
White alone, not Hispanic	69.4	65.1	61.3	57.5	53.7	50.1

1/ Includes American Indian and Alaska Native alone, Native Hawaiian and Other Pacific Islander alone, and Two or More Races

Source: Reprinted from U.S. Census Bureau, 2004, "U.S. Interim Projections by Age, Sex, Race, and Hispanic Origin," <http://www.census.gov/ipc/www/usinterimproj/>

Internet Release Date: March 18, 2004

law enforcement. To them, U.S. law enforcement may represent the negative governmental forces from which they fled, so if their experience taught them that uniformed personnel could not be trusted or were corrupt, there is little chance that they will be comfortable calling upon or assisting police officials. Language barriers will pose their own particular difficulty. Departments will need to find new ways to acquire diverse language skills, or they will not be able to do their jobs, even in regards to investigating traffic accidents or reading Miranda warnings. Languages needed by officers include Spanish, Russian, Chinese, Japanese, Vietnamese, Thai, Hmong, Farsi, Korean, and even French Caribbean to name but a few. Since most officers will not be fluent in more than one foreign language, technology may be part of the solution; with the ever-developing and improving electronic language translators that have been available for over five years becoming more important (see the links at the end of the chapter).

World Trade and Economic Patterns

World trade and economic patterns will also affect localities. As economic patterns shift, so will the tax base upon which government rests. Rapid changes in world trade patterns resulted in the U.S. steel and auto industry decline and consolidation in the 1970s, which negatively impacted U.S. cities in profound ways. Now small industrial firms are closing, in part because companies are outsourcing work to other countries where labor costs are significantly lower. While the federal government, and many state governments, can shift resources and draw upon a much more diverse tax base for income, local governments have few options. Traditionally, planning in law enforcement was predicated upon reasonably-stable municipal and county budgets. In the past two decades, however, stability has given way to widely fluctuating budget resources. Projected budget needs will continue to outpace available resources for some time to come.

Budget impacts may require the reliance upon obsolete equipment, pay cutbacks, reduced training opportunities, and **reductions in force** (**RIF**), meaning layoffs and terminations. Turnover may increase as officers pursue other career options. Finally, the quality and quantity of recruits will fall precipitously as those with higher skill and knowledge levels seek safety and economic security in another location or career or retirement. The most highly-educated officers may be the most recently hired—if RIFs occur, they generally will be the first to go because of seniority.

As local economic experience produces change and workers are displaced, unemployment will produce predictable outcomes. The population base will grow increasingly poor. Poverty and social problems related to poverty will increase. These effects are associated with emotional problems, frustration, alcohol and drug abuse, verbal outbursts, physical assaults, and domestic violence. Consequently, service demands will increase for such things as random low-level violence and drug trafficking. Neighborhoods may fall into disrepair and the general feeling of security and safety will deteriorate, thereby generating more crime opportunities (Wilson 1983). The current economic recession and unemployment rates over 9% nationally are taking their toll on the country. Many cities have unfunded pension systems, some state pension systems are financially unsound, and the national debt is reaching $14 trillion (view the National Debt Clock in the Chapter Specific links).

Shifting economic patterns may also produce an economic stimulus in some areas, however, and there are problems associated with these changes. Large numbers of new people will pose problems, and neighborhoods will grow increasingly transient in nature, which will provide widespread opportunity for household burglaries. Increased income in an area will generate a good deal of new property, and new property generates theft (which is essentially an opportunity crime). These conditions create higher demands for police service as well.

Management, supervisors, and patrol officers all need to be aware of both patterns. Because patterns will vary from location to location, management will need a steady flow of good information from line and supervision in order to assess the implications for their particular agency. Peculiar patterns will develop for each geographical area, so policies and approaches that work in one may not work in another.

One negative but possible economically-based scenario has been described by Paul Craig Roberts (2010) entitled "The Year America Dissolved." Two selected passages indicate the possible role of law enforcement agencies:

> *It was 2017. Clans were governing America… The first clans organized around local police forces. The conservatives' war on crime during the late 20th century and the Bush/Obama war on terror during the first decade of the 21st century had resulted in the police becoming militarized and unaccountable.*
>
> *As society broke down, the police became warlords. The state police broke apart, and the officers were subsumed into the local forces of their communities. The newly formed tribes expanded to encompass the relatives and friends of the police… Overwhelmed by liabilities, the government collapsed. Globalism had run its course. Life reformed on a local basis (Roberts 2010).*

NATIONAL CHANGES AND CHALLENGES

Obviously, many of the problems that impact law enforcement have international causes. However, many also have local causes and many international trends have multiple local implications. These changes relate to the kinds of crime that will occur in the future, and the processes of hiring, training, and assigning law enforcement personnel. National trends may not be noticed in all locations, and they may be more pronounced in some places over others. However, the idea that they are observable trends implies that every area of the nation will eventually be impacted by these changes in some manner.

Domestic Terror and Hate Advocates

On April 19, 1995, a bomb exploded in front of the Federal Building in Oklahoma City, killing 167 people, including several children, and injuring more than 500 others. The bomb was made of several thousand pounds of fertilizer-based explosives and was packed into a rental truck. Timothy McVeigh, a former member of the U.S. Army and Gulf War veteran, was charged, convicted, and executed (on June 11, 2001) for the act. Terry Nichols, an accomplice of McVeigh's, was convicted in federal court in 1997 and in the state court of Oklahoma in 2004 and is serving 161 life sentences consecutively. As the investigations and trials of these two men unfolded, national attention turned to the growing influence of so-called **local militias**, one of which McVeigh was said to be a member. The isolated location of Oklahoma City, in the so-called heartland of America, and its generally conservative culture combined to add to the shock of the event. People began to realize that such things could happen anywhere.

While the **mass murder** incident at Oklahoma City was shocking in and of itself, the specter of thousands of armed militia members produced serious concern for law enforcement planners. These groups of loosely-organized, poorly-disciplined armed citizens seem to represent a variety of radical antigovernment political groups. They are loosely-allied nationally and are located in nearly every state in the union. The problem these organizations pose for law enforcement is debated today, as some argue they are merely highly-patriotic people who fear the government. They tend to be secretive organizations, train in the use of combat weapons, and espouse anti-government rhetoric. Some use the FBI shootout at Ruby Ridge (Idaho) and the Branch Davidians' assault at Waco, Texas as evidence of a great government conspiracy to suppress fundamental rights of self-government.

Oklahoma City—Murra Federal Building, April 26, 1995. Search and Rescue crews work to save those trapped beneath the debris.

Source: Courtesy of FEMA

Another mass murder with domestic terror overtones occurred on November 13, 2009. Army Major Nidal Hasan (a psychiatrist and American-born Muslim) entered the Soldier Readiness Center at Ft. Hood (Texas) dressed in his uniform and armed with two semi-automatic pistols. During a 10-minute shooting spree, he killed 12 soldiers and one civilian and wounded 32 other people. Two Ft. Hood Police officers charged the location and confronted Hasan outside; he was shot four times and subdued (BBC News 2009). In October 2010 at an Article 32 hearing to determine whether Hasan would be tried at a court martial, witnesses testified that at the time of the incident, Hasan stood up and shouted "Allahu Akbar!"—Arabic for "God is great"—before he started shooting (Zucchino 2010). Reportedly, Hasan is now paralyzed and as of July 2011, he was awaiting the start of court martial proceedings. This case has raised many questions about Army personnel evaluations and the relations between service members, and the whole story may not emerge for some time.

Major Nidal Hasan

Source: © UPI /Landov

Serial killing is another form of domestic terror. One killing spree of two snipers began October 2, 2002 in the Washington, D.C. suburban county of Montgomery (MD). Within 15 hours, five fatal shootings occurred. The attacks kept the metropolitan area semi-paralyzed for days until the saga ended on October 24, when police arrested John Allen Muhammad and Lee Boyd Malvo at a highway rest area (after an observant citizen noticed the suspect's

vehicle, a description of which had been made public). A total of 10 people were killed and 3 injured (see **Figure 14-5**). Between 2003 through 2006, both Malvo and Muhammad were convicted at trial or pled guilty in multiple court cases in Maryland and Virginia. Both were sentenced to life without parole; Muhammad also received the death penalty in Virginia and was executed on November 10, 2009 (Ford 2009; Federal Bureau of Investigation 2007a and 2007b). In May 2003, another sniper case occurred on the I-270 beltway around Columbus, Ohio. It took police and the county sheriff's office some time to link the total of 24 shootings at moving vehicles, but eventually Charles A. McCoy Jr., 28, was identified and captured in Las Vegas in March 2004, two days after being identified as the primary suspect in the shootings. However, McCoy was not a serial killer, because only one of his victims died; he was sentenced in 2005 to 28 years in prison after accepting a plea agreement.

Although the D.C. Beltway shootings were solved in a relatively short time, the Ohio shootings took about nine months to solve. Unfortunately, some serial offenses take even longer to solve. For example, Gary Leon Ridgway pled guilty to 48 murders on November 5, 2003, making him the worst (known) serial killer in the nation's history. Ridgway's killings date back to the 1980s, when the remains of women, mainly runaways and prostitutes, turned up near ravines, rivers, airports, and freeways; he was dubbed the "Green River Killer" for the river near Seattle, Washington where the first bodies were found. Ridgway had been a suspect, but it took over 13 years for the evolution of DNA technology to tie him to the victims. He struck a plea bargain that resulted in a sentence of life in prison without parole (CBSNews.com 2003).

In late 2010, another serial killer case was developing in Los Angeles. Police charged one suspect with 10 counts of murder (all the victims were women). Dubbed the "Grim Sleeper" because the first seven murders tied to the suspect occurred from 1985 through 1988, the investigations yielded no suspect, and then DNA evidence linked another three murders from 2002 through 2007. In 2010, forensic analysis and undercover surveillance led to the current suspect. During a search of the suspect's residence, a "cache of about 1000 photographs and hundreds of hours of home video showing women,

FIGURE 14-5 Timeline of the 2002 Beltway Sniper killings and Investigation

October 2: James D. Martin killed while crossing a parking lot in Wheaton, Maryland.

October 3: Five more victims are murdered—James L. Buchanan, Premkumar Walekar, Sarah Ramos, and Lori Ann Lewis-Rivera in Maryland and Pascal Charlot in D.C.; all within a fifteen hour period. A multi-agency investigation is launched, led by the Montgomery County Police Department in Maryland.

October 4: A woman wounded while loading her van at Spotsylvania Mall.

October 7: A 13-year-old-boy wounded at a school in Bowie, Maryland.

October 9: Dean H. Meyers murdered near Manassas, Virginia, while pumping gas.

October 11: Kenneth Bridges shot dead near Fredericksburg, Virginia, while pumping gas.

October 14: FBI analyst Linda Franklin killed near Falls Church, Virginia.

October 17: A caller claiming to be the sniper phoned in to say that he was responsible for the murder of women during the robbery of a liquor store in Montgomery, Alabama, a month earlier.

October 19: Man wounded outside a steakhouse in Ashland, Virginia

October 20–22: Federal agents in Mobile gathered evidence from the robbery of a liquor store in Montgomery, Alabama and flew to Washington, D.C.; ATF handled the ballistic evidence and the FBI took the fingerprint evidence to the FBI Laboratory in D.C. The fingerprint database produced a match—a magazine dropped at the crime scene bore the fingerprints of Lee Boyd Malvo from a previous arrest in Washington State; there was now a suspect. The arrest record in Washington revealed another name–John Allen Muhammad–a second suspect emerged.

October 22: A bus driver, Conrad E. Johnson, killed in Aspen Hill, Maryland.

October 22: A search of another criminal records database found that Muhammad had registered a blue Chevy Caprice with the license plate of NDA-21Z in New Jersey. That description was given to the news media and shared far and wide.

October 24: Muhammad and Malvo arrested in Maryland at 3:19 a.m. at a road side rest where hours before a citizen had noticed Muhammad's vehicle. The car had a hole cut in the trunk near the license plate so that shots could be fired from within the vehicle. The FBI called the vehicle a "a rolling sniper's nest."

November 10, 2009: Muhammad executed in Virginia.

From 2003 through 2006, both Malvo and Muhammad were convicted at trial or pled guilty in multiple court cases in Maryland and Virginia. Both were sentenced to life without parole; Muhammad also received the death penalty in Virginia.

November 10, 2009: Muhammad executed in Virginia.

Sources: FBI (October 22, 2007). A Byte Out of History, The Beltway Snipers, Part 1 and A Byte Out of History, The Beltway Snipers, Part 2 (October 24, 2007); and C. Benjamin Ford (November 11, 2009). Beltway sniper executed on Tuesday evening. FairfaxTimes.com.

many of them partly or fully nude and striking sexually graphic poses" was discovered. Police feared they there were additional victims because of the long time period involved (Blankstein and Rubin 2010). In December 2010, the Los Angeles Police Department released photos of about 160 women to the public in an attempt to identify them and to determine if they were alive. By the end of 2010, 29 women had been identified, all of whom were either alive or had died of natural causes (Associated Press December 20, 2010). This case is an excellent example of how agencies today can cooperate with the media outlets and use today's social media technology (Web pages,

social networks, Amber Alerts, etc.) to solicit assistance from the public. Other agencies have successfully released photographs seeking the public's help, and of course there are also TV programs such as "America's Most Wanted" and "Unsolved Mysteries" that have assisted agencies in identifying and capturing suspects. It is expected that the use of social media and other forms of technology will be utilized in future cases investigated by law enforcement.

One of the most singularly well-known domestic terrorists in contemporary American experience was the unknown individual called the Unabomber, now known to be Ted Kaczynski, a former math professor. The name given to this domestic terrorist derives from the tendency of the terrorist, in his earliest attacks, to target university and airport settings, though he also attacked non-university individuals. Between 1978 and 1996 he struck 16 times, killing 3 and injuring 23. He followed a 1995 bomb threat with a demand that, unless his manifesto against technology was published, he would kill more people. It was published by the *Washington Post* in September 1995, and it was generally a rambling denunciation of the role of technology in our society. Partially as a result of that publication, David Kaczynski, Ted Kaczynski's brother, became suspicious of Ted Kaczynski's actions and the language used in the manifesto; David turned his brother in, resulting in an arrest in April 1996. David also hoped to be able to spare his brother's life; Ted Kaczynski was sentenced to four consecutive life terms plus 30 years with no option of parole in a federal court in Sacramento, California on May 4, 1998.

In July 1996, at the Summer Olympics in Atlanta, Georgia, a bomb exploded, killing one person and injuring more than 110 others. Later, in 1997 and 1998, bombs exploded at a building containing an abortion clinic (injuring seven), a gay and lesbian nightclub (injuring five), and another abortion clinic (killing one police officer and injuring a nurse). By May 1998, Eric Robert Rudolph was added to the FBI's Most Wanted list. For months federal agents combed the mountains of western North Carolina for Rudolph, but were unable to find him. In late May 2003, Rudolph was apprehended in Murphy, North Carolina by an officer who had found Rudolph foraging for food in garbage bins behind a grocery store at 4:30 in the morning (Seattle Times News Service 2003). In 2005, he plead guilty to four bombings and was sentenced to four consecutive life terms in prison. He is an example of another form of terror in the United States—hate.

Since the late 1980s, greater attention has been placed on **hate crimes**. A hate crime is defined generally as an offense committed against persons, property, or society that is motivated, in whole or in part, by an offender's bias or anger against an individual's or a group's immutable characteristics (e.g., race, religion, ethnic/national origin, gender, age, disability, or sexual orientation). Most states have some sort of hate crime statute, usually in the form of a **penalty enhancement**, meaning that there is an increase

in the standard criminal penalties when crimes target members of specified groups. Penalties are enhanced either through assigning a higher sentencing range for bias-motivated crimes or by increasing the level of the offense to a more serious category of crime. Hate crimes are not new, but this approach to punishing offenders for a bias-type motive is, and to some it is controversial because of the difficulty in proving motive (usually not an element of most offenses).

The FBI data for 2009 indicated a 15% decrease from 2008 reported hate crime incidents; the total was 6604 incidents involving 7789 offenses, 8336 victims, and 6225 known offenders. The bureau has compiled annual statistics on hate crime since 1991 and now publishes a separate, annual report, *Hate Crime Statistics*. Of the 6604 incidents, 61.1% were crimes against persons, 38.1% were crimes against property, and the remaining 0.8% were crimes against society. The focus of the bias motivation for the 2009 victims was (FBI 2010):

48.7% Racial Bias
18.9% Religious Bias
17.8% Sexual Orientation Bias
13.3% Ethnicity/National Origin Bias
0.02% Disability Bias

Other groups (e.g., Anti-Defamation League, Southern Poverty Law Center, and the Leadership Conference on Civil Rights) also emphasize addressing hate crimes and informing law enforcement of hate activities. These groups also support law enforcement training programs. The Southern Poverty Law Center's Intelligence Project counted 932 active hate groups in the United States in their 2009 tabulations. The center maintains a unique interactive map of the United States on its Web site depicting the type and general location of hate groups (see Chapter Specific Links). You can click on the map and a listing of hate groups according to your choice of states will be provided. The center classifies the various groups as Anti-Gay, Anti-Immigrant, Black Separatist, Christian Identity, Holocaust Denial, Ku Klux Klan, Neo-Confederate, Neo-Nazi, Racist Music, Racist Skinhead, Radical Traditional Catholicism, and White Nationalist (Southern Poverty Law Center 2010). During 2010, Southern Poverty Law Center (SPLC) came under criticism for labeling several groups as Anti-Immigrant because of their position against illegal immigration. The SPLC has been accused of becoming a propaganda arm of the "comprehensive immigration reform" advocates (Kammer 2010), and also accused of attempting to isolate and ridicule the Tea Party movement (Blaine, March 3, 2010). Of course, it must be remembered that neither the SPLC nor the authors of this text are indicating that membership in any of these groups is a criminal offense. It is not against the law to hate others; it may not be healthy, but it is not against the law unless it is a motivating factor in the commission of a criminal offense against a specific class of victim. It also is not against the law to support and defend legal immigration and speak negatively against undocumented immigration, or to seek enforcement of the country's immigration laws. The current controversies over illegal immigration and undocumented individuals are ones that put policing and law enforcement officials in the middle. Most Americans want everyone to live according to the law, but some officials argue that they need the support of the undocumented community to fight crime in their neighborhoods and to cooperate with the police. Unfortunately, illegal immigration, border security, sanctuary city policies, and deportation issues will be on-going concerns in the immediate future for those who have sworn to uphold the U.S. Constitution and enforce the nation's laws.

Immigration rally

Source: © CREATISTA/ShutterStock, Inc.

From our presentation of domestic terror and hate, we simply want you to stop and think about what types of individuals will exist in our society in the future. What can be done to lessen the likelihood of serial killers starting their activities, and how can they be caught sooner? What are the limits of hate and the inciting of others because of that hate? How will investigative techniques improve across jurisdictions in order to detect serial killings? How will law enforcement agencies balance the need to enforce the law and the need to obtain cooperation from victims and witnesses when immigration tensions exist?

Demographic and Workforce Changes

From now until 2015, the U.S. labor force is expected to undergo dramatic changes. These changes include the aging of the workforce, as the average age of workers steadily increases, along with the continuing rise in the numbers of women, minorities, and legal immigrants entering professions and the attendant changes in the work place that must result to accommodate this trend. Finally, the labor force will also experience dramatic changes in racial, cultural, language, and generational diversity. Such diversity is reflective of the trends in the population of the United States (see **Figure 14-6**).

Age Distribution

One of the major concerns for organizations, both public and private, is the changing nature of the U.S. workforce as it relates to the aging population. As the veterans or traditionalists (those born between 1922 and 1945) retire, members of the **baby boom generation** (born between 1946 and 1964) now represent nearly one-third of the population. The next generation after that, the so-called **generation X** (born between 1965 and 1980), is only half as large. **Generation Y** (born between 1981 and 2000), also called **Millennials** or Echo Boomers, are now entering the labor market as well. Today, it is common to find four generations working side-by-side in the labor force, and some say this is the first time in the history of the United States that this is occurring (Hammill 2005). Hence, there will be diverse values and attitudes toward work, family, and leisure. Generational differences need to be managed in the workplace, which constitutes a future challenge for supervisors. Since younger workers are the

FIGURE 14-6 Selected facts and projections—population of the United States

- Over four million babies are born each year in the United States and 2.4 million persons die.
- The U.S. population is growing by about 2.5 million people each year. Of that, immigration contributes over one million people to the U.S. population annually.
- The nation's Hispanic and Asian populations would triple over the next half century and non-Hispanic whites would represent about one-half of the total population by 2050.
- Overall, the country's population would continue to grow, increasing from 282.1 million in 2000 to 419.9 million in 2050. However, after 2030 the rate of increase might be the slowest since the Great Depression of the 1930s as the size of the "baby boom" population continues to decline.
- From 2000 to 2050, the non-Hispanic white population would increase from 195.7 million to 210.3 million, an increase of 7%. This group is projected to actually lose population in the 2040s and would comprise just 50.1% of the total population in 2050, compared with 69.4% in 2000.
- The U.S. fertility rate is currently 2.0 births per woman, an increase from 1.8 in 1988.
- Nearly 67 million people of Hispanic origin (who may be of any race) would be added to the nation's population between 2000 and 2050. Their numbers are projected to grow from 35.6 million to 102.6 million, an increase of 188%. Their share of the nation's population would nearly double, from 12.6 percent to 24.4%.
- The Asian population is projected to grow 213%, from 10.7 million to 33.4 million. Their share of the nation's population would double, from 3.8% to 8%.
- The black population is projected to rise from 35.8 million to 61.4 million in 2050, an increase of about 26 million, or 71%, raising their share of the country's population from 12.7% to 14.6%.
- The country's population is expected to become older. By 2030, about one in five people would be 65 or over.
- The female population is projected to continue to outnumber the male population, going from 143.7 million females and 138.4 million males in 2000 to 213.4 million females and 206.5 million males by mid-century.
- Along our coasts, where nearly half the population lives, the U.S. is among the more densely populated countries in the world.
- 46% of the U.S. population lives in coastal regions where ecosystems are the most fragile.
- California, Florida, and Texas account for one-quarter of the U.S. population and were responsible for 38% of all U.S. population growth between 1940 and 1990.

Source: U.S. Census Bureau (2004). From http://www.census.gov/Press-Release/www/releases/archives/ population/ 001720.html and Negative Population
Growth (2004). From Fast Facts About U.S. Population Growth. From http://about.com/.

traditional source of entry-level employees for most organizations, including law enforcement, some are concerned about future staffing.

Recruitment will be affected because older employees seek different job benefits. Training will change because older students learn in different ways than do younger students, and trainers also will need to appreciate the rich and diverse life experiences of older students. These differences will enhance actual job performance, but will complicate training, particularly where the age range in class is large. The process of determining promotions will also feel the affects of changing patterns as incoming cohorts of older students will seek promotion sooner and bring broader experiences to the promotion competition. The ever-increasing amount of technology being applied to law enforcement will demand that recruits be technologically-literate beyond just being able to use cell phones and play computer games.

Discipline, too, will change as a result of aging; it will need to become more a teaching tool and less a punishing tool. Law enforcement is faced with more complex, less clear tasks, along with a candidate pool less able to respond to increased hiring demands. Accordingly, termination and replacement of officers will be less and less desirable as a disciplinary strategy, with the preferred strategy becoming better training and management, with discipline only figuring to the degree it responds to these changes.

Gender and Racial Changes

Other changes in the workforce will involve the influx of many more women and minorities. In the year 2000, women occupied about one-half of the labor force; by 2009, it was 59.2%, according to the Bureau of Labor Statistics (2010). This trend will require workplace redesign. Policies for parental leave, child care, and sexual harassment are only a few of the more obvious changes that will result, especially in traditionally-male occupations such as law enforcement. Although some benefits (e.g., parental leave, flexible hours, and child care) now exist in larger agencies, they will be necessary for smaller agencies in order to recruit and retain quality employees. The way in which teams work will also change. Women tend to exhibit different management styles and are more comfortable with collaborative work approaches (Athanasaw 1997; Shipman and Kay 2009). Because collaboration and participatory management approaches dominate thinking in both public and private management literature and practice, males must learn to adopt these approaches. It is these approaches that will guide management for the next decades. It is significant to note that Problem-Oriented Policing (POP), Community-Oriented Policing (COP), and Restorative Justice all rely upon collaborative decision-making models. In the decade from 1997–2008, the gains in the percentage of women in law enforcement agencies were not substantial overall. Some gains were made at the federal and local levels of government and in the larger agencies, but the number of women in policing is only about 12% (see **Table 14-3**) (Reaves 2010 and Langton 2010).

In the year 2000, minorities made up nearly 25% of the national labor force. This will continue in future decades with more diverse cultures (including Asian, Hispanic, Middle Eastern, Caribbean, African, Native American, and African-American) entering traditional homogeneous workforces. Again, these changes will force some alterations in recruitment, training, and promotion strategies and policies. Interestingly, the percentage of minorities in sworn law enforcement positions at the local level increased from 14.6 % in 1987 to 25.3% in 2007 (Reaves 2010:14).

TABLE 14-3 Percent and Number of Female Sworn Officers, 1987–2008*

	% in 1987	% in 1998	% in 2007	% in 2008	2007 / 2008 Total Number (est.)
Federal agencies		14%		15.2%	18,200
State agencies	3.8%		6.5%		4,000
Sheriff's Offices	12.5%		11.2%		19,400
Local agencies	7.6%		12%		55,300

* Some comparisons are 1987–2007, some are 1998–2008.

Source: Data from: Langton (2010:1)

Educational Changes

Educational differences will continue to affect planning at all levels in law enforcement. Some of these problems arise from apparent contradictions in the landscape of education in the United States. By 2009, 87% of adults age 25 and over had completed at least high school, an all-time high according to the U.S. Census Bureau. Another all-time record, by 2009, about 30% of adults age 25 and over had at least a bachelor's degree (U.S. Census Bureau 2011, 149). Freshman enrollment in college in 2008 was the highest in 40 years, with minority enrollments making up three-fourths of the increase. Much of the college enrollment gains reflect the nation's rapidly changing demographics, "in which 43% of all students in K–12 are now minority. But the recession, too, is adding to the increases as more high school graduates—primarily Hispanics—enroll immediately in college rather than take their chances in the labor force" (Yen 2010).

Given changes in the labor force and in the public clientele of law enforcement agencies, agencies will be under increased pressure to address training and educational needs of employees. The increasing complexity of crime (cybercrime, cross-jurisdictional, transnational), and the emerging technological demands on law enforcement personnel to learn new skill sets (crime analysis and computer mapping), coupled with the changing enforcement approaches (COP, POP) and competition with private industry for the same labor pool, will combine to force law enforcement to address the training and education issues directly. In other words, they will have to begin including the provision of education (as distinguished from training) in hiring decisions. In fact, many departments are adopting higher educational requirements as a hiring criterion. While this number has steadily increased, education does not necessarily solve all department problems (Dantzker 1998).

Disasters and Civil Unrest

Law enforcement must also concern itself with natural disasters and the increasing lethality of social unrest. In the case of natural disasters, the nation has seen several consecutive years of wildfires, floods, tornadoes, hurricanes, and earthquakes, which destroyed wide areas of territory and disrupted normal public service. The year 2004 witnessed very diverse weather patterns throughout the United States, with some sections experiencing tornadoes, others suffering floods (including washed-out bridges), while still others had draughts; also, the state of Florida experienced an unprecedented four hurricanes that year! In the years 2009 and 2010, similar weather-related incidents occurred. Heavy snowfalls in both years crippled major cities and interrupted airline, train, and bus traffic; severe flooding caused evacuations in Massachusetts during the spring and again at the Christmas holiday season in 2010.

There are a wide range of matters that concern law enforcement in such emergencies, and a number of agencies must coordinate their emergency response. Fire services, emergency medical services (EMS), the state and federal Environmental Protection Agencies (EPA), search and rescue organizations, law enforcement agencies, National Guard units, corrections agencies, Departments of Transportation, and the Federal Emergency Management Agency (FEMA) are all likely to be involved in any major disaster. The coordination of these agencies is critical to success. Coordination requires predefined guidelines and protocols to which each agency agrees; in addition, it requires practice and training in the implementation of emergency protocols. Such disasters also impact public safety personnel's personal lives. As

agencies now prepare for coordinated efforts to respond to a terrorist threat or attack, the realization is that it is more likely that such plans would be put into operation for a natural disaster.

Natural disasters, however, may not be the most likely form of disaster, but rather only the most singularly damaging. Disasters that are the result of human actions are far more likely to cause industrial damage, for example. We can include in this list large vehicle accidents (train derailments and freeway chain reaction pile-ups, for example), plane crashes, toxic chemical spills, riots, bombings, arsons, and major gas leaks. Each of these represents a unique challenge to law enforcement, and, again, a unique set of predefined response models. However, it is important to remember that contingency plans or standard operating procedures must be flexible enough to adapt to different conditions. Moreover, plans and procedures must be practiced and reviewed on a regular basis in order to ensure currency. The purpose of disaster drills is to be able to coordinate actions of all agencies into an effective response.

Medical Issues

Until recently, law enforcement officers needed to concern themselves only with emergency aid to accident victims or getting those in custody to medical facilities if treatment was needed. Now, their environment is more complicated. In December 2010, Congress passed (and the President signed), the 9-11 Health Care Bill that provides medical coverage and compensation for first responders, workers, and others who got sick from inhaling toxic dust/materials at Ground Zero. This raises future issues that are related to other types of events. What if a weapon of mass destruction (WMD) is experienced somewhere in the United States; does this set the precedent for providing health care for everyone injured or who responds to the site and gets sick? The future holds all kinds of questions.

Medical issues have arisen in other areas too, of course. Officers need to understand the fragile nature of evidence that requires forensic work. An error in the O.J. Simpson case arose when investigating officers carried a vial of Simpson's blood around Los Angeles for an entire day, exposing it to heat and light, rather than taking it quickly to the crime lab. Preserving evidence in a crime

Flooding in New Orleans after Hurricane Katrina

Source: Courtesy of Petty Officer 2nd Class Kyle Niemi/U.S. Coast Guard. Photo courtesy of U.S. Army

scene where victim assistance is required poses additional problems. While victim treatment is essential, care must be taken not to damage evidence. In some cases, there is a great need to deal directly with emergency personnel, and the medical community in general. In rape or driving while intoxicated cases, to name only two, officers must frequently deal directly with medical facility staff. Training is necessary in order to understand the needs and interests of the medical community.

Obviously, one of the largest problems is the threat of AIDS transmission. AIDS (Auto Immune Deficiency Syndrome) is a complex disease but, essentially, it is a disease that destroys the body's ability to resist other diseases common to mankind. It is transmitted by bodily fluids, generally those such as blood or sexual fluids, and so accidental exposure to blood or tissue is a major concern for law enforcement. Officers may make contact with either in the process of arresting a suspect or assisting a victim.

It is just this sort of risk that caused the Occupational Safety and Health Administration (OSHA) to issue its guidelines for potentially infectious materials (Occupational Safety and Health Administration 2011). These guidelines are applicable to all employers, including law enforcement agencies. They cover all **blood-borne pathogens**, or pathogenic microorganisms, present in human blood. This includes not only AIDS-causing HIV (human immunodeficiency virus), but also hepatitis B virus (HBV), a pernicious and highly infectious blood disease. (A newer strain, hepatitis C, is now becoming a health and safety issue as well.) There are several serious illnesses, in fact, that can be contracted by contact with contaminated blood (U.S. Code of Federal Regulations, 29 CFR 1910.1030). The Code of Federal Regulations details the diseases covered and the precautions necessary. It is incumbent on every agency to fulfill its mission to train law enforcement officers in the appropriate protective techniques to avoid exposure to blood and to maintain and periodically update policies related to blood-borne pathogens.

AIDS and HBV are not the only medical problems looming, however. Law enforcement must also concern itself with the possible exposure to a far more problematic disease. Tuberculosis (TB) is a disease that attacks all body tissue, but the primary focus is the lungs. It is generally spread by sputum in either airborne droplets (from people spitting or sneezing) or on the ground. This disease was once thought to be conquered, but recently a new strain of the bacteria that causes TB has emerged that is immune to the drugs previously used to kill the bacteria. There is no known cure for this current strain. Law enforcement will also need to concern itself with the problem of managing holding facilities and jails in ways that do not expose those in custody to disease. As smoking in the workplace became an issue, we would expect that similar issues will become relevant to the domain of law enforcement, not only for employees, but also for those in custody.

Neighborhood Decay and Gangs

Another set of related social issues deals with the continuing decay of cities and the surrounding social fabric. Long before James Q. Wilson adopted the metaphor of "broken windows" to address the relationship between structural neglect and crime, social scientists noticed that

as inhabited areas fell into general disrepair, crime and violence followed. There is no need here to detail why this theory is reasonably correct, as it was discussed in detail in Chapter 10. The important questions deal with what this means for law enforcement.

In many ways, the overall condition of a neighborhood is related to both general criminal activity and gang activity. Indeed, addressing the issue of improving the way a neighborhood looks is central to combating gangs and crime (California Department of Justice 1993). The importance to law enforcement is obvious: Officers must take a broader view of social conditions. Instead of merely responding to a criminal event, officers must also survey the neighborhood. If there is uncollected garbage, for example, they should call the appropriate authorities. In Marysville, California, officers used a public park clean-up as a "jump start" for reviving an entire neighborhood, rescuing it from drug dealing and prostitution. By organizing citizen groups and inviting businesses to donate materials, the park was revitalized and used as a focal point to attack other criminal activity in the neighborhood. In three years, the turnaround was clear.

Neighborhood deterioration may seem like someone else's problem, but it becomes a law enforcement problem if left unchecked. If an officer sees broken windows in a home that seems inhabited, inquiry should be made as to why they are not fixed. Maybe it is an elderly person too afraid to call for assistance, or someone with a landlord who refuses to act. In the first case, officers can call city councils or service clubs for assistance, and in the second case, officers can do something directly. Someone will take action and help preserve the neighborhood if the problem is brought to the attention of appropriate agencies and pursued to resolution. If the department is fortunate enough to have community service officers, then this information should be reported to them. Follow-up should always be done.

Gangs and other outward evidence of decay cannot be addressed merely by dealing directly with those effects. The underlying conditions that give rise to such activity must be the primary focus. Because the interior regions of most cities are old and getting older, and because there are fewer and fewer government dollars for assistance in such projects, law enforcement officers should expect conditions to continue to get worse. Patrol and supervision officers can be the eyes and ears of the community as well as the department, and they can coordinate a response.

MS-13 gang members

Source: © Luis Galdamez/Landov

Gangs are an ongoing problem in the United States for many cities and counties. According to the 2009 National Youth Gang Survey, 32.4% of all cities, suburban areas, towns, and rural counties experienced gang problems in 2008 (Egley, Howell and Moore 2010:1). The Survey also found, as expected, wide discrepancies between the size of jurisdictions and reported gang problems (see **Table 14-4**)

Most indications from the National Gang Survey were that gang activity would continue to be a problem in the near future, though it must be noted that there is little agreement in either academia or in law enforcement regarding a definition for gang activity. Research suggests that gang members are no more likely to engage in drug trafficking than non-gang members, but they are more likely to engage in violence (Decker and Van Winkle 1994; Esbensen and Huizinga 1993; Klein, Maxson, and Cunningham 1991). In the 2008 National Gang Survey, it was reported that

Among respondents who reported gang activity in 2008, 44% reported an increase in gang-related aggravated assaults, 41% reported an increase

TABLE 14-4 Percentage of Law Enforcement Agencies Reporting Gang Problems, 2002–2007

	Gang Problems Reported in 2007	Gang Problems Ever Reported, 2002–2007
Larger Cities	85.7%	91.8%
Suburban Counties	50.3	65.9
Smaller Cities	34.8	52.5
Rural Counties	15.3	31.2

Source: Reprinted from National Youth Gang Center (2009). National Youth Gang Survey Analysis. http://www.nationalgang-center.gov/Survey-Analysis

in drug sales, and 41% reported an increase in firearms use compared with the previous year. Nearly one in five agencies in larger cities reported an increase in gang-related homicides in 2008. Additionally, among cities with populations of more than 250,000, the reported number of gang-related homicides increased by 10% from 2002 to 2008. Among agencies reporting a gang problem in 2008, 45% characterized their gang problem as "getting worse" (Egley, Howell and Moore 2010:2).

Another source of gang-related research is the National Gang Threat Summary, produced by the National Gang Intelligence Center. Key findings from the 2009 assessment were reported in Chapter 10; of concern here is the trend for the future, and it does not appear promising. As more gang members are prosecuted and imprisoned, the problem does not necessarily improve because of the network of prison gangs at all jurisdictional levels:

Prison gangs often control drug distribution within correctional facilities and heavily influence street-level distribution in some communities. Prison gangs exert considerable control over midlevel and retail-level drug distribution in the Southwest Region and in southern California. Their trafficking activities are facilitated through their connections to Mexican DTOs [drug trafficking organizations], which ensure access to a continuous supply of illicit drugs that are distributed through their networks in prison or are supplied to affiliated street gangs.

Local- or state-level prison gangs, particularly those operating along the U.S.–Mexico border, pose a serious concern to local law enforcement officials. Some local prison gangs along the U.S.–Mexico border maintain longstanding ties to Mexican DTOs. Local prison gangs typically operate within the department of corrections in a single state. As members are released from prison, they often settle in local communities in which they recruit and associate with local street gang members and conduct criminal activities on behalf of the prison gang. (National Gang Intelligence Center 2010:7–8).

LEGAL ISSUES

Any attempt at projecting the future is difficult business. But, much is known about the development of law and legal systems, especially in the United States. Accordingly, we can make some observations and forecasts concerning future legal restrictions that are likely to impact law enforcement.

Interrogation

One thing we should not expect to see is a fundamental change in the limits regarding interrogation. The current Supreme Court is not likely to broadly alter the current law regarding interrogation. There is little consensus by the court at the present time, and it takes consensus to create major policy shifts in the Supreme Court. Nor are they likely to reverse themselves, since the court has done this only 150 times in more than 200 years (and these reversals related to many issues besides criminal justice procedure). The next several years will probably see some new appointments to the Supreme Court because of the ages, length of service, and health of current members. That fact, too, reduces the likelihood of any major reversals in criminal interrogation guidelines.

Still, the emergence of new means of interrogation might prove very challenging to the court. For example, as computer technology becomes more powerful and easier to use, three-dimensional animation programs with integrated sound offer interesting possibilities. Law enforcement investigators could program a scenario involving their depiction of events with the face of the suspect in the scenario depicting his or her role in the crime. A fully animated depiction of how the defendant acted, and then played for the defendant, would be a powerful tool to break a refusal to confess. Is this interrogation? Is it denial of counsel?

Other problems will arise as the population becomes more diverse. Multiple language demands have already complicated interrogation of suspects and witness interviewing. Even rendering Miranda warnings will be difficult. The problems will spread to areas of the United States not yet broadly impacted, and law enforcement will need to respond with sensitivity, training, and inter-agency agreements to share language resources. Interactive, real-time language interpretation technology is progressing significantly and will be part of the solution to this issue.

There is a movement by some to require videotaping of all interrogations of felony suspects to assure that inappropriate coercion or other techniques did not occur and that any statements were knowingly and voluntarily made. Such a requirement would certainly impact law enforcement agencies significantly, but some argue persuasively that it is of little inconvenience and cost when compared to the cost of one's liberty and the price of maintaining trust in the criminal justice process. In 2009, the Indiana Supreme Court mandated a new evidence rule that applied to interrogations beginning January 1, 2011. It "prohibits the use in court of an interview of a felony suspect in police custody at a jail or police station unless video was recorded, from start to finish." Indiana's justices reportedly set rules more stringent than 15 other states that already require recordings of some or all interrogations (Murray 2009). It is expected within the next 3–5 years that most states will enact similar procedures (either through legislative enactments or judicial rules of evidence).

Criminal Law

The same problems are true of the criminal law, though there may be a shift in the policy focus on drugs. As noted elsewhere in this text, as drug arrests and incarcerations increased in the 1980s, incarcerations for violent offenses decreased while violent crime increased. Consequently, budget constraints and the resulting public outcry will likely alter the drug policy that is consuming large amounts of resources in criminal justice generally and law enforcement in particular. We can assume that some major transitions will occur on drug policy with either decriminalization or legalization and regulation replacing the current approach. While the relationship between crime and drugs is both complex and unclear, the mere cost of antidrug operations, to the exclusion of other efforts, will likely force a change in policies.

The trend in U.S. politics for harsher punishment will most likely continue for some time. Trends in attitudes about major public policy issues usually run a generation, and this is no exception. In the near future, demands for harsher punishment most likely will persist, especially for violent offenders. This will continue to push incarceration rates higher and higher, which will create long-term problems not only for corrections departments, but also for law enforcement. The only mitigating factor to alter this trend in past years has been the economic realities that affect local and state resources for jail and prison operations. Where possible, greater use of electronic monitoring is expected for non-violent offenders.

There will be a growing population of ex-cons in the cities. These individuals will have few employment skills to match a rapidly changing environment and will find, in any event, employment opportunities limited. These individuals will become increasingly hardened and networked from institutional contact. Further, absent effective social policy (i.e., reintegration efforts) to address employability problems for ex-cons, they will become a population growing in isolation from mainstream society. This will result in more criminal activity, possibly in organized structures.

New crimes should emerge from the wide variety of methods available to electronically steal both money and information. Criminal laws directed at such activities (cybercrime, identity theft, forged documents, financial fraud, etc.) will be very specific. Obtaining evidence regarding these types of offenses will demand highly-specialized knowledge by officers. This includes the ability to detect and trace remote access to networks and knowledge of operating systems, computer programming, and storage techniques. Data breaches were discussed in Chapter 11, but another problem with such loss of data occurred in a Colorado Sheriff's Office, when a database containing the personal and contact information for approximately 200,000 persons was posted to a computer system accessible to the public. The information related to confidential drug informants, suspects, victims in criminal investigations, employees, concealed carry applicants, and those serving jail sentences (Vijayan 2010).

Theft of money and information by electronic means also poses interesting problems for search and seizure law. Development of probable cause will require significant amounts of data from indirect sources. In order to obtain permission for electronic transmission interception, you will need probable cause. This means relying upon data such as import–export information, local tax information, traffic (both human and vehicular) in and out of the location under suspicion, bank transfers, trap and trace data, and other related items.

Once you have permission for electronic interception, the problem does not end. Electronic transfer is done largely over telephone lines, satellite, and dedicated cable connections. For one thing, interception of data will be made extraordinarily difficult by emerging techniques of **encryption**. Encryption is the coding of data in such a manner that only a person who possesses the code can interpret the transmission. Just as significant is the hardware and software used to intercept this information. Compatibility is essential, yet this is hard to achieve even when you know what the sender is using.

Evidence

There will be very interesting developments in evidence collection, analysis, storage, and preservation in the near future, thanks to technological advances. Officers will be able to obtain immediate confirmation of suspect identification from the scene of arrest via computer terminals (drawn from huge data banks) in their patrol cars equipped with scanning, faxing, and data transmission abilities. Interactive fingerprint scanning will produce instant results because of computer links to state and national networks. Similarly, the ability to enhance any image will dramatically improve investigation. However, the burden on officers to preserve crime scenes will increase as modern, technologically-sophisticated methods capture smaller and smaller bits of evidence. The evolution of DNA testing will similarly place burdens on officers securing a crime scene for protection without contaminating it. Each of these trends will require significant training and educational responses.

Other forms of evidence related to driving under the influence (DUI), including breath tests and blood tests, are the topics of emerging enforcement strategies. At least nine states now utilize "No Refusal" techniques for DUI enforcement. The program quickly allows officers to obtain search warrants for blood samples from suspected impaired drivers who refuse breath tests (see **Figure 14-7**).

Administrative Law and Liability

In the areas of administrative law, we expect the courts to become more and more involved in the day-to-day management of law enforcement agencies. Union issues,

Police administering horizontal gaze nystagmus

Source: © Lisa F. Young/Dreamstime.com

FIGURE 14-7 No Refusal Strategy to DUI Enforcement

The No Refusal program is an enforcement strategy that allows jurisdictions to obtain search warrants for blood samples from suspected impaired drivers who refuse breath tests. Many jurisdictions allow officers to request warrants via phone from on-call judges or magistrates. This enables law enforcement to legally acquire a proper blood sample from drivers who refuse to give a breath sample. During these specified enforcement efforts, prosecutors and judges make themselves available to streamline the warrant acquisition process and help build solid cases that can lead to impaired driving convictions. The No Refusal program should also be highly publicized to let the public know that their chances of being caught, arrested, and convicted increase during these efforts.

The NHTSA Website provides a "toolkit" to implement the program; it has sample press releases, a sample search warrant, and a blood withdrawal form.

Source: Reprinted in part from National Highway Traffic Safety Administration (2010).

---

non-union labor issues, and procedural due process issues all will generate increased numbers of court cases that will test management's approaches to decision making. In those states where public employee unions are permitted, courts and law enforcement agencies will find themselves increasingly embroiled in issues concerning unfair labor practices and contract interpretations. These issues will significantly impact the ability to implement community policing, which requires role redefinition and reassignment. Some community policing and problem-oriented policing strategies may be seen as violating labor agreements or civil service laws.

For those states where unions exist but have no legal status, courts will play an increasing role in personnel decisions. These will include reverse discrimination suits for hiring and promotion and challenges to disciplinary actions on the basis of procedural due process flaws. During 2010, the U.S. House of Representatives passed the Public Safety Employer–Employee Cooperation Act (PSEECA) in July, but the Senate version of the bill did not reach a final vote before adjournment. The legislation would have required collective bargaining for all state and local public safety forces in the United States. Obviously, a very controversial (management rights, states rights, etc.) and potentially costly (to taxpayers) piece of legislation, it will need to be resubmitted in future Congresses since it did not pass in 2010 (Govtrack.us 2010 and Sherk 2010).

The liability exposure of individual officers will continue to grow. Jury damage awards are increasing, although there is some evidence of legislatively establishing punitive limitations (financial caps) on some types of lawsuits. In communities where trust has disintegrated between officers and the people, the number of citizen complaints will continue to grow in number, absent some intervention by the department, and these will lead to more lawsuits. Similarly, there will be an increase in the number of complaints filed by officers against their departments and other officers. While sexual and racial harassment claims will make up a portion of that total, so will other issues relating to employment, including religious accommodation and claims of disabilities (due to stress-related incidents). Finally, officers and their supervisors will come under increasing scrutiny regarding excessive use of force, as was discussed in Chapter 9, and failure to train, supervise, and/or terminate. Some of this scrutiny will come from probes by the U.S. Department of Justice, Civil Rights Division; some will come from local prosecutors and grand juries; and still more will come from citizen boards and commissions. All of these argue for a strategy by law enforcement to meet these challenges, a strategy partially based on improved training and education, basic values of right and wrong in a representative democracy, community involvement, self-criticism, and self-examination. The tasks are daunting, but necessary!

AGENCY MANAGEMENT ISSUES

So, why should line officers who are not of command rank care about future problems that will affect their agency? Change at every level is essential if law enforcement is to implement and accommodate societal expectations. In order for law enforcement to meet the challenges of the next century, every officer must participate in decision-making processes. Every officer also must realize that he or she is a leader. Information gathering is essential in order to meet these challenges. The function of planning in new models of management demands participation from all levels of an organization and COP and POP incorporate collaborative decision-making throughout the department. Therefore, all levels of an organization

must participate in information acquisition and analysis, including line and supervisory personnel.

All personnel must acquire, evaluate, and share information; the key is becoming familiar with processes that are available for information acquisition and processing. Information is power, both personally and organizationally, within an organization. Information permits individuals and organizations to plan and achieve goals.

Officers, supervisors, and administrators must learn to identify a vision of where an organization has been in the past, how it has changed, and trends that seem to be developing. They must determine the preferable future of their organization and develop its personnel to achieve that future state.

LOCAL LAW ENFORCEMENT TRENDS AND PREFERABLE FUTURES

Knowledgeable and insightful managers, supervisors, and officers can use information more effectively by seeking answers to problems that confront their organization. One very useful and powerful way to encourage effective interaction and information sharing is to utilize futures research or strategic visioning techniques. One such method, called the **Nominal Group Technique (NGT)**, was developed in 1968 by Andre Delbecq (Delbecq and Van de Ven 1975; Moore 1987). It is a group process for using and sharing information, developing consensus on problems, and selecting solutions. Groups can employ this technique to make formal decisions or to merely share information informally with fellow officers. **Figure 14-8** identifies the list of 10 trends that resulted from an NGT project made up of 26 individuals (a combination of students, faculty, city officials, and police practitioners) in 1996 (even though the list is over 15 years old, it is still useful today for comparative purposes). As you review the items, think about their current impact on law enforcement activities in the United States. Note that the items listed in Figure 14-8 are the trend issues and there is little, if any, description of what direction the trend item is moving; the important aspect of this exercise was the consensus about *which* trends were important. The group could then continue to discuss the impact of trend directionality and the possible agency strategies to address those trends. This can and should be done at the local agency level.

FIGURE 14-8 Top 10 Results to the Question: "Name the Trends Affecting Law Enforcement Executives in the Next Ten Years"

Trend 1 Level of Cultural Diversity
The change in the total diversity of the community. Includes all types such as ethnicity, sexual orientation, age, and gender.

Trend 2 Change in Available Resources
Level of funding will be a question. Local, regional, and global economic trends and their effects in law enforcement.

Trend 3 Level of Economic Disparity Between Classes
Collapse of society. Rich become richer and the poor become poorer. Demands of police executive to police both divisions of the community when one can pay for services and the other cannot.

Trend 4 Court Interference with Management Decision Making
Level of influence courts and judicial system will have on the police executive. How legal will every decision need to be?

Trend 5 Change in Societal Values
Back to the values of the past. The quality of life will become more important. Morals and ethics will play a critical role.

Trend 6 Broader Leadership Responsibilities
Role as a community leader. Consolidation of services under one director. The degree of regionalization.

Trend 7 Technology Changing
Understanding and staying on the edge of technology. Finding the necessary funding.

Trend 8 Level of Public Expectations of Police Accountability
Expectation of perfection. New system of board of review, level of community involvement, and amount of hands-on by city officials.

Trend 9 Level of Ability to Communicate Effectively
Qualification level of police executive candidates.

Trend 10 Level of Public Confidence in Law Enforcement
Public's trust and confidence in law enforcement officers to do the job.

Source: Gurrela, Ruban (January 1996), California POST Command College Futures Study, Class 21.

Another approach to obtaining insight and to sharing information is called the **Delphi Technique**. Delphi is a method of soliciting and aggregating individual opinions or judgments, typically of a group of experts, to arrive at consensus views concerning such things as what may happen in the future. It can be utilized to survey the professional opinions of knowledgeable individuals or experts and usually begins with a set of questions asked in round one, with ratings or rankings of agreement used in subsequent rounds. This technique has methodological variations and can be utilized when participants are geographically distant from one another. One example, using a modified Delphi technique, identified major issues and strategies for developing more effective law enforcement (Conser et al. 2004). The questions focused primarily on the next decade and were developed and worded by a panel of individuals who were members of the Society of Police Futurists International. The items focused on various aspects of policing, but were not mutually exclusive. It was expected that some responses would overlap and some issues would be perceived as related to more than one item. The questions asked addressed (1) the mission of policing in the future, (2) providing a high quality of service to the public, (3) change in the police to meet the future challenges, (4) pressure group effects on policing, (5) professionalism, (6) ethical issues of the future, and (7) the impact of technology on policing. The responses to the questions were recorded and categorized, with similar responses being combined. Lists of statements were then compiled and submitted to respondents in round two with a request to rank them from highest or lowest value. (Note: the terminology varied according to the item; for example, some items said "most likely," others might state "highest priority," "most significant," "greatest effect," etc.) The statements were then assigned averaged (mean) scores from which further analysis and evaluation occurred. **Figure 14-9** contains the summary findings and the inferred strategies for more effective law enforcement in the future.

FIGURE 14-9 The Major Strategies for More Effective Law Enforcement

1. The Mission Challenge
During the next decade: The demands for services and responsiveness will increase; the definition of "local" will become more blurred; mobility issues and technological crime will create "jurisdictional" problems. Particular to the short term will be the need to reduce fear of crime, terrorism, and religious fanaticism (homeland security issues). There will be personnel and resource shortages.
Strategy: Increase cooperation and interoperability between agencies (possibly mergers and regionalization of operations); and improve information analysis, surveillance, and intelligence gathering at all levels of government.

2. What Must Be Done To Ensure Public Safety/Quality Service?
The police must: Improve social competence; become managerially proactive; improve technological competence; and become more dedicated to upholding constitutional rights and liberties while working with citizens to improve safety and make communities more peaceful.
　　Social Competence: Developing trust between community members and the police, realistic expectations through better communications with the public, more community oriented, represent the community.
　　Managerially proactive: Developing futures orientation; becoming more knowledgeable about the future of policing and preparing organizations for the future; being more adaptable and proactive; becoming learning organizations; more innovative; more decentralized.
　　Technological Competence: Understanding and applying technological advances, responding to technology-related crime, more proficient at database analysis, telecommunication systems, etc, to improve productivity and responsiveness.
Strategy: Move from the traditional paradigm to one of leadership, proactiveness, and community service.

3. Things that must Change
The current police culture must change: Become more adaptable to change, less resistive, less reactive, more cooperative, less pseudo-militaristic to professional service-orientation; overcome generational differences, less competitive. Employ better caliber of officer: better educated, able to think outside the box, better interpersonal skills, higher integrity, positive attitude toward problem solving, less technophobic, less xenophobic, become service professionals; racist behavior must not be tolerated.
Strategy: Change the police culture from both the top (more insightful administrators) and from the bottom (higher caliber recruits).

4. Pressure Groups' Effect on Policing
Most Significant Groups: Organized community groups; some of whom will form around critical incidents of interest to the community. Elected Officials. Special interest groups (MADD, gun control groups, domestic violence advocates, victim rights advocates, etc.). Neighborhood residents and associations. Government/Federal Agencies/Homeland Security. Police Unions.
Strategy: Recognize the power of the community and energize the leadership response of law enforcement officials.

(continued)

FIGURE 14-9 The Major Strategies for More Effective Law Enforcement (*Continued*)

5. Changes to Improve Professionalism
Current police culture must change: It restricts attracting and retaining the right people in adequate numbers; it alienates cops from the people they serve; that culture must also accept "non-traditional" candidate profiles into the ranks. Greater adherence to the constitution/principles of government/rights/liberties and greater adulation and reward for behavior supportive of public service crime prevention, and protection. Police work must be viewed as a public service. Officers need to be more personable. Higher educational standards for entry; pay and benefit package comparable to teachers in public schools are recommended.
Strategy: Greater investment in selection and training techniques and standards.

6. Most Likely Ethical Problems Facing Officers
Predominant Problems: Protecting constitutional liberties in light of powerful technologies to fight crime and thwart terrorists. Primary priority must not be "law enforcement." Immature behavior, conduct unbecoming, unprofessional demeanor. Breaking the "code of silence" or "veil of silence" of the "blue brotherhood" (or other similar labels); increased pressures on officers to report wrongdoing by other officers.
Strategy: Establish accountability mechanisms / licensing and certification revocations.

7. Technological Impacts on Policing.
Technology Challenges: Both veteran and new officers must be technologically savvy and embrace new approaches to policing. All the tools of the trade will change in the next decade and beyond: video and audio communications, weapons, investigations, forensics, vehicles, and so on will be different, improved, and more effective. Identity theft and fraud. Surveillance technology and recording and transmissions (including the use of UAV's, micro-robots and micro-cameras). Computer-related crime calls (particularly fraud and child enticement, child pornography; travelers, and harassment; eventually more commercial fraud; embezzlement calls requiring knowledge of computers.)
Strategy: Invest in and require technological competence of officers and the information technologies necessary for policing the modern world; convince funding sources and the private sector to partner in providing the technological tools necessary for public safety.

Source: Based on a survey of selected members of the Society of Police Futurists International, 2004; Conser, James A. et al, (2004), "Strategies for More Effective Law Enforcement in the Future," panel presentation, World Future Society Conference, August 1.

There are a number of tremendous challenges contained in the items identified in Figures 14-8 and 14-9. These need to be considered by every law enforcement executive and leader. There are some serious problems affecting the field as a whole today, and if the future is to be manageable, they must be addressed soon. Students considering a career in law enforcement must learn to appreciate these many debates and controversies. Remember the adage: "You can be part of the solution or you can be part of the problem."

SUMMARY

This chapter addressed many of the challenges facing the future of law enforcement. Issues that are global or international in scope—such as terrorism, genocide, immigration, and civil strive—may appear unrelated to local policing, but they are not. National problems such as racism, diversity, changing employment trends, gangs, illegal immigration, and hate groups may be visible daily but are difficult to deal with at the local level. It is much easier to recognize the impact or a consequence of these forces than it is to know how to change or prevent them. Additionally, social forces are always changing.

Your role in preparing for a career in law enforcement is to be alert to the social, political, environmental, and technological changes and challenges of the future. You must be aware that there are other issues and forces we have not addressed here. All of these factors will impact the profession of law enforcement in profound ways. You are the future employees who will address these issues!

Critical Thinking Questions

1. Why attempt to envision the future of law enforcement—either short term or long term?

2. Why should trends and incidents in foreign countries be of interest or concern to U.S. law enforcement agencies?

3. What are the changing demographic trends affecting policing and what positive or negative effects can be envisioned?

4. What economic, technological, and political changes do you envision for the United States during your lifetime?

5. Review Figure 14-8. It is the result of an exercise 15 years ago. Are the findings (results and issues) still relevant today? Describe any issues or items that you believe should be added to or deleted from the listing.

CHAPTER SPECIFIC INTERNET LINKS

FutureStates (video scenarios): http://futurestates.tv/

Hate Crime Statistics: http://www.fbi.gov/about-us/cjis/ucr/ucr

Interactive Demographic Maps: http://www.socialexplorer.com/pub/maps/home.aspx

Language Translators: http://www.miltrans.com/1stResponders.html and http://www.ojp.usdoj.gov/nij/journals/252/voice_response_print.html

Locate a Port of Entry: http://www.cbp.gov/xp/cgov/toolbox/ports/

National Debt Clock: http://www.usdebtclock.org/

School Safety and Security: http://www.schoolsecurity.org/index.html and http://nces.ed.gov/programs/crimeindicators/crimeindicators2010/ind_01.asp

Society of Police Futurists International: http://www.policefuturists.org

Southern Poverty Law Center's Hate Map: http://www.splcenter.org/intel/map/hate.jsp

Terrorism reports issued since 1979: http://www.gao.gov/docsearch/featured/terrorism.html

U.S. Census Bureau: http://www.census.gov/

World Futures Society: http://www.wfs.org

Worldwide Incidents Tracking System: https://wits.nctc.gov/FederalDiscoverWITS/index.do?N=0

Worst Killers Website: http://www.worst-killers.com/index.htm

CHAPTER GLOSSARY

Baby boom generation—those born between 1946 and 1964; the largest generation in American history.

Blood-borne pathogens—microorganisms that can cause disease that present in human blood.

Delphi Technique—a method of soliciting and aggregating individual opinions or judgments, typically of a group of experts, to arrive at consensus views concerning such things as what may happen in the future.

Encryption—the coding of data in such a manner that only a person who possesses the code can interpret the transmission.

Foresight—the ability to think and envision what may happen in the future.

Generation X—those born between 1965 and 1980; a much smaller generation than the prior one (baby boomers).

Generation Y—also called **Millennials** or Echo Boomers; those born between 1981 and 2000 and include most who are now entering the labor pool.

Hate crime—defined generally as an offense committed against persons, property, or society that is motivated, in whole or in part, by an offender's bias or anger against an individual's or a group's immutable characteristics (e.g., race, religion, ethnic/national origin, gender, age, disability, or sexual orientation).

Local militias—military-type groups of civilians organized locally for the protection of their civil and constitutional rights; usually heavily armed and may practice defensive military maneuvers.

Mass murder—generally defined as the killing of four or more persons in a single incident, usually at the same location or as a part of an on-going incident.

North American Free Trade Agreement (NAFTA)—a pact to reduce the restrictions or tariffs on trade among the countries of Mexico, Canada, and the United States.

Nominal Group Technique (NGT)—a group decision-making approach used to identify multiple problems and multiple solutions.

Penalty enhancement—an increase in the standard criminal penalties when crimes target members of specified groups; the penalties are enhanced either through assigning a higher sentencing range for bias-motivated crimes or by increasing the level of the offense to a more serious category of crime.

Reduction in force (RIF)—permanent layoffs.

Serial killing—generally defined as the killing of three or more persons on different occasions; usually separated by a period of time to distinguish that it is not an on-going incident.

CHAPTER REFERENCES AND ADDITIONAL READINGS

Associated Press (December 16, 2010). More Than 30,000 Killed in Mexico's Drug Violence. http://www.foxnews.com/world/2010/12/16/killed-mexicos-drug-violence/

Associated Press (December 20, 2010). LA Police ID 29 Women in Grim Sleeper Case Photos. wtop.com. http://www.wtop.com/?nid=104&sid=2202907

Athanasaw, Danny L., (1997) An examination of leadership styles as perceived by senior executives in the federal government, Doctoral dissertation, Nova Southeastern University.

Bayley, David H. (1986). The tactical choices of police patrol officers. *Journal of Criminal Justice* 14:329–348.

BBC News (2009). Timeline: Fort Hood shootings. http://news.bbc.co.uk/2/hi/americas/8346315.stm

Blaine, Liz (March 3, 2010). Southern Poverty Law Center Tries To 'Alinsky' The Tea Party Movement. NewsReal Blog. http://www.newsrealblog.com/2010/03/03/southern-poverty-law-center-tries-to-alinsky-the-tea-party-movement/

Bouvier, Leon F. and Lindsey Grant (1994). *How many Americans?* San Francisco: Sierra Club Books.

Bureau of Labor Statistics (2010). Women in the Labor Force: A Databook. Washington, D.C.: U.S. Department of Labor, Report 1026. http://www.bls.gov/cps/wlf-databook-2010.pdf

Burnett, John (November 8, 2010) Drugs Cross Border By Truck, Free Trade And Chance. National Public Radio http://www.npr.org/templates/story/story.php?storyId=131106638

California Department of Justice (1993). *Gangs 2000: A call to action.* Sacramento, CA: California Department of Justice.

Canton v. Harris (1989). U.S. 489:378.

CBSNews.com (2003). Gary Leon Ridgway: Green River killer. http://www.cbsnews.com/elements/2002/08/08/in_depth_us/whoswho518068_0_9_person.shtml.

Cetron, Marvin J. and Owen Davies (1994). The future face of terrorism. *The Futurist,* November–December: 10–16.

Cetron, Marvin J. and Owen Davies (2008a). 55 Trends Now Shaping the Future of Terrorism. *The Proteus Trends Series.*Vol. 1, Issue 2. http://www.carlisle.army.mil/proteus/docs/55-terror.pdf

Cetron, Marvin J. and Owen Davies (2008b). 55 Trends Now Shaping the Future of Policing. *The Proteus Trends Series.* Vol. 1, Issue 1, February. http://www.carlisle.army.mil/proteus/docs/55-policing.pdf.

Coates, Joseph F. (2002). What's next? Foreseeable terrorist acts. *The Futurist*, September–October:23–26.

Coates, Joseph F. (2004). *Were I Bin Laden.* Based on a presentation at a March 21, 2002, symposium, Analysis...Where Do We Go From Here? The Institute for Operations Research and the Management Sciences, The Washington Academy of Sciences, and the Washington, D.C. Chapter of The World Future Society, Commentary found at http://www.josephcoates.com/commentary1.html. World Future Society Web site, http://www.wfs.org/jcoates.htm.

Conser, James A., Alan Beckley, Tyree C. Blocker, Andreas Olligschlaeger, Jenny Gomery, and Shelby Williams (2004). Strategies for more effective law enforcement in the future. Panel presentation, World Future Society Conference, Washington, D.C., August 1.

Cornish, Edward (1990). Issues of the nineties. *The Futurist*, January–February:29–36.

Cornish, Edward (2010). Foresight Conquers Fear of the Future. *The Futurist,* January-February:50–51.

Corsi, Jerome (December 27, 2010). Border Wars Turn Violent in Arizona http://www.thecypresstimes.com/article/News/National_News/BORDER_WARS_TURN_VIOLENT_IN_ARIZONA/38040

Dantzker, M.L. (1998). Police education and job satisfaction: Educational incentives and recruit educational requirements. *Police Forum.* 8(3):1–4.

Day, J.C. (1996). Population projections of the United States by age, sex, race, and Hispanic origin: 1995–2050. U.S. Bureau of Census, Current Population Reports, P25-1130, p.13, Washington, D.C.: U.S. Government Printing Office.

Decker, Scott and Barrick Van Winkle (1994). Slinging dope: The role of gangs and gang members in drug sales. *Justice Quarterly.* 11(4):583–604.

Delbecq, A.L., A.H. Van de Ven, and D.H. Gustafson (1975). *Group Techniques for Program Planning: A Guide to Nominal Group and Delphi Processes.* Glenview, IL: Scott Foresman.

Egley, Arlen, Jr., and Aline K. Major (2004). Highlights of the 2002 National Youth Gang Survey. Fact Sheet. Washington D.C.: U.S. Department of Justice.

Egley, Jr., Arlen, James C. Howell, and John P. Moore (2010). Highlights of the 2008 National Youth Gang Survey. Washington, D.C.: U.S. Department of Justice, Office of Justice Programs. http://www.ncjrs.gov/pdffiles1/ojjdp/229249.pdf.

Esbensen, Finn-Aage and David Huizinga (1993). Gangs, drugs, and delinquency in a survey of urban youth. *Criminology.* 31(4): 565–86.

FBI (October 22, 2007). A Byte Out of History, The Beltway Snipers, Part 1. http://www.fbi.gov/news/stories/2007/october/snipers_102207.

FBI (October 24, 2007). A Byte Out of History, The Beltway Snipers, Part 2. http://www.fbi.gov/news/stories/2007/october/snipers_102407.

Federal Bureau of Investigation (2003). Crime in the United States. http://www.fbi.gov/ucr/03cius.htm.

Federal Bureau of Investigation (2007a). A Byte Out of History, The Beltway Snipers, Part 1. http://www.fbi.gov/news/stories/2007/october/snipers_102207.

Federal Bureau of Investigation (2007b). A Byte Out of History, The Beltway Snipers, Part 2. http://www.fbi.gov/news/stories/2007/october/snipers_102407.

Federal Bureau of Investigation (2010). Latest Hate Crime Statistics: Reported Incidents, Number of Victims Decrease. http://www.fbi.gov/news/stories/2010/november/hate_112210/hate_112210.

Finklea, Kristin M. (2010). Organized Crime in the United States: Trends and Issues for Congress. Washington, D.C.: Congressional Research Service.http://www.fas.org/sgp/crs/misc/R40525.pdf.

Finnie, Toby, Tom Petee, and John Jarvis (eds.) (2010). The Future Challenges of Cybercrime: *Proceedings of the Futures Working Group.* Federal Bureau of Investigation: Quantico, Virginia.

Ford, C. Benjamin (November 11, 2009). Beltway sniper executed on Tuesday evening. FairfaxTimes.com. http://www.fairfaxtimes.com/cms/story.php?id=587.

Ford, C. Benjamin (November 11, 2009). Beltway sniper executed on Tuesday evening. http://www.fairfaxtimes.com/cms/story.php?id=587.

Glasscock, Bruce D. (July 13, 1999). Glasscock Testimony on Decriminalization of Illegal Drugs. http://www.theiacp.org/PublicationsGuides/ResearchCenter/NationalPolicySummits/CMSDetail/tabid/398/Default.aspx?id=48.

Gore, Albert, Jr. (1990). The Critical Trends Assessment Act: Futurizing the United States government. *The Futurist*, March:22–24.

Govtrack.us (2010). Public Safety Employer-Employee Cooperation Act of 2010. S. 3991 http://www.govtrack.us/congress/billtext.xpd?bill=s111-3991.

Gurrela, Ruban (1996). California POST command college futures study. *Class 21,* January.

Hammill, Greg (2005). Mixing and Managing Four Generations of Employees. *FDU Magazine Online.* http://www.fdu.edu/newspubs/magazine/05ws/generations.htm.

Hunt, Raymond G. and John M. Magenau (1993). *Power and the Police Chief.* Newbury Park, CA: Sage Publications Inc.

Immigration and Customs Enforcement (December 14, 2009a). $26 million in counterfeits seized. News Releases, Washington, D.C. http://www.ice.gov/news/releases/0912/091214washingtondc.htm.

Immigration and Customs Enforcement (December 03, 2009b). 2 New Jersey and California businessmen plead guilty to an illegal export scheme. News Releases, Laredo, TX http://www.ice.gov/news/releases/0912/091203laredo.htm.

Immigration and Customs Enforcement (2010). Laredo couple charged with conspiring to smuggle goods to Mexico. News Releases, Laredo, TX http://www.ice.gov/news/releases/1004/100407laredo.htm.

Jamieson, D. and J. O'Mara (1991). *Managing workforce 2000: Gaining the diversity advantage.* San Francisco: Jossey-Bass Publishers.

Jensen, Carl J. and Bernard H. Levin (2007). The World of 2020: Demographic Shifts, Cultural Change, and Social Challenge. In Shafer, Joseph A. (ed.). *Policing 2020: Exploring the Future of Crime, Communities, and Policing,* FBI/PFI Futures Working Group.

Kammer, Jerry (2010). Immigration and the SPLC: How the Southern Poverty Law Center Invented a Smear, Served La Raza, Manipulated the Press, and Duped its Donors. Center for Immigration Studies. March http://www.cis.org/immigration-splc.

Kelotra, Ritu (2004). New FBI data reports increase in hate crimes for 2003. http://www.civilrights.org/hatecrimes/fbi/new-fbi-data-reports-increase-in-hate-crimes-for-2003.html.

Klein, Malcom W., Cheryl L. Maxson, and Lea C. Cunningham (1991). Crack, street gangs, and violence. *Criminology.* 29(4):623–650.

Konkler, Gerald (2010).Partnering with others to Address Cybercrime, In Finnie, Toby, Tom Petee, and John Jarvis (eds.). The Future Challenges of Cybercrime: Volume 5. *Proceedings of the Futures Working Group.* Federal Bureau of Investigation: Quantico, Virginia.

Langton, Lynn (June 2010). *Women in Law Enforcement, 1987–2008.* Washington, D.C.: U.S. Department of Justice, Bureau of Justice Statistics, NCJ 230521.

Marczak, Jason (November 3, 2010). 2010 Elections: Implications for Immigration Reform. http://www.americasquarterly.org/node/1975.

Martin, Philip and Elizabeth Midgley (2010). Population Bulletin Update: Immigration in America 2010. *Population Reference Bureau.* http://www.prb.org/pdf10/immigration-update2010.pdf.

Meade, Eric (2010). Scanning the Future of Law Enforcement: A Trend Analysis. *The Futurist.* July-August:22-25.

Moore, Carl M. (1987). *Group Techniques for Idea Building.* Newbury Park, CA: Sage Publications.

Murray, Jon (2009). State raising the bar on taped interrogations. *Indianapolis Star,* September 23, A.1.

National Commission on Terrorist Attacks Upon the United States (2004). T*he 9/11 Commission report, Authorized edition.* New York: W.W. Norton & Co.

National Gang Intelligence Center (2009). National Gang Threat Assessment 2009. Washington, D.C.: U.S. Department of Justice. 2009-M0335-001 http://www.justice.gov/ndic/pubs32/32146/32146p.pdf.

National Highway Traffic Safety Administration (2010). NHTSA No-Refusal Weekend Toolkit. U.S. Department of Transportation. http://www.nhtsa.gov/staticfiles/planners/NoRefusalWeekend/index.htm .

National Youth Gang Center (2009). National Youth Gang Survey Analysis. http://www.nationalgangcenter.gov/Survey-Analysis.

Nunez, Steve (June 16, 2010). Krentz murder report: updated story with complete notes. http://www.kgun9.com/Global/story.asp?S=12656488.

Occupational Safety and Health Administration (2011). OSHA Fact Sheet: OSHA's Bloodborne Pathogens Standard, http://www.osha.gov/OshDoc/data_BloodborneFacts/bbfact01.pdf.

Privacy Rights Clearinghouse (2010). Chronology of Data Breaches, Security Breaches 2005-Present. http://www.privacyrights.org/data-breach#CP.

Reaves, Brian A. (2010). *Local Police Departments, 2007.* Washington, D.C.: U.S. Department of Justice, Bureau of Justice Statistics, NCJ 231174.

Roberts, Paul Craig (July 26, 2010). The Year America Dissolved. http://www.counterpunch.org/roberts07262010.html.

Robers, Simone, Jijun Zhang, Jennifer Truman, and Thomas D. Snyder (2010). *Indicators of School Crime and Safety: 2010.* Washington, D.C.: U.S. Department of Education, U.S. Department of Justice.

Rowlands, David T. (November 1, 2010). Mexico: Drug wars fuelled by free trade. Green Left Weekly. http://www.bilaterals.org/spip.php?article18387.

Schafer, Joseph A. (ed.) (2007). *Policing 2020: Exploring the Future of Crime, Communities, and Policing.* FBI/PFI Futures Working Group.

Seattle Times News Service (2003). Olympic bombing suspect captured. *The Seattle Times,* June 1:1, 7.

Sherk, James, (July 2, 2010). Another Taxpayer Handout to Organized Labor. Heritage Foundation. http://www.heritage.org/Research/Commentary/2010/07/Another-taxpayer-handout-to-organized-labor.

Shipman Claire and Katty Kay (2009). Women Will Rule Business. Thursday, May 14, http://www.time.com/time/specials/packages/article/0,28804,1898024_1898023_1898078,00.html #ixzz1T4n8oxL6 .

Stephens, Gene (2010). Cybercrime in the Year 2025. In Finnie, Toby, Tom Petee, and John Jarvis (eds.). The Future Challenges of Cybercrime: Volume 5. *Proceedings of the Futures Working Group.* Federal Bureau of Investigation: Quantico, Virginia 2010.

Stout, Steve (December 15, 2010). Border Agent Killed In Shootout With 'Bandits'. http://www.kpho.com/news/26140726/detail.html

Southern Poverty Law Center (2010). Ideology. http://www.splcenter.org/get-informed/intelligence-files/ideology.

U.S. Census Bureau (2004). U.S. Interim Projections by Age, Sex, Race, and Hispanic Origin. http://www.census.gov/ipc/www/usinterimproj/.

U.S. Census Bureau (2004). http://www.census.gov/Press-Release/www/releases/archives/population/001720.html.

U.S. Code of Federal Regulations, 29 CFR 1910.1030 (1910).

U.S. Department of Justice, Office of Public Affairs (2010). Citing Conflict with Federal Law, Department of Justice Challenges Arizona Immigration Law. http://www.justice.gov/opa/pr/2010/July/10-opa-776.html.

U.S. Department of Homeland Security, Office of Inspector General (2010). Customs and Border Protection's Implementation of the Western Hemisphere Travel Initiative at Land Ports of Entry. http://www.dhs.gov/xoig/assets/mgmtrpts/OIG_11-16_Nov10.pdf.

U.S. Department of Homeland Security (2004). U.S. customs and border protection actions taken since 9.11. Fact sheet. http://www.customs.ustreas.gov/xp/cgov/newsroom/fact_sheets/09172004.xml.

U.S. Department of State (2010). Country Reports on Terrorism 2009. Washington, D.C.

U.S. Department of State, Bureau of Consular Affairs (2011). Worldwide Caution. http://travel.state.gov/travel/cis_pa_tw/pa/pa_4787.html.

U.S. Department of State, Office of the Coordinator for Counterterrorism (2004). *Patterns of global terrorism, Appendix G.* Revised June 22, 2004, http://www.state.gov/s/ct/rls/pgtrpt/2003/33777.htm.

Vijayan, Jaikumar (December 14, 2010). Sheriff's Office mistakenly posts informant, other data online. Computerworld.com http://www.computerworld.com/s/article/9201199/Sheriff_s_Office_mistakenly_posts_informant_other_data_online.

Wilson, James Q. (1983). *Thinking about crime.* New York: Basic Books.

World Future Society (2004). The art of foresight: Preparing for a changing world. A special report. *The Futurist,* May–June: 4–5.

Yen, Hope (June 16, 2010). Jump in US college enrollment highest in 40 years. http://www.boston.com/news/education/higher/articles/2010/06/16/jump_in_us_college_enrollment_highest_in_40_years/.

Zucchino, David (October 14, 2010). Survivors of Ft. Hood shootings testify. http://articles.latimes.com/2010/oct/14/nation/la-na-fort-hood-web-20101014.

Constitution of The United States

WE THE PEOPLE of the United States, in Order to form a more perfect Union, establish Justice, insure domestic Tranquility, provide for the common defence, promote the general Welfare, and secure the Blessings of Liberty to ourselves and our Posterity, do ordain and establish this Constitution for the United States of America.[*]

ARTICLE. I.

SECTION. 1.   All legislative Powers herein granted shall be vested in a Congress of the United States, which shall consist of a Senate and House of Representatives.

SECTION. 2.   [1]The House of Representatives shall be composed of Members chosen every second Year by the People of the several States, and the Electors in each State shall have the Qualifications requisite for Electors of the most numerous Branch of the State Legislature.

[2]No person shall be a Representative who shall not have attained to the Age of twenty five Years, and been seven Years a Citizen of the United States, and who shall not, when elected, be an Inhabitant of that State in which he shall be chosen.

[3][Representatives and direct Taxes shall be apportioned among the several States which may be included within this Union, according to their respective Numbers, which shall be determined by adding to the whole Number of free Persons, including those bound to service for a Term of Years, and excluding Indians not taxed, three fifths of all other Persons].[†]

The actual Enumeration shall be made within three years after the first Meeting of the Congress of the United States, and within every subsequent Term of ten Years, in such Manner as they shall by Law direct. The Number of Representatives shall not exceed one for every thirty Thousand, but each State shall have at Least one Representative; and until such enumeration shall be made, the State of New Hampshire shall be entitled to chuse three, Massachusetts eight, Rhode-Island and Providence Plantations one, Connecticut five, New-York six, New Jersey four, Pennsylvania eight, Delaware one, Maryland six, Virginia ten, North Carolina five, South Carolina five, and Georgia three.

[4]When vacancies happen in the Representation from any State, the Executive Authority thereof shall issue Writs of Election to fill such Vacancies.

---

[*] This text of the Constitution follows the engrossed copy signed by Gen. Washington and the deputies from the 12 states. The superior number preceding the paragraphs designates the number of the clause; it was not in the original.

[†] The part included in heavy brackets was changed by section 2 of the fourteenth amendment.

5The House of Representatives shall chuse their Speaker and other Officers; and shall have the sole Power of Impeachment.

SECTION. 3.   1The Senate of the United States shall be composed of two Senators from each State, [chosen by the Legislature thereof,]‡ for six Years; and each Senator shall have one Vote.

2Immediately after they shall be assembled in Consequence of the first Election, they shall be divided as equally as may be into three Classes. The Seats of the Senators of the first Classes. The Seats of the Senators of the first Class shall be vacated at the Expiration of the second Year, of the second Class at the Expiration of the fourth Year, and of the Third Class at the Expiration of the sixth year, so that one third may be chosen every second Year; [and if Vacancies happen by Resignation, or otherwise, during the Recess of the Legislature of any State, the Executive thereof may make Temporary Appointments until the next Meeting of the Legislature, which shall then fill such Vacancies].§

3No Person shall be a Senator who shall not have attained to the Age of thirty Years, and been nine Years a Citizen of the United States, and who shall not, when elected, be an Inhabitant of that State for which he shall be chosen.

4The Vice President of the United States shall be President of the Senate, but shall have no Vote, unless they be equally divided.

5The Senate shall chuse their other Officers, and also a President pro tempore, in the Absence of the Vice President, or when he shall exercise the Office of President of the United States.

6The Senate shall have the sole Power to try all Impeachments. When sitting for that Purpose, they shall be on Oath or Affirmation. When the President of the United States is tried, the Chief Justice shall preside: And no Person shall be convicted without the Concurrence of two thirds of the Members present.

Judgment in Cases of Impeachment shall not extend further than to removal from Office, and disqualification to hold and enjoy any Office of honor, Trust or Profit under the United States: but the party convicted shall nevertheless be liable and subject to Indictment, Trial, Judgment and Punishment, according to Law.

SECTION. 4.   1The Times, Places and Manner of holding Elections for Senators and Representatives, shall be prescribed in each State by the Legislature thereof; but the Congress may at any time by Law make or alter such Regulations, except as to the Places of chusing Senators.

2The Congress shall assemble at least once in every Year, and such Meeting shall [be on the first Monday in December,]ˤ unless they shall by Law appoint a different Day.

SECTION. 5.   1Each House shall be the Judge of the Elections, Returns and Qualifications of its own Members, and a Majority of each shall constitute a Quorum to do Business; but a smaller Number may adjourn from day to day, and may be authorized to compel the Attendance of absent members, in such Manner, and under such Penalties as each House may provide.

2Each House may determine the Rules of its Proceedings, punish its Members for disorderly Behaviour, and, with the Concurrence of two thirds, expel a Member.

3Each House shall keep a Journal of its Proceedings, and from time to time publish the same, excepting such Parts as may in their Judgement require Secrecy; and the Yeas and Nays of the Members of either House on any questions shall, at the Desire of one fifth of those Present, be entered on the Journal.

4Neither House, during the Session of Congress, shall, without the Consent of the other, adjourn for more than three days, nor to any other Place than that in which the two Houses shall be sitting.

SECTION. 6.   The Senators and Representatives shall receive a Compensation for their Services, to be ascertained by Law, and paid out of the Treasury of the United States. They shall in all Cases, except Treason, Felony and Breach of the Peace, be privileged from Arrest during their Attendance at the Session of their respective Houses,

---

‡ The part included in heavy brackets was changed by section 1 of the seventeenth amendment.

§ The part included in heavy brackets was changed by clause 2 of the seventeenth amendment.

ˤ The part included in heavy brackets was changed by section 2 of the twentieth amendment.

and in going to and returning from the same; and for any Speech or Debate in either House, they shall not be questioned in any other Place.

[2]No Senator or Representative shall, during the Time for which he was elected, be appointed to any civil Office under the Authority of the United States, which shall have been created, or the Emoluments whereof shall have been encreased during such time; and no Person holding any Office under the United States, shall be a Member of either House during his Continuance in Office.

SECTION.7.   [1]All Bills for raising Revenue shall originate in the House of Representatives; but the Senate may propose or concur with Amendments as on other Bills.

[2]Every Bill which shall have passed the House of Representatives and the Senate, shall, before it become a Law, be presented to the President of the United States; If he approve he shall sign it, but if not he shall return it, with his Objections to that House in which it shall have originated, who shall enter the Objections at large on their Journal, and Proceed to reconsider it. If after such Reconsideration two thirds of that House shall agree to pass the Bill, it shall be sent, together with the Objections, to the other House, by which it shall likewise be reconsidered, and if approved by two thirds of that House, it shall become a Law. But in all such Cases the Votes of both Houses shall be determined by yeas and Nays, and the Names of the Persons voting for and against the Bill shall be entered on the Journal of each House respectively. If any Bill shall not be returned by the President within ten Days (Sundays excepted) after it shall have been presented to him, the Same shall be a Law, in like Manner as if he had signed it, unless the Congress by their Adjournment prevent its Return, in which Case it shall not be a Law.

[3]Every Order, Resolution, or Vote to which the Concurrence of the Senate and House of Representatives may be necessary (except on a question of Adjournment) shall be presented to the President of the United States; and before the Same shall take Effect, shall be approved by him, or being disapproved by him, shall be repassed by two thirds of the Senate and House of Representatives, according to the Rules and Limitations prescribed in the Case of a Bill.

SECTION. 8.   [1]The Congress shall have Power To lay and collect Taxes, Duties, Imposts and Excises, to pay the Debts and provide for the common Defence and general Welfare of the United States; but all Duties, Imposts and Excises shall be uniform throughout the United States;

[2]To borrow Money on the credit of the United States;

[3]To regulate Commerce with foreign Nations, and among the several States, and with the Indian Tribes;

[4]To establish an uniform Rule of Naturalization, and uniform Laws on the subject of Bankruptcies throughout the United States;

[5]To coin Money, regulate the Value thereof, and of foreign Coin, and fix the Standard of Weights and Measures;

[6]To provide for the Punishment of counterfeiting the Securities and current Coin of the United States;

[7]To establish Post Offices and post Roads;

[8]To promote the Progress of Science and useful Arts, by securing for limited Times to Authors and Inventors the exclusive Right to their respective Writings and Discoveries;

[9]To constitute Tribunals inferior to the supreme Court;

[10]To define and punish Piracies and Felonies committed on the high Seas, and Offences against the Law of Nations;

[11]To declare War, grant Letters of Marque and Reprisal, and make Rules concerning Captures on Land and Water;

[12]To raise and support Armies, but no Appropriation of Money to that Use shall be for a longer Term than two Years;

[13]To provide and maintain a Navy:

[14]To make Rules for the Government and Regulation of the land and naval Forces;

[15]To provide for calling forth the Militia to execute the Laws of the Union, suppress Insurrections and repel Invasions;

[16]To provide for organizing, arming, and disciplining, the Militia, and for governing such Part of them as may be employed in the Service of the United States, reserving to the States respectively, the Appointment of the Officers, and the Authority of training the Militia according to the discipline prescribed by Congress;

[17]To exercise exclusive Legislation in all Cases whatsoever, over such District (not exceeding ten Miles square)

as may, by Cession of particular States, and the Acceptance of Congress, become the Seat of the Government of the United States, and to exercise like Authority over all Places purchased by the Consent of the Legislature of the Sate in which the Same shall be, for the Erection of Forts, Magazines, Arsenals, dock-yards, and other needful Buildings;-And

[18]To make all Laws which shall be necessary and proper for carrying into Execution the foregoing Powers, and all other Powers vested by this Constitution int he Government of the United States, or in any Department or Officer thereof.

SECTION. 9.   [1]The Migration or Importation of such Persons as any of the States now existing shall think proper to admit, shall not be prohibited by the congress prior to the Year one thousand eight hundred and eight, but a Tax or duty may be imposed on such Importation, not exceeding ten dollars for each Person.

[2]The Privilege of the Writ of Habeas Corpus shall not be suspended, unless when in Cases of Rebellion or Invasion the public Safety may require it.

[3]No Bill of Attainder or ex post facto Law shall be passed.

[**4]No Capitation, or other direct, Tax shall be laid, unless in Proportion to the Census or Enumeration herein before directed to be taken.

[5]No Tax or Duty shall be laid on Articles exported from any State.

[6]No Preference shall be given by any Regulation of Commerce or Revenue to the Ports of one State over those of another: nor shall Vessels bound to, or from, one State, be obliged to enter, clear, or pay Duties in another.

[7]No Money shall be drawn from the Treasury, but in Consequence of Appropriations made by Law; and a regular Statement and Account of the Receipts and Expenditures of all public Money shall be published from time to time.

[8]No Title of Nobility shall be granted by the United States: And no Person holding any Office of Profit or Trust under them, shall, without the Consent of the Congress, accept of any present, Emolument, Office, or Title, of any kind whatever, from any King, Prince, or foreign State.

** See also the sixteenth amendment.

SECTION. 10.   [1]No State shall enter into any Treaty, Alliance, or Confederation; grant Letters of Marque and Reprisal; coin Money; emit Bills of Credit; make any Thing but gold and silver Coin a Tender in Payment of Debts; pass any Bill of Attainder, ex post facto Law, or Law impairing the Obligation of Contracts, or grant any Title of Nobility.

[2]No State shall, without the Consent of the Congress, lay any Imposts or Duties on Imports or Exports, except what may be absolutely necessary for executing it's inspection Laws: and the net Produce of all Duties and Imposts, laid by any State on Imports or Exports, shall be for the Use of the Treasury of the United States; and all such Laws shall be subject to the Revision and Controul of the Congress.

[3]No State shall, without the Consent of Congress, lay any Duty of Tonnage, keep Troops, or Ships of War in time of Peace, enter into any Agreement or Compact with another State, or with a foreign Power, or engage in War, unless actually invaded, or in such imminent Danger as will not admit of delay.

ARTICLE. II.

SECTION. 1.   [1]The executive Power shall be vested in a President of the United States of America. He shall hold his Office during the Term of four Years, and, together with the Vice President, chosen for the same Term, be elected, as follows

[2]Each State shall appoint, in such Manner as the Legislature thereof may direct, a Number of Electors, equal to the whole Number of Senators and Representatives to which the State may be entitled in the Congress: but no Senator or Representative, or Person holding an Office of Trust or Profit under the United States, shall be appointed an Elector.

[The Electors shall meet in their respective States, and vote by Ballot for two Persons, of whom one at least shall not be an Inhabitant of the same State with themselves. And they shall make a List of all the Persons voted for, and of the Number of Votes for each; which List they shall sign and certify, and transmit sealed to the Seat of the Government of the United States, directed to the President of the Senate. The President of the United States shall, in the Presence of the Senate and House of

Representatives, open all the Certificates, and the Votes shall then be counted. The Person having the greatest Number of Votes shall be the President, if such Number be a Majority of the whole Number of Electors appointed; and if there be more than one who have such Majority, and have an equal Number of Votes, then the House of Representatives shall immediately chuse by Ballot one of them for President; and if no Person have a Majority, then from the five highest on the List the said House shall in like Manner chuse the President. But in chusing the President, the Votes shall be taken by States, the Representation from each State having one Vote; A quorum for this Purpose shall consist of a Member or Members from two thirds of the States, and a Majority of all the States shall be necessary to a Choice. In every Case, after the Choice of the President, the Person having the greatest Number of Votes of the Electors shall be the Vice President. But if there should remain two or more who have equal Votes, the Senate shall chuse from them by Ballot the Vice President.][††]

[3]The Congress may determine the Time of Chusing the Electors, and the Day on which they shall give their Votes; which Day shall be the same throughout the United States.

[4]No Person except a natural born Citizen, or a Citizen of the United States, at the time of the Adoption of this Constitution, shall be eligible to the Office of President; neither shall any Person be eligible to that Office who shall not have attained to the Age of thirty five Years, and been fourteen Years a Resident within the United States.

[5]In Case of the Removal of the President from Office, or of his Death, Resignation, or Inability to discharge the Powers and Duties of the said Office,[‡‡] the Same shall devolve on the Vice President, and the Congress may by Law provide for the Case of Removal, Death, Resignation or Inability, both of the President and Vice President, declaring what Officer shall then act as President, and such Officer shall act accordingly, until the Disability be removed, or a President shall be elected.

[6]The President shall, at sated Times, receive for his Services, a Compensation, which shall neither be encreased nor diminished during the Period for which he shall have been elected, and he shall not receive within that Period any other Emolument from the United States, or any of them.

[7]Before he enter on the Execution of his Office, he shall take the following Oath or Affirmation:-"I do solemnly swear (or affirm) that I will faithfully execute the Office of President of the United States, and will to the best of my Ability, preserve, protect and defend the Constitution of the United States."

SECTION. 2.   [1]The President shall be Commander in Chief of the Army and Navy of the United States, and of the Militia of the several States, when called into the actual Service of the United States; he may require the Opinion, in writing, of the principal Officer in each of the executive Departments, upon any Subject relating to the Duties of their respective Offices, and he shall have Power to grant Reprieves and Pardons for Offences against the United States, except in Cases of Impeachment.

[2]He shall have Power, by and with the Advice and Consent of the Senate, to make Treaties, provided two thirds of the Senators present concur; and he shall nominate, and by and with the Advice and Consent of the Senate, shall appoint Ambassadors, other public Ministers and Consuls, Judges of the supreme Court, and all other Officers of the United States, whose Appointments are not herein otherwise provided for, and which shall be established by Law: but the Congress may by Law vest the Appointment of such inferior Officers, as they think proper, in the President alone, in the Courts of Law, or in the Heads of Departments.

[3]The President shall have Power to fill up all Vacancies that may happen during the Recess of the Senate, by granting Commissions which shall expire at the End of their next Session.

SECTION. 3.   He shall from time to time give to the Congress Information of the State of the Union, and recommend to their Consideration such Measures as he shall judge necessary and expedient; he may, on extraordinary Occasions, convene both Houses, or either of them, and in Case of Disagreement between them, with Respect to the Time of Adjournment, he may adjourn them to such Time as he shall think proper; he shall

---

[††] This paragraph has been superseded by the twelfth amendment.

[‡‡] This provision has been affected by the twenty-fifth amendment.

receive Ambassadors and other public Ministers; he shall take Care that the Laws be faithfully executed, and shall Commission all the Officers of the United States.

SECTION. 4.   The President, Vice President and all civil Officers of the United States, shall be removed from Office on Impeachment for, and Conviction of, Treason, Bribery, or other high Crimes and Misdemeanors.

ARTICLE. III.

SECTION. 1.   The judicial Power of the United States, shall be vested in one supreme Court, and in such inferior Courts as the Congress may from time to time ordain and establish. The Judges, both of the supreme and inferior Courts, shall hold their Offices during good Behaviour, and shall, at stated Times, receive for their Services, a Compensation, which shall not be diminished during their Continuance in Office.

SECTION. 2.   [1]The judicial Power shall extend to all Cases, in Law and Equity, arising under this Constitution, the Laws of the United States, and Treaties made, or which shall be made, under their Authority;-to all Cases affecting Ambassadors, other public Ministers and Consuls;-to all Cases of admiralty and maritime Jurisdiction;-to Controversies to which the United States shall be a Party;-to Controversies between two or more States;-between a State and Citizens of another State;[§§]-between Citizens of different States,-between Citizens of the same State claiming Lands under Grants of different States, and between a State, or the Citizens thereof, and foreign States, Citizens or Subjects.

[2]In all Cases affecting Ambassadors, other public Ministers and Consuls, and those in which a State shall be Party, the supreme Court shall have original Jurisdiction. In all the other Cases before mentioned, the supreme Court shall have appellate Jurisdiction, both as to Law and Fact, with such Exceptions, and under such Regulations as the Congress shall make.

[3]The Trial of all Crimes, except in Cases of Impeachment, shall be by Jury; and such Trial shall be held in the State where the said Crimes shall have been committed; but when not committed within any State, the Trial shall be at such Place or Places as the Congress may be Law have directed.

SECTION. 3.   [1]Treason against the United States, shall consist only in levying War against them, or in adhering to their Enemies, giving them Aid and Comfort. No Person shall be convicted of Treason unless on the Testimony of two Witnesses to the same overt Act, or on confession in open Court.

[2]The Congress shall have Power to declare the Punishment of Treason, but no Attainder of Treason shall work Corruption of Blood, or Forfeiture except during the Life of the Person attainted.

ARTICLE. IV.

SECTION.1.   Full Faith and Credit shall be given in each State to the public Acts, Records, and judicial Proceedings of every other State. And the Congress may be general Laws prescribe the Manner in which such Acts, Records, and Proceedings shall be proved, and the Effect thereof.

SECTION. 2.   [1]The Citizens of each State shall be entitled to all Privileges and Immunities of Citizens in the several States.

[2]A Person charged in any State with Treason, Felony, or other Crime, who shall flee from Justice, and be found in another State, shall on Demand of the executive Authority of the State from which he fled, be delivered up, to be removed to the State having Jurisdiction of the Crime.

[3][No Person held to Service or Labour in one State, under the Laws thereof, escaping into another, shall, in Consequence of any Law or Regulation therein, be discharged from such Service or Labour, but shall be delivered up on Claim of the Party to whom such Service or Labour may be due.][¶¶]

SECTION. 3.   [1]New States may be admitted by the Congress into this Union; but no new State shall be formed or erected with in the Jurisdiction of any other State; nor any State be formed by the Junction of two or more States, or Parts of States, without the Consent of the Legislatures of the States concerned as well as of the Congress.

---

§§ This clause has been affected by the eleventh amendment.

¶¶ This paragraph has been superseded by the thirteenth amendment.

²The Congress shall have Power to dispose of and make all needful Rules and Regulations respecting the Territory or other Property belonging to the United States; and nothing in this Constitution shall be so constructed as to Prejudice any Claims of the United States, or of any particular State.

SECTION. 4.   The United States shall guarantee to every State in this Union a Republican Form of Government, and shall protect each of them against Invasion; and on Application of the Legislature, or of the Executive (when the Legislature cannot be convened) against domestic Violence.

ARTICLE. V.

The Congress, whenever tow thirds of both Houses shall deem it necessary, shall propose Amendments to this Constitution, or, on the Application of the Legislatures of two thirds of the several States, shall call a Convention for proposing Amendments, which, in either Case, shall be valid to all Intents and Purposes, as Part of this Constitution, when ratified by the Legislatures of three fourths of the several States, or by Conventions in three fourths thereof, as the one or the other Mode of Ratification may be proposed by the Congress; Provided [that no Amendment which may be made prior to the Year One thousand eight hundred and eight shall in any Manner affect the first and fourth Clauses in the Ninth Section of the first Article; and]*** that no State, without its Consent, shall be deprived of its equal Suffrage in the Senate.

ARTICLE. VI.

¹All Debts contracted and Engagements entered into, before the Adoption of this Constitution, shall be as valid against the United States under this Constitution, as under the Confederation.

²This Constitution, and the Laws of the United States which shall be made in Pursuance thereof; and all Treaties made, or which shall be made, under the Authority of the United States, shall be the supreme Law of the Land; and the Judges in every State shall be bound thereby, any Thing in the Constitution or Laws of any State to the Contrary notwithstanding.

³The Senators and Representatives before mentioned, and the Members of the several State Legislatures, and all executive and judicial Officers, both of the United States and of the several States, shall be bound by Oath or Affirmation, to support this Constitution; but no religious Test shall ever be required as a Qualification to any Office or public Trust under the United States.

ARTICLE. VII.

The Ratification of the Conventions of nine States, shall be sufficient for the Establishment of this Constitution between the States so ratifying the Same.

DONE in Convention by the Unanimous Consent of the States present the Seventeenth Day of September in the Year of our Lord one thousand seven hundred and Eighty seven and of the Independence of the United States of America the Twelfth IN WITNESS where of We have hereunto subscribed our Names.

Go WASHINGTON-
Presid^t. and deputy from Virginia.

JOHN LANGDON, MASSACHUSETTS.	**NICHOLAS GILMAN.**
NATHANEIL GORHAM, CONNECTICUT.	**RUFUS KING.**
WM. SAML. JOHNSON, NEW YORK.	**ROGER SHERMAN.**
ALEXANDER HAMILTION. NEW JERSEY.	
WILL: LIVINGSTON, DAVID BREARLEY, PENNSYLVANIA.	**WM. PATERSON, JONA: DAYTON.**
B FRANKLIN, ROBT MORRIS, THOS. FRITZSIMONS, JARED INGERSOLL, JAMES WILSON, DELAWARE.	**THOMAS MIFFLIN, GEO. CLYMER,** **GOUV MORRIS.**
GEO: READ, JOHN DICKINSON, JACO: BROOM, MARYLAND.	**GUNNING BEDFORD, jun, RICHARD BASSETT.**

*** Obsolete.

JAMES McHENRY,   DAN OF ST THOS. JENIFER,
DANL CARROLL.
VIRGINIA.

JOHN BLAIR-   JAMES MADISON Jr.
NORTH CAROLINA.

WM. BLOUNT,   RICH'D DOBBS SPAIGHT,
HU WILLIAMSON.
SOUTH CAROLINA.

J. RUTLEDGE
         CHARLES COTESWORTH PINCKNEY,
CHARLES PINCKNEY, PIERCE BUTLER.
GEORGIA.

WILLIAM FEW,   ABR BALDWIN.
Attest: WILLIAM JACKSON, SECRETARY.

RATIFICATION OF THE CONSTITUTION

The Constitution was adopted by a convention of the States on September 17, 1787, and was subsequently ratified by the several States, on the following dates: Delaware, December 7, 1787; Pennsylvania, December 12, 1787; Connecticut, January 9, 1788; Massachusetts, February 6, 1788; Maryland, April 28, 1788; South Carolina, May 23, 1788; New Hampshire, June 21, 1788. Ratification was completed on June 21, 1788.

The Constitution was subsequently ratified by Virginia, June 25, 1788; New York, July 26, 1788; North Carolina, November 21, 1789; Rhode Island, May 29, 1790; and Vermont, January 10, 1791.

AMENDMENTS TO THE CONSTITUTION OF THE UNITED STATES

The ten original amendments — The Bill of Rights — was proposed by Congress on September 25, 1789 and ratified December 15, 1791.

AMENDMENT I

Congress shall make no law respecting an establishment of religion, or prohibiting the free exercise thereof; or abridging the freedom of speech, or of the press; or the right of the people peaceably to assemble, and to petition the Government for a redress of grievances.

AMENDMENT II

A well-regulated militia, being necessary to the security of a free State, the right of the people to keep and bear arms, shall not be infringed.

AMENDMENT III

No soldier shall, in time of peace be quartered in any house, without the consent of the owner, nor in time of war, but in a manner to be prescribed by law.

AMENDMENT IV

The right of the people to be secure in their persons, houses, papers, and effects, against unreasonable searches and seizures, shall not be violated, and no warrants shall issue, but upon probable cause, supported by oath or affirmation, and particularly describing the place to be searched, and the persons or things to be seized.

AMENDMENT V

No person shall be held to answer for a capital, or otherwise infamous crime, unless on a presentment or indictment of a Grand Jury, except in cases arising in the land or naval forces, or in the militia, when in actual service in time of war or public danger; nor shall any person be subject for the same offense to be twice put in jeopardy of life or limb; nor shall be compelled in any criminal case to be a witness against himself, nor be deprived of life, liberty, or property, without due process of law; nor shall private property be taken for public use without just compensation.

AMENDMENT VI

In all criminal prosecutions, the accused shall enjoy the right to a speedy and public trial, by an impartial jury of the State and district wherein the crime shall have been committed, which district shall have been previously ascertained by law, and to be informed of the nature and cause of the accusation; to be confronted with the witnesses against him; to have compulsory process for obtaining witnesses in his favor, and to have the assistance of counsel for his defense.

AMENDMENT VII

In suits at common law, where the value in controversy shall exceed twenty dollars, the right of trial by jury shall be preserved, and no fact tried by a jury shall be otherwise reexamined in any court of the United States, than according to the rules of the common law.

AMENDMENT VIII

Excessive bail shall not be required, nor excessive fines imposed, nor cruel and unusual punishments inflicted.

AMENDMENT IX

The enumeration in the Constitution, of certain rights, shall not be construed to deny or disparage others retained by the people.

AMENDMENT X

The powers not delegated to the United States by the Constitution, nor prohibited by it to the States, are reserved to the States respectively, or to the people.

AMENDMENT XI

The judicial power of the United States shall not be construed to extend to any suit in law or equity, commenced or prosecuted against one of the United States by citizens of another State, or by citizens or subjects of any foreign state (proposed by Congress March 4, 1794 and ratified February 7, 1795).

AMENDMENT XII

The Electors shall meet in their respective States and vote by ballot for President and Vice-President, one of whom, at least, shall not be an inhabitant of the same State with themselves; they shall name in their ballots the person voted for as President, and in distinct ballots the person voted for as Vice-President, and of the number of votes for each, which lists they shall sign and certify, and transmit sealed to the seat of the Government of the United States, directed to the President of the Senate; the President of the Senate shall, in the presence of the Senate and House of Representatives, open all the certificates and the votes shall then be counted; The person having the greatest number of votes for President, shall be the President,

if such number be a majority of the whole number of Electors appointed; and if no person have such majority, then from the persons having the highest numbers not exceeding three on the list of those voted for as President, the House of Representatives shall choose immediately, by ballot, the President. But in choosing the President, the votes shall be taken by States, the representation from each State having one vote; a quorum for this purpose shall consist of a member or members from two-thirds of the States, and a majority of all the States shall be necessary to a choice. And if the House of Representatives shall not choose a President whenever the right of choice shall devolve upon them, [before the fourth day of March next following,] Altered by 20th Amendment then the Vice-President shall act as President, as in case of the death or other constitutional disability of the President. The person having the greatest number of votes as Vice-President, shall be the Vice-President, if such numbers be a majority of the whole number of electors appointed, and if no person have a majority, then from the two highest numbers on the list, the Senate shall choose the Vice-President; a quorum for the purpose shall consist of two-thirds of the whole number of Senators, and a majority of the whole number shall be necessary to a choice. But no person constitutionally ineligible to the office of President shall be eligible to that of Vice-President of the United States (proposed by Congress December 9, 1803 and ratified July 27, 1804).

AMENDMENT XIII

Section 1. Neither slavery nor involuntary servitude, except as a punishment for crime whereof the party shall have been duly convicted, shall exist within the United States, or any place subject to their jurisdiction (proposed by Congress January 31, 1865 and ratified December 6, 1865).

Section 2. Congress shall have power to enforce this article by appropriate legislation.

AMENDMENT XIV

Section 1. All persons born or naturalized in the United States, and subject to the jurisdiction thereof, are citizens of the United States and of the State wherein they reside. No State shall make or enforce any law which shall abridge the privileges or immunities of citizens of the United States; nor shall any State deprive any person of life, liberty, or property, without due process of law; nor to deny to any person within its jurisdiction the equal protection of the laws.

Section 2. Representatives shall be apportioned among the several States according to their respective numbers, counting the whole number of persons in each State, excluding Indians not taxed. But when the right to vote at any election for the choice of Electors for President and Vice-President of the United States, Representatives in Congress, the executive and judicial officers of a State, or the members of the Legislature thereof, is denied to any of the male inhabitants of such State, being twenty-one years of age, and citizens of the United States, or in any way abridged, except for participation in rebellion, or other crime, the basis of representation therein shall be reduced in the proportion which the number of such male citizens shall bear to the whole number of male citizens twenty-one years of age in such State.

Section 3. No person shall be a Senator or Representative in Congress, or Elector of President and Vice-President, or hold any office, civil or military, under the United States, or under any State, who, having previously taken an oath, as a member of Congress, or as an officer of the United States, or as a member of any State Legislature, or as an executive or judicial officer of any State, to support the Constitution of the United States, shall have engaged in insurrection or rebellion against the same, or given aid or comfort to the enemies thereof. But Congress may by a vote of two-thirds of each House, remove such disability.

Section 4. The validity of the public debt of the United States, authorized by law, including debts incurred for payment of pensions and bounties for services in suppressing insurrection or rebellion, shall not be questioned. But neither the United States nor any State shall assume or pay any debt or obligation incurred in aid of insurrection or rebellion against the United States, or any claim for the loss or emancipation of any slave; but all such debts, obligations and claims shall be held illegal and void.

Section 5. The Congress shall have the power to enforce, by appropriate legislation, the provisions of this article (proposed by Congress June 13, 1866 and ratified July 9, 1868).

AMENDMENT XV

Section 1. The right of citizens of the United States to vote shall not be denied or abridged by the United States or by any State on account of race, color, or previous condition of servitude.

Section 2. The Congress shall have the power to enforce this article by appropriate legislation (proposed by Congress February 26, 1869 and ratified February 3, 1870.)

AMENDMENT XVI

The Congress shall have power to lay and collect taxes on incomes, from whatever sources derived, without apportionment among the several States, and without regard to any census or enumeration (proposed by Congress July 2, 1909 and ratified February 3, 1913).

AMENDMENT XVII

The Senate of the United States shall be composed of two Senators from each State, elected by the people thereof, for six years; and each Senator shall have one vote. The electors in each State shall have the qualifications requisite for electors of the most numerous branch of the State Legislatures.

When vacancies happen in the representation of any State in the Senate, the executive authority of such State shall issue writs of election to fill such vacancies: Provided, That the Legislature of any State may empower the Executive thereof to make temporary appointments until the people fill the vacancies by election as the Legislature may direct.

This amendment shall not be so construed as to affect the election or term of any Senator chosen before it becomes valid as part of the Constitution (proposed by Congress May 13, 1912 and ratified April 8, 1913).

AMENDMENT XVIII

After one year from the ratification of this article the manufacture, sale, or transportation of intoxicating liquors within, the importation thereof into, or the exportation thereof from the United States and all territory subject to the jurisdiction thereof for beverage purposes is hereby prohibited.

The Congress and the several States shall have concurrent power to enforce this article by appropriate legislation.

This article shall be inoperative unless it shall have been ratified as an amendment to the Constitution by the Legislatures of the several States, as provided in the Constitution, within seven years from the date of the submission hereof to the States by the Congress (proposed by Congress December 18, 1917 and ratified January 16, 1919. Altered by Amendment 21).

AMENDMENT XIX

The right of citizens of the United States to vote shall not be denied or abridged by the United States or by any State on account of sex. Congress shall have power to enforce this article by appropriate legislation (proposed by Congress June 4, 1919 and ratified August 18, 1920).

AMENDMENT XX

Section 1. The terms of the President and the Vice-President shall end at noon on the 20th day of January, and the terms of Senators and Representatives at noon on the 3rd day of January, of the years in which such terms would have ended if this article had not been ratified; and the terms of their successors shall then begin.

Section 2. The Congress shall assemble at least once in every year, and such meeting shall begin at noon on the 3rd day of January, unless they shall by law appoint a different day.

Section 3. If, at the time fixed for the beginning of the term of the President, the President elect shall have died, the Vice-President elect shall become President. If a President shall not have been chosen before the time fixed for the beginning of his term, or if the President elect shall have failed to qualify, then the Vice-President elect shall act as President until a President shall have qualified; and the Congress may by law provide for the case wherein neither a President elect nor a Vice-President shall have qualified, declaring who shall then act as President, or the manner in which one who is to act shall be selected, and such person shall act accordingly until a President or Vice-President shall have qualified.

Section 4. The Congress may by law provide for the case of the death of any of the persons from whom the House of representatives may choose a President whenever the right of choice shall have devolved upon them, and for the case of the death of any of the persons from whom the Senate may choose a Vice-President whenever the right of choice shall have devolved upon them.

Section 5. Sections 1 and 2 shall take effect on the 15th day of October following the ratification of this article (October 1933).

Section 6. This article shall be inoperative unless it shall have been ratified as an amendment to the Constitution by the Legislatures of three-fourths of the several States within seven years from the date of its submission.

AMENDMENT XXI

Section 1. The Eighteenth article of amendment to the Constitution of the United States is hereby repealed.

Section 2. The transportation or importation into any State, Territory, or Possession of the United States for delivery or use therein of intoxicating liquors, in violation of the laws thereof, is hereby prohibited.

Section 3. This article shall be inoperative unless it shall have been ratified as an amendment to the Constitution by conventions in the several States, as provided in the Constitution, within seven years from the date of the submission hereof to the States by the Congress (proposed by Congress February 20, 1933 and ratified December 5, 1933).

AMENDMENT XXII

No person shall be elected to the office of the President more than twice, and no person who has held the office of President, or acted as President, for more that two years of a term to which some other person was elected President shall be elected to the office of President more that once.

But this Article shall not apply to any person holding the office of President when this Article was proposed by Congress, and shall not prevent any person who may be holding the office of President, or acting as President, during the term the term within which this Article becomes operative from holding the office of President or acting as President during the remainder of such term.

This article shall be inoperative unless it shall have been ratified as an amendment to the Constitution by the Legislatures of three-fourths of the several States within seven years from the date of its submission to the States by the Congress (proposed by Congress March 21, 1947 and ratified February 27, 1951).

AMENDMENT XXIII

Section 1. The District constituting the seat of Government of the United States shall appoint in such manner as Congress may direct:

A number of electors of President and Vice President equal to the whole number of Senators and Representatives in Congress to which the District would be entitled if it were a State, but in no event more than the least populous State; they shall be in addition to those appointed by the States, but they shall be considered, for the purposes of the election of President and Vice President, to be electors appointed by a State; and they shall meet in the District and preform such duties as provided by the twelfth article of amendment.

Section 2. The Congress shall have power to enforce this article by appropriate legislation (proposed by Congress June 16, 1960 and ratified March 29, 1961).

AMENDMENT XXIV

Section 1. The right of citizens of the United States to vote in any primary or other election for President or Vice President, for electors for President or Vice President, or for Senator or Representative in Congress, shall not be denied or abridged by the United States or any State by reason of failure to pay poll tax or any other tax.

Section 2. Congress shall have power to enforce this article by appropriate legislation (proposed by Congress August 27, 1962 and ratified January 23, 1964).

AMENDMENT XXV

Section 1. In case of the removal of the President from office or of his death or resignation, the Vice President shall become President.

Section 2. Whenever there is a vacancy in the office of the Vice President, the President shall nominate a Vice President who shall take the office upon confirmation by a majority vote of both houses of Congress.

Section 3. Whenever the President transmits to the President Pro tempore of the Senate and the Speaker of the House of Representatives his written declaration that he is unable to discharge the powers and duties of his office, and until he transmits to them a written declaration to the contrary, such powers and duties shall be discharged by the Vice President as Acting President.

Section 4. Whenever the Vice President and a majority of either the principal officers of the executive departments or of such other body as Congress may by law provide, transmits to the President Pro tempore of the Senate and the Speaker of the House of Representatives their written declaration that the President is unable to discharge the powers and duties of his office, the Vice President shall immediately assume the powers and duties of the office as Acting President.

Thereafter, when the President transmits to the President Pro tempore of the Senate and the Speaker of the House of Representatives his written declaration that no inability exists, he shall resume the powers and duties of his office unless the Vice President and a majority of either the principal officers of the executive departments or of such other body as Congress may by law provide, transmits within four days to the President Pro tempore of the Senate and the Speaker of the House of Representatives their written declaration that the President is unable to discharge the powers and duties of his office. Thereupon Congress shall decide the issue, assembling within forty-eight hours for that purpose if not in session. If the Congress, within twenty-one days after receipt of the latter written declaration, or, if Congress is not in session within twenty-one days after Congress is required to assemble, determines by two-thirds vote of both houses that the President is unable to discharge the powers and duties of his office, the Vice President shall continue to discharge the same as Acting President; otherwise, the President shall resume the powers and duties of his office (proposed by Congress July 6, 1965and ratified February 10, 1967).

AMENDMENT XXVI

Section 1. The right of citizens of the United States, who are 18 years of age or older, to vote shall not be denied or abridged by the United States or any state on account of age.

Section 2. The Congress shall have power to enforce this article by appropriate legislation (proposed by Congress March 23, 1971 and ratified June 30, 1971).

AMENDMENT XXVII

No law, varying the compensation for the services of the Senators and Representatives, shall take effect, until an election of Representatives shall have intervened (proposed by Congress September 25, 1789 and ratified May 8, 1992).

MAJOR EVENTS INFLUENCING THE DEVELOPMENT OF AMERICAN LAW ENFORCEMENT, 1635–2002

Law enforcement and social control in America have been influenced by a myriad of social, political, economic, and technological forces. The following chronology offers a partial list of these events and developments. The entries are not exhaustive; rather they provide reference points to help you place events into historical perspective.

1635 Citizens of Boston organize a volunteer Night Watch, the first organized law enforcement entity in colonial America.

1658 New Amsterdam (the original name for New York City) appoint eight paid watchmen to replace volunteers.

1682 William Penn publishes the first draft of *Frame of Government of Pennsylvania*. This document, which introduced concepts like trial by jury, freedom of the press, and religious tolerance, had a profound influence on the framers of the American *Constitution* and the *Bill of Rights*.

1692–1693 Salem witchcraft trials.

1702 New York passes *Act for Regulating Slaves*.

1703 Massachusetts passes a law that "forbade Indians, Negroes, and mulatto slaves and servants from being away from their homes after 9:00 pm, unless on a specific errand for their master."

1705 Virginia enacts the first slave codes in an attempt to regulate and control the behavior of its growing population of slaves.

1718–1776 England ships approximately 30,000 convicts to the colonies, a practice called transportation.

1740 South Carolina establishes a basic slave law and creates slave patrols to enforce the law. Slave patrols would eventually operate in all southern states.

1749 Philadelphia levies a tax and appoints wardens with the authority to hire night watchmen as needed.

1765 Stamp Act (which levied a tax on legal documents, newspapers, almanacs, playing cards, and dice) riots in Boston and New York.

1767–1769 "The Regulators," a South Carolina vigilante group, is the first vigilante movement in America.

1774 Political resistance to the Boston Port Bill, which required the Port to close until Boston paid restitution for the lost tea thrown overboard by colonists during the Boston Tea Party.

1775–1783 American Revolutionary War (also known as the American War of Independence).

1786 Shay's Rebellion— an armed uprising of more than 2000 western Massachusetts farmers over heavy taxation, high legal and court fees, and state government waste.

1787 The United States *Constitution* is adopted on September 17, 1787 by the Constitutional Convention in Philadelphia.

1789   *Bill of Rights* adopted.

1789   *Judiciary Act of 1789* establishes the federal judiciary. This act also creates the first federal law enforcement position, the federal marshal.

1793   *Fugitive Slave Act* creates a legal mechanism for a slaveholder to recover an escaped slave.

1794   Whiskey Rebellion takes place in Pennsylvania over the federal tax on whiskey. US Marshal Robert Forsyth was murdered, while serving papers on distillers in western Pennsylvania, becoming the first federal agent killed in the line of duty.

1794   Congress passes the *Slave Trade Act of 1794*, which forbids the importation of slaves. The *1807 Act of Congress* also forbids the importation of slaves.

1795   Demonstrations against the Jay Treaty with England take place.

1798   Virginia and Kentucky Resolutions state that certain Federal Government actions could be declared "unconstitutional" by state legislation—this is particularly directed toward the Alien and Sedition Acts (which were anti-immigrant in nature).

1799   Fries Rebellion (John Fries leads a mob to free two tax-evaders from prison).

1803   *Marbury v. Madison* establishes the principle that the Supreme Court has the final word in whether an act of Congress or state law is constitutional.

1805   The City of New Orleans establishes a "martial style" police force, which is very different from the civil style of police forces that will later develop in northern cities.

1819   The Panic of 1819 is the first major financial crisis in the United States; it is followed by a period of economic depression.

1823   Texas Rangers are established, becoming the nation's first statewide law enforcement agency.

1823   Boston appoints a city marshal.

1825   Jonathan Houghton, a night watchman, becomes Boston's first law enforcement officer killed in the line of duty.

1829   The *Metropolitan Police Act* creates the London Metropolitan Police Department, the first modern police department. It is headed by Sir Robert Peel.

1829   Pennsylvania opens Eastern State Penitentiary as part of a controversial movement to change the behavior of inmates through "confinement in solitude with labor."

1829–1850   Five major race riots in Philadelphia take place.

1831   Nat Turner, a slave, organizes and leads a slave revolt in Virginia, which resulted in the deaths of 56 whites and the beating and/or deaths of large numbers of slaves. Turner was captured and hanged. The revolt produced a strong backlash as state legislators in southern states enacted new laws to control slaves.

1832   Tariff Nullification by South Carolina brought a national crisis in federal/state relationships and authority.

1830s–1840s   The Army is involved in numerous skirmishes and small "wars" with Native Americans.

1834   Protestant mob burns the Ursuline Convent in Charlestown, MA (anti-Catholic sentiment).

1837   Irish immigrants in a funeral procession clash with a Protestant volunteer fire department brigade in Boston—15,000 people are involved.

1838   Boston creates a day police and employs six officers under the command of city marshal Francis Tukey. The force was patterned after Sir Robert Peel's London Metropolitan Police.

1841   The murder of Mary Cecilia Rogers, a popular sales clerk in a New York City cigar shop, brought attention to the poor condition of law enforcement in the city and produced widespread public demand for reform of the city's criminal justice system. Unfortunately, little reform occurred. Policing was mired in partisan politics, which prevented real reform for years to come.

1841   Houston, Texas establishes a police department, but the department remains underdeveloped until 1866, when it is reorganized. Its first black officer is hired in 1973.

1842   Dorr Rebellion occurs (over extension of suffrage to all males instead of property owners).

1844   Anti-Catholic riots in Philadelphia take place.

1844   The New York City *Municipal Police Act* establishes a police department to serve the city's 320,000 residents. The department, which numbered 1200 officers, was closely modeled after the London Metropolitan Police.

1849 Astor Place riot in New York City results in 31 killed, 150 wounded, and 86 arrested.

1850 Congress passes the *Fugitive Slave Act of 1850*, which requires the return of runaway slaves to their owners.

1850 The Los Angeles County Sheriff's Department is established and George Thompson Burrill is elected sheriff. He is allowed to hire one deputy to assist him police the massive county, which at the time included what is today Ventura, Riverside, San Bernardino, and Orange Countries. When Burrill died of illness in 1854, he was replaced by Sheriff James R. Barton, who served until 1857, when he and three members of his posse were killed in a shootout with horse thieves.

1850s American Indians are "concentrated" to certain geographical areas (reservations). The struggle and debate continues for decades.

1851 San Francisco Committee of Vigilance (vigilantism forces) is founded.

1852 Boston abolishes the office of the city marshal and establishes the office of chief of police. Francis Tukey becomes Boston's first chief of police.

1853 The Los Angeles Rangers, a volunteer California State Militia, is formed to assist the sheriff of Los Angeles County. They will eventually be assisted by volunteers of the Los Angeles Guards (1853) and volunteers of the Los Angeles City Guards (1855).

1854 Smith and Wesson begin producing revolvers. In 1856, they begin production of the Smith and Wesson Model 1, the first in a long series of revolvers adopted by the military and police departments in America and around the world.

1854 There is struggle and dissent over slavery in Kansas' application for statehood.

1854 Boston creates a central police department after the night watch and day police are disbanded. The Boston Police Department is formed under the command of Chief Robert Taylor, who is authorized to hire approximately 250 men.

1855 German tavern-keeper's revolt in Chicago takes place, with many killed and hundreds injured

1856 Supreme Court rules in *Dred Scott v Sanford* (known simple as the Dred Scott decision) that people of African descent, along with their descendents held as slaves, were not entitled to federal citizenship and were not protected by the Constitution. Moreover, Congress did not have authority to regulate slavery in the territories, nor did the territorial legislatures.

1856 The San Francisco Vigilance Committee numbers between 6000 and 8000 members. Their concerns centered on the city's crime problem, but much of their ire was focused one group: the Irish and the Democrat political machine that found its support among lower class Irish Catholics.

1858 Boston officers are required to wear uniforms for the first time. The color of the uniform is dark blue (this starts a long tradition in American policing).

1858 Boston police begin offering lodging to indigent persons, a practice that will continue until 1888.

1859 John Brown leads a raid at Harper's Ferry, Virginia.

1861 First transcontinental telegraph is opened.

1861–1865 Civil War in the United States.

1862 Boston appoints the first police officer of Irish decent, Barney McGinniskin. However, Police Chief Marshall Tukey refused to assign him to street duty and forced him to work inside the station. Tukey eventually fired McGinniskin but he was later rehired.

1863 Conscription (Draft) Riots in Boston and New York City (NYC) left many killed and hundreds injured. NYPD Police Chief John Alexander Kennedy, who had responded to an area of rioting in New York City, was severely beaten by the angry mob, as were many African-Americans, who become scapegoats and targets.

1863 President Abraham Lincoln issues the *Emancipation Proclamation*, freeing slaves.

1863 Boston police officers, who are not officially armed, begin caring 24-inch batons referred to as "night sticks."

1865 Massachusetts establishes a state police, though it remains small and rather informal until 1921, when it is modernized and expanded to a force of 50 men.

1865 President Abraham Lincoln is assassinated by John Wilkes Booth, leading to one of the biggest manhunts in American history.

1866 The Winchester Repeating Arms Company begins production of the repeating rifle; the most famous is the Model 1873, known as "the gun that won the West."

1865–1877   Reconstruction in Southern states

1865   The Ku Klux Klan (KKK) is founded in Pulaski, Tennessee by former Confederate soldiers.

1869   Los Angeles establishes police department and hires six officers.

1871   Anti-Chinese riot in Los Angeles; 23 Chinese killed.

1871   Orange Riots in NYC; 33 killed, 91 wounded.

1874   Boston police expand their mounted patrol force from one to 28 officers.

1876   Alexander Graham Bell patents the telephone.

1876   Railroad tracks are finally laid and the first train arrives in Los Angeles. However, the city was still an arid and dusty rough-and-tumble destination, a place where drought and smallpox ravaged the city's inhabitants.

1878s–1900s   Jim Crow laws are enforced in the South, codifying the segregation of the races.

1877   Great labor strikes take place in West Virginia and Pittsburgh, PA; in two days, 16 soldiers and 50 strikers are killed, and 125 locomotives, 2000 freight cars, and a depot are burned and destroyed. Many are also killed and wounded in Chicago.

1880s   The Los Angeles County Sheriff's Department begins using the Bertillion identification system, at the time considered to be a great tool for identifying suspects.

1884   Boston Police Department provides its 700 officers with Smith & Wesson .38 revolvers at a cost of $9 each.

1886   At the Haymarket Riots in Chicago, in which labor disputes fueled tensions, a bomb killed a police officer and six others.

1887   Boston Police Department hires matrons and assigns them to police stations through the city to serve as guards for women and juvenile prisoners. However, they had no power of arrest.

1893   The International Association of Chiefs of Police (IACP) is founded. It elects Chief Webber Seavey of Omaha, Nebraska to be its first President.

1896   Boston Police Department begins using bicycle-mounted police officers to patrol its parks.

1896   In *Plessy v. Ferguson,* the Supreme Court upholds separate but equal laws, which justified segregation.

1898   Manhattan, the Bronx, Brooklyn, Queens, and Richmond are consolidated to become the greater City of New York. The consolidation also witnessed the merger of 18 area police departments into a single agency, the New York Police Department (NYPD).

1900   The Los Angeles Police Department (LAPD) grows to 70 officers, one for every 1500 citizens.

1903   Boston Police Department purchases a Stanley Steamer (steam-powered vehicle) to use in support of police operations.

1905   Pennsylvania establishes the first modern state police force.

1905   August Vollmer is elected Town Marshal of Berkeley CA., beginning a long and productive career in law enforcement. He is an innovative leader, a scholar, and a driving force behind the move to professionalize policing and is today known as the "father of modern law enforcement."

1908   The City of Portland, Oregon hires Lola Greene Baldwin, a 48-year-old social worker, to perform police service as a detective primarily working with females and juveniles.

1908   Nevada establishes a State Highway Patrol and hires two officers.

1910   Alice Stebbins Wells is hired by the LAPD and becomes the first policewoman with full police powers.

1912   Margaret Q. Adams is hired by the Los Angeles County Sheriff's Department and becomes the first female deputy in the country.

1913   At the Ludlow Massacre, more than are 30 killed.

1915   The Ku Klux Klan officially organizes in Georgia (modeled after its predecessor) and is led by William Joseph Simmons. It will exist until World War II.

1917   Michigan establishes a State Police and hires 300 Troopers.

1917   New York establishes a State Police; its creation is the result of Moyca Newell and Katherine Mayo's efforts to provide police protection to rural areas of New York following the murder of one of Mrs. Newell's employees.

1917–1919   World War I: Large numbers of law enforcement officers across the country resign from their departments to serve in the war effort. At the end of the war, they are welcomed back as national heroes.

1919   During a Chicago race riot, 38 are killed and 537 injured.

1919   On September 19, 1919, approximately 1100 rank-and-file officers of Boston's 1500 member force go on strike seeking better wages and working conditions. The strike created widespread fear and disorder in the city and resulted in the mobilization of the National Guard to provide police service. All the strikers were fired, but their replacements eventually receive the benefits the strikers had sought.

1919   Boston Police Department hires its first African-American police officer, Harvey B. Yates, who serves until 1957, when he retired after 37 years of service.

1919   Chicago Crime Commission is founded by Chicago businessmen as an independent watchdog organization, and it finds widespread corruption and inefficiencies in the city's criminal justice system.

1920   *19th Amendment* gives women the right to vote.

1921   Tulsa race riot: 30 killed, 700 injured.

1922   The Cleveland Crime Survey of the administration of justice in Cleveland, Ohio, sponsored by the Cleveland Foundation, finds widespread corruption in the city's criminal justice system.

1929   The Missouri Crime Survey, a statewide survey of the Missouri criminal justice system (the first statewide survey in the nation) finds widespread corruption and inefficiencies.

1929   California establishes a Highway Patrol, and within 10 years the force had grown to 730 officers.

1931   Oregon establishes a State Police and hires 95 officers to enforce all state laws, including fish and game codes.

1931   The Wickersham Commission, officially known as the National Commission on Law Observance and Enforcement, is the first examination of the nation's criminal justice system; it finds widespread corruption and inefficiencies.

1934   Republic Steel plant in Chicago experiences union violence when the police shoot and kill 10 pickets; it is also called the Memorial Day Massacre.

1930s   Nation of Islam (Black Nationalist) movement begins.

1937   Georgia establishes a State Patrol.

1937   Oklahoma establishes a State Patrol and hires 125 troopers.

1941–1945   World War II: Many law enforcement officers are called to serve in the armed forces. They return with many new ideas about organization, leadership, and commitment to public service, which will collectively influence the future development of American policing. Moreover, prior military service becomes a prime requisite in hiring decisions well into the 1980s.

1943   Detroit race riot: 34 killed, several hundred injured

1943   Zoot-Suit Riots in Los Angeles (anti-Mexican-American sentiment).

1950s–1960s   Battle over desegregation leads to school integration and social tension.

Early 1950s   The third Klan movement is revived by Dr. Samuel Green, an Atlanta dentist.

1954   In *Brown v. Board of Education of Topeka*, the Supreme Court reverses *Plessy v. Ferguson* and rules that segregation is illegal.

1955   In Montgomery, Alabama, a boycott is staged over the segregated bus system, which is precipitated by Rosa Parks's refusal to give up her bus seat to a white person.

1955   Executive Order 10450 (November 1) required the Attorney General of the United States to prepare a list of subversive or fascist groups in America.

1955–1956   Segregationist groups called White Citizens' Councils spread throughout the South.

1956   Clinton, Texas experiences racial violence.

1957   Violence in Little Rock, Arkansas; Eisenhower orders in federal troops.

1958   John Birch Society formed in Indianapolis by Robert H.W. Welch, Jr.

1960   Racial violence in New Orleans.

1962   President John F. Kennedy sends troops to University of Mississippi in Oxford, MS to protect black student James Meredith.

1963   Birmingham, Alabama experiences a racial confrontation with police; President Kennedy denounces Governor George Wallace's stand on segregation.

1963   Civil right leader Medgar Evers is assassinated.

1963   Dr. Martin Luther King, Jr. and thousands of deminstrators march on Washington DC, where Dr. King makes his now-famous "I Have a Dream" speech.

1963 On November 21, President John F. Kennedy is assassinated in Dallas, TX, by Lee Harvey Oswald. Oswald also kills Dallas police officer J.D. Tippit. Oswald is eventually arrested, but is shot and killed two days later by Jack Ruby as he is being escorted by police. The shooting is captured on national television.

1964 There are race riots in NYC, Rochester (NY), Philadelphia, Jersey City, Paterson (NJ), Elizabeth (NJ), and Chicago; 6 people are killed, 952 injured.

1964 Civil Rights Act of 1964 passes; Title VII outlaws discrimination in employment based on race, color, religion, national origin, or sex.

1964 On October 1, The Free Speech Movement was born at Berkeley, California (led by Mario Savio and Joan Baez); the movement lasted about a year but received broad national attention and led to more "student movements."

1965 Los Angeles (Watts) race riot, in which 36 people were killed and 895 injured; the violence also spread to San Francisco, where 200 were injured and 6 killed.

1965 In February, Malcolm X is assassinated by three gunmen as he began a speech in a Harlem ballroom; he was a major leader in the Nation of Islam movement.

1965 Students for a Democratic Society (SDS) experiences phenomenal growth; led by Tom Hayden, it was essentially an anti-Vietnam movement.

1967 The President's Commission on Law Enforcement and Administration of Justice issues their summary report, *The Challenge of Crime in a Free Society*.

1967 George Lincoln Rockwell, Commander of the American Nazi Party, is killed in an ambush in front of a laundromat in Arlington, Virginia.

1967 The Youth International Party (YIPPIE) is formed; Abbie Hoffman, Jerry Rubin, and Paul Krassner were the primary leaders.

1967 150 US cities experience racial disturbances and riots.

1968 Dr. Martin Luther King, Jr. is assassinated in Memphis, TN, sparking riots in over 168 cities. James Earl Ray is eventually arrested for King's murder. He confesses and is sentenced to 99 years in prison, where he dies in 1998.

1968 While campaigning for president, Robert F. Kennedy is assassinated in Los Angeles by Sirhan Sirhan.

Sirhan is sentenced to death, but the sentence is later commuted to life in prison.

1968 Black Panther Huey Newton is convicted of voluntary manslaughter in the killing of an Oakland police officer.

1968 During August 18–29, the National Democratic Convention in Chicago becomes a "Police Riot"; over 24 "protest" organizations are represented in the crowded streets and demonstrations outside the convention. In the end, 192 officers were injured and 49 hospitalized; 425 civilians were treated at hospitals, 200 treated on the spot, and over 400 given first aid for tear gas or mace; 81 police vehicles damaged; 668 persons arrested; and much of the confrontation was televised nationwide—49 newsmen reported being hit, assaulted, or having cameras/recorders damaged by officers.

1968 Congress passes the Omnibus Crime Control and Safe Streets Act, creating the National Institute of Justice (NIJ) to support a continuing Federal criminal justice research effort to help State and local governments improve police, courts, and corrections and gain a better understanding of criminal behavior.

1969 National Institute of Justice (NIJ) is established, beginning with a budget of $2.9 million and 35 employees. NIJ joins with other Federal agencies, universities, and nonprofit organizations to foster criminological research, spur development of new knowledge in criminal justice, and increase the corps of skilled researchers and innovative practitioners.

Mid 1960s Vietnam War protest movement gains momentum, led by the Flower Power movement and the SDS.

1970 On May 4, four people are killed at Kent State University in Ohio by National Guard troops; ROTC buildings are also burned.

1970 Violence erupts at Jackson State University, Jackson, MS.

1971 At an anti-war march in Washington, DC, 12,000 are arrested.

1971 Voting age is lowered to 18 (26th Amendment).

1971 NIJ establishes the Law Enforcement Standards Laboratory under the auspices of the National Bureau of Standards to begin filling a longstanding need for scientifically-based standards for criminal justice equipment. The program continues today with the National Institute of Standards and Testing (NIST) at the US Department of Commerce.

1972   Presidential candidate George Wallace is shot in Laurel, MD.

1972   The Watergate scandal is exposed.

1972   NIJ develops soft body armor for police, which has saved thousands of officers from serious injury or even death.

1972   National Victimization Surveys are launched by the Bureau of Justice Statistics.

1973   United States involvement in Vietnam ends.

1974   Symbionese Liberation Army kidnaps Patricia Hearst.

1974   President Gerald R. Ford escapes two assassination attempts.

1974   Office of Juvenile Justice and Delinquency Prevention established.

1974   Police Foundation publishes results of Kansas City Preventive Patrol Experiment, which cast doubt on value of conventional patrol.

1976   National Organization of Black Law Enforcement Executives (NOBLE) is launched.

1976   Ten police chiefs create the Police Executive Research Forum (PERF).

1976   NIJ study of police response time shows that the time it takes to report a crime—not the speed of police response—is the major factor influencing likelihood of arrest.

1977   Research on the criminal investigation process by RAND and PERF led to "solvability" factors as a guide for prioritizing case investigations.

1979   Iranian militants seize US Embassy and take hostages.

1979   Commission on Accreditation of Law Enforcement Agencies (CALEA) is established.

1979   "Improving Policing: A Problem-Oriented Approach" by Herman Goldstein appears in the journal *Crime and Delinquency*.

1980   Racial disturbances occur in Miami.

1981   President Ronald W. Reagan is shot by John W. Hinckley, Jr. Hinckley is found not guilty by reason of insanity and is placed under institutional psychiatric care.

1985   Police storm/firebomb the home of MOVE (a radical group of Black activists) in Philadelphia; the fire spreads, killing 11 and leaving 200 homeless.

1991   Rodney King incident in Los Angeles, California leads to the indictment of four officers and widespread criticism of the LAPD.

1992   On April 29, the officers charged in the King incident were found not guilty of all but one charge against one officer. Riots erupted and lasted for 5 days resulting in more than 40 deaths, 2382 injuries, over 5000 buildings destroyed or damaged, an estimated 40,000 jobs lost and over $1 billion in property damage; 5633 people are arrested. The riots spread to other cities across the country.

1993   Two of the four officers indicted in the King incident were convicted in federal court on civil rights charges and sentenced to 30 months in prison.

1993   On February 26, bombs exploded at the World Trade Center in New York City; six people were killed and over 1000 injured.

1993   On April 19, following a 51-day standoff at Waco, Texas, the compound of the Branch Davidians, headed by David Koresh. burns to the ground after an assault by federal agents. Eighty people are believed to have died in the incident, including women and children.

1994   Nicole Simpson and Ronald Goldman are murdered; O.J. Simpson is accused but is later found not criminally guilty.

1995   On April 19, at the bombing of the Murrah Federal Building in Oklahoma City, Oklahoma, 169 people are killed and over 800 injured.

1996   National crime rate continues to drop, but juvenile violence is increasing.

1996   A bomb explodes at Summer Olympics in Atlanta, Georgia, killing one.

1996   Theodore Kaczynski, the alleged Unabomber is arrested after 18 years of incidents. He is sentenced to life in prison.

1997   Communications Decency Act ruled unconstitutional as an attempt to regulate the Internet

1997   Timothy McVeigh found guilty of the Oklahoma City Federal Building bombing and was executed in June 2001.

1997   Ramzi Ahmed Yousef and Eyad Ismoil were convicted of the NYC Trade Center Tower bombing

1997   O.J. Simpson found civilly responsible for the deaths of Nicole Simpson and Ronald Goldman

1998   A series of school violence incidents in several states where students and teachers were killed raises concerns about access to firearms by juveniles. Locations included Edinboro, Pennsylvania, Jonesboro, Arkansas, Springfield, Oregon; ages of the shooters range from 10–17.

1998   Near Jasper, Texas, African American man was beaten, chained to a pickup truck, and dragged to his death by three white men with ties to hate groups.

1998   Hate crimes statistics of the Federal Bureau of Investigation reach 7755 reported incidents involved a total of 9235 offenses, 9722 victims, and 7489 known offenders.

1999   On April 20, Columbine High School in Littleton, Colorado is the site of the worst-ever school massacre in the United States; 12 students and one teacher are killed, along with 23 wounded, before the two assailants (who were armed with guns and homemade bombs) committed suicide.

1999   NYPD officers shoot and kill unarmed Amadou Diallo in New York, heightening tensions between the community and the police.

2001   On September 11, hijackers crash two commercial jets into the twin towers of World Trade Center in New York City; another jet is crashed into the Pentagon and a fourth jet crashes in a field in rural Pennsylvania, near Shanksville. Total dead and missing numbered 2992: 2749 in New York City, 184 at the Pentagon, 40 in Pennsylvania, and 19 hijackers. Islamic al-Qaeda terrorist group is blamed. Aftermath of the 9/11 attacks puts all of the United States and other countries on alert for more possible attacks. Homeland security becomes a national priority.

2002   The Homeland Security Act creates the Department of Homeland Security; 22 federal agencies are incorporated into the new department.

TIMELINE OF CRIMINAL IDENTIFICATION IN THE UNITED STATES, 1854–2010

1854–1859   Captain Lees of the San Francisco Police Department uses a commercial photographer to make daguerreotypes (an early form of photograph using a thin brass plate) of all arrested persons.

1858   NYPD has collected over 450 photographs for its rogues' gallery.

1884   Chicago Police Department establishes its own police photograph gallery at police headquarters, believed to be the first city in the world to do so.

1888   Chicago Police Department becomes the first American city to adopt the Bertillon system of identification (which was developed by Alphonse Bertillon of the Paris Police in 1882—his "portrait parle" system was one that included a person's bodily measurements along with details about complexion; color of hair and eyes; shape of nose, ear and face; special marks and peculiarities; and photographs).

1894   The National Chiefs of Police Union (forerunner of the International Association of Chiefs of Police) petitions Congress to establish a bureau of identification of criminals at the national level.

1896   The National Chiefs of Police Union creates the National Bureau of Criminal Identification (on paper); it eventually opens in Chicago in 1897, with George Porteous, an expert in the Bertillon system, as its superintendent. A single office could now receive and respond to police requests for "Identification Wanted."

1902   The National Bureau of Criminal Identification was relocated to the Washington, DC Police Department, with Edward Evans as Superintendent.

1904   The World's Fair, held in St. Louis, MO, brings exhibitors from all over the world displaying and advocating criminal identification equipment and systems. Fingerprinting as a means of identification received great interest, and the St. Louis Police Department begins using the Henry Finger Print System.

1904   Mrs. Mary E. Holland, assistant editor of *The Detective*, is trained in the Henry System and becomes competent to install and instruct the system as an expert.

1904   The US Army and Navy and federal prisons adopt the fingerprint system over the Bertillon system.

1906   The NYPD inaugurates the use of the Henry Finger Print System.

1921   By this date, five state identification bureaus are in operation: California, Washington, Ohio, Wisconsin, and Iowa.

1923   Attorney General Harry M. Daugherty issues orders to transfer the International Association of Chiefs of Police's National Bureau of Criminal Identification to the Justice Department's Division of Identification, which became statutorily official on July 1.

1924.   State Bureaus number 23.

1935   Eye Retina Pattern identification scheme developed and offered as an adjunct to the fingerprint system.

1936   The American Dental Association, in conjunction with the US Department of Justice, begins developing a system of identification for recording dental peculiarities and records.

1936   Ophthalmologist Frank Burch proposes that individuals could be identified through iris patterns.

1939   Colonel H. Norman Schwarzkopf of the New Jersey State Police demonstrates the uses of motion pictures in making a permanent record of criminals.

1939   First color photographs appear in a wanted circular, used by the Indiana State Police.

1948   Edwin Land markets the Polaroid camera; the one-step process for developing and printing photos creates instant photography.

1959   Original version of Identi-Kit I is launched, which consisted of hand drawn foils in wooden box.

1967   Michigan State Police adopt voice print identification technology.

1970s   The FBI develops an automated search and retrieval system for fingerprint cards.

1978   The first Automated Fingerprint and Identification Systems (AFIS) are developed for digitaly scanned prints.

1987   First criminal trial in the United States where DNA (deoxyribonucleic acid) evidence is introduced takes place in Orlando, Florida.

1989   First software version of Identi-Kit is released.

1990   CODIS—a database containing the DNA signatures of convicted offender—is initiated at the Federal Bureau of Investigation as a pilot project. CODIS refers to COmbined DNA Indexing System. The DNA Identification Act of 1994 formalized the program.

1991   Facial recognition research enables real-time automated systems to be developed.

Mid-1990s   Facial thermography is developed; it detects heat patterns emitted from the skin that are created by the branching of blood vessels. The patterns, called thermograms, are highly distinctive, but further development was curtailed because of manufacturing costs of the equipment.

1995   First commercial availability of iris recognition equipment.

2003   Identi-Kit application hosted on the Internet.

2004   President Bush signs into law the "Justice for All Act of 2004," which establishes enforceable rights for victims of crimes; enhances DNA collection and analysis efforts; provides for post-conviction DNA testing; and authorizes grants to improve the quality of representation in state capital cases.

2010   City of Brockton (MA) Police Department becomes the first agency in the country to use the Mobile Offender Recognition and Identification System (MORIS)—an iPhone application that takes iris images, fingerprints, and photos of subjects on the street. This biometric data can then be uploaded on a secure network for purposes of identifying the individual in seconds.

REFERENCES

Bellis, Mary (2011). History of Photography. *About.com*. http://inventors.about.com/od/pstartinventions/a/stilphotography.htm

Cain, Steve, Lonnie Smrkovski and Mindy Wilson (2011). Voiceprint Identification. *ExpertPages.com*. http://expertpages.com/news/voiceprint_identification.htm

Cole, Simon A. (nd.). Fingerprint Identification and the Criminal Justice System:

Dilworth, Donald C. (ed.) (1977). Identification Wanted: *Development of the American Criminal Identification System, 1893–1943*. Gaithersburg, MD: International Association of Chiefs of Police.

Federal Bureau of Investigation's Biometric Center of Excellence (2011). Welcome to the Biometric Center of Excellence (BCOE) Web Site. http://www.biometriccoe.gov/

GlobalSecurity.org (2011). Emerging Biometric Technologies. http://www.globalsecurity.org/security/systems/biometrics-emerging.htm

Historical Lessons for the DNA Debate. In David Lazer (ed.). *The Technology of Justice: DNA and the Criminal Justice System*. Harvard University, John F. Kennedy School of Government. www.hks.harvard.edu/dnabook/Simon%20Cole%20II.doc

Identi-Kit Solutions (2011). Identi-Kit Timeline. http://identi-kit.com/background.html

Siuru, Bill (2010). MORISTM – The Future of Perp Identification. *Police and Security News*, 26(5):22, 25.

US Department of Justice (2011). DNA Initiative. http://www.dna.gov/info/

Selected Organizational Charts

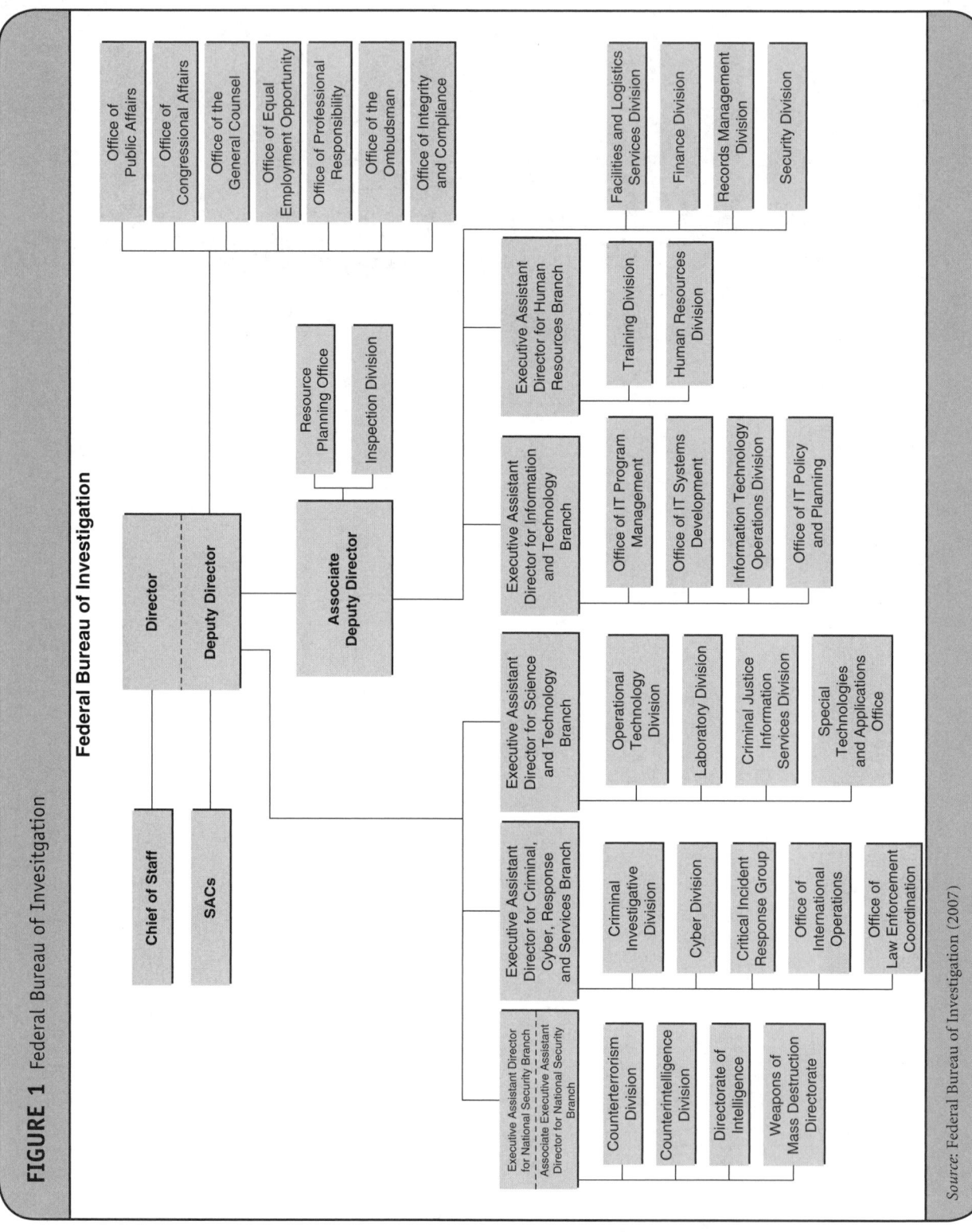

FIGURE 1 Federal Bureau of Investigation

Source: Federal Bureau of Investigation (2007)

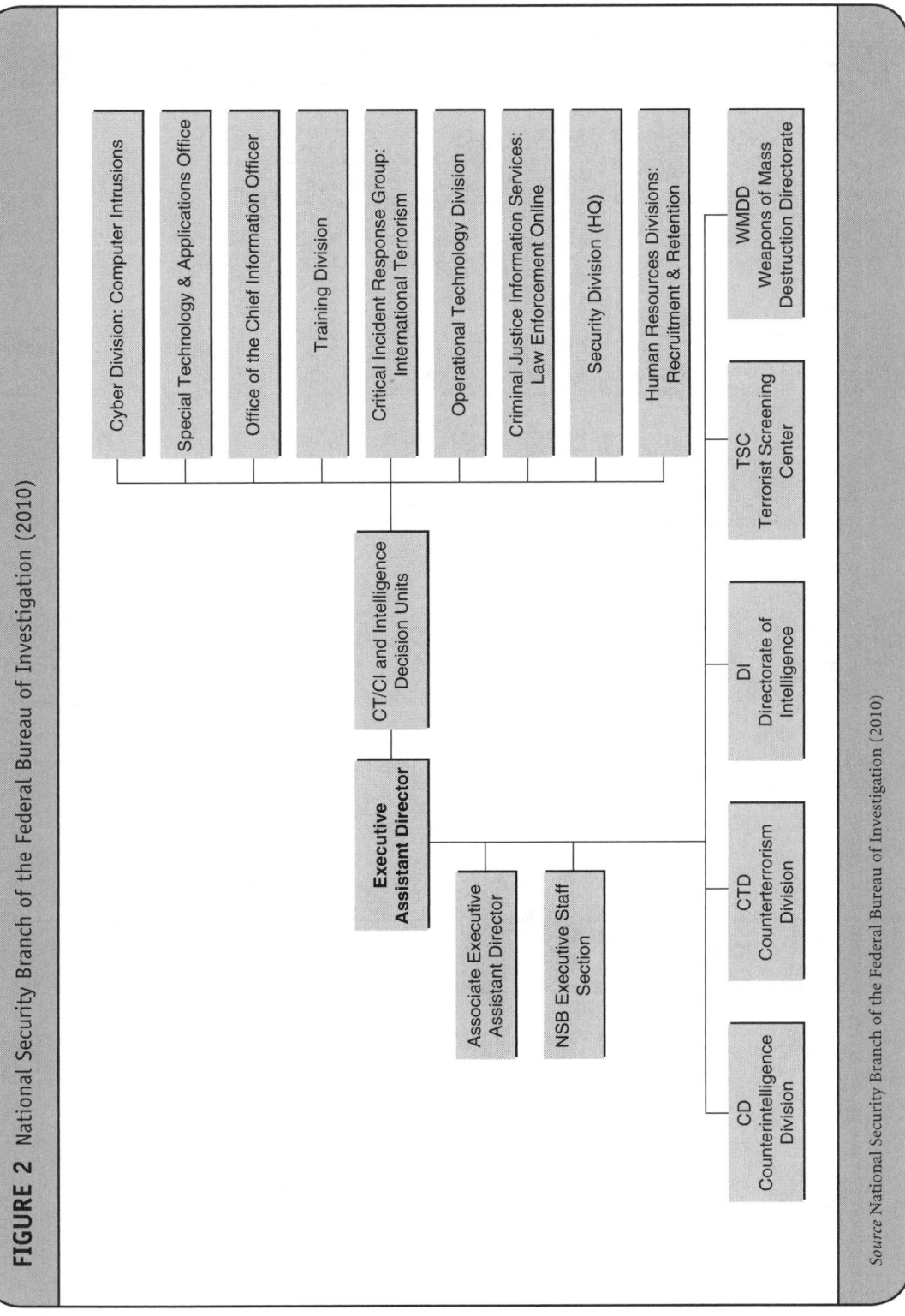

FIGURE 2 National Security Branch of the Federal Bureau of Investigation (2010)

Cyber Division: Computer Intrusions

Special Technology & Applications Office

Office of the Chief Information Officer

Training Division

Critical Incident Response Group: International Terrorism

Operational Technology Division

Criminal Justice Information Services: Law Enforcement Online

Security Division (HQ)

Human Resources Divisions: Recruitment & Retention

WMDD Weapons of Mass Destruction Directorate

CT/CI and Intelligence Decision Units

Executive Assistant Director

Associate Executive Assistant Director

NSB Executive Staff Section

CD Counterintelligence Division

CTD Counterterrorism Division

DI Directorate of Intelligence

TSC Terrorist Screening Center

Source National Security Branch of the Federal Bureau of Investigation (2010)

FIGURE 3 BOSTON POLICE DEPARTMENT ORGANIZATION CHART, September 2009

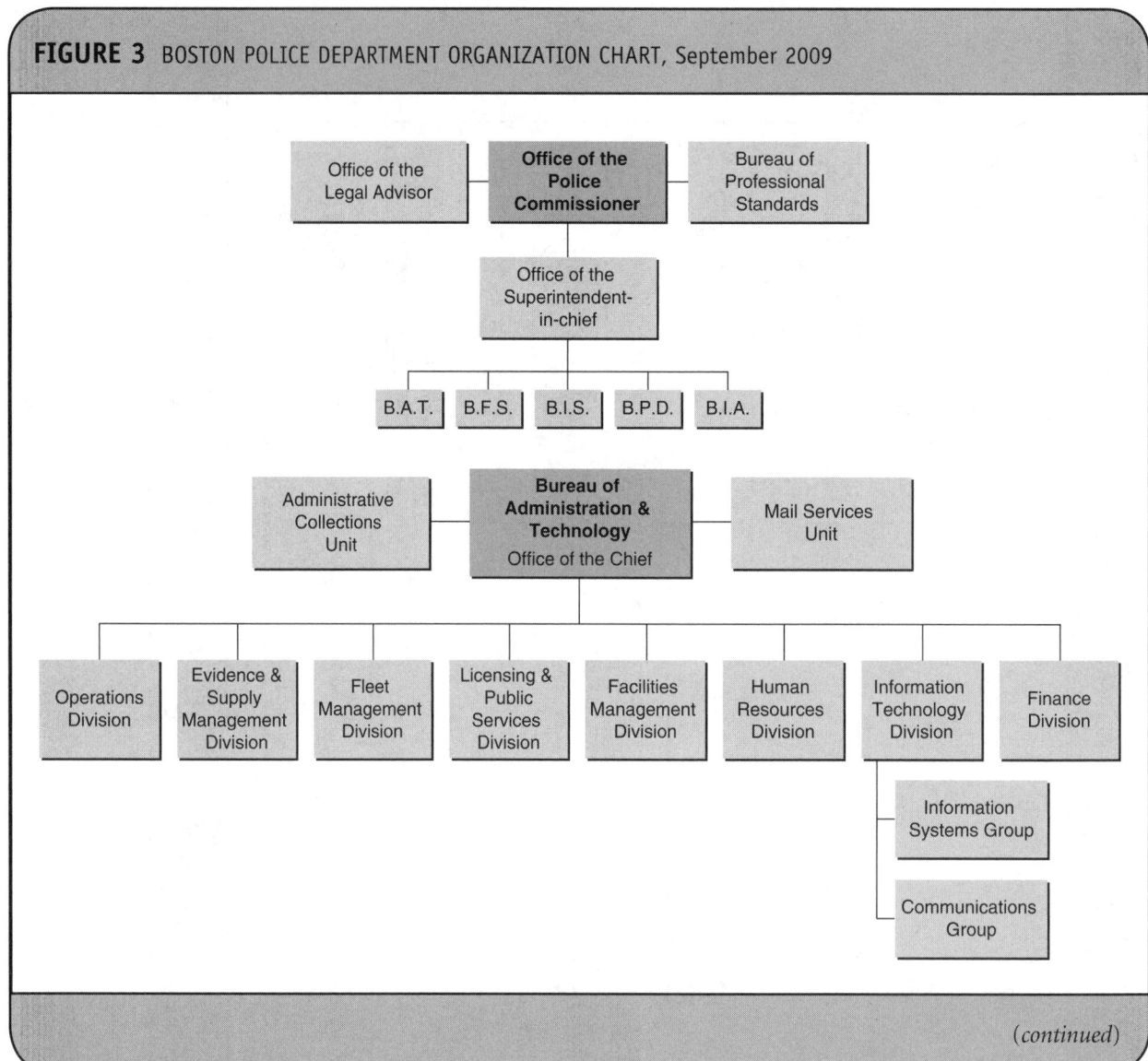

(*continued*)

FIGURE 3 BOSTON POLICE DEPARTMENT ORGANIZATION CHART, September 2009 (*Continued*)

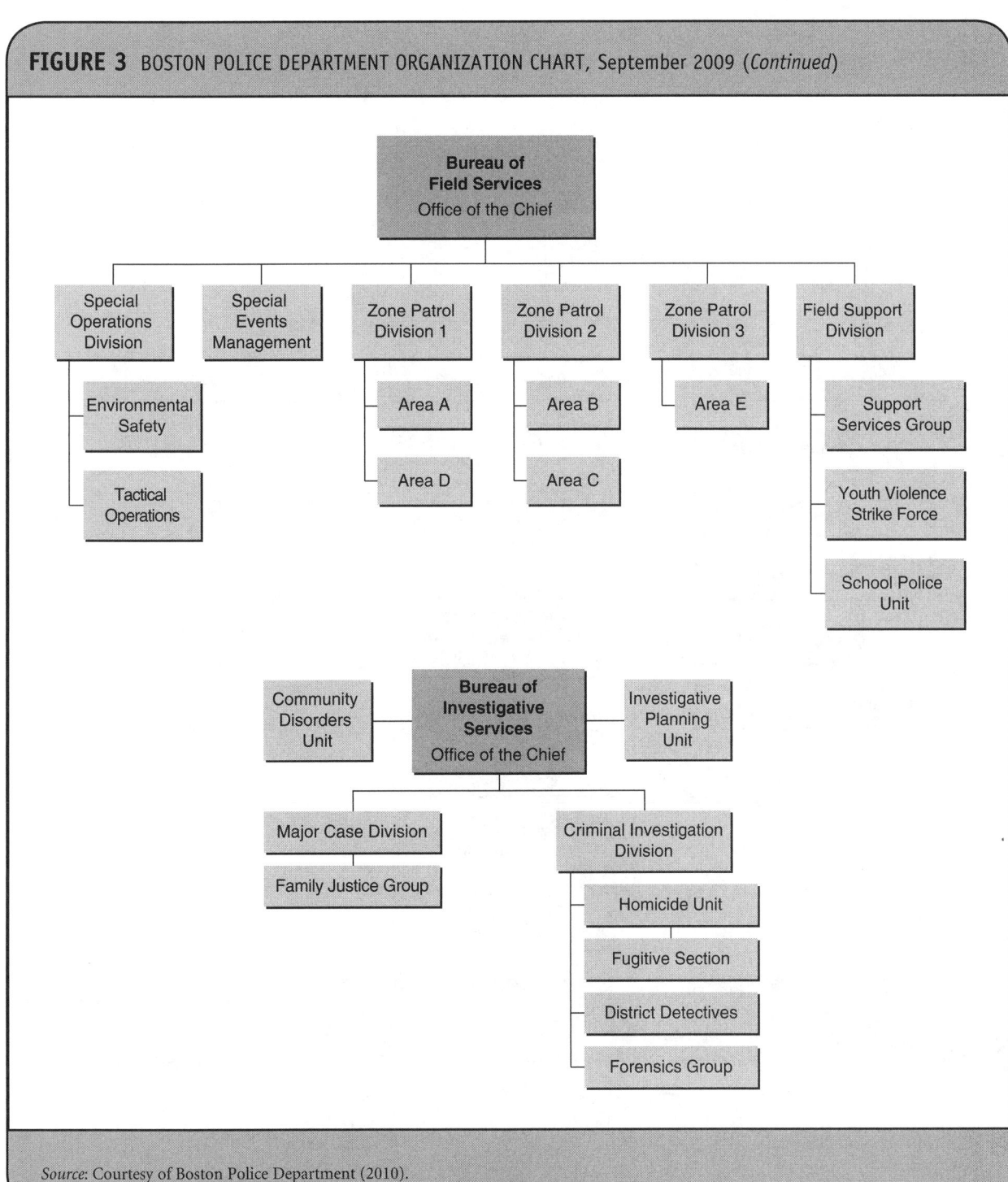

Source: Courtesy of Boston Police Department (2010).

FIGURE 4 Colorado Springs PD

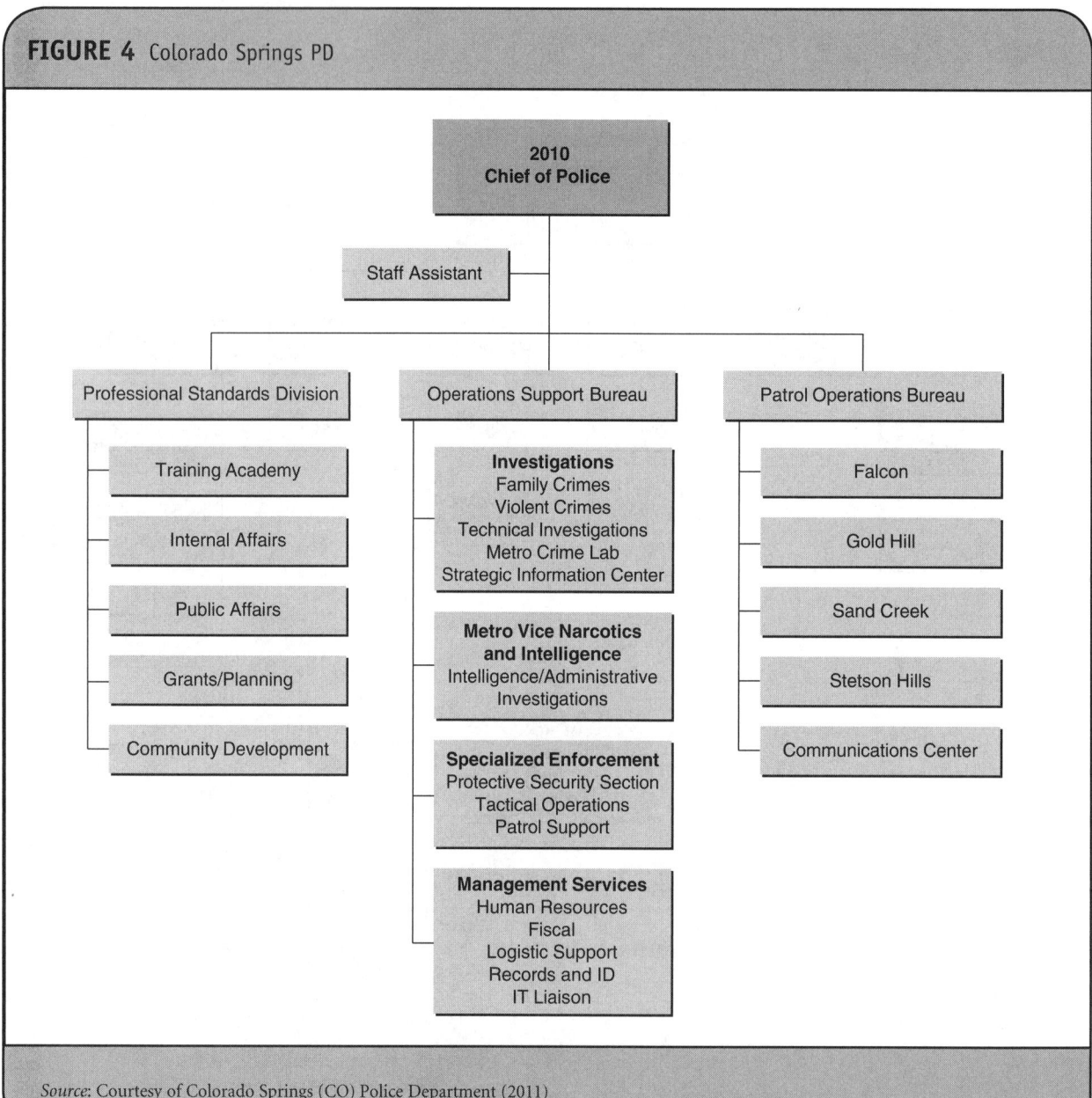

2010
Chief of Police

Staff Assistant

Professional Standards Division
- Training Academy
- Internal Affairs
- Public Affairs
- Grants/Planning
- Community Development

Operations Support Bureau

Investigations
Family Crimes
Violent Crimes
Technical Investigations
Metro Crime Lab
Strategic Information Center

**Metro Vice Narcotics
and Intelligence**
Intelligence/Administrative
Investigations

Specialized Enforcement
Protective Security Section
Tactical Operations
Patrol Support

Management Services
Human Resources
Fiscal
Logistic Support
Records and ID
IT Liaison

Patrol Operations Bureau
- Falcon
- Gold Hill
- Sand Creek
- Stetson Hills
- Communications Center

Source: Courtesy of Colorado Springs (CO) Police Department (2011)

FIGURE 5 Police Org Chart

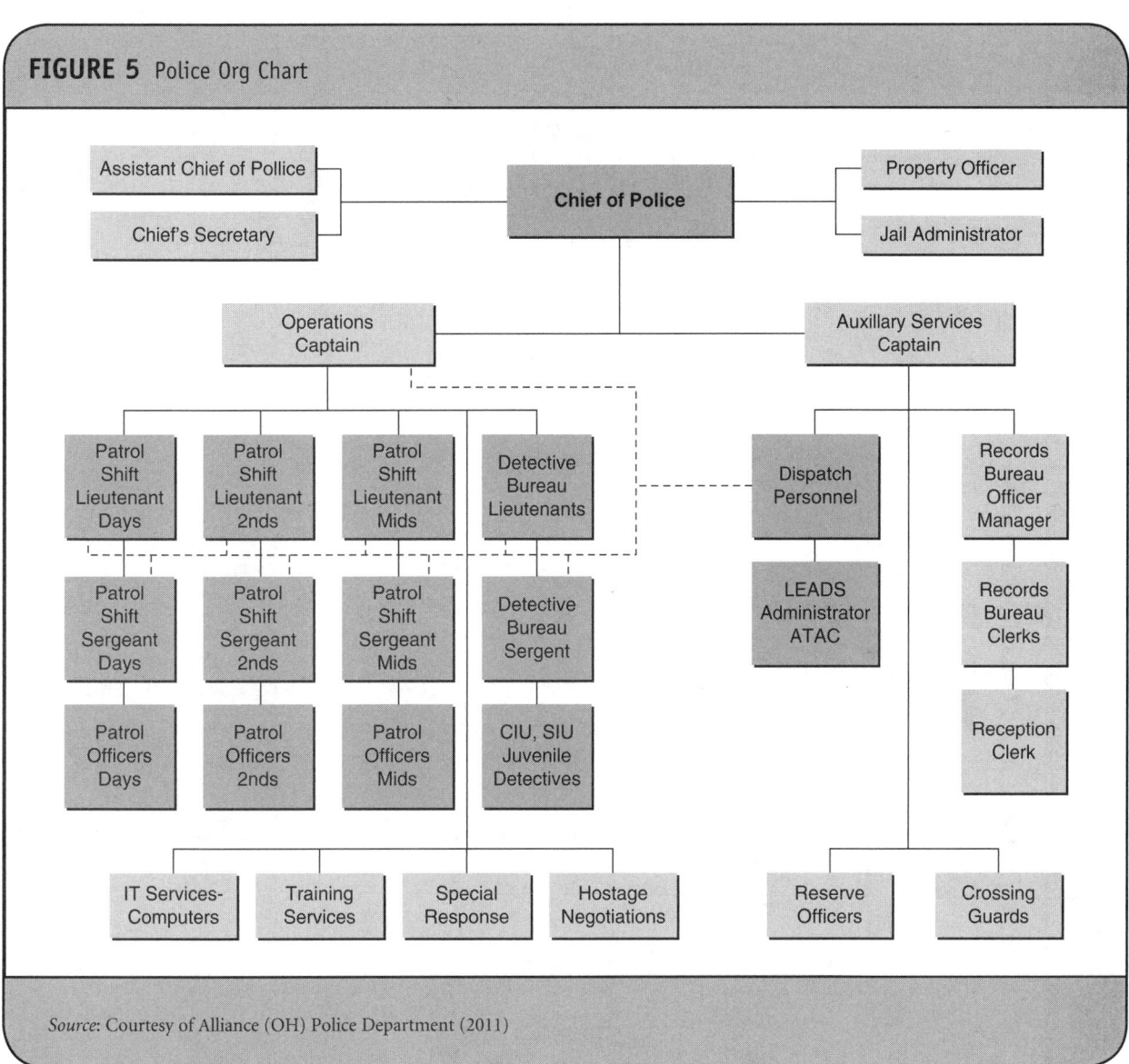

Source: Courtesy of Alliance (OH) Police Department (2011)

FIGURE 6 Monroe Org Chart

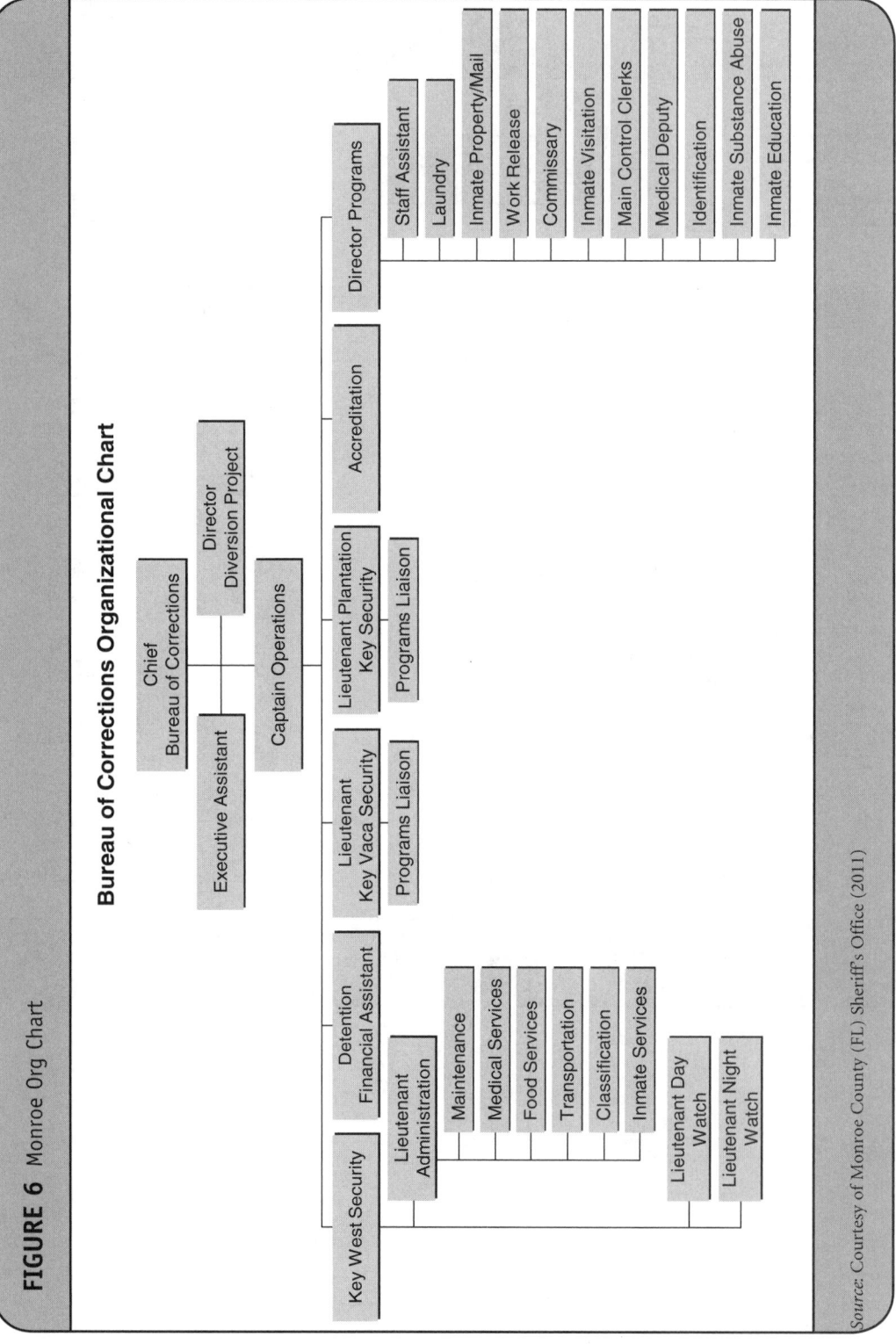

Bureau of Corrections Organizational Chart

Source: Courtesy of Monroe County (FL) Sheriff's Office (2011)

FIGURE 7 Monroe Org Chart 2010

Monroe County Sheriff's Office Organizational Chart

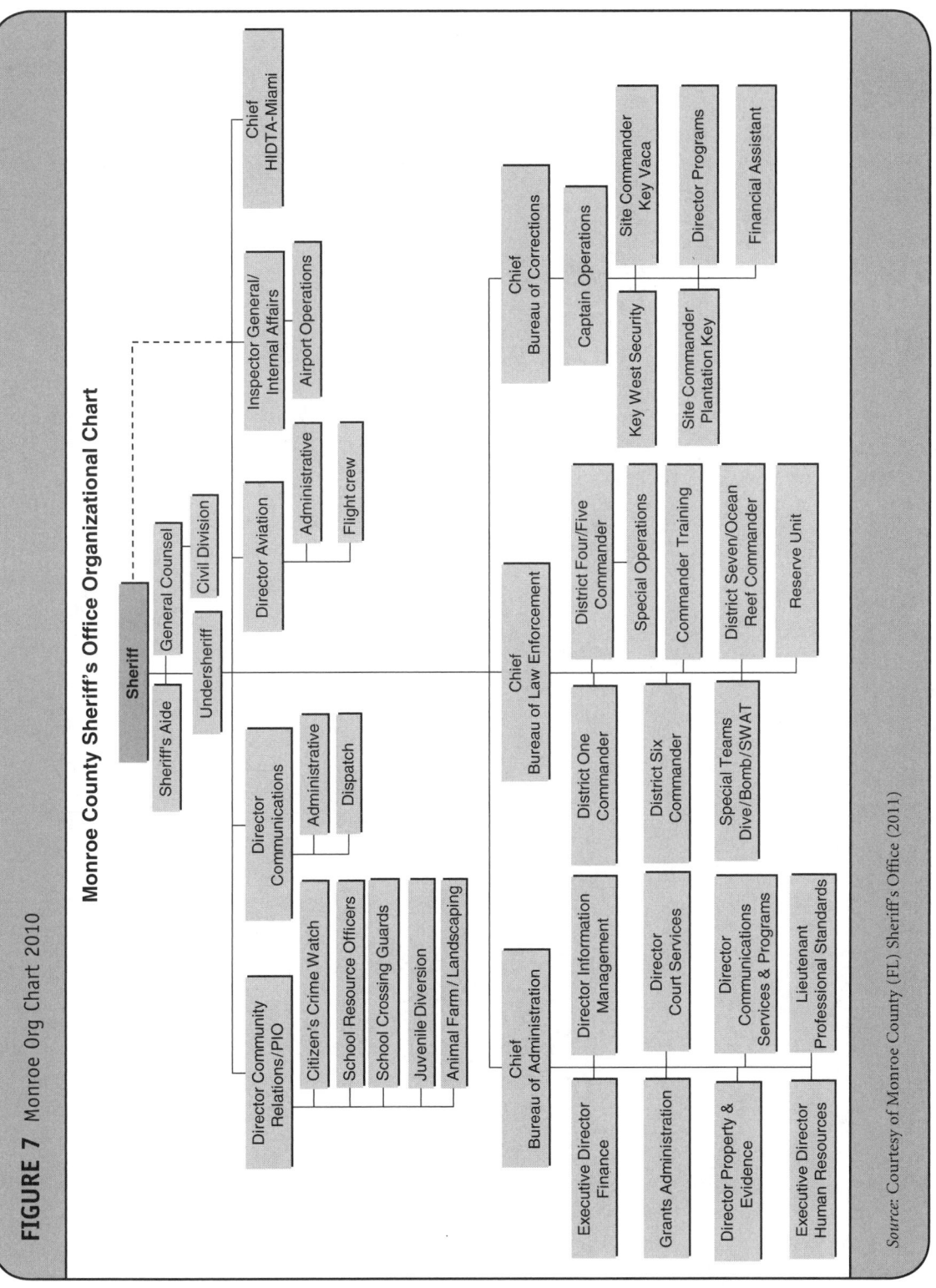

Source: Courtesy of Monroe County (FL) Sheriff's Office (2011)

Minimum Hours of Basic Training for the States of New York, California, and Florida

NEW YORK STATE

Basic Course for Police Officers Program Content (January 2009)

Part I: Administration of Justice	Required Hours
A. Introduction to Criminal Justice	
B. Jurisdictions and Responsibilities of Law Enforcement	
C. Adjudicatory Process and Court Structure - Civil & Criminal	
Total for Part I	**4**

Part II: Introduction to Law Enforcement	
A. Constitutional Law	2
B. Discretionary Powers	2
C. Ethical Awareness	12
D. Physical Fitness and Wellness	65

Part III: Laws of New York State	
A. New York State Penal Law Offenses	16
B. Justification–Use of Force & Deadly Physical Force	7
C. New York State Criminal Procedure Law	21
D. New York State Juvenile Law and Procedures	5
E. Civil Liability and Risk Management	2
F. Ancillary New York State Statutes	2
G. New York State Vehicle and Traffic Law	5

Part IV: Law Enforcement Skills	
A. Field Note-Taking	2
B. Report Writing	7
C. Communications	4
D. Observation and Patrol	4
E. Case Preparation and Demeanor in Official Proceedings	7
F. Mental Illness	14
G. Crimes in Progress	4
H. Arrest Processing	5
I. Professional Traffic Stops	5
J. Interpersonal Skills–Arrest Techniques	40
K. Emergency Medical Services	40
L. Emergency Vehicle Operation and Control	20
M. Firearms Training	40
N. Supervised Field Training Review and Orientation	160

O. Traffic Direction and Control   2
P. Traffic Enforcement   4
Q. DWI Detection and Standardized
    Field Sobriety Testing   21
R. Physical Evidence   12
S. Off-Duty and Plain Clothes Encounters   2

Part V: Community Interaction

A. Intoxication   2
B. Community Resources–Victim/Witness Services   3
C. Crime Prevention and Crime
    Against the Elderly   4
D. Cultural Diversity/Bias Related Incidents
    and Sexual Harassment   5
E. Persons with Disabilities   2
F. Community-Oriented Policing
    and Problem-Solving–Media Relations   2

Part VI Mass Casualties and Major Events

A. Standardized Response Plans for
    Unusual Events   8
B. Counter Terrorism   8
C. The Nature and Control of Civil Disorder   2

Part VII Investigations

A. Domestic Violence   14
B. Organized Crime Familiarization/
    Enterprise Corruption   2
C. Preliminary Investigation and Information
    Development   2
D. Interviewing Techniques   5
E. Common Criminal Investigation Techniques   10
F. Basic Crash Management and Reporting   14
G. Injury and Death Cases   3
H. Sex Crimes   2
I. Narcotics and Dangerous Drugs   3
J. Missing and Abducted Children/
    Missing Adult Cases   3
K. Animal Abuse Cases   2
L. Contemporary Police Problems   4
M. Human Trafficking   2
Grand Total   **639**

Source: New York State, Division of Criminal Justice Services, December 26, 2010. http://criminaljustice.state.ny.us/ops/docs/training/pubs/basicpolice/bcpooutline.

STATE OF CALIFORNIA

MINIMUM CONTENT AND HOURLY REQUIREMENTS, REGULAR BASIC COURSE (RBC)—STANDARD FORMAT (July 1, 2010)

DOMAIN	DOMAIN DESCRIPTION	MINIMUM NUMBER HOURS
01	Leadership, Professionalism & Ethics	8 hours
02	Criminal Justice System	2 hours
03	Policing in the Community	18 hours
04	Victimology/Crisis Intervention	6 hours
05	Introduction to Criminal Law	4 hours
06	Property Crimes	6 hours
07	Crimes Against Persons/Death Investigation	6 hours
08	General Criminal Statutes	2 hours
09	Crimes Against Children	4 hours
10	Sex Crimes	4 hours
11	Juvenile Law and Procedure	3 hours
12	Controlled Substances	12 hours
13	ABC Law	2 hours
14	Laws of Arrest	12 hours
15	Search and Seizure	12 hours
16	Presentation of Evidence	6 hours
17	Investigative Report Writing	52 hours
18	Vehicle Operations	24 hours
19	Use of Force	12 hours
20	Patrol Techniques	12 hours
21	Vehicle Pullovers	14 hours
22	Crimes in Progress	20 hours
23	Handling Disputes/Crowd Control	8 hours
24	Domestic Violence	10 hours
25	Unusual Occurrences	4 hours
26	Missing Persons	4 hours
27	Traffic Enforcement	16 hours
28	Traffic Collision Investigation	12 hours
29	Crime Scenes, Evidence, and Forensics	12 hours
30	Custody	2 hours
31	Lifetime Fitness	44 hours
32	Arrest Methods/Defensive Tactics	60 hours
33	First Aid and CPR	21 hours
34	Firearms/Chemical Agents	72 hours
35	Information Systems	2 hours
36	People with Disabilities	6 hours
37	Gang Awareness	2 hours

38	Crimes Against the Justice System	4 hours
39	Weapons Violations	4 hours
40	Hazardous Materials Awareness	4 hours
41	Cultural Diversity/Discrimination	16 hours
42	Emergency Management	16 hours
	Total Minimum Instructional Hours	560 hours

The minimum number of hours allocated to testing in the Course are shown below (time required for exercise testing, instructional activities, and the Work Sample Test Battery is included in instructional hours).

| TESTS | HOURS |
| Scenario Tests (40 hours tests administration; 18 hours scenario demonstration) | 58 hours |

(LDs 1, 4, 7, 20, 21, 22, 23, 25, 30, and 37)
Written Tests (25 hours test administration; 15 hours examination review) — 40 hours
Pre-Course Test (Non-scored test administered prior to instruction)
Written Tests (LDs 2, 3, 5, 6, 7, 8, 9, 10, 11, 12, 15, 16, 19, 20, 25, 26, 28, 31, 34, 36, 37, 39, 40, and 43)

POST-Constructed Comprehensive Tests
Mid-Course Proficiency Test (LDs 2, 3, 5, 6, 7, 8, 9, 10, 15, 16, 20, and 39)
End-of-Course Proficiency Test (LDs 2, 3, 5, 6, 7, 8, 9, 10, 11, 12, 15, 16, 19, 20, 25, 26, 31, 36, 37, 39, 40 and 43)

Exercise Tests (Physical Skills Pilot Tests) — 6 hours
Total Minimum Required Hours — 664 hours

Source: Peace Officer Standards and Training, State of California (December, 2010) http://www.post.ca.gov/regular-basic-course-training-specifications.aspx

FLORIDA DEPARTMENT OF LAW ENFORCEMENT
Florida CMS Law Enforcement Basic Recruit Training Program

Course Name	Course Hours
1. Introduction to Law Enforcement	11
2. Legal	69
3. Communications	76
4. Human Issues	40
5. Patrol I	58
6. Patrol II	40
7. Crime Scene Investigations	24
8. Criminal Investigations	56
9. Traffic Stops	24
10. DUI Stops	24
11. Traffic Crash Investigations	32
12. CMS Law Enforcement Vehicle Operations	48
13. CMS First Aid for Criminal Justice Officers	40
14. CMS Criminal Justice Firearms	80
15. CMS Criminal Justice Defensive Tactics	80
16. Dart-Firing Stun Gun	8
17. Criminal Justice Officer Physical Fitness Training	60
TOTAL	**770**

Source: Florida Department of Law Enforcement (December 2010) http://www.fdle.state.fl.us/Content/getdoc/eafbafaa-20c0-496c-b6ab-98cd918adccf/2009LEBRTProgramCourses.aspx

Index

Page numbers followed by *f* denote figures; those followed by *n* denote footnotes; and those followed by *t* denote tables